around the world.

crane
kerin
hartley
rudelius

marketing

eighth canadian edition

FREDERICK G. CRANE
QMA Consulting Group Limited

ROGER A. KERIN
Southern Methodist University

STEVEN W. HARTLEY
University of Denver

WILLIAM RUDELIUS
University of Minnesota

McGraw-Hill
Ryerson
Connect. Learn. Succeed.

McGraw-Hill Ryerson

Connect. Learn. Succeed.

Marketing
Eighth Canadian Edition

ISBN-13: 978-0-07-000990-5
ISBN-10: 0-07-000990-2

3 4 5 6 7 8 9 CTPS 1 9 8 7 6 5 4 3

Printed and bound in China

Care has been taken to trace ownership of copyright material contained in this text; however, the publisher will welcome any information that enables it to rectify any reference or credit for subsequent editions.

Vice-President and Editor-in-Chief: *Joanna Cotton*
Executive Sponsoring Editor: *Leanna MacLean*
Executive Marketing Manager: *Joy Armitage Taylor*
Developmental Editor: *Jennifer Cressman*
Senior Editorial Associate: *Stephanie Hess*
Photo/Permissions Researcher: *Tracy Leonard*
Manager, Editorial Services: *Margaret Henderson*
Supervising Editor: *Cathy Biribauer*
Copy Editor: *Mike Kelly*
Production Coordinators: *Jennifer Hall, Scott Morrison*
Inside Design: *Kyle Gell Design*
Composition: *Laserwords Private Limited*
Cover Design: *Valid Design & Layout/Dave Murphy*
Cover Photo: © Alex Maxim/Acclaim Images.com (iPad), Twitter, LinkedIn, WordPress, Technorati, Delicious, Yahoo and Flickr logos reproduced with permission of Yahoo! Inc. ©2010 Yahoo! Inc. YAHOO!, the YAHOO! logo, FLICKR and the FLICKR logo are registered trademarks of Yahoo! Inc.
Printer: *CTPS*

Library and Archives Canada Cataloguing in Publication Data

Marketing / Frederick G. Crane . . . [et al.].—8th Canadian ed.

Includes index.
ISBN 978-0-07-000990-5

1. Marketing—Textbooks. 2. Marketing—Canada—Textbooks. I. Crane, F. G

HF5415.M293 2011   658.8
C2010-905431-8

DEDICATION

I dedicate this book to my beautiful and beloved border collie, Ceilidh, who I lost to canine lymphoma in November 2009. For a decade, she was my constant companion and my true best friend. She loved me unconditionally and taught me so many important life lessons. She will always remain in my heart and in my soul. I miss you sweet girl!

ABOUT THE AUTHOR

Frederick G. Crane is an executive professor at the College of Business at Northeastern University, editor of the *Journal of the Academy of Business Education,* and senior fellow at the Institute for Enterprise Growth. He is a former professor of marketing and entrepreneurship at the University of New Hampshire and a former full professor at Dalhousie University. He was also the founding editor of the *Journal of Promotion Management.*

Dr. Crane grew up in a family business and also founded several of his own businesses, including successful management consulting and research firms. As a corporate consultant for more than 20 years, Dr. Crane has completed over 300 consulting assignments for companies/organizations in over two dozen countries. He has worked for both small businesses and Fortune 500 companies, assisting them with the development and execution of strategic plans, consumer research, innovation/new product development, and branding projects. He has also developed and participated in numerous corporate training and executive education programs for major corporate clients in the educational, financial services, health care, high-tech, packaged goods, pharmaceutical, and telecommunications fields.

His academic research activities have resulted in more than 100 publications, including more than a dozen books. He currently sits on the editorial boards of *Health Marketing Quarterly, Services Marketing Quarterly,* and *Journal of Hospital Marketing.* His current research stream intersects the domains of marketing, entrepreneurship, corporate venturing, and innovation. Dr. Crane has also received numerous awards for teaching excellence over the past 20 years.

BRIEF CONTENTS

CONTENTS

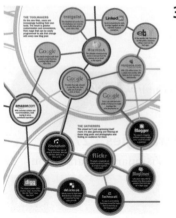

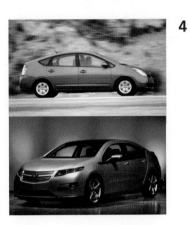

Part 2   Understanding Buyers and Markets   120

Part 3   Targeting Marketing Opportunities   200

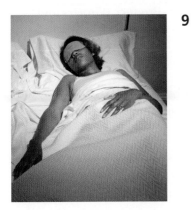

9   Market Segmentation, Targeting, and Positioning   229

Part 4   Satisfying Marketing Opportunities   252

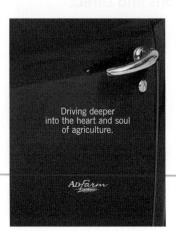

Part 5   Managing the Marketing Process 512

CURRENT, STREAMLINED COVERAGE

The Eighth Canadian Edition of *Marketing* is substantially revised, updated, and packed with new examples of marketing in Canada and around the world. You'll find new or expanded coverage of topics such as social media marketing, user-generated content, marketing metrics, Blue Oceans, Hedgehog, supplier development, green marketing, Research 3.0, bottom of the pyramid, positioning statements, feature float, mobile advertising, customer experience management, eco-consciousness, neuromarketing, and lifestyle centres.

We also overhauled our examples, cases, and pedagogy. The Eighth Canadian Edition includes nine new opening vignettes, eight new Marketing Matters boxes, and nine new Video Cases. In Appendix A, a new marketing plan focuses on Coffee Break, a fictitious specialty coffee house. A new Using Marketing Dashboards feature exposes students to the measures that marketing professionals use to track and analyze marketing phenomena and performance. Finally, a new end-of-chapter Building Your Marketing Plan feature provides students with guidance and instruction for developing their own marketing plan for a new business.

DETAILED LIST OF CHANGES

Chapter 1 – Marketing: Customer Value, Satisfaction, Relationships, and Experiences

- Chapter 1 features a new opening vignette on WildPlay Element Parks. WildPlay is also used as an example throughout the chapter. There is a new definition of marketing, new material on social media marketing including the social media marketing era, and new examples of failures in marketing. The Stratus Vineyards Video Case has also been updated.

Chapter 2– Developing Successful Marketing Strategies

- Canadian Tire is featured in this chapter's new opening vignette and new end-of-chapter Video Case. There is a new section on organizations and strategy, and new content on marketing metrics and marketing dashboards. Chapter 2 also introduces new concepts such as Hedgehog and Blue Oceans.

Chapter 3 – Scanning the Marketing Environment

- Chapter 3 features a new opening vignette on Web 2.0. There is new material on social media marketing, multicultural marketing, and small business and entrepreneurship. The latest demographic statistics on the Canadian marketplace, including population growth, ethnic diversity, and income are presented. There is also updated material on technology in marketing, and a new Video Case on Geek Squad.

Chapter 4 – Ethics and Social Responsibility in Marketing

- Chapter 4 has been revised to discuss the automotive industry and environmental issues. This chapter features new ethics codes examples, new material on corporate social responsibility (CSR), and new content on green marketing.

Chapter 5 – Consumer Behaviour

- Chapter 5 includes an updated opening vignette and new material on "buzz marketing." There is updated information on buying behaviour in subculture markets, such as French-Canadians and Chinese-Canadians. Content on consumers using the Internet and social media as part of the buying process has also been expanded. Finally, the new end-of-chapter Video Case examines how companies gain consumer insights.

Chapter 6 – Organizational Markets and Buyer Behaviour

- Chapter 6 features a new opening vignette on Bombardier. This chapter also contains new statistics on organizational/business markets in Canada, and a discussion of new concepts in business-to-business marketing such as supplier development. There is also a new end-of-chapter Video Case, which features IGLOO Software Solutions, a Canadian company marketing in the business-to-business (B2B) space.

Chapter 7 – Reaching Global Markets

- Chapter 7 provides updated trade statistics as well as new material on Canada's hottest export markets, trade groups, and e-commerce in global markets. This chapter also introduces new global business concepts such as the bottom of the pyramid market and micro-financing.

Chapter 8 – Marketing Research: From Information to Action

- Chapter 8 includes a new opening vignette on Research 3.0, which outlines all the latest in the marketing research field. This chapter also provides new examples of marketing research involving observation and ethnography. Finally, there is updated information on neuromarketing and the use of marketing dashboards as part of the marketing research function.

Chapter 9 – Market Segmentation, Targeting, and Positioning

- Chapter 9 provides new and extended content on segmentation, targeting, and positioning, including new material on writing a positioning statement. There is also a new end-of-chapter Video Case on Prince Sports to which students will relate.

Chapter 10 – Developing New Products and Services

- Chapter 10 includes a new opening vignette on Apple, Inc. as a major innovative company that excels in new product development. There is much new material on new products and services, including "newness," feature bloat, idea generation, and new-product failure examples. There is also a new Going Online box and new material on the actual product development stage of the new product process.

Chapter 11 – Managing Products and Brands

- Chapter 11 provides a new opening vignette on Gatorade and its approach to brand management. There are new examples on modifying the product, perceptual benefits of packaging, and new issues facing companies with regard to packaging and labelling. There is also an updated section on the best Canadian and global brands. Finally, the new Video Case focuses on a Canadian upstart firm marketing a new beverage called Slow Cow.

Chapter 12 – Managing Services

- Chapter 12 features a new opening vignette on authentic services featuring Cirque du Soleil. This chapter discusses new Canadian research on service quality. There is also an updated section on services in the future, and a new Marketing Matters box on how to create great service experiences.

Chapter 13 – Pricing Products and Services

- Chapter 13 contains new material on price bundling, a new Going Online box, a new Using Marketing Dashboards box, and an updated Video Case on Washburn Guitars, which requires students to apply marketing math, including break-even analysis. A new application question on the psychology of pricing has been added to the end-of-chapter material.

Chapter 14 – Managing Marketing Channels and Supply Chains

- Chapter 14 features an updated opening vignette about Apple, Inc.'s approach to creating a high-touch customer experience in a high-tech marketing channel. There is also new material on reverse logistics and a new Using Marketing Dashboards box on determining channel profitability.

Chapter 15 – Retailing

- An updated opening vignette is followed by new material on top global and Canadian retailers, online retailing (e-tailing), and vending. The retailing challenges section has been revamped and renewed to include a discussion of improving the bottom line in retailing and managing risk. Chapter 15 also provides updated material on franchising and new material on going green in retailing, including a new Making Responsible Decisions box on environmentally friendly retailing.

Chapter 16 – Integrated Marketing Communications and Direct Marketing

- Chapter 16 includes a new opening vignette on Canadian tourism, Hyundai, and Kraft Canada, and their approaches to integrated marketing communications. A new Marketing Matters box deals with combining online and traditional media to achieve successful integration of marketing communications, and a new Making Responsible Decisions box discusses privacy and online advertising. The direct marketing section has been updated to include information

related to mobile marketing, such as text and short codes. There is also a new section on Canadian legislation around privacy and direct marketing, and the new end-of-chapter Video Case features Under Armour.

Chapter 17 – Advertising, Sales Promotion, and Public Relations

- Chapter 17 offers new examples of establishing advertising objectives, using humour in advertising, and using celebrity spokespeople in advertising. There is also new material on user-generated content and mobile advertising. There is a new Using Marketing Dashboards box where students must select the best media options to reach customers, a new Marketing Matters box that discusses what Canadians really think about advertising, and a new Going Online exercise that features mobile advertising. The entire section on media alternatives has been updated, and the PR section contains an expanded discussion of sponsorships.

Chapter 18 – Personal Selling and Sales Management

- Chapter 18 includes a new and expanded section on salesforce automation and CRM. This chapter also contains a new Using Marketing Dashboards box about tracking the performance of salespeople, a new Marketing Matters box that discusses how to plug the customer into the sales solution, and a new Video Case on Xerox's approach to sales and sales management.

Chapter 19 – Pulling It All Together: The Strategic Marketing Process

- Chapter 19 features an updated opening vignette. It also presents new material on the importance of marketing metrics in the marketing planning process, as well as new content on marketing implementation. A new section on marketing evaluation includes the use of marketing ROI, metrics, and dashboards. The new end-of-chapter Video Case is on General Mills' Warm Delights product offering.

STUDENT-FRIENDLY APPROACH

Marketing has developed an excellent reputation among Canadian instructors and students as a text that delivers key marketing concepts in a student-friendly style without watering down the material. The Eighth Canadian Edition continues to be characterized by the following:

- **A high-engagement style:** An easy-to-read, high-involvement, interactive writing style that engages students through active learning techniques, timely and interesting examples, and challenging applications.

- **Personalized marketing:** A vivid and accurate description of businesses, marketing professionals, and entrepreneurs—through cases, exercises, and testimonials—that allow students to personalize marketing and identify possible career interests and role models.

- **Emphasis on marketing decision making:** The use of extended examples, cases, and videos involving people making marketing decisions, which helps students to easily relate to text concepts.

- **A strong pedagogical framework:** The use of Learning Objectives, Learning Reviews, key terms, boxed applications, and Learning Objectives in Review summaries, along with supportive student supplements, appeals to a wide range of learning styles.

Chapter-Opening Vignettes introduce students to the chapter concepts ahead, using an exciting company as an example. **Ten** vignettes are new to this edition. The new vignette in Chapter 1, for example, focuses on WildPlay Element Parks, an entrepreneurial outdoor-adventure company, with four West Coast locations that offer bungee jumping, aerial adventure tree courses, and zip-line rides. Other new vignettes highlight companies such as Canadian Tire and Apple, Inc.

chapter 1

Marketing: Customer Value, Satisfaction, Relationships, and Experiences

WILDPLAY ELEMENT PARKS: ACTIVE ADVENTURE EXPERIENCES AWAIT YOU!

Looking for an adventure? A thrilling experience? Well, Wild-Play Element Parks offers you what they call "Primal Fun and Games." WildPlay is a full-service outdoor adventure company offering customers bungee jumping, the King Swing, aerial adventure tree courses, and zip-line rides. This young, entrepreneurial start-up is capitalizing on major consumer trends: customer desire for personal and memorable experiences and customer desire to reconnect with nature.

WildPlay was started in September 2005 by two certified climbing guides, Gordon Ross and Tom Benson. These entrepreneurs spent more than 15 years leading climbing adventures and connecting people to the great outdoors. As certified climbing instructors and paragliders, both had been thinking of ways to use the power of the group experience to introduce more people to outdoor adventure activities. Additionally, the steep learning curve and high level of commitment for adventures such as climbing was a deterrent for some people and intimidating for others. Gord had discovered tree-to-tree parks during his travels to Europe and South America and was researching them with Tom as a way to deliver the outdoor experience to a broader range of people. Both recognized that this type of park would be an excellent way to realize their desire of bringing outdoor experiences to more people without the steep learning curve.

learning objectives

After reading this chapter, you should be able to:

LO1 Define marketing and identify the requirements for successful marketing to occur.

LO2 Understand the breadth and depth of marketing.

LO3 Explain how marketing discovers and satisfies consumer needs and wants.

LO4 Distinguish between marketing mix elements and environmental forces.

LO5 Describe how a market orientation focuses on creating customer value, satisfaction, and customer relationships.

LO6 Explain why some organizations have transitioned from the market orientation era to the customer experience management era.

LO7 Understand the emergence of the social media marketing era.

LO8 Understand the meaning of ethics and social responsibility and how they relate to the individual, organizations, and society.

Learning Objectives open each chapter to help students preview chapter content and study effectively.

Learning Reviews are checkpoints found at the end of each major chapter section, which pose critical-thinking and memory-recall questions. These questions help students to reflect on the text and test their comprehension of the material before moving on. (These questions were formerly known as "Concept Checks.")

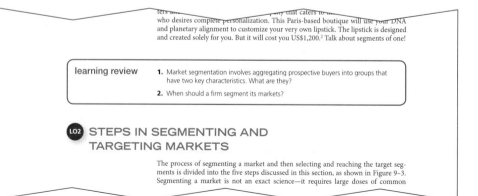

...who desires complete personalization. This Paris-based boutique will use your DNA and planetary alignment to customize your very own lipstick. The lipstick is designed and created solely for you. But it will cost you US$1,200.[2] Talk about segments of one!

learning review
1. Market segmentation involves aggregating prospective buyers into groups that have two key characteristics. What are they?
2. When should a firm segment its markets?

LO2 STEPS IN SEGMENTING AND TARGETING MARKETS

The process of segmenting a market and then selecting and reaching the target segments is divided into the five steps discussed in this section, as shown in Figure 9–3. Segmenting a market is not an exact science—it requires large doses of common

NEW! Using Marketing Dashboards boxes highlight the increasing importance of metrics in marketing. Marketing dashboards graphically portray the measures that marketers use to track and analyze marketing phenomena and performance. Students will find commonly used measures applied by successful marketers throughout the text and be exposed to their calculation, interpretation, and application. Ten new Using Marketing Dashboards boxes are interspersed throughout the text.

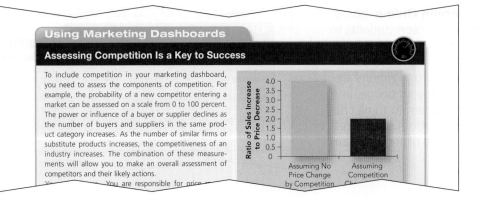

Using Marketing Dashboards

Assessing Competition Is a Key to Success

To include competition in your marketing dashboard, you need to assess the components of competition. For example, the probability of a new competitor entering a market can be assessed on a scale from 0 to 100 percent. The power or influence of a buyer or supplier declines as the number of buyers and suppliers in the same product category increases. As the number of similar firms or substitute products increases, the competitiveness of an industry increases. The combination of these measurements will allow you to make an overall assessment of competitors and their likely actions.

You are responsible for price ...

Marketing Matters boxes provide engaging, real-world examples of marketing applications in action to give students further insight into the practical world of marketing. **Thirteen** of the chapters contain new or updated Marketing Matters boxes. New topics include social media, buzz marketing, and neuromarketing. (These boxes were formerly known as "Marketing News Net.")

Marketing Matters

The Buzz about Buzz

Have you recently heard about a new product, movie, Web site, book, or restaurant from someone you know . . . or a complete stranger? If so, you may have had a buzz experience. Many Canadian marketers recognize the power of word of mouth, and there are many high-profile Canadian companies engaging in buzz marketing, including Kraft, Toyota, Molson, Coty, Nike, and even the Wine Council of Ontario. Companies can construct and operationalize their own buzz marketing campaigns or farm out the activity to buzz marketing companies such as Matchstick, Inc. of Toronto. If a company hires Matchstick, a typical buzz marketing campaign is constructed as follows: Matchstick will ... freelance basis. Th...

reach about 100 influencials in each city. The brand seeders are provided samples to give to the influencials. These influencials are encouraged (but not paid) to share their honest opinions about the brand and to disclose their relationship with Matchstick. In this way, there is transparency and this buzz is not considered stealth marketing. In short, the influencials are engaging in genuine and, hopefully, effective word-of-mouth conversations about the brand.

Word-of-mouth communication, and in particular, buzz marketing, is becoming so popular that there is even a Word of Mouth Marketing Association (**www.womma.org**), an organization dedicated to assist marketers in becoming pro...

Making Responsible Decisions boxes focus on social responsibility, sustainability, and ethics, and provide examples of how companies approach these subjects in their marketing strategy. **New** boxes in the Eighth Canadian Edition cover topics such as environmentally friendly retailing and privacy concerns in online advertising. (These boxes were formerly known as "Ethics and Social Responsibility Alert.")

Making Responsible Decisions

Environmentally Friendly Retailing Takes Off!

Sustainability has been a topic of interest for some retailers for many years. Recently, however, it has become a movement for the entire industry. What happened? A combination of factors contributed to the change: Environmental consciousness among consumers has reached an all-time high; publicity related to global warning has increased; "green" has become an important element of company image and reputation; and most environmental initiatives save retailers money!

When consumers learned that food packaging creates 50 percent of all household waste, they added packaging to their purchase decision criteria. Walmart responded by ...

Electronics retailer Best Buy recently began using solar energy in some of its stores with the goal of reducing CO_2 emissions by 8 percent by 2012. Mountain Equipment Co-op company is building on its green image by collecting rainwater to water grass at the store and to use in its toilets. When Home Depot switched its in-store light fixtures to compact fluorescent light bulbs, it saved $16 million per year. IKEA Canada no longer offers customers plastic bags in any of their stores and reserves prime parking spaces for customers driving hybrid vehicles. Other companies are using motion detectors to turn lights on and off, improving the fuel economy of delivery vehicles, and designing "zero waste" stores ...

Going Online boxes encourage students to explore digital strategies that innovative companies and organizations are employing online, and ask them to think critically about the success or failure of the company's efforts.

Going Online

IDEO—the Innovation Lab Superstar in Designing New Products

The Apple mouse. The Palm V PDA. The Crest Neat Squeeze toothpaste dispenser. The Steelcase Leap adjustable office chair. These are just some of the thousands of new products designed by an innovation lab you've probably never heard of but benefit from everyday. For David Kelley, co-founder of IDEO, product design includes both artistic and functional elements. And to foster this creativity, IDEO allows its designers and engineers much freedom—its offices look like schoolrooms; employees can hang their bicycles from the ceiling; there are rubber-band fights; and on Monday mornings, there are show-and-tell sessions.

Visit IDEO's Web site (**www.ideo.com**) to view its recent inventions and innovations for clients, such as McDonald's self-ordering kiosk, the Zyliss Mandolin fruit and vegetable slicer, LifePort's kidney transporter, Pepsi's High Visibility vending machine, and Nike's all-terrain sunglasses.

Learning Objectives in Review sections are chapter summaries that group content recaps by learning objective. These summary sections are followed by a **Focus on Key Terms** listing and **Applying Marketing Knowledge** questions.

LEARNING OBJECTIVES REVIEW

LO1 Define marketing and identify the requirements for successful marketing to occur.

Marketing is the activity for creating, communicating, delivering, and exchanging offerings that benefit the organization, its stakeholders, and society at large. For marketing to occur, it is necessary to have (a) two or more parties with unmet needs, (b) a desire and ability to satisfy them, (c) communication between the parties, and (d) something to exchange.

LO2 Understand the breadth and depth of marketing.

Marketing affects every person and organization. Both for-profit and non-profit organizations perform marketing activities. They market products, services, ideas, and experiences that ben... ...ations, and countries.

LO5 Describe how a market orientation focuses on creating customer value, satisfaction, and customer relationships.

Organizations with a market orientation focus their efforts on (a) continuously collecting information about customers' needs and competitors' capabilities, (b) sharing this information throughout the organization, and (c) using the information to create value, ensure customer satisfaction, and develop customer relationships. Organizations with a market orientation engage in customer relationship management (CRM)—the process of building and developing long-term relationships with customers by delivering customer value and satisfaction. Organizations engaging CRM understand the importance of the customer lifetime value (CLV)—the profits generated by...

NEW! At the end of each chapter, **Building Your Marketing Plan** boxes guide students through the step-by-step creation of their own marketing plan.

Building Your Marketing Plan

Does your marketing plan involve reaching global customers outside of Canada? If the answer is no, read no further and do not include a global element in your plan. If the answer is yes, try to identify the following:

1. What features of your product are especially important to potential customers.

2. In which countries these potential customers live.

3. Special marketing issues that are involved in trying to reach them.

Answers to these questions will help in developing more detailed marketing mix strategies described in later chapters.

Each chapter concludes with a **Video Case** that provides an up-close look at a company example, reinforcing the chapter content while bringing the material to life. The video segments that accompany these written cases are available for viewing on *Connect*. Geek Squad, Prince Sports, Slow Cow "anti-energy" drink, and Under Armour are just a few of the exciting new Video Cases available with the Eighth Canadian Edition. Accompanying the Video Cases are updated questions, some of which require quantitative analysis.

Video Case 9

PRINCE SPORTS, INC.: TENNIS RACQUETS FOR EVERY SEGMENT

"Over the last decade we've seen a dramatic change in the media to reach consumers," says Linda Glassel, vice president of sports marketing and brand image of Prince Sports, Inc.

Prince Sports in Today's Changing World

"Today—particularly in reaching younger consumers—we're now focusing so much more on social marketing and social networks, be it Facebook, Twitter, MySpace, and internationally with Hi5, Bebo, and Orkut," she adds.

Linda Glassel's comments are a snapshot look at what Prince Sports faces in the changing world of tennis in the 2010s.

Prince Sports is a racquet sports company whose portfolio of brands includes Prince (tennis, squash, and badminton), Ektelon (racquetball), and Viking (platform/paddle tennis). Its complete line of tennis products alone is astounding: more than 150 racquet models; more than

Taming Technology to Meet Players' Needs

Every tennis player wants the same thing: to play better. But they don't all have the same skills, or the same ability to swing a racquet fast. So adult tennis players fall very broadly into three groups, each with special needs:

- *Those with shorter, slower strokes.* They want maximum power in a lightweight frame.
- *Those with moderate to full strokes.* They want the perfect blend of power and control.
- *Those with longer, faster strokes.* They want greater control with less power.

To satisfy all these needs in one racquet is a big order.

"When we design tennis racquets, it involves an extensive amount of market research on players at all levels," explains Tyler Herring, global business director for Performance Tennis Racquets. In 2005, Prince's research led it to introduce its breakthrough O³ technology. "Our O³ technology solved an inherent contradic-

INSTRUCTOR SUPPORT

Connect

Connect is a web-based assignment and assessment platform that gives students the means to better connect with their coursework, with their instructors, and with the important concepts that they will need to know for success now and in the future. *Connect* embraces diverse study behaviours and preferences with breakthrough features that help students to master course content and achieve better results. The powerful course management tool in *Connect* also offers a wide range of exclusive features that help instructors spend less time managing and more time teaching.

With *Connect*, you can deliver assignments, quizzes, and tests online. A robust set of questions, interactives, and videos are presented and tied to the textbook's learning objectives. Track individual student performance—by question, assignment, or in relation to the class overall—with detailed grade reports. Integrate grade reports easily with Learning Management Systems (LMS) such as WebCT and Blackboard. And much more.

Connect helps you teach for today's needs:

Automatic Grading
Focus on teaching instead of administrating with electronic access to the class roster and gradebook, which easily sync with your school's course management system.

Direct Textbook and Testbank Questions
Assign students online homework, and test and quiz questions with multiple problem types, and randomized question order.

Integrated eBooks
Connect directly integrates the McGraw-Hill textbooks you already use into the engaging, easy-to-use interface.

Dedicated Canadian Support and Training
The *Connect* development team and customer service groups are located in our Canadian offices and work closely together to provide expert technical support and training for both instructors and students.

Instructor Resources
Crane *Connect* is a one-stop shop for instructor resources, including the following:

- **Instructor's Manual:** The Instructor's Manual contains learning objectives, key terms, detailed lecture notes, summaries of all boxed features, as well as answers to Learning Reviews and Applying Marketing Knowledge questions.
- **PowerPoint Presentations:** These robust presentations offer high-quality visuals that bring key marketing concepts to life. Each slide is aligned with a Learning Objective from the text. **Enhanced PowerPoints,** with additional video and ad clips embedded in the presentations, are also available.
- **Visually Enhanced Computerized Test Bank:** The Test Bank contains an extensive array of multiple choice and essay questions, each aligned with a page reference, Learning Objective, and Bloom's level of learning (knowledge, comprehension, or application). **New** for this edition, the Test Bank also offers a number

of **visually enhanced questions** which include images and figures from the text-book. The computerized test bank is available through EZ Test Online—a flexible and easy-to-use electronic testing program—that allows instructors to create tests from book-specific items. EZ Test accommodates a wide range of question types and allows instructors to add their own questions. Test items are also available in Word format (rich text format).

- **Video Cases:** A unique series of 19 contemporary marketing cases, half of which are new for this edition. Each video corresponds with a chapter-specific topic and an end-of-chapter case in the text. This series is also available on DVD.
- **Alternate Cases:** A wealth of additional cases provide even more opportunities to bring course content to life for students.
- **Video Case and Alternate Case Teaching Notes:** Helpful teaching suggestions and solutions for the Video Cases and alternate cases.
- **NEW! Brief Video Clips and Discussion Questions:** This new resource is perfect for instructors who struggle to find time to play a longer video or Video Case in class. Instructors can access short (2 to 5 minutes), engaging, and current video clips, as well as suggestions for encouraging class discussion around each clip.
- **NEW! Instructor Newsletters:** Posted to *Connect* quarterly each year, these news-letters will help provide instructors with innovative teaching resources to improve student learning, offer timely marketing examples, and make class preparation time easier.
- **Instructor's Survival Kit (ISK):** Today's students are more likely to learn and be motivated by active, participative experiences than by classic classroom lecture and discussion. To illustrate marketing concepts and encourage student participation and collaboration, the Instructor's Survival Kit contains:

  - **An In-Class Activities Guide:** These activities have received extremely positive feedback from both instructors and students. In-class activities may relate to a specific Video Case or example from the Eighth Canadian Edition text.
  - **Product Props:** *Marketing,* Eighth Canadian Edition, utilizes products from both large and small companies that will interest today's students.

- **Image Library:** A digital copy of each photo, illustration, and table from the text-book, which instructors can use to create customized PowerPoint slides or design compelling course Web sites.

Superior Service

i-Learning
ADVANTAGE
McGraw-Hill Ryerson

Your **Integrated *i*Learning Sales Specialist** is a McGraw-Hill Ryerson representative who has the experience, product knowledge, training, and support to help you assess and integrate all of the *Marketing* supplements, technology, and services into your course for optimum teaching and learning performance. Whether it's using our test bank software, helping your students improve their grades, or putting your entire course online, your *i*Learning Sales Specialist is there to help you do it. Contact your local *i*Learning Sales Specialist today to learn how to maximize all of McGraw-Hill Ryerson's resources!

*i*learning Services Program

McGraw-Hill Ryerson offers a unique *i*Services package designed for Canadian faculty. Our mission is to equip providers of higher education with superior tools and resources required for excellence in teaching. For additional information, visit www.mcgrawhill.ca/highereducation/iservices.

Teaching & Learning Conference Series

The educational environment has changed tremendously in recent years, and McGraw-Hill Ryerson continues to be committed to helping you acquire the skills you need to succeed in this new milieu. Our innovative Teaching & Learning Conference Series brings faculty together from across Canada with 3M Teaching Excellence award winners to share teaching and learning best practices in a collaborative and stimulating environment. Pre-conference workshops on general topics, such as teaching large classes and technology integration, are also offered. We will also work with you at your own institution to customize workshops that best suit the needs of your faculty at your institution.

Coursesmart

CourseSmart brings together thousands of textbooks across hundreds of courses in an eTextbook format, providing unique benefits to students and faculty. By purchasing an eTextbook, students can save up to 50 percent on the cost of a print textbook, reduce their impact on the environment, and gain access to powerful Web tools for learning including full-text search, notes and highlighting, and email tools for sharing notes between classmates. For faculty, CourseSmart provides instant access for reviewing and comparing textbooks and course materials in their discipline area without the time, cost, and environmental impact of mailing print exam copies. For further details contact your *i*Learning Sales Specialist or go to **www.coursesmart.com.**

Create Online

McGraw-Hill's Create Online gives you access to the most abundant resource at your fingertips—literally. With a few mouse clicks, you can create customized learning tools simply and affordably. McGraw-Hill Ryerson has included many of our market-leading textbooks within Create Online for eBook and print customization as well as many licensed readings and cases. For more information, go to www.mcgrawhillcreate.com.

STUDENT SUPPORT

Connect for Students

Connect provides students with a powerful tool for improving academic performance and truly mastering course material, plus 24/7 online access to an interactive and searchable eBook. Connect allows students to practise important skills at their own pace and on their own schedule. Importantly, students' assessment results and instructors' feedback are all saved online—so students can continually review their progress and plot their course to success.

ACKNOWLEDGMENTS

To ensure continuous improvement of our product, we have utilized an extensive review and development process for each of our editions. Building on that history, the Eighth Canadian Edition development process included several phases of evaluation by a broad panel of instructors. Reviewers who were vital in helping us develop this edition include:

Rick Appleby, *Okanagan College*
David Aves, *Georgian College*
Marc Boivin, *University of Calgary*
Brian Broadway, *Seneca College*
Brock Cordes, *University of Manitoba*
Rita Cossa, *McMaster University*
George Dracopolous, *Vanier College*
Armand Gervais, *Ryerson University*
Tina Grant, *Durham College*
Bob Graves, *Grant MacEwan University*
Makarand Gulawani, *Grant MacEwan University*
Dwight Heinrichs, *University of Regina*
Charles Hendriks, *York University*
Marion Hill, *Southern Alberta Institute of Technology*
Marina Jaffey, *Camosun College*
Laurie Jensen, *Mount Royal University*
Michael Johnson, *triOS College*
Melanie Lang, *University of Guelph*
Irene Lu, *Carleton University*
Zhenfeng Ma, *University of Ontario Institute of Technology*
Michael Madore, *University of Lethbridge*
Sherry McEvoy, *Fanshawe College*
Barry Mills, *College of the North Atlantic*
David Moulton, *Douglas College*
Leighann Neilson, *Carleton University*
Richard Patterson, *York University*
Brent Pearce, *Concordia University*
Keith Penhall, *Red River College*
Peter Popkowski-Leszcyc, *University of Alberta*
Diana Serafini, *Dawson College*
Janice Shearer, *Mohawk College*
Robert Soroka, *Dawson College*
Donna Stapleton, *Memorial University of Newfoundland*
Trent Tucker, *University of Waterloo*
Barb Watts, *Georgian College*
Michael Wile, *Nova Scotia Community College*

The preceding list demonstrates the amount of feedback and developmental input that went into this project; we are deeply grateful to the numerous people who have shared their ideas with us.

Thanks are due to John Shepherd of Kwantlen Polytechnic University for his contribution to the text (Appendix A). Many businesspeople and organizations also provided substantial assistance in making available information that appears in the text and supplements. Thanks to Joscelyn Chernick-Smith, Communications Advisor, Canadian Tire Corporation; Jill Skene, IGLOO Software; Wildplay Element Parks; and Cooler Solutions.

Finally, we acknowledge the professional efforts of the McGraw-Hill Ryerson Higher Education Group staff. Completion of this edition and its many supplements required the attention and commitment of many editorial, production, marketing, and research personnel. Thanks to Leanna MacLean, Executive Sponsoring Editor; Joy Armitage Taylor, Senior Marketing Manager; Cathy Biribauer, Supervising Editor; Mike Kelly, Copy Editor; and Tracy Leonard, Photo and Permissions Researcher. Finally, I really want to thank my Developmental Editor, Jennifer Cressman, for her dedication, patience, professionalism, and good humour.

I am responsible for the Canadianization of this text, so any questions or concerns about the book should be directed to me. I would like to thank my co-authors for their input, encouragement, and continued support.

I want to thank my wife Doreen, and my daughters Erinn, Jacquelyn, and Brenna, for their love and support. I love each of you so much. I also want to thank my faithful and wonderful buds, Ciara and Dex. Lastly, I want to thank my parents for their love and support.

Frederick G. Crane

Marketing: Customer Value, Satisfaction, Relationships, and Experiences

WILDPLAY ELEMENT PARKS: ACTIVE ADVENTURE EXPERIENCES AWAIT YOU!

Looking for an adventure? A thrilling experience? Well, Wild-Play Element Parks offers you what they call "Primal Fun and Games." WildPlay is a full-service outdoor adventure company offering customers bungee jumping, the King Swing, aerial adventure tree courses, and zip-line rides. This young, entrepreneurial start-up is capitalizing on major consumer trends: customer desire for personal and memorable experiences and customer desire to reconnect with nature.

WildPlay was started in September 2005 by two certified climbing guides, Gordon Ross and Tom Benson. These entrepreneurs spent more than 15 years leading climbing adventures and connecting people to the great outdoors. As certified climbing instructors and paragliders, both had been thinking of ways to use the power of the group experience to introduce more people to outdoor adventure activities. Additionally, the steep learning curve and high level of commitment for adventures such as climbing was a deterrent for some people and intimidating for others. Gord had discovered tree-to-tree parks during his travels to Europe and South America and was researching them with Tom as a way to deliver the outdoor experience to a broader range of people. Both recognized that this type of park would be an excellent way to realize their desire of bringing outdoor experiences to more people without the steep learning curve.

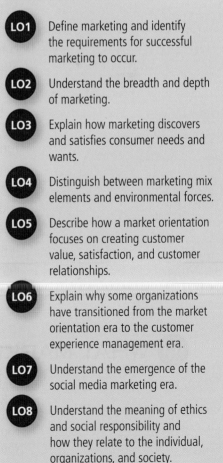

learning objectives

After reading this chapter, you should be able to:

LO1 Define marketing and identify the requirements for successful marketing to occur.

LO2 Understand the breadth and depth of marketing.

LO3 Explain how marketing discovers and satisfies consumer needs and wants.

LO4 Distinguish between marketing mix elements and environmental forces.

LO5 Describe how a market orientation focuses on creating customer value, satisfaction, and customer relationships.

LO6 Explain why some organizations have transitioned from the market orientation era to the customer experience management era.

LO7 Understand the emergence of the social media marketing era.

LO8 Understand the meaning of ethics and social responsibility and how they relate to the individual, organizations, and society.

Currently, WildPlay Element Parks have four locations. At WildPlay Nanaimo you can experience a world famous bungee jump, play in the trees (Monkido aerial adventure courses), soar on a canyon zip-line, or take the ride of your life on the King Swing. At WildPlay Whistler you can ride the ZOOM Zip Lines or experience Monkido. At WildPlay West Shore Victoria you can experience the Monkido-elevated obstacle courses in a beautiful forest suspended in the trees! And the company's newest park, WildPlay Maple Ridge, also offers the Monkido experience.

WildPlay targets corporate groups seeking team-building activities, private groups looking for group fun, and school and youth groups looking for adventurous field trips. It also targets consumers looking to host unique birthday parties and other special events. And you can have a permanent record of your adventure that includes a video recording of your bungee jump on CD-ROM!

WildPlay is also committed to the environment and to its communities. The activities the parks offer to its customers are built using environmentally sensitive methods that mitigate harm to the forest or other natural settings. The company also has a community outreach program that supports groups that promote physical fitness activities and the protection of the natural environment. The company is obviously striking a chord with customers. For example, already close to 200,000 people have taken the bungee plunge and over 100,000 have challenged themselves on the Monkido courses! And the company's intent is to continue growth through franchise opportunities across North America![1]

Marketing affects all individuals, all organizations, all industries, all countries, and our natural environment. This text seeks not only to teach you marketing concepts but also to demonstrate marketing's many applications and how it affects our lives. This knowledge should make you a better consumer, enable you to be a more informed and responsible citizen, and even help you in your career.

In this chapter and those that follow, you will feel the excitement of marketing. You will be introduced to the dynamic changes that will affect all of us in the future, and you will also meet many men and women whose marketing creativity sometimes achieved brilliant, extraordinary results. And who knows? Somewhere in these pages you may even find a career in marketing. For example, perhaps your future may involve sales for a large corporation, conducting marketing research in a consulting company, preparing advertising plans in an advertising firm, or maybe even starting your own business! You can find plenty of marketing career options by reading the "Planning a Career in Marketing" Appendix available on *Connect*™.

LO1   WHAT MARKETING IS AND WHAT IT IS NOT

Right now, we want you to take your very first marketing test. We know you are probably saying, "What a way to start off the book!" But do not get too stressed out. There is just one question, and it is the only time that we will ever ask you "not" to think before you answer. Quickly and honestly, what is the first word that comes to your mind when you hear the word "marketing"?

We are going to make an educated guess and predict that most of you will answer "advertising," "selling," or "common sense." In our classes, we have asked thousands of other students this same question and have found these to be the most typical answers. But *marketing is not advertising*. Although advertising is one of the most visible aspects of marketing, it is but one small element of marketing. *Marketing is not selling*. In fact, many marketing experts believe that effective marketing can reduce the need for selling.

Marketing is not merely common sense. While good marketers are sensible, perceptive, and intuitive, these traits alone are not sufficient for making successful marketing decisions. Effective marketing requires intimate knowledge and understanding of consumers and the marketplace, which goes beyond simple common sense.

We are very much aware of the misconceptions about marketing, including many negative ones. But marketing is not hucksterism; it is not about selling unwanted things and taking the customer's money. Nor is marketing about manipulating, fooling, or tricking the customer.[2] Therefore, in order to appreciate marketing fully, you need to understand what it is and what it is not.

Marketing: Defined

marketing
The activity for creating, communicating, delivering, and exchanging offerings that benefit the organization, its stakeholders, and society at large.

The American Marketing Association, the professional body representing marketers in Canada, the United States, and other countries around the world, states that **marketing** is the activity for creating, communicating, delivering, and exchanging offerings that benefit the organization, its stakeholders, and society at large.[3] This definition stresses the importance of delivering genuine benefits in the offerings of goods, services, ideas, and experiences marketed to customers. Also, note that the organization doing the marketing, the stakeholders affected (such as customers, employees, suppliers, and shareholders), and society should all benefit.

To serve both buyers and sellers, marketing seeks (1) to discover the needs and wants of prospective customers, and (2) to satisfy them. These prospective customers include both individuals buying for themselves or their households and organizations that buy for their own use (such as manufacturers) or for resale (such as wholesalers and retailers). You will also soon discover that marketing uses a number of terms and concepts that you'll have to know in order to truly understand marketing. For help, complete the "Going Online" exercise below.

Requirements for Marketing to Occur

For marketing to occur, at least four factors are required: (1) two or more parties (individuals or organizations) with unsatisfied needs, (2) a desire and ability on their part to be satisfied, (3) a way for the parties to communicate, and (4) something to exchange.

Going Online

Understanding Marketing: Terms and Concepts

Marketing uses a number of terms and concepts that are often difficult to remember. But the American Marketing Association is a valuable source of information on marketing. In fact, on its Web site, the AMA actually has a comprehensive dictionary containing over 4,000 marketing terms and concepts.

Go to **www.marketingpower.com** (the AMA's official Web site) and look for the Dictionary in the site's Resource Library. Search for key terms and concepts that are of interest to you. This exercise should prove invaluable to you as you attempt to gain a better understanding of the marketing discipline. There are also a number of provincial chapters of the AMA in Canada. You may also wish to check out their Web sites for the latest marketing news in Canada.

Two or More Parties with Unsatisfied Needs Suppose you have developed an unmet need—a desire for information about how computer and telecommunications are interacting to reshape the workplace—but you did not yet know that *Computer-World* magazine existed. Also unknown to you was that several copies of *Computer-World* were sitting on the magazine rack at your nearest bookstore, waiting to be purchased. This is an example of two parties with unmet needs: you, with a need for technology-related information, and your bookstore owner, needing someone to buy a copy of *ComputerWorld.*

Desire and Ability to Satisfy These Needs Both you and the bookstore owner want to satisfy these unmet needs. Furthermore, you have the money to buy the item and the time to get to the bookstore. The store's owner has not only the desire to sell *ComputerWorld* but also the ability to do so, since it is stocked on the shelves.

A Way for the Parties to Communicate The marketing transaction of buying a copy of *ComputerWorld* will never occur unless you know the product exists and its location. Similarly, the store owner will not stock the magazine unless there is a market of potential buyers nearby. When you receive a free sample in the mail or see the magazine on display in the bookstore, this communications barrier between you (the buyer) and your bookstore (the seller) is overcome.

Something to Exchange Marketing occurs when the transaction takes place and both the buyer and seller exchange something of value. In this case, you exchange your money for the bookstore's magazine. Both you and the bookstore have gained something and also given up something, but you are both better off because you have each satisfied your unmet needs. You have the opportunity to read *ComputerWorld,* but you gave up some money; the store gave up the magazine but received money, which enables it to remain in business. This exchange process and, of course, the ethical and legal foundations of exchange are central to marketing.

LO2 The Breadth and Depth of Marketing

Marketing today affects every person and organization. To understand this, let us analyze (1) what a market is, (2) who markets, (3) what they market, (4) who buys and uses what is marketed, and (5) who benefits from these marketing activities.

market
People with the desire and ability to buy a specific product.

What Is a Market? A **market** is people with the desire and ability to buy a specific product. All markets ultimately are people. Even when we say a firm bought a photocopier, we mean one or several people in the firm decided to buy it. People who are aware of their unmet needs may have the desire to buy the product, but that alone is not sufficient. People must also have the ability to buy, that is, have the authority, time, and money. People may even "buy" an idea that results in an action, such as having their blood pressure checked or turning down their thermostats to save energy.

Who Markets? Every organization markets! It is obvious that business firms involved in manufacturing (McCain Foods, General Motors of Canada, Ericsson Canada), retailing (Canadian Tire, Modrobes, The Bay), and providing services (Canadian Broadcasting Corporation, Air Canada, Via Rail, Vancouver Canucks, Scotia iTRADE.com) market their offerings. Today, many other types of marketing are also popular. For example, non-profit organizations (Winnipeg Ballet, Canadian Red Cross, Canadian Museum of Civilization, Toronto Zoo) also engage in marketing.[4] Your college or university probably has a marketing program to attract students, faculty members, and donations. Places (cities, provinces, countries) often use marketing efforts to attract tourists, conventions, or businesses. In Manitoba, for example, there is a marketing campaign called Spirited Energy designed to persuade tourists to visit the province and to convince businesses to locate there. Organizations associated

Marketing is used by non-profit organizations, causes, and places.

with special events or causes use marketing to inform and influence a target audience. These marketing activities range from government agencies such as WorkSafeBC encouraging young college and university students to keep safe in the workplace, to non-profit organizations such as the Girl Guides of Canada and 4-H Clubs of Canada using marketing to attract new members. Finally, individuals, such as politicians like Stephen Harper, often use marketing to gain attention and voter preference.

What Is Marketed?   Goods, services, ideas, and experiences are marketed. *Goods* are physical objects, such as Crest toothpaste, Nikon cameras, or Apple computers, that satisfy consumer needs. *Services* are activities, deeds, or other basic intangibles, such as airline trips on WestJet airlines, financial advice from TD Waterhouse, or long-distance telephone calls offered by the Telus Group. *Ideas* are intangibles involving thoughts about actions or causes, such as donating to the Salvation Army or to the Trans Canada Trail project. Experiences are also marketed; personal and memorable experiences such as your zip-line ride at Wildplay Element Parks!

The use of idea marketing has grown significantly over the past three decades, in particular, idea marketing that focuses on enhancing social ends is a prevalent part of today's marketplace. This is referred to as social marketing. **Social marketing** is designed to influence the behaviour of individuals by which benefits accrue to those individuals or to society in general and not to the marketer.[5] Antismoking campaigns by Health Canada or the Canadian Cancer Society are examples of social marketing. Social marketing can be conducted by for-profit and non-profit organizations or by individuals. For example, the Heart and Stroke Foundation of Nova Scotia has a social marketing campaign encouraging Nova Scotians to walk in order to improve their health. Even your friend's attempt to influence you to eat a more healthy diet could be considered social marketing. And, as we discuss later in the chapter, many marketers are now engaged in creating and delivering experiences to customers. In fact, even companies that market traditional goods and services are also now engaging in the practice of customer experience management—focusing on ensuring that your shopping experience with them is positive and satisfying and goes beyond the mere act of acquiring a new good or service.

Who Buys and Uses What Is Marketed?   Both individuals and organizations buy and use goods and services that are marketed. **Ultimate consumers** are people—whether 80 years or 8 months old—who use the goods and services purchased for a household. In contrast, **organizational buyers** are units, such as manufacturers,

social marketing
Marketing designed to influence the behaviour of individuals in which the benefits of the behaviour accrue to those individuals or to the society in general and not to the marketer.

ultimate consumers
People—whether 80 years or 8 months old—who use the goods and services purchased for a household.

organizational buyers
Those manufacturers, wholesalers, retailers, and government agencies that buy goods and services for their own use or for resale.

retailers, or government agencies, that buy goods and services for their own use or for resale. Although the terms *consumers, buyers,* and *customers* are sometimes used for both ultimate consumers and organizations, there is no consistency on this. In this book, you will be able to tell from the example whether the buyers are ultimate consumers, organizations, or both.

Who Benefits?   In our free-enterprise society, there are three specific groups that benefit from effective marketing: consumers who buy, organizations that sell, and society as a whole. True competition among products and services in the marketplace ensures that we as Canadian consumers can find value from the best products, the lowest prices, or exceptional service. Providing choices leads to consumer satisfaction and the quality of life that we have come to expect from our Canadian economic system.

Organizations that provide need-satisfying products combined with effective marketing programs—for example, McDonald's Restaurants, Tim Hortons, IBM Canada, and Microsoft Canada—have blossomed. But competition creates problems for ineffective competitors, and hundreds of Canadian businesses fail every year. Effective marketing actions result in rewards for organizations that serve customers and in thousands of marketing jobs for individuals all across the country.

Finally, effective marketing benefits society. It enhances competition, which, in turn, both improves the quality of products and services and lowers their prices. This makes countries more competitive in world markets and provides jobs and a higher standard of living for their citizens.

The Diverse Factors Influencing Marketing Activities

Although an organization's marketing activity focuses on assessing and satisfying consumer needs, countless other people, groups, and forces interact to shape the nature of its activities (Figure 1–1). Foremost is the organization itself, whose mission and

● **FIGURE 1–1**

An organization marketing department relates to many people, groups, and forces

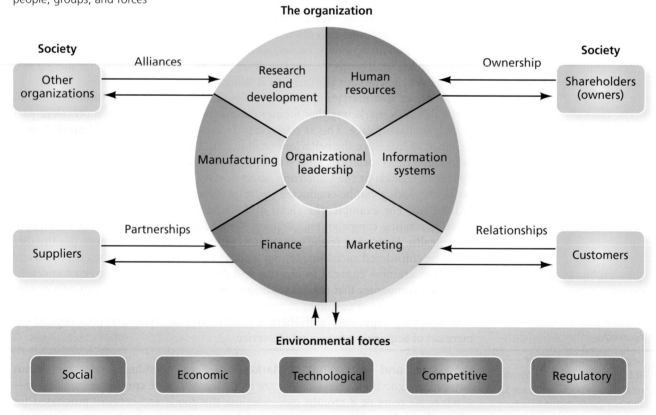

objectives determine what business it is in and what goals it seeks. Within the organization, organizational leaders are responsible for establishing these goals. And the marketing department works closely with a network of other departments and employees to help provide the customer-satisfying products required for the organization to survive and prosper.

Figure 1–1 also shows the key people, groups, and forces outside the organization that influence marketing activities. The marketing department is responsible for facilitating relationships, partnerships, and alliances with the organization's customers, its shareholders (or often representatives of groups served by a non-profit organization), its suppliers, and other organizations. Environmental forces, such as social, technological, economic, competitive, and regulatory factors, also shape an organization's marketing activities. Finally, an organization's marketing decisions are affected by and, in turn, often have an important impact on society as a whole.

The organization must strike a continual balance among the sometimes differing interests of these individuals and groups. For example, it is not possible to simultaneously provide the lowest-priced and highest-quality products to customers and pay the highest prices to suppliers, highest wages to employees, and maximum dividends to shareholders.

---

learning review

1. What is marketing?

2. Marketing focuses on _____ and _____ prospective customers' needs and wants.

3. What four factors are needed for marketing to occur?

LO3 HOW MARKETING DISCOVERS AND SATISFIES CONSUMER NEEDS

The importance of discovering and satisfying consumer needs is so critical to understanding marketing that we look at each of these two steps in detail next.

Discovering Consumer Needs

The first objective in marketing is discovering the needs of prospective customers. Sound simple? Well, it is not. In the abstract, discovering needs looks easy, but when you get down to the specifics of marketing, things can be difficult, and things can go wrong. For one thing, consumers may not always know or be able to describe what they need and want. And, as we will see later, in the case of high-technology, or new-to-world products, consumers may have no idea about how they might benefit from such products. So, even listening to customers to discover their needs does not ensure marketing success. In fact, new product development experts estimate up to 94 percent of the more than 30,000 new consumable products (food, beverage, health, beauty, and other household and pet products) introduced in North America annually do not succeed in the long run. Robert M. McMath, who has studied over 70,000 of these new-product launches, has two key suggestions to marketers: (1) focus on what the customer benefit is, and (2) learn from the past.[6]

The solution to preventing new product failures does seem embarrassingly obvious. First, find out what consumers need and want. Second, produce what they need and want, and do not produce what they do not need or want. This is far more difficult than it sounds. For example, let us look at why Coca-Cola's C2 failed. Coca-Cola spent more than $50 million to launch C2, a reduced-carb cola that still contained

Why did Coca-Cola's C2 fail? See the section "Discovering Consumer Needs."

some sugar to add taste. The company's biggest new product since Diet Coke two decades earlier, C2 was targeted to 20- to 40-year-old customers wanting some sugar in their cola while also watching calories. C2 was also sometimes priced 60 percent higher at retail than Coke, a significant issue to buyers. But the big showstopper: Many cola drinkers were disappointed in C2's taste, complaining it was flat or had an unpleasant taste![7] Firms spend billions of dollars annually on marketing and research that reduces, but does not eliminate, product failure. So meeting the needs and wants of consumers is a continuing challenge for firms.

Consumer Needs and Consumer Wants   Should marketing try to satisfy consumer needs or consumer wants? The answer is both! Heated debates rage over this question, with regard to the definitions of needs and wants and the amount of freedom given to prospective customers to make their own buying decisions.

A *need* occurs when a person feels physiologically deprived of basic necessities, such as food, clothing, and shelter. A want is a felt need that is shaped by a person's knowledge, culture, and personality. So, if you feel hungry, you have developed a basic need and desire to eat something. Let us say you then want to eat an apple or a chocolate bar because, based on your past experience and personal tastes, you know these will satisfy your hunger need. Effective marketing, in the form of creating an awareness of good products at convenient locations, can clearly shape a person's wants.

At issue is whether marketing persuades prospective customers to buy the "wrong" things—say, a chocolate bar rather than an apple to satisfy hunger pangs. Certainly, marketing tries to influence what we buy. A question then arises: at what point do we want government and society to step in to protect consumers? Most consumers would say they want government to protect us from harmful drugs and unsafe cars, but what about chocolate bars, cereals, and soft drinks? Another issue is whether marketing really makes us materialistic and desire things that we really can live without. Sometimes there are no clear-cut answers when it comes to the issue of what should be marketed, how it should be marketed, and importantly, to whom it should be marketed. This debate is most acute when it comes to marketing to children. Read the Making Responsible Decisions box on page 12, "Marketing to Canadian Children."[8] What do you think?

As shown in Figure 1–2, discovering needs involves looking carefully at prospective customers, whether they are children buying M&Ms, university or college students buying Apple iPods, or firms buying new laser printers. Principal activities of a

● **FIGURE 1–2**

Marketing's first task: discovering consumer needs

firm's marketing department are to scrutinize its consumers carefully to understand what they need, to study industry trends, to examine competitors' products, and even to analyze the needs of a customer's customer.

Satisfying Consumer Needs

target market
One or more specific groups of potential consumers toward which an organization directs its marketing program.

Marketing does not stop with the discovery of consumer needs. Because the organization obviously cannot satisfy all consumer needs, it must concentrate its efforts on certain needs of a specific group of potential consumers. This is the **target market**—one or more specific groups of potential consumers toward which an organization directs its marketing program.

LO4   **The Four Ps: Controllable Marketing Mix Factors**   Having selected the target market consumers, the firm must take steps to satisfy their needs. Someone in the organization's marketing department, often the marketing manager, must take action and develop a complete marketing program that creates, communicates, and delivers value to a target market. This happens through the use of a combination of four tools, often called the four Ps—a useful shorthand reference to them first published by Professor E. Jerome McCarthy:[9]

- *Product.* A good, service, or idea to satisfy the consumer's needs.
- *Price.* What is exchanged for the product.
- *Promotion.* A means of communication between the seller and buyer.
- *Place.* A means of getting the product into the consumer's hands.

marketing mix
The marketing manager's controllable factors; the marketing actions of product, price, promotion, and place that he or she can take to create, communicate, and deliver value.

We will define each of the four Ps more carefully later in the book, but for now, it is important to remember that they are the elements of the marketing mix, or simply the **marketing mix.** These are the marketing manager's controllable factors, the marketing actions of product, price, promotion, and place that he or she can take to create, communicate, and deliver value. The marketing mix elements are called controllable factors because they are under the control of the marketing department in an organization.

environmental forces
The uncontrollable factors involving social, economic, technological, competitive, and regulatory forces.

The Uncontrollable, Environmental Forces   There are a host of factors largely beyond the control of the marketing department and its organization. These forces can be placed into five groups (as shown in Figure 1–1): social, economic, technological, competitive, and regulatory forces. Examples are what consumers themselves want and need, changing technology, the state of the economy in terms of whether it is expanding or contracting, actions that competitors take, and government restrictions. These are the **environmental forces** in a marketing decision, the uncontrollable factors involving social, economic, technological, competitive, and regulatory forces. These five forces may serve as accelerators or brakes on marketing, sometimes expanding an organization's marketing opportunities and other times restricting them. These five environmental forces are covered in Chapter 3.

Traditionally, many marketing executives have treated these environmental forces as rigid, absolute constraints that are entirely outside their influence. Accordingly, some executives simply fail to anticipate and respond to these environmental forces. But recent studies have shown that forward-looking, action-oriented firms can take advantage of changes in the marketing environment by aligning their organizations to capitalize on such changes by introducing new technologies or competitive breakthroughs.

But Wait, What About High-Technology or New-to-World Products?   The conventional marketing process of discovering and satisfying customer needs really works well in most cases. But it does not work so well with high-technology or new-to-world products.[10] Henry Ford, famous automobile pioneer, once said, "If I asked

Making Responsible Decisions

Marketing to Canadian Children

Some experts are concerned about the effects marketing might have on Canadian children. They suggest that marketing can create excessive materialism and breed feelings of narcissism, entitlement, and dissatisfaction in today's kids. Besides attempting to make children creatures of consumption, many experts also argue that marketers may be harming the health of children. But kids represent an important target to marketers because they have their own purchasing power, they influence their parents' buying decisions, and they become the adult consumers of the future.

Some accuse marketers of encouraging kids to use "pester power"—nagging their parents into purchasing items they may not otherwise buy. Others suggest that marketers actively communicate with children hoping to develop lifetime relationships with them. According to some research, babies as young as six months of age can form mental images of corporate logos and mascots, and brand loyalties can be established as early as age two. While fast food, toy, and clothing companies have been doing this for years, adult-oriented businesses such as banks and automakers are now getting in on the act. For example, automakers actually advertise their products during children's shows on Saturday morning television. And magazines such as *Time*, *Sports Illustrated*, and *People* have all launched kid and teen editions—which feature ads for adult-related products such as minivans, hotels, and airlines.

Marketers also reach out to children on the Internet. The Internet is often part of the daily lives of children. And, unlike broadcast media, which have codes regarding marketing to kids, the Internet is totally unregulated. Moreover, sophisticated technologies make it easy to collect information from young people for marketing research, and to target individual children with personalized advertising. By creating engaging, interactive environments based on products and brand names, companies can build brand loyalties from an early age.

To market children effectively, some marketers hire researchers and psychologists to determine what makes kids tick. Marketers now have access to in-depth knowledge about children's developmental, emotional, and social needs at different ages. Using research that analyzes children's behaviour, fantasy lives, art work, and even dreams, companies are able to craft sophisticated marketing strategies to reach young people.

In addition to these concerns, many experts argue that marketers are also harming the health of children by encouraging them to consume the wrong products. The Canadian Paediatric Society suggests that the marketing of fast food, soft drinks, and candy to children has created a nation of overweight children. According to the Heart and Stroke Foundation of Canada, almost one in four Canadian children between the ages of 7 and 12 is obese.

Many Canadians are demanding restrictions on marketing to children. The Canadian Marketing Association has a code of ethics and guidelines regarding marketing to children, but many believe this does not go far enough. There are calls, for example, to ban all advertising to children. The province of Quebec has already responded with some restrictions, banning print and broadcast advertising aimed at kids under the age of 13. What is your opinion on marketing to children? What kind of restrictions should there be, if any?

the customer what they really wanted, they'd have said a faster horse!" Basically, Ford is telling marketers that when you try to discover what customers want, they will often simply ask for better versions of existing products that they already buy from you. But this approach will not help marketers who wish to produce breakthrough innovations. In essence, conventional marketing focuses on fulfilling existing market needs and not on new market creation. High-technology or new-to-world products are radically different and sometimes beyond the imagination of the customers. Often customers really do not recognize that they need or want such innovative products.

So marketers of high-technology or new-to-world products really have no market at the time of invention. But new inventions can and do create new markets and new industries. For example, the invention of the semiconductor created the computer industry in all its forms, while geneticists have created an entirely new biotechnology marketplace. Therefore, you should remember that if you wish to create something totally radical, existing customers using existing products are seldom going to be of any assistance to you. There may be no ready market for your invention, and you may never be successful in creating one. But if you do develop something that is better than all the existing technologies or products currently available, then you might become the next Henry Ford, or Bill Gates, or Steve Jobs!

● **FIGURE 1-3**
Marketing's second task:
satisfying consumer needs

The Marketing Program

Effective relationship marketing strategies help marketing managers discover what prospective customers need. They must translate this information into some concepts for products the firm might develop (Figure 1–3). These concepts must then be converted into a tangible **marketing program**—a plan that integrates the marketing mix to provide a good, service, or idea to prospective buyers. These prospects then react to the offering favourably (by buying) or unfavourably (by not buying), and the process is repeated. As shown in Figure 1–3, in an effective organization this process is continuous: consumer needs trigger product concepts that are translated into actual products that stimulate further discovery of consumer needs.

marketing program
A plan that integrates the marketing mix to provide a good, service, or idea to prospective buyers.

A Marketing Program for WildPlay Element Parks

To see some specifics of an actual marketing program, let us return to the earlier example of WildPlay Element Parks and its goal to offer outdoor experiences to its customers.[11] Figure 1–4 shows the basic features of WildPlay's marketing program.

---

learning review

4. An organization cannot satisfy the needs of all consumers, and so it must focus on one or more subgroups, which are its _____.

5. What are the four marketing mix elements that make up the organization's marketing program?

6. What are uncontrollable variables?

HOW MARKETING BECAME SO IMPORTANT

Marketing is a driving force in the modern global economy. To understand why this is so and some related ethical aspects, let us look at the (1) evolution of businesses from the production era to the customer experience management era, and (2) ethics and social responsibility in marketing.

● **FIGURE 1–4**
Marketing program for
WildPlay Element Parks

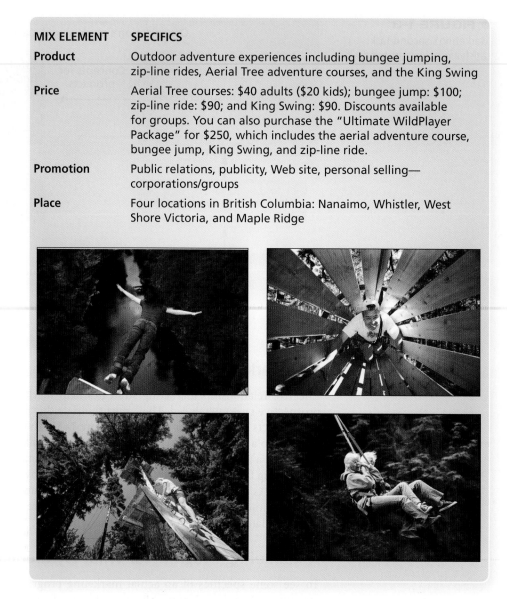

MIX ELEMENT	SPECIFICS
Product	Outdoor adventure experiences including bungee jumping, zip-line rides, Aerial Tree adventure courses, and the King Swing
Price	Aerial Tree courses: $40 adults ($20 kids); bungee jump: $100; zip-line ride: $90; and King Swing: $90. Discounts available for groups. You can also purchase the "Ultimate WildPlayer Package" for $250, which includes the aerial adventure course, bungee jump, King Swing, and zip-line ride.
Promotion	Public relations, publicity, Web site, personal selling—corporations/groups
Place	Four locations in British Columbia: Nanaimo, Whistler, West Shore Victoria, and Maple Ridge

Evolution of North American Businesses

Many organizations have experienced distinct stages in the life of their firms. We can use Pillsbury, now part of General Mills, and General Electric as examples.

Production Era   Goods were scarce in the early years in North America, and so buyers were willing to accept virtually any goods that were produced and make do with them as best they could. The central notion was that products would sell themselves, and so the major concern of business firms was production, not marketing. Robert Keith, a Pillsbury president, described his company at this stage: "We are professional flour millers. . . . Our basic function is to mill quality flour."[12] As shown in Figure 1–5, this production era generally continued through the 1920s.

Sales Era   About that time, many firms discovered that they could produce more goods than their regular buyers could consume. Competition grew. The usual solution was to hire more salespeople to find new buyers. Pillsbury's philosophy at this stage was summed up simply by Keith: "We must hire salespersons to sell it [the flour]

● **FIGURE 1-5**

Six different orientations in the history of North American business

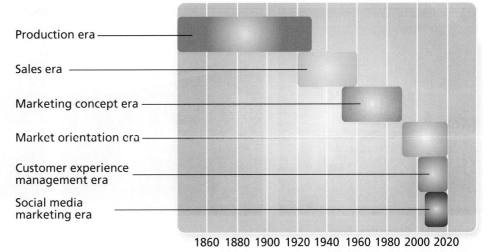

just as we hire accountants to keep our books." The role of the Pillsbury salesforce was simply to find consumers for the goods that the firm could produce best. This sales era continued into the 1950s for Pillsbury and into the 1960s for many other firms (see Figure 1-5).

Marketing Concept Era   In the 1960s, marketing became the motivating force among many firms. Then the policy became, "We are in the business of satisfying needs and wants of consumers." This is really a brief statement of what has come to be known as the **marketing concept,** which is the idea that an organization should strive to satisfy the needs of consumers, while also trying to achieve the organization's goals.

The statement of a firm's commitment to satisfying consumer wants and needs that probably launched the marketing concept appeared in a 1952 annual report of General Electric:[13] "The concept introduces . . . marketing . . . at the beginning rather than the end of the production cycle and integrates marketing into each phase of the business." This statement emphasizes that marketing ideas are fed into the production cycle from *after* an item is produced to *before* it is designed. Clearly, the marketing concept is a focus on the consumer. Unfortunately, many companies found that actually implementing the concept was very difficult.

LO5   **Market Orientation Era**   Many organizations transitioned from the marketing concept era to the market orientation era. Firms with a **market orientation** focus their efforts on (1) continuously collecting information about customers' needs and competitors' capabilities, (2) sharing this information throughout the organization, and (3) using the information to create value, ensure customer satisfaction, and develop customer relationships.

Customer value is defined as the unique combination of benefits received by the customer that include quality, price, convenience, on-time delivery, and both before-sale and after-sale service. As we point out in Chapter 5, Canadians are becoming increasingly value conscious, and Canadian companies are attempting to provide unique value that they alone can deliver to their targeted markets. This unique customer value can come in the form of best price, best product, best service, or as you will see later, the best customer experience.[14] For example, Walmart attempts to offer its customers the best price, Starbucks claims to offer its customers the best product, and Canadian Tire delivers value through exceptional customer service.

When customers believe they have received good value, they tend to be satisfied with their providers. **Customer satisfaction** is the match between customer expectations of the product and the product's actual performance. This is an important measure of the ability of a firm to successfully meet the needs of the customer. If the

---

marketing concept
The idea that an organization should strive to satisfy the needs of consumers, while also trying to achieve the organization's goals.

market orientation
Focusing efforts on (1) continuously collecting information about customers' needs and competitors' capabilities, (2) sharing this information throughout the organization, and (3) using the information to create value, ensure customer satisfaction, and develop customer relationships.

customer value
The unique combination of benefits received by the customer that include quality, price, convenience, on-time delivery, and both before-sale and after-sale service.

customer satisfaction
The match between customer expectations of the product and the product's actual performance.

What type of value do these firms offer their customers? See the text.

customer relationship management (CRM)
The process of building and developing long-term relationships with customers by delivering customer value and satisfaction.

customer lifetime value (CLV)
The profit generated by the customer's purchase of an organization's product or service over the customer's lifetime.

eCRM
A Web-centric, personalized approach to managing long-term customer relationships electronically.

interactive marketing
Involves two-way buyer–seller electronic communication in which the buyer can control the kind and amount of information received from the seller.

product fails to meet the customer's expectations, the customer will be dissatisfied. If the product performance matches expectations, the customer is satisfied. If the performance exceeds the customer's expectations, the customer is likely to be highly satisfied. Recent research involving successful Canadian and American entrepreneurs revealed that customer satisfaction is an important ingredient for the long-term success of businesses. Moreover, this same research found that customer value and satisfaction are critical for an organization in order to develop ongoing customer relationships.[15]

Therefore, it is not surprising that organizations with a market orientation actually engage in **customer relationship management (CRM)**—the process of building and developing long-term relationships with customers by delivering customer value and satisfaction. CRM involves the use of relationship-centric strategies to optimize the long-term value of an organization's selected customers. Retaining customers over time, or managing the entire customer life cycle, is a cost-effective way for firms to grow in competitive markets. Organizations engaging in CRM understand the importance of the lifetime value of a customer, not just single transactions. **Customer lifetime value (CLV)** is the profit generated by the customer's purchase of an organization's product or service over the customer's lifetime. Kimberly-Clark, for example, reports that its retained customers buy about seven boxes of Kleenex per year and will spend over $1,400 on facial tissue over a lifetime. Meanwhile, Lexus estimates that a retained and satisfied customer is worth over $600,000 in lifetime sales.[16]

To be effective, CRM requires the involvement and commitment of managers and employees throughout the organization and the growing application of information technology. In fact, technology is a key CRM enabler. And with advances in information technology and changes in customer buying behaviour—specifically, online buying—the scope of CRM has been broadened to include **eCRM**—a Web-centric, personalized approach to managing long-term customer relationships electronically.[17] Expenditures on CRM initiatives globally are expected to exceed $12 billion in 2012.[18]

An integral component of eCRM is interactive marketing. **Interactive marketing** involves two-way buyer–seller electronic communication in which the buyer can control the kind and amount of information received from the seller. For effective interactive marketing to occur, companies need to listen, understand, and respond to their customers' needs. Marketers must also treat customers as individuals and empower them to (1) influence the timing and extent of the buyer–seller interaction, and (2) have a say in the kind of products and services they buy, the information they receive, and, in some cases, even the prices they pay. Interactive marketing technology now allows for a level of customer interaction, individualization, and customer relationship management process to be carried out on a scale never before available. For example, Dove asked its customers to go online to create new ads for their Dove Cream Oil product and submit it to the company online for consideration. In this way, customers feel they are truly interacting with the company and co-participating in the type of messages the company will disseminate. Another example of interactive marketing was Sears Canada asking its customers to select the cover for its Christmas Wish Book. Canadians were invited to visit the Sears Web site and vote in an online poll for one of four potential covers for the book.

LO6   **Customer Experience Management Era**   Many experts have suggested that CRM initiatives are suffering because the focus has been on getting CRM technology in place while neglecting just how to build customer relationships.[19]

Many Canadian firms made heavy investments in CRM, including the Royal Bank, Bank of Montreal, Telus, Bell, Sears, Shoppers Drug Mart, and The Hudson's Bay Company. But they have discovered that good customer relationships really only result when companies offer their customers excellent experiences. So, CRM, with its information technology, information architecture and platforms, and other enabling processes, is necessary for customer relationship development but it is not sufficient. To be effective, CRM must include a **customer experience management (CEM)** strategy. CEM is managing the customers' interactions with the organization at all levels and at all touchpoints (direct and indirect contacts of the customer with an organization) so that the customer has a positive impression of the organization, is satisfied with the experience, and will remain loyal to the organization. In essence, it is about experience-based differentiation.

With more and more products and services becoming commoditized, most experts believe that, for the customer, it is the experience that counts, not the product or service per se. A recent study indicated that 60 percent of executives believed that improving customer experience was critical to the future growth of their companies. Yet, less than 25 percent of consumers believe organizations actually provide excellent customer experiences.[20] However, companies that do engage in CEM achieve double-digit revenue and profit growth compared to companies that do not.[21] These companies ensure that customers receive a positive, end-to-end experience with employees, Web sites, call centres, and even advertising. Hewlett-Packard (HP), for example, has a CEM group that creates and tracks customer experiences across all HP business units. And research has found that customers who feel good about their experiences with companies will become devoted loyalists to those companies.[22]

However, the transition to CEM also requires a new type of organization—a *customer-centric marketing organization (CCMO)*. In CCMO-based organizations, the customer is the focus and the company's brands, products and services, finances, leaders, and marketers are in tune and in time with the customers' needs, expectations, aspirations, and budgets.[23] Firms such as Apple, FedEx, Starbucks, and others have already made the shift to CCMO, resulting in these organizations delivering excellent customer experiences. Some organizations, such as WildPlay, actually have

customer experience management (CEM)

Managing the customers' interactions with the organization at all levels and at all touchpoints (direct and indirect contacts of the customer with an organization) so that the customer has a positive impression of the organization, is satisfied with the experience, and will remain loyal to the organization.

Pete's Frootique engages in CEM activities to retain customers for life.

"Chief Experience Officers" who oversee the creation and delivery of customer experiences. See the Marketing Matters box on page 19, titled "How Some Canadian Companies Are Creating and Managing Customer Experiences," for other Canadian companies that have recognized the need to create and manage customer experiences and have structured their organizations accordingly.[24]

LO7   **Social Media Marketing Era**   Some experts are suggesting that we are also in the midst of the emergence of the social media marketing era. In fact, some suggest that social media marketing is the biggest shift in the economy since the Industrial Revolution. There are really two distinct dimensions to **social media marketing.** First, social media marketing is about consumer-generated online-marketing efforts to promote brands and companies for which they are fans (or conversely, negatively promoting brands and companies for which they are non-fans). Second, social media marketing is the use by marketers of online tools and platforms to promote their brands or organizations. The most common tools or platforms used by both consumers and organizations are social networking sites (e.g., Facebook, MySpace, Twitter), blogs, wikis, podcasts, and other shared media sites such as YouTube.

It is the former dimension of social media marketing that is changing the rules of marketing and ushering in a new era of business. Social media creates a platform that empowers customers and provides them with an opportunity to communicate with an organization and with other customers. In fact, one author, Erik Qualman, suggests social media marketing is creating a new form of economy called *socialnomics* where consumers will no longer search for products or services, but rather will find them via social media. He suggests that social media is transforming the way we live and the way organizations do business.[25] He argues that social media platforms such as Facebook connect hundreds of millions of people to each other via instant communication and that this is creating a socio-economic shift where online communities can build or destroy brands and can make traditional marketing obsolete.

To survive in this new social media world Qualman suggests that organizations must understand, navigate, and adapt to this new landscape. Others, however, suggest that social media marketing is not necessarily a major structural shift in the marketing era but that organizations must be capable of taking advantage of social media in order to increase sales, cut marketing costs, and communicate more directly with their customers. Some organizations are heeding this advice. A recent study, in fact, showed that 25 percent of businesses, in particular small businesses and entrepreneurs, are leveraging social media as a way to connect and communicate with current and potential customers.[26]

LO8   ## Ethics and Social Responsibility: Balancing the Interests of Different Groups

As organizations have changed their orientation, society's expectations of marketers have also changed. Today, the standards of marketing practice have shifted from an emphasis on producers' interests to consumers' interests. In addition, organizations are increasingly encouraged to consider the social and environmental consequences of their actions for all parties. Guidelines for ethical and socially responsible behaviour can help managers balance consumer, organizational, and societal interests.

Ethics   Many marketing issues are not specifically addressed by existing laws and regulations. Should information about a firm's customers be sold to other organizations? Should advertising by professional service providers, such as accountants and lawyers, be restricted? Should consumers be left on their own to assess the safety of a product? These questions may not involve strict legal issues but do raise some ethical questions. **Ethics** are the moral principles and values that govern the actions and decisions of an individual or group. Ethics serve as guidelines on how to act correctly and justly. In

---

social media marketing
Consumer-generated online-marketing efforts to promote brands and companies for which they are fans (or conversely, negatively promoting brands and companies for which they are non-fans), and the use by marketers of online tools and platforms to promote their brands or organizations.

Social media is changing the way we live and the way we do business. To learn more, read the "Social Media Marketing Era" section of the text.

ethics
The moral principles and values that govern the actions and decisions of an individual or group.

Marketing Matters

How Some Canadian Companies Are Creating and Managing Customer Experiences

The Canadian marketplace has undergone tremendous change, especially with the advent of new technologies, more empowered consumers, and greater product and brand choices. But Canada's best marketers have anticipated and responded to such changes. They have understood that conventional marketing practices cannot sustain enterprise growth in the new economy. Therefore, they have created new strategies and best practices to better meet their customers' needs and to outpace their competitors. One of these strategies is customer experience management.

For example, Canadian Tire has a strong product line, resides in convenient locations, and focuses on customer service. But in order to improve the customer's experience with the company, it now offers better in-store design and better training for employees to ensure the customer enjoys a good shopping experience, especially female shoppers. Sony Canada is a company that believes in product innovation. But it also focuses on fulfilling the customer's need for a satisfying experience. Sony doesn't just sell electronics— it sells trust, and a good customer experience with the brand. And Sony's effort is paying off. Canada is the most Sony-loyal country in the world, more loyal than Japan. Sears Canada offers Canadians its famous "satisfaction

guaranteed or your money back" promise, but it also focuses on offering the customer a safe and comfortable place to shop, as well as salespeople who know their products and who want customers to have an enjoyable shopping experience. Chapters bookstores even offers musicians to play in their stores to entertain you and create ambience while you shop!

But now even small entrepreneurial companies are engaged in customer experience management. For example, independent grocers like Pete's Frootique in Halifax; The Village Grocer in Unionville, Ontario; Belbin's Grocery in St. John's; and Stong's Market in Vancouver are all in the CEM business. At Pete's Frootique, for instance, customers experience a piano player in the store, personal greetings, complimentary boxes of raisins, and even individual, fresh-cut sunflowers. Owner Pete Luckett says, "People do not go to Pete's just to buy food, they go for the experience! It's theatre, it's entertainment, it is about making people feel good." Pete says that marketing today is about getting to the customers' hearts, not their pocketbooks. He doesn't sell food commodities; he sells excitement, choice, highly personalized service, and a delightful customer experience that keeps shoppers coming back.

Chapter 4, we will discuss marketing ethics and how organizations must work to ensure that their employees not only live within the law but also practise ethical behaviour.

social responsibility
Individuals and organizations are part of a larger society and are accountable to that society for their actions.

societal marketing concept
The view that an organization should discover and satisfy the needs of its consumers in a way that also provides for society's well-being.

macromarketing
The aggregate flow of a nation's goods and services to benefit society.

micromarketing
How an individual organization directs its marketing activities and allocates its resources to benefit its customers.

Social Responsibility   While many ethical issues involve only the buyer and seller, others involve society as a whole. For example, suppose you change the oil in your old Chevy yourself and dump the used oil on a corner of your backyard. Is this just a transaction between you and the oil manufacturer? Not quite! The used oil may contaminate the soil, and so society will bear a portion of the cost of your behaviour. This example illustrates the issue of social responsibility. **Social responsibility** means that individuals and organizations are part of a larger society and are accountable to that society for their actions (also see Chapter 4). In fact, some marketing experts stress the **societal marketing concept,** the view that an organization should discover and satisfy the needs of its consumers in a way that also provides for society's well-being.[27] Many organizations, such as Stratus Vineyards (see the upcoming Video Case at the end of this chapter), have recognized they are an integral part of society and have committed to socially responsible behaviour, including sustainable business practices and green marketing.

The societal marketing concept is directly related to **macromarketing,** which looks at the aggregate flow of a nation's goods and services to benefit society.[28] Macromarketing addresses such broad issues as whether marketing costs too much, whether advertising is wasteful, and what resource scarcities and pollution side-effects result from the marketing system. Macromarketing issues are addressed in this book, but the main focus is on how an individual organization directs its marketing activities and allocates its resources to benefit its customers, referred to as **micromarketing.**

An overview of this approach appears in Chapter 2. Because of the importance of ethical and social responsibility issues in marketing today, Chapter 4 focuses on these topics, while they are also highlighted throughout the book.

---

learning review

7. The match between customer expectations of the product and the product's actual performance is called _____.

8. The process of building and developing long-term relationships with customers by delivering customer value and satisfaction is called _____.

9. Some Canadian companies are now transitioning from the market orientation era to the _____ era.

LEARNING OBJECTIVES REVIEW

 LO1 **Define marketing and identify the requirements for successful marketing to occur.**

Marketing is the activity for creating, communicating, delivering, and exchanging offerings that benefit the organization, its stakeholders, and society at large. For marketing to occur, it is necessary to have (a) two or more parties with unmet needs, (b) a desire and ability to satisfy them, (c) communication between the parties, and (d) something to exchange.

LO2 **Understand the breadth and depth of marketing.**

Marketing affects every person and organization. Both for-profit and non-profit organizations perform marketing activities. They market products, services, ideas, and experiences that benefit consumers, organizations, and countries.

LO3 **Explain how marketing discovers and satisfies consumer needs and wants.**

The first objective in marketing is discovering the needs of prospective consumers. The second objective in marketing is satisfying the needs of targeted consumers. Because an organization cannot satisfy all consumer needs, it must concentrate its efforts on certain needs of a specific group of potential consumers or target market—one or more specific groups of potential consumers toward which an organization directs its marketing program. Having selected its target market, the organization then takes action to satisfy the customers' needs by developing a unique marketing program to appeal to that market.

LO4 **Distinguish between marketing mix elements and environmental factors.**

Four elements in a marketing program designed to satisfy customer needs are product, price, promotion, and place. These elements are called the marketing mix—the four Ps—or the controllable variables because they are under the general control of the marketing department within an organization. Environmental forces, also called uncontrollable variables, are largely beyond the organization's control. These include social, technological, economic, competitive, and regulatory forces.

LO5 **Describe how a market orientation focuses on creating customer value, satisfaction, and customer relationships.**

Organizations with a market orientation focus their efforts on (a) continuously collecting information about customers' needs and competitors' capabilities, (b) sharing this information throughout the organization, and (c) using the information to create value, ensure customer satisfaction, and develop customer relationships. Organizations with a market orientation engage in customer relationship management (CRM)—the process of building and developing long-term relationships with customers by delivering customer value and satisfaction. Organizations engaging CRM understand the importance of the customer lifetime value (CLV)—the profits generated by the customer's purchase of an organization's product or service over the customer's lifetime. The concept of eCRM—a Web-centric, personalized approach to managing long-term customer relationships electronically, which includes interactive marketing—is changing the way buyers and sellers interact. Interactive marketing technology now allows for a level of customer interaction, individualization, and customer relationship management process to be carried out on a scale never before available.

 LO6 **Explain why some organizations have transitioned from the market orientation era to the customer experience management era.**

Companies have found that CRM is necessary but not sufficient in building effective relationships with customers. Accordingly, many companies have transitioned from the market orientation era to the customer experience management (CEM) era—managing the customers' interactions with the organization at all levels and at all touchpoints so that the customer has a positive impression of the organization, is satisfied with the experience, and will remain loyal to the organization. This shift also requires a new type of organization called a customer-centric marketing organization (CCMO), and some Canadian companies have already made this transition and are enjoying marketing success.

 LO7 Understand the emergence of the social media marketing era.

The social media marketing era is ushering in a major structural change in our economy. Social media marketing has two distinct dimensions: (*a*) consumer-generated online-marketing efforts to promote brands and companies for which they are fans (or conversely, negatively promoting brands and companies for which they are non-fans), and (*b*) the use by marketers of online tools and platforms such as Facebook, MySpace, Twitter, and YouTube to promote their brands or organizations. Some suggest that social media marketing is creating a new form of economy called socialnomics where consumers will no longer search for products or services, but rather will find them via social media. To survive in this new social media world organizations must understand, navigate and adapt to this new landscape.

LO8 Understand the meaning of ethics and social responsibility and how they relate to the individual, organizations, and society.

Marketing managers must balance consumer, organizational, and societal interests. This involves issues of ethics and social responsibility. Ethics are the moral principles and values that govern the actions and decisions of an individual or group. Ethics serve as guidelines on how to act correctly and justly. Social responsibility means that individuals and organizations are part of a larger society and are accountable to that society for their actions. Some marketing experts stress the societal marketing concept, the view that an organization should discover and satisfy the needs of its consumers in a way that also provides for society's well-being which includes sustainable business practices and green marketing.

FOCUSING ON KEY TERMS

customer experience management (CEM) p. 17
customer lifetime value (CLV) p. 16
customer relationship management (CRM) p. 16
customer satisfaction p. 15
customer value p. 15
eCRM p. 16
environmental forces p. 11
ethics p. 18
interactive marketing p. 16
macromarketing p. 19
market p. 6
market orientation p. 15

marketing p. 5
marketing concept p. 15
marketing mix p. 11
marketing program p. 13
micromarketing p. 19
organizational buyers p. 7
social marketing p. 7
social media marketing p. 18
social responsibility p. 19
societal marketing concept p. 19
target market p. 11
ultimate consumers p. 7

APPLYING MARKETING KNOWLEDGE

1 What value does the consumer receive by purchasing the following products or services? (*a*) Carnation Instant Breakfast, (*b*) Adidas running shoes, (*c*) Hertz Rent-A-Car, and (*d*) television home shopping programs.

2 Each of the four products, services, or programs in question 1 has substitutes. Respective examples are (*a*) a ham and egg breakfast, (*b*) regular tennis shoes, (*c*) taking a bus, and (*d*) a department store. What consumer value might these substitutes deliver instead of those mentioned in question 1?

3 What are the characteristics (e.g., age, income, education) of the target market customers for the following products or services? (*a*) *National Geographic* magazine, (*b*) *Wired* magazine, (*c*) Toronto Blue Jays baseball team, and (*d*) the Canadian Open golf tournament.

4 A university in a metropolitan area wishes to increase its evening-school offerings of business-related courses, such as marketing, accounting, finance, and management. Who are the target market customers (students) for these courses?

5 What actions involving the four marketing mix elements might be used to reach the target market in question 4?

6 What environmental forces (uncontrollable variables) must the university in question 4 consider in designing its marketing program?

7 Calculate the annual value of a specific purchase you make on a regular basis, for example, gasoline for your car. What would be the purchase value over a 10-year period? What does this tell you about the customer lifetime value concept?

8 Provide a recent example of a shopping experience where you were very satisfied and one where you were very dissatisfied with your purchase. Do you think the company was practicing customer experience management? Why or not why? Explain why you were satisfied or dissatisfied with the experience. What impact will this experience have on your future purchases from that organization?

9 Have you had any experience talking about brands that you like or dislike using social media? What have you discussed and what has been the response from others?

Building Your Marketing Plan

If your instructor assigns a marketing plan for your class, don't make a face and complain about the work—for two special reasons. First, you will get insights into trying to actually "do marketing" that often go beyond what you can get by simply reading the textbook. Second, thousands of graduating students every year get a job by showing prospective employers a portfolio of samples of their written work from university or college—often a marketing plan. This can work for you.

The Building Your Marketing Plan section at the end of each chapter suggests ways to improve and focus your marketing plan. You will use the sample marketing plan in Appendix A (following Chapter 2) as a guide, and this section after each chapter will help you apply those Appendix A ideas to your own marketing plan.

Video Case 1

STRATUS VINEYARDS: AN ECO-WINEMAKING SUCCESS STORY

Introduction

Canadians have been making wine for over two centuries. But modern-day success in the production and marketing of wines in Canada goes back only a quarter of a century. With specialty products such as icewine and new standards for quality, Canadian wine products are increasingly pleasing the palates of Canadian and global consumers. One company that is achieving success in this emerging industry is the innovative winemaker, Stratus Vineyards.

The Canadian Wine Industry

The major transformation of the Canadian wine industry largely occurred in the late 1980s and early 1990s when growers switched from producing wines made from native species grapes (Labrusca) to those made from wine-quality grapes (vinifera and French hybrid varieties). The reputation of Canadian wines was also enhanced by the introduction of a voluntary standard—Vintners Quality Alliance (VQA). The VQA symbol on a bottle of Canadian wine assures consumers of standards of production, content, varietal percentage, appellation, and vintage.

Today, Canada's emerging wine industry is characterized by new investments in world-class wineries in both Ontario and British Columbia, continued and aggressive new plantings of vinifera varietals, diversified wine offerings, new technology, expanding exports, and greater recognition of its ability to produce fine wines at competitive prices. New access for Canadian wines, especially icewine, in the European market, as well as expanding market opportunities in the United States and Asia,

are giving Canadian wines greater market exposure. In Canada, despite increasing import competition, sales of Canadian quality wines are increasing as consumers move up the quality/price scale. Finally, in spite of a world glut of wine and aggressive competition in Canada and internationally, Canada's wine industry is enjoying considerable success and facing these challenges with a degree of optimism.

There are close to 500 wineries in Canada that provide jobs, preserve valuable agricultural land, and create tourist destinations. Two provinces, Ontario and British Columbia, account for 98 percent of the volume of premium wine produced in Canada. Quebec and Nova Scotia have each developed a small, but ardent, grape wine sector. With the exception of an enthusiast in Prince Edward Island who has a vineyard and winery, there is little grape growing on a commercial scale in any other province in Canada. There are seven designated viticultural areas (VA) located in the southern areas of the provinces of Ontario and British Columbia. (The provinces of Quebec and Nova Scotia have areas in which grapes are grown, but these are not as yet officially designated as viticultural areas.)

The Canadian wine industry, although relatively small, is growing at a remarkable pace and has made a major impact on the Canadian economy. Canadians purchase over 360 million litres of wine, translating into almost $5 billion in sales. Forty percent of this total consists of Canadian brands, with imports holding on to 60 percent market share. Per capita consumption of wine also continues to rise, now averaging over 14 litres per capita. Quebec residents buy the highest amount of wine, averaging over 18 litres per adult. The overall economic impact of the wine industry in Canada is also significant. For example, the sale of just one litre of Canadian wine provides over $4 in added economic value to our economy.

Canadian wines are made as either single-varietal wines from one grape variety, or as a blend from two or more grape varieties. Figure 1 presents the grape varieties that are commonly used to produce the wide array of wine styles currently available in Canada, ranging from dry and off-dry table wines to sweet late-harvest dessert wines, of which icewine is the best known.

One of the most important wine-producing regions in Canada is the Niagara Peninsula in Ontario, where you will find one of Canada's most unique wineries, Stratus Vineyards.

Stratus Vineyards

Stratus Vineyards was established in 2000 and is located in the heart of Niagara wine country in the historic town of Niagara-on-the-Lake. One of the features of this

● FIGURE 1

The major wine styles today in Canada

STYLE	WHITE VARIETIES	RED VARIETIES
Table wines	Auxerrois	Baco Noir
	Chardonnay	Cabernet Franc
	Chenin Blanc	Cabernet Sauvignon
	Gewurztraminer	Gamay Noir
	Pinot Blanc	Maréchal Foch
	Pinot Gris	Merlot
	Riesling	Pinot Noir
	Sauvignon Blanc	Syrah/Shiraz
	Semillon	
	Viognier	
	Bordeaux Style Blends	**Bordeaux Style Blends**
Sparkling wines	Riesling	Gamay Noir
	Chardonnay/ Pinot Noir	
Dessert wines • Late Harvest • Select Late Harvest • Special Select • Botrytis Affected • Icewine	Vidal and/or Riesling	Cabernet Franc

winery that makes it very unique is its commitment to environmentally sustainable winemaking practices. Its goal is to make limited quantities of ultra-premium wine in the most eco-friendly way possible. The winery is a marvel of efficiency, sustainability, and flexibility. The fruit is handpicked before travelling up four storeys via freight elevator where it flows down a specially designed gravity-flow sorting system. This eliminates the need for pumps that can damage fragile fruit. The temperature is controlled by geothermal wells located on the vineyard property. The winery is the first building in Canada to achieve LEED (Leadership in Energy and Environmental Design) certification from the Canada Green Building Council. And, Stratus is, at present, the only winery worldwide to fully achieve this designation.

Stratus uses an old-school winemaking method. Instead of focusing on a single grape variety, Stratus uses the assemblage method to produce Stratus Red and Stratus White. The red wines use as many as seven grape varieties while the white wines use up to six. No grape varieties are listed in the bottles—you get what the winemaker crafts. In this way, the wine really represents the vineyard and not a particular grape variety. Stratus also produces a limited quantity of Cabernet Franc, Chardonnay, and Riesling, as well as a Riesling icewine.

Stratus wines are critically acclaimed and have quickly become benchmarks of quality within the Canadian wine industry. Stratus wines also bear the Vintners Quality Alliance (VQA) designation from the Niagara-on-the-Lake appellation. Stratus wines are available at the on-site winery store, online, and at select dining establishments throughout Ontario. Limited releases are also available through Ontario's LCBO as well as through select retailers across Canada and the United States.

Consistent with the quality image the winery wishes to project, Stratus uses premium packaging as well as premium pricing. For example, the company hired acclaimed graphic designer Michael Vanderbyl to create its distinctive and sophisticated label. And Stratus Red and Stratus White wines retail for about $40 a bottle, which is significantly higher than many of its domestic and foreign competitors. For instance, over 65 percent of wines made in Ontario sell for $10 or less per bottle. Only 35 percent of wines are priced over $10 a bottle, and wines costing over $20 represent less than 2 percent of total wine sales in Ontario. However, Stratus believes it is targeting a small group of upscale and discerning wine consumers who are looking for a total customer experience, rationally, emotionally, and from a sensory perspective. And, importantly, these consumers are prepared to pay for such an experience. To help provide that total experience, Stratus actually invites customers to its vineyard to try their products at their on-site retail boutique where the customer can partake in flights of wine at $10 per flight. Or they can sign up for 90-minute seminars on the art of matching wine and food at a cost of $30 per guest. Stratus also offers its customers a wine club membership; offers gift cards, and sells wine merchandise. Importantly, the company believes eco-conscious wine consumers will strongly support its environmentally sustainable business philosophy. For an overview of Stratus' marketing elements see Figure 2.

Future Driving Forces for the Canadian Wine Industry and Stratus Vineyards

As the Canadian wine industry and Stratus both look ahead to the future, there are several forces that must be considered. For example, total wine sales will continue to grow in Canada for several reasons, including the link between wine and health. Also, more and more Canadians are reaching the prime wine-consumption age (35–54), and the industry is expanding its marketing efforts to encourage wine consumption, especially in casual situations (after work, socializing at home with friends, and so on). While Canada is still a beer-drinking nation, more and more people are switching to wines as their alcohol-based beverage of choice. For example, while per capita wine consumption has increased in Canada by 3.6 litres from 1993 to 2005, per capita beer consumption declined by 3.2 litres during that same period.

The consumer is also becoming more demanding and seeking quality, consistency, and value when purchasing wine. Moreover, consumers are becoming more image or brand conscious, seeking to purchase wine that fits their self-image and the image they wish to project to others. At the same time, there will be increased competition in the marketplace by both domestic and foreign brands. In particular, while wine sales growth has been impressive in Canada over the past few years, much of that increase has been in sales of imported wine. Additionally, the retail sector will become even more polarized with price-based offerings on one end of the continuum and value-added experience offerings on the other end. Finally, the use of the Internet as a tool for consumers to search for brands and to make purchases will change the marketing landscape. At the same time, wineries are leveraging this technology in order to create two-way interaction between themselves and prospective buyers.

● **FIGURE 2**

Stratus Vineyards marketing elements

Mix Element	Specifics
Product	Premium, limited-quantity assemblaged wines in red or white; limited production of Cabernet Franc, Chardonnay, and Riesling, as well as a Riesling icewine
Price	Stratus Red and Stratus White: $44 per 750-litre bottle or $260–400 per case of six bottles
Promotion	Public relations, publicity, news releases, newsletters, hosted events, tastings and seminars at the vineyard, wine club memberships, gift cards, online promotion through its Web site, and the Wine Council of Ontario
Place	On-site retail wine store, online sales, select dining establishments in Ontario, limited releases to LCBO outlets in Ontario and select retailers elsewhere in Canada and in the U.S.

Questions

1 What is Stratus Vineyards actually marketing? Is it just wine?

2 Many Canadians say that they consider the "environmentally friendliness" of both the products they buy and the companies they buy them from. Do you think this holds true for wines? Why or why not?

3 Stratus has very limited wine-producing capacity (10,000 cases per year). Do you think they should increase that capacity and produce more wine? Why or why not?

4 How should Stratus prepare and respond to the future driving forces in the industry as outlined and discussed in the case?

2

Developing Successful Marketing Strategies

CANADIAN TIRE: THE CREATION AND GROWTH OF A VISIONARY ORGANIZATION

In 1922, two Toronto brothers, John W. and Alfred J. Billes, with a combined savings of $1,800, purchased the Hamilton Tire and Garage Ltd. at the corner of Gerrard and Hamilton streets in Toronto. In 1923, the brothers sold this venture and opened a new business called Canadian Tire Corp'n. In 1927, Canadian Tire Corporation, Limited was officially incorporated. Co-founder A.J. Billes stated that they chose the name Canadian Tire "because it sounded big." Well, the brothers did, indeed, make the business big. From humble beginnings, the organization has grown to a major corporation with five interrelated businesses that offer Canadians, coast to coast, a range of goods and services that meet life's everyday needs, including general merchandise and clothing, petroleum, and financial services. The company has more than 1,200 general merchandise and clothing stores and gas stations, and is a major financial services provider. The company employs more than 58,000 Canadians and has revenue of close to $10 billion annually.

Canadian Tire's five core businesses are Canadian Tire Retail, which is a retail chain offering automotive parts, sports and leisure, and home products; PartSource, an automotive parts specialty chain store; Canadian Tire Financial Services, which manages the second-largest MasterCard franchise; Canadian Tire Petroleum, Canada's largest independent gasoline retailer; and Mark's, a leading apparel retailer.

learning objectives

After reading this chapter, you should be able to:

LO1 Describe the kinds of organizations that exist and the three levels of strategy in them.

LO2 Describe how core values, mission, organizational culture, business, and goals are important in organizations.

LO3 Discuss how an organization sets strategic directions and tracks performance by using marketing dashboards and metrics.

LO4 Describe the strategic marketing process and its three key phases: planning, implementation, and evaluation.

LO5 Explain how the marketing mix elements are blended into a cohesive marketing program.

The company's core values include honesty, integrity, and respect. Additionally, good corporate citizenship through community support is also at the core of the culture of Canadian Tire. Its basic mission (vision) is to create sustainable growth by being a national champion and Canada's most trusted company. The organizational direction of the company is set by a focus on "creating customers for life and shareholder value." Finally, the company also establishes very specific strategic goals each year with regard to future growth, thus setting a clear direction for the organization.[1]

Chapter 2 describes how organizations such as Canadian Tire set goals to give an overall direction that is linked to their organizational and marketing strategies. For the marketing department, these strategies are converted into plans that must be implemented. The results are then evaluated to assess the degree to which they accomplish the organization's goals, consistent with its core values and mission.

TODAY'S ORGANIZATIONS

In today's global competition, it is important to recognize (1) the kinds of organizations that exist, (2) what strategy is, and (3) how this strategy relates to the three levels found in many large organizations.

LO1 Kinds of Organizations

An *organization* is a legal entity of people who share a common mission. This motivates them to develop *offerings* (products, services, ideas, experiences) that create value for both the organization and its customers by satisfying customers' needs and wants. Today's organizations can be divided into business firms and non-profit organizations. A *business firm* is a privately owned organization that serves its customers in order to earn a profit. Business firms must earn profits to survive. **Profit** is the money left after a business firm's total expenses are subtracted from its total revenue and is the reward for the risk it undertakes in marketing its offerings.

profit
The money left after a business firm's total expenses are subtracted from its total revenue; the reward for the risk it undertakes in marketing its offerings.

In contrast to business firms, a *non-profit organization* is a non-governmental organization that serves its customers but does not have profit as an organizational goal. Instead, its goals may be operational efficiency or client satisfaction. Regardless, it also must receive sufficient funds to continue operations. For simplicity, in the rest of the book we use the terms *firm, company, corporation,* and *organization* interchangeably to cover both business and non-profit operations.

Organizations that develop similar offerings, when grouped together, create an *industry,* such as the computer industry or the automobile industry. As a result, organizations make strategic decisions that reflect the dynamics of the industry to create a compelling and sustainable advantage for their offerings relative to those of competitors to achieve a superior level of performance.[2] The foundation of much of an organization's marketing strategy is having a clear understanding of the industry within which it competes.

What Is Strategy?

An organization has limited human, financial, technological, and other resources available to produce and market its offerings—it can't be all things to all people! Every organization must develop strategies to help focus and direct its efforts to accomplish

strategy
An organization's long-term course of action designed to deliver a unique customer experience while achieving its goals.

its goals. However, the definition of strategy has been subject to debate among management and marketing theorists.[3] For our purpose, **strategy** is an organization's long-term course of action designed to deliver a unique customer experience while achieving its goals.[4] Whether explicit or implicit, all organizations set a strategic direction. And marketing helps not only to set this direction but also to move the organization there.

Structure of Today's Organizations

Large organizations can be extremely complex. They usually consist of three organizational levels whose strategy is linked to marketing as shown in Figure 2–1.

corporate level
Level at which top management directs overall strategy for the entire organization.

Corporate Level   The corporate level is where top management directs overall strategy for the entire organization. "Top management" usually means the board of directors and senior management officers with a variety of skills and experiences that are invaluable in establishing overall strategy.

The president or chief executive officer (CEO) is the highest ranking officer in the organization and is usually a member of its board of directors. This person must possess leadership skills and expertise ranging from overseeing the organization's daily operations to spearheading strategy planning efforts that may determine its very survival.

In recent years many large firms have changed the title of the head of marketing from vice president of marketing to chief marketing officer (CMO). These CMOs have an increasingly important role in top management because of their ability to think strategically. Most bring multi-industry backgrounds, cross-functional management expertise, analytical skills, and intuitive marketing insights to their job, which enables them to create and deliver value to the organization and its customers. The Marketing Matters box describes the breadth of responsibilities of three key marketing executives—with various titles—in widely different firms. But whatever their titles, the head of marketing in today's organizations not only frame marketing strategy but also see that it is implemented to achieve critical marketing goals.[5]

● **FIGURE 2–1**
The board of directors oversees the three levels of strategy in organizations: corporate, business unit, and functional

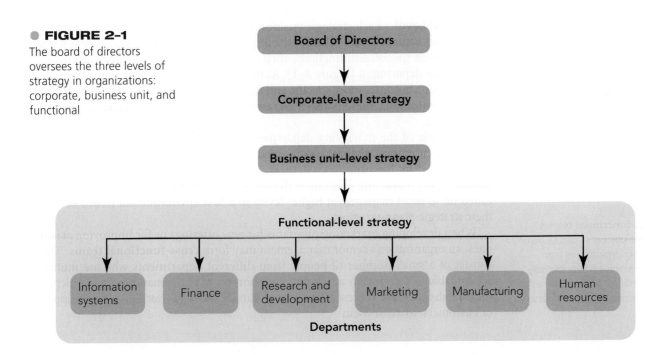

Marketing Matters

Chief Marketing Officers in the Executive Suites—and What They Do Every Day

Key marketing executives—often titled chief marketing officers (CMOs)—have an increasingly important role in top management because of their ability to think strategically. Most bring multi-industry backgrounds, cross-functional management expertise, analytical skills, and intuitive marketing insights to their job, which enables them to create and deliver value to the organization and its customers. Below are three marketing executives who have significant strategic responsibilities within their organizations.

 Cammie Dunaway is executive vice president of sales and marketing for Nintendo and is responsible for leading Nintendo's worldwide branding efforts and product marketing initiatives. She oversees product planning and positioning as well as the execution of customer acquisition and retention strategies for Nintendo's products.

 Eduardo Conrado is vice president of global marketing and portfolio management for Motorola Networks. He is responsible for portfolio management, global marketing, product positioning, pricing, and the publication of systems road maps in cooperation with engineering division product management teams, among other responsibilities.

 Leslie Short is president of marketing, advertising, and public relations for FUBU The Collection and FB Entertainment. She develops marketing and advertising plans, coordinates all public relations initiatives, executes promotional events, and oversees the development of corporate and international licensees.

strategic business unit (SBU)
A subsidiary, division, or unit of an organization that markets a set of related offerings to a clearly defined group of customers.

strategic business unit level
A business unit level where managers set a more specific strategic direction for their businesses to exploit value-creating opportunities.

functional level
The level in an organization where groups of specialists actually create value for the organization.

cross-functional teams
A small number of people from different departments in an organization who are mutually accountable to accomplish a task or common set of performance goals.

Strategic Business Unit Level　Some multimarket, multiproduct firms, such as Johnson & Johnson and General Electric, really manage a portfolio or group of businesses.[6] Each group is called a **strategic business unit (SBU),** which is a subsidiary, division, or unit of an organization that markets a set of related offerings to a clearly defined group of customers. At the **strategic business unit level,** managers set a more specific strategic direction for their businesses to exploit value-creating opportunities. For less complex firms with a single business focus, the corporate and business unit levels may merge.

Functional Level　Each strategic business unit has a **functional level,** where groups of specialists actually create value for the organization. The term *department* generally refers to these specialized functions, such as the marketing department or information systems department (Figure 2–1). At the functional level, the organization's strategic direction becomes more specific and focused. Just as there is a hierarchy of levels within organizations, there is also a hierarchy of strategic directions set by managers at each level.

A key role of the marketing department is to look outward, keeping the organization focused on creating customer value both for it and for customers. This is accomplished by listening to customers, developing and producing offerings, and implementing marketing program activities. In large organizations marketing may be called on to assist managers at higher levels to assess environmental trends or aid in their strategic planning efforts.

When developing marketing programs for new offerings or for improving existing ones, an organization's senior management may form **cross-functional teams.** These consist of a small number of people from different departments who are mutually accountable to accomplish a task or a common set of performance goals. Sometimes these teams will have representatives from outside the organization, such as suppliers or customers, to assist them.

learning review

1. What is the difference between a business firm and a non-profit organization?

2. What is strategy?

3. What are examples of a functional level in an organization?

LO2 STRATEGY IN VISIONARY ORGANIZATIONS

Management experts stress that to be successful, today's organizations must be forward looking. They must both anticipate future events and respond quickly and effectively. This requires a visionary organization to specify its foundation (why does it exist?), set a direction (what will it do?), and formulate strategies (how will it do it?) as shown in Figure 2–2.[7] An organization's foundation is its philosophical reason for being—why it exists. So its senior managers must identify its core values and describe its mission and organizational culture—its purpose for being. Next, these managers can set the direction for the organization by defining its business and specifying its long-term and short-term goals.

Organizational Foundation: Why Does It Exist?

An organization's foundation is its philosophical reason for being—why it exists—and rarely changes.[8] Successful visionary organizations use this foundation to guide and inspire their employees through three elements: core values, mission, and organizational culture.

Core Values   An organization's **core values** are the fundamental, passionate, and enduring principles that guide its conduct over time.[9] A firm's founders or senior management develop these core values, which are consistent with their essential beliefs and character.[10] They capture the firm's heart and soul and serve to inspire and motivate its stakeholders—employees, shareholders, board of directors, suppliers, distributors, unions, government, local communities, and customers. Core values also are timeless and should not change due to short-term financial, operational, or marketing concerns. Finally, core values guide the organization's conduct. To be effective, an organization's core values must be communicated to and supported by its top management and employees; if not, they are just hollow words.[11]

Mission   By understanding its core values, an organization can take steps to define its **mission,** a statement of the organization's function in society, often identifying its customers, markets, products, and technologies. Today, often used interchangeably

core values

An organization's core values are the fundamental, passionate, and enduring principles that guide its conduct over time.

mission

A statement of the organization's function in society, often identifying its customers, markets, products, and technologies.

● **FIGURE 2-2**

Today's visionary organization uses key elements to (1) establish a foundation and (2) set a direction using (3) its strategies that enable it to develop and market its offerings successfully.

Organizational foundation (why)	Organizational direction (what)	Organizational strategies (how)

• Core values
• Mission (vision)
• Organizational culture
	• Business
	• Goals (objectives)
	  ○ Long-term
	  ○ Short-term
		• By level • By offering
		  ○ Corporate ○ Product
		  ○ SBU ○ Service
		  ○ Functional ○ Idea
		                   ○ Experience

(**+** between first and second box; **=** between second and third box)

with *vision*, a mission statement should be clear, concise, meaningful, inspirational, and long-term.[12] This inspiration and focus appears in the mission of many organizations, including:

- *Canadian Red Cross.* To improve the lives of vulnerable people by mobilizing the power of humanity in Canada and around the world.
- *Tim Hortons.* Our guiding mission is to deliver superior quality products and services for our customers and communities through leadership, innovation and partnerships.
- *RBC.* Always earning the right to be our clients' first choice.
- *Canadian Tire.* To create sustainable growth by being a national champion and Canada's most trusted company. We will grow from our strengths—leveraging our brands, core capabilities, assets, and extraordinary people.

Each statement exhibits the qualities of a good mission: a clear, challenging, and compelling picture of an envisioned future.

Recently, organizations have added a social element to their mission statements to reflect an ideal that is morally right and worthwhile.[13] Stakeholders, particularly customers, employees, and now society, are asking organizations to be exceptional citizens by providing long-term value while solving society's problems.[14]

Organizational Culture   An organization must be connected with all of its stakeholders. Thus, an important corporate-level marketing function is communicating its core values and mission to them. Some organizations print these statements on cards or placards. Whether at the corporate, strategic business unit, or functional level, an **organizational culture** exists, which is a set of values, ideas, attitudes, and norms of behaviour that is learned and shared among the members of an organization.

Organizational Direction: What Will It Do?

As shown in Figure 2–2, the organization's foundation enables it to set a direction, in terms of (1) the "business it is in" and (2) its specific goals.

Business   A **business** describes the clear, broad, underlying industry or market sector of an organization's offering. To help define its business, an organization can start by looking at the set of organizations that sell similar offerings—those that are in direct competition with each other, such as "the automobile business" or "the personal computer business." The organization can then begin to answer the questions, "What do we do?" or "What business are we in?"

To help us, Professor Theodore Levitt argues in his now-famous "Marketing Myopia" article that railroads in the first half of the twentieth century defined their business too narrowly, proclaiming, "We are in the railroad business!" This myopic focus caused these firms to lose sight of who their customers were and what they needed. Thus, railroads only saw other railroads as direct competitors and failed to develop strategies to compete with airlines, barges, pipelines, trucks, bus lines, and cars—offerings that carried both goods and people. As a result, many railroads eventually merged or went bankrupt. Railroads would probably have fared better if they had realized they were in "the transportation business."[15]

With today's increased global competition, many organizations are rethinking their *business model*, the strategies an organization develops to provide value to the customers it serves. Technological innovation is often a trigger for the business model change. Canadian newspapers, for example, are looking for a new business model as former subscribers get their news online and buy cars from online auto sales directories rather than using newspaper want ads. Other organizations have also seen their business models evolve. For example, Disney is no longer a theme park or movie

organizational culture
A set of values, ideas, attitudes, and norms of behaviour that is learned and shared among the members of an organization.

business
The clear, broad, underlying industry or market sector of an organization's offering.

In the first half of the twentieth century, what "business" did railroads believe they were in? The text reveals their disastrous error.

goals or objectives
Statements of an accomplishment of a task to be achieved, often by a specific time.

market share
The ratio of sales revenue of the firm to the total sales revenue of all firms in the industry, including the firm itself.

business company; rather it is an entertainment business company, creating fun, fantasy, and experiences for its customers in a variety of ways.

Goals   **Goals** or **objectives** (terms used interchangeably in this textbook) are statements of an accomplishment of a task to be achieved, often by a specific time. For example, Kodak may have the goal of being the top seller of digital cameras by 2012 (currently, it is third). Goals convert an organization's mission and business into long- and short-term performance targets to measure how well it is doing (see Figure 2–2).

Useful criteria for writing effective goals are given by the acronym SMART:

- *Specific.* Be a precise description of what is to be achieved
- *Measurable.* Be a quantitative value to show attainment
- *Attainable.* Be achievable, but challenging
- *Relevant.* Be pertinent to the organization's mission
- *Time-based.* Have a deadline for completion

Business firms can pursue several different types of goals:

- *Profit.* Classic economic theory assumes a firm seeks to maximize long-run profit, achieving as high a financial return on its investment as possible.
- *Sales revenue.* If profits are acceptable, a firm may elect to maintain or increase its sales level, even though profitability may not be maximized. Canadian Tire's goal over the next five years is to increase top-line growth (sales) as well as improve its profitability.
- *Market share.* A firm may choose to maintain or increase its market share, sometimes at the expense of greater profits if industry status or prestige is at stake. **Market share** is the ratio of sales revenue of the firm to the total sales revenue of all firms in the industry, including the firm itself.
- *Unit sales.* Sales revenue may be deceiving because of the effects of inflation, and so a firm may choose to maintain or increase the number of units it sells, such as cars, cases of breakfast cereal, or TV sets.
- *Quality.* A firm may target the highest quality products or services in its industry, as 3M does with its Six Sigma program; Loblaws' goal is to offer customers high-quality food products and a quality shopping experience.
- *Customer satisfaction.* Customers are the reasons the organization exists, and so their satisfaction is of vital importance. At IBM Canada, based in Markham, Ontario, customer satisfaction is tracked just the same as financial revenue figures. At Maritime Life Assurance Company in Halifax, Nova Scotia, yearly bonuses paid to employees are based on customer satisfaction data.
- *Employee welfare.* A firm may recognize the critical importance of its employees by having an explicit goal stating its commitment to provide good employment opportunities and working conditions. Crystal Decisions Inc. owns a chalet at a Whistler resort that its employees can use; Pfizer Canada offers daycare facilities to its employees; and BC Biomedical offers flex-work opportunities.
- *Social responsibility.* A firm may seek to balance conflicting goals of consumers, employees, and shareholders to promote the overall welfare of all these groups, even at the expense of profits. Firms marketing on a global basis are often confronted with the notion of being "good global citizens." The Making Responsible Decisions box, "The Global Dilemma: How to Achieve Sustainable Development," deals with the concept of sustainable development, an issue relevant to global marketers.[16]

Many Canadian private organizations that do not seek profits also exist. Examples include museums, such as the Montreal Museum for Fine Arts; symphony orchestras, such as the Edmonton Symphony Orchestra; hospitals, such as Saint Joseph's

Making Responsible Decisions

The Global Dilemma: How to Achieve Sustainable Development

Corporate executives and world leaders are increasingly asked to address the issue of "sustainable development." This term was formally defined in a 1987 United Nations report as meeting present needs "without compromising the ability of future generations to meet their own needs." What often happens is the achievement of profits for a firm and economic development for a country by adding jobs in highly polluting industries, thereby pushing cleanup actions into the future.

Eastern Europe and the nations of the former Soviet Union provide an example. Tragically, poisoned air and dead rivers are the legacies of seven decades of communist rule. With more than a third of the households of many of these nations below the poverty level, should the immediate goal be a cleaner environment or more food, clothing, housing, and consumer goods? What should the heads of

these governments do? What should Western firms trying to enter these new, growing markets do? What will be the impact on future generations?

3M developed an innovative program called Pollution Prevention Pays (3P) to reduce harmful environmental impacts, making a profit doing so. 3M estimates that the 3P program in the last quarter century has cut its pollution by 1.6 billion pounds while saving almost $900 million in raw materials and avoiding fines. The company's current environmental goal is to improve energy efficiency per pound of product by 20 percent while reducing waste per pound by 25 percent.

Should the environment or economic growth come first? What are the societal tradeoffs? Will profit-making firms adopt and implement a 3P kind of program?

Hospital in Hamilton, Ontario; and research institutes, such as the Conference Board of Canada and the Fraser Institute in Vancouver. These organizations strive to serve consumers, members, or patrons with the greatest efficiency and the least cost.

Although technically not falling under the definition of "non-profit organization," government agencies also perform marketing activities in trying to achieve their goal of serving the public good. For example, Industry Canada is a federal government department responsible for fostering a competitive, knowledge-based Canadian economy. The department works with Canadians in all parts of the country and throughout the economy to improve conditions for investment, improve Canada's innovation performance, increase Canada's share of global trade, and build a fair, efficient, and competitive marketplace. Some of their marketing initiatives include promoting investment and trade, promoting tourism, and facilitating small business development.

Organizational Strategies: How Will It Do It?

As shown in Figure 2–2, the organizational foundation sets the "why" of organizations and organizational direction sets the "what." To convert these into actual results, the organizational strategies are concerned with the "how." These organizational strategies vary in at least two ways, partly depending on the level in the organization and the offerings it provides customers.

Variation by Level   Moving from the corporate to the strategic business unit to the functional level involves creating increasingly detailed strategies and plans. For example, at the corporate level, top management may struggle with writing a meaningful mission statement, while at the functional level the issue may involve whether Joan or John makes a sales call tomorrow.

Variation by Offering   Organizational strategies also vary by the organization's offering. The strategy will be far different when marketing a very tangible physical product (a heart pacemaker), a service (a WestJet flight), an idea (donation to the Canadian Red Cross), or an experience (bungee jumping at WildPlay Element Parks).

LO3 SETTING STRATEGIC DIRECTIONS

Setting strategic directions involves answering two other difficult questions: (1) Where are we now? (2) Where do we want to go?

A Look Around: Where Are We Now?

Asking an organization where it is at the present time involves identifying its competencies, customers, and competitors. More detailed approaches of assessing "where are we now?" include both SWOT analysis, discussed later in this chapter, and environmental scanning (Chapter 3).

competencies
An organization's special capabilities, including skills, technologies, and resources, that distinguish it from other organizations and provide value to its customers.

competitive advantage
A unique strength relative to competitors, often based on quality, time, cost, innovation, customer intimacy, or customer experience management.

quality
Those features and characteristics of a product that influence its ability to satisfy customer needs.

benchmarking
Discovering how others do something better than your own firm so that you can imitate or leapfrog competition.

Competencies   Senior managers of an organization must ask a critical question: "What do we do best?" The answer involves a frank assessment of the organization's core **competencies,** which are its special capabilities, including the skills, technologies, and resources that distinguish it from other organizations and that provide value to its customers. Exploiting these competencies can lead to success, particularly if other organizations cannot copy them.[17] Competencies should be distinctive enough to provide a **competitive advantage,** a unique strength relative to competitors that is often based on quality, time, cost, innovation, customer intimacy, or customer experience management.[18]

For example, if 3M has a goal of generating a specific portion of its sales from new products, it must have a supporting competency in research and development and new-product marketing. Canadian Tire believes one of its competitive advantages is its ability to stay close to the customer (customer intimacy). It is able to do so, in part, because of its strategic retail locations. In fact, 92 percent of the Canadian population lives within 15 minutes of a Canadian Tire store, and more than 40 percent of Canadian adults shop there every week. Once the customer is in the store, Canadian Tire associates attempt to provide outstanding customer service.

Another strategy is to develop a competency in producing high-quality products. **Quality** here means those features and characteristics of a product that influence its ability to satisfy customer needs. Firms often try to improve quality through benchmarking—discovering how others do something better than your own firm so that you can imitate or leapfrog the competition. **Benchmarking** can also involve studying operations in completely different businesses and applying this new knowledge to your own business. And, as we saw in Chapter 1, developing a competency to deliver an excellent customer experience is now an extremely important mission for many firms competing in the new customer experience management economy.

Today, an organization must leverage its core competencies in order to clearly differentiate itself from its competitors. One emerging notion being used is the "Hedgehog Concept." The Greek parable of the hedgehog and the fox says that "the fox knows many things but the hedgehog knows one big thing." An organization using the Hedgehog Concept develops a simple, excellent offering that captures the imagination of its employees and its customers. To become a hedgehog an organization must ask itself three basic questions: (1) What can we be the best at in the world? (2) What drives our economic engine? (3) What are we deeply passionate about?[19]

Customers   A sound strategic direction is set by knowing in complete detail who an organization's customers and prospective customers are and the type of products and services (value) they are seeking. Moreover, where, how, and in what form they want this value delivered must also be known. Without such intimate knowledge, an organization's strategic direction may be misaligned and finite corporate resources wasted. In order to stay close to their customers and to understand their needs, every employee at R.C. Purdy's Chocolates of Vancouver actually serves customers.

Competitors   In today's globalized economy, a given organization is likely to face a complex array of competitors. Successful organizations continuously assess both who the competitors are and how they are behaving in order to respond with their own competitive strategies. One competitive strategy an organization can utilize is to go outside its currently defined industry and swim in "Blue Oceans." In fact, some experts suggest there are times when an organization must swim out of a "red ocean of bloody competition" and into a "blue ocean having less competition."[20] Red oceans represent an organization's existing industry whose boundaries are well defined and accepted by its sellers and buyers. Here, an organization competes for market share. Over time, the number of competitors increases and they begin to look alike so that their offerings and brands become commodities—barely distinguishable to consumers. So the ocean (market) becomes blood red as competitors (sharks) eat each other up battling for market share. Blue oceans, on the other hand, denote all industries (1) not yet in existence or (2) that are created by expanding industry boundaries. An organization that follows a blue ocean strategy reduces or eliminates some factors an industry competes on while raising and creating value to buyers on other factors. This creates a leap in value for both the organization and its customers.[21] A good example of a blue ocean strategy is Apple, Inc. avoiding the highly competitive red ocean music business with its unique iPod and iTunes concept and effectively redefining how people listen to and buy music.

Growth Strategies: Where Do We Want to Go?

Knowing where the organization is at the present time enables managers to set a direction for the firm and start to allocate resources to move toward that direction. Two techniques to aid in these decisions are (1) business portfolio analysis and (2) market-product analysis.

Business Portfolio Analysis   The Boston Consulting Group's (BCG) *business portfolio analysis* uses quantified performance measures and growth targets to analyze a firm's business units (called strategic business units, or SBUs, in the BCG analysis) as though they were a collection of separate investments.[22] While used at the strategic business unit level here, this BCG analysis has also been applied at the product line or individual product or brand level. Using this approach, an organization classifies its SBUs according to the growth-share matrix as shown in Figure 2–3.

The vertical axis, the *market growth rate,* provides a measure of market attractiveness. The horizontal axis, *relative market share,* serves as a measure of the organization's strength in the market. The growth-share matrix reveals four types of SBUs:

- *Cash cows* are low-growth, high-share businesses that require less investment to maintain market share.
- *Stars* are high-growth, high-share businesses that require heavy investment to finance their rapid growth. When their growth slows, they are likely to become cash cows.
- *Question marks* are low-share businesses in high-growth markets that require major investments to hold share, and even more investment to increase it. Management needs to make decisions about which question marks to build into stars and which ones to phase out or eliminate.

● **FIGURE 2-3**

Boston Consulting Group
portfolio analysis

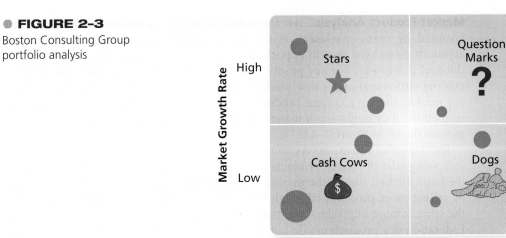

- *Dogs* are low-growth, low-share businesses. They may generate enough cash to maintain themselves but do not hold promise to become real winners for the organization.

To illustrate, notice that there are ten circles in the growth-share matrix in Figure 2–3. These circles represent a company's ten current SBUs. The company has two stars, two cash cows, three question marks, and three dogs. The area of each circle in Figure 2–3 is proportional to the corresponding SBU's dollar sales. The company is in reasonable shape in terms of revenue and growth, but not in great shape. The company is faced with a number of strategic decisions in terms of its future growth. For example, (1) it could invest in some question marks to make them stars; (2) it could invest in the current stars in the hope they will become cash cows; (3) it could simply milk the cash cows and make little or no investment in the question marks or stars; (4) it could eliminate some dogs; (5) it could use revenue from the cash cows to fuel the growth of the stars or question marks; or (6) it could use some combination of the above actions.

Once an SBU is classified, the company must determine what role each SBU will play in the company's future growth. One of four strategies can be pursued for each SBU. The company can invest more in the SBU to *build* its share. It can invest enough to *hold* share. It can *harvest* the SBU, milking it for short-term revenue. Or it can *divest* the SBU.

It should be noted that, as time passes, SBUs change their positions in the growth-share matrix, with each SBU having its own lifecycle. For example, question marks often move counter-clockwise around the growth-share matrix to become stars, then cash cows, and finally dogs. Therefore, a company is often compelled to add new units or products to prevent a stall in growth. Moreover, because most firms have limited influence on market growth rates, their main strategic alternative is to try to change their relative market share in given markets.

The strength of the business portfolio analysis lies in forcing a company to place each of its SBUs in the growth-share matrix, which, in turn, suggests which units or products will be cash producers and cash users in the future. However, there are problems or weaknesses with the business portfolio analysis approach including the fact that it is often difficult to get needed information on market growth and market share and generally difficult to include competitive information into the analysis. It can also be time consuming, and by the time decisions are made, market conditions have may changed.

Market-Product Analysis   An alternative to business portfolio analysis, and one favoured by many marketers, is the use of market-product analysis. With this approach, firms view growth opportunities in terms of markets and products. Let us think of it this way: For any product, there is both a current market (consisting of existing customers) and a new market (consisting of potential customers). And for any market, there is a current product (what they are now using) and a new product (something they might use if it were developed). These four market-product strategies are shown in Figure 2–4.[23]

For example, a firm can try to use *market penetration*—a marketing strategy of increasing sales of present products in existing markets. There is no change in either the basic product line or the market served, but increased sales are possible—either by selling more products (through better promotion or distribution) *or* by selling the same amount of product at a higher price to its existing customers. For example, Fédération des producteurs de lait du Québec promotes the consumption of two glasses of milk daily in order to increase their market penetration in the beverage market in Quebec.[24]

Market development is a marketing strategy of selling existing products to new markets. This could be new geographic markets, such as opening a new Tim Hortons location where no outlet currently exists, or selling to a new market segment that currently does not consume your product. For example, a firm that sells mainly to women, such as Weight Watchers, now sells to the overweight male market.

Product development is a marketing strategy of selling new products to existing markets. For example, Coca-Cola currently serves customers in the Canadian market with its traditional carbonated soft drink products but now offers Canadians a new line of chai tea.[25]

Diversification is a marketing strategy of developing new products and selling them in new markets. This is the riskiest growth strategy because the organization cannot use its expertise with current products or knowledge of its existing markets. There are, however, varying degrees of diversification: related diversification and unrelated diversification. *Related diversification* occurs when new products and new markets have something in common with the firm's existing operations. For example, McDonald's Canada could buy out and operate Red Lobster restaurants. In this case, it remains in the restaurant industry, just a different sector of it. *Unrelated diversification* means the new products and new markets have nothing in common with existing operations. In this case, McDonald's Canada might diversify into completely new business areas such as financial services. To see how some firms grow using multiple market-product strategies, read the accompanying Marketing Matters box, "Growing by Using Multiple Market-Product Strategies."[26]

● **FIGURE 2-4**
Four market-product strategies

Markets	PRODUCTS	
	Current	**New**
Current	**Market Penetration** Selling more products in existing markets	**Product Development** Selling new products in existing markets
New	**Market Development** Selling existing products in new markets (either geographic or new segments)	**Diversification** Selling a new product in new markets

Marketing Matters

Growing by Using Multiple Market-Product Strategies

Most firms do not rely solely on a single growth path, or on one market-product strategy. In fact, most firms simultaneously pursue multiple growth paths, or multiple market-product strategies. For example, as you read in the Video Case 1 vignette at the end of Chapter 1, Stratus Vineyards is using market penetration to enter the Canadian wine market. It is also using market development (growing new markets in the U.S.) and new product development (offering new products such as icewine to existing customers). Second Cup also pursues a multi-prong growth path. It uses a market penetration strategy, allowing customers to use its Café Card (pre-loaded payment card) to pay for their orders, thus providing greater convenience and encouraging greater consumption by existing customers. Second Cup also offers new in-store products, such as its new line of music CDs by Canadian artists. McCain, a Canadian and global leader in the frozen food category, also uses a multi-prong growth path. The New Brunswick–based company continues to penetrate the Canadian market, both the consumer product and food service segments. In fact, it is the largest french fry provider to the food service and

institutional market segment. It also grows by constantly launching new products to meet the changing needs of its customers. The company also continues to develop new markets (market development) with a presence in over 100 countries. Finally, McCain uses a diversification strategy, branching out from the frozen foods category into the ready-to-serve beverage market.

One of the reasons why firms do not or cannot rely on a single growth path or one market-product strategy is because that single strategy may, eventually, lead to stalled growth. For example, some firms work on market penetration as their initial primary growth strategy. But, if successful, sometimes additional penetration is not possible or might be cost prohibitive. Heinz Canada, for instance, has 90 percent share of the jarred baby food market in Canada and cannot cost-effectively increase its market penetration. Therefore, the company focuses on maintaining this penetration while developing new products and new markets. Ultimately, successful firms understand the importance of using multiple market-product strategies in order to sustain their growth.

A campaign to promote increased milk consumption in Quebec is an example of the market penetration marketing strategy.

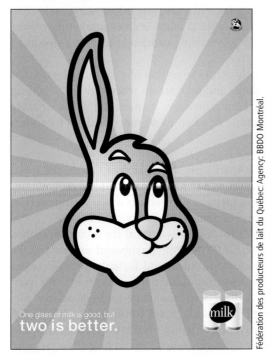

Fédération des producteurs de lait du Québec. Agency: BBDO Montréal.

The product development marketing strategy involves selling new products to existing markets, as Coca-Cola did when introducing a new line of chai tea.

An effective marketing dashboard, like this one for Oracle, helps managers assess a business situation at a glance.

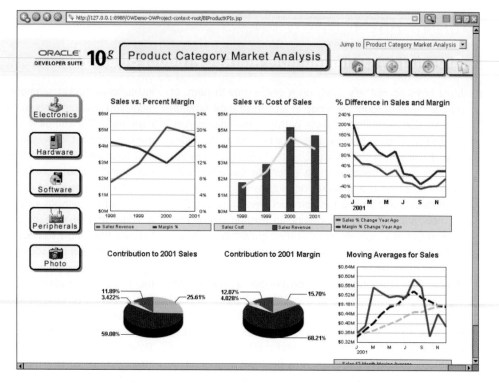

Tracking Strategic Performance with Marketing Dashboards and Metrics

Although marketing managers can set strategic directions for their organizations, how do they know if they are making progress in getting there? One answer is to measure performance by using marketing dashboards and metrics.

marketing dashboard
The visual computer display of the essential information related to achieving a marketing objective.

Car Dashboards and Marketing Dashboards　A **marketing dashboard** is the visual computer display of the essential information related to achieving a marketing objective.[27] Often it is an Internet-based display with real-time information and active hyperlinks to provide further detail. An example is when a chief marketing officer wants to see hourly what effect a new TV advertising campaign has on a product's sales.

The idea of a marketing dashboard really comes from that of a car's dashboard. On a car's dashboard we glance at the fuel gauge and take action when our gas is getting low. With a marketing dashboard, a marketing manager glances at a graph or table and makes a decision whether to take action, or often to do more analysis to understand the problem better.[28]

marketing metric
A measure of the quantitative value or trend of a marketing activity or result.

Dashboards, Metrics, and Plans　The marketing dashboard of Oracle (pictured above) shows graphic displays of key performance measures of a product category such as sales versus cost of sales.[29] Each performance variable is a **marketing metric,** a measure of the quantitative value or trend of a marketing activity or result.[30]

The choice of which marketing metrics to display is critical for a busy manager, who can be overwhelmed with too much information. Dashboard designers take great care to show graphs and tables in easy-to-understand formats to enable clear interpretation at a glance.[31] The Oracle marketing dashboard presents several marketing metrics on the computer screen. A three-step "challenge-findings-action" format is utilized for the Using Marketing Dashboards boxes featured throughout the textbook. This format stresses the importance of using marketing dashboards and the metrics contained within them to measure or evaluate marketing strategies and

Using Marketing Dashboards

Which Provinces Are Underperforming?

Three years ago, you started your own company to sell a snack that includes a top-secret ingredient you discovered while travelling in the Amazon after graduation. The snack is really delicious and adds IQ and strength with every bite!

Your Challenge   The snack is sold in all ten provinces. Your goal is 10 percent growth annually. You want to get 2012 off to a fast start. You want to act quickly to solve any sales problems. You know that pockets of sales stagnation or decline (0 percent or negative growth) are offset by growth markets with greater than 10 percent growth.

Studying a table of sales and percent change versus a year ago in each of the ten provinces would work but would be very time consuming. A good graphic is better. You choose the following marketing metric, where "sales" is measured in units:

$$\text{Annual \% Sales Change} = \frac{(\text{2011 Sales} - \text{2010 Sales} \times 100)}{\text{2010 Sales}}$$

You want to act quickly to improve sales. In your map, growth that is greater than 10 percent is GREEN, 0 to 10 percent growth is ORANGE, and decline is RED. Notice that you (1) picked a metric and (2) made your own rules that GREEN is good, ORANGE is bad, and RED is very bad.

Your Findings   At a glance you see that sales growth in Atlantic Canada and Alberta is weaker than the 10 percent target, and sales are declining in other provinces, too.

Your Action   Marketing is often about grappling with sales shortfalls. You'll need to start by trying to identify and correct the problems in the provinces that are underperforming—in this case, Atlantic Canada and Alberta are declining, and sales are weaker than what you want in Saskatchewan and Manitoba.

You'll want to do the marketing research to see if the problem starts with (1) an external factor, such as changing consumer tastes, or (2) an internal factor, such as a breakdown in your distribution system.

marketing program actions. You will have an opportunity to use a marketing dashboard in this chapter for a snack company you started after your graduation (see the Using Marketing Dashboards box).

---

learning review

6. What is business portfolio analysis?

7. What are the four market-product strategies?

8. What is a marketing dashboard?

LO4 THE STRATEGIC MARKETING PROCESS

After the organization assesses where it is at and where it wants to go, other questions emerge:

1. How do we allocate our resources to get where we want to go?
2. How do we convert our plan to actions?
3. How do our results compare with our plans, and do deviations require new plans?

strategic marketing process
Process whereby an organization allocates its marketing mix resources to reach its target markets.

marketing plan
A road map for the marketing activities of an organization for a specified future period of time, such as one year or five years.

This same approach is used in the **strategic marketing process,** whereby an organization allocates its marketing mix resources to reach its target markets. This process is divided into three phases: planning, implementation, and evaluation (Figure 2–5).

The strategic marketing process is so central to the activities of most organizations that they formalize it as a **marketing plan,** which is a road map for the marketing activities of an organization for a specified future period of time, such as one year or five years. Appendix A at the end of this chapter provides guidelines for writing a marketing plan and also presents a sample marketing plan for a new coffee house located in Surrey, B.C. The sequence of activities that follow parallels the elements of the marketing plan that appears in Appendix A.

Strategic Marketing Process: The Planning Phase

As shown in Figure 2–5, the planning phase of the strategic marketing process consists of the three steps shown at the top of the figure: (1) situation analysis, (2) market-product focus and goal setting, and (3) the marketing program. Let us use the recent marketing planning experiences of several companies to look at each of these steps.

● FIGURE 2-5
The strategic marketing process

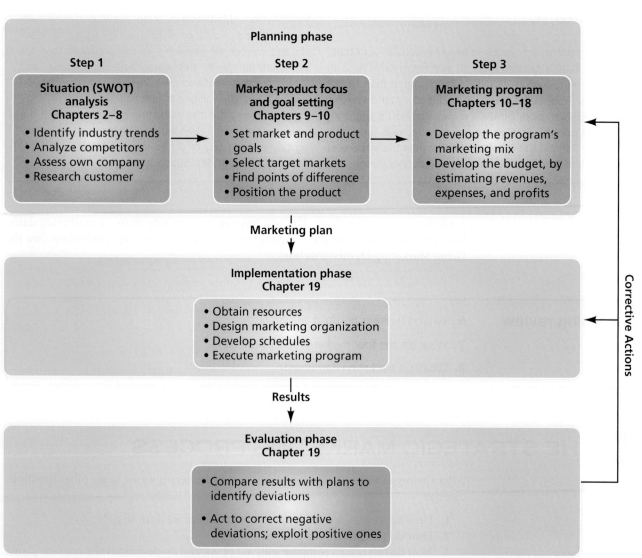

Figure 2–5 also shows how the strategic marketing process integrates the chapters in this book. Chapters 2 through 8 provide the information for the situation (SWOT) analysis, step 1 of the planning phase. Step 2, developing a market-product focus and goals for the product, is covered in Chapters 9 and 10. The elements of the marketing program in step 3—the 4Ps—are discussed in Chapters 10 through 18. The book concludes with Chapter 19, which ties together the planning, implementation, and evaluation phases of the strategic marketing process.

Step 1: Situation (SWOT) Analysis   The essence of **situation analysis** is taking stock of where the firm or product has been recently, where it is now, and where it is headed in terms of the organization's plans and the external factors and trends affecting it. The situation analysis box in Figure 2–5 is the first of the three steps in the planning phase.

An effective shorthand summary of the situation analysis is a **SWOT analysis,** an acronym describing an organization's appraisal of its internal **S**trengths and **W**eaknesses and its external **O**pportunities and **T**hreats. Both the situation and SWOT analyses can be done at the level of the entire organization, the business unit, the product line, or the specific product. As an analysis moves from the level of the entire organization to the specific product, it, of course, gets far more detailed. For small firms or those with basically a single product line, an analysis at the firm or product level is really the same thing.

The SWOT analysis is based on an exhaustive study of the four areas shown in step 1 of the planning phase of the strategic marketing process (see Figure 2–5). Knowledge of these areas forms the foundation on which the firm builds its marketing program:

- Identifying trends in the firm's industry.
- Analyzing the firm's competitors.
- Assessing the firm itself.
- Researching the firm's present and prospective customers.

Let us assume that you are responsible for growing the Ben & Jerry's ice cream brand in Canada. This product is widely available in the United States and many other countries but has only limited market coverage via its franchised Scoop Shops in Canada; in fact, the scoop stores can only be currently found in Ontario, Quebec, Alberta, and British Columbia. But the good news is that the brand is also available through supermarkets and grocery stores in Canada. Given your task, the first thing you might want to do is a SWOT analysis. One is completed for you and shown in Figure 2–6. Note that your SWOT table has four cells formed by the combination of internal versus external factors (the rows) and favourable versus unfavourable factors (the columns) that summarize Ben & Jerry's strengths, weaknesses, opportunities, and threats. This SWOT analysis can identify opportunities to grow the brand as well as possibly eliminate Ben & Jerry's flavours that will not meet Canadian customers' tastes. Those that do not will wind up in the "Flavor Graveyard." Go online and check it out!

A SWOT analysis helps a firm identify the strategy-related factors in these four cells that can have a major effect on the firm. The goal is not simply to develop the SWOT analysis but to translate the results of the analysis into specific actions to help the firm grow and succeed. The ultimate goal is to identify the *critical* factors affecting the firm and then build on vital strengths, correct glaring weaknesses, exploit significant opportunities, and avoid disaster-laden threats. That is a big order.

The Ben and Jerry's SWOT analysis in Figure 2–6 can be the basis for these kinds of specific actions. An action in each of the four cells might be the following:

- *Build on a strength.* Find specific efficiencies in distribution with Unilever's (the parent company of Ben & Jerry's) existing ice cream brands.
- *Correct a weakness.* Recruit experienced managers from other consumer product firms to help stimulate growth in the supermarket segment. Locate bright,

situation analysis
Taking stock of where the firm or product has been recently, where it is now, and where it is headed in terms of the organization's plans and the external factors and trends affecting it.

SWOT analysis
An acronym describing an organization's appraisal of its internal **S**trengths and **W**eaknesses and its external **O**pportunities and **T**hreats.

● FIGURE 2-6
Ben & Jerry's: a SWOT analysis
to get it growing in Canada

Location of Factor	TYPE OF FACTOR	
	Favourable	Unfavourable
Internal	**Strengths** • Prestigious brand name • Major share of the super-premium ice cream market • Can complement Unilever's existing ice cream brands	**Weaknesses** • Danger that B&J's social responsibility actions may add costs, reduce focus on core business • Need for experienced managers to help growth • Flat sales and profits in recent years
External	**Opportunities** • Growing demand for quality ice cream • Increasing demand for frozen yogourt and other low-fat desserts • Success of many firms in extending successful brand in one product category to others	**Threats** • Consumer concern about fatty desserts; B&J customers are the type who read new nutritional labels • Competes with Haagen-Dazs brand • Downturn in Canadian economy

assertive Canadian entrepreneurs who wish to own their own business and would do well operating a Ben & Jerry's Scoop Shop.

• *Exploit an opportunity.* Develop a new line of low-fat frozen yogourts to respond to consumer health concerns.

• *Avoid a disaster-laden threat.* Focus on physical markets only where there is high consumer discretionary income and desire for a premium ice cream product.

Step 2: Market-Product Focus and Goal Setting   Determining which products will be directed toward which customers (step 2 of the planning phase in Figure 2–5) is essential for developing an effective marketing program (step 3). This decision is often based on **market segmentation,** which involves aggregating prospective buyers into groups, or segments, that (1) have common needs and (2) will respond similarly to a marketing action. Ideally, a firm can use market segmentation to identify the segments on which it will focus its efforts—its target market segments—and develop one or more marketing programs to reach them.

As always, understanding the customer is essential. In the case of Medtronic, executives researched a potential new market in Asia by talking extensively with doctors in India and China. They learned that these doctors saw some of the current state-of-the-art features of heart pacemakers as unnecessary and too expensive. Instead, they wanted an affordable pacemaker that was reliable and easy to implant. This information led Medtronic to develop and market a new product, the Champion heart pacemaker, directed at the needs of this Asian market segment.

Goal setting involves setting measurable marketing objectives to be achieved. Such objectives would be different depending on the level of marketing involved. For a specific market, the goal may be to introduce a new product, such as Toyota's launch of its hybrid car, the Prius. For a specific brand or product, the goal may be to create a

market segmentation
Aggregating prospective buyers into groups, or segments, that (1) have common needs and (2) will respond similarly to a marketing action.

Going Online

Ben & Jerry's Flavours: From Chocolate Fudge Brownie Ice Cream and One Sweet Whirled Novelty Bars to . . . the Flavor Graveyard

Ben & Jerry's markets its flavours of ice cream, frozen yogourt, sorbet, and novelty bars in response to both consumer . . . ahem! . . . tastes and important causes it supports, a practice continued even after being sold to Unilever in 2000. For more than a decade, the brownies for Ben & Jerry's popular Chocolate Fudge Brownie ice cream have been supplied by Greyston Bakery, a non-profit organization that trains, employs, and houses low-income people in the area. Recently, Ben & Jerry's teamed up with the award-winning Dave Matthews Band and SaveOurEnvironment.org to fight global warming by creating the One Sweet Whirled ice cream flavour in pints and novelty bars. But not all flavours last. The ones that don't survive wind up in Ben & Jerry's "Flavor Graveyard." To see Ben & Jerry's current flavours as well as those "dearly departed flavours" in the Flavor Graveyard, visit "Flavors" at **www.benjerry.com**. Which flavours have been "laid to rest"?

promotional campaign or pricing strategy that will get more consumers to purchase. For an entire marketing program, the objective is often a series of actions to be implemented over several years.

Using the strategic marketing process shown in Figure 2–5, let us examine Medtronic's five-year plan to reach the "affordable and reliable" segment of the pacemaker market:[32]

- *Set marketing and product goals.* The chances of new-product success are increased by specifying both market and product goals. Based on their market research showing the need for a reliable yet affordable pacemaker, Medtronic executives set the following as their goal: design and market such a pacemaker in the next three years that could be manufactured in China for the Asian market.
- *Select target markets.* The Champion pacemaker will be targeted at cardiologists and medical clinics performing heart surgery in India, China, and other Asian countries.

points of difference
Characteristics of a product that make it superior to competitive substitutes.

- *Find points of difference.* **Points of difference** are those characteristics of a product that make it superior to competitive substitutes. Just as a competitive advantage is a unique strength of an entire organization compared with its competitors, points of difference are the unique characteristics of one of its products that make it superior to the competitive products it faces in the marketplace. For the Champion pacemaker, the key points of difference are not the state-of-the-art features that drive up production costs and are important to only a minority of patients. Instead, they are high quality, long life, reliability, ease of use, and low cost.
- *Position the product.* The pacemaker will be "positioned" in cardiologists' and patients' minds as a medical device that is high quality and reliable with a long, nine-year life. The name Champion is selected after testing acceptable names among doctors in India, China, Pakistan, Singapore, and Malaysia.

Details in these four elements of step 2 provide a solid foundation to use in developing the marketing program, the next step in the planning phase of the strategic marketing process.

LO5 **Step 3: Marketing Program**   Activities in step 2 tell the marketing manager which customers to target and which customer needs the firm's product offerings can satisfy—the *who* and *what* aspects of the strategic marketing process. The *how* aspect—step 3 in the planning phase—involves developing the program's marketing mix and its budget.

● **FIGURE 2-7**
Elements of the marketing
mix that comprise a cohesive
marketing program

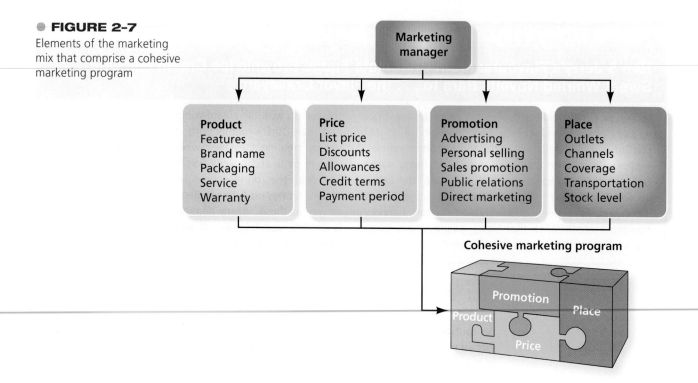

Figure 2–7 shows components of each marketing mix element that are combined to provide a cohesive marketing program. For the five-year marketing plan of
Medtronic, these marketing mix activities include the following:

- *Product strategy.* Offer a Champion brand heart pacemaker with features needed
  by Asian patients at an affordable price.
- *Price strategy.* Manufacture Champion to control costs so that it can be priced
  below $1,000 (in Canadian dollars)—a fraction of the price of the state-of-the-art
  pacemakers offered in Western markets.
- *Promotion strategy.* Feature demonstrations at cardiologist and medical conventions across Asia to introduce the Champion and highlight the device's features
  and application.
- *Place (distribution) strategy.* Search out, utilize, and train reputable medical distributors across Asia to call on cardiologists and medical clinics.

Putting this marketing program into effect requires that the firm commit time and
money to it in the form of a sales forecast and budget that must be approved by top
management.

learning review

9. What is the difference between a strength and an opportunity in a SWOT
analysis?

10. What is market segmentation?

11. What are points of difference, and why are they important?

Strategic Marketing Process: The Implementation Phase

As shown in Figure 2–5, the result of the tens or hundreds of hours spent in the planning phase of the strategic marketing process is the firm's marketing plan. Implementation, the second phase of the strategic marketing process, involves carrying out the marketing plan that emerges from the planning phase. If the firm cannot put the marketing plan into effect—in the implementation phase—the planning phase was a waste of time. Figure 2–5 also shows the four components of the implementation phase: (1) obtaining resources, (2) designing the marketing organization, (3) developing schedules, and (4) actually executing the marketing program designed in the planning phase.

Obtaining Resources   As you have discovered, most companies have numerous options for growth. But such growth requires an investment. Corporate leadership within an organization determines the best options for growth and how they should be funded. For example, Starbucks Coffee wants to obtain greater market penetration in Canada, which, for them, requires more advertising spending. Sheila Murray, brand and category director at Starbucks, had to determine how much to spend and then obtain funding from the company to run a new national radio and print ad campaign. Similarly, Zipcar, North America's largest car-sharing provider, wants to attract more customers and generate more revenue in Canada. To execute this plan, it is using its financial resources to hire experienced marketing managers in Canada.[33]

Designing the Marketing Organization   A marketing program needs a marketing organization to implement it. Figure 2–8 shows the organization chart of a typical manufacturing firm, giving some details of the marketing department's structure. Four managers of marketing activities are shown to report to the vice-president of marketing. Several regional sales managers and an international sales manager may report to the manager of sales. This marketing organization, as a part of the corporate team, is responsible for converting marketing plans to reality.

● **FIGURE 2-8**

Organization of a typical manufacturing firm, showing a breakdown of the marketing department

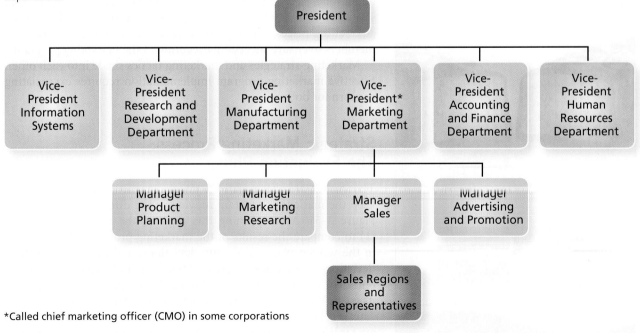

*Called chief marketing officer (CMO) in some corporations

More recently, a number of large consumer products firms changed the title of the head of the marketing department from "vice-president of marketing" to "chief marketing officer" (CMO), but the responsibilities have stayed largely the same.[34] And, as we saw in Chapter 1, many organizations are placing more emphasis on their marketing organization as they attempt to become more customer-centric, creating customer-centric marketing organizations (CCMOs). In CCMO-based organizations, marketing executives take on even more responsibility and leadership in terms of crafting the organization's growth. For example, at Pitney Bowes, marketers have tremendous clout and exercise it by planning, implementing, and evaluating all the marketing programs within the company.[35]

Developing Schedules   Effective implementation requires developing appropriate schedules and determining specific deadlines for the creation and execution of marketing activities. For example, ads to be run during a Super Bowl take several months of planning in order to ensure that they are ready to air on television during the game. Marketers also have to make the ad space purchase before the network deadline otherwise the ads will not run.

marketing strategy

The means by which a marketing goal is to be achieved, usually characterized by a specified target market and a marketing program to reach it.

marketing tactics

Detailed day-to-day operational decisions essential to the overall success of marketing strategies.

3 Musketeers has a specific target market and a specific marketing program to reach it.

Executing the Marketing Program   Marketing plans are meaningless pieces of paper without effective execution of those plans. This effective execution requires attention to detail for both marketing strategies and marketing tactics. A **marketing strategy** is the means by which a marketing goal is to be achieved, usually characterized by a specified target market and a marketing program to reach it. Although the term *marketing strategy* is often used loosely, it implies both the end sought (target market) and the means to achieve it (marketing program). For example, at Mars Incorporated, the company targets health-conscious females by advertising its 3 MUSKETEERS® Bar which has "45 percent less fat than average of the leading chocolate brands." It uses clever television ads to promote this product benefit and is achieving good sales results using this strategy.[36] You can actually watch those television ads online at **www.3musketeers.com.**

To implement a marketing program successfully, hundreds of detailed decisions are often required. These decisions, called **marketing tactics,** are detailed day-to-day operational decisions essential to the overall success of marketing strategies. At many Canadian companies, this might involve writing ads, setting prices, training salespeople, and working with channel members to ensure successful execution of the marketing program.

Marketing strategies and marketing tactics shade into each other. Effective marketing program implementation requires excruciating concern for both.

Strategic Marketing Process: The Evaluation Phase

The evaluation phase of the strategic marketing process seeks to keep the marketing program moving in the direction set for it (see Figure 2–5). Accomplishing this requires the marketing manager (1) to compare the results of the marketing program with the goals in the written plans to identify deviations, and (2) to act on these deviations—correcting negative deviations and exploiting positive ones. For example, sometimes the marketing program falls short of its goals. When this occurs, managers need to take corrective actions. This is called *correcting a negative deviation.* But when actual results are far better than the plan called for, creative managers find ways to exploit the situation. This is called *exploiting a positive deviation.*

This one tastes *light & fluffy.*   This one tastes *free.*

45% LESS FAT
3 Musketeers
BUY ONE GET ONE FREE.

There are numerous tools available to the marketer in the evaluation phase of the marketing process in order to assess properly the success or failure of marketing programs including marketing ROI, marketing dashboards, and marketing metrics. These will be discussed in greater detail in Chapter 19.

---

learning review   **12.** What is the evaluation phase of the strategic marketing process?

13. How do the goals set for a marketing program in the planning phase relate to the evaluation phase of the strategic marketing process?

LEARNING OBJECTIVES REVIEW

 Describe the kinds of organization that exist and the three levels of strategy in them.

An organization is a legal entity of people who share a common mission. There are two kinds. One is a business firm that is a privately owned organization that serves its customers in order to earn a profit so that it can survive. The other is a non-profit organization that is a non-governmental organization that serves its customers but does not have profit as an organizational goal. Most large business firms and non-profit organizations are divided into three levels of strategy: (*a*) the corporate level, where top management directs overall strategy for the entire organization; (*b*) the strategic business unit level, where managers set a more specific strategic direction for their businesses to set value-creating opportunities; and (*c*) the functional level, where groups of specialists actually create value for the organization.

LO2 **Describe how core values, mission, organizational culture, business, and goals are important in organizations.**

Organizations exist to accomplish something for someone. To give organizations direction and focus, they continuously assess their core values, mission, organizational culture, business, and goals. Today's organizations specify their foundation, set a direction, and formulate strategies—"why," "what," and "how" factors, respectively. Core values are the organization's fundamental, passionate, and enduring principles that guide its conduct over time—what Enron forgot when it lost sight of its responsibilities to its stakeholders. The organization's mission is a statement of its function in society, often identifying its customers, markets, products, and technologies. Organizational culture is a set of values, ideas, attitudes, and norms of behaviour that is learned and shared among the members of an organization. To answer the question, "What business are we in?" an organization defines its "business"—the clear, broad, underlying industry category or market sector of its offering. Finally, the organization's goals (or objectives) are statements of an accomplishment of a task to be achieved, often by a specific time.

LO3 **Discuss how an organization sets strategic directions and tracks performance by using marketing dashboards and metrics.**

Managers of an organization ask two key questions to set a strategic direction. The first question, "Where are we now?" requires an organization to (*a*) re-evaluate its competencies to ensure that its special capabilities still provide a competitive advantage; (*b*) assess its present and prospective customers to ensure they have a satisfying customer experience—the central goal of marketing today; and (*c*) analyze its current and potential competitors from a global perspective to determine whether it needs to redefine its business. The second question, "Where do we want to go?" requires an organization to set a specific direction and allocate resources to move it in that direction. Business portfolio analysis and market-product analysis are two useful techniques to do this. Then, tracking strategic directions can be accomplished with marketing dashboards and marketing metrics.

LO4 **Describe the strategic marketing process and its three key phases: planning, implementation, and evaluation.**

An organization uses the strategic marketing process to allocate its marketing mix resources to reach its target markets. This process consists of three phases, which are usually formalized in a marketing plan. The planning phase consists of (*a*) a situation (SWOT) analysis of the organization's strengths, weaknesses, opportunities, and threats; (*b*) a market-product focus through market segmentation, points of difference analysis, and goal setting; and (*c*) a marketing program that specifies the budget and activities (marketing strategies and tactics) for each marketing mix element. The implementation phase carries out the marketing plan that emerges from the planning phase. It has four key elements: obtaining resources, designing the marketing organization, developing schedules, and executing the marketing program. The evaluation phase compares the results from the implemented marketing program with the marketing plan's goals, and involves correcting negative deviations from the goals and/or exploiting positive deviations.

LO5 Explain how the marketing mix elements are blended into a cohesive marketing program.

A marketing manager uses information obtained during the SWOT analysis, market-product focus, and goal-setting steps in the planning process to develop marketing strategies and marketing tactics for each marketing mix element for a given product, which are then implemented, as specified in the marketing plan, as a marketing program.

FOCUSING ON KEY TERMS

benchmarking p. 35
business p. 32
competencies p. 35
competitive advantage p. 35
core values p. 31
corporate level p. 29
cross-functional teams p. 30
functional level p. 30
goals p. 33
marketing dashboard p. 40
marketing metric p. 40
marketing plan p. 42
marketing strategy p. 48
marketing tactics p. 48

market segmentation p. 44
market share p. 33
mission p. 31
objectives p. 33
organizational culture p. 32
points of difference p. 45
profit p. 28
quality p. 35
situation analysis p. 43
strategic business unit (SBU) p. 30
strategic business unit level p. 30
strategic marketing process p. 42
strategy p. 29
SWOT analysis p. 43

APPLYING MARKETING KNOWLEDGE

1 (a) Explain what a mission statement is. (b) Explain how it gives a strategic direction to its organization. (c) Create a mission statement for your own career.

2 What competencies best describe (a) your college or university, (b) your favourite restaurant, and (c) the company that manufactures the computer you own or use most often?

3 Assume you were starting a new business. In terms of competition, would you rather enter a red ocean or blue ocean? Why?

4 Why does a product often start as a question mark and then move counter-clockwise around BCG's growth-share matrix shown in Figure 2–3?

5 Many Canadian universities have traditionally offered an undergraduate degree in liberal arts (the product) to full-time 18- to 22-year-old students (the market). How might such an institution use the four market-product expansion strategies shown in Figure 2–4 to compete in the twenty-first century?

6 What is the main result of each of the three phases of the strategic marketing process: (a) planning, (b) implementation, and (c) evaluation?

7 Select one strength, one weakness, one opportunity, and one threat from the SWOT analysis for Ben & Jerry's shown in Figure 2–6, and suggest a specific possible action that Unilever might take to exploit or address each one.

8 The goal-setting step in the planning phase of the strategic marketing process sets quantified objectives for use in the evaluation phase. What actions are suggested for a marketing manager if measured results are below objectives? Above objectives?

Building Your Marketing Plan

1. Read Appendix A, "Creating an Effective Marketing Plan." Then write a 600-word executive summary for the Coffee Break Coffee House marketing plan using the numbered headings shown in the plan. When you have completed the draft of your own marketing plan, use what you learned in writing an executive summary for the coffee house to write a 600 word summary to go in front of your own marketing plan.

2. Using Chapter 2 and Appendix A as guides, give focus to your marketing plan by (a) writing your mission statement in 25 words or less, (b) listing three nonfinancial goals and three financial goals, (c) writing your competitive advantage in 35 words or less, and (d) doing a SWOT analysis table.

Video Case 2

CANADIAN TIRE

Background

Canadian Tire is an iconic corporation with five inter-related businesses that offer Canadians, coast to coast, a range of goods and services that meet life's everyday needs, including general merchandise and clothing, petroleum, and financial services. The company operates more than 1,200 general merchandise and clothing stores and gas stations, and also is a major financial services provider. The company employs 58,000 Canadians and has revenue of close to $10 billion annually. According to Canadian Tire, the company offers goods and services that meet life's everyday needs people under one of the nation's most-trusted brands—the red triangle. In fact, Canadian Tire consistently ranks among the top 10 brands in Canada. Moreover, 90 percent of Canadians live within 25 kilometres of a Canadian Tire store, and 90 percent of Canadians shop at a Canadian Tire store at least once a year. Finally, Canadian Tire is one of the most-shopped general merchandise retailers in Canada.

Canadian Tire's Core Businesses

Canadian Tire has five core businesses:

- **Canadian Tire Retail (CTR)** is a retail chain that offers automotive parts, sports and leisure goods, and home products. Canadian Tire Retail and its Associate Dealers together form Canada's most-shopped general merchandise retailer, with more than 480 stores from coast-to-coast. Canadian Tire offers customers a large selection of national and retail brands through three specialty categories in which the organization is the market leader: automotive parts, accessories, and service; sports and leisure products; and home products. CTR serves over 180 million customers a year. The corporation believes that CTR is the main engine of it corporate growth.
- **PartSource** is an automotive parts specialty chain with more than 85 stores designed to meet the needs of major purchasers of automotive parts—professional automotive installers and serious do it yourselfers.
- **Canadian Tire Financial Services** manages over four million Canadian Tire MasterCard accounts and markets related to financial products and services for retail and petroleum customers. Canadians can also access financial services online at **www.ctfs.com.** One in five Canadian households has a Canadian Tire credit card.
- **Canadian Tire Petroleum** is one of the country's largest and most-productive independent retailers of gasoline, operating more than 280 gas bars, more than 280 convenience stores and kiosks, and more than 70 car washes.

- **Mark's,** one of the country's leading apparel retailers, operates more than 375 stores in Canada. Under the Clothes That Work™ marketing strategy, Mark's sells apparel and footwear in work, work-related, casual, and active-wear categories, as well as health-care and business-to-business apparel. The Web site, **www.marks.com,** offers Canadians the opportunity to shop for Mark's products online. Mark's is the largest industrial apparel and footwear retailer and the second-largest casual pants and jeans retailer in Canada. It is also the seventh-largest seller of women's wear in Canada. Many of Mark's stores are co-located with CTR stores. And the company recently launched new clothes vending machines!

Canadian Tire's Strategic Goals/Objectives

In 2010, Canadian Tire set some very specific strategic goals and objectives. They include the following:

1. *Strengthen the core—create a great CTR with a strong automotive division.* Specific activities to achieve this goal include rolling out new-concept stores, including small-market stores; enhancing its customer loyalty program; developing a customer-centric retailing approach; and improving customer experience at the store level.

2. *Align business units to support core CTR growth, including automotive, and deliver strong performance.* Specific activities to achieve this goal include opening new or rebranded outlets at Petroleum, PartSource and Mark's; testing new credit cards and financing programs to drive new avenues of growth and to support CTR marketing initiatives; bringing more auto parts closer to customers by building new PartSource hub stores; and piloting store rebranding of "Mark's Work Wearhouse" to "Mark's."

3. *To become a high-performing, customer-focused organization.* Specific activities to achieve this goal include completing centralization of key corporate centre functions across the company; simplifying pricing, promotional planning, and vendor engagement; upgrading technology infrastructure to reduce risk and lower operating costs; incorporating business sustainability as an inherent part of business strategy; and growing Canadian Tire Jumpstart Charities to support community-based programs to assist financially challenged families and kids.

Canadian Tire's Performance

The year 2009 was characterized by a slowing economy, which impacted almost every Canadian retailer. Figure 1 shows Canadian Tire's financial performance comparing 2008 and 2009. Figure 2 shows the performance of each business unit.

As you can see in Figure 1, the company's performance has declined in 2009 compared to 2008 on three key metrics of performance. Figure 2 reveals why Canadian Tire insists that CTR is a core component of their overall business. It accounts for 63 percent of overall revenue and 55 percent of overall earnings before taxes. However, it is interesting to note that the financial services unit, while representing only 10 percent of overall gross operating revenue, represents 27 percent of overall earnings before taxes.

Conclusions

Canadian Tire is optimistic about its future growth. It believes one of its greatest assets is its brand. It further believes that sustaining its brand will require each of its non-core business units—PartSource, Financial Services, Petroleum, and Mark's—to make a substantial contribution to the core business unit, Canadian Tire Retail (CTR). Canadian Tire insists that the strategic alignment of these units with the CTR core will provide it with a sustainable competitive advantage and unique position among Canadian retailers.

Questions

1 Canadian Tire has articulated three strategic goals/objectives (see above). Do you agree with these goals/objectives? If so, how best can they be achieved? If you do not agree, what should be the company's strategic objectives?

2 You learned in this chapter that part of determining growth strategies is determining where the company wants to go. Using the market-product analysis (see Figure 2–4) map out the growth strategies for each of Canadian Tire's business units.

3 Another thing you learned in this chapter is the importance of tracking performance by using marketing dashboards and metrics. Take a look at Figure 2 in this case. What can you glean from this data in terms of the performance of each business unit?

4 Now, again looking at the data in Figure 2, calculate the rate of return (percentage-wise) that each business unit is contributing to earnings before taxes for each business unit. What does this reveal? Does this impact on your decision about where to grow the business? Does this data affirm Canadian Tire's belief that CTR is and should be its "core business"?

5 Canadian Tire is known for having the first and most-enduring loyalty program in Canada—Canadian Tire Money. How can the company leverage this program to achieve additional market growth?

● **FIGURE 1**
Canadian Tire financial performance (2008 vs. 2009)

	2008	2009	Change
Retail sales (millions)	10,614.4	10,020.9	(5.6%)
Gross operating revenue	9,121.3	8,686.5	(4.8%)
Earnings before income taxes	543.0	479.2	(11.8%)

● **FIGURE 2**
Financial performance for each business unit (2009)

	Gross Operating Revenue (millions)	% of Overall Revenue	Earnings before Taxes (millions)	% of Overall Earnings before Taxes
Canadian Tire Retail[1]	5,552.2	63%	261.6	55%
Canadian Tire Financial Services	910.0	10%	131.9	27%
Canadian Tire Petroleum	1,515.0	17%	24.2	5%
Mark's Work Wearhouse	834.0	10%	61.5	13%
Totals	8,811.2	100%	479.2	100%

[1] Includes PartSource.

A

Creating an Effective Marketing Plan

"New ideas are a dime a dozen," observes Arthur R. Kydd, "and so are new products and new technologies." Kydd should know. As chief executive officer of St. Croix Venture Partners, he and his firm have provided the seed money and venture capital to launch more than 60 start-up firms in the last 25 years. Today, those firms have more than 5,000 employees. Kydd elaborates:

> I get 200 to 300 marketing and business plans a year to look at, and St. Croix provides start-up financing for only two or three. What sets a potentially successful idea, product, or technology apart from all the rest is markets and marketing. If you have a real product with a distinctive point of difference that satisfies the needs of customers, you may have a winner. And you get a real feel for this in a well-written marketing or business plan.[1]

This appendix (1) describes what marketing and business plans are, including the purposes and guidelines in writing effective plans, and (2) provides a sample marketing plan.

MARKETING PLANS AND BUSINESS PLANS

After explaining the meanings, purposes, and audiences of marketing plans and business plans, this section describes some writing guidelines for them and what external funders often look for in successful plans.

Meanings, Purposes, and Audiences A *marketing plan* is a road map for the marketing activities of an organization for a specified future period of time, such as one year or five years.[2] It is important to note that no single generic marketing plan applies to all organizations and all situations. Rather, the specific format for a marketing plan for an organization depends on the following:

- *The target audience and purpose.* Elements included in a particular marketing plan depend heavily on (1) who the audience is, and (2) what its purpose is. A marketing plan for an internal audience seeks to point the direction for future marketing activities and is sent to all individuals in the organization who must implement the plan or who will be affected by it. If the plan is directed to an external audience, such as friends, banks, venture capitalists, or potential investors, for the purpose of raising capital, it has the additional function of being an important sales document. In this case, it contains elements such as the strategic plan/focus, organization, structure, and biographies of key personnel that would rarely appear in an internal marketing plan. Also, the financial information is far more detailed when the plan is used to raise outside capital. The elements of a marketing plan for each of these two audiences are compared in Figure A–1 on page 54.
- *The kind and complexity of the organization.* A small neighbourhood restaurant has a somewhat different marketing plan from that of Nestlé, which serves international markets. The restaurant's plan would be relatively simple and directed at serving customers in a local market. In Nestlé's case, because there is a hierarchy of marketing plans, various levels of detail would be used—such as the entire organization, the business unit, or the product/product line.
- *The industry.* Both the restaurant that serves a local market and Medtronic that sells heart pacemakers globally analyze competition. Not only are their geographic thrusts far different, but the complexities of their offerings and hence the time periods likely to be covered by their plans also differ. A one-year marketing plan may be adequate for the restaurant, but Medtronic may need a five-year planning horizon because product-development cycles for complex, new medical devices may be three or four years.

In contrast to a marketing plan, a *business plan* is a road map for the entire organization for a specified future period of time, such as one year or five years.[3] A key difference between a marketing plan and a business plan is that the business plan contains details on the research and development (R&D), operations, and manufacturing activities of the organization. Even for a manufacturing business, the marketing plan is probably 60 or 70 percent of the entire business plan. For such businesses as a small restaurant or an auto repair shop, marketing and business plans are virtually identical. The elements of a business plan typically targeted at internal and external audiences appear in the two right-hand columns in Figure A–1.

The Most-Asked Questions by Outside Audiences   Lenders and prospective investors reading a business or marketing plan that is used to seek new capital are probably the toughest audiences to satisfy. Their most-asked questions include the following:

1. Is the business or marketing idea valid?
2. Is there something unique or distinctive about the product or service that separates it from substitutes and competitors?
3. Is there a clear market for the product or service?
4. Are the financial projections realistic and healthy?
5. Are the key management and technical personnel capable, and do they have a track record in the industry in which they must compete?
6. Does the plan clearly describe how those providing capital will get their money back and make a profit?

Rhonda M. Abrams, author of *The Successful Business Plan,* observes that "within the first five minutes of reading your . . . plan, readers must perceive that the answers to these questions are favourable."[4] While her comments apply to plans seeking to raise capital, the first five questions just listed apply equally well to plans for internal audiences.

Writing and Style Suggestions   There are no magic one-size-fits-all guidelines for writing successful marketing and business plans. Still, the following writing and style guidelines generally apply:[5]

● **FIGURE A–1**

Elements in typical marketing and business plans targeted at different audiences

Element of the plan	Marketing plan		Business plan	
	For internal audience (to direct the firm)	For external audience (to raise capital)	For internal audience (to direct the firm)	For external audience (to raise capital)
1. Executive summary	✔	✔	✔	✔
2. Description of company		✔		✔
3. Strategic plan/focus		✔		✔
4. Situation analysis	✔	✔	✔	✔
5. Market-product focus	✔	✔	✔	✔
6. Marketing program strategy and tactics	✔	✔	✔	✔
7. R&D and operations program			✔	✔
8. Financial projections	✔	✔	✔	✔
9. Organization structure		✔		✔
10. Implementation plan	✔	✔	✔	✔
11. Evaluation and control	✔		✔	
Appendix A: Biographies of key personnel		✔		✔
Appendix B, etc.: Details on other topics	✔	✔	✔	✔

- Use a direct, professional writing style. Use appropriate business terms without jargon. Present and future tenses with active voice ("I will write an effective marketing plan.") are generally better than past tense and passive voice ("An effective marketing plan was written by me.").
- Be positive and specific to convey potential success. At the same time, avoid superlatives ("terrific," "wonderful"). Specifics are better than glittering generalities. Use numbers for impact, justifying projections with reasonable quantitative assumptions, where possible.
- Use bullet points for succinctness and emphasis. As with the list you are reading, bullets enable key points to be highlighted effectively.
- Use A-level (the first level) and B-level (the second level) headings under the numbered section headings to help readers make easy transitions from one topic to another. This also forces the writer to organize the plan more carefully. Use these headings liberally, at least one every 200 to 300 words.
- Use visuals, where appropriate. Photos, illustrations, graphs, and charts enable massive amounts of information to be presented succinctly.
- Aim for a plan 15 to 35 pages in length, not including financial projections and appendixes. An uncomplicated small business may require only 15 pages, while a high-technology start-up may require more than 35 pages.
- Use care in layout, design, and presentation. Laser printers give a more professional look than do ink-jet printers. Use 11- or 12-point type (you are now reading 10.5-point type) in the text. Use a serif type (with "feet," like that you are reading now) in the text because it is easier to read, and sans serif (without "feet") in graphs and charts, as in Figure A–1. A bound report with an attractive cover and clear title page adds professionalism.

These guidelines are used, where possible, in the sample marketing plan that follows.

SAMPLE FIVE-YEAR MARKETING PLAN FOR COFFEE BREAK COFFEE HOUSE

To help interpret the marketing plan for Coffee Break Coffee House that follows, we suggest some guidelines.

Interpreting the Marketing Plan

The sample marketing plan for Coffee Break, a specialty coffee house on Kwantlen Polytechnic University's Surrey campus, was written by Professor John Shepherd of Kwantlen Polytechnic University. The invaluable assistance provided by Aina Adashynski, Belinda Kaplan, Catherine Wilkinson, and Connie Shepherd during the preparation of the plan is greatly appreciated.

Notes in the margins next to the plan fall into two categories:

1. *Substantive notes* are shaded blue and elaborate on the significance of an element in the marketing plan and are keyed to chapter references in this text.
2. *Writing style, format, and layout notes* are shaded in pink and explain the editorial or visual rationale for the element.

A Closing Word of Encouragement

Writing an effective marketing plan is hard—but challenging and satisfying—work. However, dozens of the authors' students have used effective marketing plans they wrote for class in their interviewing portfolio to show prospective employers what they could do and to help them get their first job.

Blue boxes explain significance of Marketing Plan elements.

Pink boxes give writing style, format, and layout guidelines.

The Table of Contents provides quick access to the topics in the plan, usually organized by section and subsection headings.

Seen by many experts as the single most important element in the plan, the Executive Summary "sells" the plan to readers through its clarity and brevity.

The Company Description highlights the recent history of the organization.

Marketing Plan
Coffee Break Coffee House

Table of Contents

1. Executive Summary

The following plan outlines the marketing strategy and tactics for *Coffee Break,* a specialty coffee house opening on *Kwantlen Polytechnic University*'s Surrey campus in autumn 2010. Located in a residential area, the Surrey campus has two existing restaurants, a cafeteria and a student association café. There are several additional restaurants within easy walking distance.

Coffee Break will target a combined student and staff population of 11,000 with a take-out coffee counter and coffee house. *Coffee Break* will have four distinguishing features: a coffee take-out counter, a comfortable atmosphere created by a skilled serving team, excellent beverages, and the use of on-campus promotional activities to build awareness and a steady clientele.

In addition to securing a suitable location, *Coffee Break* must expand the campus food services market by attracting student beverage purchases now spent in local restaurants. Unless campus amenities, such as *Coffee Break,* can provide reasons for students to remain on campus after hours, the market is inherently limited by the number of days that classes are in session each year.

2. Company Description

Coffee Break is opening a 60-seat coffee house adjacent to the central courtyard of the *Kwantlen Polytechnic University*'s Surrey campus. The coffee house will target the 10,000 students, 900 staff, and visitors of the campus with a selection of specialty coffees, teas, beverages, and healthy snacks.

Kwantlen Polytechnic University has a student population of 17,000 spread over four campuses that service the growing municipalities of Surrey, Langley, Delta, and Richmond. The main *Kwantlen* campus is near the western boundary of Surrey, a municipality of 400,000 people located southeast of the City of Vancouver. Originally a college, *Kwantlen Polytechnic* has grown rapidly over the past 20 years and is now a university.

Coffee Break will be known for its warm, inviting atmosphere, a fun place for students between 18 and 25 years of age to relax and meet with friends. A coffee take-out counter at the front will focus on fast turnaround times for students and staff who desire a quick coffee or a snack between classes.

The café will offer a wide selection of coffees, teas, and other refreshments, along with light food items such as wraps, pastries, and vegetarian dishes. *Coffee Break* will focus on providing quality coffee and superior customer service. The restaurant's menu prices will match those of its on-campus competitors.

The interior of the coffee house will resemble a neighbourhood pub with lots of wood and a youthful spin. Features will include comfortable chairs of a variety of types, an outside view of the campus courtyard, and the aroma of fine coffee. Warm colours, local art, evening entertainment, theme nights, and light background music will create a fun, enjoyable atmosphere.

Customer service will be emphasized. Serving staff will be hired based on their warm, friendly personalities and carefully trained in the arts of service and fine coffee. Staff will be recognized for outstanding performance and every effort will be made for them to feel an integral part of the team.

Coffee Break's focus on atmosphere, service, fine coffee, and ongoing promotional activities will expand the size of the food-services pie on campus by giving students another reason to linger on campus after class. This plan describes how *Coffee Break* can establish a leading position on the Surrey campus and develops a business model that can be franchised to other medium-sized college and university campuses.

3. Strategic Focus and Plan

Core Values

The core values of *Coffee Break* are as follows:
1. To respect our customers and fellow workers.
2. A commitment to providing our customers with a superior quality product, delivered with a smile.

Mission

The mission of Coffee Break is to create a social place where people leave their worries at the door, enjoy the best coffee on campus, and meet fellow students in a relaxed atmosphere.

Non-Financial Objectives

1. To open the first *Coffee Break* restaurant in August 2010.
2. To become known as the best student employer on campus.
3. To become the place for students to relax and meet with friends on campus.
4. To open three *Coffee Break* restaurants at other western Canadian colleges or universities within five years.

The Strategic Focus and Plan sets the strategic direction for the entire organization, a direction with which proposed actions of the marketing plan must be consistent. This section is not included in all marketing plans. See Chapter 2.

The qualitative Mission statement focuses the activities of Coffee Break for the stakeholder groups to be served. See Chapter 2.

The Objectives sections set both the nonfinancial and financial targets—where possible in quantitative terms—against which the company's performance will be measured. See Chapter 2.

> Lists use parallel construction to improve readability—in this case a series of infinitives starting with "To .-.-."

Financial Objectives

1. To reach the break-even point for the Kwantlen coffee house by the end of its first year of operations (e.g., $230,000 in annual sales).
2. To achieve the revenue target of $300,000 and an operating profit of $46,500 during the 2010–2011 fiscal year.
3. To finance future expansion using internally generated funds.

Competencies and Competitive Advantage

The core competency of *Coffee Break* is its management's expertise and focus in the unique needs of the post-secondary market. This capability will enable the business to create a student-centred atmosphere, where learners can drink a good cup of coffee or other beverage in a friendly, youth-focused atmosphere.

Management will achieve service and product excellence by carefully selecting the staff, conducting ongoing staff training, providing leadership by example, and creating a supportive environment where employees feel valued.

> The SWOT Analysis identifies strengths, weaknesses, opportunities, and threats to provide a solid foundation as a springboard to identify subsequent actions in the marketing plan. See Chapter 2.

4. SWOT and Market Analysis

SWOT Analysis

The SWOT analysis is summarized in Figure 1, showing the internal and external factors that could affect the restaurant's competitive success.

> The text discussion of Figure 1 (the SWOT Analysis table) elaborates on its more important elements. This "walks" the reader through the information from the vantage of the plan's writer. In brief plans this accompanying discussion is sometimes omitted, but is generally desirable to give the reader an understanding of what the company sees as the critical SWOT elements.

In the company's favour are internal factors such as the strength of the concept, detailed planning, and a management team with restaurant experience. Favourable external factors include a growing population base in *Kwantlen*'s service area and limited on-campus competition.

Coffee Break faces adverse factors, both internally and externally. Business start-ups are risky propositions, particularly in the food-services sector. Securing a good on-campus location near high pedestrian areas is crucial. Staffing the coffee house with qualified service and food preparation staff will be a challenge.

Industry Analysis

Coffee is the second-largest commodity in the world in market value. Discovered in Ethiopia, the coffee plant was first chewed as a stimulant. Coffee houses spread to Europe in the 1600s and became popular meeting places for people of all social classes. Both Lloyds of London and the London Stock Exchange started in coffee houses.

> The Industry Analysis section provides the backdrop for the subsequent, more detailed analysis of competition, the company, and the company's customers. Without an in-depth understanding of the industry, the remaining analysis may be misdirected. See Chapter 2.

Each long table, graph, or photo is given a figure number and title. It then appears as soon as possible after the first reference in the text, accommodating necessary page breaks. Short tables or graphs that are less than 3 cm are often inserted in the text without figure numbers because they do not cause serious problems with page breaks.

FIGURE 1: *Coffee Break* SWOT Analysis

Internal Factors	Strengths	Weaknesses
Management	Experienced and entrepreneurial management	Competitive market for qualified and experienced staff.
Offering	Quality coffee, good service, and a student-friendly atmosphere.	Wide range of nearby specialty coffee and fast food restaurants.
Marketing	Low-cost promotional activities targeted to each market segment.	A limited marketing budget.
Human Resources	Practices that attract and retain quality serving staff.	A highly competitive job market for quality service staff.
Manufacturing	Partnerships with post-secondary culinary arts programs.	Limited access to experienced and talented chefs.
Product Development	Partnerships with post-secondary culinary arts programs.	Limited in-house capacity for new menu item development.
External Factors	Opportunities	Threats
Consumer/Social	Significant, underserved customer demographic. Retail location key.	Price sensitive and seasonal market.
Competition	Limited on-campus competition.	Wide range of specialty coffee and fast food restaurants within walking distance.
Technological	No fundamental changes expected.	Product and process innovations by specialty coffee and fast food chains.
Socio-demographic	Continued population growth expected in the Kwantlen service area.	Disposable income of students affected by availability of work and tuition fees.
Legal/Regulatory	Health regulations benefit well-managed operations.	Few barriers for entry.

Effective tables seek to summarize a large amount of information in a short amount of space.

Even though relatively brief, this in-depth treatment of the coffee industry demonstrates to the plan's readers the company's understanding of the industry in which it competes. It gives both external and internal readers confidence that the company thoroughly understands its own industry.

Coffee farming is labour intensive, as 4,000 handpicked beans are needed to produce a pound of the coffee. The best coffees use beans from the *arabica* plant, which is grown in the tropics at altitudes around 1,500 metres. The plant is delicate, requiring a steady temperature year-round and tender loving care. Coffees are judged by their aroma, body, acidity, and flavour.

Over the past 30 years, specialty coffee houses have transformed the industry. According to Barney McKenzie, co-founder of Vancouver-based *Bean Around the World,* the specialty coffee boom should have peaked around 1997.

However, social trends such as less tolerance for alcohol as a social lubricant, a focus on a healthier lifestyle, and a greater sophistication among consumers have transformed specialty coffee houses into a mainstream product. Nearly 20 percent of adult Americans drink a cup of specialty coffee each day, and the market for specialty coffees experienced sales growth of 5 to 10 percent per year until the 2008 recession.

Specialty coffee retailers were hit hard by the recent recession. For example, the *Starbucks* chain has shut down over a thousand stores since July 2008. Moreover, fast food chains, such as *McDonald's,* are moving aggressively into the market with new offerings and multi-million dollar advertising budgets.

While coffee houses still sell 49 percent of specialty coffee servings in the U.S., hamburger chains sell 11 percent and doughnut chains were 19 percent. The dividing line both in quality and in price is blurring between traditional and specialty brands. According to *Leaky Bucket Report, Starbucks* faces a "price-value problem" and "credible threats from *McDonald's* and *Dunkin' Donuts.*"

While coffee is the most popular beverage, it is facing competition from energy drinks. Stimulant energy drinks such as *Red Bull* were a US$1.3 billion market in 2004 and growing at 40 percent per year. Energy drinks target consumers under 30 with active lifestyles and a desire for an energy kick.

Energy drinks and teas have become attractive substitutes to coffee among younger people. According to a *Restaurants and Institutions* article, Generation Y is more adventuresome in their tea preferences, drinking more green tea, herbal teas, and chai than other age groups.

Greater Vancouver Specialty Coffee Retail Market

Greater Vancouver has a sophisticated and highly competitive coffee market. In the 2008 Yellow Pages, there were listings for 220 coffee houses and coffee specialty bars with City of Vancouver addresses. Roughly 100 of these retailers were independents and the remainder were chain operations.

The largest player is *Starbucks* with 76 outlets, followed by *Blenz Coffee* with 18 outlets, *Tim Hortons* with 7 outlets, and several smaller chains. Regional chains include *Blenz Coffee, Bean Around the World,* and *Caffè Artigiano.*

Surrey Specialty Coffee Retail Market

In comparison, the City of Surrey, with roughly 70 percent of the City of Vancouver's population, has 53 restaurants listed under the Coffee Houses & Specialty Bars, and Coffee – Retail categories of the Yellow Pages. The majority of listings are either *Starbucks* (17) or *Tim Hortons* (14). There are two local chains: *Java Hut* (3) and *Esquires Coffee* (4). The remaining 15 listings are single-store operations.

The different number of coffee houses servicing the Vancouver and Surrey markets is hard to explain. Median family and individual incomes are similar, though there are a larger number of low-income households in Surrey. Vancouver is more urbanized than Surrey, which has several town centres embedded in suburban sprawl.

According to 2006 Census, the provincial electoral district that surrounds *Kwantlen Polytechnic University*'s Surrey campus is largely composed of visible minorities and recent immigrants. The largest ethnic group are South Asians (55 percent)

As with the Industry Analysis, the Competitive Analysis demonstrates that the company has a realistic understanding of who its major competitors are and what their marketing strategies are. Again, a realistic assessment gives confidence to both internal and external readers that subsequent marketing actions in the plan rest on a solid foundation. See Chapters 2, 3, 8, and 9.

followed by residents of European descent (31 percent). This ethnic mix may be significant as India is a tea region. Five times more tea than coffee is consumed per capita in India.

Competitive Analysis—On-Campus Restaurants

The *Chartwells College & University Dining Division* of the Compass Group recently lost its food-services contract at the *Kwantlen* campuses. In April 2010, *Kwantlen* announced that Sodexo Canada was the successful bidder for the institutional food-services contract. The contract is still in the process of being negotiated and its impact on campus food services is currently unknown. Sodexo, headquartered in France, has revenue of €14.7 billion a year and has won numerous industry awards.

The facility is a standard college cafeteria with plastic seating and is overdue for a renovation. *Starbucks* specialty coffees were added to the menu in September 2009 with a wide range of lattes, iced coffees, cappuccinos, and espresso drinks available on request. Demand for the 50 to 60 specialty brews steadily grew during the autumn semester. Coffee is the most popular hot beverage. Tea is much less popular. The cafeteria also provides a selection of breakfast items, along with soups, burgers and fries, daily entree features, chili, wraps, sandwiches, pizzas, pastries, muffins, and pre-packaged salads.

According to Belinda Kaplan, manager of food services, most coffee is sold during the following times: 9 to 10 a.m., 11 a.m. to 1 p.m., and 5 to 6:30 p.m. The busiest days in cafeteria are Monday through Thursday. Friday is the slowest weekday, and Saturdays are very slow. The cafeteria is open from 7 a.m. to 9 p.m., Monday to Thursday, and for reduced hours on Friday and Saturday.

The *GrassRoots Café* is operated by the *Kwantlen Student Association (KSA)* on the Surrey campus. The student association is located in part of a campus building that includes student offices, a café, and a fitness centre.

GrassRoots offers a trendier food menu, including wraps, burgers, pasta, stir-fry, soups, salads, bagels, a line of vegetarian items, muffins, and dessert items. The prices of its menu items are similar to those in the cafeteria, mainly in the $5 to $7 range.

The café has a pleasant atmosphere, with students at the front counter, who may connect better with the students than the older staff in the cafeteria. *GrassRoots Café* is open from 8 a.m. to 8 p.m., Monday to Thursday, and until 5 p.m. on Friday. The sitting area contains a mixture of couches, bar stools, and chairs surrounding round and rectangular tables. A big-screen TV at one end of the room is used for movie nights, and an open mike is available. While the KSA received a liquor licence in 2009, it has not emphasized that aspect of the business. According to Catherine Wilkinson, the KSA commercial services manager, most coffee sales are made before and between classes. The majority of coffee sales occur during the following times: 9:30 to 10:30 a.m.,

11:30 a.m. to 1:00 p.m., 1:45 to 2:15 p.m., and 5:30 to 6:30 p.m. Coffee sales average $500 per weekday.

Sales volume is highly seasonal. Daily sales during the summer semester are roughly a quarter of those during the autumn and spring semesters. According to a recent edition of the student newspaper, the 2010 budget for the *Grassroots Café* is $286,000 in annual sales.

The *GrassRoots Café* relies heavily on word of mouth among students and discount coupons for faculty and staff. KSA is actively involved in student orientation at the beginning of each semester. The cafeteria doesn't actively promote its services.

Both campus restaurants would benefit from improved signage, as they are not visible from the central courtyard. The university cafeteria is on the second floor of a building and *GrassRoots Café* at the edge of the campus. Both restaurants have ample floor space—1,400 square feet for the café and 3,200 for the cafeteria. However, limited food preparation and storage space are a challenge for the *GrassRoots Café*. A visit to both restaurants on a Tuesday, at 11 a.m., revealed comparable traffic at their front counters and a similar number of people seated.

Competitive Analysis—Off-Campus Restaurants

Kwantlen's Surrey campus is located on 72nd Avenue, near Surrey's Newton Town Centre. According to the City of Surrey, the avenue is a busy street with a daily traffic count (in both directions for a typical weekday) of 30,000 vehicles.

Direct competition for *GrassRoots Café* and the cafeteria are five pizza and ethnic restaurants (e.g., *Urban Masala, Great Pizza, Gulberg Restaurant, Ocean Park Pizza,* and *Yellow Chilli Restaurant*) adjacent to the Surrey campus. The menu items at these restaurants are significantly cheaper than those found on campus.

Kwantlen students frequently meet off campus at *Tim Hortons, Starbucks,* or *KFC*, a short drive away in the Strawberry Hill Shopping Mall. *Tim Hortons* is a doughnut shop, with a dedicated clientele who line up each morning for their coffee at the take-out window. *Tim Hortons* caters to people interested in a coffee, snack, or light meal. Given its relatively inexpensive menu and adequate seating, it is popular among the students.

The nearest *Starbucks* is attached to a *Chapters* bookstore in the Strawberry Hill Shopping Mall. The coffee house has limited seating but a better selection of specialty coffee and teas. A larger Starbucks is slightly farther away on Scott Road.

Customer Analysis—Canadian and U.S. Markets

According to the *2003 Canadian Coffee Drinking Study,* coffee was Canada's most popular beverage with 63 percent of adults drinking coffee on a daily basis. The average

> These two sections use a "block" style and do *not* indent each paragraph, although an extra space separates each paragraph. Compare this page with the previous page, which has indented paragraphs. Most readers find that indented paragraphs in market plans and long reports are easier to follow.

Canadian coffee drinker consumed 2.6 cups a day. Men and women were equally likely to drink coffee.

Most coffee was consumed earlier in the day, half during breakfast and an additional 16 percent during the morning hours. People drank a further 9 percent during lunches, 10 percent in the afternoons, 8 percent during supper, and 7 percent in evening hours.

Coffee was consumed by Canadians at home (66 percent), at work (12 percent), at eateries (16 percent), and at institutions such as public libraries (5 percent). Roughly half of Canadians drank a specialty coffee during the year and 6 percent drank such brews on a daily basis. Canadians reported drinking iced coffee (24 percent) and cappuccinos (32 percent) during that year. According to the *US National Coffee Association's 2008 Annual Coffee Study,* 17 percent of adult Americans drank gourmet coffee on a daily basis. Americans in the 18-to-24 age group were "the fastest-growing segment of coffee drinkers" according to the report, drinking an average of 3.2 cups a day.

An article in *Automatic Merchandiser* suggests that coffee drinkers in the 18-to-34 age group are more likely to visit coffee houses and less likely to prepare coffee at home. It suggested that the message of marketers should stress the "coffee house experience" and "energy boost" among younger consumers.

Another article in *Dairy Foods* explored the young adult market, stating that many young people do not use either ground or instant coffee. This age group is driving the markets for coffee beverages (such as coffee-milk beverages), organic coffees, and ethical coffees. These consumers are more likely to drink iced coffee, lattes, flavoured coffees, espressos, or cappuccinos than other age groups.

A personal conversation with a counter person at a nearby *Starbucks* store suggested that lattes (i.e., coffees or other beverages with hot milk) are very popular for women during the winter months, though they are considered "girlie drinks" by men. Blended ice drinks are very popular among both men and women during the summer months.

Customer Analysis—Campus Market

The coffee house's primary market will be students at the Surrey campus of *Kwantlen Polytechnic University.* Surrey lacks a central downtown core and its businesses are spread among six different townships. As a result, most students either drive or catch a ride to the Surrey campus each day.

The student registrations at the campus for the 2008/09 academic year were 10,042, a figure that has grown 5 percent over the past three years. Student numbers are highly seasonal, with peak figures during the September to April semesters. Student enrollments for the summer semester are roughly one-third of enrollments during the regular academic year.

Satisfying customers and providing genuine value to them is why organizations exist in a market economy. This section addresses the question of "Who are the customers for Coffee Break?" citing relevant survey data. See Chapters 5, 6, 7, 8, and 9.

According to the *2008 Fall Registration Survey,* one-third of the students are new to *Kwantlen* each autumn, highlighting the need for regular promotional activities. Primary residence figures illustrate that 79 percent of *Kwantlen* students live within the university's service area, which includes the cities of Surrey, Langley, Delta, and Richmond. Less than 5 percent of the student population are international students. The age profile of the student body is heavily weighted to recent high school graduates, with 48 percent of students between 18 and 21 years of age.

FIGURE 2: Kwantlen Student Age Profile, 2008/09

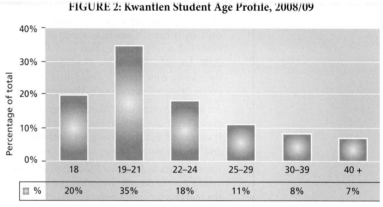

%	20%	35%	18%	11%	8%	7%
Age groups	18	19–21	22–24	25–29	30–39	40 +

Age groups (years)

The registration survey asked the students why they selected the institution. The most common reasons were selection of programs, affordable tuition, proximity to home, and program reputation. Most students were either preparing for a specific occupation (51 percent) or planning to transfer to another college or university (31 percent).

Unfortunately, the survey reported on the student population as a whole. No figures were available for the Surrey campus. Limited funds and lack of free time are issues facing *Kwantlen* students. Many of the students are employed part-time while attending the university—48 percent reported working 10 to 29 hours a week and 14 percent in excess of 30 hours.

The major ethnic groups at *Kwantlen* are Caucasian (47 percent), East Asian (19 percent), South Asian (18 percent), Southeast Asian (6 percent), and other (10 percent). As many South Asians live in the City of Surrey, their percentage of the Surrey campus student population is higher than indicated by the figures above.

A *Florida State University* study stressed the importance of a social space in the lives of post-secondary students. Eighty percent of students reported their favourite

> This section demonstrates the company's insights into major trends that have a potentially large impact.

social place as off campus, mainly in coffee shops and restaurants. These places help students find companionship, relax, and adjust to academic life. Over 70 percent of university students visit their social place at least once a week and nearly a quarter visit daily. Important features for favoured social places are location, atmosphere, and the opportunity to meet other students.

A secondary market for *Coffee Break* is the staff and faculty of *Kwantlen Polytechnic University*. There were 1,600 *Kwantlen* employees, of which, 56 percent reported Surrey as their primary campus, suggesting a head count of 900 at that location.

While faculty (40 percent of total staff) workloads are often spread over multiple campuses, support staff and administration are typically stationed at a specific campus. Eighty-five percent of employees had worked at *Kwantlen* for over 2 years and 44 percent for more than 10 years. Given the long service of many *Kwantlen* employees, many are nearing retirement. For example, 29 percent of faculty, 19 percent of staff, and 23 percent of administration employees are 55 years of age or older.

<u>Market Potential</u>

The combined daily sales of the two existing restaurants are probably in the range of $5,000 per weekday, from September to April, when the institution's classes are in session. A ballpark estimate of coffee sales is in the range of 25 percent of total food and beverage sales, perhaps $1,250 per day.

If a conservative estimate is made, based on 25 percent of people on campus buying one cup a day at $2.00 per cup, this results in an estimate of $5,000 in potential daily coffee sales. Clearly, there must be a lot of leakage of food-services sales to nearby restaurants. Based on this estimate and the number of school days per year, a total market potential of $800,000 of annual coffee sales appears reasonable.

5. Market-Product Focus and Goal Setting

This section outlines the marketing objectives for *Coffee Break,* the target markets, points of difference, and restaurant positioning.

<u>Marketing and Product Objectives</u>

One-Year Marketing Objectives
- To create awareness of the *Coffee Break* concept on campus among 80 percent of students, staff and faculty.
- To stimulate trial and repeat purchases by 40 percent of consumers in all target market segments.
- To become recognized among *Kwantlen* students and staff for its prompt and friendly service and the best coffee on campus.
- To be the most popular place on campus for students to relax and meet with friends.

Size of headings should give a professional look to the report and not overwhelm the reader. These two headings are too large.

As noted in Chapter 10, the chances of success for a new product are significantly increased if objectives are set for the product itself and if target market segments are identified for it. This section makes these explicit for Coffee Break. The objectives also serve as the planned targets against which marketing activities are measured in program implementation and evaluation.

This section identifies the specific niches or target markets toward which the company's products are directed. When appropriate and when space permits, this section often includes a market-product grid. See Chapter 9.

An organization cannot grow by offering only "me-too" products or services. The greatest single factor in a new product's or service's failure is the lack of significant "points of difference" that set it apart from competitors' substitutes. This section makes these points of difference explicit. See Chapter 10.

Five-Year Marketing Objectives
- To become known as the employer of choice at all college and university campuses where *Coffee Break* has operations.
- To establish coffee houses in three other medium-sized colleges or universities in Western Canada.

Marketing and Product Objectives

Coffee Break's primary market is the 10,000 students enrolled in courses at the Surrey campus between September and April. One-third as many students are enrolled during the summer semester. The take-out window will service students looking for a quick coffee or snack between classes. The coffee house will serve students looking for a place to socialize, eat light meals, or do school work.

The venture's secondary market is the 900 employees working at the Surrey campus. Roughly 40 percent are faculty, who spend little time on campus when classes are not in session. The remaining 60 percent of support staff and administrators have a fairly regular work week on campus. A warm, inviting atmosphere should attract employees looking for a place to relax and socialize with colleagues. Employees could become a steady clientele of a take-out coffee counter if the service was prompt, the location was convenient, and the price was right.

Finally, depending on the exact location of the coffee house, a tertiary market could be the high school students and staff of the 1,500-student Princess Margaret Secondary School, a few hundred metres east of the campus, along 72nd Avenue. Partnerships between the two institutions, such as an enrichment program, already result in some mixing of the student populations.

Points of Difference

Coffee Break will have three distinguishing characteristics.
1. A comfortable, youth-oriented atmosphere created by serving teams with a "can do" attitude, regular entertainment, and a warm decor.
2. Hot and cold beverages prepared by staff with a passion for excellence.
3. The skillful use of advertising, promotions, and publicity to establish a brand identity, create a sense of excitement, and target specific market segments.

Positioning

Coffee Break is positioned in the middle of the specialty coffee spectrum in pricing and product quality. The restaurant's differentiation will be its student-focused atmosphere and friendly well-trained staff. *Coffee Break* will raise the competitive bar for customer service and beverage quality on campus.

A positioning strategy helps communicate the company's unique points of difference of its products to prospective customers in a simple, clear way. This section describes this positioning. See Chapters 9 and 10.

Everything that has gone before in the marketing plan sets the stage for the marketing mix actions—the 4 Ps—covered in the marketing program. See Chapters 10 through 19.

To improve readability, each numbered section usually starts on a new page. (This is not always done in this plan to save space.)

This section describes in detail key elements of the company's product strategy. See Chapters 10, 11, and 12.

The Price Strategy section makes the company's price point very clear, along with its price position relative to potential substitutes. When appropriate and when space permits, this section might contain a break-even analysis. See Chapter 13.

6. Marketing Program

Coffee Break must reduce the leakage of student spending on food in off-campus restaurants and counter competitive reactions from the two existing restaurants.

More fundamentally, *Coffee Break* must collaboratively work with university administration and other partners to provide students and staff with more reasons to stay on campus after class. Otherwise, *Coffee Break* market will be limited to the 150 days when classes are in session between September to April and a summer session of 60 days.

Product Strategy

The retailing concept is based on *The Beanery Coffee House*, a 60-seat specialty coffee house on the UBC campus. *The Beanery* is like a two-storey house of about 2,000 square feet. Spread among several rooms are sofas, places to study, computers, a piano, a pool table, and a television, a relaxing environment like someone's home. *The Beanery* offers a variety of beverages, sandwiches, wraps, salads, and light snacks.

A *Florida State University* study summarized the design elements that create a warm atmosphere for students. Features include comfortable chairs, furniture that students can rearrange, wood furniture, an outside view, and pleasant food smells. The layout should allow students to rearrange the furniture to create "temporary territories." Students like to "anchor themselves against walls" and look outside to people watch.

Coffee Break will provide a variety of seating, ranging from bar stools to sofas to places to spread out and do homework. Lighting will be adequate in study areas so that students can read and use their computers. Tables that are square or rectangular are easier to assemble for group projects and socializing.

The aroma of baked goods and coffee is important in creating a coffee house atmosphere. Coffee shops vent smells into the seating areas and outside to draw people in. A "soft and cozy atmosphere" can be created by using soft lighting and through the colour and texture of the flooring, walls, and furnishings. Amenities such as a pool table, dart boards, a book/magazine exchange, local art, and background music help create the right atmosphere and acoustic privacy for conversations.

Coffee Break will add to its menu a limited selection of South Asian cuisine and attempt to recruit servicing staff fluent in the major Indian dialects.

Price Strategy

The strategy of *Coffee Break* is to match the prices of on-campus restaurants and to offer similar prices as specialty coffee shops such as *Starbucks* (see Figure 3). The goal is to avoid price competition with existing on-campus restaurants.

GrassRoots Café will distribute discount coupons to *Kwantlen* staff and will not charge for coffee refills. *Coffee Break* will provide similar incentives.

FIGURE 3: Price Ranges for Coffee near Campus

Beverages	Cafeteria	GrassRoots	Tim Hortons	Starbucks	McDonald's
Regular Coffee	$1.75–$2.20	$1.75–$2.50	$1.16–$1.67	$1.65–$2.10	$1.19–$1.59
Tea	$1.40	$1.50	$1.16–$1.67	$1.85–$2.45	$1.19
Flavoured and Specialty Coffees	$2.45–$3.75	$3.75–$4.75	$1.47–$2.32	$3.50–$5.00	–
Iced Coffees	$2.70–$4.45	$4.75	$1.89–$3.09	$3.45–$4.55	$1.59–$1.99
Espresso or Americano	$2.15–$3.10	$1.75–$2.50	$1.19–$1.59	$1.60–$2.05	–
Cappuccino	$3.10–$4.10	–	$2.04–$3.14	$3.05–$4.05	–

Promotion Strategy

Print Material. The plan is designed to create local awareness and build a consistent identity among the university community. Print materials, menus, and signage will have the same style of lettering. A logo (two people with an arm on each others' shoulder) and a common theme—**where good friends gather**—will be used. Standard templates for menus, print advertisements, and brochures will be prepared.

Publicity. Prior to opening, interviews are planned with the editorial staffs of campus newspapers such as the *Kwantlen Chronicle* and *The Runner*. Management will seek interviews with reporters from local community newspapers.

Grand Opening. After a few weeks of limited hours and staff training at the end of summer, the Grand Opening is scheduled for September 2010. *Coffee Break* will partner with a suitable charity such as *SPCA* to use the Grand Opening as a fundraising event. A local radio station could co-sponsor the fundraiser, supplying live broadcasting on location during the event.

Advertisements. A small advertisement will be placed in each edition of the two *Kwantlen* newspapers, *Kwantlen Chronicle* and *The Runner*.

Student Orientation. Student orientations are held in September and January each year for new students. *Coffee Break* will staff a table and hand out student discount coupons at the beginning of each semester. Staff coupons will be distributed twice each year.

Sponsorships. A small budget will be available to sponsor sports teams and campus events.

Coffees of the World. Coffee Break will bring in specialty coffees, hold coffee tasting events, and create a coffee passport program, where a patron receives a stamp

---

Elements of the Promotion Strategy are highlighted in terms of the key promotional activities the company is emphasizing. For space reasons, the company's online strategies are not shown in the plan. See Chapters 16, 17, and 18.

The higher-level "A heading" of Promotion Strategy above has a more dominant typeface and position than the lower-level "B heading" of Student Orientation. These headings introduce the reader to the sequence and level of topics covered. The organization of this textbook uses this kind of structure and headings.

whenever a coffee from another country is consumed. Patrons with enough stamps receive a certificate.

Entertainment, Coffee Workshops, and Theme Nights. Kwantlen marketing students could help organize special events and promotions to gain applied work experience. Events could include coffee appreciation workshops, entertainment from local musicians, and cultural events organized by local ethnic groups.

Fantasy Getaways. Two fantasy getaway events are planned for the first year during the dreary winter months—*Amazon Adventure* and *African Escape. Amazon Adventure* would involve a special tasting of coffees from South America. *Coffee Break* staff, through the local consulate, will invite local Brazilian groups to display their traditional dances, music, and cuisine.

The Place Strategy is described here. See Chapters 14 and 15.

Place (Distribution) Strategy

The location of the coffee house is vital, particularly for the coffee take-out window. The ideal location is on the ground floor of one the buildings facing the central courtyard. Successful specialty coffee houses are typically located in high pedestrian traffic areas, allowing people to people watch. Outside tables allow people to take advantage of sunny days, an attractive amenity during the summer months.

Securing such a location will not be easy, given the space constraints on campus and the alternative uses for such locations such as campus bookstores, etc. However, given the desire of the university administration to improve on-campus facilities and amenities, an acceptable location might be found.

If adequate retail space is not available on campus, a market likely exists for an express coffee take-out service, much like the express Tim Hortons outlet at the Vancouver International Airport. The retail space for take-out coffee counter should be easier to lease and less costly to operate than a full coffee house.

All the marketing mix decisions covered in the just-described marketing program have both revenue and expense effects. These are summarized in this section of the marketing plan. See Appendix B.

7. Sales Forecast

The sales forecast of $300,000 during year one is based on $1,500 per day during the academic year and one-third that figure during the summer semester. Sales are split between coffee sales and other beverages, snack, and light meal menu items.

Cost of goods sold is budgeted at 32.5 percent of sales, rent at $3,500 per month, and other costs at $2,000 per month, including marketing costs. Schedules showing breakdowns of start-up costs, along with pro-forma income statements (see Figure 4), balance sheets, and monthly cash flow forecasts are found in the financials section of the business plan.

The financial projections are often based on judgment forecasts. Gross revenue and then operating profit—critical to the coffee house's survival—are also projected. Often, multiple forecasts using different forecast scenarios are included in the appendix to the plan.

FIGURE 4: *Coffee Break* **Pro-forma Income Statement (year ended August 31, 2011)**

Revenues and Expenses	Budget
Revenues	$300,000
Cost of Sales	97,500
Gross Profit	202,500
Employee Wages and Benefits	90,000
Rent and Common Area Costs	42,000
Other Operating Expenses	24,000
Total Operating Expenses	156,000
Operating Profit	46,500

As most operating expenses are fixed costs and cost of goods sold is a variable cost, the estimated break-even point of *Coffee Break* is:

$$\text{Break-even point (\$ sales)} = \text{Fixed costs}/(1 - \%\text{ variable costs})$$
$$= \$156,000/(1 - 32.5\%) = \$231,000 \text{ in annual sales}$$

While this sales amount suggests a comfortable safety margin, there is a tendency for new ventures to underestimate costs. A common rule of thumb used in the specialty coffee industry is a break-even point of ten times the commercial rent payment. This ballpark figure suggests that *Coffee Break* will break even on $300,000 of sales.

8. Implementation Plan

The Implementation Plan shows how the company will turn plans into results. Action-item lists are often used to set deadlines and assign responsibilities for the many tactical marketing decisions needed to enter a new market. See Chapter 19.

Marketing Organization

The manager of the coffee house will have overall responsibility for all marketing and promotional activities.

As additional coffee houses are added to the chain, a group management position will be created to develop and oversee the implementation of chain-wide marketing program activities. The division of marketing responsibilities between the individual coffee house managers and the group manager will be specified in their job descriptions. Separate annual budgets for local and group-wide marketing activities will be prepared by managers each year.

Marketing Budget

The marketing budget for 2010–2011 is outlined in Figure 5.

Marketing Activities Plan

Marketing activities will support the two-phase opening of the first *Coffee Break* outlet. The take-out window will open during the late summer before students arrive

FIGURE 5: *Coffee Break* Marketing Budget
(year ended August 31, 2011)

Marketing Costs	Budget
Advertising – Campus Newspapers	$500
Give-Away Items – Certificates, Small Prizes, etc.	500
Grand Opening Celebration	2,500
Entertainment, Theme Nights, etc.	2,000
Printing – Posters, Coupons, Promotional Materials, etc.	500
Sponsorships	500
Marketing Budget – Year One	**$6,500**

on campus. After staff training is complete, the Grand Opening of the coffee house is planned for the second week of September 2010.

A more detailed implementation plan for marketing and promotional activities, during year one, can be found in Figure 6.

FIGURE 6: *Coffee Break* Marketing Activities Plan
(year ended August 31, 2011)

When	Who	What
August 2010	Manager	Limited hours – coffee take-out window Distribution of staff coupons
September 2010	Manager	Student orientation week activities Grand Opening (second week of classes)
October 2010	Manager and staff	Tastes of the World (coffee and biscotti)
November 2010	Manager and staff	Tastes of the World (coffees and biscotti) Fantasy getaway – Amazon Adventure
December 2010	Manager and staff	Tastes of the World (coffee and biscotti) End of Classes Party
January 2011	Manager and staff	Tastes of the World (coffee and biscotti) Fantasy getaway – African Escape
February 2011	Manager and staff	Student orientation week activities Tastes of the World (coffees and biscotti) Valentine's Day Coffee and Chocolate
March 2011	Manager and staff	Tastes of the World (coffees and biscotti)
April 2011	Manager and staff	Tastes of the World (coffees and biscotti) End of Classes Party
May 2011	Manager and staff	Limited hours of operation Tastes of the World (coffee and biscotti)
June to August	Manager	Limited hours of operation Planning for the upcoming year

> The essence of the Evaluation Phase is comparing actual sales with the targeted values set in the plan and taking appropriate actions. See Chapter 19.

9. Evaluation Phase

Annual budgets will be prepared for *Coffee Break.* Actual sales and expenses will be compared to budgeted figures and variances investigated. Weekly sales by category will be tracked and the results of each promotional activity evaluated.

For each institution, *Coffee Break* will create an advisory board composed of students, faculty, and staff members. Each group will meet with *Coffee Break* staff on a monthly basis, over coffee, to identify problem areas and to evaluate how well the restaurant is meeting the needs of the campus community.

On the new Web, users are increasingly building their own tools. The result is greater customization and convenience, from maps that can be easily programmed to ads that change with every new blog post

craigslist

The classified-ad service has 23 employees but receives more traffic than all but seven other sites

Linked in

Social networking for suits. It brings together an élite clientele of global executives

e

At the auctio are the po ratings w bae

Google

The search empire built itself around a social function: counting links between Web sites

WIKIPEDIA

The ultimate crowdsourcing model, it showed that the masses are as smart as the experts

myspace.com
a place for friends

With 120 million users, it's a whole new society, with features that maximize individuality

Google
AdSense

Provides free ads relevant to your Web site, then pays you if people click on them

Google
Maps

Users can add their own points of interest to create mashups like *www.beerhunter.ca*

amazon.com

With customer reviews and recommendations, book buying is now a communal experience

THE GATHERERS

The crowd isn't just expressing itself more; it's also gathering and filtering all those blog posts and photographs and finding an audience for them

Blogg

The popular bl software servic every would-be a publish

iStockphoto

This photo store taps an army of amateurs, who can sell their shots for as little as $1

flickr

The photo-scrapbook site helped popularize tagging as a way to organize information

Bloglin

Lets users subsc various sites the updates from on a sing

digg

The crowd as news editor: readers "digg" stories they like and "bury" ones they don't

del.icio.us

Allows users to share their Web-browser bookmarks,

Technorati

chapter 3

Scanning the Marketing Environment

WEB 2.0 IS ALL ABOUT YOU!

The Web is changing at an extraordinary pace, and each year new change provides more customization and convenience for you. If you use Twitter, MySpace, Facebook, Second Life, or any one of hundreds of new products on the Web, you are already part of the new world of the Web!

Not long ago the Web simply provided a modern channel for traditional businesses. Music led the way with file-sharing services such as Napster and eventually online stores such as iTunes. The entire entertainment industry followed by offering books, movies, television, radio, and photography on the Web. The digital revolution allowed all of these businesses to benefit from the technical aspects of the Web.

Now the term Web 2.0 is used to describe the changes in the World Wide Web that reflect the growing interest in collaboration, open sharing of information, and customer control. Many products and services such as podcasts, webblogs, videologs, social networking, bookmarking, wikis, folksonomy, and RSS feeds are already available, and many more are in development.

As the focus moves from providing a new channel for existing businesses to empowering individual consumers with customized products, suddenly the Web is all about you! You can create your own video and post it on YouTube, sell your photos on iStockphoto, build a social networking site on Ning, publish your ideas at Blogger, find the right mate online at Match.com, and buy or sell products on eBay or Craigslist. How did this happen? The marketing environment changed!

learning objectives

After reading this chapter, you should be able to:

LO1 Explain how environmental scanning provides information about social, economic, technological, competitive, and regulatory forces.

LO2 Describe how social forces, such as demographics, and cultural and economic forces, such as macroeconomic conditions and consumer income, affect marketing.

LO3 Describe how technological changes are impacting marketers and customers.

LO4 Discuss the forms of competition that exist in a market, key components of competition, and the impact of small businesses as competitors.

LO5 Explain the major legislation that ensures competition and protects consumers in Canada.

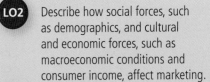

First, technologies such as high-speed Internet, high-resolution displays, file-transfer software, and mobile communications were developed. Second, the regulatory environment changed to allow the exchange and sale of copyrighted materials such as songs and movies. Third, competitive forces by companies such as Apple, Google, eBay, Microsoft, and Amazon gave the Web worldwide exposure. Finally, consumers changed, making it clear that they want "a tool for bringing together the small contributions of millions of people and making them matter." The future promises to be even more exciting. Some experts are suggesting that Web 3.0 will be even more innovative, including allowing you to have your very own intelligent personal assistant available 24/7 to help you find and obtain the products, services, and information that you want and need.[1]

Many businesses operate in environments where important forces change. Anticipating and responding to changes such as those taking place on the Web often means the difference between marketing success and failure. This chapter describes how the marketing environment has changed in the past and how it is likely to change in the future.

LO1 THE IMPORTANCE OF ENVIRONMENTAL SCANNING

environmental scanning
The process of continually acquiring information on events occurring outside the organization to identify and interpret potential trends.

Changes in the marketing environment are a source of opportunities and threats to be managed. The process of continually acquiring information on events occurring outside the organization to identify and interpret potential trends is called **environmental scanning.** Environmental scanning is critically important to marketers who wish to ensure that they remain aligned with the evolving marketplace. Companies that fail to engage in environmental scanning do so at their peril and perhaps truncate their future growth.

Tracking Environmental Trends

Environmental trends typically arise from five sources: social, economic, technological, competitive, and regulatory forces. As shown in Figure 3–1 and described later in this chapter, these forces affect the marketing activities of a firm in numerous ways. To illustrate how environmental scanning is used, consider the following trend:

> Statistics Canada revealed that coffee consumption in Canada has risen to over 92 litres, up 9 litres from its most recent low. Beer, wine, and bottled water all saw increases in consumption as well. But tea and soft drink consumption actually declined.[2]

What types of businesses are likely to be influenced by this trend? How will they be affected? What caused this trend? And how can businesses respond?

Clearly, many players in the Canadian beverage industry are affected by these trends. Obviously, coffee manufacturers, coffee shops, and supermarkets would be affected positively and would benefit from this trend. So too would producers and retailers of beer, wine, and bottled water. On the other hand, producers and retailers of teas and soft drinks would be adversely affected by these trends. The key to environmental scanning is not only identifying this trend but also determining why it is occurring. There may be many reasons, some influenced by marketers, some not. For example, perhaps the coffee manufacturers and retailers have simply done a better job

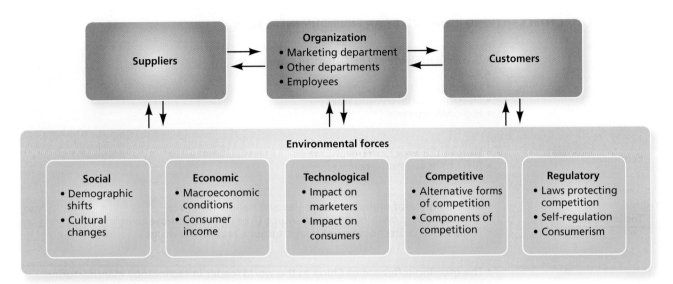

● FIGURE 3-1

Environmental forces affecting the organization as well as its suppliers and customers

marketing their beverage compared to their competitors? In fact, after steady declines in coffee consumption in recent years, coffee producers began offering new flavours and seasonal blends, coffee shops automated to prepare drinks faster, and supermarkets added coffee boutiques and gourmet brands to try to reverse the trend. These actions appear to have worked. On the other hand, perhaps changes in consumer needs and wants are responsible for this trend. For example, many college and university students often complain about being tired and fatigued, and coffee is known to provide a boost of energy to the user. So perhaps this group turned to coffee for this particular reason. It seems plausible since consumption of coffee by 18- to 24-year-olds is now at a record high. It could also be that companies like Starbucks have been able to capitalize on the trend of consumers seeking experiences and have focused on marketing coffee as an experience and not just a beverage.

But for tea the story is a little different. Even though tea consumption is down slightly, it remains the fourth-most popular beverage in Canada (behind coffee, milk, and tap water). Still, the Tea Association of Canada is hoping to increase tea consumption by capitalizing on Canadians' concern for health. It hopes that reports that specialty teas are linked to good health will help increase overall tea consumption.[3]

This example of one single trend in the beverage industry illustrates how successful scanning works: identifying trends, understanding the reasons behind the trends, and taking action to respond to such trends.

Will the reported healthful benefits of drinking specialty teas lead to increased tea consumption in Canada?

An Environmental Scan of Canada

What other trends might affect marketing in the future? A firm conducting an environmental scan of the marketplace might uncover key trends, such as those listed in Figure 3–2 for each of the five environmental forces.[4] Although the list of trends is far from complete, it reveals the breadth of an environmental scan—from the growing diversity of the Canadian population, to the shift to the experience economy, to the increasing use of new technologies. These trends affect consumers and the businesses and organizations that serve them. Such trends are covered as the five environmental forces are described in the following pages.

ENVIRONMENTAL FORCE   **TREND IDENTIFIED BY AN ENVIRONMENTAL SCAN**

Social
- Growing diversity of the Canadian population
- Aging
- Obesity
- Electronic social communities
- Eco-consciousness

Economic
- Shift to the experience economy
- Growth in electronic commerce

Technological
- Increasing use of digital technologies and nanotechnology
- The dramatic growth of the open source (free) software movement
- Advances in biotechnology, cosmetic surgery, and cancer drugs

Competitive
- The growing influence of China as the world leader in technology manufacturing
- Mergers and acquisitions to create scale and improve competitiveness
- Increased focus on empowering workers to improve performance

Regulatory
- New legislation related to digital copyright, intellectual property protection, and consumer privacy
- Increased emphasis on free trade
- Deregulation of industries to encourage competition

● **FIGURE 3–2**
An environmental scan of Canada's marketplace

L02 SOCIAL FORCES

social forces
Forces of the environment that include the demographic characteristics of the population and its values.

demographics
The study of the characteristics of a human population. These characteristics include population size, growth rate, gender, marital status, ethnicity, income, and so forth.

The **social forces** of the environment include the demographic characteristics of the population and its values. Changes in these forces can have a dramatic impact on marketing strategy.

Demographics

Demographics is the study of the characteristics of a human population. These characteristics include population size, growth rate, gender, marital status, ethnicity, income, and so forth. Several organizations, such as the United Nations, monitor the world population profile, while other organizations, such as Statistics Canada, provide information on the Canadian population.

The World Population at a Glance   The most recent estimates indicate that there are over 6 billion people in the world today and that the population is likely to grow to 9 billion by 2050. While this growth has led to the term population explosion, the increases have not occurred worldwide—they are primarily in the developing countries of Africa, Asia, and Latin America. In fact, India is predicted to have the world's largest population in 2050 with 1.5 billion people, and China will be a close second with 1.3 billion people. Moreover, as Figure 3–3 reveals, just ten countries will account for over 56 percent of the world's population by 2050.[5]

Another important global trend is the shifting age structure of the world population. It is expected that the number of people older than 65 will more than double in the coming decades, while the number of youth will grow at a much lower rate. Again, the magnitude of this trend varies by region, and the developed countries such

● FIGURE 3-3

Top ten most populous
countries by 2050

Country	Populations (millions)	Cumulative Percentage of World Population
India	1,531,438	17.2%
China	1,395,182	32.8%
USA	408,695	37.4%
Pakistan	348,700	41.3%
Indonesia	293,797	44.6%
Nigeria	258,478	47.5%
Bangladesh	254,599	50.4%
Brazil	233,140	53.0%
Ethiopia	170,987	54.9%
Democratic Republic of Congo	151,644	56.6%

as Canada are expected to face a high growth rate of the elderly age group. For example, by 2050, over 32 percent of the Canadian population will be 60 years of age or older.[6] Global income levels and living standards have also been increasing, although the averages across countries are very different. Per capita income, for example, ranges from $43,000 in Luxembourg, to $24,000 in Canada, to $800 in Afghanistan.

For marketers, such trends have many implications. Obviously, the relative size of such countries as India and China will mean they represent huge markets for many product categories. Elderly populations in the developed countries are likely to save less and begin spending their funds on health care, travel, and other retirement-related products and services. Economic progress in the developing countries will lead to growth in entrepreneurship; new markets for infrastructure related to manufacturing, communication, and distribution; and the growth of exports.

The Canadian Population Studies of the demographic characteristics of the Canadian population suggest several important trends. By 2011, the Canadian population is estimated to be 34 million; by 2050, it is expected to be 39 million.[7] But it is a population that is growing older and more ethnically diverse. The median age will rise from 37 years of age to almost 46 years of age by 2050.[8] With Canada's declining birth rate, the principal source of growth in the Canadian population will be from immigration, which will add even more diversity to the Canadian population. If current trends in life expectancy, birth rates, and immigration continue, niche markets based on age, life stage, family structure, geographic location, and ethnicity will become increasingly important.

baby boomers
The generation of those born between 1946 and 1964.

Generational Cohorts A major reason for the greying of Canada is that the **baby boomers**—the generation of those born between 1946 and 1964—are growing older. As the baby boomers have aged, their participation in the workforce and their earnings have increased, making them an important consumer market. This group accounts for the majority of the purchases in most consumer product and service categories. In the future, baby boomers' interests will reflect concern for their children, their grandchildren, their own health, and their retirement, and companies will need to position products to respond to these interests. Generally, baby boomers are receptive to anything that makes them look and feel younger. Olay's Total Effects product line, for example, includes anti-aging moisturizers, cleansing cloths, and restoration treatments designed for this age group. This aging baby boomer group is also starting to experience health problems related to aging, such as incontinence and erectile dys-function (ED). In fact, there is a heated ED marketing war in Canada as drug compa-nies vie for a share of this growing market.

Generation X
The population of those born between 1965 and 1976.

The baby boom cohort is followed by **Generation X,** which includes the popula-tion of those born between 1965 and 1976. This group represents about 15 percent of the Canadian population. This period is also known as the "baby bust" because the number of children born each year declined during that period. This generation of consumers is self-reliant, entrepreneurial, supportive of ethnic diversity, and better educated than any previous generation. Generation Xers are not prone to extrava-gance and are likely to pursue lifestyles that are a blend of caution, pragmatism, and traditionalism. For example, Generation Xers are saving, planning for retirement, and taking advantage of retirement plans much earlier than did the boomer generation. As the baby boomers move into grandparenthood, Generation X is becoming the new parent market. In response, some brands that Generation X helped popularize are expanding their offerings. Tommy Hilfiger and DKNY, for example, have launched children's lines for the babies of Generation X parents.

Generation Y
Those born between 1977 and 1994.

The generational cohort labelled **Generation Y** includes those born between 1977 and 1994. This was a period of increasing births, which resulted from baby boomers having children, and is often referred to as the "echo-boom" or "baby boomlet." Gen-eration Y exerts influence on music, sports, computers, video games, and especially wireless phones. Generation Y views wireless communication as a lifeline to friends and family and has been the first to use text messaging, wireless phone games, and built-in cameras. This is also the group that includes recent and future 21-year-olds—the beginning of adult responsibilities and many new consumer activities.

Because the members of each generation are distinctive in their attitudes and consumer behaviour, marketers have been studying the many groups or cohorts that make up the marketplace and have developed *generational marketing* programs for them. For example, Toyota Canada recently developed a spin-off company to develop and market a new brand of vehicles called Scion to appeal to the Generation Y group, while still marketing their traditional brands, such as the Toyota Camry, to the baby boomers. In addition, global marketers have discovered that many of the Canadian generational differences also exist outside of Canada.[9]

The Canadian Family   The types of families in Canada are changing in both size and structure. The average family size in Canada is about three persons. In 1971, one in three Canadian families consisted of the once-typical scenario of a husband work-ing outside the home, with a wife inside the home with their children. Today, only one in seven families falls into this category. The dual-income family is the norm in Canada, representing almost 65 percent of all husband–wife families.

blended family
Family formed by the merging into a single family of two previously separated units.

About 50 percent of all first marriages in Canada end in divorce. Thus, the single-parent family is also becoming more typical and is more socially acceptable. But the majority of divorced people eventually remarry, giving rise to the **blended family,** one formed by the merging into a single family of two previously separated units. Today, many Canadians are finding themselves as a step-parent, step-child, step-sibling, or some other member of a blended family. In fact, Hallmark Cards specially designs cards and verses for such blended families. But many people do not remarry, and single-parent families now represent almost 20 percent of all family units in Canada.

census metropolitan areas (CMAs)
Geographic labour markets having a population of 100,000 persons or more.

Population Shifts   Since the mid-1970s, there has been a major shift in the Canadian population from rural to urban areas. In fact, more than 80 percent of Canadians are urban dwellers. Most Canadians live in **census metropolitan areas (CMAs),** geographic labour markets having a population of 100,000 persons or more. About 65 percent of the Canadian population is located in just the top 27 CMAs in the country, which include such cities as Toronto, Montreal, Vancouver, Ottawa, Calgary, and Edmonton. Moreover, four major urban regions are emerg-ing in Canada, representing over 50 percent of the Canadian population. These important regions are the Golden Horseshoe in Ontario (Oshawa, Toronto, Hamilton, St. Catharines–Niagara, Kitchener, Guelph, and Barrie); Montreal and adjacent regions (Salaberry-de-Valleyfield, Saint-Jean-sur-Richelieu, Saint-Hyacinthe, Sorel, Joliette, and Lachute); British Columbia's Lower Mainland and southern Vancouver Island; and the Calgary–Edmonton corridor. With the concentration of the population in or near the CMAs and key urban regions, marketers can reach large segments of the Canadian population efficiently and effectively.

Ethnic Diversity   While we often think of Canada as consisting of French and English Canadians, close to three out of ten Canadians are of neither French nor British descent. While the majority of the non-British, non-French populations are of European descent, there has been a major growth in other ethnic groups and visible minorities in Canada. In fact, more than 100 different ethnic groups are represented in Canada. And close to 70 percent of all immigrants to Canada are now classified as visible minorities, primarily people from China, Southeast Asia, Africa, and India. Visible minorities are projected to represent between 21 and 25 percent of the Canadian population by 2017. The largest groups will be South Asians, Chinese, and blacks. Specifically, there will be close to 2 million South Asians, 2 million Chinese, and over 1 million blacks in Canada by 2017.[10]

Much of the ethnic population in Canada can be found in major metropolitan cities, such as Toronto, Vancouver, Montreal, Calgary, and Edmonton. In fact, by 2017, visible minorities will represent the majority of the population of Vancouver, and shortly thereafter this also will be the case for Toronto.[11] Moreover, the average age of these ethnic populations will be much lower than that of other Canadians, thus making them an important part of Canada's future consumer growth.

Marketers have recognized the growing ethnic diversity in Canada and have developed **ethnic marketing** (sometimes called *multicultural marketing*) programs, which are combinations of the marketing mix that reflect the unique attitudes, race or ancestry, communication preferences, and lifestyles of ethnic Canadians. For example, TD Canada Trust has obtained the largest share of the ethnic market in the financial services sector by targeting ethnic groups through community events and in-branch promotions. The Royal Bank has an ethnic marketing program to reach South Asians and Chinese communities across Canada and the company believes much of its future growth will come from ethnic or multicultural markets. And Scotiabank also targets to ethnic markets through community involvement and sponsorships.

Many other Canadian companies also engage in ethnic marketing, including Walmart, Sears Canada, IKEA, and The Brick. For example, Walmart runs ads targeted specifically to ethnic markets using ethnic television and speaking to these customers in native languages such as Chinese, Italian, Portuguese, and Spanish.[12] For more about the challenges and pitfalls of ethnic marketing in Canada, read the accompanying Marketing Matters box, "The Follies of Multicultural Marketing in Canada."[13]

ethnic marketing
Combinations of the marketing mix that reflect the unique attitudes, race or ancestry, communication preferences, and lifestyles of ethnic Canadians.

Culture

culture
The set of values, ideas, and attitudes that are learned and shared among the members of a group.

A second social force, **culture**, incorporates the set of values, ideas, and attitudes that are learned and shared among the members of a group. Because many elements of culture influence consumer buying patterns, monitoring national and global cultural trends is important in marketing. Cross-cultural analysis needed for global marketing is discussed in Chapter 7. Some noteworthy cultural trends in Canada are discussed here.

Changing Attitudes and Values   In recent years, Canadians have experienced notable cultural changes that have affected consumer attitudes and values. Attitudes toward work, lifestyles, and consumption are evolving. For example, more than 65 percent of Canadian women work outside the home. In fact, women now make up close to half of the Canadian labour force. But with more working women, the

The Follies of Multicultural Marketing in Canada

According to Sachi Mukerji, managing partner of Monsoon Communications, there are three basic follies of multicultural marketing. Not knowing your audience is the first great folly of modern Canadian *multicultural* marketing. Second is not taking the numbers seriously. Third, too many marketers continue to see multicultural marketing only as a simple creative adaptation.

Mukerji suggests that too many marketers simply do not have a deep and rich understanding of the multicultural audiences they are seeking and tend to paint multicultural markets with a broad brush. For example, South Asians are often lumped together yet there is great diversity in South Asian value systems, family structures, psychographics, and purchasing influences. Additionally, while Statistics Canada has confirmed that South Asian and Chinese communities are dominating the changing face of Canada, many marketers have not responded to these new emerging markets. Mukerji suggests that South Asians, in particular, are coming to Canada in large numbers and in five years will outnumber the Chinese in Canada. Yet, the largest and fastest-growing multicultural segment is really not on the radar for most national marketing companies. Companies that have recognized this market segment, unfortunately,

are typically only making simple marketing adaptations to appeal to this segment. Often the core national strategy is modified to include culturally oriented catch phrases and imagery. But this is not sufficient. For example, a quick advertising solution is typically used when a real marketing solution based on customer needs is the real answer. For that, marketers have to get away from their desks and get into the marketplace, yet few are doing so. If marketers did so they would realize that there are cultures within cultures and a variety of family, religious, language, and social pillars that are driving purchase behaviour.

Mukerji suggests that there are a few things marketers can do to improve their multicultural marketing efforts. One, start to customize, not generalize, and do not believe you can get away with building stereotypes. You may do your brand more harm than good. Two, build a relationship with your ethnic Canadian customers. Acknowledge them as Canadians while respecting them for being different in their culture and value systems. Three, do not be in a hurry. Results may not be obtained in the first year. But, if you do it right your return on investment will materialize by years two and three. Four, spend your resources in gaining knowledge of these ethnic markets, including good field research.

number of tasks to do is expanding, while the time available to do them is shrinking. This has led to the phenomenon of time poverty. Therefore, many Canadian consumers, particularly working women, are living harried lives and want to do business with companies that can offer them greater convenience. Many businesses are responding by offering express lanes of checkouts, longer store hours, drive-through windows, delivery services, and electronic shopping. Sobeys Inc., a major supermarket, offers its time-pressed shoppers the convenience of one-stop shopping, including groceries, in-store pharmacies, wellness centres, and banking services. The Hudson's Bay Company offers its customers the option of shopping in its retail stores or on the Internet via its online store at HBC.com. The Bay and Imperial Oil have teamed up to allow customers to use The Bay and Zellers credit cards at Esso stations across Canada. Esso even allows customers to pay for their purchases with its electronic "Speedpass" payment system.

Companies are also creating new products to meet the convenience imperative demanded by consumers. From soup to desserts, products now come in hands-free versions for easier consumption. The concept of "dashboard dining" is now a major trend in the food industry with car-friendly products and packaging popping up everywhere. The Campbell Soup Company, for example, now offers "Soup at Hand" for the busy commuter.

Many Canadians are changing their attitudes toward health. Fitness activity and sports participation are on the rise. Many Canadians are also changing their eating habits. For example, Statistics Canada reports that Canadians are consuming less sugar, less fat, and fewer calories in their diets. Many Canadians are also drinking healthier beverages, including bottled water and juices, instead of traditional soft drinks.[14]

Health-conscious Canadians are also buying more health supplements and medical self-diagnostic kits. For example, sales of multivitamins and calcium supplements are soaring, and brands such as Centrum, Shoppers Drug Mart's Life brand, and Roots Canada's vitamin lines are enjoying growth. LifeScan Canada is doing well with its self-testing kits that can monitor cholesterol or test for colorectal cancer.

However, while some Canadians are trying to be healthier, the medical community suggests that obesity is becoming a major public health threat. In fact, obesity in Canada is reaching epidemic proportions and is even showing up in young children. Some firms are responding to this trend by marketing plus sized clothing. In fact, Canadian retailers report clothing sales to larger women are growing faster than the overall rate.

value consciousness
The concern for obtaining the best quality, features, and performance of a product or service for a given price.

Another change in the attitudes of Canadians is the trend toward **value consciousness**—the concern for obtaining the best quality, features, and performance of a product or service for a given price. Innovative marketers have responded to this new orientation in numerous ways. Holiday Inn Worldwide offers customers Holiday Inn Express hotels, which feature comfortable accommodations with room rates lower the traditional Holiday Inns. Sobeys Inc., one of Canada's top food retailers, offers customers its Compliments Value brand of products, which is a private-label, value-based line. Canada's major banks offer lower-interest credit cards, some with value-added enhancements, such as frequent flyer programs and cash-back offers. Even Canada's sports, restaurant, and entertainment industries are appealing to the value-conscious customer.

Another emerging consumer trend is *eco-consciousness* or *going green.* Many Canadians are more sensitive about the impact their consumption has on their natural environment, and they make their buying decisions accordingly. This may mean buying more environmentally safe or more environmentally friendly products, buying products that can be reused or recycled, or actually reducing consumption altogether. The Hotel Association of Canada, for instance, says six in ten Canadians look for an environmentally friendly hotel as part of their travel plans. Air Canada is working with Toronto-based Zerofootprint on a program that allows customers to contribute to an environmentally friendly project to cancel out their share of carbon dioxide generated by their flights. Air Canada patrons can go online to calculate the amount of carbon dioxide their trip will generate and the cost to offset it, which can then be added to their ticket purchase. A trip from Vancouver to Montreal (return), for example, would cost the flyer an extra $12.80, and this offset amount would go to planting trees, restoring ecosystems, and assisting in green community developments.

Canadians are spending more of their dining-out budget at ethnic restaurants.

This trend toward eco-consciousness has opened up numerous opportunities for creative businesspeople, who are called *ecopreneurs,* entrepreneurs who see business opportunities through an environmental lens. As noted in the Video Case in Chapter 1, Stratus Vineyards began with this perspective and has found customers who appreciate this philosophy and buy its products. Another example of an eco-based business is Vancouver-based Earthcycle Packaging. It has created an eco-friendly package made from a renewable resource called palm fibre, which composts in less than 90 days and provides a healthy contribution to soil. Finally, Evergreen Memories of Dryden, Ontario, is a business built on providing "green gifts" to customers, including tree seedlings that couples can give as favours to guests attending their weddings. In Chapter 4, we will examine more fully the growing importance of preserving the ecological environment and its effects on both consumer and corporate behaviour.

Responding to consumer demand for value, Sobeys offers a value-based line of products that come with a low-price guarantee.

Finally, another important trend is that Canadians are becoming more experiential. As the chapter opener points out, Canadians are willing to try new things, and are seeking new experiences. For example, spending on foreign travel is up, spending on entertainment and dining outside the home is also up, in particular, spending on ethnic foods. Canadians looking to spice up their lives are flocking to a new generation of ethnic restaurants. Spending on Chinese, Japanese, and Greek food has increased dramatically. Food chains such as Manchu Wok, Edo Japan, and Mr. Greek have all reported major jumps in revenue.[15] This trend is consistent with discussions in previous chapters of this text regarding the emerging customer experience era.

---

learning review

1. Describe three generational cohorts.

2. Why are many companies developing multicultural marketing programs?

3. What is a census metropolitan area?

ECONOMIC FORCES

economy
Pertains to the income, expenditures, and resources that affect the cost of running a business and household.

The second component of the environmental scan, the **economy,** pertains to the income, expenditures, and resources that affect the cost of running a business and household. We will consider two aspects of these economic forces: a macroeconomic view of the marketplace and a microeconomic perspective of consumer income.

Macroeconomic Conditions

Of particular concern at the macroeconomic level is the inflationary or recessionary state of the economy, whether actual or perceived by consumers or businesses. In an inflationary economy, the cost to produce and buy products and services escalates as prices increase. From a marketing standpoint, if prices rise faster than consumer incomes do, the number of items consumers can buy decreases. Whereas inflation is a period of price increases, recession is a time of slow economic activity. Businesses decrease production, unemployment rises, and many consumers have less money to spend. The Conference Board of Canada's report, *Canadian Outlook Long-Term Economic Forecast* (through the year 2030), indicates modest economic growth, stable inflation, strong commodity prices, and a strong Canadian dollar.

Assessing consumer expectations of an inflationary and recessionary economy is an important element of environmental scanning. Consumer spending, which accounts for two-thirds of Canadian economic activity, is affected by expectations of the future. Surveys of consumer expectations are tracked over time by researchers, who ask such questions as "Do you expect to be better off or worse off financially a year from now?" Surveyors record the share of positive and negative responses to this question and related ones to develop an index, sometimes called a consumer confidence or consumer sentiment index. The higher the index, the more favourable are consumer expectations. Many firms evaluate such indexes in order to plan production levels. Chrysler LLC, for example, uses such indexes to plan its automobile production levels in order to avoid overproducing cars during a recessionary economy.

Consumer Income

The microeconomic trends in terms of consumer income are also important issues for marketers. Having a product that meets the needs of consumers may be of little value if they are unable to purchase it. A consumer's ability to buy is related to income, which consists of gross, disposable, and discretionary components.

gross income
The total amount of money made in one year by a person, household, or family unit.

Gross Income   The total amount of money made in one year by a person, household, or family unit is referred to as **gross income.** Average gross family income in Canada is slightly over $76,000. But family income in Canada varies by province as well as by the education level and profession of the head(s) of the family. For example, the majority of families earning above the average income of $76,000 are headed by university graduates. Average gross family income also varies by province and territory. Do the Going Online exercise, "Family Income in Canada by Province and Territory," to learn about family income in Canada.

disposable income
The money a consumer has left after paying taxes to use for such necessities as food, shelter, clothing, and transportation.

Disposable Income   The second income component, **disposable income,** is the money a consumer has left after paying taxes to use for such necessities as food, shelter, clothing, and transportation. Thus, if taxes rise at a faster rate than does disposable income, consumers must economize. The average Canadian household saw about 20 percent of their expenditures go to personal income tax, while food, shelter, clothing, and transportation accounted for almost 45 percent of total household expenditures. The cost of transportation has now outstripped the cost of food, with transportation accounting for over 14 percent of total household expenditures, while food accounted for only 11 percent. However, the proportion of income spent on necessities varies by household income level. For example, the lowest one-fifth of income households in Canada spent over half their household income on food, shelter, and clothing while the top one-fifth of income household spent 27 percent.[16]

discretionary income
The money that remains after paying for taxes and necessities.

Discretionary Income   The third component of income is **discretionary income,** the money that remains after paying for taxes and necessities. Discretionary income is used for luxury items, such as vacations at a Four Seasons resort. An obvious problem in defining discretionary versus disposable income is determining whether something is a luxury or a necessity. Observation can be a way to make this determination; if a family has Royal Doulton china, Rolex watches, and Lexus automobiles, one could assume that they have, or had, discretionary income. Still, it is important to note that a product defined as a necessity by one individual may be viewed as a luxury by another. For example, some Canadians view a microwave oven as a necessity, while others see it as a luxury item.

LO3 TECHNOLOGICAL FORCES

technology
Inventions or innovations from applied science or engineering research.

Our society is in a period of dramatic technological change. **Technology,** the third environmental force, refers to inventions or innovations from applied science or engi-neering research. For example, nanotechnology, the science of unimaginably small electronics, has led to smaller microprocessors, efficient fuel cells, and major advances in biomedicine, including implantable health monitoring systems. New computer technology and robotics have also led to a host of new products, including "smart cars" that can park themselves.

New technologies are also dramatically changing marketing practices and forever altering the way consumers shop and what they buy. Business experts agree that new technologies are enabling marketers and, more importantly, are empowering custom-ers. Let's see how!

Technology's Impact on Marketers

intranet
An Internet/Web-based network used within the boundaries of an organization.

extranet
An Internet-based technology that permits communication between a company and its suppliers, distributors, and other partners.

marketspace
An information- and communication-based electronic exchange environment.

e-business
All electronic-based company activities, both within and outside the company.

e-commerce
Specific buying and selling processes on the Internet.

e-marketing
Also called *online marketing*, the marketing component of e-commerce.

The transformative power of technology and its impact on marketers may be best illustrated by the widespread adoption and use of *information and communication technologies (ICTs)*. One of the most important ICTs that has changed the marketing landscape is the Internet. In fact, over 80 percent of all Canadian firms use the Internet, creating business efficiencies and enabling firms to engage in new levels of interactive marketing (Chapter 1) not imaginable a decade ago. Many have applied Internet-based technology internally, through an intranet. An **intranet** is basically a private Internet that may or may not be connected to the public Internet. Many companies also use an **extranet,** an Internet-based technology that permits communication between a com-pany and its suppliers, distributors, and other partners (such as advertising agencies).

The Internet and other ICTs have also given rise to the new **marketspace,** an information- and communication-based electronic exchange environment. In this new marketspace, Canadian companies can engage in e-business, e-commerce, e-marketing, and social media marketing. **E-business** is a broad concept that includes all electronic-based company activities, both within and outside the company. **E-commerce** is a more narrow activity involving specific buying and selling processes on the Internet.

E-marketing, or *online marketing*, is simply the marketing component of e-commerce. In Canada, it appears that buying online outstrips marketing online. For example, while 45 percent of Canadian firms make purchases online themselves, less than 10 percent are actually engaged in online selling to other businesses (*business-to-business marketing*, or B2B) or to final consumers (*business-to-consumer*, or B2C). Still, e-marketing has been growing steadily over the past five years in Canada with the value of sales transacted online now exceeding $40 billion. The bulk of these sales, however, continue to be B2B transactions, not B2C.[17] But experts suggest that even though actual online B2C sales are not a substantial part of overall B2C retail sales (less than 2% of the total), the online environment clearly influences off-line consumer purchase behaviour.[18] Marketers are well aware of this fact and leverage the Internet to grow awareness of their brands and to communicate the benefits of their brands to the customer. This is particularly true with the application of social media marketing. Many companies, large and small, now have a presence on online social communities and networks such as Facebook, MySpace, and Twitter.

Just some of the growing e-marketing platforms and techniques that marketers are using include e-mail marketing, search-engine marketing, in-game ads/advergaming, mobile marketing, interactive Web sites, and electronic classifieds. For example, Canada, is one of the world leaders when in comes to e-mail marketing. High delivery rates (93%), opening rates (55%), and click-through rates (8%) establish Canada as one of the best markets in terms of e-mail marketing results.[19] *Search-engine marketing (SEM)* is growing at a double-digit rate with Google, Yahoo, MSN, and AOL dominating the field. Companies recognize that having a search-engine marketing strategy is necessary to reach online customers. Many marketers use *search-engine optimization (SEO)* so that when you search for information or items online, the resultant listings for certain keywords are the ones you see first.

Many Canadian companies also market their products by advertising in video games (in-game ads) or by creating actual games built around their brand (advergames). In-game advertising, especially to players who play online, is growing substantially. Gaming Web sites reach almost 50 percent of the total Internet universe.[20] Companies place their products within the games and/or allow users to click on ads to view them. Advergames are actual video games built for and around the specific marketer's brand.

Mobile marketing, particularly by cellular or wireless phones, is a core emerging digital platform for marketers. Almost 65 percent of Canadians have access to wireless phones, and they use them for more than simple phone conversations.[21] Most wireless phones in Canada are multi-use devices and can be used for voice, text, photos, Internet, and e-mail purposes. Many marketers engage in text-message marketing (via short message service, or SMS) over wireless phones. A key aspect of mobile marketing is known as *short codes.* Short codes allow mobile device users to interact with marketers via a five- or six-digit code that often spells a word or brand name.[22] Other marketers use mobile technology to reach consumers with actual video content. Additionally, many marketers use the power of the Internet to develop interactive Web sites (many with video content), while other marketers have developed electronic classified ad sites. We will discuss many of these concepts further when we cover marketing communications topics in Chapters 16 to 18. Finally, there is a new tool available for marketers wishing to stay in contact with their highly mobile customers. Twitter is a microblogging site that uses a short messaging service. For example, skateboard entrepreneur Tony Hawk stashed 60 decks in cities around the world and sent out tweets to the more than 677,000 people who follow Hawk on Twitter. His scavenger hunt helped promote his line of skateboards—the Birdhouse brand. In no time at all, the skateboards were located. The media picked up the story and photos of happy hunters appeared everywhere. All of this without a planning session or a budget! This successful Twitter program was replicated again when Tony launched his new video game, Tony Hawk: Ride.[23]

To see how entrepreneurs and other marketers leverage new technologies like Twitter, read the text.

Technology's Impact on Customers

The new marketspace may have enabled marketers with new and innovative ways to market, but it has also clearly empowered consumers. Armed with the power of the Internet, consumers research companies and brands and communicate to others their experiences with those companies and brands.

The Internet has become an integral part of the lives of Canadians. Over 22 million Canadians are now part of the Internet or online universe. They are spending between 13 and 14 hours per week, or about 2 hours per day on the Internet.[24] The Internet is the third-highest media consumed in Canada, behind television and radio only. The Internet is influencing the way consumers buy products, do their banking, communicate, consume media, and play games. High-speed penetration (broadband) and wireless access via new technology devices such as mobile phones and PDAs (such as the Apple iPad and RIM Blackberry) are allowing Canadian consumers to take the Internet experience to the next level. For example, over 18 million Canadians have a wireless device, mainly a cellular or mobile phone, and over 25 percent of these customers use their wireless phone or PDA to log on to the Internet.[25] Even portable game consoles like Sony PSP and Nintendo Wii are Internet-compatible and can be used as mobile devices.

Other customer-driven Internet-based platforms include social media such as online social networks and communities, blogs, and other consumer-generated content sites. For example, it is estimated that close to 1 million Canadians have a personal **blog** on the Internet—a personal Web site or Web page that contains the online personal journal of an individual.[26] These blogs often contain personal reflections, comments, and experiences of the writer, including how they feel about certain companies and brands. In addition to blogs, there has been tremendous growth in other consumer-or user-generated content on the Internet. *User-generated content (UGC),* also called *user-created media,* encompasses a variety of tools and media. This includes online social networks and communities such as MySpace and Facebook, where users create personal Web pages full of self-designed and self-authored content to share with others in their network or community. For example, if Facebook were a country it would be the third largest in the world with over 500 million users. Other online networks include YouTube, which features consumer-produced videos that are posted and shared among users. Many such videos feature user-created ads or spoofs of commercial ads. And, as mentioned earlier, technologies like Twitter are allowing consumers to stay connected in real-time with each other and the brands they buy. In essence, 24/7 consumers can receive and send world news, news about purchases, or simple updates to and from family and friends. To learn more about the emergence of social media and its impact on customers and marketers, read the Marketing Matters box, "The Emergence of Social Media."[27]

The interesting thing about UGC is that smart, forward-thinking marketers were the ones who created the platforms, architecture, and virtual spaces to allow consumers to express themselves. In doing so, these entrepreneurs created their own new businesses—and consumers have benefited by having new venues to express themselves—and gained greater control over their marketing environment.

Other marketers have created *consumer-to-consumer (C2C) marketing* sites, allowing consumers to buy and sell products and services among themselves. The best example is eBay, which allows consumers to engage in online buying and selling, on a global, 24/7 basis. Other sites, such as Craigslist, also facilitate C2C marketing on a more local or regional level.

Finally, many empowered customers have actually managed to create a new form of marketing called *customer-to-business (C2B) marketing,* where proactive customers initiate communication and interact with companies online, providing suggestions and feedback on their experiences. Of course, many forward-thinking companies have encouraged and enabled such behaviour, so much so that C2B activity now extends to the customer actually making new product suggestions, providing advice on advertising and promotion activities, and even assisting in determining price points for products and services. Some consumers are now being compensated if their suggestions and advice positively impact on the company's bottom line.

In addition to the Internet, other technologies have empowered Canadian consumers and given them greater control over their environment. For example, Canadian

blog
A personal Web site or Web page that contains the online personal journal of an individual.

Marketing Matters

The Emergence of Social Media

As you read in Chapter 1, some experts have suggested that we have entered the social media marketing era and the rules of the marketing game have now changed. In fact, Erik Qualman, author of *Socialnomics,* argues that social media is transforming how we live and how organizations conduct business. And for the doubters out there he provides some amazing statistics regarding the impact of social media. For example, he says that 96 percent of Gen Y'ers belong to a social network; social media has overtaken porn as the #1 activity on the Web; and one out of eight couples meet via social media. To illustrate the growth of social media, Qualman points out that radio took 38 years to reach 50 million users, TV took 13 years, the Internet took 4 years, and the iPod took 3 years. Yet, Facebook took 9 months to add 100 million users! He suggests that if Facebook was a country it would be the world's third largest with a user base of 500 million users. QZone, China's version of Facebook, also has a large user base of over 300 million. Qualman also presents statistics that reveal that Russia has the most engaged social media audience with visitors spending almost 7 hours per month on social networks.

Social media has become so popular, according to Qualman, that most Generation Y'ers and Generation Z'ers (people born mid-1990s onward) believe e-mail is now passé. Additionally, the second-largest search engine in the world is now YouTube, and there are over 200 million blogs on the Web. And, about 35 percent of bloggers actually post opinions about products and brands! Another interesting trend is that over 80 percent of companies looking to find new employees are using LinkedIn.

Qualman suggests that social media is having such a big impact on business because of its speed in engaging word-of-mouth communication, something he calls "world of mouth." Importantly, 25 percent of search results for the world's top brands are actually links to user-generated content. And while less than 15 percent of social media users trust advertisements, almost 80 percent of social media users trust peer recommendations found in social media sites. Another tangible signal that social media is impacting consumers' lives as well as affecting business is that major newspapers are experiencing record declines in circulation while consumers are finding the news and other content they want online. He suggests that successful companies will use social media more like Dale Carnegie, listening first, selling second. And, successful companies using social media will act more like party planners, aggregators, and content providers. To Qualman, social media is a revolution and marketers better recognize this revolution or they will be left behind!

consumers can more easily control the media they watch and the advertising within that media. With PVRs (personal video recorders), you can decide when you want to watch television programs and you can also eliminate the advertising content. You can also select to watch television over the Internet via IPTV, or download media content on your wireless phone or MP3 player, on your own terms and conditions. You can also listen to commercial-free radio via satellite radio providers such as XM or Sirius.

COMPETITIVE FORCES

competition
Alternative firms that could provide a product to satisfy a specific market's needs.

The fourth component of the environmental scan, **competition**, refers to the alternative firms that could provide a product to satisfy a specific market's needs. There are various forms of competition, and each company must consider its present and potential competitors in designing its marketing strategy.

LO4 Alternative Forms of Competition

There are four basic forms of competition that form a continuum from pure competition to monopolistic competition to oligopoly to pure monopoly. Chapter 13 contains further discussions on pricing practices under these four forms of competition.

At one end of the continuum is *pure competition,* in which every company has a similar product. Companies that deal in commodities common to agribusiness (for example, wheat, rice, and grain) often are in a pure competition position, in which distribution (in the sense of shipping products) is important but other elements of marketing have little impact.

In the second point on the continuum, *monopolistic competition,* many sellers compete with their products on a substitutable basis. For example, if the price of coffee rises too much, consumers may switch to tea. Coupons or sales are frequently used marketing tactics.

Oligopoly, a common industry structure, occurs when a few companies control the majority of industry sales. Because there are few sellers in an oligopolistic situation, price competition among firms is not desirable because it would lead to reduced revenue for all producers. Instead, nonprice competition is common, which means competing on other dimensions of the marketing mix, such as product quality, distribution, and/or promotion. Canada is sometimes referred to by some economists as the "land of oligopoly" because it has several major industries that can be considered oligopolistic, including the airline industry and the banking industry.

The final point on the continuum, *monopoly,* occurs when only one firm sells the product or service. It has been common for producers of goods and services considered essential to a community: water, electricity, or telephone service. Typically, marketing plays a small role in a monopolistic setting because it is regulated by a province or the federal government. Government control usually seeks to ensure price protection for the buyer.

Components of Competition

In developing a marketing program, companies must consider the factors that drive competition: entry, bargaining power of buyers and suppliers, existing rivalries, and substitution possibilities.[28] Scanning the environment requires a look at all of them. These factors relate to a firm's marketing mix decisions and may be used to create a barrier to entry, increase brand awareness, or intensify a fight for market share. Read the accompanying Using Marketing Dashboards box for ideas about assessing the components of competition.[29]

barriers to entry
Business practices or conditions that make it difficult for new firms to enter a market.

Entry   In considering the competition, a firm must assess the likelihood of new entrants. Additional producers increase industry capacity and tend to lower prices. A company scanning its environment must consider the possible **barriers to entry** for other firms, which are business practices or conditions that make it difficult for new firms to enter a market. Barriers to entry can be in the form of capital requirements, advertising expenditures, product identity, distribution access, or switching costs. The higher the expense of the barrier, the more likely it will deter new entrants.

Power of Buyers and Suppliers   A competitive analysis must consider the power of buyers and suppliers. Powerful buyers exist when they are few in number, there are low switching costs, or the product represents a significant share of the buyer's total costs. This last factor leads the buyer to exert significant pressure for price competition. A supplier gains power when the product is critical to the buyer and when it has built up the switching costs.

Existing Competitors and Substitutes   Competitive pressures among existing firms depend on the rate of industry growth. In slow-growth settings, competition is more heated for any possible gains in market share. High fixed costs also create competitive pressures for firms to fill production capacity. For example, airlines offer discounts for making early reservations and charge penalties for changes or cancellations in an effort to fill seats, which represent a high fixed cost.

Using Marketing Dashboards

Assessing Competition Is a Key to Success

To include competition in your marketing dashboard, you need to assess the components of competition. For example, the probability of a new competitor entering a market can be assessed on a scale from 0 to 100 percent. The power or influence of a buyer or supplier declines as the number of buyers and suppliers in the same product category increases. As the number of similar firms or substitute products increases, the competitiveness of an industry increases. The combination of these measurements will allow you to make an overall assessment of competitors and their likely actions.

Your Challenge   You are responsible for price recommendations for an existing product that has been very successful during the past year. In general, you believe that there is a strong relationship between price and sales, and that a reduction in price would lead to an increase in sales. That is:

Sales Increase (%) = Price Reduction (%) ×
Ratio of Sales Increase to Price
Reduction

Your goal is to increase sales by 10 percent.

Your Findings   After studying the prices of similar products and their sales you estimate that a 1 percent decrease in price will lead to a 4 percent increase in sales. This calculation, however, ignores the likely reaction of competitors. That is, when a firm lowers its price, competitors may reduce price also, changing the ratio of sales increase to price reduction for the product. Based on your assessment of the components of competition you estimate that competitors will meet half of your price reduction.

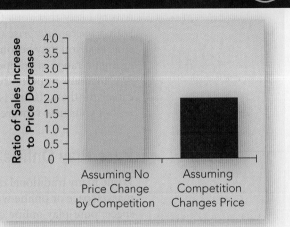

Your Action   The information about competition allows you to adjust your estimates. Because competitors will meet half of your price reduction, the increase in sales will probably be about half of your original estimate. So, the ratio of sales increase to price reduction will change from 4-to-1 to 2-to-1. To achieve the 10 percent increase in sales, you estimate that a 5 percent price reduction is needed (5% × 2/1).

This use of marketing metrics shows how assessment of competition can allow higher precision in the actions taken by marketing managers.

Note: The ratio of the unit amount of increase in sales for each unit decrease in price is often referred to as price elasticity, and is discussed in Chapter 13.

Small Businesses as Competitors

While large companies provide familiar examples of the forms and components of competition, small businesses make up the majority of the competitive landscape for most businesses. In fact, in Canada there are over 2.7 million small- and medium-sized enterprises (SMEs), and they generate half of the country's total gross domestic product (GDP), employ six out of ten Canadians, and create the bulk of all new jobs. Economic growth in Canada is largely tied to the activities of SMEs, and entrepreneurs who start new businesses provide new competition for existing large companies. A small business is a firm that has fewer than 100 employees while a medium-sized business has more than 100 but less than 500 employees. Currently, 98 percent of all businesses in Canada are small businesses. Moreover, SMEs not only play a significant role in our economy but also are a significant source of innovation, including new products, new services, and new technologies. For example, you can check out some of the finalists for Dell's Global Small Business Excellence Awards—small businesses that leverage technology and innovation to grow. Some of these firms include Hour-Zero Crisis Consulting Ltd., Edmonton, a firm specializing in K-12 school emergency preparedness;

WildPlay Element Parks of British Columbia, an adventure recreation company (featured in Chapter 1); and Jolera, Inc., Toronto, a global provider of IT solutions. SMEs participate in every sector but are dominant players in several key areas including retail, construction, professional services, accommodation, and food service. It is very likely that your first marketing job may be working with a SME, or perhaps with a *micro-enterprise* (firm with fewer than five employees). It is also entirely possible that you may become a self-employed entrepreneur and find yourself competing against a range of competitors of all sizes, both here and globally. In fact, 40 percent of Canadians indicate that starting their own company would be the most rewarding career for them. If this is in your future, marketing will play a critical role in the success of your new venture.[30]

Pure-Play Online Competitors

While many traditional companies (bricks and mortar) also have a presence in the new marketspace or online world, there are a host of companies that exist only in this new space: pure-play online competitors. Many of these competitors are also small, entrepreneurial start-ups that target specialized or niche markets.

---

learning review

4. What is the difference between a consumer's disposable income and discretionary income?

5. How does technology impact customer value?

6. In pure competition, there are a _____ number of sellers.

LO5 REGULATORY FORCES

regulation
Restrictions that provincial and federal laws place on business with regard to the conduct of its activities.

For any organization, the marketing and broader business decisions are constrained, directed, and influenced by regulatory forces. **Regulation** consists of restrictions that provincial and federal laws place on business with respect to the conduct of its activities. Regulation exists to protect companies as well as consumers. Much of the regulation from the federal and provincial levels has been passed to ensure competition and fair business practices. For consumers, the focus of legislation is to protect them from unfair trade practices and ensure their safety.

Protecting Competition and Consumers

Legislation and regulations exist in Canada at all three levels of government—federal, provincial, and municipal—to protect and encourage a competitive environment, which is deemed desirable because it permits the consumer to determine which competitor will succeed and which will fail.

The Competition Act   The key legislation designed to protect competition and consumers in Canada is the *Competition Act*. The purpose of the *Competition Act* is:

> to maintain and encourage competition in Canada in order to promote the efficiency and adaptability of the Canadian economy, in order to expand opportunities for Canadian participation in world markets while at the same time recognizing the role of foreign competition in Canada, in order to ensure that small- and medium-sized enterprises have an equitable opportunity to

participate in the Canadian economy and in order to provide consumers with competitive prices and product choices.[31]

Competition Act
The key legislation designed to protect competition and consumers in Canada.

In essence, the **Competition Act** is designed to protect and to balance the interests of competitors and consumers. The Bureau of Competition Policy, which is part of Industry Canada, is responsible for administering and enforcing the provisions of the *Competition Act*. The *Competition Act* contains both criminal and non-criminal provisions.

Criminal offences under Part VI of the *Competition Act* include conspiracy (e.g., price fixing), bid rigging, discriminatory and predatory pricing, price maintenance, and misleading or deceptive marketing practices, such as double ticketing or bait-and-switch selling.

Non-criminal reviewable matters under Part VIII of the *Competition Act* include mergers, abuse of dominant position, refusal to deal, consignment selling, exclusive dealing, tied selling, market restriction, and delivered pricing. The Director of the Bureau of Competition Policy refers these matters to the Competition Tribunal under non-criminal law standards. The tribunal was established when the *Competition Act* took effect, and is governed by the *Competition Tribunal Act*. The tribunal adjudicates all reviewable matters under the *Competition Act*.

Industry Canada is responsible for most of the legislation affecting business practices in Canada. Figure 3–4 lists the more significant federal legislation that protects competition and consumers in Canada. Marketers must also be cognizant of the fact that in addition to federal laws and regulations, there are many more at the provincial level. Many provinces have their own departments of consumer affairs in order to administer any such legislation and regulations enacted on the provincial government level.

However, the laws and regulations at the provincial level tend to vary from province to province. Therefore, a marketer may find it necessary to adapt some aspect of the marketing mix or some broader business practice, depending on the province. For example, in Quebec, there are specific laws dealing with store signage, packaging, and labelling. Additionally, advertising directed toward children is prohibited in Quebec. Many provinces, including Quebec, also have consumer protection acts and/or business or trade practices acts.

● **FIGURE 3–4**
Major federal legislation designed to protect competition and consumers

Bank Cost Borrowing Act	Hazardous Products Act
Bankruptcy Act	Income Tax Act
Bills of Exchange Act	Industrial Design Act
Board of Trade Act	Maple Products Industry Act
Broadcasting Act	Motor Vehicle Safety Act
Canada Agricultural Products Standards Act	Official Languages Act
	Patent Act
Canada Cooperative Association Act	Personal Information Protection and Electronic Documents Act
Canada Corporations Act	
Canada Dairy Products Act	Precious Metals Marketing Act
Canadian Human Rights Act	Privacy Act
Competition Act	Small Loans Act
Consumer Packaging and Labelling Act	Standards Council of Canada Act
Copyright Act	Textile Labelling Act
Criminal Code	The Interest Act
Department of Consumer and Corporate Affairs Act	Timber Marketing Act
	Trade-marks Act
Electricity Inspection Act and Gas Inspection Act	True Labelling Act
	Weights and Measures Act
Fish Inspection Act	Winding-up Act
Food and Drugs Act	

Self-Regulation

The government has provided much legislation to create a competitive business climate and protect the consumer. An alternative to government control is **self-regulation,** where an industry attempts to police itself. The Canadian Broadcasting Association, whose members include major television networks and radio stations across the country, has a code of ethics that helps govern the conduct of its members in terms of protecting the consumer against deceptive trade practices, such as misleading advertising. Similarly, the Advertising Standards Council, the self-regulatory arm of the Canadian Advertising Foundation, has established the Canadian Code of Advertising Standards for its members to follow. The members of this organization consist of major advertising agencies that are responsible for allocating the bulk of advertising dollars in Canada. The Canadian Radio-television and Telecommunications Commission (CRTC), the federal agency responsible for licensing and regulating broadcasting in Canada, is in favour of greater industry self-regulation.

The Canadian Marketing Association, whose members represent 80 percent of direct-marketing sales in Canada, has mandated that its members comply with the consumer's right to privacy and honour consumers who request not to be contacted by telephone or mail for selling purposes. Critics argue that telemarketers in Canada demonstrate what is wrong with self-regulation efforts—noncompliance by members and enforcement.

Another well-known self-regulatory group is the Better Business Bureau (BBB). This organization is a voluntary alliance of companies whose goal is to help maintain fair business practices. Although the BBB has no legal power, it does try to use "moral suasion" to get members to comply with its regulations.

Consumerism

Regulation by government and self-regulation by industry help in protecting the consumer in the marketplace. But the consumer can also play a direct and active role. **Consumerism** is a movement to increase the influence, power, and rights of consumers in dealing with institutions. Modern consumerism in Canada and the United States really began in the 1960s. U.S. President John F. Kennedy, in a speech entitled "Consumer Bill of Rights," outlined four basic consumer rights: (1) the right to safety, (2) the right to be informed, (3) the right to choose, and (4) the right to be heard. Although not passed as laws, these proclaimed rights serve as the basis for modern consumerism. Shortly after President Kennedy's Consumer Bill of Rights was unveiled in the United States, the Canadian government formed the Department of Consumer and Corporate Affairs, making it the agency responsible for protecting consumers and regulating corporate activities.

Canada also has many independent consumer organizations that advance the cause of consumerism. The Consumers Association of Canada (CAC) is the largest consumer group working on behalf of the Canadian consumer. The CAC serves as a channel for supplying consumers' views to government and industry, providing consumer information, and studying consumer problems and presenting recommended solutions to those problems. In addition to ensuring that the four original consumer rights are protected, the consumer movement also includes consumer demands for environmentally safe products and ethical and socially responsible business practices, including the right to privacy.

The *Privacy Act (PA)* and *Personal Information Protection and Electronic Documents Act (PIPEDA)* were enacted by the federal government to protect Canadian citizens' privacy and to ensure that information on individuals is collected, used, and disclosed legally and ethically. However, recent research shows that 80 percent of Canadians are unaware of this legislation, yet Canadian consumers are concerned about their privacy.[32] Canadian companies that have collected or are collecting customer information should be proactive and responsible to ensure customer privacy.

Making Responsible Decisions

Protecting Canadian Consumers' Privacy

While new legislation is in place to protect consumer privacy in Canada, some argue that companies should go beyond the legal letter of the law to ensure consumer rights with regard to privacy. Amanda Malthy, an authority on privacy, and vice-president of public affairs and communications at the Canadian Marketing Association, has some advice for marketers in terms of the ethical and responsible use of consumer information. She suggests that every organization should designate a privacy officer who will be responsible for ensuring that the organization complies with privacy laws. She also suggests that companies should clearly identify how they intend to use customer data, now and in the future, and receive consent from the customer for the collection, use, and disclosure of personal information. If marketing lists are to be made available to third parties, companies must obtain consent from customers. The collection of personal information should also be limited to that which is necessary for the purposes identified by the organization, such as maintaining service records.

Marketers are also obligated to keep personal information on customers as accurate, complete, and up-to-date as possible. Safeguards should be in place for protecting customer information to ensure against unauthorized access, alteration, or use. Organizations should be prepared to publicize their information-handling practices through all customer touchpoints in their business. All staff should also be trained regarding the privacy policies of the organization. Consumers should be made aware that they have a right to know if the marketer holds personal information about them, and such information needs to be made available to the customer on request. The consumer also has a right to correct erroneous information. Finally, an organization must establish formal inquiry and complaint-handling mechanisms and make sure that these procedures are known to the consumers who inquire or complain.

Maltby suggests that all organizations need to adhere to these principles in order to comply with the law. Moreover, they should go beyond the minimal requirements set by law in order to ensure consumer rights to privacy as well as give consumers confidence in the organization's ability to safeguard personal information. What are your thoughts regarding consumer privacy rights in Canada? Do Maltby's principles go far enough? What other obligations do firms have regarding the protection of customer privacy?

In fact, some experts suggest this should be top priority for organizations. See the Making Responsible Decisions box, "Protecting Canadian Consumers' Privacy," for a discussion of this topic.[33]

learning review

7. The _____ Act is the most important legislation designed to protect competition and consumers in Canada.

8. An alternative to legislation protecting competition and consumers is self-_____.

9. What is consumerism?

LEARNING OBJECTIVES REVIEW

LO1 **Explain how environmental scanning provides information about social, economic, technological, competitive, and regulatory forces.**

Many businesses operate in environments where important forces change. Environmental scanning is the process of acquiring information about these changes to allow marketers to identify and interpret trends. There are five environmental forces that businesses must monitor: social, economic,

technological, competitive, and regulatory. By identifying trends related to each of these forces, businesses can develop and maintain successful marketing programs. Several trends that most businesses are monitoring include the growing diversity of the Canadian population, the increasing use of electronic information and communication technologies, and new legislation related to consumer privacy.

LO2 Describe how social forces, such as demographics, and culture and economic forces, such as macro-economic conditions and consumer income, affect marketing.

Demographic information helps describe the world population; the Canadian population; generational cohorts, such as baby boomers, Generation X, and Generation Y; the structure of the Canadian family; and ethnic diversity. Ethnic diversity, for example, has led to ethnic marketing programs in Canada. Cultural trends in Canada indicate that many individuals are suffering from time poverty and are more interested in health and fitness. Still, obesity persists and is a public health problem. Economic forces include the strong relationship between consumers' expectations about the economy and their spending habits.

LO3 Describe how technological changes are impacting marketers and customers.

New technologies have dramatically changed marketing practices and have altered the way consumers shop and what they buy. Some of these new technologies include information and communication technologies (ICTs) such as the Internet. The Internet has given rise to a new marketspace where marketers and consumers can engage in electronic commerce and information sharing.

LO4 Discuss the forms of competition that exist in a market, key components of competition, and the impact of small businesses as competitors.

There are four forms of competition: pure competition, monopolistic competition, oligopoly, and monopoly. The key components of competition include the likelihood of new competitors, the power of buyers and suppliers, and the presence of competitors and possible substitutes. While large companies are often used as examples of marketplace competitors, there are over two million small- and medium-sized enterprises in Canada that have a significant impact on the economy and the competitive landscape. Also, traditional marketers must now contend with new pure-play online competition.

LO5 Explain the major legislation that ensures competition and protects consumers in Canada.

Regulation exists to protect competition and consumers. The key legislation in Canada that ensures a competitive marketplace and consumer protection is the *Competition Act.* Self-regulation through such organizations as the Canadian Marketing Association and the Better Business Bureau provides an alternative to federal and provincial regulations.

FOCUSING ON KEY TERMS

baby boomers   p. 79
barriers to entry   p. 90
blended family   p. 80
blog   p. 88
census metropolitan areas (CMAs)   p. 80
competition   p. 89
Competition Act   p. 93
consumerism   p. 94
culture   p. 81
demographics   p. 78
discretionary income   p. 85
disposable income   p. 85
e-business   p. 86
e-commerce   p. 86
e-marketing   p. 86

economy   p. 84
environmental scanning   p. 76
ethnic marketing   p. 81
extranet   p. 86
Generation X   p. 80
Generation Y   p. 80
gross income   p. 85
intranet   p. 86
marketspace   p. 86
regulation   p. 92
self-regulation   p. 94
social forces   p. 78
technology   p. 86
value consciousness   p. 83

APPLYING MARKETING KNOWLEDGE

1 For many years, Gerber has manufactured baby food in small, single-serving containers. In conducting an environmental scan, identify three trends or factors that might significantly affect this company's future business, and then propose how Gerber might respond to these changes.
2 Describe the new features you would add to an automobile designed for an aging baby boomer. In what magazines would you advertise to appeal to this target market?

3 How have social media tools such as Facebook and MySpace changed the way that companies market? How has social media changed how you shop and buy?
4 Historically, a couple of large firms dominated the Canadian brewing industry (Labatt and Molson). But now, these companies face competition from many regional brands and micro-breweries. In terms of the continuum of competition, how would you explain this change?

5 What role does marketing play now in the deregulated Canadian airline industry? What elements of the marketing mix are more or less important now?

6 The Johnson Company manufactures buttons and pins with slogans and designs. These pins are inexpensive to produce and are sold in retail outlets, such as discount stores, hobby shops, and bookstores. Little equipment is needed for

a new competitor to enter the market. What strategies should Johnson consider to create effective barriers to entry?

7 Today's consumer is more value-conscious. How could a retail home improvement centre sell the same products but still offer the consumer greater perceived value? What specific things could the retailer do?

Building Your Marketing Plan

Your marketing plan will include a situation analysis based on internal and external factors that are likely to affect your marketing program.

1. To summarize information about external factors, create a table similar to Figure 3–2 and identify three trends related to each of the five forces (social,

economic, technological, competitive, and regulatory) that relate to your product or service.

2. When your table is completed, describe how each of the trends represents an opportunity or a threat for your business.

Video Case 3

GEEK SQUAD: A NEW BUSINESS FOR A NEW ENVIRONMENT

"As long as there's innovation there is going to be new kinds of chaos," explains Robert Stephens, founder of the technology support company Geek Squad. The chaos Stephens is referring to is the difficulty we have all experienced trying to keep up with the many changes in our environment, particularly those related to computers, technology, software, communication, and entertainment. Generally, consumers have found it difficult to install, operate, and use many of the electronic products available today. "It takes time to read the manuals," continues Stephens. "I'm going to save you that time because I stay home on Saturday nights and read them for you!"

The Company

The Geek Squad story begins when Stephens, a native of Chicago, passed up an Art Institute scholarship to pursue a degree in computer science. While Stephens was a computer science student he took a job fixing computers for a research laboratory, and he also started consulting. He could repair televisions, computers, and a variety of other items, although he decided to focus on computers. His experiences as a consultant led him to realize that most people needed help with technology and that they saw value in a service whose employees would show up at a specified time, be friendly, use understandable language,

and solve the problem. So, with just $200, Stephens formed Geek Squad in 1994.

Geek Squad set out to provide timely and effective help with all computing needs regardless of the make, model, or place of purchase. Geek Squad employees were called "agents" and wore uniforms consisting of black pants or skirts, black shoes, white shirts, black clip-on ties, a badge, and a black jacket with a Geek Squad logo to create a "humble" attitude that was not threatening to customers. Agents drove black-and-white Volkswagen Beetles, or Geekmobiles, with a logo on the door, and charged fixed prices for services, regardless of how much time was required to provide the service. The "house call" services ranged from installing networks, to debugging a computer, to setting up an entertainment system, and cost from $100 to $300. "We're like *Dragnet;* we show up at people's homes and help, offers Stephens. "We're also like *Ghostbusters,* and there's a pseudo-government feel to it like *Men in Black.*"

In 2002, Geek Squad was purchased by leading consumer electronics retailer Best Buy for about $3 million. Best Buy had observed very high return rates for most of its complex products. Shoppers would be excited about new products, purchase them and take them home, get frustrated trying to make them actually work, and then return them to the store demanding a refund. In fact, Best

Buy research revealed that consumers were beginning to see service as a critical element of the purchase. The partnership was an excellent match. Best Buy consumers welcomed the help. Stephens became Geek Squad's chief inspector and a Best Buy vice president and began putting a Geek Squad "precinct" in every Best Buy store, creating some stand-alone Geek Squad stores, and providing 24-hour telephone support. There are now more than 2,000 agents in the United States, Canada, the United Kingdom, and China, and return rates have declined by 25 to 35 percent. Geek Squad customer materials now suggest that the service is "Saving the World One Computer at a Time. 24 Hours a Day. Your Place or Ours!"

The Changing Environment

Many changes in the environment occurred to create the need for Geek Squad's services. Future changes are also likely to change the way Geek Squad operates. An environmental scan helps understand the changes.

The most obvious changes may be related to technology. Wireless broadband technology, high-definition televisions, products with Internet interfaces, and a general trend toward computers, phones, entertainment systems, and even appliances being interconnected are just a few examples of new products and applications for consumers to learn about. There are also technology-related problems such as viruses, spyware, lost data, and "crashed" or inoperable computers. New technologies have also created a demand for new types of maintenance such as password management, operating system updates, disk cleanup, and "defragging."

Another environmental change that contributes to the popularity of Geek Squad is the change in social factors such as demographics and culture. In the past many electronics manufacturers and retailers focused primarily on men. Women, however, are becoming increasingly interested in personal computing and home entertainment, and according to the Consumer Electronics Association, they are likely to outspend men in the near future. Best Buy's consumer research indicates that women expect personal service during the purchase and installation after the purchase—exactly the service Geek Squad is designed to provide. Our culture is also embracing the Geek Squad concept. If you follow television programming you may have noticed the series *Chuck* where one of the characters works for the "Nerd Herd" at "Buy More" and drives a car like a Geekmobile on service calls!

Competition, economics, and the regulatory environment have also had a big influence on Geek Squad. As discount stores such as Walmart and PC makers such as Dell began to compete with Best Buy, Circuit City, and CompUSA, new services such as in-home installation were needed to create value for customers. Now, just as changes in competition created an opportunity for Geek Squad, it is also leading to another level of competition as Circuit City has introduced its own computer support service called Firedog, Dell has introduced Dell-On-Call, and cable companies are offering their own services. The economic situation for electronics continues to improve as prices decline and median income in the U.S., particularly for women, is increasing. In 2007, consumers purchased 16 million high-definition televisions, but household penetration is still below 40 percent. Finally, the regulatory environment continues to change with respect to electronic transfer of copyrighted materials such as music, movies, and software. Geek Squad must monitor the changes to ensure that its services comply with relevant laws.

The Future for Geek Squad

The combination of many positive environmental factors helps explain the extraordinary success of Geek Squad. Today, it repairs more than 3,000 PCs a day and generates more than $1 billion in revenue. Since Geek Squad services have a high-profit margin they contribute to the overall performance of Best Buy, and they help generate traffic in the store and create store loyalty. To continue to grow, however, Geek Squad will need to continue to scan the environment and try new approaches to creating customer value.

One possible new approach is to find additional locations that are convenient to consumers. For example, Geek Squad locations are being tested in some FedEx/Kinko stores and in some Office Depot stores. Another possible approach is to create new houses that are designed for the newest consumer electronics products. To test this idea Best Buy has created partnerships with home builders to wire new houses with high-speed cables and networking equipment that Geek Squad agents can use to create ideal computer and entertainment systems. Geek Squad is also using new technology to improve. Agents now use a smart phone to access updated schedules, log in their hours, and run diagnostics tests on client's equipment. Finally, to attract the best possible employees, Geek Squad and Best Buy are trying a "results-only work environment" that has no fixed schedules and no mandatory meetings. By encouraging employees to make their own work-life decisions, the Geek Squad hopes to keep morale and productivity high.

Other changes and opportunities are certain to appear soon. Despite the success of the Geek Squad, and the potential for additional growth, however, Robert Stephens is modest and claims, "Geeks may inherit the Earth, but they have no desire to rule it!"

Questions

1 What are the key environmental factors that created an opportunity for Robert Stephens to start the Geek Squad?

2 What changes in the purchasing patterns of (*a*) all consumers, and (*b*) women made the acquisition of Geek Squad particularly important for Best Buy?

3 Based on the case information and what you know about consumer electronics, conduct an environmental scan for Geek Squad to identify key trends. For each of the five environmental forces (social, economic, technological, competitive, and regulatory), identify trends likely to influence Geek Squad in the near future.

4 What promotional activities would you recommend to encourage consumers who use independent installers to switch to Geek Squad?

chapter 4

Ethics and Social Responsibility in Marketing

CANADIAN AUTOMAKERS MAKE A COMMITMENT TO CANADA

Canadian automobile manufacturers have a long-standing tradition of social responsibility and dedication to the country. They are involved in multifaceted efforts to support the communities in which they operate and to protect the natural environment of Canada. They have a history of supporting countless charities and other worthy causes and have even established specific foundations to support these charities and causes.

For example, General Motors of Canada is committed to being a good corporate citizen, and its philanthropic contributions are evidence of that citizenship. Some of the organizations that GM supports are MADD, Junior Achievement, the United Way, Scouts Canada, and Girl Guides Canada. It also provides postsecondary education scholarships and bursaries for students across Canada. The Partners for the Advancement of Collaborative Engineering Education (PACE), a corporate alliance between General Motors, EDS, and Sun Microsystems, also provides funding to prepare mechanical designers, engineers, and analysts with the skills to compete in the future. GM has already given a half-billion dollars to Canadian universities coast-to-coast.

Improved global environmental quality is also a goal at General Motors of Canada. Accordingly, it has established the "General Motors Environmental Principles." As a responsible corporate citizen, General Motors is dedicated to protecting human health, natural resources, and

learning objectives

After reading this chapter, you should be able to:

LO1 Explain the differences between legal and ethical behaviour in marketing.

LO2 Identify factors that influence ethical and unethical behaviour in marketing.

LO3 Describe the different concepts of social responsibility.

LO4 Recognize unethical and socially irresponsible consumer behaviour.

the global environment. This dedication reaches farther than compliance with the law to encompass the integration of sound environmental practices into its business decisions.

Ford Motor Company of Canada has also made a commitment to the Canadian environment with its "Build for Today—Preserve for Tomorrow" program. This program includes a focus on sustainable technology solutions, green vehicles, and smarter manufacturing. Its facilities are ISO 14001–certified, and the company has made a major commitment to the 3Rs (reduce, reuse, recycle).

Nissan Canada developed the Nissan Canada Foundation as a signal of its commitment to the Canadian community. This foundation was established to help Canadian senior citizens, who represent a substantial portion of the population. Nissan raises funds and provides grants and vehicles to nonprofit organizations that serve the senior citizens of our country, including Meals on Wheels.

Toyota Canada believes that environmental stewardship and community involvement go hand in hand. Toyota has developed an "Earth Charter" that guides its corporate behaviour. It is also an ISO 14001–certified company and a leader in the hybrid vehicle category. It is also a major sponsor of the Special Olympics.[1] Unfortunately, as we have seen lately, Toyota ran into some safety issues with some of their vehicles, necessitating recalls and repairs and much inconvenience for their customers. The company has established policies to deal with these recalls, including setting up a toll-free information line and providing ongoing information to consumers on its Web site (**www.toyota.ca**).

This chapter focuses on ethics and social responsibility in marketing. You will see that some Canadian companies recognize that while ethically and socially responsible behaviour often comes with a price tag, the price for unethical and socially irresponsible behaviour is often much higher. In essence, in this marketplace, companies can "do well by doing good." Importantly, as is the case with Toyota, when things go wrong with a company's product or service, responsive remedial action is required in order to rebuild customer trust.

NATURE AND SIGNIFICANCE OF MARKETING ETHICS

ethics
The moral principles and values that govern the actions and decisions of an individual or group.

As defined in Chapter 1, **ethics** are the moral principles and values that govern the actions and decisions of an individual or group.[2] Simply put, ethics serve as guidelines on how to act correctly and justly when faced with moral dilemmas. For marketing managers, ethics concern the application of moral principles and values to marketing decision making.

 ## Ethical/Legal Framework in Marketing

A good starting point for understanding the nature and significance of ethics is the distinction between legality and ethicality of marketing decisions. Figure 4–1 helps you visualize the relationship between laws and ethics.[3] While ethics deal with personal and moral principles and values, **laws** are society's values and standards that are enforceable in the courts.[4]

laws
Society's values and standards that are enforceable in the courts.

● **FIGURE 4–1**
Classifying marketing decisions according to ethical and legal relationships

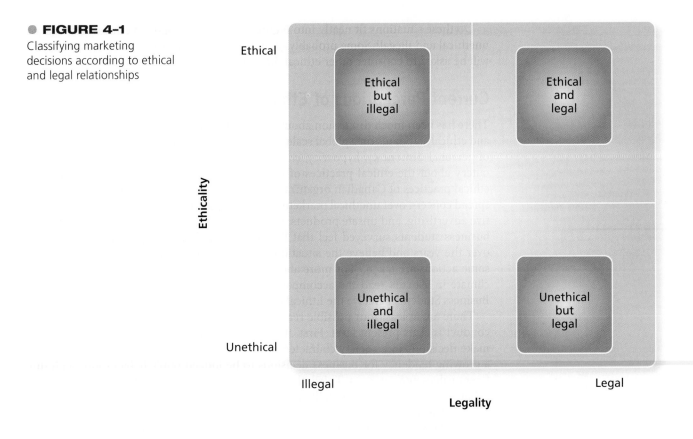

In general, what is illegal is also unethical. For example, deceptive advertising is illegal. It is also unethical because it conflicts with the moral principles of honesty and fairness. But not all unethical conduct is illegal. For instance, price gouging is usually not illegal but is often viewed as unethical. Marketing managers often find themselves in many situations where they must make judgments in defining ethical and legal boundaries. For some, the distinction between ethics and laws can sometimes lead to the rationalization that if a behaviour is within legal limits, then it is not really unethical. For example, a group of Canadian business students surveyed were asked, "Is it okay to charge a higher price than normal when you know the customer really needs the product and will pay the higher price?" Almost 35 percent of the business students who took part in the survey responded yes.[5] How would you have answered this question?

Now consider the following situations. After reading each, assign it to the cell in Figure 4–1 that you think best fits the situation along the ethical–legal continuum.

1. Several companies meet and agree to bid rigging for sealed tendered government contract work. Bid rigging is illegal under the *Competition Act* because it eliminates free and open competition.
2. A company uses a technique called "slugging," or selling under the guise of research. Once prospective customers agree to take part in the research, the salespeople switch to their sales pitch.
3. A real estate agent sells a high-rise condo unit to a customer, primarily because the customer loves the city view from the condo windows. The agent knows that in one year another high-rise will be built, effectively blocking the view so important to the customer. The agent decides not to give that information to the customer.
4. A company interviews a very qualified female for a business sales position. She is more qualified than any males who have been interviewed. However, the company knows that some male purchasing agents prefer to deal with a male salesperson, and so they hire a less qualified male applicant.

Do these situations fit neatly into Figure 4–1 as clearly defined ethical and legal or unethical and illegal? Some probably do not. As you read further in this chapter, you will be asked to consider other ethical dilemmas.

Current Perceptions of Ethical Behaviour

There has been much discussion about the possible deterioration of personal morality and ethical standards on a global scale. The news media offer well-publicized examples of personal dishonesty, hypocrisy, cheating, and greed. There also has been a public outcry about the ethical practices of businesspeople, and public cynicism about the ethical practices of Canadian organizations is on the rise.[6] In particular, there is widespread concern over unethical marketing practices, such as price fixing, bribery, deceptive advertising, and unsafe products. Recent Canadian research also shows that most business students surveyed feel that the ethical standards of business have declined over the years and believe the situation is not likely to improve in the future unless some actions are taken.[7] For more about how Canadian students perceive the ethical climate in Canada read the accompanying Marketing Matters box, "How Canadian Business Students Perceive the Ethical Climate in Canada."

There are at least four possible reasons why the state of perceived ethical business conduct is at its present level. First, there is increased pressure on businesspeople to make decisions in a society characterized by diverse value systems. Second, there is a growing tendency for business decisions to be judged publicly by groups with different values and interests. Third, the public's expectations regarding ethical business behaviour have increased. Finally, and most disturbing, ethical business conduct may have declined. EthicScan Canada, an organization that monitors the ethical performance of hundreds of Canadian companies, seems to have confirmed this decline.[8]

---

learning review
1. What are ethics?
2. What are laws?

UNDERSTANDING ETHICAL MARKETING BEHAVIOUR

Researchers have identified numerous factors that influence ethical marketing behaviour.[9] Figure 4–2 presents a framework that shows these factors and their relationships.

● **FIGURE 4–2**
A framework for understanding ethical behaviour

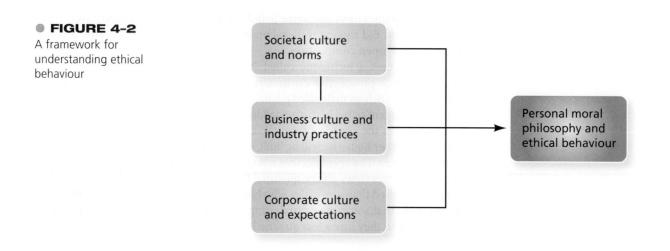

Marketing Matters

How Canadian Business Students Perceive the Ethical Climate in Canada

A recent study of Canadian, American, and British MBA students revealed that respondents in all three countries believe there are ethical standards that should be followed in business. However, most believe that current ethical standards fail to meet the needs of business and society. In fact, only 28 percent of Canadian MBA students feel that current ethical standards in Canada meet the needs of business and society. Moreover, close to 50 percent believe business ethics have deteriorated over the years.

More unfortunate is that less than 30 percent of Canadian respondents believe business ethics will actually improve in the future, unless some action is taken. Most Canadian respondents believe that they can determine what is ethical business behaviour and what is unethical. But more than six in ten respondents actually believe you

can be taught business ethics. And eight in ten state that they want a required an ethics course to be taught in business schools. The overwhelming majority of all respondents in the study, including Canadian respondents, believe that they could learn something of value in such a course.

While respondents do not believe ethical standards in Canadian business have deteriorated to a point of "anything goes," they are concerned about the ethical climate in Canada. They believe that it is possible to improve business ethics, but ethical training of Canada's future business leaders will be required. These students are receptive to such training and believe it will be a catalyst to improving the ethical conduct of business in the future. What are your thoughts? Do you think courses in business ethics will help improve the ethical climate in Canada?

LO2 Societal Culture and Norms

As described in Chapter 3, culture incorporates the set of values, ideas, and attitudes that are learned and shared among members of a group. Culture also serves as a socializing force that dictates what is morally right and just. This means that moral standards are relative to particular societies. These standards often reflect the laws and regulations that affect social and economic behaviour, which can create moral dilemmas.[10] For example, restraining trade, price fixing, deceiving buyers, or marketing unsafe products are behaviours that are considered morally wrong in Canada. Furthermore, the unauthorized use of intellectual property, such as another's ideas, copyright, trademark, or patent, is also considered both illegal and unethical in Canada.

Outside Canada, however, is another story.[11] Unauthorized use of copyrights, trademarks, and patents is routine in some countries, such as China, Mexico, and Korea, and costs the authorized owners billions of dollars annually. In Korea, for instance, copying is partly rooted in its society's culture. According to international trade officials, many Koreans have the idea that the thoughts of one person should benefit all, and the Korean government rarely prosecutes infringements. Copyright infringement in the global software and music industries is particularly widespread with the explosive growth of the Internet. Copies of software and music can be distributed and downloaded quickly and globally, with a click of the mouse, and many individuals in some countries do not feel it is illegal or unethical to engage in such conduct.

Business Culture and Industry Practices

Societal culture provides a foundation for understanding moral and ethical behaviour in business activities. *Business cultures* "comprise the effective rules of the game, the boundaries between competitive and unethical behaviour, [and] the codes of conduct in business dealings."[12] Consumers have witnessed numerous instances where business cultures in the brokerage (insider trading), insurance (deceptive sales practices), and defence (bribery) industries went awry. Business culture affects ethical conduct both in the exchange relationship between sellers and buyers and in the competitive behaviour among sellers.

Ethics of Exchange   The exchange process is central to the marketing concept. Ethical exchanges between sellers and buyers should result in both parties being better off after a transaction.[13]

caveat emptor
The legal concept of "let the buyer beware" that was pervasive in Canadian business culture before the 1960s.

Prior to the 1960s, the legal concept of **caveat emptor**—let the buyer beware—was pervasive in Canadian business culture. The growth and strength of the consumer movement resulted in this concept becoming an unacceptable marketplace philosophy. A codification of ethics between buyers and sellers was established, with consumers recognizing their rights to safety, to be informed, to choose, and to be heard.

The right to safety manifests itself in industry and federal safety standards for most products sold in Canada. However, even the most vigilant efforts to ensure safe products cannot foresee every possibility. This is illustrated, as mentioned in the chapter opener, by Toyota's recent safety issues with some of its vehicles. There are also other examples. For instance, consider Mattel's experience with its Cabbage Patch Snack-time Kids doll. The doll was designed to "eat" plastic french fries, celery, and other tidbits by drawing them into its motorized mouth. Despite exhaustive laboratory and in-home testing, Mattel executives did not consider that a child's hair might become caught in the doll's mouth and cause harm. Unfortunately, this happened. Mattel immediately pulled the dolls from store shelves, refunded buyers, and discontinued the product.

The right to be informed means that marketers have an obligation to give consumers complete and accurate information about products and services. This right also applies to the solicitation of personal information over the Internet and its subsequent use by marketers. While most Web sites collect personal information, such as consumer e-mail addresses, telephone numbers, shopping habits, and financial data, many of these sites fail to properly inform consumers about what is done with this information once obtained. Recently, Facebook found itself in hot water with its users when it was discovered that the company intended to use personal data on its users to attract advertisers. User furor over this practice caused Facebook to change its mind. This type of practice is relatively common. Thus, in an effort to ensure that consumer information is properly obtained over the Internet and that consumers are fully informed about its use, the Canadian government uses legislation such as the *Personal Information Protection and Electronic Documents Act (PIPEDA),* which requires marketers to seek the consent of individuals prior to collecting, using, and disclosing their personal information.

Relating to the right to choose, many supermarket chains now demand "slotting allowances" from manufacturers, in the form of cash rebates or free goods, to stock new products. This practice could limit the number of new products available to consumers and interfere with their right to choose. One critic of this practice remarked, "If we had had slotting allowances a few years ago, we might not have had granola, herbal tea, or yogourt."[14]

Finally, the right to be heard means that consumers should have access to company and/or public policymakers regarding comments or complaints about products and services. Many Canadian companies have set up consumer service departments to deal with customer comments and complaints. In fact, it was consumer complaints about late-night and repeated calls by telemarketers that led to greater limitations on telemarketing practices.

Ethics of Competition   Business culture also affects ethical behaviour in competition. Two kinds of unethical behaviour are most common: (1) economic espionage, and (2) bribery.

economic espionage
The clandestine collection of trade secrets or proprietary information about a company's competitors.

Economic espionage is the clandestine collection of trade secrets or proprietary information about a company's competitors. This practice is illegal and unethical and includes such activities as trespassing, theft, fraud, wire tapping, and searching a competitor's trash. Many Canadian and American firms have uncovered espionage in some form, costing them billions of dollars a year.[15] This practice is most prevalent in high-technology industries, such as electronics, specialty chemicals, industrial equipment, aerospace, and pharmaceuticals, where technical know-how and secrets separate industry leaders from followers.

But espionage can occur anywhere, including the toy industry and even the cookie industry! Procter & Gamble charged that competitors photographed its plants and production lines, stole a sample of its cookie dough, and infiltrated a confidential sales presentation to learn about its technology, recipe, and marketing plan. The competitors paid Procter & Gamble $120 million in damages after a lengthy dispute.

The second form of unethical competitive behaviour is giving and receiving bribes and kickbacks. Bribes and kickbacks are often disguised as gifts, consultant fees, and favours. This practice is more common in business-to-business and government marketing than in consumer marketing.

In general, bribery is most evident in industries experiencing intense competition and in countries in earlier stages of economic development. Bribery on a worldwide scale is monitored by Transparency International. Recent results of the organization's Corruption Perceptions Index (CPI) reveal the worst offenders in term of the use of bribery were Russia, China, and India. Complete the Going Online exercise and view the other country rankings, including Canada's.

Corporate Culture and Expectations

A third influence on ethical practices is corporate culture. *Corporate culture* is a set of values, ideas, and attitudes that is learned and shared among the members of an organization. The culture of a company demonstrates itself in the dress ("We don't wear ties"), sayings ("The IBM Way"), and manner of work (team efforts) of employees. Culture is also apparent in the expectations for ethical behaviour present in formal codes of ethics and the ethical actions of top management and co-workers.

code of ethics
A formal statement of ethical principles and rules of conduct.

Codes of Ethics   A **code of ethics** is a formal statement of ethical principles and rules of conduct. Research shows that ethics codes are commonplace in corporate Canada.[16] Ethics codes typically address such issues as contributions to government officials and political parties; relations with customers, competitors, and suppliers; conflicts of interest; and accurate recordkeeping. Nexen, Inc., a global energy company, has developed an international code of ethics for doing business at home and broad, while Mars Canada provides ethical guidance to its employees through its *Five Principles,* which all employees must follow when conducting business.

Going Online

The Corruption Perceptions Index

The use of bribery as a means to win and retain business varies widely by country. Transparency International, based in Germany, periodically polls employees of multinational firms and institutions as well as political analysts and ranks countries on the basis of their perceived level of bribery to win or retain business. To obtain the most recent ranking, visit the Transparency International Web site at **www.transparency.org**. Click on the Corruption Perception Index (CPI).

Scroll through the Corruption Perceptions Index to see where Canada stands in the worldwide rankings. How about our neighbours, the United States and Mexico? Any surprises?

The Canadian Marketing Association (CMA), the largest marketing organization in Canada, whose members include Microsoft Canada, Bank of Montreal, The Shopping Channel, and Bell Canada, has a code of ethics that is compulsory for all members to follow. The purpose of the CMA code of ethics is shown in Figure 4–3. For a copy of the complete code of ethics, visit **www.the-cma.org**. Additionally, the American Marketing Association (AMA), which represents marketing professionals in Canada and the United States, also has a statement of ethics. The preamble to their code is also found in Figure 4–3. For a copy of the AMA's complete statement of ethics, visit **www.marketingpower.com**.

However, an ethics code is rarely enough to ensure ethical behaviour. One of the reasons for this is the lack of specificity of ethics codes. Ultimately, it is the employee who often judges whether a specific behaviour is really unethical.

Ethical Behaviour of Management and Co-workers   A second reason for violating ethics codes rests in the perceived behaviour of top management and co-workers. Observing peers and top management and gauging responses to unethical behaviour play an important role in individual actions. For example, what message do employees receive when they see personnel being rewarded for engaging in unethical behaviour and see others punished for refusing to engage in unethical behaviour? Clearly, ethical dilemmas often bring personal and professional conflict. In some cases, **whistle-blowers,** employees who report unethical or illegal actions of their employers, face

whistle-blowers
Employees who report unethical or illegal actions of their employers.

● **FIGURE 4–3**
Excerpt from the Canadian Marketing Association's Code of Ethics and Standards of Practice and from the American Marketing Association's Code of Ethics. The full documents are available at **www.the-cma.org** and at **www.marketingpower.com**.

Purpose of Canadian Marketing Association Code of Ethics and Standards of Practice

The CMA Code of Ethics and Standards of Practice (the "Code") is designed to establish and maintain standards for the conduct of marketing in Canada.

Marketers acknowledge that the establishment and maintenance of high standards of practice are a fundamental responsibility to the public, essential to winning and holding consumer confidence, and the foundation of a successful and independent marketing industry in Canada.

Members of the Canadian Marketing Association recognize an obligation—to the consumers and the businesses they serve, to the integrity of the discipline in which they operate and to each other—to practice to the highest standards of honesty, truth, accuracy, fairness and professionalism.

American Marketing Association Statement of Ethics: ETHICAL NORMS AND VALUES FOR MARKETERS

Preamble

The American Marketing Association commits itself to promoting the highest standard of professional ethical norms and values for its members. Norms are established standards of conduct that are expected and maintained by society and/or professional organizations. Values represent the collective conception of what people find desirable, important and morally proper. Values serve as the criteria for evaluating the actions of others. Marketing practitioners must recognize that they not only serve their enterprises but also act as stewards of society in creating, facilitating and executing the efficient and effective transactions that are part of the greater economy. In this role, marketers should embrace the highest ethical norms of practicing professionals and the ethical values implied by their responsibility toward stakeholders (e.g., customers, employees, investors, channel members, regulators and the host community).

recrimination. To protect them, some firms have appointed ethics officers who are responsible for safeguarding such individuals.

At other firms, such as Manulife, there is a culture that encourages employees to come forward and report ethical breaches; employees know that they will not be stigmatized for reporting unethical conduct. Additionally, senior management fosters ethical behaviour in other ways. Every day, for example, Manulife employees receive a daily prompt when they sign on to their computers and are taken to the company's intranet where they receive ethics reminders. The company also has a global ethics hotline that pops up as an autolaunch feature upon computer start-up.[17]

Personal Moral Philosophy and Ethical Behaviour

Ultimately, ethical choices are based on the personal moral philosophy of the decision maker. Moral philosophy is learned through the process of socialization with friends and family and by formal education. It is also influenced by the societal, business, and corporate cultures in which a person finds himself or herself. Moral philosophies are of two types: (1) moral idealism, and (2) utilitarianism.[18]

moral idealism
A personal moral philosophy that considers certain individual rights or duties as universal, regardless of the outcome.

utilitarianism
A personal moral philosophy that focuses on the "greatest good for the greatest number" by assessing the costs and benefits of the consequences of ethical behaviour.

What does 3M's Scotchgard have to do with ethics, social responsibility, and a $200 million loss in annual sales? Read the text to find out.

Moral Idealism   **Moral idealism** is a personal philosophy that considers certain individual rights or duties as universal (e.g., right to freedom) regardless of the outcome. This philosophy is favoured by moral philosophers and consumer interest groups. For example, the right to know applies to probable defects in an automobile that relate to safety.

This philosophy also applies to ethical duties. A fundamental ethical duty is to do no harm. Adherence to this duty prompted a decision by 3M executives to phase out production of a chemical 3M has manufactured for nearly 40 years. The substance, used in far-ranging products from pet food bags, candy wrappers, carpeting, and 3M's popular Scotchgard fabric protector had no known harmful health or environmental effects. However, the company discovered that the chemical appeared in minuscule amounts in humans and animals around the world and accumulated in tissue. Believing that the substance could be possibly harmful in large doses, 3M voluntarily stopped its production, resulting in a $200 million loss in annual sales.[19]

Utilitarianism   An alternative perspective on moral philosophy is **utilitarianism,** which is a personal moral philosophy that focuses on "the greatest good for the greatest number" by assessing the costs and benefits of the consequences of ethical behaviour. If the benefits exceed the costs, then the behaviour is ethical. If not, then the behaviour is unethical. This philosophy underlies the economic tenets of capitalism and, not surprisingly, is embraced by many business executives and students.[20]

Utilitarian reasoning was apparent in Nestlé Canada's original decision to add peanut product additives to some of the company's chocolate snacks. However, some consumers, albeit only a small percentage of Canadians, are severely allergic to peanuts. Still, Nestlé was intent on pursuing this strategy until many Canadians protested the move. In the end, Nestlé decided to cancel the proposed practice and took out advertising in major newspapers to announce its decision. While the vast majority of Canadians may have enjoyed the newly formulated snacks, and certainly would not have been harmed by them, protestors believed that some consumers may have been harmed by this proposed practice. The views of the protestors prevailed in this case, even though Nestlé could have used the "greatest good for the greatest number" argument.[21]

An appreciation for the nature of ethics, coupled with a basic understanding of why unethical behaviour arises, alerts a person to when and how ethical issues exist in marketing decisions. Ultimately, ethical behaviour rests with the individual, but the consequences affect many.

LO3 UNDERSTANDING SOCIAL RESPONSIBILITY IN MARKETING

As we noted in Chapter 1, the societal marketing concept stresses marketing's social responsibility by not only satisfying the needs of consumers but also providing for society's welfare. As defined in Chapter 1, *social responsibility* means that individuals and organizations are part of a larger society and are accountable to that society for their actions. In the context of corporate behaviour, social responsibility is sometimes referred to as *corporate social responsibility (CSR)*. Like ethics, agreement on the nature and scope of social responsibility is often difficult to come by, given the diversity of values present in different societal, business, and corporate cultures.[22]

Concepts of Social Responsibility

Figure 4–4 shows three concepts of social responsibility: (1) profit responsibility, (2) stakeholder responsibility, and (3) societal responsibility.

Profit Responsibility   **Profit responsibility** holds that companies have a simple duty—to maximize profits for their owners or shareholders. This view is expressed by Nobel Laureate Milton Friedman, who said, "There is one and only one social

profit responsibility
Idea that companies have a simple duty—to maximize profits for their owners or shareholders.

● **FIGURE 4–4**
Three concepts of social responsibility

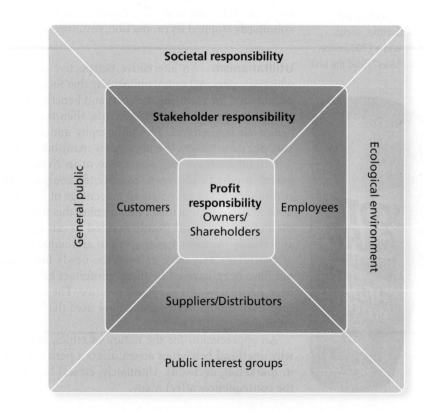

responsibility of business—to use its resources and engage in activities designed to increase its profits so long as it stays within the rules of the game, which is to say, engages in open and free competition without deception or fraud."[23] Genentech had sales of over $1.6 billion in 2006, an increase of 39 percent. Its colon-cancer drug, Avastin, had a sales increase of over 96 percent and it was a very profitable drug for the company. However, the firm charges patients over $47,000 for a ten-month treatment regime. Consumer groups call this price immoral as there is no other drug alternative, and Genentech has a monopoly. The company counters by saying that it provides free drugs to patients without insurance and who meet an income cap requirement.[24]

stakeholder responsibility
Focuses on the obligations an organization has to those who can effect achievement of its objectives, including customers, employees, suppliers, and distributors.

Stakeholder Responsibility Frequent criticism of the profit view has led to a broader concept of social responsibility. **Stakeholder responsibility** focuses on the obligations an organization has to those who can effect achievement of its objectives. These constituencies include customers, employees, suppliers, and distributors. Source Perrier S.A., the supplier of Perrier bottled water, exercised this responsibility when it recalled 160 million bottles of water in 120 countries after traces of a toxic chemical were found in 13 bottles. The recall cost the company $35 million, and $40 million more was lost in sales. Even though the chemical level was not harmful to humans, Source Perrier's president believed he acted in the best interests of the firm's consumers, distributors, and employees by removing "the least doubt, as minimal as it might be, to weigh on the image of the quality and purity of our product."[25]

societal responsibility
Refers to obligations that organizations have to (1) the preservation of the ecological environment, and (2) the general public.

triple-bottom-line
Recognition of the need for organizations to improve the state of people, the planet, and profit simultaneously, if they are to achieve sustainable, long-term growth.

Societal Responsibility An even broader concept of social responsibility has emerged in recent years. **Societal responsibility** refers to obligations that organizations have to (1) the preservation of the ecological environment, and (2) the general public. Today, emphasis is placed on what is termed the **triple-bottom-line**— recognition of the need for organizations to improve the state of people, the planet, and profit simultaneously, if they are to achieve sustainable, long-term growth. Growing interest in green marketing, cause marketing, social audits, and sustainable development reflect this recognition.

As we saw in Chapter 3, many Canadians are becoming more eco-conscious and sensitive to the impact their consumption has on the ecological environment. And, as you have read so far, many Canadian companies, too, have recognized the growing importance of preserving the ecological environment and have responded by engaging in **green marketing**—marketing efforts to produce, promote, and reclaim environmentally sensitive products. Green marketing can take many forms.[26] For example, Richard Branson, CEO of Virgin, is spending $3 billion in profits from his transport businesses to invest in commercial ventures designed to produce renewable energy in order to fight global warming. The Canadian aluminum industry recycles nearly two-thirds of all aluminum cans for reuse. The Food and Consumer Products Manufacturers of Canada has a program known as the Grocery Industry Packaging Stewardship Initiative, which is designed to promote responsible waste and product recycling. Black's Photography of Ontario has factored the environment into everything it does, from product conception to manufacturing, distribution, and sales. It even offers information to consumers through its online e-newsletter about how to respect the natural environment when taking pictures. Teknion Corporation, a Canadian manufacturer of office systems and furniture products, uses its GreenWorks employee teams to find ways to green its manufacturing and administrative facilities. Such efforts have led to not only more responsible environmental practices but also cost savings to the company of over $3 million. Finally, Mercedes-Benz has designed its S-class sedans and 500/600 SEC luxury coupes to be entirely recyclable. These voluntary responses to environmental issues have been implemented with little or no additional cost to consumers.

green marketing
marketing efforts to produce, promote, and reclaim environmentally sensitive products.

A global undertaking to further green marketing efforts is the ISO 14001 initiative developed by the International Standards Organization (ISO) in Geneva, Switzerland.

Which of the three concepts of social responsibility do you think Perrier applied when it learned of quality problems with its popular water? Read the text to learn how the company responded to this problem and its reasoning.

ISO 14001
Worldwide standards for environmental quality and green marketing practices.

cause marketing
Occurs when the charitable contributions of a firm are tied directly to the customer revenues produced through the promotion of one of its products.

social audit
A systematic assessment of a firm's objectives, strategies, and performance in the domain of social responsibility.

sustainable development
Conducting business in a way that protects the natural environment while making economic progress.

ISO 14001 consists of worldwide standards for environmental quality and green marketing practices. These standards are embraced by more than 100 countries, including Canada, members of the European Union, and most Pacific Rim countries.[27]

Socially responsible efforts on behalf of the general public are also becoming more common. A formal practice is **cause marketing,** which occurs when the charitable contributions of a firm are tied directly to the customer revenues produced through the promotion of one of its products.[28] This definition distinguishes cause marketing from a firm's standard charitable contributions, which are outright donations. For example, Procter & Gamble raises funds for the Special Olympics when consumers purchase selected company products, and MasterCard International links usage of its card with fundraising for institutions that combat cancer, heart disease, child abuse, drug abuse, and muscular dystrophy. Avon Products, Inc., focuses on different issues in different countries: breast cancer in the United States, Canada, Philippines, Mexico, Venezuela, Malaysia, and Spain; programs for women who care for senior citizens in Japan; emotional and financial support for mothers in Germany; and AIDS in Thailand. Cause marketing programs incorporate all three concepts of social responsibility by addressing public concerns, satisfying customer needs, and enhancing corporate sales and profits.[29]

The Social Audit

Converting socially responsible ideas into actions involves careful planning and monitoring of programs. Many companies develop, implement, and evaluate their social responsibility efforts by means of a **social audit,** which is a systematic assessment of a firm's objectives, strategies, and performance in the domain of social responsibility. Frequently, marketing and social responsibility programs are integrated, as is the case with McDonald's. The company's concern for the needs of families with children who are chronically or terminally ill was converted into Ronald McDonald Houses around the world. These facilities, located near treatment centres, enable family members to stay together during a child's care. In this case, McDonald's is contributing to the welfare of a portion of its target market.

A social audit consists of five steps:[30]

1. Recognition of a firm's social expectations and the rationale for engaging in social responsibility endeavours.
2. Identification of social responsibility causes or programs consistent with the company's mission.
3. Determination of organizational objectives and priorities for programs and activities it will undertake.
4. Specification of the type and amount of resources necessary to achieve social responsibility objectives.
5. Evaluation of social responsibility programs and activities undertaken and assessment of future involvement.

Corporate attention to social audits will increase as companies seek to achieve sustainable development and improve the quality of life in a global economy.[31] **Sustainable development** involves conducting business in a way that protects the natural environment while also making economic progress. Ecologically responsible initiatives, such as green marketing, represent one such initiative. Other initiatives

Marketing and social responsibility programs are often integrated, as is the case with McDonald's. Its concern for ill children is apparent in the opening of another Ronald McDonald House for children and their families.

McDonald's
www.mcdonalds.com

related to working conditions at offshore manufacturing sites that produce goods for North American companies focus on quality-of-life issues. Public opinion surveys show that Canadian consumers are concerned about working conditions under which products are made in Asia and Latin America.[32] Some companies, such as Reebok, Nike, Liz Claiborne, Levi Strauss, and Mattel, have responded by imposing codes of conduct to reduce harsh or abusive working conditions at offshore manufacturing facilities. Reebok, for example, now monitors the production of its sporting apparel and equipment to ensure that no child labour is used in making its products.

Companies that demonstrate societal responsibility are often rewarded for their efforts. For example, some research has shown that these companies (1) benefit from favourable word-of-mouth among consumers, and (2) typically outperform less responsible companies on financial performance.[33] However, other research has shown that some corporate social responsibility (CSR) behaviour is going unnoticed and/or is not impacting on the consumers' choice of companies or brands purchased. For example, over 75 percent of leading Canadian companies are actively engaged in CSR initiatives, but only one-third of Canadian consumers are aware of any companies that do so. Additionally, research shows that while Canadian consumers "say" they are concerned about whether companies are being socially responsible, it does not often match their purchase behaviour. Specifically, researchers have found that lower prices, convenience, and customer service often trump whether a company engages in CSR when a consumer makes a buying decision.[34]

Still, many companies continue to engage in socially responsible activities and are receiving recognition for their efforts. For example, *CorporateKnights*, a Canadian magazine for responsible business, prepares an annual list of Canada's best corporate citizens, and widely disseminates this list. Some of the companies recognized include Hydro One, Petro-Canada, Canadian National Railway, Vancouver City Savings, Telus, and Loblaw Companies Ltd. In addition, the magazine publishes an annual list of the "Most Sustainable International Companies." Recently, the top 100 companies listed included several Canadian companies including Encana Corp., Telus, Toronto-Dominion Bank, and Transcanada Corp.[35]

You should be mindful, however, that many environmentalists suggest that some companies claim to be green and/or to engage in sustainable development, but their actual behaviour indicates otherwise. These companies are often labelled *greenwashers*. **Greenwashing,** a modification of the term whitewashing, is defined as disinformation disseminated by an organization so as to present an environmentally responsible public image. Greenwashing is considered a deceptive marketing practice but its prevalence is hotly debated. However, most experts agree that it does exist and therefore it can be difficult for the consumer to determine which companies are really green and which are not. Some suggest that greenwashing is common in food marketing where claims of environmental friendliness or sustainable agricultural practices can attract consumers to the products being offered.

LO4 Turning the Table: Consumer Ethics and Social Responsibility

Consumers also have an obligation to act ethically and responsibly in the exchange process and in the use and disposition of products. Unfortunately, consumer behaviour is sometimes spotty on both counts.

Unethical practices of consumers are a serious concern to marketers.[36] These practices include filing warranty claims after the claim period; misredeeming coupons; making fraudulent returns of merchandise; providing inaccurate information on credit applications; tampering with utility meters; tapping cable TV lines; illegally downloading music, movies, and software from the Internet; and submitting phony insurance claims. Some consumers routinely redeem coupons for unpurchased products or use coupons destined for other products. Electrical utilities lose 1 to 3 percent of yearly revenues due to meter tampering, while retailers lose billions of dollars yearly from shoplifting. Illegal downloading is also a major problem in Canada. A recent Canadian study indicated that neither the illegal downloading of copyrighted music, movies, and TV shows nor the illegal file swapping of such is considered a "big deal" among most Canadians. While most Canadians believe that stealing or shoplifting a DVD is a serious offence, they do not feel the same way about illegal downloads.[37] The cost to marketers in lost sales revenue and prevention expenses is huge.

Consumer purchase, use, and disposition of environmentally sensitive products relates to consumer social responsibility. Research indicates that consumers are generally sensitive to ecological issues.[38] Furthermore, some research indicates that seven in ten Canadians are willing to pay more for an environmentally friendly product.[39] However, as in the case of patronizing companies who engage in CSR initiatives over those who do not, some research indicates that some consumers may be unwilling to sacrifice convenience and pay potentially higher prices to protect the environment, and may lack the knowledge to make informed decisions dealing with the purchase, use, and disposition of products.[40] For example, some research suggests that Canadians will buy the new, small Smart cars not because they are green per se, but because they sell for under $20,000, are convenient to use, are easy to park, and use little fuel.[41]

Many marketers suggest that consumers must become more educated when it comes to environmentally conscious behaviour. *Corporate Knights,* for example, has prepared numerous reports for consumers to inform individuals and encourage green behaviour. These guides include advice on how to choose and use environmentally friendly products, as well as recommended choices in various product categories such as automobiles, appliances, and consumer packaged goods.[42] It is also important for consumers to be proactive and to conduct their own research concerning the credibility of companies that make green or sustainable development claims.

In the end, both marketers and consumers are responsible and accountable for ethical and socially responsible behaviour.

Are Canadian consumers buying this car because they are eco-minded? Or because it is a practical choice? Read the text.

---

learning review

6. What is meant by social responsibility?

7. Marketing efforts to produce, promote, and reclaim environmentally sensitive products are called _____.

8. What is a social audit?

LEARNING OBJECTIVES REVIEW

LO1 **Explain the differences between legal and ethical behaviour in marketing.**

A good starting point for understanding the nature and significance of ethics is the distinction between legality and ethicality of marketing decisions. Whereas ethics deal with personal moral principles and values, laws are society's values and standards that are enforceable in the courts. This distinction can lead to the rationalization that if a behaviour is within reasonable ethical and legal limits, then it is not really illegal or unethical. Judgment plays a large role in defining ethical and legal boundaries in marketing. Ethical dilemmas arise when acts or situations are not clearly ethical and legal or unethical and illegal.

LO2 **Identify factors that influence ethical and unethical behaviour in marketing.**

Four factors influence ethical marketing behaviour. First, societal culture and norms serve as socializing forces that dictate what is morally right and just. Second, business culture and industry practices affect ethical conduct both in the exchange relationships between buyers and sellers and the competitive behaviour among sellers. Third, corporate culture and expectations are often defined by corporate ethics codes and the ethical behaviour of top management and co-workers. Finally, an individual's personal moral philosophy, such as moral idealism or utilitarianism, will dictate ethical choices. Ultimately, ethical behaviour rests with the individual, but the consequences affect many.

LO3 **Describe the different concepts of social responsibility.**

Social responsibility means that individuals and organizations are part of a larger society and are accountable to that society for their actions. In a corporate behaviour context, social responsibility is called corporate social responsibility (CSR). There are three concepts of social responsibility. First, profit responsibility holds that companies have a simple duty: to maximize profits for their owners or shareholders. Second, stakeholder responsibility focuses on the obligations an organization has to those who can affect the achievement of its objectives. Those constituencies include consumers, employees, suppliers, and distributors. Finally, societal responsibility focuses on obligations that organizations have to the preservation of the ecological environment and the general public, including placing an emphasis on the triple-bottom-line and engaging in green marketing and sustainable development activities. Companies placing greater emphasis on societal responsibility today can reap the rewards of positive word-of-mouth from their consumers and favourable financial performance. However, they must do more to make consumers aware of their corporate social responsibility initiatives.

LO4 Recognize unethical and socially irresponsible consumer behaviour.

Consumers, like marketers, have an obligation to act ethically and responsibly in the exchange process and in the use and disposition of products. Unfortunately, consumer behaviour is sometimes spotty on both counts. Unethical consumer behaviour includes filing warranty claims after the claim period; misredeeming coupons; pirating music, movies, and software from the Internet; and submitting phony insurance claims, among other behaviours. Consumer purchase, use, and disposition of environmentally sensitive products relate to consumer social responsibility. Even though consumers are sensitive to ecological issues, they may be unwilling to sacrifice convictions and pay potentially higher prices to protect the environment, and may lack the knowledge to make informed decisions dealing with the purchase, use, and disposition of products. Greater consumer education about environmentally conscious behaviour is required.

FOCUSING ON KEY TERMS

cause marketing p. 112
caveat emptor p. 106
code of ethics p. 107
economic espionage p. 106
ethics p. 102
green marketing p. 111
greenwashing p. 114
ISO 14001 p. 112
laws p. 102

moral idealism p. 109
profit responsibility p. 110
social audit p. 112
societal responsibility p. 111
stakeholder responsibility p. 111
sustainable development p. 112
triple-bottom-line p. 111
utilitarianism p. 109
whistle-blowers p. 108

APPLYING MARKETING KNOWLEDGE

1 What concepts of moral philosophy and social responsibility are applicable to the practices of the Canadian automakers described in the introduction to this chapter? Why?

2 Where would the following situations fit in Figure 4–1? (*a*) Exaggerating the performance of a product to get a sale, and (*b*) selling a used automobile knowing it had a major mechanical problem and not telling the buyer.

3 A recent survey of Canadian business students asked, "Is calling your office pretending to be sick in order to take the day off ethical or unethical behaviour?" How would you respond to this question?

4 Compare and contrast moral idealism and utilitarianism as alternative personal moral philosophies.

5 How would you evaluate Milton Friedman's view of the social responsibility of a firm?

6 The text lists several unethical practices of consumers. Can you name others? Why do you think consumers engage in unethical conduct?

7 Cause marketing programs have become popular. Describe two such programs that you are familiar with.

Building Your Marketing Plan

Consider these potential stakeholders that may be affected in some way by the marketing plan on which you are working: shareholders (if any), suppliers, employees, customers, and society in general. For each group of stakeholders:

1. Identify what, if any, ethical and social responsibility issues might arise.

2. Describe, in one or two sentences, how your marketing plan addresses each potential issue.

STARBUCKS CORPORATION: SERVING MORE THAN COFFEE

Wake up and smell the coffee—Starbucks is everywhere! As the world's number-one specialty coffee retailer, Starbucks serves more than 25 million customers in its stores every week. The concept of Starbucks goes far beyond being a coffee house or coffee brand. It represents the dream of its founder, Howard Schultz, who wanted to take the experience of an Italian—specifically, Milan—espresso bar to every corner of every city block in the world. So, what is the *Starbucks experience?* According to the company:

> You get more than the finest coffee when you visit Starbucks. You get great people, first-rate music, a comfortable and upbeat meeting place, and sound advice on brewing excellent coffee at home. At home you're part of a family. At work you're part of a company. And somewhere in between there's a place where you can sit back and be yourself. That's what a Starbucks store is to many of its customers—a kind of "third place" where they can escape, reflect, read, chat, or listen.

But there is more. Starbucks has embraced corporate social responsibility like few other companies. A recent "Starbucks Corporate Social Responsibility Annual Report" described the company's views on social responsibility:

> Starbucks defines corporate social responsibility as conducting our business in ways that produce social, environmental, and economic benefits to the communities in which we operate. In the end, it means being responsible to our stakeholders.

There is a growing recognition of the need for corporate accountability. Consumers are demanding more than "product" from their favourite brands. Employees are choosing to work for companies with strong values. Shareholders are more inclined to invest in businesses with outstanding corporate reputations. Quite simply, being socially responsible is not just the right thing to do—it can distinguish a company from its industry peers. Starbucks not only recognizes the central role that social responsibility plays in its business but also takes constructive action to be socially responsible.

The Company

Starbucks is the leading retailer, roaster, and brand of specialty coffee in the world, with more than 13,000 retail locations in North America, Latin America, Europe, the

Middle East, and the Pacific Rim. Beginning in 1971 with a single retail location in Seattle, Washington, Starbucks grew to become a Fortune 500 company in 2003 with annual sales exceeding $4 billion. In addition, Starbucks is ranked as one of the "Ten Most Admired Companies in America" and one of the "100 Best Companies to Work For" by *Fortune* magazine. It has been recognized as one of the "Most Trusted Brands" by *Ad Week* magazine. Starbucks ranked 21st in *Business Ethics* magazine's list of the "100 Best Citizens" in 2003. Starbucks' performance can be attributed to a passionate pursuit of its mission and adherence to six guiding principles. The Starbucks mission and guiding principles both appear in Figure 1.

Commitment to Corporate Social Responsibility

Starbucks continually emphasizes its commitment to corporate social responsibility. Speaking at the annual shareholders meeting in March 2004, Howard Schultz said:

> From the beginning, Starbucks has built a company that balances profitability with a social conscience. Starbucks business practices are even more relevant today as consumers take a cultural audit of the goods and services they use. Starbucks is known not only for serving the highest quality coffee, but for enriching the daily lives of its people, customers, and coffee farmers. This is the key to Starbucks' ongoing success and we are pleased to report our positive results to shareholders and partners [employees].

Each year, Starbucks makes public a comprehensive report on its corporate social responsibility initiatives. A central feature of this annual report is the alignment of the company's social responsibility decisions and actions with the Starbucks mission statement and guiding principles. The Starbucks 2003 Corporate Social Responsibility Report, titled "Living Our Values," focused on six topical areas: (*a*) partners, (*b*) diversity, (*c*) coffee, (*d*) customers, (*e*) community and environment, and (*f*) profitability.

Partners

Starbucks employs more than 145,000 people around the world. The company began considering its employees as partners following the creation of Starbucks stock

● **FIGURE 1**
Starbucks mission statement
and guiding principles

Establish Starbucks as the premier purveyor of the finest coffee in the world while maintaining our uncompromising principles as we grow.

The following six principles will help us measure the appropriateness of our decisions:

1. Provide a great work environment and treat each other with respect and dignity.
2. Embrace diversity as an essential component in the way we do business.
3. Apply the highest standards of excellence to the purchasing, roasting, and fresh delivery of our coffee.
4. Develop enthusiastically satisfied customers all the time.
5. Contribute positively to our communities and our environment.
6. Recognize that profitability is essential to our future success.

option plan in 1991, called "Bean Stock." The company believes that giving eligible full- and part-time employees an ownership in the company and sharing the rewards of Starbucks' financial success has made the sense of partnership real. In addition, the company has one of the most competitive employee benefits and compensation packages in the retail industry. Ongoing training, career advancement opportunities, partner recognition programs, and diligent efforts to ensure a healthy and safe work environment have all contributed to the fact that Starbucks has one of the lowest employee turnover rates within the restaurant and fast food industry.

Diversity

Starbucks strives to mirror the customers and communities it serves. On a quarterly basis, the company monitors the demographics of its workforce to determine whether they reflect the communities in which Starbucks operates. In 2003, Starbucks' U.S. workforce comprised 63 percent women and 24 percent visible minorities. The company also is engaged in a joint venture called Urban Coffee Opportunities (UCO) created to bring Starbucks stores to diverse neighbourhoods. There were 52 UCO locations employing almost 1,000 Starbucks partners at the end of 2003.

Supplier diversity is also emphasized. To do business with Starbucks as a diverse supplier, that company must be 51 percent owned, operated, and managed by women, minorities, or socially disadvantaged individuals and meet Starbucks requirements of quality, service, value, stability, and sound business practice. The company spent $80 million with diverse suppliers in 2003, $95 million with diverse suppliers in 2004.

Coffee

Starbucks' attention to quality coffee extends to its coffee growers located in more than 20 countries. Sustainable

development is emphasized. This means that Starbucks pays coffee farmers a fair price for the beans; that the coffee is grown in an ecologically sound manner; and that Starbucks invests in the farming communities where its coffees are produced.

One longstanding initiative is Starbucks' partnership with Conservation International, a nonprofit organization dedicated to protecting soil, water, energy, and biological diversity worldwide. Starbucks is particularly focused on environmental protection and helping local farmers earn more for their crops. In 2003, Starbucks invested more than $1 million in social programs, notably health and education projects, that benefited farming communities in nine countries, from Columbia to Indonesia.

Customers

Starbucks served customers in 40 countries in 2007. The company and its partners are committed to providing each customer the optimal Starbucks experience every time they visit a store. For very loyal Starbucks customers, that translates into 18 visits per month on average.

Making a connection with customers at each store and building the relationship a customer has with Starbucks baristas, or coffee brewers, is important in creating the Starbucks experience. Each barista receives 24 hours of training in customer service and basic retail skills, as well as "Coffee Knowledge" and "Brewing the Perfect Cup" classes. Baristas are taught to anticipate the customers' needs and to make eye contact while carefully explaining the various coffee flavours and blends. Starbucks also enhances the customer relationship by soliciting feedback and responding to patrons' experiences and concerns. Starbucks Customer Relations reviews and responds to every inquiry or comment, often within 24 hours in the case of telephone calls and e-mails.

Community and Environment

Efforts to contribute positively to the communities it serves and the environments in which it operates are emphasized in Starbucks' guiding principles. "We aren't in the coffee business, serving people. We are in the people business, serving coffee," says Howard Schultz. Starbucks and its partners have been recognized for volunteer support and financial contributions to a wide variety of local, national, and international social, economic, and environmental initiatives. For example, the "Make Your Mark" program rewards partners' gifts of time for volunteer work with charitable donations from Starbucks. In addition, Starbucks is a supporter of CARE International, a nonprofit organization dedicated to fighting global poverty.

Starbucks is also committed to environmental responsibility. Starbucks has been a long-time involvement with Earth Day activities. It has instituted companywide energy and water conservation programs and waste reduction, recycling, and reuse initiatives proposed by partner *Green Teams*.

Profitability

At Starbucks, profitability is viewed as essential to its future success. When the Starbucks' guiding principles were conceived, profitability was included but intentionally placed last on the list. This was done not because profitability was the least important. Instead, it was believed that adherence to the five other principles would ultimately lead to good financial performance. In fact, it has.

Questions

1 How does Starbucks' approach to social responsibility relate to the three concepts of social responsibility described in the text?

2 What role does sustainable development play in Starbucks' approach to social responsibility?

Consumer Behaviour

GETTING TO KNOW THE AUTOMOBILE CUSTOM(H)ER AND INFLUENC(H)ER

Who buys more than 55 percent of all new cars sold in Canada and influences most of the rest of car-buying decisions made by Canadian households? Women. Yes, women.

Women are a driving force in the Canadian automotive industry. Enlightened carmakers have hired women designers, engineers, and marketing executives to better understand and satisfy this valuable car-buying consumer and influencer. What have they learned? Women and men think and feel differently about key elements of the new-car-buying decision process and experience.

- *The sense of styling.* Women and men care about styling. For men, styling is more about a car's exterior lines and accents. Women are more interested in interior design and finishes. Designs that fit their proportions, provide good visibility, offer ample storage space, and make for effortless parking are particularly important.
- *The need for speed.* Both genders want speed, but for different reasons. Men think about how many seconds it takes to get from zero to 100 kilometres per hour. Women want to feel secure that the car has enough acceleration to outrun an 18-wheeler trying to pass them on a highway entrance ramp.

learning objectives

After reading this chapter, you should be able to:

 LO1 Describe the stages in the consumer purchase decision process.

LO2 Distinguish among three variations of the consumer purchase decision process: routine, limited, and extended problem solving.

LO3 Identify the major psychological influences on consumer behaviour.

LO4 Identify the major socio-cultural influences on consumer behaviour.

- *The substance of safety.* Safety for men is about features that help avoid an accident, such as antilock brakes and responsive steering. For women, safety is about features that help you survive an accident, including passenger airbags and reinforced side panels.
- *The shopping experience.* The new-car-buying experience differs between men and women. Generally, men decide upfront what car they want and set out alone to find it. By contrast, women approach it as an intelligence-gathering expedition. They actively seek information and postpone a purchase decision until all options have been evaluated. Women frequently visit auto-buying Web sites, read online auto magazines such as *Canadian Driver,* and scan car advertisements. Still, recommendations of friends and relatives matter most. Women typically shop at three dealerships before making a purchase decision—one more than men. While only a third of women say that price is the most influential factor when they shop for a new car, 71 percent say price determines the final decision.

Carmakers have learned that women, more than men, dislike the car-buying experience. In particular, women dread the price negotiations that are often involved in buying a new car. Not surprisingly, 76 percent of women car buyers take a man with them to finalize the terms of sale.[1]

consumer behaviour
The actions that a person takes in purchasing and using products and services, including the mental and social processes that precede and follow these actions.

This chapter examines **consumer behaviour,** the actions that a person takes in purchasing and using products and services, including the mental and social processes that precede and follow these actions. This chapter shows how the behavioural sciences help answer such questions as why people choose one product or brand over another, how they make these choices, and how companies use this knowledge to provide value to consumers.

LO1 CONSUMER PURCHASE DECISION PROCESS

purchase decision process
The stages a buyer passes through in making choices about which products and services to buy.

Behind the visible act of making a purchase lies an important decision process that must be investigated. The stages that a buyer passes through in making choices about which products and services to buy is the **purchase decision process.** This process has the five stages shown in Figure 5–1: (1) problem recognition, (2) information search, (3) alternative evaluation, (4) purchase decision, and (5) post-purchase behaviour.

Problem Recognition

Problem recognition, the initial step in the purchase decision, is perceiving a difference between a person's ideal and actual situations that is big enough to trigger a decision.[2] This can be as simple as finding an empty milk carton in the refrigerator; noting, as a first-year university student, that your high school clothes are not in the style that other students are wearing; or realizing that your laptop computer may not be working properly.

In marketing, advertisements or salespeople can activate a consumer's decision process by showing the shortcomings of competing (or currently owned) products. For instance, an advertisement for an MP3 player could stimulate problem recognition because it emphasizes "maximum music from one device."

| Problem recognition | → | Information search | → | Evaluation of alternatives | → | Purchase decision | → | Post-purchase behaviour |

● **FIGURE 5–1**
Purchase decision process

Information Search

After recognizing a problem, a consumer begins to search for information, the next stage in the purchase decision process. First, you may scan your memory for previous experiences with products or brands.[3] This action is called *internal search*. For frequently purchased products, such as shampoo and conditioner, this may be enough. Or a consumer may undertake an *external search* for information.[4] This is especially needed when past experience or knowledge is insufficient, the risk of making a wrong purchase decision is high, and the cost of gathering information is low. The primary sources of external information are (1) *personal sources,* such as relatives and friends whom the consumer trusts; (2) *public sources,* including various product-rating organizations, such as *Consumer Reports,* government agencies, and TV "consumer programs"; and (3) *marketer-dominated sources,* such as information from sellers that includes advertising, company Web sites, salespeople, and point of purchase displays in stores.

Suppose you are considering buying an MP3 player. You will probably tap several information sources: friends and relatives, MP3 advertisements, brand and company Web sites, and stores carrying MP3 players (for demonstrations). You might also study comparable evaluation of various MP3 players as found in *Consumer Reports,* published in either hard copy or found online. In fact, online information search has become very popular, with recent research indicating that the Internet is one of the primary information-gathering and search tools used by Canadian consumers.[5] Also, as you have already learned from previous chapters, more and more often, consumers are relying on social media for information on products, services, and brands, and paying very close attention to what others are saying about various brands on these social media sites.

Alternative Evaluation

The information search stage clarifies the problem for the consumer by (1) yielding brand names, (2) suggesting criteria to use to judge the various brands, and (3) developing consumer value perceptions. The brands that you become aware of during your search become part of your *awareness set.* The criteria you consider when evaluating MP3 players are called **evaluative criteria**—factors that represent both the objective attributes of a brand (such as locate speed) and the subjective ones (such as brand prestige) you use to compare different products and brands.[6] Only the brands that meet your criteria become part of your evoked set, or **consideration set**—the group of brands that a consumer would consider acceptable from among all the brands of which he or she is aware.[7]

Consumers often have several criteria for evaluating brands. Knowing this, companies seek to identify the most important evaluative criteria that consumers use when judging brands and often display these criteria in advertisements. The goal is to create in the consumer's mind the best brand or best value for the money sought by him or her and other consumers. For example, if you were buying a new MP3 player, your selection criteria might consist of price, sound quality, ease of use, or some combination of these and other criteria. Companies developing MP3 players would have to demonstrate to you that their brands meet your criteria and do so better than do the competitors.

evaluative criteria
Factors that represent both the objective attributes of a brand (such as locate speed) and the subjective ones (such as brand prestige) you use to compare different products and brands.

consideration set
The group of brands that a consumer would consider acceptable from among all the brands of which he or she is aware.

A satisfactory or unsatisfactory consumption or use experience is an important factor in post-purchase behaviour. Marketer attention to this stage can pay huge dividends, as described in the text.

Purchase Decision

Having examined the alternatives in the consideration set, you are almost ready to make a purchase decision. Two choices remain: (1) from whom to buy, and (2) when to buy. For a product like an MP3 player, the information search process probably involves visiting retail stores, seeing different brands in catalogues, and viewing an MP3 player on a seller's Web site. The choice of which seller to buy from will depend on such considerations as the terms of sale, past experience buying from the seller, and the return policy. Often, a purchase decision involves a simultaneous evaluation of both product attributes and seller characteristics. For example, you might choose the second-most preferred brand of MP3 player at a store with a liberal refund and return policy versus the most preferred brand at a store with more conservative policies.

Deciding when to buy is frequently determined by a number of factors. For instance, you might buy sooner if one of your preferred brands is on sale or its manufacturer offers a rebate. Other factors, such as the store atmosphere, pleasantness of the shopping experience, salesperson persuasiveness, time pressure, and financial circumstances, could also affect whether a purchase decision is made or postponed.[8]

Post-Purchase Behaviour

After buying a product, the consumer compares it with his or her expectations and is either satisfied or dissatisfied. If the consumer is dissatisfied, marketers must decide whether the product was deficient or consumer expectations were too high. Product deficiency may require a design change; if expectations are too high, perhaps the company's advertising or the salesperson oversold the product's features.

Sensitivity to a customer's consumption or use experience is extremely important in a consumer's value perception. For example, research indicates that satisfaction or dissatisfaction does affect consumer value perceptions.[9] Furthermore, studies show that satisfaction or dissatisfaction affects consumer communications and repeat-purchase behaviour. Satisfied buyers tell three other people about their experiences. Dissatisfied buyers complain to nine people.[10] Satisfied buyers also tend to buy from the same seller each time a purchase occasion arises. The financial impact of repeat-purchase behaviour is significant.[11] Accordingly, such firms as General Electric (GE), Johnson & Johnson, Coca-Cola, and British Airways focus attention on post-purchase behaviour to maximize customer satisfaction and retention. These firms, among many others, provide toll-free telephone numbers, offer liberalized return and refund policies, and engage in staff training to handle complaints, answer questions, and record suggestions. Many forward-thinking firms are also monitoring what is being said about their brands on social media sites in order to gauge customer satisfaction.

Often, a consumer is faced with two or more highly attractive alternatives, such as a Zune or Sony MP3 player. If you choose the Zune, you may think, "Should I have purchased the Sony?" This feeling of post-purchase psychological tension or anxiety is called **cognitive dissonance.** To alleviate it, consumers often attempt to applaud themselves for making the right choice. So, after your purchase, you may seek information to confirm your choice by asking friends such questions as, "Don't you like my new MP3 player?" or by reading ads of the brand you chose. You might even look for negative features about the brand you did not buy and decide that that brand was not right for you. Firms often use ads or follow-up calls from salespeople in this post-purchase stage to assure buyers that they made the right decision. For many years, Buick ran an advertising campaign with the message, "Aren't you really glad you bought a Buick?"

cognitive dissonance
Feeling of post-purchase psychological tension or anxiety.

Involvement and Problem-Solving Variations

Sometimes, consumers do not engage in the five-stage purchase decision process. Instead, they skip or minimize one or more stages, depending on the level of **involvement,** the personal, social, and economic significance of the purchase to the consumer.[12] High-involvement purchase occasions typically have at least one of three characteristics: The item to be purchased (1) is expensive, (2) can have serious personal consequences, or (3) could reflect on one's social image. For these occasions, consumers engage in extensive information search, consider many product attributes and brands, form attitudes, and participate in word-of-mouth communication. Low-involvement purchases, such as toothpaste and soap, are barely involving to most of us, but audio and video systems and automobiles are very involving. There are three general variations in the consumer purchase decision process based on consumer involvement and product knowledge. Figure 5–2 shows some of the important differences between the three problem-solving variations.[13]

Extended Problem Solving   In extended problem solving, each of the five stages of the consumer purchase decision process is used in the purchase, including considerable time and effort on external information search and in identifying and evaluating alternatives. Several brands are in the consideration set, and these brands are evaluated on many attributes. Extended problem solving exists in high-involvement purchase situations for such items as automobiles and elaborate audio systems.

Limited Problem Solving   In limited problem solving, consumers typically seek some information or rely on a friend to help them evaluate alternatives. In general, several brands might be evaluated using a moderate number of different criteria. You might use limited problem solving in choosing a toaster, a restaurant for lunch, and other purchase situations in which you have little time or effort to spend.

Routine Problem Solving   For such products as table salt and milk, consumers recognize a problem, make a decision, and spend little effort seeking external information and evaluating alternatives. The purchase process for such items is virtually a

involvement
The personal, social, and economic significance of the purchase to the consumer.

● **FIGURE 5–2**
Comparison of problem-solving variations

CHARACTERISTICS OF THE CONSUMER PURCHASE DECISION PROCESS	EXTENDED PROBLEM SOLVING	LIMITED PROBLEM SOLVING	ROUTINE PROBLEM SOLVING
Number of brands examined	Many	Several	One
Number of sellers considered	Many	Several	Few
Number of product attributes evaluated	Many	Moderate	One
Number of external information sources used	Many	Few	None
Time spent searching	Considerable	Little	Minimal

HIGH   **CONSUMER INVOLVEMENT**   LOW

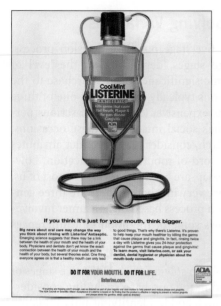

If you think it's just for your mouth, think bigger.

DO IT FOR YOUR MOUTH. DO IT FOR LIFE.
listerine.com

What does this ad for CoolMint Listerine have to do with consumer involvement? Read the text to find out.

habit and typifies low-involvement decision making. Routine problem solving is typically the case for low-priced, frequently purchased products.

Involvement and Marketing Strategy   Low and high consumer involvement has important implications for marketing strategy. If a company markets a low-involvement product and its brand is a market leader, attention is placed on (1) maintaining product quality, (2) avoiding stock-out situations so that buyers do not substitute a competing brand, and (3) advertising messages that reinforce a consumer's knowledge or assure buyers they made the right choice. Market challengers have a different task. They must break buying habits and use free samples, coupons, and rebates to encourage trial of their brand. Advertising messages will focus on getting their brand into a consumer's consideration set. For example, Campbell's V8 vegetable juice advertising message—"I could have had a V8!"—was targeted at consumers who routinely purchased fruit juices and soft drinks. Challengers can also link their brand attributes with high-involvement issues. Listerine does this by linking regular use of its mouthwash with oral care and good health.

Marketers of high-involvement products recognize that their consumers constantly seek and process information about objective and subjective brand attributes, form evaluative criteria, rate product criteria for various brands, and combine these ratings for an overall brand evaluation—like that described in the MP3 player purchase decision. Market leaders freely supply consumers with product information through advertising and personal selling and create chat rooms on their company or brand Web sites. Market challengers capitalize on this behaviour through comparative advertising that focuses on existing product attributes and often introduces novel evaluative criteria for judging competing brands. Increasingly, challengers benefit from Internet search engines, such as Bing and Google, that assist buyers of high-involvement products.

Situational Influences

situational influences

Have an impact on your purchase decision process: (1) the purchase task, (2) social surroundings, (3) physical surroundings, (4) temporal effects, and (5) antecedent states.

Often the purchase situation will affect the purchase decision process. Five **situational influences** have an impact on your purchase decision process: (1) the purchase task, (2) social surroundings, (3) physical surroundings, (4) temporal effects, and (5) antecedent states.[14] The purchase task is the reason for engaging in the decision in the first place. Information searching and evaluating alternatives may differ, depending on whether the purchase is a gift, which often involves social visibility, or for the buyer's own use. Social surroundings, including the other people present when a purchase decision is made, may also affect what is purchased. Physical surroundings, such as decor, music, and crowding in retail stores, may alter how purchase decisions are made. Temporal effects, such as time of day or the amount of time available, will influence where consumers have breakfast and lunch and what is ordered. Finally, antecedent states, which include the consumer's mood or the amount of cash on hand, can influence purchase behaviour and choice.

Figure 5–3 shows the many influences that affect the consumer purchase decision process. The decision to buy a product also involves important psychological and socio-cultural influences, the two important topics discussed in the remainder of this chapter. Marketing mix influences are described in Chapters 10 through 18.

---

learning review

1. What is the first stage in the consumer purchase decision process?

2. The brands that a consumer considers buying out of the set of brands in a product class which the consumer is aware of is called the _____.

3. What is the term for post-purchase anxiety?

● **FIGURE 5-3**

Influences on the consumer
purchase decision process

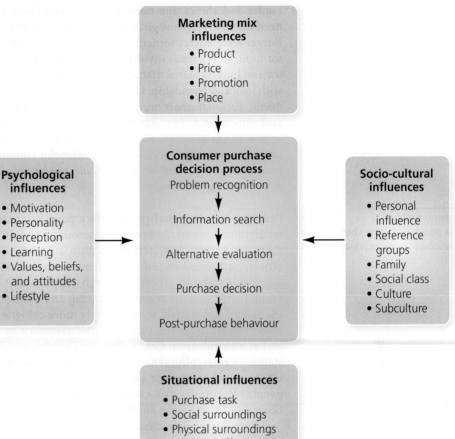

PSYCHOLOGICAL INFLUENCES ON CONSUMER BEHAVIOUR

LO3

Psychology helps marketers understand why and how consumers behave as they do.
In particular, such concepts as motivation and personality; perception; learning; values, beliefs, and attitudes; and lifestyle are useful for interpreting buying processes and
directing marketing efforts.

Motivation and Personality

Motivation and personality are two familiar psychological concepts that have specific
meanings and marketing implications. They are both used frequently to describe why
people do some things and not others.

motivation

The energizing force that causes
behaviour that satisfies a need.

Motivation   **Motivation** is the energizing force that causes behaviour that satisfies a
need. Because consumer needs are the focus of the marketing concept, marketers try
to arouse these needs.

An individual's needs are boundless. People possess physiological needs for such
basics as water, sex, and food. They also have learned needs, including esteem,
achievement, and affection. Psychologists point out that these needs are hierarchical;
that is, once physiological needs are met, people seek to satisfy their learned needs.

Figure 5–4 shows one need hierarchy and classification scheme that contains five need classes.[15] *Physiological needs* are basic to survival and must be satisfied first. A Burger King advertisement featuring a juicy hamburger attempts to activate the need for food. *Safety needs* involve self-preservation and physical well-being. Smoke detector and burglar alarm manufacturers focus on these needs. *Social needs* are concerned with love and friendship. Dating services and fragrance companies try to arouse these needs. *Personal needs* are represented by the need for achievement, status, prestige, and self-respect. The American Express Gold Card and Harry Rosen men's wear appeal to these needs. Sometimes, firms try to arouse multiple needs to stimulate problem recognition. For example, Michelin combines security with parental love to promote tire replacement. *Self-actualization* needs involve personal fulfillment, such as completing your degree.

personality

A person's consistent behaviours or responses to recurring situations.

Personality　　**Personality** refers to a person's consistent behaviours or responses to recurring situations. Although numerous personality theories exist, most identify key traits—enduring characteristics within a person or in his or her relationships with others. Such traits include assertiveness, extroversion, compliance, dominance, and aggression, among others. Research suggests that compliant people prefer known brand names and use more mouthwash and toilet soaps. In contrast, aggressive types use razors, not electric shavers, apply more cologne and after-shave lotions, and purchase signature goods, such as Birks' jewellery in its famous blue box, or clothing and accessories from Gucci, Yves St. Laurent, and Donna Karan, all as indicators of status.[16] Cross-cultural analysis also suggests that residents of different countries have a **national character,** or a distinct set of personality characteristics common among people of a country or society.[17] For example, Canadians are more deliberate and cautious about purchasing anything without examining it.

national character

A distinct set of personality characteristics common among people of a country or society.

self-concept

The way people see themselves and the way they believe others see them.

These personality characteristics are often revealed in a person's **self-concept,** which is the way people see themselves and the way they believe others see them. Marketers recognize that people have an actual self-concept and an ideal self-concept. The *actual self* refers to how people actually see themselves. The *ideal self* describes how people would like to see themselves. These two self "images" are reflected in the products and brands a person buys, including automobiles, home appliances and furnishings, magazines, clothing, grooming products, and leisure products, and,

● **FIGURE 5-4**

Hierarchy of needs

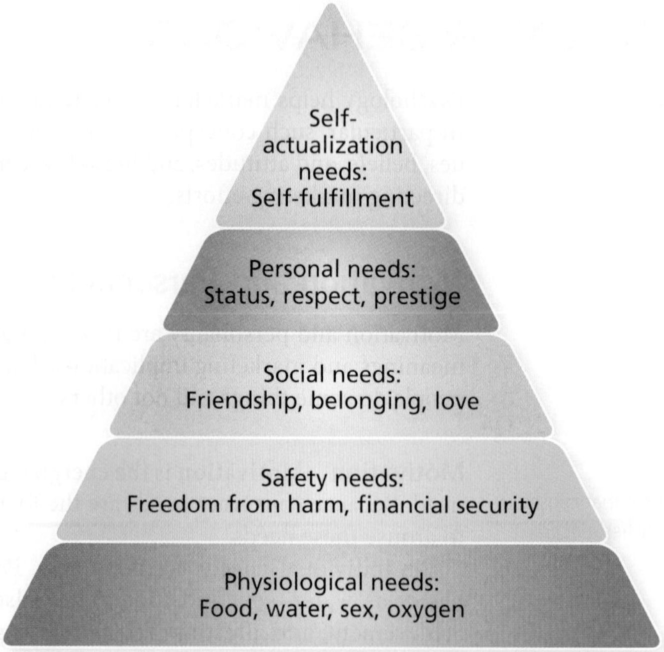

Self-actualization needs: Self-fulfillment

Personal needs: Status, respect, prestige

Social needs: Friendship, belonging, love

Safety needs: Freedom from harm, financial security

Physiological needs: Food, water, sex, oxygen

frequently, in the stores a person shops. The importance of self-concept is summed up by a senior executive at Lenovo, a global supplier of notebook computers: "The notebook market is getting more like cars. The car you drive reflects you, and notebooks are becoming a form of self-expression as well."[18]

Perception

One person sees a Cadillac as a mark of achievement; another sees it as ostentatious. This is the result of **perception**—the process by which an individual selects, organizes, and interprets information to create a meaningful picture of the world.

Selective Perception Because the average consumer operates in a complex environment, the human brain attempts to organize and interpret information through a filtering process called *selective perception*. The four stages of selective perception are selective exposure, selective attention, selective comprehension, and selective retention. First, consumers are not exposed to all information or messages in the marketplace. In other words, there is *selective exposure*. For example, you may watch CTV, but not CBC television. In doing so, you do not expose yourself to any information broadcast on the CBC network. Because of selective exposure, marketers must work to determine where consumers are most likely to be exposed to information.

But even if a consumer is exposed to a message, either by accident or design, the consumer may not attend to that message. In general, with *selective attention*, the consumer will pay attention only to messages that are consistent with their attitudes and beliefs and will ignore those that are inconsistent. Consumers are also more likely to attend to messages when they are relevant or of interest to them. For example, consumers are likely to pay attention to an ad about a product they just bought or to an ad for a product they are interested in buying.

perception
The process by which an individual selects, organizes, and interprets information to create a meaningful picture of the world.

Why does the Good Housekeeping seal for Clorox's Fresh Step Crystals cat litter appear in the ad, and why does Mary Kay, Inc. offer a free sample of its Velocity brand fragrance through its Web site? The answers appear in the text.

Clorox Fresh Step
www.freshstep.com

Mary Kay Velocity
www.mkvelocity.com

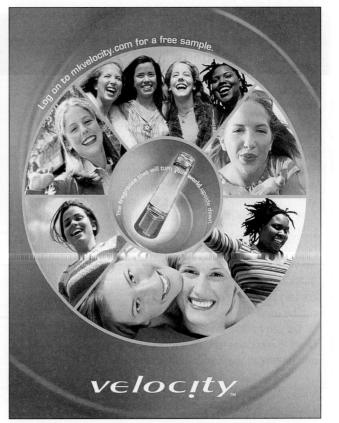

Selective comprehension involves interpreting information so that it is consistent with one's attitudes and beliefs. A marketer's failure to understand this can have disastrous results. For example, Toro introduced a small, lightweight snowblower called the Snow Pup. Even though the product worked, sales failed to meet expectations. Why? Toro later found out that consumers perceived the name to mean that Snow Pup was a toy or too light to do any serious snow removal. When the product was renamed Snow Master, sales increased sharply.[19]

Selective retention means that consumers do not remember all the information they see, read, or hear, even minutes after exposure to it. This affects the internal and external information search stage of the purchase decision process. This is why furniture and automobile retailers often give consumers product brochures to take home after they leave the showroom.

Because perception plays such an important role in consumer behaviour, it is not surprising that the topic of subliminal perception is a popular item for discussion. **Subliminal perception** means that you see or hear messages without being aware of them. The presence and effect of subliminal perception on behaviour is a hotly debated issue, with more popular appeal than scientific support. Indeed, evidence suggests that such messages have limited effects on behaviour.[20] If these messages did influence behaviour, would their use be an ethical practice? (See the accompanying Making Responsible Decisions box, "The Ethics of Subliminal Messages.)"[21]

subliminal perception

Means that you see or hear messages without being aware of them.

perceived risk

The anxiety felt because the consumer cannot anticipate the outcomes of a purchase but believes that there may be negative consequences.

Perceived Risk　　Perception plays a major role in the perceived risk in purchasing a product or service. **Perceived risk** represents the anxieties felt because the consumer cannot anticipate the outcomes of a purchase but believes that there may be negative consequences. Examples of possible negative consequences are the size of the financial outlay required to buy the product (Can I afford $200 for those skis?), the risk of physical harm (Is bungee jumping safe?), and the performance of the product

Making Responsible Decisions

The Ethics of Subliminal Messages

For almost 50 years, the topic of subliminal perception and the presence of subliminal messages embedded in commercial communications has sparked debate. To some, the concept of subliminal messages is a hoax. To others, the possibility of a person being influenced without their knowledge is either an exciting or a frightening concept. Many experts suggest that the use of subliminal messages by marketers, effective or not, is deceptive and unethical.

But there are marketers who occasionally pursue opportunities to create these messages. For example, a recent book by August Bullock, *The Secret Sales Pitch: An Overview of Subliminal Advertising,* is devoted to this topic. Bullock identifies images and advertisements that he claims contain subliminal messages, and describes techniques that can be used for conveying these messages.

Do you believe that attempts to implant subliminal messages in electronic and print media are a deceptive practice and unethical, regardless of their intent?

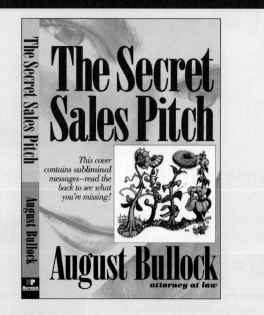

(Will the hair colouring work?). A more abstract form is psychosocial (What will my friends say if I wear that sweater?). Perceived risk affects information search because the greater the perceived risk, the more extensive the external search phase is likely to be.

Recognizing the importance of perceived risk, companies develop strategies to reduce the consumer's risk and encourage purchases. These strategies and examples of firms using them include the following:

- *Obtaining seals of approval.* Canadian Standards Association (CSA) seal or the Good Housekeeping seal for Fresh Step Crystals cat litter.
- *Securing endorsements from influential people.* Athletes promoting milk consumption.
- *Providing free trials of the product.* Sample packages of General Mills Cheerios Snack Mix or Mary Kay's Velocity fragrance.
- *Giving extensive usage instructions.* Clairol Haircolouring.
- *Providing warranties and guarantees.* Kia Motors' 10-year, 160,000-kilometre warranty.

Learning

Much consumer behaviour is learned. Consumers learn which sources to use for information about products and services, which evaluative criteria to use when assessing alternatives, and, more generally, how to make purchase decisions. **Learning** refers to those behaviours that result from (1) repeated experience, and (2) thinking.

learning
Those behaviours that result from (1) repeated experience, and (2) thinking.

Behavioural Learning   *Behavioural learning* is the process of developing automatic responses to a situation built up through repeated exposure to it. Four variables are central to how consumers learn from repeated experience: drive, cue, response, and reinforcement. A *drive* is a need that moves an individual to action. Drives, such as hunger, might be represented by motives. A *cue* is a stimulus or symbol perceived by consumers. A *response* is the action taken by a consumer to satisfy the drive, and a *reinforcement* is the reward. Being hungry (drive), a consumer sees a cue (a billboard), takes action (buys a hamburger), and receives a reward (it tastes great!).

Marketers use two concepts from behavioural learning theory. *Stimulus generalization* occurs when a response elicited by one stimulus (cue) is generalized to another stimulus. Using the same brand name for different products is an application of this concept, such as Tylenol Cold & Flu and Tylenol PM. *Stimulus discrimination* refers to a person's ability to perceive differences in stimuli. Consumers' tendency to perceive all light beers as being alike led to Budweiser Light commercials that distinguished among many types of "lights" and Bud Light.

Cognitive Learning   Consumers also learn through thinking, reasoning, and mental problem solving without direct experience. This type of learning, called *cognitive learning*, involves making connections between two or more ideas, or simply observing the outcomes of others' behaviours and adjusting your own accordingly. Firms also influence this type of learning. Through repetition in advertising, such messages as "Advil is a headache remedy" attempt to link a brand (Advil) and an idea (headache remedy) by showing someone using the brand and finding relief.

Brand Loyalty   Learning is also important because it relates to habit formation—the basis of routine problem solving. Furthermore, there is a close link between habits and **brand loyalty**, which is a favourable attitude toward and consistent purchase of a single brand over time. Brand loyalty results from the positive reinforcement of previous actions. A consumer reduces risk and saves time by consistently purchasing the

brand loyalty
A favourable attitude toward and consistent purchase of a single brand over time.

same brand of shampoo and has favourable results—healthy, shining hair. There is evidence of brand loyalty in many commonly purchased products in Canada and the global marketplace. However, the incidence of brand loyalty appears to be declining in North America, Mexico, European Union nations, and Japan.[22]

Values, Beliefs, and Attitudes

Values, beliefs, and attitudes play a central role in consumer decision making and all related marketing actions.

values
Personally or socially preferable modes of conduct or states of existence that are enduring.

Values **Values** are personally or socially preferable modes of conduct or states of existence that are enduring. In essence, values are ideas that people hold to be important or believe to be good. Values vary by level of specificity. We speak of Canadian core values, including material well-being and humanitarianism. We also have personal values, such as thriftiness and ambition. Marketers are concerned with both but focus mostly on personal values.

beliefs
A consumer's subjective perception of how well a product or brand performs on different attributes.

Beliefs **Beliefs** are a consumer's subjective perception of how well a product or brand performs on different attributes. Beliefs are based on personal experience, advertising, and discussions with other people.

attitude
A learned predisposition to respond to an object or class of objects in a consistently favourable or unfavourable way.

Attitudes An **attitude** is a "learned predisposition to respond to an object or class of objects in a consistently favourable or unfavourable way."[23]

Attitudes are shaped by our values and beliefs. For example, personal values affect attitudes by influencing the importance assigned to specific product attributes. Suppose thriftiness is one of your personal values. When you evaluate cars, fuel economy (a product attribute) becomes important. If you believe (a belief) that a specific car has this attribute, you are likely to have a favourable attitude toward it.

Attitudes toward Colgate toothpaste and Extra Strength Bayer Aspirin were successfully changed by these ads. How? Read the text to find out how marketers can change consumer attitudes toward products and brands.

Colgate-Palmolive
www.colgate.ca

Bayer Corporation
www.bayer.ca

Attitude Change   Marketers use three approaches to try to change consumer attitudes toward products and brands, as shown in the following examples.[24]

1. *Changing beliefs about the extent to which a brand has certain attributes.* To allay consumer concern that aspirin use causes an upset stomach, Bayer Corporation successfully promoted the gentleness of its Extra Strength Bayer Plus Aspirin.
2. *Changing the perceived importance of attributes.* Pepsi-Cola made freshness an important product attribute when it stamped freshness dates on its cans. Prior to doing so, few consumers considered cola freshness an issue.
3. *Adding new attributes to the product.* Colgate-Palmolive included a new antibacterial ingredient, tricloson, in its Colgate Total toothpaste and spent $100 million marketing the brand. The result? Colgate replaced Crest as the market leader for the first time in 25 years.

Lifestyle

lifestyle
A mode of living that is identified by how people spend their time and resources, what they consider important in their environment, and what they think of themselves and the world around them.

Lifestyle is a mode of living that is identified by how people spend their time and resources, what they consider important in their environment, and what they think of themselves and the world around them. The analysis of consumer lifestyles, called *psychographics,* has produced many insights into consumer behaviour. For example, lifestyle analysis has proven useful in segmenting and targeting consumers for new and existing products and services (Chapter 9).

Psychographics, in essence, the practice of combining psychology and demographics, is often used to uncover consumer motivations for buying and using products and services. There are several well-known psychographic systems developed by various researchers, including (1) the VALS system developed by SRI Consulting Business Intelligence (SRIC-BI), (2) Monitor MindBase developed by Yankelovich Partners, and (3) PRIZM developed by Claritas. Until recently, these psychographic systems have been American-based. But VALS is now available for the Japanese and British markets, and PRIZM has been adapted for the Canadian market by Environics Analytics and is called PRIZM C2. PRIZM C2 classifies Canadian neighbourhoods into 66 lifestyle types (clusters) and includes such groups as Les Chics and Lunch at Tim's

 FIGURE 5–5

Example of PRIZM C2 Psychographic Segments © 2008 Environics Analytics Group Ltd. PRIZM is a registered trademark of Claritas Inc., used with permission.

Working-class old and young industrial towns and cities

Located in industrial towns and cities across southern Ontario, Lunch at Tim's consists of high school-educated, blue collar workers living in older homes and small apartment buildings. They're the kind of tight-knit communities where residents like to socialize at local eateries. Few clusters rank higher in the popularity of pizza parlours, Chinese restaurants and doughnut shops. Residents also like to wind down after work by watching TV, playing video games and going snowboarding. They'll occasionally splurge on a visit to a casino, but these working-class folks are more concerned about hanging on to their paycheques than gambling them away. As they put it: "I am willing to work at a boring job as long as the pay is good."

46
Lunch at Tim's
U4 Urban Mix

Lower-Middle $45,488
Young & Mature
Low

(Figure 5–5). Check out which group or cluster you might belong to by following the directions provided in the Going Online exercise.

Given our globalized economy, one firm set out to determine if discernible lifestyle segments cut across cultures, regardless of differences in geographics, languages, or other factors. Global Scan, developed by BSBW, is a psychographics system based on surveys of 15,000 consumers in 14 countries (Australia, Canada, Columbia, Finland, France, Germany, Hong Kong, Indonesia, Japan, Mexico, Spain, the United Kingdom, the United States, and Venezuela). It measures more than 250 values and attitudes, in addition to demographics, media usage, and buying preferences. BSBW discovered that five global lifestyle segments emerged: strivers, achievers, pressured, adapters, and traditionals. These segments exist in all 14 countries, but the percentage of the population in each group varies by country. Still, this psychographic system allows global marketers insight into how to segment and target consumers in these different countries.

learning review	**4.** The problem with the Toro Snow Pup was an example of selective _____.
	5. What three attitude-change approaches are most common?
	6. What does lifestyle mean?

LO4 SOCIO-CULTURAL INFLUENCES ON CONSUMER BEHAVIOUR

Socio-cultural influences, which evolve from a consumer's formal and informal relationships with other people, also exert a significant impact on consumer behaviour. These involve personal influence, reference groups, family, social class, culture, and subculture.

Personal Influence

A consumer's purchases are often influenced by the views, opinions, or behaviours of others. Two aspects of personal influence are important to marketing: opinion leadership and word-of-mouth activity.

Opinion Leadership   Individuals who exert direct or indirect social influence over others are called **opinion leaders.** Opinion leaders are considered to be knowledgeable about users of particular products and services, and so their opinions influence others' choices. Opinion leadership is widespread in the purchase of cars and trucks, clothing and accessories, club membership, consumer electronics, vacation locations, and financial investments.

opinion leaders
Those knowledgeable about users of particular products and services, and so their opinions influence others' choices.

About 10 percent of adults are considered opinion leaders.[25] Identifying, reaching, and influencing opinion leaders is a major challenge for companies. Some firms use sports figures or celebrities as spokespersons to represent their products, for example, Wayne Gretzky promoting Ford or Mike Weir with Sears. Others promote their products in those media believed to reach opinion leaders. Still others use more direct approaches such as actually inviting people deemed opinion leaders to try their products and services or providing such products and services for free to the opinion leaders in the hope that they will influence others to purchase.

word of mouth
The influencing of people during conversations.

Word of Mouth   The influencing of people during conversations is called **word of mouth.** Word of mouth is the most powerful and authentic information source for consumers because it typically involves friends viewed as trustworthy. Canadian research illustrates well the importance of word of mouth. For example, the Canadian Mood & Mindset online survey reveals that we do rely on each other for recommendations about products.[26] For services, word of mouth plays an even stronger role, with 70 percent of Canadians saying that they used word of mouth when selecting a bank, and 95 percent relied on word of mouth when choosing a physician.[27]

The power of personal influence has prompted firms to promote positive word of mouth and to retard negative word of mouth. For instance, "teaser" advertising campaigns are run in advance of new-product introductions to stimulate conversations. Other techniques, such as advertising slogans, music, and humour, also heighten positive word of mouth. Many commercials shown during the Grey Cup or Super Bowl games, for instance, are created expressly to initiate conversations about the advertisements and featured product or service the next day.

buzz marketing
Popularity created by consumer word of mouth.

viral marketing
The online version of word of mouth, involving the use of messages "infectious" enough that consumers wish to pass them along to others through online communication.

Increasingly, companies are working hard to stimulate positive consumer word of mouth about their products or services. This is called **buzz marketing**—popularity created by consumer word of mouth. The use of buzz marketing is becoming increasingly popular with Canadian marketers. In fact, according to the Canadian Marketing Association, buzz marketing is now closely linked to business and brand growth. For more insight into this phenomenon, read the Marketing Matters box.[28]

The electronic or online version of word of mouth is called **viral marketing.** This involves the use of messages "infectious" enough that consumers wish to pass along

Marketing Matters

The Buzz about Buzz

Have you recently heard about a new product, movie, Web site, book, or restaurant from someone you know . . . or a complete stranger? If so, you may have had a buzz experience. Many Canadian marketers recognize the power of word of mouth, and there are many high-profile Canadian companies engaging in buzz marketing, including Kraft, Toyota, Molson, Coty, Nike, and even the Wine Council of Ontario. Companies can construct and operationalize their own buzz marketing campaigns or farm out the activity to buzz marketing companies such as Matchstick, Inc. of Toronto. If a company hires Matchstick, a typical buzz marketing campaign is constructed as follows: Matchstick will hire "brand seeders" on a freelance basis. These seeders are close in age or lifestyle to the relevant product category's target consumer. Seeders are paid by Matchstick to identify potential influencers, or "influencials"—individuals who are naturally enthusiastic toward the brand and who will gladly spread the word about the brand. Matchstick does market research to identify potential influencials and passes this information along to the seeders. Several dozen seeders will

reach about 100 influencials in each city. The brand seeders are provided samples to give to the influencials. These influencials are encouraged (but not paid) to share their honest opinions about the brand and to disclose their relationship with Matchstick. In this way, there is transparency and this buzz is not considered stealth marketing. In short, the influencials are engaging in genuine and, hopefully, effective word-of-mouth conversations about the brand.

Word-of-mouth communication, and in particular, buzz marketing, is becoming so popular that there is even a Word of Mouth Marketing Association (**www.womma.org**), an organization dedicated to assist marketers in becoming proficient at developing and harnessing word-of-mouth communication. The association also has an ethics code that defines best practices, unacceptable practices, and baseline rules for word-of-mouth activities. Sean Moffitt, one of Canada's word-of-mouth experts, is the author of a popular blog, "Buzz Canuck." He tells us that word of mouth can be the most important source of new business and most brands can benefit from buzz marketing.

to others through online forums, social networks, chat rooms, bulletin boards, blogs, message board threads, instant messages, and e-mails. Many companies actively encourage viral marketing while many others use special software to monitor online messages and find out what consumers are saying about their products and services. Ontario-based Brandimensions, for example, collects online conversations for its clients, including the Royal Bank, Chrysler, and Fox, in order to determine what is being said about their products and services and who is saying it.

On the other hand, rumours about Kmart (snake eggs in clothing), McDonald's (worms in hamburgers), Corona Extra beer (contaminated beer), and Snickers candy bars in Russia (a cause of diabetes) have resulted in negative word of mouth, none of which was based on fact. Overcoming or neutralizing negative word of mouth, especially electronic or Internet-based word of mouth, is difficult and costly. Marketers have found that supplying factual information, providing toll-free numbers for consumers to call the company, giving appropriate product demonstrations, and monitoring and responding to word-of-mouth activity on the Internet have proven helpful.

Reference Groups

reference groups
People to whom an individual looks as a basis for self-appraisal or as a source of personal standards.

Reference groups are people to whom an individual looks as a basis for self-appraisal or as a source of personal standards. Reference groups affect consumer purchases because they influence the information, attitudes, and aspiration levels that help set a consumer's standards. For example, one of the first questions one asks others when planning to attend a social occasion is, "What are you going to wear?" Reference groups have an important influence on the purchase of luxury products but not of necessities—reference groups exert a strong influence on the brand chosen when its use or consumption is highly visible to others.

Consumers have many reference groups, but three groups have clear marketing implications. A *membership group* is one to which a person actually belongs, including fraternities and sororities, social clubs, and the family. Such groups are easily identifiable and are targeted by firms selling insurance, insignia products, and charter vacations. An *aspiration group* is one that a person wishes to be a member of or wishes to be identified with, such as a professional society. Firms frequently rely on spokespeople or settings associated with their target market's aspiration group in their advertising. A *dissociative group* is one that a person wishes to maintain a distance from because of differences in values or behaviours.

Family Influence

Family influences on consumer behaviour result from three sources: consumer socialization, passage through the family life cycle, and decision making within the family or household.

consumer socialization
The process by which people acquire the skills, knowledge, and attitudes necessary to function as consumers.

Consumer Socialization   The process by which people acquire the skills, knowledge, and attitudes necessary to function as consumers is **consumer socialization.**[29] Children learn how to purchase (1) by interacting with adults in purchase situations, and (2) through their own purchasing and product usage experiences. Research shows that children evidence brand preferences at age two, and these preferences often last a lifetime.[30] As discussed in Chapter 1, this leads many companies to target children at a very young age in the hopes of developing customers for life.

family life cycle
The distinct phases that a family progresses through from formation to retirement, each phase bringing with it identifiable purchasing behaviours.

Family Life Cycle   Consumers act and purchase differently as they go through life. The **family life cycle** concept describes the distinct phases that a family progresses through from formation to retirement, each phase bringing with it identifiable purchasing behaviours.[31] Figure 5–6 illustrates the traditional progression as well as contemporary variations of the family life cycle. Today, the traditional family—married couples with children younger than 18 years—constitutes less than one-third of all

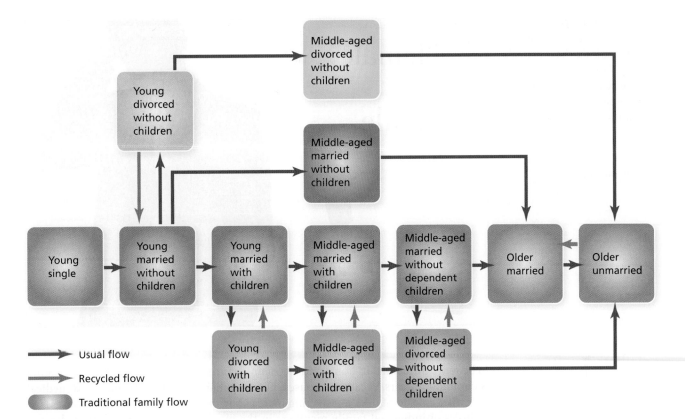

● FIGURE 5–6
Modern family life cycle

households. The remaining households include single parents; unmarried couples; divorced, never-married, or widowed individuals; and older married couples whose children no longer live at home.

Young singles' buying preferences are for nondurable items, including prepared foods, clothing, personal care products, and entertainment. They represent a target market for recreational travel, automobile, and consumer electronics firms. Young married couples without children are typically more affluent than young singles because usually both spouses are employed. These couples exhibit preferences for furniture, housewares, and gift items for each other. Young marrieds with children are driven by the needs of their children. They make up a sizable market for life insurance, various children's products, and home furnishings. Single parents with children are the least financially secure of households with children. Their buying preferences are affected by a limited economic status and tend toward convenience foods, child care services, and personal care items.

Middle-aged married couples with children are typically better off financially than their younger counterparts. They are a significant market for leisure products and home improvement items. Middle-aged couples without children typically have a large amount of discretionary income. These couples buy better home furnishings, status automobiles, and financial services. Persons in the last two phases—older married and older unmarried—make up a sizable market for prescription drugs, medical services, vacation trips, and gifts for younger relatives.

Family Decision Making   A third influence in the decision-making process occurs within the family.[32] Two decision-making styles exist: spouse-dominant and joint decision making. With a joint decision-making style, most decisions are made by both husband and wife. Spouse-dominant decisions are those for which either the husband or the wife is responsible. Research indicates that wives tend to have the most say when purchasing groceries, children's toys, clothing, and medicines. Husbands tend

The Haggar Clothing Co. recognizes the important role women play in the choice of men's clothing. The company directs a large portion of its advertising toward women because they influence and purchase men's clothing.

Haggar Clothing Co.
www.haggar.com

to be more influential in home and car maintenance purchases. Joint decision making is common for cars, vacations, houses, home appliances and electronics, and medical care. As a rule, joint decision making increases with the education of the spouses.

Roles of individual family members in the purchase process are another element of family decision making. Five roles exist: (1) information gatherer, (2) influencer, (3) decision maker, (4) purchaser, and (5) user. Family members assume different roles for different products and services. This knowledge is important to firms. For example, many wives either influence or make outright purchases of men's clothing. Knowing this, Haggar Clothing, a men's wear marketer, advertises in women's magazines, such as *Vanity Fair* and *Redbook*. Even though women are often the grocery decision maker, they are not necessarily the purchaser. More than 40 percent of all food-shopping dollars are spent by male customers. Increasingly, preteens and teenagers are the information gatherers, influencers, decision makers, and purchasers of products and services for the family, given the prevalence of working parents and single-parent households. Children under 12 directly influence billions of dollars in annual family purchases. Teenagers also influence billions of dollars in annual family purchases and spend millions of their own money annually. These figures help explain why, for example, Nabisco, Johnson & Johnson, Apple, Kellogg, P&G, Sony, and Oscar Mayer, among countless other companies, spend close to billions annually in media that reach preteens and teens.

Social Class

social class
The relatively permanent, homogeneous divisions in a society into which people sharing similar values, lifestyles, interests, and behaviour can be grouped.

A more subtle influence on consumer behaviour than direct contact with others is the social class to which people belong. **Social class** may be defined as the relatively permanent, homogeneous divisions in a society into which people sharing similar values, interests, and behaviour can be grouped. A person's occupation, source of income (not level of income), and education determine his or her social class. Generally speaking, three major social class categories exist—upper, middle, and lower—with subcategories within each. This structure has been observed in Canada, the United States, the United Kingdom, Western Europe, and Latin America.[33]

To some degree, persons within social classes exhibit common attitudes, lifestyles, and buying behaviours. Compared with the middle classes, people in the lower classes have a more short-term time orientation, are more emotional than rational in their reasoning, think in concrete rather than abstract terms, and see fewer personal opportunities. Members of the upper classes focus on achievements and the future and think in abstract or symbolic terms.

Companies use social class as a basis for identifying and reaching particularly good prospects for their products and services. In general, people in the upper classes are targeted by companies for such items as financial investments, expensive cars, and evening wear. The middle classes represent a target market for home improvement centres, automobile parts stores, and personal hygiene products. Firms also recognize differences in media preferences among classes: lower and working classes prefer sports and scandal magazines; middle classes read fashion, romance, and celebrity (e.g., *People*) magazines; and upper classes tend to read literary, travel, and news magazines, such as *Maclean's*.

Culture and Subculture

As described in Chapter 3, culture incorporates the set of values, ideas, and attitudes that are learned and shared among members of a group. This we often refer to as, say, Canadian culture, American culture, British culture, or Japanese culture. (Cultural underpinnings of Canadian buying patterns are described in Chapter 3, while Chapter 7 explores the role of culture in global marketing.)

Subgroups within the larger, or national, culture with unique values, ideas, and attitudes are referred to as **subcultures.** Subcultures can be identified by age (e.g., baby boomers versus Generation X), geography (e.g., Western Canadian versus Atlantic Canadian), and ethnicity. Here, we focus on ethnic subcultures.

An *ethnic subculture* is a segment of a larger society whose members are thought, by themselves and/or by others, to have a common origin and to participate in shared activities believed to be culturally significant. Common traits, such as customs, language, religion, and values, hold ethnic subcultures together.

Canada has traditionally thought of itself as a cultural mosaic, a pluralist society, rather than a melting pot. In this case, ethnic groups did not necessarily join the mainstream culture. This was referred to as the *salad bowl phenomenon,* where a potpourri of people mix but do not blend. However, new Canadian research indicates that Canada's ethnic population is becoming integrated into the cultural mainstream in a single generation. This has implications for marketers wanting to appeal to ethnic Canadians and for ethnic media attempting to reach ethnic groups. Assimilation means a possible loss of ethnic markets.[34]

French-Canadian Subculture There are over seven million French-speaking Canadians, about 25 percent of the total Canadian population. The overwhelming majority of French Canadians live in Quebec. Some suggest that the average French Quebecer has more in common with the average English-speaking Canadian than ever before. However, consumer research shows that French-speaking Quebecers do differ from other Canadians on a variety of dimensions, including consumption behaviour.[35] PRIZM C2, the psychographic system mentioned earlier in the chapter, has found that French-speaking Quebecers are very different from other Canadians. In fact, 15 of the 66 segments or clusters in the PRIZM C2 system are distinctly Quebecois, including Les Chics, Mini Van & Vin Rouge, and Quebec Rustics. In fact, because of the distinct differences, Environics has created PRIZM QC, which captures and illustrates these differences. Moreover, other research has also confirmed that French Canadians are different from other Canadians in many ways.

For example, if you checked the iPod of a young French-Canadian living in Montreal, you would likely find music from France, Quebec, the U.S., the rest of Canada, and even Italy. When Quebecers are asked what is most important to them, they are more likely than other Canadians to say "enjoying life" and "seeking happiness." In fact, Quebecers enjoy living in the moment and are prone to seeking instant gratification. They are also more tolerant and open-minded than English Canadians

subcultures
Subgroups within the larger, or national, culture with unique values, ideas, and attitudes.

on a variety of issues. For instance, French Canadians are more likely to believe that everybody should be free to do their own thing, compared with English Canadians.

More Quebecers also say they feel the need to be closer to nature. In fact, Quebec has the highest percentage of hunters and fishers in the world. Quebecers also like to be comfortable at home and in their backyards. Yet, Quebecers do not appear too keen to fix things around the house; just 22 percent say that they only do do-it-your-self projects if they absolutely have to. They are also less likely than English Canadians to own power tools.

Quebecers are very loyal to their province. In fact, 41 percent of Quebecers claim they identify first and foremost with their province, while 32 percent do so with Canada. Quebecers are also loyal to their heritage and are also keen to understand their roots.

More so than other Canadians, French Canadians feel a need to be with people whose outlook on life and sense of values are similar to their own. French Canadians say they feel closer to people who have the same religious, national, or ethnic background as their own. However, interestingly enough, many Quebecers feel closer to Americans than to the rest of Canada. Furthermore, French Quebecers have seemingly moved away from their Catholic roots with almost one-quarter (22 percent), significantly more than any other region of the country, saying their belief in God has declined over the years.

Quebecers also like to talk. They call radio stations and they chat online. In fact, Yahoo! Canada's French-language portal is very busy in Quebec. Quebecers are also obsessed with the lives of their stars, big and small.

Quebecers tend to have eccentric tastes and they enjoy shopping. They are also more brand loyal than are other Canadians. Also, two-thirds of Quebecers feel the need to add their own touch to the things they buy, compared with 48 percent of English Canadians.

Quebecers are more likely to say they follow their instincts than listen to experts. Yet, Quebecers like advertising more than do other Canadians. But they are no more likely to believe its claims than are English Canadians, and they are more likely than other Canadians to say that they have been offended by an ad. Furthermore, most Quebecers simply ignore online advertising and believe such ads to be of little use while also being invasive.

Quebecers prefer to plan their shopping, and more Quebecers shop with a grocery list compared with other Canadians. Quebecers use coupons more than do English Canadians, but they do not appear to think of themselves as bargain hunters. They do, however, feel a greater need to evaluate the quality and value of the products they buy. Metro-Richelieu, a Quebec grocery chain, has found that Quebecers do consult the chain's weekly circulars. The firm has also found that Metro's Econo-Metro plan, a program that offers discount coupons and weekly money-saving tips, has also been a hit with Quebecer shoppers.

Quebecers like to buy things that pleasure the senses. For example, they like fine restaurants and fine wines and like to use bath additives and perfume. Quebecois women are also very fashion-conscious, and upscale brands, such as Prada, Coach, Lancome, and Seven Jeans, sell well in Quebec. In fact, Quebecers compare with New Yorkers in terms of their fashion sense. They also enjoy looking good and young and many say they will do whatever they can to look as young as possible.

The financial services industry is different in Quebec. More than 60 percent of the province's financial services market remains in the hands of two players that are almost nonexistent in English Canada: the Mouvement Desjardins (the federation of Quebec credit unions) and the National Bank. Both players deploy integrated and Quebec-specific communications that resonate in this market. However, the personal savings rate is lower in Quebec than in the rest of Canada, and there is a greater proportion of the population in Quebec with less than $50,000 in their RRSPs than anywhere else in Canada. This may be explained by their desire to live life in the here and now.

While the province of Quebec has the highest percentage of alcohol drinkers and the most relaxed drinking laws in Canada, it also has the lowest percentage of excessive drinkers and the fewest alcohol-related problems. Finally, Quebecers are ahead of the curve when it comes to social media and the creation of user-generated content online.

To be successful in marketing to French Canadians living in Quebec, marketers must be sensitive to the wants and needs of Quebecois consumers and appreciate the inherent differences between them and other Canadians. In addition to cultural and lifestyle differences, there are also other issues that marketers must address. Commercial advertising to children is prohibited, and there are greater restrictions on alcohol advertisements. Provincial regulations require that labels and packages be in both French and English, while storefront signage may be only in French.

Acadian Subculture   Many Canadians assume that French Canadians are basically the same. Even though the majority of French-speaking Canadians reside in Quebec, another special group of French-speaking Canadians live outside of Quebec. These people are the Acadians, most of whom live in New Brunswick and are proud of their distinctive heritage. The Acadians are often referred to as the "forgotten French market."

Acadians are different from French Quebecers in many ways. In terms of consumption, Acadians are very fashion-oriented and tend to dine out more often than their French counterparts in Quebec. Acadians are very price-conscious. They also prefer companies that speak to them in their language, which is slightly different from French Quebecois.

Chinese-Canadian Subculture   The Chinese-Canadian market currently represents almost 4 percent of Canada's population, but it is one of the fastest-growing subcultures in Canada. This ethnic group is composed predominantly of immigrants from Hong Kong, mainland China, and Taiwan and is concentrated largely in Toronto and Vancouver.

Chinese-Canadian consumers spend over $20 billion each year. In general, these consumers are relatively young, educated, and affluent. They tend to spend their money on homes and home furnishings, automobiles, kids' education, investments, high-tech gadgets, travelling, and gifts. They like to do business within their own communities and prefer media in their own languages. They have strong allegiance to brands and are very family-oriented. Because they live in close-knit communities, word of mouth is extremely important to them. They also place great value on business success and financial stability.[36]

However, like other Canadians, Chinese-Canadians are not one monolithic group. In fact, recent research has broken this market into eight psychographic segments including the Top Gun Metros (owners of new castles), Ethnic Cruisers, Up the Ladders, and Empty Nesters.[37] Many Canadian firms have recognized the importance of this emerging market and its relevant segments and are successful marketing to them, including firms such as Rogers Wireless, RBC, and BMW.

Other Ethnic Subcultures   Many other ethnic Canadians can be found in large metropolitan centres or clustered in certain geographic areas. Kitchener-Waterloo has a large German-Canadian population, Winnipeg is home to many Ukrainian-Canadians, and Toronto has a large number of Italian-Canadians. Marketers must appreciate the fact that these ethnic Canadians may carry with them distinctive social and cultural behaviours that might affect their buying patterns. Subcultural research and sensitivity can aid organizations in developing effective marketing strategies designed to appeal to these groups.

---

learning review

7. What are the two primary forms of personal influence?

8. Which types of reference groups are marketers concerned with?

9. What is an ethnic subculture?

LEARNING OBJECTIVES REVIEW

LO1 **Describe the stages in the consumer purchase decision process.**

The consumer purchase decision process consists of five stages. They are problem recognition, information search, alternative evaluation, purchase decision, and post-purchase behaviour. Problem recognition is perceiving a difference between a person's ideal and actual situation that is big enough to trigger a decision. Information search involves remembering previous purchase experiences (internal search) and external search behaviour, such as seeking information from other sources. Alternative evaluation clarifies the problem for the consumer by (*a*) yielding brand names that might meet the criteria, (*b*) suggesting the evaluative criteria to use for the purchase, and (*c*) developing consumer value perceptions. The purchase decision involves the choice of an alternative, including from whom to buy and when to buy. Post-purchase behaviour involves the comparison of the chosen alternative with a consumer's expectations, which leads to satisfaction or dissatisfaction and subsequent purchase behaviour.

LO2 **Distinguish among three variations of the consumer purchase decision process: routine, limited, and extended problem solving.**

Consumers do not always engage in the five-stage purchase decision process. Instead, they skip or minimize one or more stages depending on the level of involvement—the personal, social, and economic significance of the purchase. For low-involvement purchase occasions, consumers engage in routine problem solving. They recognize a problem, make a decision, and spend little effort seeking external information and evaluating alternatives. For high-involvement purchase occasions, each of the five stages of the consumer purchase decision process is used, including considerable time and effort on external information search and in identifying and evaluating alternatives. With limited problem solving, consumers typically seek some information or rely on a friend to help them evaluate alternatives.

LO3 **Identify the major psychological influences on consumer behaviour.**

Psychology helps marketers understand why and how consumers behave as they do. In particular, psychological concepts, such as motivation and personality; perception; learning; values, beliefs, and attitudes; and lifestyle are useful for interpreting buying processes. Motivation is the energizing force that stimulates behaviour to satisfy a need. Personality refers to a person's consistent behaviours or responses to recurring situations. Perception is the process by which an individual selects, organizes, and interprets information to create a meaningful picture of the world. Consumers filter information through selective attention, selective exposure, selective comprehension, and selective retention.

Much consumer behaviour is learned. Learning refers to those behaviours that result from (*a*) repeated experience, and (*b*) reasoning. Brand loyalty results from learning. Values, beliefs, and attitudes are also learned and influence how consumers evaluate products, services, and brands. A more general concept is lifestyle. Lifestyle, also called psychographics, combines psychology and demographics and focuses on how people spend their time and resources, what they consider important in their environment, and what they think of themselves and the world around them.

LO4 **Identify the major socio-cultural influences on consumer behaviour.**

Socio-cultural influences, which evolve from a consumer's formal and informal relationships with other people, also affect consumer behaviour. These involve personal influence, reference groups, the family, social class, culture, and subculture. Opinion leadership and word-of-mouth behaviour are two major sources of personal influence on consumer behaviour. Reference groups are people to whom an individual looks as a basis for self-approval or as source of personal standards. Family influences on consumer behaviour result from three sources: consumer socialization, passage through the family life cycle, and decision making within the family or household. A more subtle influence on consumer behaviour than direct contact with others is the social class to which people belong. Persons within social classes tend to exhibit common values, attitudes, beliefs, lifestyles, and buying behaviours. Finally, a person's culture and subculture have been shown to influence product preferences and buying patterns.

FOCUSING ON KEY TERMS

attitude p. 132
beliefs p. 132
brand loyalty p. 131
buzz marketing p. 135
cognitive dissonance p. 124
consideration set p. 123
consumer behaviour p. 122
consumer socialization p. 136
evaluative criteria p. 123
family life cycle p. 136
involvement p. 125
learning p. 131

lifestyle p. 133
motivation p. 127
national character p. 128
opinion leaders p. 134
perceived risk p. 130
perception p. 129
personality p. 128
purchase decision process p. 122
reference groups p. 136
self-concept p. 128
situational influences p. 126
social class p. 138

APPLYING MARKETING KNOWLEDGE

1   Outline the consumer purchase decision process you used to select your college or university. Discuss your perceived problem, information sources used, awareness set, evaluative criteria, consideration set, and how happy you are with your decision.

2   Suppose research at Panasonic reveals that prospective buyers are anxious about buying expensive high-definition television sets. What strategies might you recommend to the company to reduce consumer anxiety?

3   A Porsche salesperson was taking orders on new cars because he was unable to satisfy the demand with the limited number of cars in the showroom and lot. Several persons had backed out of the contract within two weeks of signing the order. What explanation can you give for this behaviour, and what remedies would you recommend?

4   Which social class would you associate with each of the following items or actions: (*a*) tennis club membership, (*b*) an arrangement of plastic flowers in the kitchen, (*c*) *True Romance* magazine, (*d*) *Maclean's* magazine, (*e*) formally dressing for dinner frequently, and (*f*) being a member of a bowling team.

5   Assign one or more levels of the hierarchy of needs and the motives described in Figure 5–4 to the following products: (*a*) life insurance, (*b*) cosmetics, (*c*) the *Financial Post,* and (*d*) hamburgers.

6   With which stage in the family life cycle would the purchase of the following products and services be most closely identified: (*a*) bedroom furniture, (*b*) life insurance, (*c*) a Caribbean cruise, (*d*) a house mortgage, and (*e*) children's toys?

7   "The greater the perceived risk in a purchase situation, the more likely that cognitive dissonance will result." Does this statement have any basis given the discussion in the text? Why?

Building Your Marketing Plan

To do a consumer analysis of the product—the good, service, idea, or experience—in your marketing plan:

1. Identify the consumers who are most likely to buy your product—the primary target market—in terms of (*a*) their demographic characteristics and (*b*) any other kinds of characteristics you believe are important.

2. Describe (*a*) the main points of difference of your product for this group and (*b*) what problem it helps solve for the consumer, in terms of the first stage in the consumer purchase decision process in Figure 5–1.

3. Identify the one or two key influences for each of the four outside boxes in Figure 5–3: (*a*) marketing mix, (*b*) psychological, (*c*) socio-cultural, and (*d*) situational influences.

This consumer analysis will provide the foundation for the marketing mix actions you develop later in your plan.

Video Case 5

COOLER SOLUTIONS

Background

As you learned in this chapter, consumer behaviour is defined as the actions a person takes in purchasing and using products and services, including the mental and social processes that precede and follow these actions. You also learned that behavioural sciences can help answer such questions as why people choose one product or brand over another, how they make these choices, and how companies can use this knowledge to provide value to consumers. One Canadian company, Cooler Solutions, is assisting marketers to better understand customers so that they can better meet customer needs.

Cooler Solutions: The Company

When a consumer engages in the purchase decision process there are many influences, psychological and social, that impact that process. Cooler Solutions, a Toronto-based enterprise, is an innovation, product design, and market research company that assists its clients to better understand the consumer purchase decision process. Cooler Solutions provides what it calls "deep down" consumer insights with regard to consumer behaviour in the marketplace so that companies might discover market opportunities to introduce better or new solutions to customer problems.

Cooler Solutions' Approach

Cooler Solutions offers three distinct but connected business solutions to their clients. One is called "Cooler Innovation Thinking," or CIT. CIT is a three-phase system designed to promote a culture of sustained innovation within a company. It involves architecture, methodology, and culture. First, Cooler Solutions works to align the client's vision, values, and strategy with the innovative outcomes the client is seeking. This is called innovation architecture. Second, this architecture is then integrated with methodologies used within the client's company and is designed to ensure that innovation is part of the mindset within the company. Also, Cooler Solutions helps the client develop a process for developing and bringing innovation to the marketplace. Third, Cooler Solutions develops the internal capabilities of the client to foster and sustain innovation. This includes human resource acquisition, training and development, and creating an innovation climate within the company.

Cooler Solutions also offers a "product design" solution for its clients. The company has a staff of industrial designers, project managers, and "problem solvers" that work with clients to develop better product designs by using consumer behaviour research in the earliest stages of the design process. Cooler Solutions focuses its design on enhancing the users' experience. In addition to developing new product solutions, Cooler Solutions also performs existing product "renovation"—retooling and redesigning existing products by using field research, including ethnography. This approach focuses on observing how customers interact with products in the marketplace as well as in their use environment.

This is where Cooler Solutions third business solution—Cooler Ethnography—comes into play. Cooler Solutions' trained personnel go into the marketplace to observe and interact with customers, focusing on "seeing products through the eyes of the consumer." Ethnography has the advantage of observing consumers in their "real life situations." The goal is to uncover what consumers buy, how they buy, why they buy, and how they use those products. Importantly, the company focuses on trying to discover if there is "something missing in the product experience." In other words, Cooler Solutions is attempting to determine if certain consumer needs are going unmet and then attempts to provide new solutions to meet those needs. This is often referred to as identifying "white space opportunities"—market opportunities not previously isolated or uncovered. The company then works with its clients to develop and introduce new products, services, or experiences to exploit these identified opportunities. It is also important to note that unlike traditional marketing research firms that might use surveys to obtain information from consumers, Cooler Solutions uses "collaborative ideation"—working closely with customers to uncover unmet needs and aspirations of the customer and co-create solutions to meet those needs and aspirations.

According to Cooler Solutions, ethnography identifies product and service gaps in the marketplace, providing insight that is immediately actionable. Practical big-picture information is generated by analyzing and interacting with customers in the field. It seeks answers to critical questions such as why customers use something one way and not the other, and what would make the use situation ideal.

Examples of Observing and Understanding Consumer Behaviour and Its Results

Cooler Solutions has worked with many clients, assisting them with product design, service design, and brand improvements. For example, Cooler Solutions worked with OfficeMax Inc., a leader in both business-to-business office products solutions and retail office products. The company provides office supplies and in-store print and document services in more than 900 stores. Interacting with consumers in the field, the company uncovered an opportunity for OfficeMax to design and launch a new private-label brand of office furniture and accessories. The result was higher margin products that continue to build customer loyalty.

Cooler Solutions also worked with Spin Master Toys, an innovative toy manufacturer with a leading brand of remote control toys called Air Hogs. Spin Master wanted to improve a specific Air Hogs product and to engage customers to build their 10-year-old legacy brand. Cooler Solutions focused its ethnography on Spin Master Toys' target market, boys aged 8 to 12 years. The researchers observed the children while playing and also had the children keep detailed play diaries. Cooler Solutions learned how boys and their parents related to Air Hogs, and gained insight into the kinds of toys that resonated with this age group.

Using ethnographic research the company was able to design an integrated nursing hub and low-cost surgical display solution for the London Health Science Centre. London Health Science Centre is a leading medical research centre in Ontario. The centre uses computers in the operating room to assist with surgery and for patient data. Through ethnographic research, Cooler Solutions learned that nurses needed to look at the computer monitor and the operating room simultaneously. The solution was a design that allows the nurse to watch the monitor and patient while providing compact vertical storage and surfaces for information display.

Finally, Cooler Solutions worked with Coleman to discover the key needs of everyday grillers. Designers and researchers conducted in-field user observation to uncover key insights. These insights were then translated into valuable design features. The new Coleman Even Heat barbeque grill was improved in three main areas: cooking performance, durability, and maintenance.

In terms of improved cooking performance, researchers observed that most barbeques suffered from inaccurate temperature control, resulting in inconsistent and often over-cooked meals. To address this, Cooler Solutions' design team focused on developing a grill that distributes heat evenly for consistent cooking and fewer flare-ups, and a built-in timer with bell was included to remind grillers when their food is ready. Further, users noted their frustration at unexpected propane shortages. As a solution, the Coleman barbeque has a fuel gauge monitor so that propane levels can easily be checked before and after cooking.

In terms of durability, the researchers uncovered some other key insights. For example, cooking elicited a deep sense of nostalgia, passion, and even competitiveness among avid barbeque users, the majority of whom were male. These dedicated grillers insisted on "nothing fancy" but rather appreciated a basic and simple look. Cooler Solutions' resulting barbeque design is simple and clean with no fuss. The double-lined cast lid sides not only stabilize the lid and improve heat retention, but also impart an aesthetic of protection and masculinity. Grillers also valued durability and complained of unreliable igniters that broke easily, often spurring users to resort to hand-held lighters. The new Coleman barbeque features the InstaStart electronic ignition that offers faster, safer, and more dependable ignition.

Finally, the in-field research revealed that proper barbeque maintenance was often neglected. Grill experts confirmed that dirty barbeques are less efficient and can even pose certain health hazards. However, in assessing the market, Cooler Solutions' team recognized that little has been done to facilitate the grill-cleaning regimen. In response, Coleman's new barbeque has easy-to-remove grates and removable grease trays for a quicker and more thorough cleanup. Further, instructions on proper barbeque maintenance were made available online through the Coleman and Canadian Tire Web sites.

Cooler Solutions—Socially Responsible and Sustainable Design

The company is also very committed to socially responsible behaviour and sustainable design. One example of this is the company's design and development of the Dignity Toilet. It is a storage and disposal system that addresses health, dignity, and compliance. In many locations around the globe, waste storage and disposal can become a great health concern, often causing infection and disease. During times of disaster or at any time the displacement of people occurs, food and shelter do not complete basic needs. The Dignity Toilet provides storage of solid waste for four people for 7 to 10 days. The storage vessel is then removed from its seating dock and taken to a controlled area where it is manually augered into the soil. When its contents are released, it is mixed with the soil for natural decomposition. Cooler Solutions' Dignity Toilet design won the HIDO International Design Award.

Conclusions

Cooler Solutions uses novel approaches to understand what consumers do in the marketplace, how they do it, and why they do it. This understanding of consumer behaviour has helped the company provide real insight to its clients and enabled those same clients to provide new and/or better solutions to consumers. This innovative field research is intended not only to uncover what, how, and why consumers do what they do but also to gain glimpses into what consumers "might like to do," presently and in the future. If the old saying is true that "consumers are a moving target," Cooler Solutions is working to find ways to stay ahead of consumers, anticipating their needs and designing solutions to satisfy those needs.

Questions

1 What do you think about Cooler Solutions process for understanding consumer behaviour? Are there any limitations and/or pitfalls with this approach?

2 Are there other ways you might suggest that could also offer insight into consumer behaviour?

3 Select a product or service. Then, go into the field and observe consumers buying and/or using that product or service. Then, engage them and discuss what, how, and why they purchased what they did and how they intend to use that purchase. Prepare a one- to two-page report indicating what you discovered. In this report, outline opportunities to improve the consumer's buying or use experience. Also, indicate if you have uncovered new market opportunities for the company behind the product or service (e.g., a new use, a new solution, a new customer).

chapter 6

Organizational Markets and Buyer Behaviour

BOMBARDIER: PLANES, TRAINS, WORLDWIDE

Bombardier is headquartered in Montreal and is a global transportation company with a presence in more than 60 countries on five continents. It operates two industry-leading businesses: aerospace and rail transportation. Specifically, the company manufactures and markets commercial and business jets as well as rail transportation equipment, systems, and services to "organizational or business customers" such as government entities and private businesses around the world. Therefore, Bombardier is considered a player in the business-to-business (B2B) arena. The company employs over 66,000 employees and posts revenues of almost $20 billion.

Bombardier Aerospace competes in global markets and is ranked as the third-largest civil aircraft manufacturer in the world. It manufactures and markets a portfolio of products including business aircraft (Learjet, Challenger, and Global aircraft brands), commercial aircraft (CSeries, CRJ, and Q-Series brands), amphibious aircraft (Bombardier 415), jet travel solutions (Flexjet), specialized aircraft solutions (aircraft modified for special missions), and aircraft services and training (aircraft parts, maintenance, and training and support). Bombardier Transportation is a leading rail-equipment manufacturing and servicing company. It manufactures and markets a portfolio of products including rail vehicles (automated people movers, monorails, light-rail vehicles, rapid transit, commuter trains, and high-speed trains), propulsion and controls

learning objectives

After reading this chapter, you should be able to:

 LO1 Distinguish among industrial, reseller, and government organizational markets.

LO2 Describe the key characteristics of organizational buying that make it different from consumer buying.

LO3 Explain how buying centres and buying situations influence organizational purchasing.

LO4 Recognize the importance and nature of online buying in industrial, reseller, and government organizational markets.

(application for trolley buses to freight locomotives), bogies (products for an entire range of rail vehicles), transportation systems (customized "design-build-operate-maintain" system solutions), rail control solutions (signalling), and services (fleet maintenance and refurbishment).

Because the company competes in the B2B marketplace, it recognizes that demand for its products is often contingent on you, the end customer. For example, demand for aircraft purchases is largely determined by air travel demand by passengers such as you. If airline passengers decide to travel less, then demand for Bombardier aircraft by the commercial airlines that purchase Bombardier planes will decline. This is why players in the B2B space must keep in touch and monitor drivers of demand in both the consumer and business marketplaces. Moreover, because Bombardier competes on a global basis it must determine where growth in demand, geographically, will come from in coming years. For example, Bombardier is forecasting that over the next 20 years there will be significant growth in markets outside North America and Europe, specifically in China and India. Marketers at Bombardier play a significant role in the company in helping to determine what types of products will be in demand (types of planes, types of rail transport), where the products will be in demand geographically, by what type of customers, and how to market to them.[1]

This chapter focuses on organizational markets and buyer behaviour, including the types of organizational buyers; key characteristics of organizational buying, including online buying; some typical buying decisions in organizational or business markets; and how firms like Bombardier can be successful in marketing to business customers.

LO1 THE NATURE AND SIZE OF ORGANIZATIONAL MARKETS

business marketing
The marketing of goods and services to companies, governments, and not-for-profit organizations for use in the creation of goods and services that they can produce and market to others.

organizational buyers
Those manufacturers, wholesalers, retailers, and government agencies that buy goods and services for their own use or for resale.

Business marketing is the marketing of goods and services to companies, governments, and not-for-profit organizations for use in the creation of goods and services that they can produce and market to others. This is also sometimes referred to as *business-to-business, or B2B, marketing.* Because many Canadian business school graduates take jobs in firms that engage in business marketing, it is important to understand the fundamental characteristics of organizational buyers and their buying behaviour.

Organizational buyers are those manufacturers, retailers, and government agencies that buy goods and services for their own use or for resale. For example, all these organizations buy computers and telephone services for their own use. However, manufacturers buy raw materials and parts that they reprocess into the finished goods they sell, whereas retailers resell goods they buy without reprocessing them. Organizational buyers include all the buyers in a nation, except the ultimate consumers. These organizational buyers purchase and lease tremendous volumes of capital equipment, raw materials, manufactured parts, supplies, and business services. In fact, because they often buy raw materials and parts, process them, and sell the upgraded product several times before it is purchased by the final organizational buyer or ultimate consumer, the aggregate purchases of organizational buyers in a year are far greater than those of ultimate consumers.

Organizational buyers are divided into three markets: (1) industrial, (2) reseller, and (3) government markets.

Industrial Markets

industrial firm
An organizational buyer that, in some way, reprocesses a good or service it buys before selling it again to the next buyer.

There are thousands of firms in the industrial, or business, market in Canada. **Industrial firms,** in some way, reprocess a good or service they buy before selling it again to the next buyer. This is certainly true of a steel mill that converts iron ore into steel. It is also true (if you stretch your imagination) of a firm selling services, such as a bank that takes money from its depositors, reprocesses it, and "sells" it as loans to its commercial borrowers.

There has been a marked shift in the scope and nature of the industrial marketplace. Service industries are growing; they currently make the greatest contribution to Canada's gross domestic product (GDP). Because of the importance of service firms, service marketing is discussed in detail in Chapter 12. Industrial firms and primary industries currently account for about 21 percent of Canada's GDP. Nevertheless, primary industries (e.g., farming, mining, fishing, and forestry) and the manufacturing sector are important components of Canada's economy. There are about 40,000 manufacturers in Canada whose estimated value of shipments is over $600 billion.[2]

For an understanding of the role of manufacturing in the Canadian economy, read the accompanying Marketing Matters box, "The Importance of Canada's Manufacturing Sector."

Reseller Markets

resellers
Wholesalers or retailers that buy physical products and sell them again without any processing.

Wholesalers and retailers that buy physical products and sell them again without any reprocessing are **resellers.** Over 200,000 retailers and over 65,000 wholesalers are currently operating in Canada. Some of the largest retailers in Canada include The Hudson's Bay Co., Sears Canada, and Costco. Some major wholesalers are Cargill, Medis Health, and Federated Co-Operatives. These companies participate in B2B marketing. In later chapters, we see how manufacturers use wholesalers and retailers in their distribution ("place") strategies as channels through which their products reach ultimate consumers. In this chapter, we look at resellers mainly as organizational buyers in terms of (1) how they make their own buying decisions, and (2) which products they choose to carry.

Government Markets

government units
The federal, provincial, and local agencies that buy goods and services for the constituents they serve.

Government units are the federal, provincial, and local agencies that buy goods and services for the constituents they serve. Their annual purchases vary in size from the billions of dollars for a federal department, such as National Defence, to millions or thousands of dollars for a local university or school. The bulk of the buying at the federal government level is done by Service Canada. Most provincial governments have a government services department that does the buying on the provincial level. Hundreds of government departments, including agencies and Crown corporations, such as CBC, VIA Rail, and the Royal Canadian Mint, must purchase goods and services to operate. The federal government is a large organizational consumer, making total purchases of goods and services amounting to over $300 billion annually.[3]

Global Organizational Markets

Industrial, reseller, and government markets also exist on a global scale. In fact, many of Canada's top exporters, including Bombardier, Canadian Pacific, DuPont Canada, Maple Leaf Foods, and Pratt & Whitney, focus on organizational customers, not ultimate consumers.

Marketing Matters

The Importance of Canada's Manufacturing Sector

While Canada has been transitioned to a services-based economy, the manufacturing sector still plays an important role in the national economy. According to the Canadian Manufacturers & Exporters (CME-MEC), manufacturing employs over 2 million Canadians directly, and another 2.5 million depend on the sector for their livelihood. Directly, manufacturing accounts for 21 percent of Canada's economic activity. But when spinoffs are included, such as the purchases of goods and services in Canada, manufacturers drive 55 percent of the economy. Every $1 of manufacturing in Canada generates $3 in total economic activity. Pay in the manufacturing sector is 25 percent above the national average. And more manufacturers (83 percent) have employee-training programs than any other sector of the economy.

Nearly 70 percent of all goods manufactured in Canada are exported, and manufactured products account for 90 percent of Canada's merchandise exports. Manufacturers perform 75 percent of private sector research and

development (R&D) in Canada and 30 percent of business investment in nonresidential construction, machinery, and equipment.

Because of the importance of the manufacturing sector in Canada, RFPSOURCE.ca was developed. It is an e-marketplace that matches products and services with thousands of business opportunities posted by domestic and foreign corporations and governments. Through an international tender feeding system, small and medium-size companies can source bids, post opportunities, and pursue strategic partnerships, all within a secure online environment. Businesses can also participate in the RFPSource Tradeshow, a unique tool for businesses to profile their products and services through the creation of a virtual trade booth. You can visit the site at **www.rfpsource.ca.** You can also visit the Canadian Manufacturers & Exporters site at **www.cme-mec.ca.**

Most world trade involves manufacturers, resellers, and government agencies buying goods and services for their own use or for resale to others. The exchange relationships often involve numerous transactions spanning the globe. For example, Honeywell's Micro Switch Division sells its fibre-optic technology and products to manufacturers of data communication systems worldwide, through electronic component resellers in more than 20 countries, and directly to national governments in Europe and elsewhere. Europe's Airbus Industrie, the world's largest aircraft manufacturer, sells its passenger airplanes to Air Canada, which flies Canadian businesspeople to Asia. Ontario-based Inco, one of the world's largest nickel producers, is a global business participant, marketing its products to customers around the world. In fact, it exports 90 percent of its products to global organizational markets.

MEASURING DOMESTIC AND GLOBAL INDUSTRIAL, RESELLER, AND GOVERNMENT MARKETS

The measurement of industrial, reseller, and government markets is an important step for a firm interested in gauging the scope and size of one, two, or all three of these markets in Canada and around the world. The North American Free Trade Agreement (NAFTA) partners, Canada, Mexico, and the United States, now have common systems for measuring economic activities in organizational markets. One is a supply-oriented (production) industry classification system called the *North American Industry Classification System (NAICS)*. The other is a demand-based classification framework called the *North American Product Classification System (NAPCS)*. They are complementary but independent classification systems.[4]

The NAICS divides the economy into sectors using a six-digit coded system. The first two digits designate sectors, the third digit designates subsectors, the fourth digit designates industry groups, and the fifth digit designates industries. The sixth digit is used to designate national industries. NAICS in Canada consists of 20 sectors,

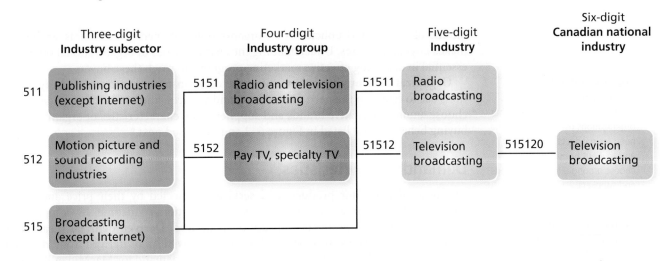

Three-digit **Industry subsector**		Four-digit **Industry group**		Five-digit **Industry**		Six-digit **Canadian national industry**
511	Publishing industries (except Internet)	5151	Radio and television broadcasting	51511	Radio broadcasting	
512	Motion picture and sound recording industries	5152	Pay TV, specialty TV	51512	Television broadcasting	515120 Television broadcasting
515	Broadcasting (except Internet)					

● **FIGURE 6–1**

NAICS breakdown for information and cultural industries sector: NAICS code 51 (abbreviated)

103 subsectors, 328 industry groups, 728 industries, and 928 national industries. Figure 6–1 illustrates how the NAICS works with an abbreviated breakdown for the Canadian information and cultural industries sector (code 51).

To complement the NAICS, the three countries have also developed the NAPCS, an integrated demand-based classification framework that classifies both goods and services according to how they are principally used. NAPCS can be used by researchers to coordinate the collection, tabulation, and analysis of data on the value of products produced by both goods- and services-producing industries and on the prices charged for those products. The long-term objective of NAPCS is to develop a market-oriented, or demand-based, hierarchical classification system for products (goods and services) that (a) is not industry-of-origin based but can be linked to the NAICS industry structure, (b) is consistent across the three NAICS countries, and (c) promotes improvements in the identification and classification of service products across international classification systems.

These systems allow marketers to examine organizational markets in terms of size and growth as well as to identify customers and competition. However, there are some limitations with the systems. For example, with the NAICS, each organization is assigned one code based on its principal economic activity. So, large firms that engage in many different activities are still assigned only one code. Hence, there will be a few large and complex enterprises whose activities may be spread over the different sectors in such a way that classifying them to one sector might misrepresent the range of their activities.

learning review

1. What are the three main types of organizational buyers?

2. What is the North American Industry Classification System (NAICS)?

3. What is the North American Product Classification System (NAPCS)?

LO2 CHARACTERISTICS OF ORGANIZATIONAL BUYING

Organizations are different from individuals, and so buying for an organization is different from buying for yourself or your family.[5] True, in both cases, the objective in making the purchase is to solve the buyer's problem—to satisfy a need or want. But unique objectives and policies of an organization put special constraints on how it makes buying decisions. Understanding the characteristics of organizational buying is essential in designing effective marketing programs to reach these buyers.

Organizational buying behaviour is the decision-making process that organizations use to establish the need for products and services, and to identify, evaluate, and choose among alternative brands and suppliers. Key characteristics of organizational buying behaviour are listed in Figure 6–2 and discussed next.[6]

organizational buying behaviour
The decision-making process that organizations use to establish the need for products and services, and to identify, evaluate, and choose among alternative brands and suppliers.

Demand Characteristics

Consumer demand for products and services is affected by their price and availability and by consumers' personal tastes and discretionary income. By comparison, demand for business products and services is derived. **Derived demand** means that the demand for business products and services is driven by, or derived from, demand for consumer products and services. For example, the demand for MacMillan Bloedel's pulp and paper products is based on consumer demand for newspapers, Pizza Pizza's "keep warm" pizza-to-go boxes, Federal Express packages, and disposable diapers. Derived demand is often based on expectations of future consumer demand. For instance, Whirlpool purchases parts for its washers and dryers in anticipation of consumer demand, which is affected by the replacement cycle for these products and by consumer income.

derived demand
Demand for business products and services is driven by, or derived from, demand for consumer products and services.

Ultimately, most demand is derived from consumer demand, the exception being demand derived from government purchases. Therefore, because of the importance of the concept of derived demand, business marketers are always paying close attention to consumer demand forecasts and reports.[7]

● **FIGURE 6-2**
Key characteristics of organizational buying behaviour

CHARACTERISTICS	DIMENSIONS
Market characteristics	• Demand for business products and services is derived. • Few customers typically exist, and their purchase orders are large.
Product or service characteristics	• Products or services are technical in nature and purchased on the basis of specifications. • There is a predominance of raw and semifinished goods purchased. • Heavy emphasis is placed on delivery time, technical assistance, postsale service, and financing assistance.
Buying process characteristics	• Technically qualified and professional buyers exist and follow established purchasing policies and procedures. • Buying objectives and criteria are typically spelled out, as are procedures for evaluating sellers and products (services). • Multiple buying influences exist, and multiple parties participate in purchase decisions. • Reciprocal arrangements exist, and negotiation between buyers and sellers is commonplace. • Online buying over the Internet is widespread.
Marketing mix characteristics	• Direct selling to organizational buyers is the rule, and physical distribution is very important. • Advertising and other forms of promotion are technical in nature. • Price is often negotiated, evaluated as part of broader seller and product (service) qualities, typically inelastic owing to derived demand, and frequently affected by trade and quantity discounts.

Size of the Order or Purchase

The size of the purchase involved in organizational buying is typically much larger than that in consumer buying. The value of a single purchase made by an organization often runs into the thousands or millions of dollars. For example, Motorola was awarded an $88 million contract to install a cellular phone system in Brazil.[8] With so much money at stake, most organizations place constraints on their buyers in the form of purchasing policies or procedures. Buyers must often get competitive bids from at least three prospective suppliers when the order is above a specific amount, such as $5,000. When the order is above an even higher amount, such as $50,000, it may require the review and approval of a vice-president or even the president of the company. Knowing how the size of the order affects buying practices is important in determining who participates in the purchase decision and who makes the final decision, as well as the length of time required to arrive at a purchase agreement.

Number of Potential Buyers

Firms selling consumer products or services often try to reach thousands or millions of individuals or households. For example, your local supermarket or bank probably serves thousands of people, and Kelloggs Canada tries to reach more than 10 million Canadian households with its breakfast cereals and probably succeeds in selling to a third or half of these in any given year. In contrast, firms selling to organizations are often restricted to far fewer buyers. Bombardier can sell its business jets to a few thousand organizations throughout the world, and B. F. Goodrich sells its original equipment tires to fewer than 10 car manufacturers.

Organizational Buying Objectives

Organizations buy products and services for one main reason: to help them achieve their objectives. For business firms, the buying objective is usually to increase profits through reducing costs or increasing revenues. Mac's buys automated inventory systems to increase the number of products that can be sold through its convenience stores and to keep them fresh. Nissan Motor Company switched its advertising agency because it expects the new agency to devise a more effective ad campaign to help it sell more cars and increase revenues. To improve executive decision making, many firms buy advanced computer systems to process data. The objectives of non-profit firms and government agencies are usually to meet the needs of the groups they serve. Thus, a hospital buys a high-technology diagnostic device to serve its patients better. Understanding buying objectives is a necessary first step in marketing to organizations. Recognizing the high costs of energy, Sylvania promotes to prospective buyers cost savings and increased profits made possible by its fluorescent and halogen lights. Many companies today have broadened their buying objectives to include environmental considerations. For example, The Home Depot no longer purchases lumber from companies that harvest timber from the world's endangered forests.[9] Successful business marketers recognize that understanding buying objectives is a necessary first step in marketing to organizations.

Organizational Buying Criteria

organizational buying criteria
The objective attributes of the supplier's products and services and the capabilities of the supplier itself.

In making a purchase, the buying organization must weigh key buying criteria that apply to the potential supplier and what it wants to sell. **Organizational buying criteria** are the objective attributes of the supplier's products and services and the capabilities of the supplier itself. These criteria serve the same purpose as the evaluative criteria used by consumers and described in Chapter 5. Seven of the most commonly used criteria are (1) price, (2) ability to meet the quality specifications required for the item, (3) ability to meet required delivery schedules, (4) technical capability, (5) warranties and claim policies in the event of poor performance, (6) past performance on previous contracts, and (7) production facilities and capacity.[10] Suppliers that meet or exceed these criteria create customer value.

ISO 9000 standards
Registration and certification of a manufacturer's quality management and quality assurance system.

Organizational buyers who purchase products and services in a global marketplace often supplement their buying criteria with supplier ISO 9000 certification. **ISO 9000 standards,** developed by the International Standards Organization (ISO) in Geneva, Switzerland, refer to standards for registration and certification of a manufacturer's quality management and assurance system based on an on-site audit of practices and procedures. ISO certification is administered in Canada by SCC (Standards Council of Canada: **www.scc.ca**). Many Canadian companies that market globally have achieved this certification.[11]

supplier development
The deliberate effort by organizational buyers to build relationships that shape suppliers' products, services, and capabilities to fit a buyer's needs and those of its customers.

Many organizational buyers today are transforming their buying criteria into specific requirements that are communicated to prospective suppliers. This practice, called **supplier development,** involves the deliberate effort by organizational buyers to build relationships that shape suppliers' products, services, and capabilities to fit a buyer's needs and those of its customers.[12] For example, consider Deere & Company, the maker of John Deere farm, construction, and lawn-care equipment. Deere employs 94 supplier-development engineers who work full-time with the company's suppliers to improve their efficiency and quality and reduce their costs. According to a Deere senior executive, "Their quality, delivery, and costs are, after all, our quality, delivery, and costs."[13] Harley-Davidson also emphasizes supplier collaboration in its product design.[14]

With many Canadian manufacturers using a "just-in-time" (JIT) inventory system that reduces the inventory of production parts to those to be used within hours or days, on-time delivery is becoming an even more important buying criterion and, in some instances, a requirement. Caterpillar trains its key suppliers at its Quality Institute in JIT inventory systems and conducts supplier seminars on how to diagnose, correct, and implement continuous quality improvement programs. The just-in-time inventory system is discussed further in Chapter 14.

Buyer–Seller Relationships and Supply Partnerships

Another distinction between organizational and consumer buying behaviour lies in the nature of the relationship between organizational buyers and suppliers. Specifically, organizational buying is more likely to involve complex negotiations concerning delivery schedules, price, technical specifications, warranties, and claim policies. These negotiations also can last for an extended period of time. This was the case when the Lawrence Livermore National Laboratory acquired two IBM supercomputers—each with capacity to perform 360 trillion mathematical operations per second—at a cost of $290 million.[15]

reciprocity
An industrial buying practice in which two organizations agree to purchase each other's products and services.

Reciprocal arrangements also exist in organizational buying. **Reciprocity** is a business buying practice in which two organizations agree to purchase each other's products and services. Industry Canada frowns on reciprocal buying because it restricts the normal operation of the free market. However, the practice exists and can limit the flexibility of organizational buyers in choosing alternative suppliers.

Long-term relationships are also prevalent.[16] For example, Kraft announced it would spend $1.7 billion over seven years for global information technology services from Electronic Data Systems. Hewlett-Packard is also engaged in a 10-year, $3 billion contract to manage Procter & Gamble's information technology in 160 countries.[17]

supply partnership
A relationship that exists when a buyer and its supplier adopt mutually beneficial objectives, policies, and procedures for the purpose of lowering the cost and/or increasing the value of products and services delivered to the ultimate consumers.

In some cases, buyer–seller relationships develop into supply partnerships.[18] A **supply partnership** exists when a buyer and its supplier adopt mutually beneficial objectives, policies, and procedures for the purpose of lowering the cost and/or increasing the value of products and services delivered to the ultimate consumer.

Making Responsible Decisions

Sustainable Procurement for Sustainable Growth

Manufacturers, retailers, wholesalers, and government agencies are increasingly sensitive to how their buying decisions affect the environment. Concerns about the depletion of natural resources; air, water, and soil pollution; and the social consequences of economic activity have given rise to the concept of sustainable procurement. Sustainable procurement aims to integrate environmental considerations into all stages of an organization's buying process with the goal of reducing the impact on human health and the physical environment.

Starbucks is a pioneer and global leader in sustainable procurement. The company's attention to quality coffee extends to its coffee growers located in more than 20 countries. This means that Starbucks pays coffee farmers a fair price for the beans, that the coffee is grown in

an ecologically sound manner, and that Starbucks invests in the farming communities where its coffees are produced. In this way, Starbucks focuses on the sustainable growth of its suppliers.

Intel, the world's largest manufacturer of microprocessors and the "computer inside" most personal computers, is a case in point. Intel supports its suppliers by offering them quality management programs and by investing in supplier equipment that produces fewer product defects and boosts supplier productivity. Suppliers, in turn, provide Intel with consistently high-quality products at a lower cost for its customers, the makers of personal computers, and finally you, the ultimate customer. Retailers, too, are forging partnerships with their suppliers. Walmart and Zellers have such a relationship with Procter & Gamble for ordering and replenishing P&G's products in their stores. By using computerized cash register scanning equipment and direct electronic linkages to P&G, these retailers can tell P&G what merchandise is needed, along with how much, when, and to which store to deliver it on a daily basis. Because supply partnerships also involve the physical distribution of goods, they are again discussed in Chapter 14 in the context of supply chains.

Supply partnerships often include provisions for what is called *sustainable procurement*. This buying practice is described in the accompanying Making Responsible Decisions box.[19] Because supply partnerships also involve the physical distribution of goods, they are again discussed in Chapter 14 in the context of supply chain management.

The Buying Centre: A Cross-Functional Group

For routine purchases with a small dollar value, a single buyer or purchasing manager often makes the purchase decision alone. In many instances, however, several people in the organization participate in the buying process. The individuals in this group, called a **buying centre,** share common goals, risks, and knowledge important to a purchase decision. For most large multistore chain resellers, such as Sears or Zellers, the buying centre is highly formalized and is called a *buying committee*. However, most industrial firms or government units use informal groups of people or call meetings to arrive at buying decisions.

The importance of the buying centre requires that a firm marketing to many business firms and government units understand the structure, technical and business functions, and behaviour of these groups. Four questions provide

buying centre
The group of people in an organization who participate in the buying process and share common goals, risks, and knowledge important to a purchase decision.

guidance in understanding the buying centre in these organizations:[20]

1. Which individuals are in the buying centre for the product or service?
2. What is the relative influence of each member of the group?
3. What are the buying criteria of each member?
4. How does each member of the group perceive our firm, our products and services, and our salespeople?

Answers to these questions are difficult to come by, particularly when dealing with industrial firms, resellers, and governments outside Canada.[21] For example, Canadian firms are often frustrated by the fact that Japanese buyers "ask a thousand questions" but give few answers, sometimes rely on third-party individuals to convey views on proposals, are prone to not "talk business," and often say yes to be courteous when they mean no. Firms in the global chemical industry recognize that production engineering personnel have a great deal of influence in Hungarian buying groups, while purchasing agents in the Canadian chemical industry have relatively more influence in buying decisions.

People in the Buying Centre   The composition of the buying centre in a given organization depends on the specific item being bought. Although a buyer or purchasing manager is almost always a member of the buying centre, individuals from other functional areas are included, depending on what is to be purchased. In buying a million-dollar machine tool, the president (because of the size of the purchase) and the production vice-president or manager would probably be members. For key components to be incorporated in a final manufactured product, a cross-functional group of individuals from research and development (R&D), engineering, and quality control are likely to be added. For new word-processing equipment, experienced secretaries who will use the equipment would be members. Still, a major question in penetrating the buying centre is finding and reaching the people who will initiate, influence, and actually make the buying decision.

Roles in the Buying Centre   Researchers have identified five specific roles that an individual in a buying centre can play.[22] In some purchases, the same person may perform two or more of these roles.

- *Users* are the people in the organization who actually use the product or service, such as a nurse who will use a new PDA medical device.
- *Influencers* affect the buying decision, usually by helping define the specifications for what is bought. The information systems manager would be a key influencer in the purchase of new computer servers.
- *Buyers* have formal authority and responsibility to select the supplier and negotiate the terms of the contract. The purchasing manager probably would perform this role in the purchase of the new servers.
- *Deciders* have the formal or informal power to select or approve the supplier that receives the contract. Whereas in routine orders the decider is usually the buyer or purchasing manager, in important technical purchases, it is more likely to be someone from R&D, engineering, or quality control. The decider for a key component being incorporated in a final manufactured product might be any of these three people.
- *Gatekeepers* control the flow of information in the buying centre. Purchasing personnel, technical experts, and administrative assistants can all keep salespeople or information from reaching people performing the other four roles.

	BUY-CLASS SITUATION	
BUYING CENTRE DIMENSION	**NEW BUY**	**STRAIGHT/MODIFIED REBUY**
People involved	Many	Few
Decision time	Long	Short
Problem definition	Uncertain	Well-defined
Buying objective	Good solution	Low-price supplier
Suppliers considered	New/present	Present
Buying influence	Technical/operating personnel	Purchasing agent

● **FIGURE 6-3**
How the buying situation affects buying centre behaviour

buy classes
Three types of organizational buying situations: new buy, straight rebuy, and modified rebuy.

Buying Situations and the Buying Centre   The number of people in the buying centre largely depends on the specific buying situation. Researchers who have studied organizational buying identify three types of buying situations, called **buy classes.** These buy classes vary from the routine reorder, or *straight rebuy,* to the completely new purchase, termed *new buy.* In between these extremes is the *modified rebuy.* Some examples will clarify the differences.[23]

- *Straight rebuy.* Here, the buyer or purchasing manager reorders an existing product or service from the list of acceptable suppliers, probably without even checking with users or influencers from the engineering, production, or quality control departments. Office supplies and maintenance services are usually obtained as straight rebuys.
- *Modified rebuy.* In this buying situation, the users, influencers, or deciders in the buying centre want to change the product specifications, price, delivery schedule, or supplier. Although the item purchased is largely the same as with the straight rebuy, the changes usually necessitate enlarging the buying centre to include people outside the purchasing department.
- *New buy.* Here, the organization is a first-time buyer of the product or service. This involves greater potential risks in the purchase, and so the buying centre is enlarged to include all those who have a stake in the new buy. Procter & Gamble's purchase of a multi-million dollar fibre-optic network to link its corporate offices from Corning, Inc. represented a new buy.[24]

Figure 6–3 summarizes how buy classes affect buying centre tendencies in different ways.[25]

The marketing strategies of sellers facing each of these three buying situations can vary greatly because the importance of personnel from functional areas, such as purchasing, engineering, production, and R&D, often varies with (1) the type of buying situation, and (2) the stage of the purchasing process.[26] If it is a new buy for the manufacturer, you should be prepared to act as a consultant to the buyer, work with technical personnel, and expect a long time for a buying decision to be reached. However, if the manufacturer has bought the component part from you before (a straight or modified rebuy), you might emphasize a competitive price and a reliable supply in meetings with the purchasing agent.

learning review

4. What one department is almost always represented by a person in the buying centre?

5. What are the three types of buying situations or buy classes?

CHARTING THE ORGANIZATIONAL BUYING PROCESS

Organizational buyers, like consumers, engage in a decision process when selecting products and services. As defined earlier in this chapter, organizational buying behaviour is the decision-making process that organizations use to establish the need for products and services, and to identify, evaluate, and choose among alternative brands and suppliers. There are important similarities and differences between the two decision-making processes. To better understand the nature of organizational buying behaviour, we first compare it with consumer buying behaviour and then describe an actual organizational purchase in detail.

Stages in the Organizational Buying Process

As shown in Figure 6–4 (and covered in Chapter 5), the five stages a student might use in buying an MP3 player also apply to organizational purchases. However, comparing the two right-hand columns in Figure 6–4 reveals some key differences. For example, when an MP3 player manufacturer buys earphones for its units from a supplier, more individuals are involved, supplier capability becomes more important, and the post-purchase evaluation behaviour is more formalized.

● **FIGURE 6–4**

Comparing the stages in consumer and organizational purchases

STAGE IN THE BUYING DECISION PROCESS	CONSUMER PURCHASE: MP3 PLAYER FOR A STUDENT	ORGANIZATIONAL PURCHASE: EARPHONES FOR AN MP3 PLAYER
Problem recognition	Student does not like the features of the portable CD player now owned and desires a new MP3 player.	Marketing research and sales departments observe that competitors are improving the earphones on their MP3 models. The firm decides to improve the earphones on its own new models, which will be purchased from an outside supplier.
Information search	Student uses own and friends' past experience, ads, the Internet, and *Consumer Reports* to collect information and uncover alternatives.	Design and production engineers draft specifications for earphones. The purchasing department identifies suppliers of MP3 player earphones.
Alternative evaluation	Alternative MP3 players are evaluated on the basis of important attributes desired in a MP3 player, and several stores are visited.	Purchasing and engineering personnel visit with suppliers and assess (1) facilities, (2) capacity, (3) quality control, and (4) financial status. They drop any suppliers not satisfactory on these factors.
Purchase decision	A specific brand of MP3 player is selected, the price is paid, and the student leaves the store.	They use (1) quality, (2) price, (3) delivery, and (4) technical capability as key buying criteria to select a supplier. Then they negotiate terms and award a contract.
Post-purchase behaviour	Student re-evaluates the purchase decision, may return the MP3 player to the store if it is unsatisfactory, and looks for supportive information to justify the purchase.	They evaluate suppliers using a formal vendor rating system and notify the supplier if earphones do not meet their quality standard. If the problem is not corrected, they drop the firm as a future supplier.

The earphone-buying decision process is typical of the steps made by organizational buyers. Let us now examine in detail the decision-making process for a more complex product—machine vision systems.

Buying a Machine Vision System

Machine vision is widely regarded as one of the keys to the factory of the future. The chief elements of a machine vision system are its optics, light source, camera, video processor, and computer software. Vision systems are mainly used for product inspection. They are also becoming important as one of the chief elements in the information feedback loop of systems that control manufacturing processes. Vision systems, selling for around $25,000, are mostly sold to original equipment manufacturers (OEMs) who incorporate them in still larger industrial automation systems that sell for $200,000 to $300,000.

Finding productive applications for machine vision involves the constant search for technology and designs that satisfy user needs. The buying process for machine vision components and assemblies is frequently a new buy because many machine vision systems contain elements that require some custom design. Let us track five purchasing stages that a company, such as the Industrial Automation Division of Siemens, a large German industrial firm, would follow when purchasing components and assemblies for the machine vision systems it produces and installs.

Problem Recognition   Sales engineers constantly canvass industrial automation equipment users, such as Ford Motor Company, Grumman Aircraft, and many Asian and European firms, for leads on upcoming industrial automation projects. They also keep these firms current on Siemens' technology, products, and services. When a firm needing a machine vision capability identifies a project that would benefit from Siemens' expertise, company engineers typically work with the firm to determine the kind of system required to meet the customer's need.

make-buy decision
An evaluation of whether components and assemblies will be purchased from outside suppliers or built by the company itself.

After a contract is won, project personnel must often make a **make-buy decision**— an evaluation of whether components and assemblies will be purchased from outside suppliers or built by the company itself. (Siemens produces many components and assemblies.) When these items are to be purchased from outside suppliers, the company engages in a thorough supplier search and evaluation process.

Information Search   Such companies as Siemens employ a sophisticated process for identifying outside suppliers of components and assemblies. For standard items, such as connectors, printed circuit boards, and components—for example, resistors and capacitors—the purchasing agent consults the company's purchasing databank, which contains information on hundreds of suppliers and thousands of products. All products in the databank have been prenegotiated as to price, quality, and delivery time, and many have been assessed using **value analysis**—a systematic appraisal of the design, quality, and performance of a product to reduce purchasing costs.

value analysis
A systematic appraisal of the design, quality, and performance of a product to reduce purchasing costs.

For one-of-a-kind components or assemblies, such as new optics, cameras, and light sources, the company relies on its engineers to keep current on new developments in product technology. This information is often found in technical journals and industry magazines or at international trade shows where suppliers display their most recent innovations. In some instances, supplier representatives might be asked to make presentations to the buying centre at Siemens. Such a group often consists of a project engineer; several design, system, and manufacturing engineers; and a purchasing agent.

Alternative Evaluation   Three main buying criteria are used to select suppliers: price, performance, and delivery. Other important criteria include assurance that a supplier will not go out of business during the contractual period, assurance that

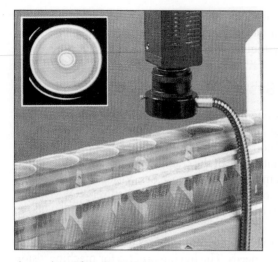

The purchase of machine vision systems involves a lengthy organizational buying process.

bidders' list
A list of firms believed to be qualified to supply a given item.

the supplier will meet product quality and performance specifications, and service during the contractual period. Typically, two or three suppliers for each standard component and assembly are identified from a **bidders' list**—a list of firms believed to be qualified to supply a given item. This list is generated from the company's purchasing databank as well as from engineering inputs. Specific items that are unique or one-of-a-kind may be obtained from a single supplier after careful evaluation by the buying centre.

Firms selected from the bidders' list are sent a quotation request from the purchasing agent, describing the desired quantity, delivery date(s), and specifications of the components or assemblies. Suppliers are expected to respond within 30 days.

Purchase Decision   Unlike the short purchase stage in a consumer purchase, the period from supplier selection to order placement to product delivery can take several weeks or even months. Even after bids for components and assemblies are submitted, further negotiation concerning price, performance, and delivery terms is likely. Sometimes, conditions related to warranties, indemnities, and payment schedules have to be agreed on. The purchase decision is further complicated by the fact that two or more suppliers of the same item might be awarded contracts. This practice can occur when large orders are requested. Furthermore, suppliers who are not chosen are informed why their bids were not selected.

Post-Purchase Behaviour   As in the consumer purchase decision process, postpurchase evaluation occurs in the organizational purchase decision process, but it is formalized and often more sophisticated. All items purchased are examined in a formal product-acceptance process. The performance of the supplier is also monitored and recorded. Performance on past contracts determines a supplier's chances of being asked to bid on future purchases, and poor performance may result in a supplier's name being dropped from the bidders' list.

The preceding example of an organizational purchase suggests four lessons for marketers to increase their chances of selling products and services to organizations. Firms selling to organizations must (1) understand the organization's needs, (2) get on the right bidders' list, (3) find the right people in the buying centre, and (4) provide value to the organizational buyer.

---

learning review   **6.** What is a make-buy decision?

7. What is a bidders' list?

 ONLINE BUYING IN ORGANIZATIONAL MARKETS

Organizational buying behaviour and business marketing continues to evolve with the application of *information communication technologies (ICTs),* including the Internet. Organizations dwarf consumers in terms of both online transactions made and purchase volume.[27] In fact, organizational buyers account for about 80 percent of the total worldwide dollar value of all online transactions. It is projected that online organizational buyers around the world will purchase between $8 trillion and $10 trillion worth of products and services in 2010. Organizational buyers in North America will account for about 60 percent of these purchases.

Prominence of Online Buying in Organizational Markets

Online buying in organizational markets is prominent for three major reasons.[28] First, organizational buyers depend heavily on timely supplier information that describes product availability, technical specifications, application uses, price, and delivery schedules. This information can be conveyed quickly via Internet technology. Second, this technology has been shown to reduce buyer order processing costs substantially. At General Electric, online buying has cut the cost of a transaction from $50 to $100 per purchase to about $5. Third, business marketers have found that online technology can reduce marketing costs, particularly sales and advertising expense, and broaden their potential customer base for many types of products and services. For these reasons, online buying is popular in all three kinds of organizational markets. For example, airlines order more than $400 million in spare parts from the Boeing Web site each year.

Customers of Provigo, a large Canadian food wholesaler, can buy online, while provincial and municipal governments across Canada also engage in online purchasing. Online buying can assume many forms. Organizational buyers can purchase directly from suppliers. For instance, a buyer might acquire a dozen desktop photocopiers from Xerox.ca. This same buyer might purchase office furniture and supplies online through a reseller, such as Office Depot at officedepot.ca. Increasingly, organizational buyers and business marketers are using e-marketplaces and online auctions to purchase and sell products and services.

E-Marketplaces: Virtual Organizational Markets

e-marketplaces

Online trading communities that bring together buyers and supplier organizations.

A significant development in organizational buying has been the creation of online trading communities, called **e-marketplaces,** that bring together buyers and supplier organizations. These online communities go by a variety of names, including B2B exchanges and e-hubs, and make possible the real-time exchange of information, money, products, and services.

E-marketplaces can be independent trading communities or private exchanges.[29] Independent e-marketplaces act as a neutral third party and provide an Internet-technology trading platform and a centralized market that enable exchanges between buyers and sellers. They charge a fee for their services and exist in settings that have one or more of the following features: (1) thousands of geographically dispersed buyers and sellers, (2) volatile prices caused by demand and supply fluctuations, (3) time sensitivity due to perishable offerings and changing technologies, and (4) easily comparable offerings between a variety of suppliers. Well-known independent e-marketplaces include PlasticsNet (plastics), FreeMarkets (industrial parts, raw material, and commodities), Empori.com, and XSAg.com (both agricultural products). Small business buyers and sellers, in particular, benefit from independent e-marketplaces. These e-marketplaces offer them an economical way to expand their customer base and reduce the cost of products and services. eBay launched eBayBusiness to serve the small businesses market in Canada and the United States. You can learn about how B2B exchanges work and about eBayBusiness by doing the Going Online exercise, eBay Means Business, Too.[30]

Large companies tend to favour private exchanges that link them with their network of qualified suppliers and customers. Private exchanges focus on streamlining a company's purchase transactions with its suppliers and customers. Like independent e-marketplaces, they provide a technology trading platform and central market for buyer–seller interactions. They are not a neutral third party, however, but represent the interests of their owners. For example, Worldwide Retail Exchange performs the buying function for its 62 retail members, including Best Buy, The Gap, Radio Shack, Safeway, Target, and Walgreens. The Global Healthcare Exchange and its Canadian counterpart, GHX Canada, engage in the buying and selling of health care products for 1,400 hospitals and more than 100 health care suppliers, such as Abbott

Laboratories, Johnson & Johnson, and U.S. Surgical. These private exchanges have saved their members millions of dollars due to efficiencies in purchase transactions.

Online Auctions in Organizational Markets

Online auctions have grown in popularity among organizational buyers and business marketers. Many e-marketplaces offer this service. Two general types of auctions are common: (1) a traditional auction, and (2) a reverse auction.[31] Figure 6–5 shows how buyer and seller participants and price behaviour differ by type of auction. Let us look at each auction type more closely to understand the implications of each for buyers and sellers.

traditional auction

A seller puts an item up for sale, and would-be buyers are invited to bid in competition with each other.

In a **traditional auction** a seller puts an item up for sale and would-be buyers are invited to bid in competition with each other. As more would-be buyers become involved, there is an upward pressure on bid prices. Why? Bidding is sequential.

Prospective buyers observe the bids of others and decide whether to increase the bid price. The auction ends when a single bidder remains and "wins" the item with its highest price. For example, eBayBusiness uses a traditional auction. Traditional auctions are also used to dispose of excess merchandise. For example, Dell Inc. sells surplus, refurbished, or closeout computer merchandise at its dellauction.com Web site.

reverse auction

A buyer communicates a need for a product or service, and would-be suppliers are invited to bid in competition with each other.

A reverse auction works in the opposite direction from a traditional auction. In a **reverse auction,** a buyer communicates a need for a product or service and would-be suppliers are invited to bid in competition with each other. As more would-be suppliers become involved, there is a downward pressure on bid prices for the buyer's business. Why? Like traditional auctions, bidding is sequential, and prospective suppliers observe the bids of others and decide whether to decrease the bid price. The

Going Online

eBay Means Business, Too

eBay, Inc., is a true Internet phenomenon. By any measure, it is the predominant person-to-person trading community in the world.

eBay has a trading platform for the millions of small businesses in Canada, the United States, and around the world. When you go to the eBayBusiness Web site (**www.ebaybusiness.com**) or the Canadian site (**http://business.shop.ebay.ca**), you will find a homepage structured for the small business marketplace. The site is easy for small business buyers and sellers to navigate and features many industry marketplaces and a dozen cross-industry products, such as office equipment, metalworking, and professional photography. Transactions on eBayBusiness exceed sales of $2 billion annually.

eBay is always updating its industry marketplaces. Go to the industry listing on the homepage. What types of industries are most prominent? Are products for all three kinds of organizational markets—industrial, reseller, and government—available?

● **FIGURE 6-5**
How buyer and seller
participants and price
behaviour differ by type of
online auction

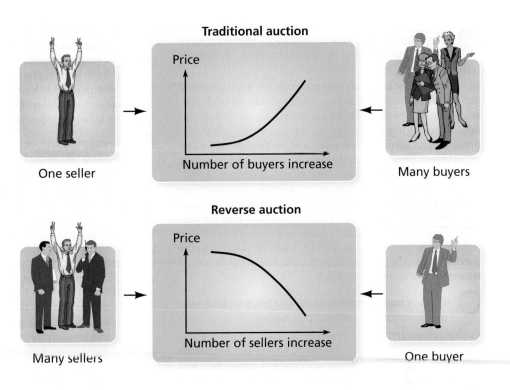

● **FIGURE 6-5**
How buyer and seller
participants and price
behaviour differ by type of
online auction

auction ends when a single bidder remains and "wins" the business with its lowest price. Reverse auctions benefit organizational buyers by reducing the cost of their purchases. As an example, United Technologies Corp., estimates that it has saved $600 million on the purchase of $6 billion in supplies using online reverse auctions.[32]

Clearly, buyers welcome the lower prices generated by reverse auctions. Some suppliers also favour reverse auctions because they give them a chance to capture business that they might not have otherwise had because of a long-standing purchase relationship between the buyer and another supplier. On the other hand, suppliers say that reverse auctions put too much emphasis on prices, discourage consideration of other important buying criteria, and threaten supply partnership opportunities.[33]

---

learning review

8. What are e-marketplaces?

9. In general, which type of online auction creates upward pressure on bid prices, and which type creates downward pressure on bid prices?

LEARNING OBJECTIVES REVIEW

LO1 **Distinguish among industrial, reseller, and government organizational markets.**

There are three different organizational markets: industrial, reseller, and government. Industrial firms, in some way, reprocess a product or service they buy before selling it to the next buyer. Resellers—wholesalers and retailers—buy physical products and sell them again without any reprocessing.

Government agencies, at the federal, provincial, and local levels, buy goods and services for the constituents they serve. The North American Industry Classification System (NAICS) and the North American Product Classification System (NAPCS) provides common industry definitions for Canada, Mexico, and the United States, which facilitate the measurement of economic activity for these three organizational markets.

Describe the key characteristics of organizational buying that make it different from consumer buying.

Seven major characteristics of organizational buying make it different from consumer buying. These include demand characteristics, size of the order or purchase, number of potential buyers, buying objectives, buying criteria, buyer–seller relationships and supply partnerships, and multiple buying influences within organizations. The organizational buying process itself is more formalized, more individuals are involved, supplier capability is more important, and the post-purchase evaluation behaviour often includes performance of the supplier and the item purchased. Figure 6–4 details how the purchase of an MP3 player differs between a consumer purchase and an organizational purchase. The case study describing the purchase of machine vision systems by an industrial firm illustrates this process in greater depth.

LO3 **Explain how buying centres and buying situations influence organizational purchasing.**

Buying centres and buying situations have an important influence on organizational purchasing. A buying centre consists of a group of individuals who share common goals, risks, and knowledge important to a purchase decision. A buyer or purchasing manager is almost always a member of a buying centre. However, other individuals may affect organizational purchasing due to their unique roles in a purchase decision. Five specific roles that a person may play in a buying centre include user, influencer, buyer, decider, and gatekeeper. The specific buying situation will influence the number of people in and the different roles played in a buying centre. For a routine reorder of an item—a straight rebuy situation—a purchasing manager or

buyer will typically act alone in making a purchasing decision. When an organization is a first-time purchaser of a product or service—a new buy situation—a buying centre is enlarged and all five roles in a buying centre often emerge. A modified rebuy buying situation lies between these two extremes. Figure 6–3 offers additional insights into how buying centres and buying situations influence organization purchasing.

LO4 **Recognize the importance and nature of online buying in industrial, reseller, and government organizational markets.**

Organizations dwarf consumers in terms of online transactions made and purchase volume. Online buying in organizational markets is popular for three reasons. First, organizational buyers depend on timely supplier information that describes product availability, technical specifications, application uses, price, and delivery schedules. This information can be conveyed quickly via Internet technology. Second, this technology substantially reduces buyer order processing costs. Third, business marketers have found that Internet technology can reduce marketing costs, particularly sales and advertising expense, and broaden their customer base. Two developments in online buying have been the creation of e-marketplaces and online auctions. E-marketplaces provide a technology trading platform and a centralized market for buyer–seller transactions and make possible the real-time exchange of information, money, products, and services. These e-marketplaces can be independent trading communities, such as freemarkets, or private exchanges, such as the worldwide retail exchange. Online traditional and reverse auctions represent a second major development. With traditional auctions, the highest-priced bidder "wins." Conversely, the lowest-priced bidder "wins" with reverse auctions.

FOCUSING ON KEY TERMS

bidders' list p. 160
business marketing p. 148
buy classes p. 157
buying centre p. 155
derived demand p. 152
e-marketplaces p. 161
government units p. 149
industrial firm p. 149
ISO 9000 standards p. 154
make-buy decision p. 159

organizational buyers p. 148
organizational buying behaviour p. 152
organizational buying criteria p. 153
reciprocity p. 154
resellers p. 149
reverse auction p. 162
supplier development p. 154
supply partnership p. 154
traditional auction p. 162
value analysis p. 159

APPLYING MARKETING KNOWLEDGE

1 Describe the major differences among industrial firms, resellers, and government units in Canada.
2 Explain how the North American Industry Classification System (NAICS) might be helpful in understanding industrial, reseller, and government markets, and discuss the limitations inherent in this system.
3 List and discuss the key characteristics of organizational buying that make it different from consumer buying.

4 What is a buying centre? Describe the roles assumed by people in a buying centre and what useful questions should be raised to guide any analysis of the structure and behaviour of a buying centre.
5 Effective marketing is of increasing importance in today's competitive environment. How can firms more effectively market to organizations?

6 A firm that is marketing multi-million dollar wastewater treatment systems to cities has been unable to sell a new type of system. To date, the firm's marketing efforts have been directed to city purchasing departments to be included on approved bidders' lists. Talks with city-employed personnel have indicated that the new system is very different from current systems and therefore city sanitary and sewer department engineers, directors of these two departments, and city council members are unfamiliar with the workings of the system. Consulting engineers, hired by cities to work on the engineering and design features of these systems and paid on a percentage of system cost, are also reluctant to favour the new system. (*a*) What roles do the various individuals play in the purchase process for a wastewater treatment system? (*b*) How could the firm improve the marketing effort behind the new system?

Building Your Marketing Plan

Your marketing plan may need an estimate of the size of the market potential or industry potential (see Chapter 9) for a particular product-market in which you compete. Use these steps:

1. Define the product-market precisely, such as ice cream manufacturing.

2. Visit the Industry Canada site at **www.ic.gc.ca/cis-sic/cis-sic.nsf/IDE/cis31152defe.html**.

3. On the left-hand side you will see a menu that you can use to access information on ice cream manufacturing (e.g., click on "Performance" and you will find "Net Revenues").

4. Check out the type of data available there that will allow you to assess the market potential for an ice cream manufacturing business.

Video Case 6

IGLOO SOFTWARE

Background

IGLOO Software was founded in 2008. It is a Kitchener, Ontario–based developer of online communities and social networking solutions for organizations (businesses, non-profit, and government entities). IGLOO software is designed to allow organizations to use the power of social networking to improve internal collaboration and communications with external partners. Basically, IGLOO's software is delivered through an SaaS (software as a service). IGLOO's communities are built into their client's existing hardware, and then hosted through the Internet to allow seamless integration globally. The service is entirely virtual, allowing it to be installed with zero upfront technology investment costs, and it is fully compatible with BlackBerry, iPhone, e-mail, and existing social networking services.

IGLOO Solutions

The company, IGLOO Software, believes that business is driven by social interactions. According to IGLOO, organizations do not build products, negotiate deals, or make service calls—people do. IGLOO further believes that organizations have been using social interactions as a vital business tool for decades, long before anyone had ever heard of Facebook, LinkedIn, or Twitter. These include interactions ranging from telephone conversations to face-to-face meetings to the business conversations that happen in the hallway or after work. All of these are early forms of social interactions in the workplace and are still being used today.

IGLOO suggests that e-mail is the number-one collaboration, knowledge sharing, and social networking tool at work, with more than 90 billion messages sent and received daily. But according to IGLOO, this heavy reliance on e-mail hampers productivity and cripples the pace of innovation through the duplication of daily business activities.

Therefore, IGLOO's software solutions help organizations create vital connections between people, processes, and information through the creation of online business communities. Companies use online communities to improve collaboration, to share knowledge, and to drive employee engagement across geographically dispersed project teams, departments, and business units—inside and out.

How IGLOO Software Works

Basically, IGLOO's model is based on the concept that incorporating a social software solution into any organization will allow its members to:

- Make timely and informed business decisions quickly and easily;
- Promote the sharing of knowledge and ideas to maximize the impact of intellectual capital;
- Transcend borders, disciplines, and economic boundaries;
- Encourage participation, communication, and collaboration across the entire organization; and
- Raise awareness and involvement of key stakeholder groups to improve policies, procedures, methodologies, and outcomes.

IGLOO's online community solutions are designed to give their clients greater control over the way their clients work and access knowledge. According to the company, every solution powered by IGLOO software comes complete with an integrated suite of content management, collaboration, and knowledge sharing tools, within one secure social business platform.

IGLOO Workplace Communities are developed to be internally focused and used to connect their clients' workforces across geographically dispersed project teams, departments, and business units. IGLOO Marketplace Communities are externally focused and used to extend collaboration, knowledge sharing, and networking beyond their clients' firewalls to their customers, partners, and suppliers.

IGLOO solutions are designed to give their clients control and the power to change the way their clients work. According to IGLOO, their solutions enable all types of enterprises to quickly and easily create online communities for almost any project, team, or business activity—with no new IT investment required.

IGLOO solutions are designed to help organizations with vital tasks such as sales and marketing, customer engagement, employee productivity, and research and development. For example, in terms of sales and marketing, IGLOO solutions allow organizations to connect sales and marketing teams to unify the organizational message and to drive leads and grow revenue. IGLOO solutions are designed to improve customer engagement, including speeding up response times and enhancing customer interactions, which are drivers of customer loyalty. The company's solutions are also built to facilitate and promote employee productivity as well as reward knowledge sharing and collaboration. Finally, IGLOO solutions are designed to enhance their clients' research and development efforts, including increasing the ability to find and capitalize on new ideas to achieve new growth targets.

According to IGLOO, its goal is to assist organizations with workplace communities and marketplace communities. In terms of workplace communities, IGLOO strives to connect an organization's workforce across time and space. In regard to marketplace communities, IGLOO attempts to extend an organization's network beyond its firewall to connect to customers, suppliers, and partners to deepen relationships.

Examples of IGLOO at Work

To better understand what IGLOO does, consider the following three examples. TEMS is an organization that provides emergency management consulting and IT solutions during natural disasters. When the recent earthquake hit Haiti, IGLOO worked with TEMS to create a community to coordinate relief efforts. Within 48 hours, the "Haiti Community" was launched online. It quickly became the clearinghouse for those involved in the relief efforts, including government agencies, universities, hospitals, and even the United Nations. MIN, or the Manufacturing Innovation Network, also worked with IGLOO. MIN is an innovation cluster comprised of manufacturers, academic institutions, and others who wish to promote innovation as a source of competitive advantage. IGLOO helped MIN create an online innovation network complete with news, expert bloggers, company directories, trade events, and more. Finally, IGLOO worked with The BlackBerry Partners Fund. This is a $150 million venture-capital fund focused on supporting applications and services designed for the BlackBerry platform. It required a publicly accessible Web site to promote the fund globally and a private online community for the investment committee to oversee funding applications and competitions. IGLOO designed an integrated solution for content management, collaboration, and secure storage for The BlackBerry Partners Fund.

Marketing at IGLOO Software

Currently, IGLOO's marketing approach consists of online and print advertising, strategic partnerships, and sponsorship activities. IGLOO uses its own medium—its social networking platforms—to reach possible end users.

Pricing

A basic IGLOO solution costs $199 per month. This is geared toward small business customers. The company also has an "enterprise" solution for $999 per month, which is targeted toward Global 1000 companies and large government agencies.

Questions

1 Given IGLOO Software Solutions' products and the type of customers it sells to, who do you think are the members of the buying centre or buying committee when a company like IGLOO comes calling?

2 What would be important buying criteria that would drive the decision for an organization/business customer to buy or not to buy IGLOO's solutions?

3 As you know, in B2B marketing, a company selling in this space is faced with a customer considering a make-buy decision. How can IGLOO ensure that the customer arrives at a "buy" decision?

4 What marketing activities would you recommend to ensure that IGLOO is successful in this B2B space?

chapter 7

Reaching Global Markets

CANADIAN COMPANIES COMPETE SUCCESSFULLY IN THE GLOBAL MARKETPLACE

Many Canadian marketers have recognized the vast potential of global markets. Over 99 percent of the world's population lives outside of Canada, and collectively, these potential customers possess tremendous purchasing power. Not only are global markets substantial in size, but many are also growing faster than comparable markets in Canada. Moreover, increased free trade among nations has opened up these global markets and given Canadian companies an opportunity to compete worldwide.

Accordingly, many Canadian firms are seizing opportunities in global markets. For example, British Columbian hemlock producers have successfully penetrated the Japanese home construction market where their product is now the preferred choice for post-and-beam home construction. ADI International Inc. of Fredericton, New Brunswick, competes successfully in global markets based on innovative technology. The company is a world leader in providing water treatment systems that remove arsenic from drinking water. Currently, over 95 percent of its sales come from export markets. RIM's BlackBerry is used by millions of subscribers around the world and the brand has achieved global and pop-culture stardom.

Inniskillin Wines of Ontario has also achieved much success in European markets with its VQA icewine. Positioned as a unique, high-quality dessert beverage, the product has been well received by the upscale and discerning European wine consumer. In less than 10 years, Toronto-based Spin Master Toys grew to become one of the top 10 global toy manufacturers. It has achieved its global success by developing innovative products and utilizing strong licensing arrangements with some leading global brands, including McDonald's, Disney, and Hershey. Finally, G.A.P Adventures of Toronto is an adventure-travel company offering unique sustainable travel adventures in over 100 countries and on all seven continents. CEO Bruce Poon Tip believed that travellers around the world wanted authentic adventures such as trekking, diving, and wildlife experiences. He was correct. He has grown the company from a one-person operation to a company with over 500 employees on several continents. The company serves 60,000 customers worldwide each year. For his efforts, Bruce has been recognized as Canada's Entrepreneur of the Year.[1] G.A.P Adventures has also been named one of Canada's 50 Best Managed Companies and Canada's Top 100 Employers.

As this chapter illustrates, pursuit of global markets by Canadian and foreign marketers ultimately results in greater world trade activity and positive economic impact on participating countries, companies, and global consumers. This chapter will also describe the challenges involved in global marketing and how market-driven companies meet those challenges.

LO1 DYNAMICS OF WORLD TRADE

The dollar value of world trade has more than doubled in the past decade and will exceed $20 trillion in 2012. Manufactured goods and commodities account for about 75 percent of world trade. Service industries, including telecommunications, transportation, insurance, education, banking, and tourism, represent the other 25 percent of world trade.[2]

World Trade

All nations and regions of the world do not participate equally in world trade. World trade activities reflect interdependencies among industries, countries, and regions and manifest themselves in country, company, industry, and regional exports and imports.

Global Perspective   Figure 7–1 shows the top ten exporters and importers in the world (merchandise only, not services). Canada makes the list in both categories.[3] The top ten exporters and importers—Germany, China, United States, Japan, France, Netherlands, Italy, United Kingdom, Belgium, and Canada—account for more than 50 percent of total world merchandise export and import value.

Not all trade involves the exchange of money for goods or services. In a world where 70 percent of all countries do not have convertible currencies or where government-owned enterprises lack sufficient cash or credit for imports, other means of payment are used. An estimated 15 to 20 percent of world trade involves **countertrade,** the practice of using barter rather than money for making global sales.[4]

Countertrade is popular with many Eastern European nations, Russia, and Asian countries. For example, the Malaysian government exchanged 20,000 tonnes of rice for an equivalent amount of Philippine corn. Volvo of North America delivered

countertrade

The practice of using barter rather than money for making global sales.

Rank	Exporters	Export Value in Billions of Dollars	Rank	Importers	Import Value in Billions of Dollars
1	Germany	1,326	1	United States	2,020
2	China	1,218	2	Germany	1,058
3	United States	1,162	3	China	956
4	Japan	713	4	Japan	621
5	France	553	5	United Kingdom	620
6	Netherlands	551	6	France	615
7	Italy	492	7	Italy	504
8	United Kingdom	438	8	Netherlands	492
9	Belgium	431	9	Belgium	413
10	Canada	419	10	Canada	390

● **FIGURE 7–1**

Top ten global exporters and importers (merchandise)

trade feedback effect

A country's imports affect its exports and exports affect its imports.

gross domestic product (GDP)

The monetary value of all goods and services produced in a country during one year.

balance of trade

The difference between the monetary value of a nation's exports and imports.

automobiles to the Siberian police force when Siberia had no cash to pay for them. It accepted payment in oil, which it then sold for cash to pay for media advertising.

A global perspective on world trade views exports and imports as complementary economic flows: A country's imports affect its exports and exports affect its imports. Every nation's imports arise from the exports of other nations. As the exports of one country increase, its national output and income rise, which, in turn, leads to an increase in the demand for imports. This nation's greater demand for imports stimulates the exports of other countries. Increased demand for exports of other nations energizes their economic activity, resulting in higher national income, which stimulates their demand for imports. This phenomenon is called the **trade feedback effect** and is one argument for free trade among nations.

Canadian Perspective Canada's **gross domestic product (GDP),** the monetary value of all goods and services produced in a country during one year, is valued at over $1.5 trillion. Canada exports a significant percentage of the goods and services it produces. In fact, it exports more than 35 percent of GDP, making it an important trading nation.[5]

The difference between the monetary value of a nation's exports and imports is called the **balance of trade.** When a country's exports exceed its imports, it incurs a surplus in its balance of trade. When imports exceed exports, a deficit has occurred. As shown in Figure 7–1, the largest exporting nations are also the world's largest importing nations. For some, like the United States, this results in a trade deficit or negative balance of trade. Canada, on the other hand, maintains an overall surplus or positive balance of trade at this time. Currently, Canada's top exports include industrial products, machinery, energy products, automotive products, and forestry products. However, Canada has also increased its exportation of services (now totalling over $70 billion), including travel services, communication services, computer services, financial services, and management services.[6]

Almost every Canadian is affected by Canada's trading activity. The effects vary from the products we buy (Samsung computers from Korea, Waterford crystal from Ireland, and Lindemans wine from Australia) to those we sell (Moosehead beer to Sweden, Inniskillin icewines to the EU, and Bombardier aircraft to Norway) to the additional jobs and improved standard of living that can result from world trade.

World trade flows to and from Canada reflect demand and supply interdependencies for goods and services among nations and industries. While Canada trades with dozens of other countries, the three largest importers of Canadian goods and services are the United States (about 80 percent), Japan, and the European Union (EU). These countries are also the top three exporters to Canada. The EU and Japan enjoy trade surpluses with our country, while the United States incurs a trade deficit.[7]

Trade is so important to Canada that it is one of the federal government's key priorities. It is so critical to the growth of the Canadian economy that the government established what it calls Team Canada Inc. (TCI), a network of more than 20 federal departments and agencies that work to help Canadian firms find new global markets and assist them in competing in those markets. Some of Canada's hottest export markets recently by identified by Team Canada are discussed in the Marketing Matters box, "Canada's Hottest Export Markets," on page 174.[8]

Competitive Advantage of Nations

As companies in many industries find themselves competing against foreign competitors at home and abroad, government policy-makers around the world are increasingly asking why some companies and industries in a country succeed globally while others lose ground or fail. Michael Porter suggests a "diamond" to explain a nation's competitive advantage and why some industries and firms become world leaders.[9] He identified four key elements, which appear in Figure 7-2:

1. *Factor conditions.* These reflect a nation's ability to turn its natural resources, education, and infrastructure into a competitive advantage. Consider Holland, which exports 59 percent of the world's cut flowers. The Dutch lead the world in the cut-flower industry because of their research in flower cultivation, packaging, and shipping—not because of their weather.

● **FIGURE 7-2**

Porter's "diamond" of national competitive advantage

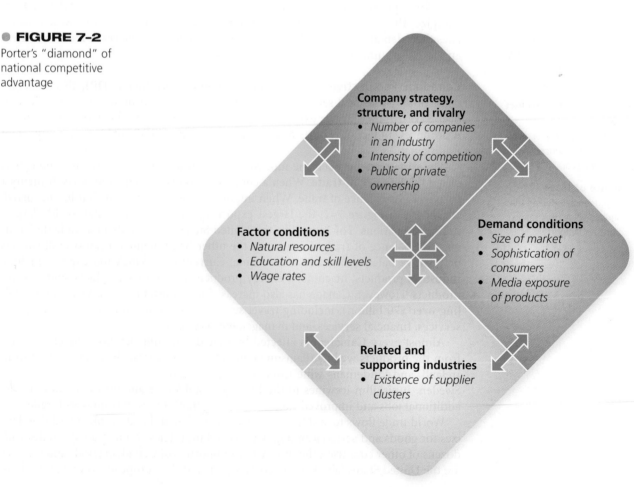

Sharp and Dior have succeeded in the global marketplace as well as in their domestic markets.

2. *Demand conditions.* These include both the number and sophistication of domestic customers for an industry's product. Japan's sophisticated consumers demand quality in their TVs and radios, thereby making Japan's producers, such as Sony, Sanyo, Matsushita, and Hitachi, some of the world leaders in the electronics industry.

3. *Related and supporting industries.* Firms and industries seeking leadership in global markets need clusters of world-class suppliers that accelerate innovation. The German leadership in scientific and industrial instrumentation relates directly to the cluster of supporting German precision engineering suppliers.

4. *Company strategy, structure, and rivalry.* These factors include the conditions governing the way a nation's businesses are organized and managed, along with the intensity of domestic competition. The Italian shoe industry has become a world leader because of intense domestic competition among such firms as MAB, Bruno Magli, and Rossimoda, which has made shoes for Christian Dior and Anne Klein Couture.

In Porter's study, case histories of firms in more than 100 industries were analyzed. While the strategies employed by the most successful global competitors were different in many respects, a common theme emerged—a firm that succeeds in global markets has first succeeded in intense domestic competition. Hence, competitive advantage for global firms grows out of relentless, continuing improvement, innovation, and change.

It is important to note, however, that it is not essential to be a giant company to compete successfully in global markets. Numerous small Canadian firms succeed in global markets because they find niche markets, sell innovative products, successfully leverage technology or licensing arrangements, or establish unique market positioning. In fact, Porter's study for the Canadian government on Canada's global competitiveness recommended, among other things, that Canadian firms should utilize these strategies as opposed to attempting to sell price-oriented commodities in global markets. He believes that by investing in research and development (R&D), and enhancing domestic competition, Canadian firms can improve their global competitiveness.[10]

---

learning review

1. What is the trade feedback effect?

2. What variables influence why some companies and industries in a country succeed globally, while others lose ground or fail?

LO2 MARKETING IN A BORDERLESS ECONOMIC WORLD

Global marketing has and continues to be affected by a growing borderless economic world. Four trends in the past decade have significantly influenced the landscape of global marketing:

Trend 1: Gradual decline of economic protectionism by individual countries.

Trend 2: Formal economic integration and free trade among nations.

Trend 3: Global competition among global companies for global customers.

Trend 4: Development of networked global marketspace.

Marketing Matters

Canada's Hottest Export Markets

Globally oriented Canadian companies are looking beyond this country to find new markets to exploit. International Trade Canada, a federal agency that is part of the federal government's Team Canada Inc. network, has identified several markets that it believes offer the best opportunities for Canadian companies seeking growth in global markets. They include China, India, and Mexico.

Canada currently exports more than $10 billion of goods and services to China, and China's import rate is growing at about 20 percent. China's burgeoning wealth and appetite for consumer products and natural resources make it an attractive market for many Canadian companies. For example, China has a need for better infrastructure, which means demand for transportation systems, water-supply systems, and telecommunications systems. Rising health concerns in China are also boosting demand for medical equipment, including imaging, diagnostics, and cancer treatment, a sector in which Canada is a world leader. Finally, China is looking for management services providers to help it improve in the areas of marketing, human resource management, and venture financing.

India has an import growth rate at over 20 percent, and Canada already exports more than $2 billion of goods and services to that country. But research suggests that India's economic growth rate will make it one of the top five economies within 30 years. It already has the fifth-largest telecommunications network and a customer base of over 250 million. This means big opportunities for exporters of telecommunications products. India is also looking to extend electricity to all its 1.3 billion people by 2012, which will drive demand in the power generation sector. The country is also looking to improve its transportation infrastructure including roads, railways, seaports, and airports.

Finally, Mexico is one of Canada's NAFTA partners and currently buys more than $6 billion in Canadian goods and services. Its import rate is growing at over 10 percent. The country has a major demand for energy, including natural gas, a sector where Canada competes well. Telecommunications deregulation is also creating demand in the information and communications technology (ICT) sector. Finally, Mexico's booming auto industry is creating major sales opportunities for auto parts.

Decline of Economic Protectionism

protectionism

The practice of shielding one or more industries within a country's economy from foreign competition through the use of tariffs or quotas.

tariff

A government tax on goods or services entering a country, which primarily serves to raise prices on imports.

quota

A restriction placed on the amount of a product allowed to enter or leave a country.

Protectionism is the practice of shielding one or more industries within a country's economy from foreign competition through the use of tariffs or quotas. The economic argument for protectionism is that it limits the outsourcing of jobs, protects a nation's political security, discourages economic dependency on other countries, and encourages the development of domestic industries. Read the accompanying Making Responsible Decisions box, "Global Ethics and Global Economics—The Case of Protectionism," and ask yourself whether protectionism has an ethical and social responsibility dimension.[11]

Tariffs and quotas discourage world trade, as depicted in Figure 7–3. **Tariffs,** which are government taxes on goods or services entering a country, primarily serve to raise prices on imports. The average tariff on manufactured goods in industrialized countries is 4 percent. However, wide differences exist across nations. For example, European Union countries have a 10 percent tariff on cars imported from Japan, which is about four times higher than the tariff imposed by the United States on Japanese cars.

The effect of tariffs on world trade and consumer prices is substantial. Consider rice exports to Japan. Experts claim that if the Japanese rice market were opened to imports by lowering tariffs, lower prices would save Japanese consumers over $8 billion annually. Similarly, tariffs imposed on bananas by European Union countries cost consumers $4 billion a year. Ecuador (the world's largest banana exporter), Mexico, Guatemala, and Honduras have negotiated a reduction in this levy.

A **quota** is a restriction placed on the amount of a product allowed to enter or leave a country. Quotas can be mandated or voluntary, and may be legislated or negotiated by governments. Import quotas seek to guarantee domestic industries access to a certain percentage of their domestic market. For example, there is a limit on imported television sets to the United Kingdom and Italian quotas on Japanese motorcycles. Canada also imposes quotas, which ultimately result in Canadian consumers usually paying higher prices for various goods.

Every country engages in some form of protectionism. However, protectionism has declined over the past 50 years due, in large part, to the *General Agreement on Tariffs and Trade (GATT)*. This international treaty was intended to limit trade barriers and promote world trade through the reduction of tariffs, which it did. However, GATT did not explicitly address nontariff trade barriers, such as quotas, and world trade in services, which often sparked heated trade disputes between nations.

● **FIGURE 7–3**

How protectionism affects world trade

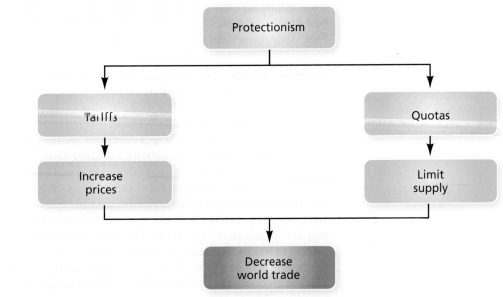

Global Ethics and Global Economics—The Case of Protectionism

World trade benefits from free and fair trade among nations. Nevertheless, governments of many countries continue to use tariffs and quotas to protect their various domestic industries. Why? Protectionism earns profits for domestic producers and tariff revenue for government. There is a cost, however. Protectionist policies cost Japanese consumers between $75 billion and $110 billion annually. Canadian consumers pay billions each year in higher prices because of tariffs and other protective restrictions.

Sugar and textile import quotas in the United States, automobile and banana import tariffs in many European countries, beer import tariffs in Canada, and rice import tariffs in Japan protect domestic industries but also interfere with world trade for these products. Regional trade agreements, such as those found in the provisions of the European Union and the North American Free Trade Agreement, may also pose a situation whereby member nations can obtain preferential treatment in quotas and tariffs but nonmember nations cannot.

Protectionism, in its many forms, raises an interesting global ethical question. Is protectionism, no matter how applied, an ethical practice?

As a consequence, the major industrialized nations of the world formed the *World Trade Organization (WTO)* in 1995 to address a broad array of world trade issues.[12] There are more than 150 WTO member countries, including Canada, accounting for more than 90 percent of world trade. The WTO is a permanent institution that sets rules governing trade among its members through panels of trade experts who decide on trade disputes between members and issue binding decisions. The WTO reviews more than 200 disputes annually. For instance, the WTO denied Kodak's multi-million dollar damage claim that the Japanese government protected Fuji Photo from import competition. In another decision, the WTO allowed the United Kingdom, Ireland, and the European Union to reclassify U.S.-produced local area network (LAN) computer equipment as telecommunications gear. The new classification effectively doubled the import tariff on these American goods.

Rise of Economic Integration

In recent years, a number of countries with similar economic goals have formed transnational trade groups or signed trade agreements for the purpose of promoting free trade among member nations and enhancing their individual economies. Three of the best-known examples are the European Union (or simply EU), the North American Free Trade Agreement (NAFTA), and Asian free trade areas.

European Union The European Union consists of 27 member countries that have eliminated most barriers to the free flow of goods, services, capital, and labour across their borders (Figure 7–4). This single market houses more than 500 million consumers. In addition, 16 countries have adopted a common currency called the *euro*. Adoption of the euro has been a boon to electronic commerce in the EU by eliminating the need to continually monitor currency exchange rates.

The EU creates abundant marketing opportunities because firms no longer find it necessary to market their products and services on a nation-by-nation basis. Rather, pan-European marketing strategies are possible due to greater uniformity in product and packaging standards; fewer regulatory restrictions on transportation, advertising, and promotion imposed by countries; and removal of most tariffs that affect pricing practices. For example, Colgate-Palmolive Company now markets its Colgate toothpaste with one formula and package across EU countries at one price. Similarly, Black & Decker—the maker of electrical hand tools, appliances, and other consumer

● FIGURE 7-4

The countries of the European Union in 2010

**European Union
www.europa.eu.int**

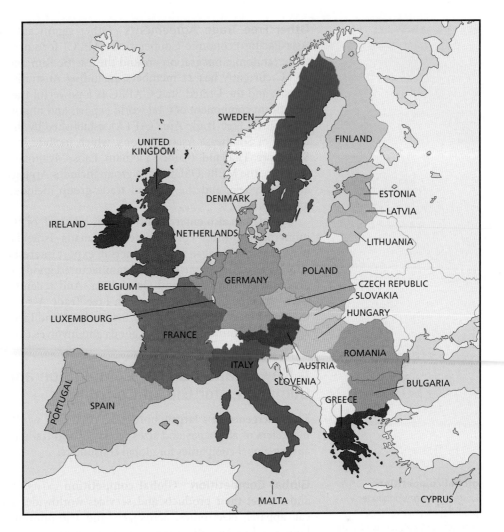

products—now produces 8, not 20, motor sizes for the European market, resulting in production and marketing cost savings. These practices were previously impossible because of different government and trade regulations. Europe-wide distribution from fewer locations is also feasible, given open borders. French tire maker Michelin has closed 180 of its European distribution centres and now uses just 20 to serve all EU countries.

North American Free Trade Agreement   The North American Free Trade Agreement lifted many trade barriers among Canada, Mexico, and the United States and created a marketplace with more than 450 million consumers. Negotiations are under way to expand NAFTA to create a 34-country Free Trade Area of the Americas. This agreement would include the United States, Canada, Mexico, Latin America, and the Caribbean countries.

NAFTA has stimulated trade flows among member nations as well as cross-border retailing, manufacturing, and investment. For example, NAFTA paved the way for Walmart to move to Mexico, and for Mexican supermarket giant Gigante to move into the United States. Whirlpool Corporation's Canadian subsidiary stopped making washing machines in Canada and moved that operation to Ohio. Whirlpool then shifted the production of kitchen ranges and compact dryers to Canada. Ford invested $60 million in its Mexico City manufacturing plant to produce smaller cars and light trucks for global sales.

Other Free Trade Agreements   Other significant trade agreements include the Asia-Pacific Economic Cooperation (APEC) forum, which was established to promote economic integration around the Pacific Rim and to sustain economic growth. APEC currently has 21 members, including Australia, Canada, China, Japan, Peru, Russia, and the United States. APEC is a powerful trading group and accounts for a significant component of total world exports and imports. Another trade agreement is the ASEAN Free Trade Area (AFTA), established by the member nations of the Association of Southeast Asian Nations, which include Indonesia, Malaysia, Philippines, Singapore, Thailand, Brunei, Vietnam, Laos, Myanmar, and Cambodia. And in South America, the MERCOSUR trade group includes Argentina, Brazil, Paraguay, Uruguay, and Venezuela, and the Andean trade group includes Bolivia, Columbia, Ecuador, and Peru.

Canada has also entered into various bilateral, or two-way, trade agreements with numerous countries. For example, the Canada–Israel Free Trade Agreement improves market access for agri-food products of export interest to both Canada and Israel and eliminates tariffs on virtually all manufactured goods. Canada also has bilateral trade agreements with Chile and Costa Rica. And recently, Canada entered into a new trade agreement with the European Free Trade Association (EFTA), which includes the countries of Iceland, Norway, Switzerland, and Liechtenstein. This Canada–EFTA agreement eliminates tariffs on goods and involves over $11 billion in bilateral trade.

A New Reality: Global Competition among Global Companies for Global Consumers

The emergence of a largely borderless economic world has created a new reality for marketers of all shapes and sizes. Today, world trade is driven by global competition among global companies for global consumers.

global competition
Exists when firms originate, produce, and market their products and services worldwide.

Global Competition   **Global competition** exists when firms originate, produce, and market their products and services worldwide. The automobile, pharmaceutical, apparel, electronics, aerospace, and telecommunication fields represent well-known industries with sellers and buyers on every continent. Other industries that are increasingly global in scope include soft drinks, cosmetics, ready-to-eat cereals, snack chips, and retailing.

Global competition broadens the competitive landscape for marketers. The familiar "cola war" waged by Pepsi-Cola and Coca-Cola in Canada has been repeated around the world, including India, China, and Argentina. Procter & Gamble's Pampers and Kimberly-Clark's Huggies have taken their disposable diaper rivalry from Canada to Western Europe. Boeing and Europe's Airbus vie for lucrative commercial aircraft contracts on virtually every continent.

strategic alliances
Agreements among two or more independent firms to cooperate for the purpose of achieving common goals, such as a competitive advantage or customer value creation.

Collaborative relationships also are becoming a common way to meet the demands of global competition. Global **strategic alliances** are agreements among two or more independent firms to cooperate for the purpose of achieving common goals, such as a competitive advantage or customer value creation. For instance, several of the world's largest telecommunication equipment makers, including Ericsson (Sweden), Nortel (Canada), Siemens (Germany), and 3Com (USA), formed Juniper Networks, Inc., an alliance created to build devices to speed global Internet communications. General Mills and Nestlé of Switzerland created Cereal Partners Worldwide for the purpose of fine-tuning Nestlé's European cereal marketing and distribution of General Mills cereals worldwide. This global alliance produces more than $1 billion in sales in 130 countries.[13]

Global Companies   Three types of companies populate and compete in the global marketplace: (1) international firms, (2) multinational firms, and (3) transnational firms.[14] All three employ people in different countries, and many have administrative,

Pepsi-Cola, now available in more than 190 countries and territories, accounts for a quarter of all soft drinks sold internationally. This Brazilian ad—"How to make jeans last 10 years"—features the popular Diet Pepsi brand targeted at weight-conscious consumers.

PepsiCo, Inc.
www.pepsico.com

marketing, and manufacturing operations (often called *divisions* or *subsidiaries*) around the world. However, a firm's orientation toward and strategy for global markets and marketing defines the type of company it is or attempts to be.

An *international firm* engages in trade and marketing in different countries as an extension of the marketing strategy in its home country. Generally speaking, these firms market their existing products and services in other countries the same way they do in their home country. Avon, for example, successfully distributes its product line through direct selling in Asia, Europe, and South America, employing virtually the same marketing strategy used in North America.

A *multinational firm* views the world as consisting of unique parts, and markets to each part differently. Multinationals use a **multidomestic marketing strategy,** which means that they have as many different product variations, brand names, and advertising programs as countries in which they do business. For example, Lever Europe, a division of Unilever, markets its fabric softener known as Snuggle in Canada in ten European countries under seven brand names, including Kuschelweich in Germany, Coccolino in Italy, and Mimosin in France. These products have different packages, different advertising programs, and occasionally different formulas. Procter & Gamble markets Mr. Clean, its multipurpose cleaner, in North America and Asia. But you will not find Mr. Clean in other parts of the world. In Latin America, Mr. Clean is Mastro Limpio. Mr. Clean is Mr. Proper in Europe, Africa, and the Middle East.

A *transnational firm* views the world as one market and emphasizes cultural similarities across countries or universal consumer needs and wants more than differences. Transnational marketers employ a **global marketing strategy**—the practice of standardizing marketing activities when there are cultural similarities and adapting them when cultures differ. This approach benefits marketers by allowing them to realize economies of scale from their production and marketing activities.

Global marketing strategies are popular among many business-to-business marketers, such as Caterpillar and Komatsu (heavy construction equipment), and Texas Instruments, Intel, Hitachi, and Motorola (semiconductors). Consumer goods marketers also successfully execute this strategy, including such global companies as Timex, Seiko, and Swatch (watches); Coca-Cola and Pepsi-Cola (cola soft drinks); Mattel and LEGO (children's toys); Gillette (personal care products); L'Oréal and Shiseido (cosmetics); and McDonald's (quick-service restaurants). Each of these

multidomestic marketing strategy
Use of as many different product variations, brand names, and advertising programs as countries in which they do business.

global marketing strategy
The practice of standardizing marketing activities when there are cultural similarities and adapting them when cultures differ.

global brand
A brand marketed under the same name in multiple countries with similar and centrally coordinated marketing programs.

companies markets a **global brand**—a brand marketed under the same name in multiple countries with similar and centrally coordinated marketing programs.[15] Global brands have the same product formulation or service concept, deliver the same benefits to consumers, and use consistent advertising across multiple countries and cultures. This is not to say that global brands are not sometimes tailored to specific cultures or countries. However, adaptation is only used when necessary to better connect the brand to consumers in different markets. Consider McDonald's.[16] This global marketer has adapted its proven formula of "food, fun, and families" across more than 100 countries. Although the Golden Arches and Ronald McDonald appear worldwide, McDonald's tailors other aspects of its marketing program. It serves beer in Germany, wine in France, and coconut, mango, and tropical mint shakes in Hong Kong. Hamburgers are made with different meat and spices in Japan, Thailand, India, and the Philippines. But McDonald's world-famous french fry is standardized. Its french fry in Beijing, China, tastes like that in Paris, France, which tastes like that in your neighbourhood.

global consumers
Consumer groups living in many countries or regions of the world that have similar needs or seek similar features and benefits from products or services.

Global Consumers   Global competition among global companies often focuses on the identification and pursuit of global consumers. **Global consumers** consist of consumer groups living in many countries or regions of the world who have similar needs or seek similar features and benefits from products or services.[17] For example, evidence suggests the emergence of a global middle-income class, a youth market, and an elite segment, each consuming or using a common assortment of products and services, regardless of geographic location. A variety of companies have capitalized on the global consumer. Whirlpool, Sony, and IKEA have benefited from the growing global middle-income class desire for kitchen appliances, consumer electronics, and home furnishings, respectively. Levi's, Nike, Coca-Cola, and Benetton have tapped the global youth market, a market consisting of 500 million 13- to 19-year-olds in Europe, North America, South America, and the industrialized nations of Asia and the Pacific Rim who are remarkably similar in terms of buying behaviour. Finally, DeBeers, Chanel, Gucci, Rolls Royce, and Sotheby's and Christie's, the world's largest fine art and antique auction houses, cater to the elite segment for luxury goods worldwide.

Emergence of a Networked Global Marketspace

The use of Internet technology as a tool for exchanging goods, services, and information on a global scale is the fourth trend affecting world trade. More than 1.7 billion businesses, educational institutions, government agencies, and households worldwide

Nestlé features multiple country and language Web sites that customize content and communicate with consumers in their native tongue. The Web site for China shown here is an example. Read the text to learn how many Web sites and languages Nestlé uses.

Nestlé S. A.
www.nestle.com

currently have access to the Internet, but that number will rise to over 2 billion by 2011.[18] The broad reach of this technology suggests that its potential for promoting world trade is huge.

The networked global marketspace enables the exchange of goods, services, and information from companies *anywhere* to customers anywhere at any time and at a lower cost. Companies engaged in business-to-business marketing (B2B) are leading the charge in terms of global e-commerce. Ninety percent of global e-commerce revenue arises from business-to-business transactions among a dozen countries in North America, Western Europe, and the Asia/Pacific Rim region. Industries that have benefited from this technology include industrial chemicals and controls; maintenance, repair, and operating supplies; computer and electronic equipment and components; aerospace parts; and agricultural and energy products. The United States, Canada, the United Kingdom, Germany, Sweden, Japan, China, and Taiwan are among the most active participants in worldwide business-to-business e-commerce.

Marketers recognize that the networked global marketspace offers unprecedented access to prospective buyers on every continent. Companies that have successfully capitalized on this access manage multiple country and language Web sites that customize content and communicate with consumers in their native tongues. Nestlé, the world's largest packaged food manufacturer, coffee roaster, and chocolate maker, is a case in point. The company operates 65 individual country Web sites in 20 languages that span five continents.

---

learning review

3. What is protectionism?

4. Among which countries was the North American Free Trade Agreement designed to promote free trade?

5. What is the difference between a multidomestic marketing strategy and a global marketing strategy?

LO3 A GLOBAL ENVIRONMENTAL SCAN

Global companies conduct continuing environmental scans of the five sets of environmental forces described in Figure 3–1 on page 77 (social, economic, technological, competitive, and regulatory forces). This section focuses on three kinds of uncontrollable environmental variables—cultural, economic, and political-regulatory—that affect global marketing practices in strikingly different ways from those in domestic markets.

Cultural Diversity

cross-cultural analysis

Involves the study of similarities and differences among consumers in two or more nations or societies.

Marketers must be sensitive to the cultural underpinnings of different societies if they are to initiate and consummate mutually beneficial exchange relationships with global consumers. A necessary step in this process is **cross-cultural analysis,** which involves the study of similarities and differences among consumers in two or more nations or societies.[19] A thorough cross-cultural analysis involves an understanding of and an appreciation for the values, customs, symbols, and languages of other societies.

Values As defined in Chapter 5, values are personally or socially preferable modes of conduct or states of existence that are enduring. Understanding and working with these aspects of a society's values are important factors in global marketing. For example,

- McDonald's does not sell beef hamburgers in its restaurants in India because the cow is considered sacred by almost 85 percent of the population. Instead,

McDonald's sells the McMaharajah: two all-mutton patties, special sauce, lettuce, cheese, pickles, and onions on a sesame-seed bun.

- Germans have not been overly receptive to the use of credit cards, such as Visa or MasterCard, and installment debt to purchase goods and services. Indeed, the German word *Schuld* is the same for debt as well as for guilt.

These examples illustrate how cultural values can influence behaviour in different societies. Cultural values become apparent in the personal values of individuals that affect their attitudes and beliefs and the importance assigned to specific behaviours and attributes of goods and services. These personal values affect consumption-specific values, such as the use of installment debt by Germans, and product-specific values, such as the importance assigned to credit card interest rates.

customs

Norms and expectations about the way people do things in a specific country.

Customs   **Customs** are the norms and expectations about the way people do things in a specific country. Clearly, customs can vary significantly from country to country. For example, 3M Company executives were perplexed when the company's Scotch-Brite floor-cleaning product initially produced lukewarm sales in the Philippines. When a Filipino employee explained that consumers there customarily clean floors by pushing coconut shells around with their feet, 3M changed the shape of the pad to a foot, and sales soared! Some other customs are unusual to Canadians. Consider, for example, that in France, men use more than twice the number of cosmetics than women do and that Japanese women give Japanese men chocolates on Valentine's Day.

Customs also relate to the nonverbal behaviour of individuals in different cultural settings. For example, in many European countries, it is considered impolite not to have both hands on the table in business meetings. A simple gesture in a commercial, such as pointing a finger, is perfectly acceptable in Western culture, but is perceived as an insult in Middle and Far Eastern countries. Direct eye contact is viewed positively in North and Latin America but negatively in Japan. Casual touching is also inappropriate in Japan, while men hold hands in Middle Eastern countries as a sign of friendship. Business executives in Japan like to hold their opinions, listen longer, and pause before responding in meetings. Sometimes, the silence is misread by North American executives as lack of response.[20]

cultural symbols

Things that represent ideas and concepts.

semiotics

The field of study that examines the correspondence between symbols and their role in the assignment of meaning for people.

Cultural Symbols   **Cultural symbols** are things that represent ideas and concepts. Symbols or symbolism play an important role in cross-cultural analysis because different cultures ascribe different meanings to things. So important is the role of symbols that a field of study, called **semiotics,** has emerged that examines the correspondence between symbols and their role in the assignment of meaning for people. By adroitly using cultural symbols, global marketers can tie positive symbolism to their products and services to enhance their attractiveness to consumers. However, improper use of symbols can spell disaster. A culturally sensitive global marketer will know that[21]

- North Americans are superstitious about the number 13, and Japanese feel the same way about the number 4. *Shi,* the Japanese word for four, is also the word for death. Knowing this, Tiffany & Company sells its fine glassware and china in sets of five, not four, in Japan.
- "Thumbs-up" is a positive sign in Canada. However, in Russia and Poland, this gesture has an offensive meaning when the palm of the hand is shown, as AT&T learned. The company reversed the gesture depicted in ads, showing the back of the hand, not the palm.

Cultural symbols evoke deep feelings. Consider how executives at Coca-Cola Company's Italian office learned this lesson. In a series of advertisements directed at Italian vacationers, the Eiffel Tower, the Empire State Building, and the Tower of Pisa were turned into the familiar Coca-Cola bottle. However, when the white marble columns in the Parthenon that crowns Athens' Acropolis were turned into Coca-Cola bottles, the Greeks were outraged. Greeks refer to the Acropolis as the "holy rock,"

What cultural lesson did Coca-Cola executives learn when they used the Parthenon in a global advertising campaign?

and a government official said the Parthenon is an "international symbol of excellence" and that "whoever insults the Parthenon insults international culture." Coca-Cola apologized for the ad.[22]

Global markets are also sensitive to the fact that the "country of origin or manufacture" of products and services can symbolize superior or poor quality in some countries. For example, Russian consumers believe products made in Japan and Germany are superior in quality to products from North America and the United Kingdom. Japanese consumers believe Japanese products are superior to those made in Europe and North America. However, recently, Canadian firms marketing in Japan have discovered that Japanese like the "Canadian-ness" of products, and so brands and labels that say "Canada" add cachet for Japanese consumers.[23]

Language   Global marketers should know not only the native tongues of countries in which they market their products and services but also the nuances and idioms of a language. Even though about 100 official languages exist in the world, anthropologists estimate that at least 3,000 different languages are spoken. There are 20 official languages spoken in the European Union, and Canada has two official languages (English and French). Seventeen major languages are spoken in India alone.

English, French, and Spanish are the principal languages used in global diplomacy and commerce. However, the best language to communicate with consumers is their own, as any seasoned global marketer will attest to. Unintended meanings of brand names and messages have ranged from the absurd to the obscene:

- When the advertising agency responsible for launching Procter & Gamble's successful Pert shampoo in Canada realized that the name means "lost" in French, it substituted the brand name Pret, which means "ready."
- In Italy, Cadbury Schweppes, the world's third-largest soft drink manufacturer, realized that its Schweppes Tonic Water brand had to be renamed Schweppes Tonica because "il water" turned out to be an idiom for bathroom.

In Canada, all packages and labels must be printed in both English and French, and most major companies also run their ads in both languages. Here are both the English and French versions of a service ad for Hewlett-Packard. The company's Web site is multilingual, too.

Hewlett-Packard
www.hp.com/canada

- The Vicks brand name common in North America is German slang for sexual intimacy; therefore, Vicks is called Wicks in Germany.

back translation
Retranslating a word or phrase into the original language by a different interpreter to catch errors.

Experienced global marketers use **back translation,** where a translated word or phrase is retranslated into the original language by a different interpreter to catch errors. For example, IBM's first Japanese translation of its "Solutions for a small planet" advertising message yielded "Answers that make people smaller." The error was caught and corrected. Nevertheless, unintended translations can produce favourable results. Consider Kit Kat bars marketed by Nestle worldwide. Kit Kat is pronounced "kitto katsu" in Japanese, which roughly translates to "I hope you win." Japanese teens eat Kit Kat bars for good luck, particularly when taking crucial school exams.

The use of language in global marketing is assuming greater importance in an increasingly networked and borderless economic world. For example, Oracle Corporation, a leading worldwide supplier of software, now markets its products by language groups instead of through 145 country-specific efforts. The French group markets to France, Belgium, Switzerland, and Canada. A Spanish-language group oversees Spain and Latin America. Eight other language groups—English, Japanese, Korean, Chinese, Portuguese, Italian, Dutch, and German—cover Oracle's top revenue-producing countries.[24]

Cultural Ethnocentricity   The tendency for people to view their own values, customs, symbols, and language favourably is well known. However, the belief that aspects of one's culture are superior to another's is called *cultural ethnocentricity* and is a sure impediment to successful global marketing.

An outgrowth of cultural ethnocentricity exists in the purchase and use of goods and services produced outside of a country. Global marketers are acutely aware that certain groups within countries disfavour imported products, not on the basis of price, features, or performance, but purely because of their foreign origin. **Consumer ethnocentrism** is the tendency to believe that it is inappropriate, indeed immoral, to purchase foreign-made products.[25] Ethnocentric consumers believe that buying imported products is wrong because such purchases are unpatriotic, harm domestic industries, and cause domestic unemployment.[26]

consumer ethnocentrism
The tendency to believe that it is inappropriate, indeed immoral, to purchase foreign-made products.

Economic Considerations

Global marketing is also affected by economic considerations. Therefore, a scan of the global marketplace should include (1) a comparative analysis of the economic development in different countries, (2) an assessment of the economic infrastructure in these countries, (3) measurement of consumer income in different countries, and (4) recognition of a country's currency exchange rates.

Stage of Economic Development   There are about 200 independent countries in the world today, each of which is at a slightly different point in terms of its stage of economic development. However, they can be classified into two major groupings that will help the global marketer better understand their needs:

- *Developed* countries have somewhat mixed economies. Private enterprise dominates, although they have substantial public sectors as well. Canada, the United States, Japan, and most of Western Europe can be considered developed.
- *Developing* countries are in the process of moving from an agricultural to an industrial economy. There are two subgroups within the developing category: (1) those that have already made the move, and (2) those that remain locked in a preindustrial economy. Such countries as Brazil, China, India, Poland, Hungary, Israel, Venezuela, Singapore, and South Africa fall into the first group. In the second group are Afghanistan, Sri Lanka, Tanzania, and Chad, where living standards are low and improvement will be slow.

bottom of the pyramid
The largest, but poorest socio-economic group of people in the world consisting of 4 billion people who reside in developing countries and live on less than $2 per day.

About 86 percent of the world's population of roughly 7 billion people reside in developing countries and have only one-fifth of the total world income. Four billion of these people live on less than $2 per day. In global marketing terms, they are viewed as being at the **bottom of the pyramid,** which is the largest, but poorest socioeconomic group of people in the world.[27]

Today, global companies are choosing to serve people at the bottom of the pyramid by being responsive to their conditions and needs. Motorola is an example. The company developed a low-cost cellphone with battery life as long as 500 hours for rural villagers without regular electricity and an extra-loud volume for use in noisy markets. Motorola's cellphone, a no-frills design is priced at $40, has standby time of two weeks, and conforms to local language and customs. Motorola has been successfully selling this cellphone design in rural areas across China, India, and Turkey. Still, the task facing global marketers is not easy. A country's stage of economic development affects and is affected by other economic factors, as described next.

Economic Infrastructure   The *economic infrastructure*—a country's communications, transportation, financial, and distribution systems—is a critical consideration in determining whether to try to market to a country's consumers and organizations. Parts of the infrastructure that North Americans or Western Europeans take for granted can be huge problems elsewhere—not only in the developing nations but also in Eastern Europe, the Indian subcontinent, and China, where such an infrastructure is assumed to be in place. Consider, for instance, the transportation and distribution systems in these countries. Two-lane roads that limit average speeds to 55 or 65 kilometres per hour are commonplace—and a nightmare for firms requiring prompt truck delivery. In China, the bicycle is the preferred mode of transportation. This is understandable because China has few navigable roads outside its major cities, where 80 percent of the population lives. In India, Coca-Cola uses large tricycles to distribute cases of Coke along narrow streets in many cities. Wholesale and retail institutions tend to be small and are operated by new owner-managers still learning the ways of a free market system.

The communication infrastructures in these countries also differ. This infrastructure includes telecommunications systems and networks in use, such as Internet, telephones, cable television, broadcast radio and television, computers, satellites, and wireless telephones. In general, the communication infrastructure in many developing countries is limited or antiquated compared with that of the developed countries.

Even the financial and legal systems can cause problems. Formal operating procedures among financial institutions and private properties did not exist under communism and are still limited. As a consequence, it is estimated that two-thirds of the commercial transactions in Russia involve nonmonetary forms of payment. The legal red tape involved in obtaining title to buildings and land for manufacturing, wholesaling, and retailing operations also has been a huge problem. Nevertheless, the Coca-Cola Company invested $750 million from 1991 through 1998 to build bottling and distribution facilities in Russia, Allied Lyons spent $30 million to build a plant to make Baskin-Robbins ice cream, and Mars opened a $200 million candy factory outside Moscow.[28]

Consumer Income and Purchasing Power   A global marketer selling consumer goods must also consider what the average per-capita or household income is among a country's consumers and how the income is distributed to determine a nation's purchasing power. Per-capita income varies greatly between nations. Average yearly per-capita income in EU countries is more than $30,000 and is less than $300 in some developing countries, such as Vietnam. A country's income distribution is important because it gives a more reliable picture of a country's purchasing power. Generally speaking, as the proportion of middle-income-class households in a country increases, the greater a nation's purchasing power tends to be. Figure 7–5 shows the worldwide disparity in the percentage distribution of households by level of purchasing power.

The Coca-Cola Company has made a huge financial investment in bottling and distribution facilities in Russia.

The Coca-Cola Company
www.thecoca-colacompany.com

In established market economies, such as those in North America and Western Europe, 65 percent of households have an annual purchasing capability of $20,000 or more. In comparison, 75 percent of households in the developing countries of South Asia have an annual purchasing power of less than $5,000.[29]

Seasoned global marketers recognize that people in the developing countries often have government subsidies for food, housing, and health care that supplement their income. Accordingly, people with seemingly low incomes are potentially promising

● **FIGURE 7–5**

How purchasing power differs around the world

Percentage Distribution of Households by Annual Purchasing Power Level

Less than $5,000 $5,000 to $9,999

$10,000 to $19,999 $20,000 and above

	Less than $5,000	$5,000 to $9,999	$10,000 to $19,999	$20,000 and above
South Asia	75%	21%	4%	1%
Sub-Saharan Africa	75%	16%	7%	2%
East Asia/Pacific	73%	17%	7%	4%
Former socialist economies	21%	32%	30%	17%
Middle Eastern crescent	22%	32%	28%	18%
Latin America	24%	23%	26%	27%
Established market economies	8%	3% 24%		65%

0%   20%   40%   60%   80%   100%

Note: Consumption is in U.S. dollars on a purchase-power-parity basis. Percentages may add to more than 100 percent due to rounding.

customers for a variety of products. For example, a consumer in South Asia earning the equivalent of $250 per year can afford Gillette razors. When that consumer's income rises to $1,000, a Sony television becomes affordable, and a new Volkswagen or Nissan can be bought with an annual income of $10,000. In the developing countries of Eastern Europe, a $1,000 annual income makes a refrigerator affordable, and $2,000 brings an automatic washer within reach.

microfinance
The practice of offering small, collateral-free loans to individuals who otherwise would not have access to the capital necessary to begin small businesses or other income-generating activities.

Efforts to raise household incomes in developing countries are evident in the growing popularity of microfinance. **Microfinance** is the practice of offering small, collateral-free loans to individuals who otherwise would not have access to the capital necessary to begin small businesses or other income-generating activities. An example of microfinance is found in Hindustan Lever's initiative in India. The company realized it could not sell to the rural poor in India unless it found ways to distribute its products such as soap, shampoos, and laundry detergents. Lever provided startup loans to women to buy stocks of products to sell to local villagers. Today, thousands of women entrepreneurs sell Lever products in 100,000 villages in India and account for about 15 percent of the company's rural sales in that country. Equally important, these women now have a source of income, whereas before they had nothing.[30]

Income growth in the developing countries of Asia, Latin America, and Eastern Europe is expected to stimulate world trade well into the twenty-first century. The number of consumers in these countries earning the equivalent of $10,000 per year is expected to surpass the number of consumers in North America, Japan, and Western Europe combined by 2015.

Currency Exchange Rates   Fluctuations in exchange rates among the world's currencies are of critical importance in global marketing. Such fluctuations affect everyone—from international tourists to global companies.

currency exchange rate
The price of one country's currency expressed in terms of another country's currency.

A **currency exchange rate** is the price of one country's currency expressed in terms of another country's currency, such as the Canadian dollar expressed in Japanese yen or Swiss francs. Failure to consider exchange rates when pricing products for global markets can have dire consequences.

Exchange-rate fluctuations have a direct impact on the sales and profits made by global companies. When foreign currencies can buy more Canadian dollars, for example, Canadian products are less expensive for foreign customers. Short-term fluctuations, however, can have a significant effect on the profits of global companies. Hewlett-Packard gained nearly a half million dollars of additional profit through exchange rate fluctuation in one year. On the other hand, Honda lost over $400 million on its European operations due to currency swings in the Japanese yen compared with the euro and the British pound. Severe and protracted fluctuations in a country's currency can affect trade as well. For example, Procter & Gamble briefly suspended product shipments to Turkey, one of its largest export markets, because of instability of the Turkish currency.

Political-Regulatory Climate

The political and regulatory climate for marketing in a country or region of the world lies not only in identifying the current climate but also in determining how long a favourable or unfavourable climate will last. An assessment of a country or regional political-regulatory climate includes an analysis of its political stability and trade regulations.

Political Stability   Trade among nations or regions depends on political stability. Billions of dollars have been lost in the Middle East and Africa as a result of internal political strife and war. Such losses encourage careful selection of politically stable countries and regions of the world for trade.

Political stability in a country is affected by numerous factors, including a government's orientation toward foreign companies and trade with other countries. These factors combine to create a political climate that is favourable or unfavourable for marketing and financial investment in a country or region of the world. Marketing managers monitor political stability using a variety of measures and often track country risk ratings supplied by such agencies as the PRS Group. Visit the PRS Group Web site shown in the accompanying Going Online box, "Checking a Country's Political Risk Rating," to see the most recent political risk ratings for countries.

Trade Regulations   Countries have a variety of rules that govern business practices within their borders. These rules often serve as trade barriers.[31] For example, Japan has some 11,000 trade regulations. Japanese car safety rules effectively require all automobile replacement parts to be Japanese and not North American or European; public health rules make it illegal to sell aspirin or cold medicine without a pharmacist present. The Malaysian government has advertising regulations stating that "advertisements must not project or promote an excessively aspirational lifestyle," Greece bans toy advertising, and Sweden outlaws all advertisements to children. Until recently, the EU banned Canadian icewine from its markets because the icewine's alcohol content was beyond accepted levels.

Trade regulations also appear in free trade agreements among countries. European Union nations abide by some 10,000 rules that specify how goods are to be made and marketed. For instance, the rules for a washing machine's electrical system are detailed on more than 100 typed pages. There are also regulations related to contacting consumers via telephone, fax, and e-mail without their prior consent. The European Union's ISO 9000 quality standards, though not a trade regulation, have the same effect on business practice. These standards, described in Chapter 6, involve registration and certification of a manufacturer's quality management and quality assurance system. Many European companies require suppliers to be ISO 9000 certified as a condition of doing business with them. Certified companies have undergone an on-site audit that includes an inspection of its facilities to ensure that documented quality control procedures are in place and that all employees understand and follow them.

---

learning review

6. Semiotics involves the study of _____.

7. When foreign currencies can buy more U.S. dollars, are American products more or less expensive for a foreign consumer?

Going Online

Checking a Country's Political Risk Rating

The political climate in every country is regularly changing. Governments can make new laws or enforce existing policies differently. Numerous consulting firms prepare political risk analyses that incorporate a variety of variables, such as the risk of internal turmoil, external conflict, government restrictions on company operations, and tariff and nontariff trade barriers.

The PRS Group maintains multiple databases of country-specific information and projections, including country political risk ratings. These ratings can be accessed at **www.prsgroup.com**. Click "Intl. Country Risk Guide," and then click "Table 1: Country Risk, Ranked by Composite Rating" (you will need to give your name and e-mail

address to obtain the table). Which three countries have the highest rating (lowest risk), and which three have the lowest rating (highest risk)? Which countries have risk ratings closest to Canada?

LO4 COMPARING GLOBAL MARKET ENTRY STRATEGIES

Once a company has decided to enter the global marketplace, it must select a means of market entry. Four general options exist: (1) exporting, (2) licensing, (3) joint venture, and (4) direct investment.[32] As Figure 7–6 demonstrates, the amount of financial commitment, risk, marketing control, and profit potential increases as the firm moves from exporting to direct investment.

Exporting

exporting

Producing goods in one country and selling them in another country.

Exporting is producing goods in one country and selling them in another country. This entry option allows a company to make the least number of changes in terms of its product, its organization, and even its corporate goals. Host countries usually do not like this practice because it provides less local employment than under alternative means of entry.

Indirect exporting is when a firm sells its domestically produced goods in a foreign country through an intermediary. It involves the least amount of commitment and risk but will probably return the least profit. This kind of exporting is ideal for the company that has no overseas contacts but wants to market abroad. The intermediary is often a distributor that has the marketing know-how and the resources necessary for the effort to succeed.

Direct exporting occurs when a firm sells its domestically produced goods in a foreign country without intermediaries. Most companies become involved in direct exporting when they believe their volume of sales will be sufficiently large and easy to obtain that they do not require intermediaries. For example, the exporter may be approached by foreign buyers that are willing to contract for a large volume of purchases. Direct exporting involves more risk than indirect exporting for the company but also opens the door to increased profits.

● **FIGURE 7–6**

Alternative global market entry strategies

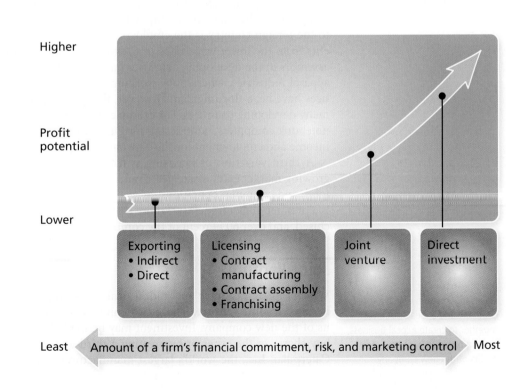

McDonald's uses franchising as a market-entry strategy, and more than 60 percent of the company's sales came from foreign operations

McDonald's
www.mcdonalds.com

licensing
Offering the right to a trademark, patent, trade secret, or other similarly valued items of intellectual property in return for a royalty or a fee.

joint venture
An arrangement in which a foreign company and a local firm invest together to create a local business, sharing ownership, control, and profits of the new company.

Novartis Consumer Health Canada markets its cough remedy product, Buckley Mixture, using an indirect exporting strategy in the Australian market and a direct exporting strategy for the United States market. Reif Estate Winery in Niagara-on-the-Lake and Andrés Wines of Grimsby, Ontario, both engage in exporting their Canadian wines to the European Union as well as other foreign markets, where sales have grown significantly.

Licensing

Under **licensing,** a company offers the right to a trademark, patent, trade secret, or other similarly valued items of intellectual property in return for a royalty or a fee. In international marketing, the advantages to the company granting the licence are low risk and a capital-free entry into a foreign country. The licensee gains information that allows it to start with a competitive advantage, and the foreign country gains employment by having the product manufactured locally.

There are some serious drawbacks to this mode of entry, however. The licensor forgoes control of its product and reduces the potential profits gained from it. In addition, while the relationship lasts, the licensor may be creating its own competition. Some licensees are able to modify the product somehow and enter the market with product and marketing knowledge gained at the expense of the company that got them started. To offset this disadvantage, many companies strive to stay innovative so that the licensee remains dependent on them for improvements and successful operation. Finally, should the licensee prove to be a poor choice, the name or reputation of the company may be harmed.

Two variations of licensing, *contract manufacturing* and *contract assembly,* represent alternative ways to produce a product within the foreign country. With contract manufacturing, a Canadian company may contract with a foreign firm to manufacture products according to stated specifications. The product is then sold in the foreign country or exported back to Canada. With contract assembly, the Canadian company may contract with a foreign firm to assemble (not manufacture) parts and components that have been shipped to that country. In both cases, the advantage to the foreign country is the employment of its people, and the Canadian firm benefits from the lower wage rates in the foreign country. Contract manufacturing and assembly in the developing countries had sparked controversy in the toy, textile, and apparel industries, where poor working conditions, low pay, and child labour practices have been documented. However, this practice has been an economic boon to many developing countries. For example, Taiwan makes more than half of the world's notebook computers, contracting for Dell and IBM, and this has generated personal income and employment for the Taiwanese people.

A third variation of licensing is *franchising.* Franchising is one of the fastest-growing market entry strategies. Franchises include soft-drink, motel, retailing, fast-food, and car rental operations, as well as a variety of business services. McDonald's is a premier global franchiser: more than 70 percent of the company's stores are franchised, and over 60 percent of the company's sales come from foreign operations.[33]

Joint Venture

When a foreign country and a local firm invest together to create a local business, it is called a **joint venture.** These two companies share ownership, control, and profits of the new company. Investment may be made by having either of the companies buy shares in the other or by creating a third and separate entity. This was done by Caterpillar, Inc., the world's largest manufacturer of earth-moving and construction equipment when it created NEVAMASH with its joint-venture partner, Kirovsky Zvod, a large Russian manufacturer of heavy equipment.

The advantages of this option are twofold. First, one company may not have the necessary financial, physical, or managerial resources to enter a foreign market alone. Ford and Volkswagen formed a joint venture to make four-wheel-drive vehicles in Portugal. Second, a government may require or strongly encourage a joint venture before it allows a foreign company to enter its market. This is the case in China. Today, more than 50,000 Chinese–foreign joint ventures operate in China.[34]

The disadvantages arise when the two companies disagree about policies or courses of action for their joint venture or when governmental bureaucracy bogs down the effort. For example, Canadian firms often prefer to reinvest earnings gained, whereas some foreign companies may want to spend those earnings. Or a Canadian firm may want to return profits earned to Canada, while the local firm or its government may oppose this—the problem now faced by many potential joint ventures in Eastern Europe, Russia, Latin America, and South Asia.

Direct Investment

direct investment

A domestic firm actually investing in and owning a foreign subsidiary or division.

The biggest commitment a company can make when entering the global market is **direct investment,** which entails a domestic firm actually investing in and owning a foreign subsidiary or division. Examples of direct investment are Toyota's automobile plant in Ontario and Hyundai's plant in Quebec. Many Canadian-based companies are also switching to this mode of entry. Alcan Aluminium built a recycling plant in Worrington, England, and Ganong Brothers owns a plant that manufactures chocolates in Thailand. And New Brunswick–based McCain Foods, a global leader in the frozen-food industry has 55 production facilities on six continents. It is the world's largest processor of frozen french fries, producing, in fact, one-third of all frozen french fries in the world.

For many firms, direct investment often follows one of the other three market entry strategies. For example, Ernst & Young, an international accounting and management consulting firm, entered Hungary first by establishing a joint venture with a local company. Ernst & Young later acquired the company, making it a subsidiary with headquarters in Budapest. Following the success of its European and Asian exporting strategy, Harley-Davidson now operates wholly owned subsidiaries in Germany, Italy, and Japan.

The advantages to direct investment include cost savings, better understanding of local market conditions, and fewer local restrictions. Firms entering foreign markets using direct investment believe that these advantages outweigh the financial commitments and risks involved.

---

learning review

8. What mode of entry could a company follow if it has no previous experience in global marketing?

9. How does licensing differ from a joint venture?

 LO5 CRAFTING A WORLDWIDE MARKETING PROGRAM

The choice of a market entry strategy is a necessary first step for a marketer when joining the community of global companies. The next step involves the challenging task of designing, implementing, and controlling marketing programs worldwide.

Successful global marketers standardize global marketing programs whenever possible and customize them wherever necessary. The extent of standardization and customization is often rooted in a careful global environment scan supplemented with judgment based on experience and marketing research.

Product and Promotion Strategies

Global companies have five strategies for matching products and their promotion efforts to global markets. As Figure 7–7 shows, the strategies focus on whether a company extends or adapts its product and promotion message for consumers in different countries and cultures.

A product may be sold globally in one of three ways: (1) in the same form as in its home market, (2) with some adaptations, or (3) as a totally new product:[35]

1. *Product extension.* Selling virtually the same product in other countries is a product extension strategy. It works well for such products as Coca-Cola, McCain frozen french fries, Gillette razors, Wrigley's gum, Levi's jeans, Sony consumer electronics, Harley-Davidson motorcycles, and Nokia cellphones. As a general rule, product extension seems to work best when the consumer market target for the product is alike across countries and cultures—that is, consumers share the same desires, needs, and uses for the product.

2. *Product adaptation.* Changing a product in some way to make it more appropriate for a country's climate or consumer preferences is a product adaptation strategy. Gerber baby food comes in different varieties in different countries. Vegetable and Rabbit Meat is a favourite in Poland. Freeze-Dried Sardines and Rice is popular in Japan. Maybelline's makeup is formulaically adapted in labs to suit local skin types and weather across the globe, including an Asia-specific mascara that does not run during the rainy season.

3. *Product invention.* Alternatively, companies can invent totally new products designed to satisfy common needs across countries. Black & Decker did this with its Snake Light Flexible Flashlight. Created to address a global need for portable lighting, the product became a bestseller in North America, Europe, Latin America, and Australia, and is the most successful new product developed by Black & Decker. Similarly, Whirlpool developed a compact, automatic clothes washer specifically for households in the developing countries with annual household incomes of $2,000. Called Ideale, the washer features bright colours because washers are often placed in a home's living areas, not hidden in

● **FIGURE 7-7**

Five product and promotion strategies for global marketing

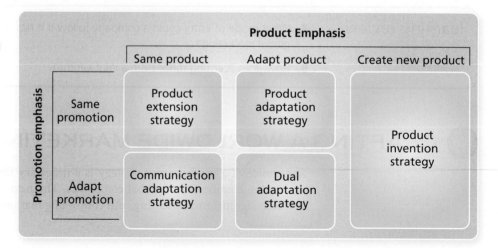

laundry rooms (which do not exist in many homes in the developing countries). Demand for this product exceeded forecasts when it was introduced in Brazil, China, and India.

An identical promotion message is used for the product extension and product adaptation strategies around the world. Gillette uses the same global message for its men's toiletries: "Gillette, the Best a Man Can Get."

Global companies may also adapt their promotion message. For instance, the same product may be sold in many countries but advertised differently. As an example, L'Oréal, a French health and beauty products marketer, introduced its Golden Beauty brand of sun-care products through its Helena Rubenstein subsidiary in Western Europe with a communication adaptation strategy. Recognizing the cultural and buying motive differences related to skin care and tanning, Golden Beauty advertising features dark tanning for northern Europeans, skin protection to avoid wrinkles among Latin Europeans, and beautiful skin for Europeans living along the Mediterranean Sea, even though the products are the same.

Other companies use a dual adaptation strategy by modifying both their products and promotion messages. Nestlé does this with Nescafé coffee. Nescafé is marketed using different coffee blends and promotional campaigns to match consumer preferences in different countries. For example, Nescafé, the world's largest brand of coffee, generally emphasizes the taste, aroma, and warmth of shared moments in its advertising around the world. However, Nescafé is advertised in Thailand as a way to relax from the pressures of daily life.

These examples illustrate the simple rule applied by global companies: Standardize product and promotion strategies whenever possible and customize them wherever necessary. This is the art of global marketing.[36]

Distribution Strategy

Distribution is of critical importance in global marketing. The availability and quality of retailers and wholesalers, as well as transportation, communication, and warehousing facilities, are often determined by a country's stage of economic development. Figure 7–8 outlines the channel through which a product manufactured in one country must travel to reach its destination in another country. The first step involves the seller; its headquarters is the starting point and is responsible for the successful distribution to the ultimate consumer.

The next step is the channel between two nations, moving the product from one country to another. Intermediaries that can handle this responsibility include resident buyers in a foreign country, independent merchant wholesalers who buy and sell the product, or agents who bring buyers and sellers together.

Once the product is in the foreign nation, that country's distribution channels take over.[37] These channels can be very long or surprisingly short depending on the product line. In Japan, fresh fish go through three intermediaries before getting to a retail outlet. Conversely, shoes go through only one intermediary. In other cases, the channel does not even involve the host country. Procter & Gamble sells its soap door to door in the Philippines because there are no other alternatives in many parts of

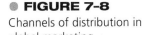

● FIGURE 7-8

Channels of distribution in global marketing

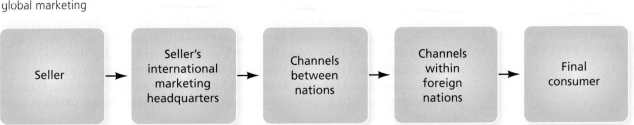

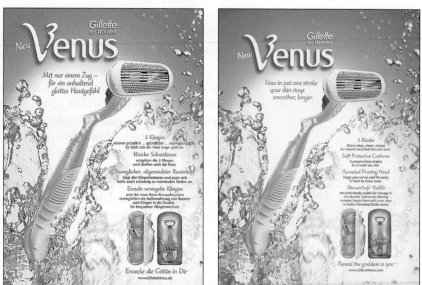

Gillette delivers the same global message whenever possible, as shown in the Gillette for Women Venus ads from Greece, Germany, and Canada.

The Gillette Company
www.gillette.com

dumping
Occurs when a firm sells a product in a foreign country below its domestic price or below its actual cost.

grey market
A situation where products are sold through unauthorized channels of distribution.

that country. The sophistication of a country's distribution channels increase as its economic infrastructure develops. Supermarkets facilitate selling products in many nations, but they are not popular or available in many others where culture and lack of refrigeration dictate shopping on a daily rather than a weekly basis. For example, when Coke and Pepsi entered China, both had to create direct-distribution channels, investing in refrigerator units for small retailers.

Pricing Strategy

Global companies also face many challenges in determining a pricing strategy as part of their worldwide marketing effort. Individual countries, even those with free trade agreements, may impose considerable competitive, political, and legal constraints on the pricing latitude of global companies. For example, antitrust authorities in Germany limited Walmart from selling some items below cost to lure shoppers. Without this practice, Walmart was unable to compete against German discount stores. This, and other factors, led Walmart to leave Germany.[38] Of course, economic factors, such as the costs of production, selling, and tariffs, plus transportation and storage costs, also affect global pricing decisions.

Pricing too low or too high can have dire consequences. When prices appear too low in one country, companies can be charged with dumping, a practice subject to severe penalties and fines. **Dumping** is when a firm sells a product in a foreign country below its domestic price or below its actual cost. This is often done to build a company's share of the market by pricing at a competitive level. Another reason is that the products being sold may be surplus or cannot be sold domestically and, therefore, are already a burden to the company. The firm may be glad to sell them at almost any price.

When companies price their products very high in some countries but competitively in others, they face a grey-market problem. A **grey market,** also called *parallel importing,* is a situation where products are sold through unauthorized channels of distribution. A grey market comes about when individuals buy products in a lower-priced country from a manufacturer's authorized retailer, ship them to higher-priced countries, and then sell them below the manufacturer's suggested retail price through unauthorized retailers. Many well-known products have been sold through grey markets, including Olympus cameras, Seiko watches, Chanel perfume, and Mercedes-Benz cars.

> **learning review**
>
> **10.** Products may be sold globally in three ways. What are they?
>
> **11.** What is dumping?

LEARNING OBJECTIVES REVIEW

LO1 **Describe the scope and nature of world trade from a global perspective and its implications for Canada.**

A global perspective on world trade views exports and imports as complementary economic flows: A country's imports affect its exports, and exports affect its imports. World trade flowing to and from Canada reflects demand and supply interdependencies for goods among nations and industries. Canada is a trading nation and currently maintains a surplus in its balance of trade. The largest importers of Canadian goods and services are the United States, Japan, and the EU.

LO2 **Identify the major trends that have influenced the landscape of global marketing in the past decade.**

Four major trends have influenced the landscape of global marketing. First, there has been a gradual decline of economic protectionism by individual countries, leading to a reduction in tariffs and quotas. Second, there is growing economic integration and free trade among nations, reflected in the creation of the European Union and the North American Free Trade Agreement. Third, there is increased global competition among global companies for global consumers, resulting in firms adopting global marketing strategies and promoting global brands. And finally, a networked global marketspace has emerged using Internet technology as a tool for exchanging goods, services, and information on a global scale.

LO3 **Identify the environmental factors that shape global marketing efforts.**

Three major environmental factors shape global marketing efforts. First, there are cultural factors, including values, customs, cultural symbols, and language. Economic factors also shape global marketing efforts. These include a country's stage of economic development and economic infrastructure, consumer income and purchasing power, and currency exchange rates. Finally, political-regulatory factors in a country or region of the world create a favourable or unfavourable climate for global marketing efforts.

LO4 **Name and describe the alternative approaches companies use to enter global markets.**

Companies have four alternative approaches for entering global markets. These are exporting, licensing, joint venture, and direct investment. Exporting involves producing goods in one country and selling them in another country. Under licensing, a company offers the right to a trademark, patent, trade secret, or similarly valued items of intellectual property in return for a royalty or fee. In a joint venture, a foreign company and a local firm invest together to create a local business. Direct investment entails a domestic firm actually investing in and owning a foreign subsidiary or division.

LO5 **Explain the distinction between standardization and customization when companies craft worldwide marketing programs.**

Companies distinguish between standardization and customization when crafting worldwide marketing programs. Standardization means that all elements of the marketing program are the same across countries and cultures. Customization means that one or more elements of the marketing program are adapted to meet the needs or preferences of consumers in a particular country or culture. Global marketers apply a simple rule when crafting worldwide marketing programs: standardize marketing programs whenever possible and customize them wherever necessary.

FOCUSING ON KEY TERMS

back translation p. 184
balance of trade p. 171
bottom of the pyramid p. 185
consumer ethnocentrism p. 184
countertrade p. 170
cross-cultural analysis p. 181
cultural symbols p. 182
currency exchange rate p. 187
customs p. 182
direct investment p. 191
dumping p. 194

exporting p. 189
global brand p. 180
global competition p. 178
global consumers p. 180
global marketing strategy p. 179
grey market p. 194
gross domestic product (GDP) p. 171
joint venture p. 190
licensing p. 190
microfinance p. 187
multidomestic marketing strategy p. 179

APPLYING MARKETING KNOWLEDGE

1 What is meant by this statement: "Quotas are a hidden tax on consumers, whereas tariffs are a more obvious one"?

2 Is the trade feedback effect described in the text a long-run or short-run view on world trade flows? Explain your answer.

3 Because English is the official language in Australia, some Canadian global companies might select it as an easy market to enter. Others believe that this similarity in language could make it harder to enter that market successfully. Who is right? Why?

4 How successful would a television commercial in Japan be if it featured a husband surprising his wife in her dressing area

on Valentine's Day with a small box of chocolates containing four candies? Why?

5 As a novice in global marketing, which alternative for global market entry strategy would you be likely to start with? Why? What other alternatives do you have for a global market entry?

6 Coca-Cola is sold worldwide. In some countries, Coca-Cola owns the bottling facilities; in others, it has signed contracts with licensees or relies on joint ventures. When selecting a licensee in each country, what factors should Coca-Cola consider?

Building Your Marketing Plan

Does your marketing plan involve reaching global customers outside of Canada? If the answer is no, read no further and do not include a global element in your plan. If the answer is yes, try to identify the following:

1. What features of your product are especially important to potential customers.

2. In which countries these potential customers live.

3. Special marketing issues that are involved in trying to reach them.

Answers to these questions will help in developing more detailed marketing mix strategies described in later chapters.

Video Case 7

CNS BREATHE RIGHT® STRIPS: GOING GLOBAL

"It's naive to treat 'international' as one big market—particularly within OTC," explains Marti Morfitt, president and CEO of CNS, the company that manufactures Breathe Right® nasal strips. "There are many discrete, unique markets, and local expertise is needed to understand the dynamics within each and address them effectively."

"OTC" refers to over-the-counter medical products, such as aspirin or cough syrup, that customers can buy without a doctor's prescription. Breathe Right nasal strips qualify as an OTC product. But that does not mean there is not a lot of technology and medical science behind it.

Breathe Right nasal strips are innovative adhesive strips with patented dual flex bars inside. When attached to the nose, they gently lift and hold open nasal passages, making it easier to breathe. Breathe Right strips are used for a variety of reasons, all to help breathe better through

the nose: athletes hoping to play their best (particularly when wearing mouth guards); snorers (and their spouses hoping for a quiet night's sleep); and allergy, sinusitis, and cold sufferers looking for drug-free relief from nasal congestion.

How It All Began

Breathe Right strips were invented by Bruce Johnson, a chronic nasal congestion sufferer. At times, Johnson put straws or paper clips in his nose at night to keep his nasal passages open. He eventually came up with a prototype for Breathe Right strips. He brought his invention to CNS, Inc., which recognized its market potential.

CNS took the strips to the U.S. Food and Drug Administration for approval of claims for relief of snoring and nasal congestion. CNS, a small company, had a limited marketing budget. However, it got a big public relations break when Jerry Rice, the wide receiver for the National Football League's San Francisco 49ers, wore a Breathe Right strip on national TV and scored two touchdowns during the 49ers' 1995 Super Bowl victory. Demand for the strips soared.

"What really helped sales of Breathe Right strips was that CNS had done a very effective job of getting press kits in the hands of news and sports media," says Morfitt. "When people on television asked, 'What is that funny looking thing on his nose?' the reporters could talk about how the strip was an effective consumer product for everyone. And a $1.4 million business turned into a $45 million business in just one year," she explains.

The Decision To Go Global

As awareness and trial were building domestically, CNS began to get inquiries from people in other countries asking where they could buy these strips. In 1995, CNS decided to take advantage of the global interest and introduce Breathe Right strips internationally.

What countries did CNS choose to enter with its Breathe Right strips? "Countries we focus on are those with a large OTC market, high per-capita spending in the OTC market, and future prospects for growth," says Kevin McKenna, vice-president for international at CNS. All these factors relate to market size. "But the real key to success in a market is a local partner that is entrepreneurial and has an ability to execute in terms of achieving distribution and sales."

Importance of Local Partners

Dynamic world market changes in the last 30 years have influenced opportunities for global sales of Breathe Right strips. Key trends include increased availability of OTC products formerly available only by prescription and a global push toward self-care, spurred by the increasing cost of health and medical care. Additionally, OTC products have extended beyond the traditional boundary of the pharmacy and into grocery and other channels; and the role of the pharmacist has expanded from that of medical professional to one that includes selling and marketing OTC products to consumers.

At the same time, changes were taking place within CNS. When Morfitt joined CNS in 1998, she began pulling together a new management group with extensive experience in marketing consumer packaged goods, including globally. CNS began seeking "hungry" international partners who would bring greater localized market expertise and direct-selling capabilities than past partners. Morfitt also wanted partners with demonstrated entrepreneurial spirit to match that of the new management team.

The company's partner in Italy, BluFarm Group, uses its local knowledge and direct selling skills to partner with pharmacists to teach them how to increase sales of Breathe Right strips in their stores. In Italy, as throughout

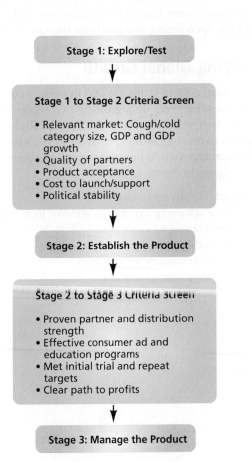

Stage 1: Explore/Test

Stage 1 to Stage 2 Criteria Screen

- Relevant market: Cough/cold category size, GDP and GDP growth
- Quality of partners
- Product acceptance
- Cost to launch/support
- Political stability

Stage 2: Establish the Product

Stage 2 to Stage 3 Criteria Screen

- Proven partner and distribution strength
- Effective consumer ad and education programs
- Met initial trial and repeat targets
- Clear path to profits

Stage 3: Manage the Product

much of Europe, OTC products, such as antacids, aspirin, and nasal strips, are typically placed behind pharmacy counters and therefore not visible to customers. The only way to sell a product is for a customer to ask for it by name. BluFarm Group recognized the importance of in-store advertising and sales execution to build awareness and created point-of-sale materials, such as window and counter displays (see photo) to let customers know that Breathe Right strips were available in the store. "BluFarm's ability to capture consumers' awareness of Breathe Right strips as they walk in the retailer's door has beneficial results for CNS, BluFarm, pharmacists, and consumers," says McKenna.

"Working with an experienced local partner helps overcome surprises in global markets," says Nick Naumann, senior marketing communications manager at CNS. One surprise: universal product codes (UPCs) on packaging are not "universal"—they are used only in the United States and Canada. "Different forms of those codes in other countries can take a few weeks to six months or more of government review to obtain," he says.

Even the same packaging colours do not work around the globe. Research with domestic consumers revealed that they wanted darker packaging to suggest the strips' use at night by snorers and those with stuffed noses. "'Too grim and negative' Asian and European consumers told us," says Naumann. Breathe Right strips in those countries have a lighter, airier look than the domestic packages, to convey the open feeling one gets from the nasal strips.

Managing Global Growth

Today, Breathe Right strips are sold in over 25 countries, and global sales make up a growing percentage of CNS business each year. To ensure the Breathe Right brand continues to meet growth expectations, CNS now uses a three-stage approach to penetrate and develop new markets, as shown in Figure 1:

- Stage 1: Explore/test the concept
  — Use screening criteria to identify high-potential markets
  — Identify potential partners
  — Validate concept with research
  — Develop strategy and launch test market

- Stage 2: Establish the product
  — Penetrate the marketplace
  — Refine messages for local market
  — Evaluate partnership and marketing strategies
- Stage 3: Manage the product
  — Achieve sustainability/profitability
  — Exploit new product and new use opportunities

Overall, this approach starts with what works domestically and extends it into new markets, paying close attention to local needs and customs. Throughout the three stages, CNS conducts market research and makes financial projections.

As shown in the figure, at each stage of the market development process, performance must be met for the product to enter the next stage. Once success with Breathe Right nasal strips is established in a country, the groundwork is laid and international partners have the ability to introduce other Breathe Right products, such as Snore Relief™ Throat Spray and Vapor Shot™ personal vaporizer.

Looking Forward

"We believe the Breathe Right brand has great potential, both domestically and around the world," says Morfitt. "Growth will come both from further expansion of Breathe Right nasal strips and from other drug-free, better-breathing line extensions," says Morfitt.

Questions

1 What are the advantages and disadvantages for CNS taking Breathe Right strips into international markets?
2 What are the advantages to CNS of (*a*) using its three-stage process to enter new global markets, and (*b*) having specific criteria to move through the stages?
3 Using the CNS criteria, with what you know, which countries should have highest priority for CNS?
4 Which single segment of potential Breathe Right strip users would you target to enter new markets?
5 Which marketing mix variables should CNS emphasize the most to succeed in a global arena? Why?

chapter 8

Marketing Research: From Information to Action

THE FUTURE OF MARKETING RESEARCH: RESEARCH 3.0

Simon Chadwick, CEO of Peanut Labs, suggests that the way we think of and use marketing research in the future will be much different than today. Chadwick suggests that the new marketing research model of the future, what he terms "Research 3.0," will have a molecular structure with primary research in the centre and a surrounding collection of other types of data gathering or sources of data, including ethnography, secondary research, Web-based listening posts like social media, Web and customer relationship management analytics, knowledge mining, and data mining. With Research 3.0, marketing research transitions from being merely about conducting "a survey" toward a broader, holistic approach in which a marketing research project is not about a single survey. Instead it will encompass a number of different methods and sources and will have an emphasis that goes beyond simple data collection to robust data synthesis.

He suggests that with Research 3.0 we will make the jump from a type of interrogation (we ask, you answer) to being more of having a dialogue with consumers. In essence, it will involve much more watching and listening. With Research 3.0, marketing research will stretch to capture insight from the countless forums through which consumers can express themselves, from the product reviews they post online to their tweets, blog postings, and chat discussions. With so much information available from so many types of sources, future marketing researchers will have to become "integrators

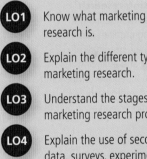

learning objectives

After reading this chapter, you should be able to:

LO1 Know what marketing research is.

LO2 Explain the different types of marketing research.

LO3 Understand the stages in the marketing research process.

LO4 Explain the use of secondary data, surveys, experiments, and observation in marketing research.

LO5 Explain how a marketing information system can trigger marketing actions.

of information." They will have to mine for insights and then become proficient storytellers to communicate those insights.

Chadwick also suggests that Research 3.0 will rely on more novel approaches such as ethnography, social networks and other Web-based communities and panels, trend experts, buzz networks, blog mining, and neurolinguistics. "Virtual venues" for conducting research will also be commonplace. Online technologies will facilitate a variety of interaction not generally possible in traditional settings, and this will lead to a more robust research experience, and richer data. In the Research 3.0 world more emphasis will be placed on the use of online focus groups and one-on-ones, online tracking studies, more qualitative research to gain deeper consumer insights, and then combining of qualitative and quantitative approaches to yield valid and reliable results. Finally, this new Research 3.0 will require new talent beyond statisticians and methodologists, such as renaissance men and women, video gamers, writers, and data miners. Research 3.0 will embrace a type of marketing research that is more relevant to businesses, shed new light on challenging marketing problems, and be a fun domain in which to work.[1] This chapter examines the concept of marketing research and its link to successful marketing decision making.

LO1 WHAT IS MARKETING RESEARCH?

marketing research
The process of defining a marketing problem and opportunity, systematically collecting and analyzing information, and recommending actions to improve an organization's marketing activities.

Marketing research is the process of defining a marketing problem or opportunity, systematically collecting and analyzing information, and recommending actions to improve an organization's marketing activities.[2] Broadly speaking, assessing the needs and wants of consumers and providing information to help design an organization's marketing program to satisfy them is the principal role that marketing research performs. This means that marketing research attempts to identify and define both marketing problems and opportunities and to generate and evaluate marketing actions. Although marketing research can provide few answers with complete assurance, it can reduce risk and uncertainty to increase the likelihood of the success of marketing decisions. It is a great help to the marketing managers who must make final decisions. Conducted properly, marketing research can solve most marketing-related problems that an executive might have. However, marketing research should not be designed to simply replace an executive's good sense, experience, or intuition but rather should be used in conjunction with those skills and as a way of taking out some of the guesswork in the marketing decision-making process.

LO2 TYPES OF MARKETING RESEARCH

To understand the variety of research activity, it is helpful to categorize different types of marketing research. Marketing research is often classified on the basis of either technique or function. Surveys, experiments, and observation are a few research techniques with which you may be familiar. However, categorizing research by its purpose or function shows how the nature of the marketing problem influences the choice of research techniques. The nature of the problem will determine whether the research is (1) exploratory, (2) descriptive, or (3) causal.

Exploratory Research

Exploratory research is preliminary research conducted to clarify the scope and nature of the marketing problem. It is generally carried out to provide the researcher with a better understanding of the dimensions of the problem. Exploratory research is often conducted with the expectation that subsequent and more conclusive research will follow.

For example, the Dairy Farmers of Canada, an association representing dairy producers in the country, wanted to discover why milk consumption was declining in Canada. They conducted a search of existing literature on milk consumption, talked to experts in the field, and even conducted preliminary interviews with consumers to get ideas about why consumers were drinking less milk. This exploratory research helped the association to crystallize the problem and identify issues for more detailed follow-up research. We examine exploratory research as an integral component of the basic marketing research process later in this chapter.

Descriptive Research

Descriptive research is research designed to describe the basic characteristics of a given population or to profile particular marketing situations. Unlike exploratory research, with descriptive research, the researcher has a general understanding of the marketing problem and is seeking conclusive data that answer the questions necessary to determine a particular course of action. Examples of descriptive research would include profiling product purchasers (e.g., the Canadian shopper at the health food store), describing the size and characteristics of markets (e.g., the Canadian pizza restaurant market), detailing product usage patterns (e.g., ATM usage by Canadian bank customers), or outlining consumer attitudes toward particular brands (e.g., Canadian attitudes toward national, private, and generic brands).

Magazines, radio stations, and television stations almost always do descriptive research to identify the characteristics of their audiences in order to present them to prospective advertisers. As a follow-up to its exploratory research, the Dairy Farmers of Canada conducted descriptive research to determine the demographic characteristics

The Dairy Farmers of Canada conducted three types of marketing research in an effort to solve the problem of decline in milk consumption. For details, read the text.

Dairy Farmers of Canada
www.dairyfarmers.org

Dairyville   By Dairy Farmers of Canada

I should cut down on milk. My wife thinks I'm having an affair with a dietitian.

Fact: Milk is recommended for its many vital nutrients.

of milk consumers, current usage patterns, and consumer attitudes toward milk consumption.

Causal Research

Causal research is research designed to identify cause-and-effect relationships among variables. In general, exploratory and descriptive research normally precede causal research. With causal research, there is typically an expectation about the relationship to be explained, such as predicting the influence of a price change on product demand. In general, researchers attempt to establish that one event (e.g., a price change) will produce another event (e.g., a change in demand). Typical causal research studies examine the effect of advertising on sales, the relationship between price and perceived quality of a product, and the impact of a new package on product sales. When the Dairy Farmers of Canada conducted its descriptive research on milk consumers, it discovered that many believed milk was too fattening and too high in cholesterol. The association felt that these beliefs might be related to the overall decline in milk consumption in Canada. To test this assumption, the association ran a television advertising campaign to demonstrate that milk was a healthful product and essential to a person's diet. In its tracking studies, it found that the ad campaign did change consumer attitudes toward milk, which, in turn, was causally related to a subsequent increase in milk consumption. We refer to causal research later in this chapter when we deal with experiments as a basic research technique.

---

learning review

1. What is marketing research?

2. What is the difference among exploratory, descriptive, and causal research?

LO3 THE MARKETING RESEARCH PROCESS

Marketing research should always be conducted on the basis of the *scientific method,* a process of systematically collecting, organizing, and analyzing data in an unbiased, objective manner. Marketing research must meet two basic principles of the scientific method—reliability and validity. *Reliability* refers to the ability to replicate research results under identical environmental conditions. In other words, if a research project were to be conducted for the second, third, or fourth time, the results should be the same. Marketers need to have reliable information to make effective decisions. If the results of a study are not reliable, the research can do more harm than no research at all. *Validity* involves the notion of whether the research measured what was intended to be measured. In other words, does the research tell marketers what they need to know? You should keep the concepts of reliability and validity in mind as we discuss the marketing research process.

Figure 8–1 outlines the basic marketing research process. The figure is perhaps an oversimplification of the process, as marketing research does not always follow such a neat and ordered sequence of activities. However, all marketing research consists of four basic stages: (1) defining the problem, (2) determining the research design, (3) collecting and analyzing data, and (4) drawing conclusions and preparing a report.

In reviewing Figure 8–1, you can see that the researcher has a number of decisions and choices to make during the stages of the process. For example, the red boxes in Figure 8–1 indicate stages in the process where a choice of one or more techniques or methods must be made. The dotted line indicates the researcher's choice to bypass the exploratory research stage of the process.

● **FIGURE 8-1**

The basic marketing
research process

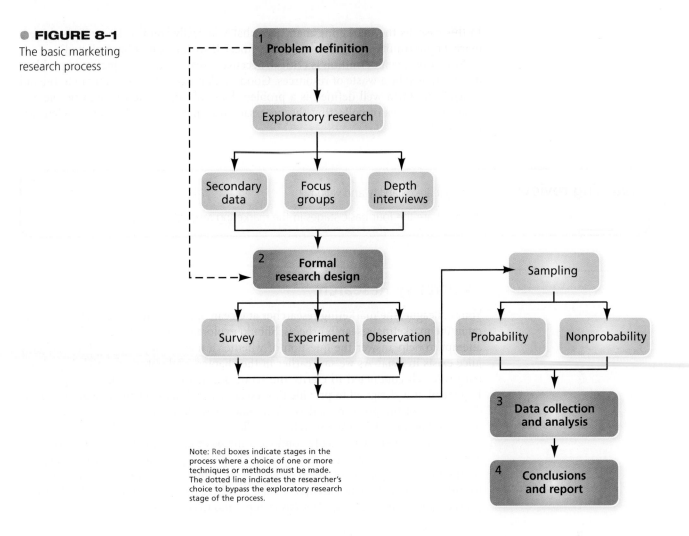

Note: Red boxes indicate stages in the
process where a choice of one or more
techniques or methods must be made.
The dotted line indicates the researcher's
choice to bypass the exploratory research
stage of the process.

LO4 PROBLEM DEFINITION

The first step in the marketing research process is to properly define the scope and nature of the marketing problem to be investigated. In general, the term *problem* suggests that something has gone wrong. In reality, to the marketing researcher, the word *problem* may also mean something to explore or an opportunity to define, or a current marketing situation to monitor or evaluate. Sometimes, the problem is obvious, but in other cases, the problem may be more difficult to identify and define. In either case, the marketing researcher must fully understand and properly identify the problem at hand.

The marketing research process is often initiated by the marketing manager, who will approach the marketing researcher with a problem that requires information for decision making. For example, suppose you were the marketing manager for cranberry juice at Ocean Spray. You want to know if Asian consumers who have never heard of cranberries would buy cranberry juice. You also have other problems. The word "cranberry" is not part of any foreign language, and so you would have to find a name for it and its juice. Also, if you are going to take the product to Asia, you have to find a way to encourage consumers there to try the new product.[3] The marketing researcher has to fully understand these problems. The researcher must also remember that the best place to begin a research project is at the end. In other words, the researcher must know what is to be accomplished through the research process.

In this case, as the marketing manager, what you really want to know is: Is there a market opportunity in Asia for cranberry juice? If so, how can it be exploited?

Proper problem definition is critical, because research based on incorrect problem definition will be a waste of resources. Good marketing researchers adhere to the old adage "a problem well defined is a problem half-solved." If the research problem is clear, the chances of collecting the necessary information to solve the problem are increased.

---

learning review

3. What are reliability and validity?

4. What are the four basic stages in the marketing research process?

Exploratory Research

Your colleague, the marketing researcher at Ocean Spray, has to make a decision early on in the marketing research process. Should exploratory research be conducted in an attempt to help answer the question of whether a market opportunity for cranberry juice exists in Asia? As we saw earlier in the chapter, exploratory research is preliminary research conducted to clarify the scope and nature of the marketing problem. In general, it is designed to provide the researcher with a better understanding of the dimensions of the problem and is often conducted with the expectation that subsequent and more conclusive research may follow.

Most researchers will usually conduct some basic exploratory research during the early stage of the research process. The extent of the exploratory research will depend on the magnitude of the problem as well as its complexity. If the researcher decides to conduct exploratory research, he or she has three basic techniques to choose from: (1) secondary data analysis, (2) focus groups, and (3) depth interviews.

secondary data
Facts and figures that have been recorded before the project at hand.

primary data
Facts and figures that are newly collected for the project.

Secondary Data   Exploratory research almost always involves the use of **secondary data** (or historical data)—data previously collected and assembled for some project other than the one at hand. **Primary data,** on the other hand, are data gathered and assembled specifically for the project at hand. As a rule, researchers gather secondary data before collecting primary data. In general, secondary data can be obtained more quickly and at a lower cost compared with primary data. However, there can be problems with secondary data. The required information may not exist, and if it does, it may not be current or particularly pertinent to the problem at hand. Still, most researchers agree that investigating secondary data sources can save researchers from "reinventing the wheel."

Researchers examine secondary data both inside and outside the organization. Internal secondary data include financial statements, research reports, customer letters, and customer lists. What did your colleague in marketing research at Ocean Spray discover during the secondary data search efforts? She discovered that Ocean Spray did attempt to introduce a bland cranberry juice in Japan—named "Cranby"—but the attempt fizzled, and the product was pulled off the market. As a marketing manager, this information does provide some background, but you still have more questions than answers about the possible marketing opportunity in Asia.

Sources of external secondary data can be wide and varied. One key Canadian source of marketing data is Statistics Canada (**www.statcan.gc.ca**). This federal government agency provides census data as well as numerous other reports on Canadian households and businesses, most of which are available through its searchable online database.

Should Ocean Spray introduce cranberry juice in Asia when consumers there have never heard of cranberries? See the text.

Ocean Spray
www.oceanspray.com

focus groups
An informal session of six to ten customers—past, present, or prospective—in which a discussion leader, or moderator, asks their opinions about the firm's and its competitors' products.

In addition to Statistics Canada there are numerous other sources of secondary data including business directories, business periodicals, newspapers, magazines, and trade associations. Finally, there are many online databanks that provide specialized data services. Figure 8–2 provides some key sources of secondary data.

One emerging type of secondary data that is available to marketers is called *single source data.* This is integrated information from multiple sources that allows marketers to examine customers' household demographics and lifestyles, product purchases, media habits, and responses to sales promotions, such as coupons and free samples. For example, if you have a loyalty card with a particular retailer, your purchase data is captured by the checkout scanner and can be archived in a marketing information system where it can be examined along with your personal information to determine how the company can better market its product or services. If you purchase online, your purchase data is also captured and stored along with your personal information. This information can then be used to tailor offerings to you based on your past purchase behaviour. We will discuss the use of integrated data when we examine marketing information systems later in this chapter.

Getting back to our marketing researcher at Ocean Spray and the cranberry juice in Asia question, she discovers some external secondary data, specifically a study on Taiwan consumers that shows increased consumption of juice beverages. Still, the study is not specific to cranberry juice and is about four years old. As marketing manager, you realize you still have a high degree of uncertainty about the possible marketing opportunity in Asia. So you ask your colleague in marketing research to continue the exploratory stage of the marketing process.

Focus Groups   A very popular exploratory research technique designed to obtain primary data is the use of focus groups. **Focus groups** are informal interview sessions in which six to ten persons, relevant to the research project, are brought together in a room with a moderator to discuss topics surrounding the marketing research problem. The moderator poses questions and encourages the individuals to answer in their own words and to discuss the issues with each other. Often, the focus-group sessions are watched by observers through one-way mirrors, and/or the sessions are videotaped. (Of course, participants should be informed they are being observed and/or taped.)

Many companies are also conducting online focus groups where participants and the moderator interact in an online setting. Companies can present online participants with audio or video material for respondent evaluation, and even present them with virtual product concepts to evaluate. Focus group sessions often provide the marketer with valuable information for decision making or can uncover other issues that should be researched in a more quantitative fashion.[4]

For example, Canada's military ran focus groups in cities across Canada to find out what images should appear in the Army's next recruitment campaign. The research revealed that prospective recruits, particularly young men 18 to 24 years of age, wanted more reality in military ads. Importantly, they wanted to see action rather than a soft pitch about career opportunities. As a result of the focus groups, the ad program called "Fight" was developed. The centrepiece was two stark 60-second TV spots. In one, soldiers rescue flood victims in Manitoba. In the other, tanks patrol

Selected Statistics and Trade Sources	**Business/Trade Magazines**
Canadian Trade Index (**www.ctidirectory.com**)	*Advertising Age*
Conference Board of Canada (**www.conferenceboard.ca**)	*American Demographics*
	Business Week
Financial Post's Canadian Demographics: Key census data at the municipal level	*Canadian Business*
	Forbes
Fraser's Canadian Trade Directory (**www.frasers.com**)	*Fortune*
Industry Canada Strategis Web site (**www.strategis.ic.gc.ca**): Includes Canadian Company Capabilities, online directory, Canadian Patent Database, Canadian Trademark Database	*Harvard Business Review*
	The Globe and Mail Report on Business
	Marketing Magazine
	Marketing News
Scott's Directories (**www.scottsinfo.com**)	*Profit Magazine*
Statistics Canada (**www.statcan.gc.ca**): Online database, including census data, plus guidebooks such as the *Market Research Handbook*	*Progressive Grocer*
	Sales and Marketing Management
	Small Business Canada Magazine
	Strategy Magazine
Marketing Journals	**Other Sources (including Online Databases)**
Canadian Journal of Marketing Research	ABI Inform / Proquest
Journal of Advertising	AC Nielsen Canada (**www.acnielsen.ca**)
Journal of Consumer Research	Blue Book of Canadian Business (**www.cbr.ca**)
Journal of Marketing	Dialog (**www.dialog.com**)
Journal of Marketing Research	Dun & Bradstreet Canada (**www.dnb.ca**)
Journal of Retailing	Hoover's (**www.hoovers.com**)
	Interactive Advertising Bureau of Canada (**www.iabcanada.com**)
	LexisNexis (**www.lexis-nexis.com**)

● **FIGURE 8-2**
Sources of secondary data

war-torn streets, a nail bomb explodes, and soldiers do battle in Afghanistan. Both end with the superimposed tag line: "Fight fear, fight distress, fight chaos... Fight with the Canadian Forces." The ads clearly struck a nerve. The number of applicants rose 40 percent to 40,000, and Canadian Forces signed up 12,862 full-time and reserve members—about 400 more than the target.[5]

depth interviews
Detailed, individual interviews with people relevant to a research project.

Depth Interviews   Another exploratory research technique used to obtain primary data involves the use of depth interviews. **Depth interviews** are detailed individual interviews with people relevant to a research project. The researcher questions the individual at length in a free-flowing conversational style to obtain information that may help solve the marketing problem being investigated. Sometimes these interviews can take a few hours, and they are often recorded on audio- or videotape.

Hamburger Helper did not fare too well with consumers when General Mills first introduced it. Initial instructions called for cooking separately a half pound of hamburger, which was later mixed with the noodles. Depth interviews revealed that consumers did not think the recipe called for enough meat and that they did not want the hassle of cooking in two different pots. So the Hamburger Helper product manager changed the recipe to call for a full pound of meat and to allow users to prepare the meal in one dish; this converted a potential failure into a success.

Researchers have also become creative in devising other exploratory research techniques. For example, finding "the next big thing" for consumers has become the obsession in many industries. In order to unearth the next big thing, marketing researchers have developed some unusual techniques, sometimes referred to as "fuzzy front-end" methods. These techniques are designed to identify elusive consumer tastes or trends far before typical consumers have themselves recognized them. For example, having consumers take a photo of themselves every time they snack resulted in General Mills' Homestyle Pop Secret popcorn, which delivers the real butter and bursts of salt in microwave popcorn that consumers thought they could only get from the stovetop variety.[6]

Other unusual techniques are also being used to try to spot trends early. For example, Teenage Research Unlimited had teenagers complete a drawing to help discover what teenagers like, wear, listen to, and read.[7] Another company, Trend Hunter uses *trend hunting*—the practice of identifying, emerging shifts in social behaviour that are driven by changes in pop culture, which can lead to new products. Trend Hunter has identified over 47,000 "micro trends" through its global network of 27,000 spotters and features several of these trends on its daily Trend Hunter TV broadcast via its Web site (see **www.trendhunter.com/tv**).[8]

---

learning review

5. What are secondary data?

6. What are focus groups?

FORMAL RESEARCH DESIGN

After identifying and clarifying the marketing problem, with or without exploratory research, the researcher must determine the basic framework for finding a solution to the problem. At the formal research design stage, the researcher produces a plan that outlines the method and procedures for collecting and analyzing the required information. The plan includes the objectives of the research, the sources of information to be used, the research methods (e.g., survey, experiment), the sampling plan, and the schedule and cost of the research.

In selecting basic research methods, the researcher must make decisions. In general, the objectives of the research, available data sources, nature of the information required, and timing and cost considerations will determine which research method will be chosen. The basic methods the researcher can choose for descriptive and causal research include: (1) survey, (2) experiment, and (3) observation.

Survey

survey
A research technique used to generate data by asking people questions and recording their responses on a questionnaire.

The most common research method of generating new or primary data is the use of surveys. A **survey** is a research technique used to generate data by asking people questions and recording their responses on a questionnaire. Surveys can be conducted by personal interview (face-to-face), by mail, by telephone, or online. In choosing these alternatives, the marketing researcher has to make important trade-offs (as shown in Figure 8–3) in order to balance, for instance, cost against the expected quality of information obtained. For example, personal interview (face-to-face) surveys have the major advantage of enabling the interviewer to be flexible in asking probing questions or getting reactions to visual materials but are very costly to conduct. Mail surveys are usually biased because those likely to respond have had especially positive or negative experiences with a given product, service, or brand. While telephone surveys allow flexibility, they are increasingly difficult to complete because respondents may hang up on the interviewer. Also, with many unlisted telephone numbers, it is becoming increasingly more difficult to obtain representative samples. Online surveys are somewhat restrictive in that they are limited to respondents having the technology.[9] Still, as Internet penetration grows, so too will the use of online surveys. Some of you are probably already familiar with popular online survey sites such as Zoomerang or Survey Monkey.

Basis of Comparison	Mail Surveys	Telephone Surveys	Personal Interview	Online Surveys
Cost per completed survey	Not very expensive	Moderately expensive	Most expensive	Very inexpensive
Ability to probe and ask complex questions	Little to none	Some, interviewer can probe and elaborate	Much, interviewer is face-to-face	Depends, can go back and ask respondent to clarify responses
Opportunity for interviewer to bias results	None	Some, because of voice and gender	Significant, voice, appearance, gender present	Little, if done correctly
Anonymity given to respondent	Complete, unless coded instrument is used	Some, because of telephone contact	Little, because of face-to-face contact	Some, e-mail/ user name may be known
Response rate	Poor or fair	Fair, refusal rates are increasing	Good	Very good, if done correctly
Speed of data collection	Poor	Good	Good	Very good

● **FIGURE 8–3**

Comparing mail, telephone, personal, and online surveys

The high cost of reaching respondents in their homes through personal interview surveys has led to an increase in the use of *mall intercept interviews*, which are personal interviews of consumers at shopping centres. These face-to-face interviews reduce the cost of personal visits to consumers in their homes while providing flexibility to show respondents visual cues, such as ads or actual product samples. However, a critical disadvantage of mall intercept interviews is that the people selected for the interviews may not be representative of the consumers targeted for the interviews, causing possible bias in results.

Sometimes, marketers will survey over time the same sample of people, commonly known as a survey *panel*. A panel can consist of a sample of consumers, stores, or experts, from which researchers can take a series of measurements. For example, a consumer's switch from one brand of breakfast cereal to another can be measured with panel data. The use of panels is becoming more popular with marketers as they attempt to obtain ongoing information about their constituents. Panel data are often incorporated into marketing information systems, which are discussed later in the chapter. These online panels give marketers immediate access to their consumers.

When marketers decide to use surveys to ask questions, they assume that (1) the right questions are being asked, (2) people will understand the questions being asked, (3) people know the answers to the questions, (4) people will answer the questions truthfully, and (5) the researchers themselves will understand the answers provided. Marketers must concern themselves not only with asking the right questions but also with how to word those questions properly. Proper phrasing of a question is vital to uncovering useful marketing information.

Figure 8–4 shows typical problems to guard against in wording questions to obtain meaningful answers from respondents. For example, in the question about whether you eat at fast-food restaurants regularly, the word "regularly" is ambiguous. Two people might answer "yes" to the question, but one might mean "once a day" while the other means "once or twice a year." Both answers appear as "yes" to the researcher who tabulates them, but they suggest that dramatically different marketing actions be directed to each of these two prospective consumers. Therefore, it is essential that marketing research questions be worded precisely so that all respondents interpret

● **FIGURE 8-4**
Typical problems in wording questions

PROBLEM	SAMPLE QUESTION	EXPLANATION
Leading question	Why do you like Wendy's fresh meat hamburgers better than those of competitors?	Consumer is led to make statements favouring Wendy's hamburgers
Ambiguous question	Do you eat at fast-food restaurants regularly? ☐ Yes ☐ No	What is meant by word *regularly*—once a day, once a month, or what?
Unanswerable question	What was the occasion for your eating your first hamburger?	Who can remember the answer? Does it matter?
Two questions in one	Do you eat Wendy's hamburgers and chili? ☐ Yes ☐ No	How do you answer if you eat Wendy's hamburgers but not chili?
Nonexhaustive question	Where do you live? ☐ At home ☐ In dormitory	What do you check if you live in an apartment?
Non–mutually exclusive answers	What is your age? ☐ Under 20 ☐ 20–40 ☐ 40 and over	What answer does a 40-year-old check?

Wendy's changes continuously in response to changing customer wants while keeping its "Fresh, hot'n juicy®" image.

Wendy's Restaurants
www.wendys.com

the same question similarly. Marketing researchers must also take great care not to use "leading" questions (wording questions in a way to ensure a particular response), which can lead to a very distorted picture of the respondents' actual feelings or opinions.

In Figure 8–5, we can see the number of different formats that questions can take in a survey instrument. The questions presented are taken from a Wendy's survey that assessed fast-food preferences among present and prospective consumers. Question 1 is an example of an *open-end question,* which the respondent can answer in his or her own words. In contrast, questions in which the respondent simply checks an answer are *closed-end* or *fixed alternative questions.* Question 2 is an example of the simplest fixed alternative question, a *dichotomous question* that allows only a "yes" or "no" answer. A fixed alternative question with three or more choices uses a scale. Question 5 is an example of a question that uses a *semantic differential scale,* a five-point scale in which the opposite ends have one- or two-word adjectives that have opposite meanings. For example, depending on how clean the respondent believes that Wendy's is, he or she would check the left-hand space on the scale, the right-hand space, or one of the three intervening points. Question 6 uses a *Likert scale,* in which the respondent is asked to indicate the extent to which he or she agrees or disagrees with a statement.

The questionnaire in Figure 8–5 is an excerpt of a precisely worded survey that provides valuable information to the marketing researcher at Wendy's. Questions 1 to 8 inform the researcher about the likes and dislikes in eating out, frequency of eating out at fast-food restaurants generally and at Wendy's specifically, and sources of information used in making decisions about fast-food restaurants. Question 9 gives details about the personal or household characteristics, which can be used in trying to segment the fast-food market, a topic discussed in Chapter 9.

Surveys of distributors—retailers and wholesalers in the marketing channel—are also very important for manufacturers. A reason given for the success of many Japanese consumer products in Canada, such as Sony Walkmans and Toyota automobiles, is the emphasis that Japanese marketers place on obtaining accurate information from their distributors.

1. What things are most important to you when you decide to eat out and go to a fast-food restaurant?

_____

_____

_____

2. Have you eaten at a fast-food restaurant in the past month?

☐ Yes   ☐ No

3. If you answered yes to question 2, how often do you eat fast food?

☐ Once a week   ☐ 2 to 3 times a month   ☐ Once a month or less

4. How important is it to you that a fast-food restaurant satisfies you on the following characteristics? [Check the box that describes your feelings for each item listed]

CHARACTERISTIC	VERY IMPORTANT	SOMEWHAT IMPORTANT	IMPORTANT	UNIMPORTANT	SOMEWHAT UNIMPORTANT	VERY UNIMPORTANT
• Taste of food	☐	☐	☐	☐	☐	☐
• Cleanliness	☐	☐	☐	☐	☐	☐
• Price	☐	☐	☐	☐	☐	☐
• Variety of menu	☐	☐	☐	☐	☐	☐

5. For each of the characteristics listed below, check the space on the scale that describes how you feel about Wendy's. Mark an X on only **one** of the five spaces listed for each item listed.

CHARACTERISTIC	CHECK THE SPACE THAT DESCRIBES THE DEGREE TO WHICH WENDY'S IS . . .
• Taste of food	Tasty ____ ____ ____ ____ ____ Not tasty
• Cleanliness	Clean ____ ____ ____ ____ ____ Dirty
• Price	Inexpensive ____ ____ ____ ____ ____ Expensive
• Variety of menu	Broad ____ ____ ____ ____ ____ Narrow

● **FIGURE 8–5**

To obtain the most valuable information from consumers, the Wendy's survey utilizes nine different kinds of questions discussed in the text

As the chapter opener indicated, new technologies, including the Internet, have revolutionized the traditional concept of surveys. In addition to online research, marketers can survey respondents via electronic kiosks in shopping centres. Respondents read questions on-screen and key their answers into a computer with a touch screen. Marketers can also utilize fully automated telephone systems to conduct surveys. An automated voice questions respondents over the telephone, who then key in their replies on a touch-tone telephone. Marketers are also using wireless phones to send text surveys, and even conducting surveys via iPods and other hand-held wireless devices.

Experiment

experiment

Obtaining data by manipulating factors under tightly controlled conditions to test cause and effect.

Another method that can be used by marketing researchers to generate primary data is the experiment. Marketing experiments offer the potential for establishing cause-and-effect relationships (causal research). An **experiment** involves the manipulation

6. Check one box that describes your agreement or disagreement with each statement listed below:

STATEMENT	STRONGLY AGREE	AGREE	DON'T KNOW	DISAGREE	STRONGLY DISAGREE
• Adults like to take their families to fast-food restaurants	☐	☐	☐	☐	☐
• Our children have a say in where the family chooses to eat	☐	☐	☐	☐	☐

7. How important are each of the following sources of information to you when selecting a fast-food restaurant to eat at? [Check one box for each source listed]

SOURCE OF INFORMATION	VERY IMPORTANT	SOMEWHAT IMPORTANT	NOT AT ALL IMPORTANT
• Television	☐	☐	☐
• Newspapers	☐	☐	☐
• Radio	☐	☐	☐
• Billboards	☐	☐	☐
• Flyers	☐	☐	☐

8. How often do you eat out at each of the following fast-food restaurants? [Check one box for each source listed]

RESTAURANT	ONCE A WEEK OR MORE	2 TO 3 TIMES A MONTH	ONCE A MONTH OR LESS
• Burger King	☐	☐	☐
• McDonald's	☐	☐	☐
• Wendy's	☐	☐	☐

9. Please answer the following questions about you and your household. [Check only one for each item]

a. What is your gender? ☐ Male ☐ Female

b. What is your marital status? ☐ Single ☐ Married ☐ Other (widowed, divorced, etc.)

c. How many children under age 18 live in your home? ☐ 0 ☐ 1 ☐ 2 ☐ 3 or more

d. What is your age? ☐ Under 25 ☐ 25–44 ☐ 45 or older

e. What is your total annual individual or household income?
☐ <$15,000 ☐ $15,000–49,000 ☐ $50,000 or more

● **FIGURE 8-5**
(*Continued*)

of an independent variable (cause) and the measurement of its effect on the dependent variable (effect) under controlled conditions.

In marketing experiments, the independent variables are often one or more of the marketing mix variables—sometimes called the marketing *drivers*—such as product features, price, or promotion used. An ideal dependent variable usually is a change in purchases by an individual, household, or entire organization. If actual purchases cannot be used as a dependent variable, factors that are believed to be highly related to purchases, such as preferences in a taste test or intentions to buy, are used.

Experiments can be conducted in the field or in a laboratory. In *field experiments,* the research is conducted in the real world, such as in a store or bank, or on the street, wherever the behaviour being studied occurs naturally. Field experiments can be expensive but are a good way to determine people's reactions to changes in the elements of the marketing mix. Test marketing is probably the most common form of field experiments. For example, suppose you wanted to know if Asian consumers would buy cranberry juice when they had never tasted cranberries? Perhaps

How might Walmart have done early marketing research to help develop its supercentres, which have achieved international success? For its unusual research, see the text.

your marketing research colleague might recommend taste tests in Asia to gauge consumers' responses to the product. In fact, many food companies use test marketing. Walmart, for instance, opened three experimental stand-alone supercentres to gauge consumer acceptance before deciding to open others. Today, Walmart operates over 1,000 supercentres around the world.

Because marketers cannot control all the conditions in the field, they sometimes turn to a laboratory setting. Laboratories are not the real world but do offer highly controlled environments. Unlike in the field, the marketer has control over all the factors that may impact the behaviour under investigation.

For example, in a field experiment, the marketer may wish to examine the impact of a price reduction on the sales of a particular product. The competition, however, may see the price reduction and offer its own price deal, thus interfering with the possible results of the field experiment. This does not occur in a laboratory setting. Many companies are using laboratory settings where they can control conditions but can do so in a real-world fashion, such as simulated supermarkets. Here, they can experiment with changes in aisle displays, packaging changes, or other variables that may affect buyer behaviour without the fear of other extraneous factors influencing the results.

Today, the Internet has also opened up opportunities to do creative online market testing of products, packaging, advertising, and so on. For example, Coca-Cola used online research to test consumer responses to proposed new Fruitopia flavours, and Breyers asked for consumer feedback on proposed new ice cream flavours. Ipsos Canada, a major Canadian research firm, argues that online market testing can be fast and very effective. Using online technology, Ipsos assists their clients by conducting virtual reality testing of product concepts where consumers can view the products online, click on features, and rank preferences. With online panels, companies also have the added advantage of ready-made beta-test samples for new concepts, products, and services. In fact, you recently used an online panel to test your current format of your super snack bar against a proposed new format and the results are shown in the Using Marketing Dashboard box. What conclusions can you draw from the results?

Observation

observation
Watching, either mechanically or in person, how people behave.

Another basic research method used to obtain primary data is observation. In general, **observation** involves watching, either mechanically or in person, how people behave. In some circumstances, the speed of events or the number of events being observed make mechanical or electronic observation more appropriate than personal observation. Retailers, for example, can use electronic cameras to count the number of customers entering or leaving a store.

A classic form of mechanical observation is Nielsen Media Research's *people meter*, which is a box attached to television sets, cable boxes, and satellite dishes in selected households in Canada and the United States in order to determine the size of audiences watching television programs delivered by the networks. When a household member watches TV, he or she is supposed to push a button on a remote and push it again when viewing stops. The information is transmitted and analyzed by Nielsen in order to measure who in the household is watching what program on every TV set owned.

This information is used to calculate ratings for each TV program, which, in turn, is used to set advertising rates for such programs. But people meters have limitations—as with all observations collected mechanically. Critics do not believe the devices

Using Marketing Dashboards

Making Sense of Online Panel Results

While you are happy with the results of sales, overall, with your new super snack bar, your R&D and food science group within the company have developed a new bar format that they feel might better appeal to your current user group. The existing bar format looks like a dark-chocolate bar with a smooth, pressed, and tabbed (easy-to-break in pieces) appearance. But some of your people think a new format, a light, granular-looking (similar to granola), non-tabbed appearance may have appeal with current users. So you present both formats to your online panel. You ask them to rate the two formats on several attributes known to be important to the buyers and then ask if they have a preference for one format over the other. Below are the results.

Your Findings: Online Panel Results (N = 300 users)
Question: Which format for the super snack bar, if any, do you prefer?

	Format A – Current Product	**Format B – New Format**
Perceived taste	4.6	4.1
Perceived healthfulness	4.5	4.0
Perceived IQ/strength delivery	4.4	3.9
Perceived energy delivery	4.6	4.3
Perceived convenience	4.9	3.3
Overall preference	80%	20%

Scale: 1–5 (1 = very unlikely to deliver on this attribute, 5 = very likely to deliver on this attribute)

Your Action It is clear that your current users prefer the current format of your super snack bar (80% vs. 20%), and all users expressed a strong preference one way or another. It is also clear that the current format is also ranked higher on all attributes compared to the new format. The perceived convenience score between the two formats is particularly large. Thus, it appears the current tabbed format is strongly preferred. Yet, there is a distinctive 20 percent of your panel that has expressed a preference for the proposed new format. You have to consider whether to add this new format (a new offering, line-extension), which means new production issues, and securing channel members cooperation to handle a new SKU (stock-keeping unit). You have to consider whether introducing the new format (while retaining the existing format) will improve your top-line revenue numbers as well as your bottom-line profitability.

accurately measure who is watching a given TV program or what is actually watched. Moreover, people meters cannot measure large segments of the population that watch TV programs at parties, hotels, or sports bars. A new *portable people meter (PPM)* is now being introduced by BBM Canada. This device, which is the size of a pager, is carried by consumers and automatically detects audible codes in TV programming at both in-home and outside venues. Each night, participants place the meter into a base station, which then transmits the data for analysis.[10]

Nielsen also uses an electronic meter to record Internet user behaviour. These data are collected by tracking the actual mouse clicks made by users as they surf the Internet via a meter installed on their home or work computers. Nielsen has been able to identify the Web sites that have the largest audiences, the top advertising banners viewed, the top Internet advertisers, and global Internet usage for selected countries. Nielsen is also implementing a new measurement program called *Anytime Anywhere Media Measurement (A2/M2)*, which will measure all types of viewing behaviour from a variety of devices and sources such as DVR and VOD, and Internet-delivered TV shows on computers via iTunes, streaming media, smartphones, etc.

Watching consumers in person or by videotaping them are other observational approaches used to collect primary data. For example, Procter & Gamble watched women do their laundry, clean the floor, put on makeup, and so on, because 80 percent of the customers who buy its products are women! Gillette marketing researchers actually videotaped consumers brushing their teeth in their own bathrooms to find out how they really brush—not just how they say they brush. The result: Gillette's new Oral-B CrossAction toothbrush that is supposed to do a better job! [11]

ethnographic research
Observational approach to discover subtle emotional reactions as consumers encounter products in their "natural use environment."

A specialized observational approach is **ethnographic research,** in which anthropologists and other trained observers seek to discover subtle emotional reactions as consumers encounter products in their "natural use environments," such as in homes, cars, or hotels. For example, Office Max used this anthropological method to observe how its shoppers interacted with its stores. The result: Office Max moved products that consumers bought in tandem closer together, thus increasing sales. Kraft launched Deli Creations, which are sandwiches made with its Oscar Meyer meats, Kraft cheeses, and Grey Poupon mustard, after spending several months with consumers in their kitchens. Kraft discovered that consumers wanted complete, ready-to-serve meals that are easy to prepare—and it had the products to create them.[12]

Finally, before Moen Inc. put its new massaging shower head, the Revolution, on the market, it wanted to find out what consumers thought about the new product design. But Moen did not want to just give consumers the shower head and later ask them if they liked it or not. The company wanted to see the consumers actually using the product . . . in the shower. So it hired QualiData Research Inc. to do some ethnographic research. QualiData enlisted 20 nudists as their volunteers and paid them $250 each to answer questions about their lifestyles, and to allow QualiData to install a tiny video camera in the shower of each volunteer in order to watch them use the new showerhead. As a result of the research, the product was redesigned and has become a major new product success for Moen.[13]

Another creative approach to obtaining observational data is the hiring of *mystery shoppers.* Companies hire people to pose as real customers and have them go through an exchange process and record their observations in detailed reports. For example, a mystery shopper might be paid to travel to a vacation resort, eat at restaurants, play golf, open up bank accounts, test-drive new cars at auto dealers, or shop for groceries or clothes. The information they provide based on their observations often gives marketers unique insight that cannot be obtained any other way. There are Canadian mystery shopping companies, just in case you want a job like this!

How do you do marketing research on something like toothbrushes? For some creative answers, see the text.

Personal observation is both useful and flexible, but it can be costly and unreliable, especially when different observers report different conclusions in watching the same activities. Also, although observation can reveal what people do, it cannot determine why they do it, such as why they are buying or not buying a product. To determine why consumers behave as they do, marketing researchers must talk with consumers and record their responses. This is usually accomplished through the use of surveys.

Many marketers, however, feel that traditional marketing research methods do not go far enough in really understanding consumers. And, as previous chapters have pointed out, understanding the customer's experience with products and brands has become more important for marketers. Therefore, marketers are developing new and innovative ways to conduct research that goes a little deeper. One new concept is known as *neuromarketing,* which measures brain activity to discover how consumers respond to brands and advertising. For a peek at this new method, read the accompanying Marketing Matters box that discusses neuromarketing and whether it might become the holy grail of marketing research.[14]

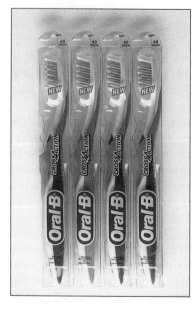

Is There an Optimal Research Design?

In short, there is no optimal research design. A researcher may choose among a variety of alternative methods for solving a particular marketing problem. A good marketing researcher understands that there is likely to be more than one

Marketing Matters

Neuromarketing: The Holy Grail of Marketing Research?

Thirty men and women study a sporty silver test model of a 2011 Hyundai. They are asked to stare at specific parts of the vehicle, including the bumper, the windshield, and the tires. Electrode-studded caps on their heads capture the electrical activity in their brains as they view the car for an hour. That information is recorded in a hard drive each person wears on a belt. Their brain activity is supposed to show preferences that could lead to purchasing decisions. "We want to know what consumers think about a car before we start manufacturing thousands of them," says Dean Macko, manager of brand strategy at Hyundai Motors. Macko expects the carmaker will tweak the exterior based on the electroencephalograph reports, which track activity in all parts of the brain.

Neuromarketing, or brain-wave marketing, is becoming popular as a marketing research tool. Using EEGs and/or MRIs to track electrical activity and blood flow in consumers' brains is thought to guide marketers to develop the right products, right brands, and right ads to boost sales. For example, executives at PepsiCo's Frito-Lay unit use neuromarketing to test commercials, products, and packaging. According to Frito-Lay Chief Marketing Officer Ann Mukherjee, brain-imaging tests can be more accurate than focus groups. Frito-Lay brain-tested a commercial that traditional focus groups panned. The spot for Cheetos featured a woman taking revenge on someone in a laundromat by putting the orange snack food in a dryer full of white clothes. Participants said they didn't like the prank, probably because they didn't want to look

too mean-spirited to other focus group members. But EEG tests showed brain activity that suggested women loved the ad. The snack-food marketer then started airing the prank ad. Yahoo has a 60-second television commercial that features happy, dancing people around the world. Before spending the money to air the ad on prime-time and cable TV, as well as online, Yahoo ran it by EEG-cap-wearing consumers. The brain waves showed stimulation in the limbic system and frontal cortices of their brains, where memory and emotional thought occurs. The ad, which is part of Yahoo's new $100 million branding campaign, was rolled out to bring more users to the search engine. A few years ago the cost of renting brain-imaging machines kept many marketers from dabbling in neuromarketing. Today, there are several companies offering EEG and MRI testing devices and thus the costs have come down significantly. A marketer can hook 30 consumers up to an EEG device for $50,000. An MRI trial with 20 people would cost more like $40,000.

However, there are skeptics of neuromarketing. For example, Craig Bennett, a neuroscientist, wrote a report about running a dead Atlantic salmon through an MRI machine. The result showed signals of brain activity similar to the ones neuromarketers see when testing commercials on consumers. "You could say the salmon liked one brand of peanut butter over another brand," says Bennett. "But it was dead." So, the question is: Will neuromarketing become the holy grail of marketing research?

way to tackle a problem. The ability to select the most appropriate research design develops with experience. Inexperienced researchers often embrace the survey method as the best design because they are most familiar with this method. More experienced researchers, on the other hand, recognize the value of other methods and can often put together creative research designs that can solve marketing problems more quickly and less expensively. Experienced researchers often note that the proper definition of marketing plays a central role in determining the most appropriate research design.

Sampling

sampling
The process of gathering data from subsets of a total population.

Although sampling is an inherent component of the research design stage, it is a distinctive aspect of the research process. The researcher's sampling plan indicates who is to be sampled, how large a sample is needed, and how the sampling units will be selected. Rarely does a research project involve a complete census of every person in the research population. This is because of the time and cost involved in conducting a census. Thus, sampling is used. **Sampling** is the process of gathering data from a subset of the total population rather than from all members (census) of that particular population. A *sample*, then, is a subset from a larger population.

If proper statistical procedures are followed, a researcher does not need to select every member in a population, because a properly selected sample should be representative of the population as a whole. However, errors can and do occur in sampling, and the reliability of the data obtained through sampling can sometimes become an issue. Thus, the first and most critical sampling question for researchers to ask is: Who is to be sampled?

Another key question concerns the sample size: How big should the sample be? As mentioned, it is usually unrealistic to expect a census of the research population be conducted. In general, larger samples are more precise than smaller ones, but proper sampling can allow a smaller subset of the total population to provide a reliable measure of the whole.

The final question in the sampling plan concerns how to select the sampling units. There are two basic sampling techniques: probability and nonprobability sampling. **Probability sampling** involves precise rules to select the sample such that each element of the population has a specific known chance of being selected. For example, if your university wants to know how last year's 1,000 graduates are doing, it can put their names in a bowl and randomly select 100 names of graduates to contact. The chance of being selected—100/1000 or 0.10 is known in advance, and all graduates have an equal chance of being contacted. This procedure helps select a sample (100 graduates) that should be representative of the entire population (the 1,000 graduates) and allows conclusions to be drawn about the entire population.

Nonprobability sampling involves the use of arbitrary judgment by the marketing researcher to select the sample so that the chance of selecting a particular element of the population is either unknown or zero. If your university decided to talk to 100 of last year's graduates but only those who lived closest to the university, many class members would be arbitrarily eliminated. This has introduced a bias, or possible lack of representativeness, which may make it dangerous to draw conclusions about the entire population of the graduating class. Nonprobability samples are often used when time and budgets are limited and are most often used for exploratory research purposes. In general, marketing researchers use data from such samples with caution.

probability sampling
Using precise rules to select the sample such that each element of the population has a specific known chance of being selected.

nonprobability sampling
Using arbitrary judgments to select the sample so that the chance of selecting a particular element may be unknown or zero.

---

learning review

7. What is a survey?

8. Which research method offers the potential for establishing cause-and-effect relationship?

9. What is sampling?

DATA COLLECTION AND ANALYSIS

Once the research design has been formalized, the process of gathering or collecting data begins. Sometimes referred to as *fieldwork,* data collection at this stage of the research process includes all the activities that the researcher (and staff) undertakes to obtain data from the identified sources or respondents. Because there are several research methods that could be used by the researcher, this means there may be multiple ways to collect the data. For example, with the survey method, data may be collected by telephone, mail, or personal interview.

However the data are collected, it is important to minimize errors in the process. Most research experts agree that the data collection stage of the research process is one of the major sources of error in marketing research. Some of the errors that occur are a result of a variety of problems ranging from failure to select the right respondents to incorrect recording of observations. Competent and well-trained researchers inside the organization or those employed by outside research companies can go a long way in ensuring proper data collection.

The next step for the marketing researcher is data analysis. Mark Twain once observed, "Collecting data is like collecting garbage. You've got to know what you're going to do with the stuff before you collect it." In essence, the marketing researcher must know *why* the data are being collected and *how* to analyze them effectively in order for the data to have any value in decision making.

The level of analysis conducted on the data depends on the nature of the research and the information needed to provide a solution to the marketing problem. For survey data, frequency analysis is completed—calculating the responses question by question. The researcher may then wish to identify patterns in the data or examine how data pertaining to some questions may relate to data obtained from asking other questions. Probably the most widely used technique for organizing and analyzing marketing data is cross-tabulation. This method is particularly useful for market segmentation analysis.

CONCLUSIONS AND REPORT

At this stage of the process, the marketing researcher, often in conjunction with marketing management, must review the analysis and ask: What does this information tell us? A critical aspect of the marketing researcher's job is to interpret the information and make conclusions with regard to managerial decision making. The researcher must prepare a report to communicate the research findings. Included in this report should be suggestions for actions that might be taken by the organization to solve the marketing problem.

The researcher must be careful not to overwhelm management with technical terminology. Rather, the report should highlight the important results and conclusions in a clear and concise manner. Ultimately, the marketing researcher and management must work closely together to ensure proper interpretation of the research results. In addition, management must make a commitment to act—to make decisions based on the research and their good judgment and knowledge of the situation. In other words, someone must "make something happen" to see that a solution to the marketing problem gets implemented. Failure to act on the research findings creates an appearance that the marketing research effort is of little value. Finally, once implemented, the proposed solution should be monitored to ensure that intended results do occur.

ETHICAL ISSUES IN THE MARKETING RESEARCH PROCESS

According to the Marketing Research and Intelligence Association (MRIA), Canada's national association for professional marketing researchers, nine out of ten Canadians support marketing and survey research and believe that it serves a valuable societal purpose. However, unethical practices by some individual organizations are threatening the goodwill that Canadians have toward research.[15] Ethical issues can arise in the marketing researchers' relationships with all parties involved in the research process, including the respondents, the general public, their organizations, and/or clients. Professional marketing researchers must make ethical decisions regarding the collecting, using, and reporting of research data. Examples of unethical behaviour include failure to report problems with research results because of incomplete data, reporting only favourable results, using deception to collect information, and breaching the confidentiality of

Making Responsible Decisions

A New Charter of Respondent Rights

The Marketing Research and Intelligence Association (MRIA), Canada's national association for professional marketing researchers, has developed the world's first Charter of Respondent Rights. The MRIA states that Canadians who participate in research by providing their opinions to researchers should be respected in terms of their time and their privacy. The Charter sets out nine rights of respondents, and all MRIA members must adhere to this Charter and its nine article components. The MRIA believes this Charter (reprinted below) will help protect the relationship between researchers and the general public.

Charter of Respondent Rights   Your participation in legitimate marketing, social or public opinion research is very important to us. We value your honest feedback and your time. Your opinions help companies develop new products, make existing ones better, and improve customer service. Your views also assist government and non-profit organizations in advancing laws and policies that are in the public interest.

Our relationship with you is based on respect, trust and goodwill. When you participate in research conducted by our firm, or by any other corporate member of the Marketing Research and Intelligence Association (MRIA), you can be assured that:

Article 1 You will always be told the first name of the person contracting you, the research company's name and the nature of the study.

Article 2 You can verify that the research you have been invited to participate in is legitimate in one of two ways.

You can either obtain a registration number and the MRIA's toll-free telephone number for any research registered with MRIA's Research Registration System or you can obtain the contact information of the research director who is conducting the study.

Article 3 You will not be sold anything or asked for money.

Article 4 Your privacy and the privacy of your answers will be respected and strictly preserved in accordance with the organization's privacy policy and applicable federal and provincial laws.

Article 5 You will be contacted at reasonable times, but it the time is inconvenient, you may ask to be re-contacted at a more convenient time.

Article 6 You are entitled to know the approximate duration of the interview.

Article 7 Your decision to participate in a study, answer specific questions, or discontinue your participation will be respected without question.

Article 8 You will be informed in advance if the interview will be recorded and the intended use of the recording. You may choose not to proceed with the interview if you do not want it to be recorded.

Article 9 You are assured that the highest standards of professional conduct will be upheld throughout all stages of the study.

respondents.[16] Many companies are also collecting clickstream data when consumers go online, and sometimes these data are used for marketing purposes without the knowledge and consent of the consumer. The MRIA has developed formal ethical standards, guidelines, and policies for all its members to adhere to with regard to all aspects of marketing research. An example of the organization's efforts to respect respondent's time and privacy, and to honour their societal contribution by providing feedback to marketing researchers, is the world's first charter of respondent rights as outlined in the Making Responsible Decisions box, "A New Charter of Respondent Rights."[17]

LO5 USING A MARKETING INFORMATION SYSTEM TO TRIGGER MARKETING ACTIONS

Today's marketing managers can be drowned in such an ocean of data that they need to adopt strategies for dealing with complex, changing views of the competition, the market, and the consumer. The Internet and the PC power of today provide a gateway to exhaustive data sources that vary from well organized and correct to disorganized and incorrect.

The Marketing Manager's View of Sales "Drivers"

Figure 8–6 shows a marketing manager's view of the product or brand "drivers," the factors that influence buying decisions of a household or organization and, hence, sales. These drivers include both the controllable marketing mix factors, such as product and distribution, as well as the uncontrollable factors, such as competition and the changing tastes of households or organizational buyers.

Understanding these drivers involves managing this ocean of data. Sometimes, hundreds of thousands of bits of data are created each week. Sources feeding this database ocean range from internal data about sales and customers to external data from syndication services and TV ratings. The marketer's task is to convert this data ocean into useful information on which to base informed decisions. In practice, some market researchers distinguish *data*—the facts and figures—from *information*—the distilled facts and figures whose interpretation leads to marketing actions.

Current information about products, competitors, and customers is almost always accessed and analyzed by computer. So, today, these activities fall under the broader term of a *marketing information system,* which involves people, computers, and communication systems to satisfy an organization's needs for data storage, processing, access, and marketing decision making.

Key Elements of a Marketing Information System

Figure 8–7 shows the key elements of a marketing information system. At the bottom of Figure 8–7, the marketer queries the databases in the marketing information system with marketing questions that need answers. These questions go through statistical models that analyze the relationships existing among the data. The databases form the core, or *data warehouse,* where the ocean of data is collected and stored. After the search of this data warehouse, the models select and link the pertinent data, often presenting them in tables and graphics for easy interpretation. Marketers can also use

 **FIGURE 8-6**

Product and brand drivers: factors that influence sales

SOURCE: Used by permission of Ford Consulting Group, Inc.

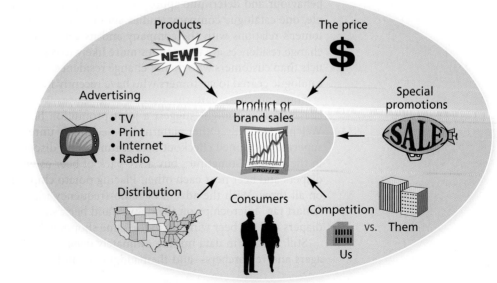

● **FIGURE 8-7**
How marketing researchers
and managers use information
technology to turn
information into action

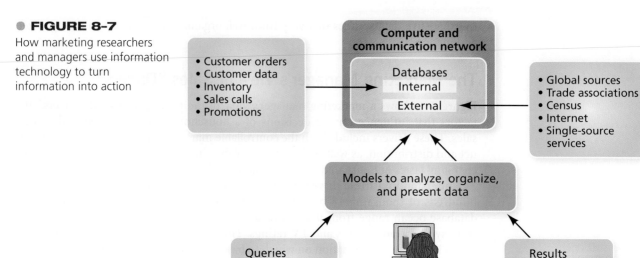

● **FIGURE 8-7**
How marketing researchers
and managers use information
technology to turn
information into action

sensitivity analysis to query the database with "what if" questions to determine how a hypothetical change in a driver, such as advertising, can affect sales.

Data Mining: Searching the Data Ocean

Traditional marketing research typically involves identifying possible drivers and then collecting data: Increasing couponing (the driver) during spring will increase trial by first-time buyers (the result). Marketing researchers then try to collect information to attempt to verify the truth of the relationship.

data mining
The extraction of hidden predictive information from large databases.

In contrast, **data mining** is the extraction of hidden predictive information from large databases. Catalogue companies, such as Sears Canada and Lands' End, use data mining to find statistical links that suggest particular marketing actions. Data mining, in fact, often plays a critical role in a company's customer relationship management (CRM) efforts. Through data mining, a company can monitor customer behaviour and determine appropriate strategies based on that behaviour. For example, one catalogue company studies about 3,500 variables over the lifetime of a customer's relations with the company and its catalogue. It found that customers who change residences are three times more likely to buy new tables and decorative products than customers who do not change residences. So the company actually created a catalogue geared to customers who have recently moved.

Some purchase patterns are common sense. Peanut butter and grape jelly purchases link and might suggest a joint promotion between Kraft peanut butter and Welch's grape jelly. Other patterns link seemingly unrelated purchases. For example, a supermarket mined checkout data scanners and discovered that men buying diapers in the evening sometimes buy a six-pack of beer as well. So the supermarket placed diapers and beer near each other. Placing potato chips between them increased sales on all three. With the advent of radio-frequency identification devices (RFID) with "smart tag" microchips on the diapers and beer, supermarkets will really know if the diapers and the beer wind up in the same shopping bag—at 10 o'clock in the evening.

Still, success in data mining ultimately depends on humans—the marketing managers and researchers—and their judgments in how to select, analyze, and interpret the information. Additionally, new techniques and methods are always emerging and marketing researchers must keep abreast of such developments. The MRIA provides the latest news in marketing research on its Web site. Check out the accompanying Going Online box, "The Latest News in Marketing Research," to keep yourself up-to-date on the latest developments.

---

learning review

10. What does a marketing manager mean when she talks about a sales "driver"?

11. How does data mining differ from traditional marketing research?

Going Online

The Latest News in Marketing Research

Go to the Marketing Research and Intelligence Association's Web site to check out all the latest news in marketing research (**www.mria-arim.ca**). On the site, you will find the link for the latest news.

LEARNING OBJECTIVES REVIEW

 LO1   Know what marketing research is.

Marketing research is the process of defining a marketing problem or opportunity, systematically collecting and analyzing information, and recommending actions to improve an organization's marketing activities. Marketing research is used by executives to aid in the decision-making process.

 LO2   Explain the different types of marketing research.

There are three basic types of marketing research: (*1*) exploratory research, which is preliminary research conducted to clarify the scope and nature of the marketing problem; (*2*) descriptive research, which is research designed to describe basic characteristics of a given population or to profile particular marketing situations; and (*3*) causal research, which is research designed to identify cause-and-effect relationships among variables.

LO3   Understand the stages in the marketing research process.

The four basic stages in the marketing research process generally are: (*1*) defining the problem, (*2*) determining the research design, (*3*) collecting and analyzing data, and (*4*) drawing conclusions and preparing a report. The first stage—problem definition—is critical, because research based on incorrect problem definition will be a waste of resources. At the research design stage, the researcher produces a plan that outlines the methods and procedures for collecting and analyzing the required information. The plan includes the objectives of the research, the sources of information to be used, the research methods, the sampling plan, and the schedule and cost of the research.

LO4   Explain the use of secondary data, surveys, experiments, and observation in marketing research.

The marketing research can utilize secondary data—data previously collected and assembled for some other project than the one at hand. These data consist of information from both inside and outside the organization that may provide some insight into the marketing problem and its solution. If it does not, the marketing researcher may turn to the collecting of primary data—new data gathered and assembled specifically for the project—which can be obtained via surveys, experiments, and observation. A survey generates data by asking people questions and recording their responses on a questionnaire. An experiment involves the manipulation of an independent variable (e.g., price) and measuring its effect on the dependent variable (e.g., purchase behaviour). Observation involves watching, either mechanically or in person, how people actually behave. Research is being conducted more and more often via the Internet (online research) because it can be cheaper, faster, and better. And researchers are also using more creative approaches to research, including ethnographic research and neuromarketing research.

 LO5   Explain how a marketing information system can trigger marketing actions.

Today's marketing managers are often overloaded with data—from internal data to those provided on, say, TV viewing habits or on grocery purchases from the scanner data at checkout counters. This can involve millions of bits of new information in a week or a month. A marketing information system enables massive amounts of marketing data to be stored, processed, and accessed. Using this system, databases are queried using data mining to find statistical relationships to aid in marketing decisions and actions.

FOCUSING ON KEY TERMS

data mining   p. 222
depth interviews   p. 208
ethnographic research   p. 216
experiment   p. 212
focus groups   p. 207
marketing research   p. 202
nonprobability sampling   p. 218

observation   p. 214
primary data   p. 206
probability sampling   p. 218
sampling   p. 217
secondary data   p. 206
survey   p. 209

APPLYING MARKETING KNOWLEDGE

1 Is it possible to make effective marketing decisions without marketing research?

2 Why is the problem definition stage of the marketing research process probably the most important stage?

3 You plan to open an ice cream shop in your town. What type of exploratory research would you conduct to help determine its feasibility? You find the exploratory research does not answer all your questions. You decide to do a survey to determine whether you should open the shop. What kind of questions will you ask? Whom do you ask?

4 Suppose you are trying to determine the top three favourite department stores in your area. You show customers at a shopping mall a list of department stores and ask them to rank their three favourite stores from 1 to 3 (with 1 being the favourite). What problems can occur with the survey?

5 Your university bookstore wants to find out students' opinions about the store's merchandise, prices, and customer service. What type of marketing research would you recommend to the store?

6 You are a marketing researcher observing what people do when selecting bread in a supermarket. You are behind a one-way mirror, and the customers do not know they are being observed. During the course of the day, you observe several people shoplifting a smaller snack product near the bread section. You know personally two of the shoplifters you see. What are the ethical problems you face in this situation?

7 You plan to open a new rent-a-car business. You have drafted a survey you want to distribute to airline passengers. The survey will be left at the airports, and respondents will mail the surveys back in a prepaid envelope. Some of the questions you plan to use are shown below. Use Figure 8–4 to (*a*) identify the problem with each question, and (*b*) correct it. (Note: Some questions may have more than one problem.)

   a. Do you own your own car or usually rent one?
     ☐ Yes   ☐ No

   b. What is your age?   ☐ 21–30   ☐ 30–40   ☐ 41–50   ☐ 50+

   c. How much did you spend on rental cars last year?
     ☐ $100 or less   ☐ $101–$400   ☐ $401–$800
     ☐ $800–$1,000   ☐ $1,000 or more

   d. What is a good daily rental car rate? _____

8 Suppose the government of British Columbia hired you to develop a new tourism ad campaign for the province. You have developed two ad concepts. But you need to test customer response to the ads online. How would you go about the testing? And what would you measure?

Building Your Marketing Plan

To help you collect the most useful data for your marketing plan, develop a three-column table:

1. In column 1, list the information you would ideally like to have to fill holes in your marketing plan.

2. In column 2, identify the source for each bit of information in column 1, such as a Web search, talking to prospective customers, looking at internal data, and so forth.

3. In column 3, set a priority on information you will have time to spend collecting by ranking them: 1 = most important, 2 = next most important, and so forth.

MYSTERY SHOPPING AS A MARKETING RESEARCH TOOL

Introduction

Mystery shopping is the practice of using trained field workers to play the role of shoppers to anonymously collect data on a "shopping experience" in order to evaluate an organization's customer service, operations, employee integrity, merchandising, and product or service quality. Mystery shopping is a form of direct observational research. Often used in banking, retailing, travel, hotels, and restaurants, mystery shoppers enter the marketplace, posing as real customers. They collect data on customer service and the customer experience, and findings are then reported back to the commissioning organization. Mystery shopping goes by many names: secret shopping, mystery customers, spotters, anonymous audits, virtual customers, or performance audits. Mystery shopping is often used to fill in a gap of critical information between operations and marketing. In particular, mystery shopping is used on the front line to collect data that helps determine what happens to customers and prospects when they visit or call on a company to purchase products or services. Mystery shopping is a $1 billion industry and there are Canadian companies that supply mystery shoppers to clients coast-to-coast.

Marketing Research versus Mystery Shopping

Marketing research is the process of obtaining knowledge and gaining an understanding about what people think, feel, and do to meet their needs, desires, and preferences related to buying products and services. Marketing research is used to identify and define marketing opportunities and problems; generate, refine, and evaluate marketing actions; monitor marketing; and improve understanding of marketing as a process. In plain English, it is determining what real customers, real prospects, and other specific groups of people think about companies, services, products, and marketing communications.

Though many marketing research firms conduct mystery shopping, mystery shopping is not marketing research per se. In other words, it is research but it is not pure marketing research. It is actually more closely related to operations research. Mystery shopping complements marketing research, but it is different in critical ways. For example, mystery shoppers must follow specific guidelines on what to do during an evaluation and must shop at specified locations they may not normally visit. On the other hand, marketing research study participants are not given such evaluation guidelines in advance.

Mystery shopping is typically more operational in nature than marketing research and is most often used for quality control, training, and incentive purposes. Marketing research is used most often to determine real customer and prospect opinions, perceptions, needs, and wants. Mystery shoppers are recruited based on specific profiles that closely match a company's real customers. Marketing research study participants are sampled at random from a qualified population to represent a larger population. Mystery shoppers are asked to be objective and explain observations. Marketing research study participants are encouraged to give their subjective opinions freely. Mystery shopping reports on specific visits or calls—each evaluation can be used independently to make improvements to operations and training. Mystery shopping is not predictive of every customer's experience unless sufficient samples are taken and data are analyzed in aggregate.

Mystery shopping should not be used alone to determine customer satisfaction—it can complement, but not replace traditional customer satisfaction research. You can't predict or measure customer satisfaction using mystery shopping because customer satisfaction is a subjective topic based on what real customers think. Mystery shoppers are not real customers—they know what to evaluate before entering the store and they may not typically visit the store they are evaluating.

Types of Mystery Shopping Methods

As with marketing research, there are many different types of data collection methods for mystery shopping. Some of the common mystery shopping data collection methods include in-person/on-site shopping, telephone shopping, e-commerce Web site shopping, hidden video/audio recording, full narrative shopping (qualitative), checklist shopping (quantitative), purchase and returns shopping, and discrimination (matched-pair) testing.

The Benefits of a Mystery Shopping Program

A mystery shopper program can monitor and measure service performance, improve customer retention, make employees aware of what is important in serving customers, reinforce positive employee/management actions with incentive-based reward systems, provide feedback from the front line operations, monitor facility conditions, ensure product/service delivery quality, support promotional programs, audit pricing and merchandising compliance, provide data for competitive analyses, complement other forms of marketing research data, identify training needs and sales opportunities, ensure positive customer relationships on the front line, and enforce employee integrity.

Designing Mystery Shopping Questionnaires/Evaluation Forms

Questionnaires for mystery shopping evaluations should be designed to provide objective, observational feedback with a system to allow for checks and balances. Criteria to be evaluated must be objective rather than subjective. Typical retail mystery shopping questionnaires cover the following: greeting, customer service, facility cleanliness and orderliness, speed of service, product quality, and employee product knowledge.

Unlike marketing research questionnaires that often employ Likert scales for ratings, mystery shopping questionnaires typically use only binary ("yes" and "no") questions. For certain questions, mystery shoppers may be required to provide open-ended narratives for clarification of observations. Multiple-response questions are used to allow mystery shoppers to check off the features and benefits that are mentioned during the shop. Most mystery shopping questionnaires include a "general comments" section that encourages mystery shoppers to remark on anything they find significant or interesting during the shop.

For mystery shopping questionnaires, some questions may be more important than others—a point/scoring system for questions can emphasize the most important issues. If using a scoring system, which is often recommended, appropriate weighting of questions is critical. Some questions may not need to have points allocated to them at all, but may be necessary for background on the shop experience. Mystery shoppers' evaluations may be questioned and/or appealed once the facility knows that a mystery shop has occurred.

How to Make the Most of a Mystery Shopping Program

With a mystery shopping program, companies can establish customer service guidelines, and monitor and reward excellent performance. As management guru Tom Peters says, "What gets measured gets done."

Once shopper reports are compiled, sharing those results with operations, training, and other key personnel is the important next step in a program's success. Results of mystery shopping programs can be used to reward company personnel for a job well done while identifying areas where training may improve customer service and sales.

Mystery shopping can also be used as a marketing and training tool to help ensure a company's communications, service, and operational objectives are being carried out on the front line. An established, ongoing program, where employees know that any customer may be the mystery shopper, is more effective and objective than sporadic audits.

Questions

1 How does the use of mystery shoppers relate to observational research discussed in the chapter, including ethnographic research?

2 What are the strengths and pitfalls of using mystery shopping to evaluate likely customer experience with an organization?

3 Suppose that a hotel, hospital, and supermarket each hired you to be a mystery shopper. Construct a basic evaluation instrument that you would use to examine the performance of those organizations in terms of customer service and measuring your overall customer experience with those organizations.

4 What are the ethical issues involved in a company hiring mystery shoppers to measure the performance of their employees with regard to delivering a good customer experience?

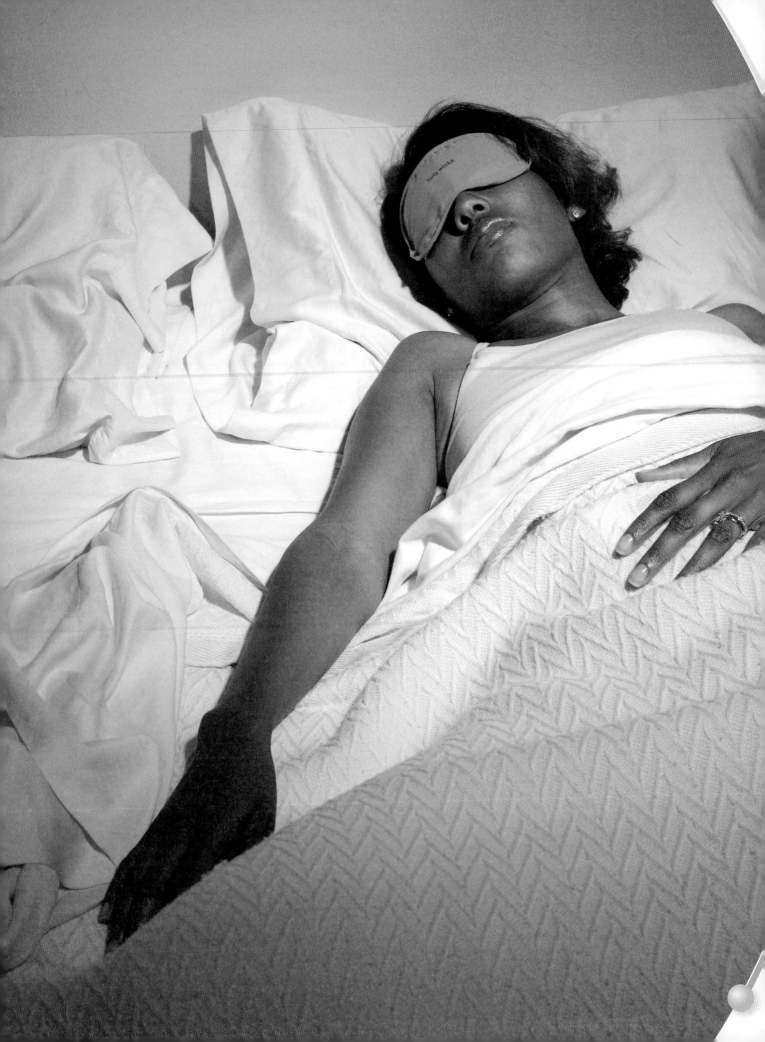

Market Segmentation, Targeting, and Positioning

HAD A GOOD NIGHT SLEEP LATELY? IF NOT, IT MIGHT NOT BE YOUR MATTRESS. IT COULD BE YOUR BED PILLOW!

Canadian consumers spend hundreds of millions of dollars annually on bedding, including mattresses, bed pillows, sheets, and comforters. Yet many Canadians complain about the quality of their sleep. The solution for many is to buy a new mattress. Many sleep experts, however, suggest that people may be simply sleeping on the wrong bed pillow!

Even though you might not give a lot of thought to your bed pillow, the bedding industry is constantly trying to create and provide you with the best pillow for your particular needs. In fact, sleep scientists believe that they have found the correct pillow for each sleeper depending on how the person sleeps—or the person's preferred sleep position. In short, the market is divided or segmented into three basic types of sleepers: side sleepers, back sleepers, and stomach sleepers. The bedding industry recommends a particular bed pillow type based on your sleep position. For example, if you sleep on your side, a firm pillow provides more cushion between your head, shoulders, and mattress. Feather, fluffy-filled hollofil or regular polyester or foam latex make the firmest pillow.

learning objectives

After reading this chapter, you should be able to:

LO1 Explain what market segmentation is and when to use it.

LO2 Identify the five steps involved in segmenting and targeting markets.

LO3 Recognize the different factors used to segment consumer and organizational (business) markets.

LO4 Know how to develop a market-product grid to identify a target market and recommend resulting actions.

LO5 Explain how marketing managers position products in the marketplace.

LO6 Describe three approaches to developing a sales forecast for a company.

If you sleep on your back, a medium-firm pillow provides a natural cushioning between head and mattress. Down/feather, medium-filled hollofil, or bonder polyester offers the most comfort for back sleepers. If you sleep on your stomach, a soft pillow gives less cushioning between head and mattress. Down, down/feather, or lightly filled hollofil polyester is best for the stomach sleeper.

So, what is your preferred sleep position: side, back, or stomach? Yes, we know you might change your sleep position through the night. But sleep scientists have discovered that people do have a preferred sleep position. Does the pillow you have on your bed actually match your sleep position? If not, this might explain why your sleep is not restful.

Now, do you want to estimate the relative sizes of the three segments of sleepers? You would want to know this if you were a bed pillow manufacturer who wanted to produce the right type and right number of pillows for the sleepers out there. Well, the answer is: 73 percent of people sleep on their side, 22 percent sleep on their back, and 5 percent sleep on their stomach.[1]

What this example illustrates is that even for a simple product like bed pillows, there is not a "one size/one type fits all" marketing solution. Different sleepers do have different needs. This is the essence of market segmentation: designing and delivering products and services to satisfy the needs of different customers. After we discuss more fully why markets need to be segmented, we will discuss the steps used in segmenting markets, the process of selecting a target segment(s), and how to position a product or service offering effectively in the marketplace. We will then discuss forecasting sales for given segments or targets.

LO1 WHY SEGMENT MARKETS?

One of the oldest stories about the need for market segmentation comes from the early automobile industry. Henry Ford developed his Model T, a car he felt would satisfy the needs of everyone. Ford said, "They can have it in any colour, as long as it's black." His strategy was simple: focus in the economies of scale created by mass production. Ford's strategy was also known as a mass marketing strategy. In contrast, General Motors began producing different models of cars, each available in different colours, designed to appeal to the preferences of different consumers. This strategy enabled GM to surpass Ford and become the leading automaker. In short, most companies segment markets because of an almost unassailable premise: People are different, and people who are different are likely to have different needs and wants. Accordingly, smart marketers segment markets so that they can respond more effectively to the specific needs and wants of groups of potential buyers and thus increase its sales and profits. Not-for-profit organizations also segment the clients they serve to satisfy client needs more effectively while achieving the organization's goals. Let's now talk in more detail about (1) what market segmentation is, and (2) when it is necessary to segment markets.

What Market Segmentation Means

The fact that people are different is not necessarily a comfortable notion for marketers. In fact, it would be easier for marketers if people were all the same. But they are not. So, market segmentation involves aggregating prospective buyers into groups that

● **FIGURE 9–1**

Market segmentation—
linking market needs to an
organization's marketing
program

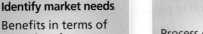

Identify market needs

Benefits in terms of
- Product features
- Expense
- Quality
- Savings in time and
  convenience

→ Process of
segmenting and
targeting markets →

**Execute marketing
program**

A marketing mix in terms of
- Product
- Price
- Promotion
- Place

market segments

The relatively homogeneous
groups of prospective buyers
that result from the market
segmentation process.

(1) have common needs, and (2) will respond similarly to a marketing action. **Market segments** are the relatively homogeneous groups of prospective buyers that result from the market segmentation process. Each market segment consists of people who are relatively similar to each other in terms of their consumption behaviour.

The existence of different market segments has caused firms to use a marketing strategy of **product differentiation.** This strategy involves a firm using different marketing mix activities, such as product features and advertising, to help consumers perceive the product as being different from and better than competing products. The perceived differences may involve physical features or nonphysical ones, such as image or price.

product differentiation

Strategy that involves a firm using
different marketing mix activities,
such as product features and
advertising, to help consumers
perceive the product as being
different from and better than
competing products.

Segmentation: Linking Needs to Actions The process of segmenting a market and selecting specific segments as targets is the link between the various buyers' needs and the organization's marketing program (Figure 9–1). Market segmentation is only a means to an end: to lead to tangible marketing actions that can increase sales and profitability.

Market segmentation first stresses the importance of grouping people or organizations in a market according to the similarity of their needs and the benefits they are looking for in making a purchase. Second, such needs and benefits must be related to specific marketing actions that the organization can take. These actions may involve separate products or other aspects of the marketing mix, such as price, advertising, or distribution strategies.

market-product grid

A framework to relate the market
segments of potential buyers
to products offered or potential
marketing actions by the firm.

Using Market-Product Grids A **market-product grid** is a framework to relate the market segments of potential buyers to products offered or potential marketing actions by the firm. The market-product grid in Figure 9–2 shows different market segments for bed pillows discussed in the chapter opener. The market segments appear in the horizontal rows while the product offerings appear in the vertical columns. Also notice in this market-product grid analysis that the estimated market size of each sleeper segment is also provided. This provides the bed pillow manufacturers

● **FIGURE 9–2**

Market-product grid showing
the types of bed pillow
segments and their relative
sizes as percentage of total
market

Market Segments	Bed Pillow Products		
	Firm Pillows	Medium Pillows	Soft Pillows
Side Sleepers	73%		
Back Sleepers		22%	
Stomach Sleepers			5%

an indication of the relative attractiveness of given segments and an idea about the type and amount of pillows that should be produced to cater to those segments.

When to Segment Markets

A business firm goes to the trouble and expense of segmenting its markets when it expects that this will increase its sales, profit, and return on investment. When expenses are greater than the potentially increased sales from segmentation, a firm should not attempt to segment its market. However, three specific situations that illustrate effective use of market segmentation are the cases of (1) one product and multiple market segments, (2) multiple products and multiple market segments, and (3) "segments of one," or mass customization.

One Product and Multiple Market Segments   When a firm produces only a single product or service and attempts to sell it to two or more market segments, it avoids the extra costs of developing and producing additional versions of the product, which often entail extremely high research, engineering, and manufacturing expenses. In this case, the incremental costs of taking the product into new market segments are typically those of a separate promotional campaign or a new channel of distribution. Although these expenses can be high, they are rarely as large as those for developing an entirely new product.

Movies, magazines, and books are single products frequently directed to two or more distinct market segments. Movie companies often run different TV commercials or magazine ads featuring different aspects of a newly released film (love, or drama, or spectacular scenery) that are targeted to different market segments. Many Canadian magazines produce separate editions usually targeting unique geographic and demographic segments using a special mix of editorial content and advertisements. *Maclean's* produces 15 different editions, and *Reader's Digest* produces nine.

Although multiple TV commercials for movies and separate covers or advertisements for magazines or books are expensive, they are minor compared with the costs of producing an entirely new movie, magazine, or book for another market segment.

Multiple Products and Multiple Market Segments   Reebok, a major athletic apparel manufacturer, offers different styles of shoes, each targeted at a different type of user. This is an example of multiple products aimed at multiple market segments. Manufacturing these different styles of shoes is clearly more expensive than producing only a single style but seems worthwhile if it serves customers' needs better, does not reduce quality or increase price, and adds to the sales revenues and profits.

Some marketers also often engage in what are called two-tier marketing strategies—or "Tiffany/Walmart strategies." This means that firms offer different variations of the same basic product or service to both high-end and low-end segments. Gap's Banana Republic chain sells blue jeans for $58, whereas its Old Navy stores sell a slightly different version for $22. The Walt Disney Company carefully markets two distinct Winnie-the-Poohs, such as the original line-drawn figures on fine china sold at Nordstrom and a cartoon-like Pooh on polyester bedsheets sold at Walmart.

Segments of One: Mass Customization   Canadian marketers are rediscovering today what their ancestors running the corner general store knew a century ago: Every customer is unique, has unique wants and needs, and desires special tender loving care or a particular customer experience from the marketer. Economies of scale in manufacturing and marketing during the past century made mass-produced goods so affordable that most customers were willing to compromise their individual tastes and settle for standardized products. Today's Internet environment, coupled with flexible manufacturing and marketing processes, have made *mass customization* possible, that is, tailoring goods or services to the tastes of individual customers on a high-volume scale.

Customization for segments
of one.

Mass customization is the next step beyond *build-to-order (BTO)*, manufacturing a product only when there is an order from a customer. Dell Computer uses BTO systems that trim work-in-progress inventories and shorten delivery times to customers. Dell's three-day deliveries are made possible by restricting its computer line to only a few basic modules and stocking a variety of each. This gives customers a good choice with quick delivery—Dell PCs can be assembled in four minutes. Most Dell customization comes from loading the unique software each customer selects.

There are even companies that will customize products or services for you, individually, on a much smaller scale. For example, you can go online right now and order custom M&Ms candies especially made for you, including even having your name printed on the candy, and have them delivered right to your door. But the latest trend is for companies to offer consumers what is called *ultra-customization*. Ultra-customization allows you to hand-pick your entertainment packages, personalize your next vacation, design your own clothes, customize your Web site, and choose exactly the information you want to be exposed to, including receiving customized newsletters and magazines. *By Terry* is a company that caters to the very affluent consumer who desires complete personalization. This Paris-based boutique will use your DNA and planetary alignment to customize your very own lipstick. The lipstick is designed and created solely for you. But it will cost you US$1,200.[2] Talk about segments of one!

---

learning review

1. Market segmentation involves aggregating prospective buyers into groups that have two key characteristics. What are they?

2. When should a firm segment its markets?

LO2 STEPS IN SEGMENTING AND TARGETING MARKETS

The process of segmenting a market and then selecting and reaching the target segments is divided into the five steps discussed in this section, as shown in Figure 9–3. Segmenting a market is not an exact science—it requires large doses of common

● **FIGURE 9-3**

The five key steps in segmenting and targeting markets link market needs of customers to the organization's marketing program

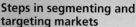

Identify market needs

→

Steps in segmenting and targeting markets
1 Group potential buyers into segments
2 Group products to be sold into categories
3 Develop a market-product grid and estimate size of markets
4 Select target markets
5 Take marketing actions to reach target markets

→

Execute marketing program

sense and managerial judgment. As shown in the nearby Marketing Matters box, segmentation is not easy but is central to successful marketing.[3]

So, now let us have you put on your entrepreneur's hat to use the market segmentation process to choose target markets and take useful marketing actions. Suppose that you own a Wendy's fast-food restaurant next to a large urban university that offers both day and evening classes. Your restaurant specializes in the Wendy's basics: hamburgers, french fries, Frosty desserts, and chili. Even though you are part of a chain and have some restrictions on menu and decor, you are free to set your hours of business and to undertake local advertising. How can market segmentation help?

Step 1: Group Potential Buyers into Segments

It is not always a good idea to segment a market. Grouping potential buyers into meaningful segments involves meeting some specific criteria that answer the questions: "Would segmentation be worth doing?" and "Is it possible?" If so, the next step is to find specific variables that can be used to create the various segments.

 Criteria to Use in Forming the Segments   A marketing manager should develop market segments that meet five main criteria:

- *Potential for increased profit.* The best segmentation approach is the one that maximizes the opportunity for future profit and return on investment (ROI). If this potential is maximized without segmentation, do not segment. For not-for-profit organizations, the criterion is the potential for serving client users more effectively.
- *Similarity of needs of potential buyers within a segment.* Potential buyers within a segment should be similar in terms of a marketing action, such as product features sought or advertising media used.
- *Difference of needs of buyers among segments.* If the needs of the various segments are not very different, combine them into fewer segments. A different segment usually requires a different marketing action, which, in turn, means greater costs. If increased sales do not offset extra costs, combine segments and reduce the number of marketing actions.
- *Potential of a marketing action to reach a segment.* Reaching a segment requires a simple but effective marketing action. If no such action exists, do not segment.
- *Simplicity and cost of assigning potential buyers to segments.* A marketing manager must be able to put a market segmentation plan into effect. This means being able to recognize the characteristics of potential buyers and then assigning them to a segment without encountering excessive costs.

Ways to Segment Consumer Markets   Figure 9–4 shows the main dimensions used to segment Canadian consumer markets. These include geographic, demographic, psychographic, and behavioural segmentation. By examining Figure 9–4, you

Marketing Matters

Segmentation Is Not Easy

Most marketing experts agree that segmentation is central to successful marketing. However, these experts also suggest that segmentation is perhaps the most difficult task in marketing and perhaps the worst practised. Professor Marc Meyer, in his recent book, *The Fast Path to Corporate Growth,* argues that most marketers create segmentation schemes that are simply too complicated. He suggests that we should keep it simple—segmentation is about "users" and "uses." Meyer says that a simple grid based on users and uses can be very revealing and can lead to actionable marketing activities. (Remember our simple grid for bed pillows earlier in this chapter?) Professor Meyer suggests that there are no monolithic markets anymore. And, importantly, market segments are always changing; new users and new uses for products emerge over time. Therefore, segmentation must be an ongoing exercise.

Professor Malcolm McDonald suggests that poor segmentation leads to poor targeting and poor positioning. He suggests that we must identify customer needs and the benefits they seek when they buy products and services, group customers together into segments based on similar needs and benefits, and properly identify each needs-based segment using demographics and behavioural dimensions

so that segments are distinct and actionable. He suggests that in order to do so we must understand exactly what is purchased including why, where, when, and how, as well as the actual use of the product. McDonald says that if segmentation is done properly, it is easy to determine which targets to pursue and how to position products and services effectively to appeal to those targets.

Professor Roger Best also argues that understanding customer needs is the first step in market segmentation. Too many marketers, he suggests, start with demographics, lifestyle, and usage behaviours. But this is the wrong approach. There are simply too many variables, and too many meaningless combinations. Instead, the market segmentation process should start with customers with like needs. Then, for each needs-based segment, we can determine the demographics, lifestyle, and usage behaviours that make one segment meaningfully different from another. But good segmentation is built first and foremost around customer needs.

Segmentation is the cornerstone of a successful marketing strategy. But it requires experience, skill, and creativity. Done correctly it creates opportunities for enterprise growth and profitability.

can also see that a number of variables can be used within each dimension for segmentation purposes. What you should remember is that segmenting markets is not a pure science—it requires large doses of common sense and managerial judgment. A marketer may have to use several dimensions and multiple variables within each dimension to form proper market segments. Let us take a look at how some marketers might segment consumer markets using the information in Figure 9–4.

- *Geographic segmentation.* Using geographic segmentation, a marketer segments based on where consumers live. Geographic variables, such as countries, regions, provinces, counties, cities, or even neighbourhoods, could be used. Marketers often find that Canadians differ in terms of needs or preferences based on the region in which they live. This is a form of geographic segmentation. For example, Colgate-Palmolive markets Arctic Power, its cold-water detergent, on an energy cost saving dimension in Quebec, but as a clothes saver (cold-water washing is easier on clothes) in western Canada.

- *Demographic segmentation.* One of the most common ways to segment consumer markets is to use demographic segmentation, or segmenting a market based on population characteristics. This approach segments consumers according to such variables as age, gender, income, education, occupation, and so forth. Cyanamid Canada Inc. uses age as a segmentation variable, producing and marketing its vitamins to various age groups, including children, young adults, and older Canadians. Centrum Select, for instance, is specifically designed for adults over 50. Trimark Investments of Ontario segments the financial services market by gender, targeting males and females with different products and different advertising

Main Dimensions	Variables	Typical Breakdowns
Geographic segmentation	Region	Atlantic, Quebec, Ontario, Prairies, British Columbia
	City or census metropolitan area (CMA) size	Under 5,000; 5,000–19,999; 20,000–49,999; 50,000–99,999; 100,000–249,999; 250,000–499,999; 500,000–999,999; 1,000,000–3,999,999; 4,000,000+
	Density	Urban; suburban; rural
	Climate	East; West
Demographic segmentation	Age	Infant; under 6; 6–11; 12–17; 18–24; 25–34; 35–49; 50–64; 65+
	Gender	Male; female
	Family size	1–2; 3–4; 5+
	Life stage	Infant; preschool; child; youth; collegiate; adult; senior
	Birth era	Baby Boomer (1946–1964); Generation X (1965–1976); Baby Boomer/Generation Y (1977–1994)
	Marital status	Never married; married; separated; divorced; widowed
	Income	Under $10,000; $10,000–$19,999; $20,000–$29,999; $30,000–$39,999; $40,000–$54,999; $55,000–$74,999; $75,000+
	Occupation	Professional; managerial; clerical; sales; labourers; students; retired; housewives; unemployed
	Education	Grade school or less; some high school; high school graduate; some university; university graduate
	Race	White; Black; Asian; Native; other
	Home ownership	Own home; rent home
Psychographic segmentation	Personality	Gregarious; compulsive; extroverted; introverted
	Lifestyle PRIZM C2	Cosmopolitan Elite; Suburban Gentry; Grads & Pads; Les Chics; Lunch at Tim's; and so on
Behavioural segmentation	Benefits sought	Quality; service; low price
	Usage rate	Light user; medium user; heavy user
	User status	Nonuser; ex-user; prospect; first-time user; regular user
	Loyalty status	None; medium; strong

● **FIGURE 9-4**

Segmentation variables and breakdowns for Canadian consumer markets

campaigns. General Electric uses family size as a segmentation variable, targeting smaller families with compact microwaves and larger families with extra-large refrigerators. You should note, however, that a single demographic variable may not be sufficient in understanding and segmenting a given market.[4] Thus, many marketers combine a number of demographic variables that might clearly distinguish one segment from another. For example, cosmetics companies, such as Clinique, combine gender, income, and occupation in order to examine market segments for different lines of cosmetic products.

• *Psychographic segmentation.* Marketers use psychographic segmentation when they segment markets according to personality or lifestyle. It has been found that people who share the same demographic characteristics can have very different psychographic profiles. As we saw in Chapter 5, personality traits have been linked to product preferences and brand choice. In addition, a person's lifestyle (his or her activities, interests, and opinions) also affects the types of products, the brands of products, and how they may be purchased. Remember the PRIZM C2 lifestyle segments or clusters from Chapter 5? Well, for example, the Grads & Pads segment consists of young midscale urban singles with liberal lifestyles. They are night owls and like to drink beer, tequila, and rum. In contrast, the Cosmpolitan Elite are affluent middle-aged or older city dwellers who possess Canada's wealthiest lifestyle. They own luxury import autos, send their kids to private school, and own private cottages. Les Chics, on the other hand, are sophisticated urban Quebec couples or singles who live in expensive homes, like to party, and buy expensive perfume and wine.[5]

- *Behavioural segmentation.* When marketers use consumers' behaviour with or toward a product to segment the market, they are using behavioural segmentation. A powerful form of behavioural segmentation is to divide the market according to the benefits consumers seek from a product category. Using *benefits sought,* the marketer examines the major benefits consumers look for in the product category, the kinds of consumers who look for each benefit, and the major brands that deliver each benefit. For example, Telus Mobility and Bell Mobility both market their wireless communications products and services to young adults under 24 years of age who want text messaging "rather than talk" in order to ensure privacy. On the other hand, Rogers Wireless targets CEOs of large businesses who want to improve employee productivity through the use of wireless technology. Another example is Schick marketing its Intuition razor to Canadian women who seek the convenience benefit of a one-step lather-and-shave design while it also markets its Quattro to women who want the benefit of a truly long-lasting shave.

usage rate

Quantity consumed or patronage—store visits—during a specific period; varies significantly among different customer groups.

80/20 rule

A concept that suggests 80 percent of a firm's sales are obtained from 20 percent of its customers.

Wireless communications providers target young adults seeking specific benefits from wireless technology.

Another behavioural segmentation variable often used by marketers is **usage rate**—quantity consumed or patronage during a specific period, which varies significantly among different customer groups. Air Canada, for example, focuses on usage rate for its frequent-flyer program, which is designed to encourage passengers to use its airline repeatedly. Usage rate is sometimes referred to in terms of the **80/20 rule,** a concept that suggests that 80 percent of a firm's sales are obtained from 20 percent of its customers. The percentages in the 80/20 rule are not really fixed; rather, the rule suggests that a small fraction of customers provide a large fraction of sales. For example, Air Canada pays special attention to the business travel segment that comprises only 20 percent of the airline seats but 40 percent of overall revenues.

Research shows that the fast-food market can also be segmented into light, medium, or heavy users. For every $1 spent by a light user in a fast-food restaurant, each heavy user spends about $5.[6] This is the reason for the emphasis in almost all marketing strategies on effective ways to reach heavy users of products and services. Thus, as a Wendy's restaurant owner, you want to keep the heavy-user segment constantly in mind. With advances in information technology, marketers are now able to conduct detailed segmentation studies. Some Canadian telecommunications companies, for example, can now segment on the basis of more than 100 criteria, from calling patterns to promotional response.

Variables to Use in Forming Segments for Wendy's   Now, in determining one or two variables to segment the market for your Wendy's restaurant, very broadly, we find two main markets: students and nonstudents. To segment the students, we

Phone. Walkie-talkie. And free text, too.
You're always with your friends when you're Solo.

Solo
SANYO   mobile   solomobile.ca

Colors are better when they're green.

Ready For Real Business **xerox**

What variables might Xerox use to segment the organizational markets for its answer to colour copying problems? For the possible answer and related marketing actions, see the text.

Xerox Corporation
www.xerox.com

could try a variety of demographic variables, such as age, gender, year in school, or university major, or psychographic variables, such as personality or lifestyle. But none of these variables really meets the five criteria listed previously—particularly the fourth criterion: leading to a feasible marketing action to reach the various segments. Four student segments that *do* meet these criteria include the following:

- Students living in dormitories (residence halls, fraternity houses).
- Students living near the university in apartments.
- Day commuter students living outside the area.
- Night commuter students living outside the area.

These segmentation variables are really a combination of where the student lives and the time he or she is on campus (and near your restaurant). For nonstudents who might be customers, similar variables might be used:

- Faculty and staff members at the university.
- People who live in the area but are not connected with the university.
- People who work in the area but are not connected with the university.

Ways to Segment Organizational (Business) Markets   Variables for segmenting organizational (business) markets are shown in Figure 9–5. A product manager at Xerox responsible for its office laser printer might use a number of these segmentation variables, as follows:

- *Geographic segmentation.* The product manager might segment on the basis of region or actual location of the potential customer. Firms located in a census metropolitan area (CMA) might receive a personal sales call, whereas those outside the CMA might be contacted by phone.
- *Demographic segmentation.* Firms might be categorized by the North American Industry Classification System (NAICS). Manufacturers, for example, with global

● **FIGURE 9-5**
Dimensions used to segment Canadian organizational markets

MAIN DIMENSIONS	VARIABLES	TYPICAL BREAKDOWNS
Geographic segmentation	Region	Atlantic, Quebec, Ontario, Prairies, British Columbia
	Location	In CMA; not in CMA
Demographic segmentation	NAICS code	2-digit: section; 3-digit: subsection; 4-digit: Industry Group
	Number of employees	1–19; 20–99; 100–249; 250+
	Annual sales volume	Less than $1 million; $1–10 million; $10–100 million; over $100 million
Behavioural segmentation	Benefits sought	Quality; customer service; low price
	Usage rate	Light user; medium user; heavy user
	User status	Nonuser; ex-user; prospect; first-time user; regular user
	Loyalty status	None, medium, strong
	Purchase method	Centralized; decentralized; Individual; group
	Type of buy	New buy; modified rebuy; straight rebuy

customers might have different printing needs than do retailers or lawyers serving local customers.

- *Behavioural segmentation.* The market might also be segmented on the basis of benefits sought. Xerox may decide to focus on firms looking for quality product and good customer service as opposed to those looking for simply low prices. The product manager might also segment the market on the basis of usage rate, recognizing that larger, more globally oriented firms are more likely to be heavy users.

Some experts have combined geographic, demographic, and behavioural segmentation variables used in segmenting organizational (business) markets to produce a segmentation concept known as firmographics. *Firmographics* involves both organizational or business characteristics—such as location, size of firm, industry category, corporate activities, business objectives, and buying objectives—and characteristics of the composition of the organization—such as the income distribution of employees, age, gender, and education of the workforce. Organizations with distinguishing firmographics are then grouped into market segments.[7]

Step 2: Group Products to Be Sold into Categories

As important as grouping customers into segments is finding a means of grouping the products you are selling into meaningful categories. If the firm has only one product or service, this is not a problem, but when it has dozens or hundreds, these must be grouped in some way so that buyers can relate to them. This is why department stores and supermarkets are organized into product groups, with the departments or aisles containing related merchandise. Likewise, manufacturers have product lines that are the groupings they use in the catalogues sent to customers.

What are the groupings for your Wendy's restaurant? It could be the item purchased, such as a Frosty, chili, hamburgers, and french fries, but this is where judgment—the qualitative aspect of marketing—comes in. Students really buy an eating experience, or a meal that satisfies a need at a particular time of day, and so the product grouping can be defined by meal or time of day such as breakfast, lunch, between-meal snack, dinner, and after-dinner snack. These groupings are more closely related to the way purchases are actually made and permit you to market the entire meal, not just your french fries or Frosty. To examine how Apple Inc. grouped its products to be sold into specific categories over its 30-year history, see the Going Online exercise.

 ## Step 3: Develop a Market-Product Grid and Estimate Size of Markets

As you recall from earlier in the chapter a key step in the segmentation process is developing a market-product grid: labelling the markets (or horizontal rows) and products (or vertical columns), as shown in Figure 9–6. In addition, the size of the market in each cell, or the market-product combination, must be estimated. For your restaurant, this involves estimating the number of, or sales revenue obtained from, each kind of meal that can reasonably be expected to be sold to each market segment. This is a form of the usage rate analysis discussed earlier in the chapter.

Going Online

Apple Inc. Product Groupings

In its 30-year history, Apple Inc. has developed hundreds of products. Visit **www.apple-history.com**, look for "Family" (for family of products) on the right-hand side and hit the Family tab. There you will see Apple's approach to grouping its products from computers to its iPod line.

● **FIGURE 9-6**

Selecting a target market for your fast-food restaurant next to an urban university (target market is shaded)

MARKETS	PRODUCTS: MEALS				
	BREAK-FAST	LUNCH	BETWEEN-MEAL SNACK	DINNER	AFTER-DINNER SNACK
STUDENT					
Dormitory	0	1	3	0	3
Apartment	1	3	3	1	1
Day commuter	0	3	2	1	0
Night commuter	0	0	1	3	2
NONSTUDENT					
Faculty or staff	0	3	1	1	0
Live in area	0	1	2	2	1
Work in area	1	3	0	1	0

Key: 3 = Large market; 2 = Medium market; 1 = Small market; 0 = No market.

The market sizes in Figure 9–6 may be simple "guesstimates" if you do not have time for formal marketing research (as discussed in Chapter 8). But even such crude estimates of the size of specific markets using a market-product grid are far better than the usual estimates of the entire market. Estimating the size of given market segments is very helpful when completing Step 4 of the segmentation process: determining which target markets to select.

Step 4: Select Target Markets

A firm must take care to choose its target market segments carefully. If it chooses too narrow a group of segments, it may fail to reach the volume of sales and profits it needs. If it selects too broad a group of segments, it may spread its marketing efforts so thin that the extra expenses more than offset the increased sales and profits.

Criteria to Use in Choosing the Target Segments   Two different kinds of criteria are present in the market segmentation process: (1) those to use in dividing the market into segments (discussed earlier), and (2) those to use in actually choosing the target segments. Even experienced marketing executives often confuse these two different sets of criteria. The five criteria to use in actually selecting the target segments apply to your Wendy's restaurant in this way:

- *Market size.* The estimated size of the market in the segment is an important factor in deciding whether it is worth going after. There is really no market for breakfasts among campus students (see Figure 9–6), so why devote any marketing effort toward reaching a small or non-existent market?
- *Expected growth.* Although the size of the market in a segment may be small now, perhaps it is growing significantly or is expected to grow in the future. For example, the segment using drive-through ordering is growing three times faster than the eat-inside segment. So having a fast-service drive-through facility may be critical for your restaurant's success.
- *Competitive position.* Is there a lot of competition in the segment now or is there likely to be in the future? The less the competition, the more attractive the segment is. For example, if the university cafeterias announce a new policy of "no meals on weekends," this segment is suddenly more promising for your restaurant.
- *Cost of reaching the segment.* A segment that is inaccessible to a firm's marketing actions should not be pursued. For example, the few nonstudents who live in the area may not be economically reachable with ads in newspapers or other media. As a result, do not waste money trying to advertise to them.

A late night oasis on the highway of hunger.

Wendy's Late Night Pick-up Window is open 'til midnight or later. So, you can get a *hot 'n juicy Classic Single, Classic Double with cheese or Classic Triple with cheese,* and eat great, even late.

How can Wendy's target different market segments, such as drive-through customers, with different advertising programs? For the answer, see the text and Figure 9–7.

- *Compatibility with the organization's objectives and resources.* If your restaurant does not have the cooking equipment to make breakfasts and has a policy against spending more money on restaurant equipment, then do not try to reach the breakfast segment.

As is often the case in marketing decisions, a particular segment may appear attractive according to some criteria and very unattractive according to others.

Choose the Segments   Ultimately, a marketing executive has to use these criteria to choose the segments for special marketing efforts. As shown in Figure 9–6, let us assume you have written off the breakfast market for two reasons: too small market size and incompatibility with your objectives and resources. In terms of competitive position and cost of reaching the segment, you choose to focus on the four student segments and not the three nonstudent segments (although you are certainly not going to turn away business from the nonstudent segments). This combination of market-product segments—your target market—is shaded in Figure 9–6. In some cases, after selecting target markets, a firm may discover some segments may be too costly or unprofitable to serve. This may lead to de-selection of certain customers or segments, as the Making Responsible Decisions box, "De-selection of Customers or Customer Segments," points out.

Step 5: Take Marketing Actions to Reach Target Markets

The purpose of developing a market-product grid is to trigger marketing actions to increase revenues and profits. This means that someone must develop and execute an action plan.

Making Responsible Decisions

De-selection of Customers or Customer Segments

Obviously, every organization has a right to determine the customer segments it wants to serve. And no one will dispute that organizations can do so as long as they are not discriminating against customers on the basis of race, ethnicity, or gender. However, as you have learned in this chapter, not all customers have the same value to an organization. In fact, in a world of high-technology and sophisticated segmentation analysis, many organizations are now able to discern the true costs and bottom-line value of individual consumers and/or given customer segments.

In most cases, good segmentation analysis reveals these hard numbers to show the real costs and contribution margins of certain customers. When this information is presented to executives, they may have to make some tough decisions. In some cases, it might mean to de-market or de-select certain customers. In other words, a firm might "fire" or quit the customer or invoke such practices as charging additional fees or restricting access to certain customer service levels, which might force some customers to find another alternative to do business with.

One bank, for example, determined through detailed segmentation analysis that certain customers were clearly

less profitable, or even unprofitable, to serve compared with others. They started to charge a fee to those high-cost, low-profit customers if they used a teller at a branch or if they phoned a call centre for customer assistance. Many of these customers, upon finding charges of $2 per contact, decided to leave the bank, which is exactly what the bank intended. Others simply complained about unfair treatment and sought to have those fees removed from their statements. Another financial services company, finding that only their business-to-business (B2B) segment was highly profitable, simply stopped serving the business-to-consumer (B2C) market segment and informed those customers that they were exiting the B2C segment of the market, thus forcing this segment to find a new provider.

What do you think about the de-selection of customers or customer segments? Does a company have the right to de-select customers after segmentation analysis reveals that these customers are more costly to serve and/or contribute less to the profitability of the organization compared with other customers? If so, who will serve these customers?

Your Wendy's Segmentation Strategy   With your Wendy's restaurant, you have already reached one significant decision: There is a limited market for breakfast, and so you will not open for business until 10:30 a.m. In fact, Wendy's first attempt at a breakfast menu was a disaster and was discontinued in 1986. Wendy's evaluates possible new menu items continuously, to compete not only with McDonald's and Burger King but also with a complex array of supermarkets, convenience stores, and gas stations that sell reheatable packaged foods as well as new "easy-lunch" products.

Another essential decision is where and what meals to advertise to reach specific market segments. An ad in the student newspaper could reach all the student segments, but you might consider this "shotgun approach" too expensive and want a more focused "rifle approach" to reach smaller segments. If you choose three segments for special actions (Figure 9–7), advertising actions to reach them might include the following:

- *Day commuters* (an entire market segment). Run ads inside commuter buses and put flyers under the windshield wipers of cars in parking lots used by day commuters. These ads and flyers promote all the meals at your restaurant to a single segment of students—a horizontal cut through the market-product grid.
- *Between-meals snacks* (directed to all four student markets). To promote eating during this downtime for your restaurant, offer "Ten percent off all purchases between 2:00 and 4:30 p.m. during the winter term." This ad promotes a single meal to all four student segments—a vertical cut through the market-product grid.
- *Dinners to night commuters.* The most focused of all three campaigns, this ad promotes a single meal to a single student segment. The campaign might consist of a windshield flyer offering a free Frosty with a coupon when the customer buys a drive-through meal between 5:00 and 7:00 p.m.

Depending on how your advertising actions work, you can repeat, modify, or drop them and design new campaigns for other segments you feel are worth the effort. This example of advertising your Wendy's restaurant is just a small part of a complete marketing program using all the elements of the marketing mix. In other words, other changes in your marketing mix elements may be required to appeal to particular

● **FIGURE 9-7**

Advertising actions to reach specific student segments

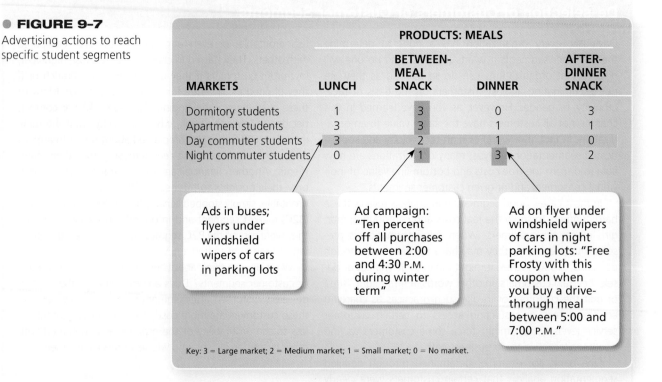

MARKETS	LUNCH	BETWEEN-MEAL SNACK	DINNER	AFTER-DINNER SNACK
Dormitory students	1	3	0	3
Apartment students	3	3	1	1
Day commuter students	3	2	1	0
Night commuter students	0	1	3	2

PRODUCTS: MEALS

Ads in buses; flyers under windshield wipers of cars in parking lots

Ad campaign: "Ten percent off all purchases between 2:00 and 4:30 P.M. during winter term"

Ad on flyer under windshield wipers of cars in night parking lots: "Free Frosty with this coupon when you buy a drive-through meal between 5:00 and 7:00 P.M."

Key: 3 = Large market; 2 = Medium market; 1 = Small market; 0 = No market.

segments. For the night commuter, for example, having a late-night drive-through window that is open past 11 p.m. would be an important marketing mix decision.

---

learning review

3. What are some criteria used to decide which segments to choose for targets?

4. In a market-product grid, what factor is estimated or measured for each of the cells?

LO5 POSITIONING THE PRODUCT

product positioning
The place an offering occupies in consumers' minds on important attributes relative to competitive products.

When a company introduces a new product, a decision critical to its long-term success is how prospective buyers view it in relation to those products offered by its competitors. **Product positioning** refers to the place an offering occupies in consumers' minds on important attributes relative to competitive products. In contrast, **product repositioning** involves *changing* the place an offering occupies in a consumer's mind relative to competitive products.

product repositioning
Changing the place an offering occupies in a consumer's mind relative to competitive products.

Two Approaches to Product Positioning

There are two main approaches to positioning a new product in the market. *Head-to-head positioning* involves competing directly with competitors on similar product attributes in the same target market. Using this strategy, Dollar competes directly with Avis and Hertz. *Differentiation positioning* involves seeking a less competitive, smaller market niche in which to locate a brand, usually stressing the unique aspects of the product. For example, the irreverent underwear company, Ginch Gonch of Vancouver, does not compete head-to-head against the larger players in the mainstream underwear market. Instead, it markets its brands (brands that cannot be mentioned in this text) to a niche market of upwardly mobile 18- to 40-year-old men and women who are not afraid to show their underwear.[8] Similarly, Leading Brands of Vancouver avoids competing against bigger national brands by positioning its unique TrueBlue blueberry drink to the health-conscious consumer.[9] Finally, entrepreneur Frank D'Angelo makes his living producing niche products. For example, he produces Copperhead—a premium beer that sells for $42 for a 12-pack—avoiding the buck-a-beer trend in the Canadian brewing industry. He also sells Duh! Premium Old Fashioned Soda and Pulp Fusion, a high-protein breakfast replacement drink. The success of these products, he argues, is because they are not "me-toos" and are positioned as premium niche products.[10] Companies also follow a differentiation positioning strategy among brands within their own product line to try to minimize cannibalization of a brand's sales or shares.

Competing based on differentiation positioning with premium products in niche markets.

Writing a Positioning Statement

Marketing managers often convert their positioning ideas for an offering into a succinct written positioning statement. The positioning statement is used not only internally within the marketing department but also for others, outside it, such as research companies and marketing communications firms working for the company.[11] Here is the Volvo positioning statement for the North American market:

> For upscale families who desire a carefree driving experience, Volvo is a premium-priced automobile that offers the upmost in safety and dependability.

This focuses Volvo's North American marketing strategy and has led to adding side-door airbags for its cars. Also, Volvo advertising almost always mention safety and dependability, as seen in its "Volvo for life" campaign.

Product Positioning Using Perceptual Maps

A key to positioning a product or brand effectively is discovering the perceptions of its potential customers. In determining its positioning in the hearts or minds of customers, companies take four steps:

1. Identify the important attributes for a product or brand class.
2. Discover how target customers rate competing products or brands with respect to these attributes.
3. Discover where the company's product or brand is on these attributes in the hearts or minds of potential customers.
4. If necessary, reposition the company's product or brand in the hearts or minds of potential customers.

From these data, it is possible to develop a **perceptual map,** a means of displaying or graphing in two dimensions the location of products or brands in the hearts or minds of consumers to enable a manager to see how consumers perceive competing products or brands, as well as its own product or brand.

Repositioning Chocolate Milk for Adults   Figure 9–8 shows the positions that consumer beverages might occupy in the minds of adults. Note that even these positions vary from one consumer to another. But for simplicity, let's assume these are the typical positions on the beverage perceptual map of adults.

Dairies, struggling to increase milk sales, hit on a wild idea: Target adults by positioning chocolate milk to the location of the star shown in the perceptual map in Figure 9–9, the position of letter "B." Their arguments are nutritionally powerful. For

perceptual map
A means of displaying or graphing in two dimensions the location of products or brands in the minds of consumers to enable a manager to see how consumers perceive competing products or brands relative to its own and then take marketing actions.

● **FIGURE 9-8**
Using positioning and perceptual maps to increase milk sales to adults

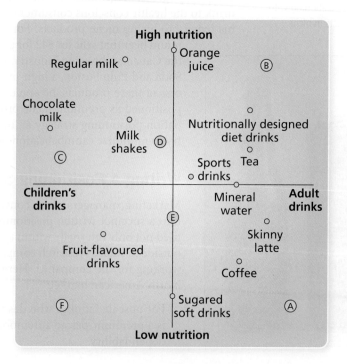

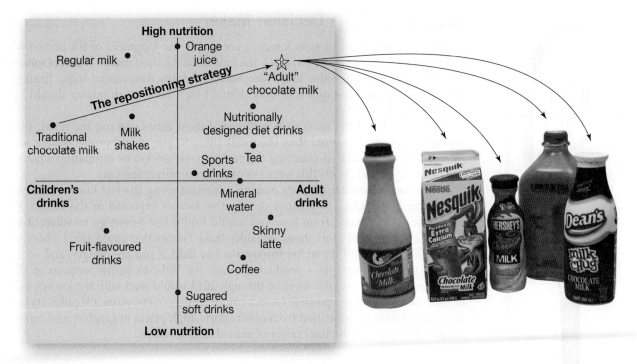

● **FIGURE 9–9**

The strategy dairies are using to reposition chocolate milk to reach adults: Have adults view chocolate milk both as more nutritional and "more adult."

women, chocolate milk provides calcium, critically important in female diets. And dieters get a more filling, nutritious beverage than with a soft drink for about the same calories.[12] The result: Chocolate milk sales increased dramatically, much of it because of adult consumption.[13] Part of this is due to giving chocolate milk "nutritional respectability" for adults, but another part is due to the innovative packaging that enables many new chocolate milk containers to fit in a car's cup holders.

LO6 SALES FORECASTING TECHNIQUES

Forecasting or estimating potential sales is critical when segmenting and selecting target markets. Good sales forecasts are also important for a firm as it schedules production.[14]

market (industry) potential
The maximum total sales of a product by all firms to a segment during a specified time period under specified environmental conditions and marketing efforts of the firms.

The term **market potential,** or **industry potential,** refers to the maximum total sales of a product by all firms to a segment during a specified time period under specified environmental conditions and marketing efforts of the firms. For example, the market potential for cake mix sales to Canadian consumers in 2011 might be 1.5 million cases—what Pillsbury, Betty Crocker, Duncan Hines, and other cake mix producers would sell to Canadian consumers under the assumptions that (1) past patterns of dessert consumption continue, and (2) the same level of promotional effort continues relative to other desserts. The term **sales forecast,** or **company forecast,** refers to the total sales of a product that a firm expects to sell during a specified time period under specified environmental conditions and its own marketing efforts. For example, Betty Crocker might develop a sales forecast of 500,000 cases of cake mix for consumers in 2011, assuming consumers' dessert preferences remain constant and competitors do not change prices.

sales (company) forecast
The total sales of a product that a firm expects to sell during a specified time period under specified environmental conditions and its own marketing efforts.

Three main sales forecasting techniques are often used: (1) judgments of the decision maker, (2) surveys of knowledgeable groups, and (3) statistical methods.

How might a marketing manager for Wilson tennis racquets forecast sales through 2013? Use a lost-horse forecast, as described in the text.

direct forecast
Estimating the value to be forecast without any intervening steps.

lost-horse forecast
Making a forecast using the last known value and modifying it according to positive or negative factors expected in the future.

survey of buyers' intentions forecast
Asking prospective customers if they are likely to buy a product during some future time period.

salesforce survey forecast
Asking the firm's salespeople to estimate sales during a coming period.

trend extrapolation
Extending a pattern observed in past data into the future.

linear trend extrapolation
The pattern is described with a straight line.

Judgments of the Decision Maker

Probably 99 percent of all sales forecasts are simply the judgment of the person who must act on the results of the forecast—the individual decision maker. A **direct forecast** involves estimating the value to be forecast without any intervening steps. Examples appear daily: How many quarts of milk should I buy? How much money should I get out of the ATM?

You probably get the same cash withdrawal most times you use the ATM. But if you need to withdraw more than the usual amount, you would probably take some intervening steps (such as counting the cash in your pocket or estimating what you will need for special events this week) to obtain your direct forecast.

A **lost-horse forecast** involves making a forecast using the last known value and modifying it according to positive or negative factors expected in the future. The technique gets its name from how you would find a lost horse: go to where it was last seen, put yourself in its shoes, consider those factors that could affect where you might go (to the pond if you are thirsty, the hay field if you are hungry, and so on), and go there. For example, a product manager for Wilson's tennis racquets in 2010 who needed to make a sales forecast through 2013 would start with the known value of 2009 sales and list the positive factors (more tennis courts, more TV publicity) and the negative ones (competition from other sports, high prices of graphite and ceramic racquets) to arrive at the final series of annual sales forecasts.

Surveys of Knowledgeable Groups

If you wonder what your firm's sales will be next year, ask people who are likely to know something about future sales. Two common groups that are surveyed to develop sales forecasts are prospective buyers and the firm's salesforce.

A **survey of buyers' intentions forecast** involves asking prospective customers if they are likely to buy a product during some future time period. For industrial products with few prospective buyers, this can be effective. There are only a few hundred customers in the entire world for Boeing's largest airplanes, and so Boeing surveys them to develop its sales forecasts and production schedules.

A **salesforce survey forecast** involves asking a firm's salespeople to estimate sales during a coming period. Because these people are in contact with customers and are likely to know what customers like and dislike, there is logic to this approach. However, salespeople can be unreliable forecasters—painting too rosy a picture if they are enthusiastic about a new product and too grim a forecast if their sales quota and future compensation are based on it.

Statistical Methods

The best-known statistical method of forecasting is **trend extrapolation,** which involves extending a pattern observed in past data into the future. When the pattern is described with a straight line, it is **linear trend extrapolation.** Suppose that in early 2000 you were a sales forecaster for the Acme Corporation and had actual sales running from 1988 to 1999 (Figure 9–10). Using linear trend extrapolation, you draw a line to fit the past data and project it into the future to give the forecast values shown for 2000 to 2012.

If in 2008 you want to compare your forecasts with actual results, you are in for a surprise—illustrating the strength and weakness of trend extrapolation. Trend extrapolation assumes that the underlying relationships in the past will continue into the future, which is the basis of the method's key strength: simplicity. If this assumption proves correct, you have an accurate forecast. However, if this proves wrong, the forecast is likely to be wrong. In this case, your forecasts from 2001 through 2008 were too high, as shown in Figure 9–10, largely because of fierce competition.

● **FIGURE 9-10**

Linear trend extrapolation of sales revenues of Acme Corporation, made at the start of 2000

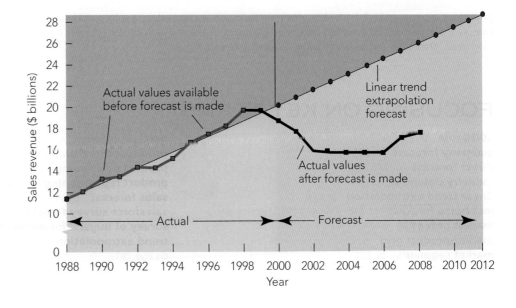

learning review

5. Why do marketers use perceptual maps in product positioning decisions?

6. What are the three kinds of sales forecasting techniques?

7. How do you make a lost-horse forecast?

LEARNING OBJECTIVES REVIEW

LO1 **Explain what market segmentation is and when to use it.**

Market segmentation involves aggregating prospective buyers into groups that (*a*) have common needs, and (*b*) will respond similarly to a marketing action. Organizations go to the trouble and expense of segmenting their markets when it increases their sales, profits, and ability to serve customers better.

LO2 **Identify the five steps involved in segmenting and targeting markets.**

Step 1 is to group potential buyers into segments. Buyers within a segment should have similar characteristics to each other and respond similarly to marketing actions, such as a new product or a lower price. Step 2 involves putting related products to be sold into groups. In step 3, organizations develop a market product grid with estimated size of markets in each of the market-product cells of the resulting table. Step 4 involves selecting the target market segments on which the organization should focus. Step 5 involves taking marketing mix actions—often in the form of a marketing program—to reach the target market segments.

LO3 **Recognize the different factors used to segment consumer and organizational (business) markets.**

Factors used to segment consumer markets include customer characteristics (geographic, demographic, psychographic, and behavioural variables). Organizational markets use related variables, often combining them to create what is called firmographics.

LO4 **Know how to develop a market-product grid to identify a target market and recommend resulting actions.**

Organizations use five key criteria to segment markets, whose groupings appear in the rows of the market-product grid. Groups of related products appear in the columns. After estimating the size of market in each cell in the grid, they select the target market segments on which to focus. They then identify marketing mix actions—often in a marketing program—to reach the target market most efficiently.

LO5 **Explain how marketing managers position products in the marketplace.**

Marketing managers often locate competing products on two-dimensional perceptual maps to visualize the products in the hearts or minds of consumers. They then try to position new products or reposition existing products in this space to attain the maximum sales and profits.

LO6 **Describe three approaches to developing a sales forecast for a company.**

One approach uses subjective judgments of the decision maker, such as direct or lost-horse forecasts. Surveying knowledgeable groups is a second method. It involves obtaining such information as the intentions of potential buyers or estimates of the salesforce. Statistical methods involving extending a pattern observed in past data into the future is a third example. The best-known example is linear trend extrapolation.

FOCUSING ON KEY TERMS

80/20 rule p. 237
company forecast p. 245
direct forecast p. 246
industry potential p. 245
linear trend extrapolation p. 246
lost-horse forecast p. 246
market potential p. 245
market-product grid p. 231
market segments p. 231

perceptual map p. 244
product differentiation p. 231
product positioning p. 243
product repositioning p. 243
sales forecast p. 245
salesforce survey forecast p. 246
survey of buyers' intentions forecast p. 246
trend extrapolation p. 246
usage rate p. 237

APPLYING MARKETING KNOWLEDGE

1 What variables might be used to segment these consumer markets? (*a*) lawn mowers, (*b*) frozen dinners, (*c*) dry breakfast cereals, and (*d*) soft drinks.

2 What variables might be used to segment these industrial markets? (*a*) industrial sweepers, (*b*) photocopiers, (*c*) computerized production control systems, and (*d*) car rental agencies.

3 In Figure 9–6, the dormitory market segment includes students living in university-owned residence halls, sororities, and fraternities. What market needs are common to these students that justify combining them into a single segment in studying the market for your Wendy's restaurant?

4 You may disagree with the estimates of market size given for the rows in the market-product grid in Figure 9–6. Estimate the market size, and give a brief justification for these market

segments: (*a*) dormitory students, (*b*) day commuters, and (*c*) people who work in the area.

5 Suppose you want to increase revenues for your fast-food restaurant even further. Referring to Figure 9–7, what advertising actions might you take to increase revenues from (*a*) dormitory students, (*b*) dinners, and (*c*) after-dinner snacks from night commuters?

6 Find examples of some good positioning statements used by successful Canadian companies. Why would you deem the ones you have located as being "good" examples?

7 For which of the following variables would linear trend extrapolation be more accurate: (*a*) annual population of Canada, or (*b*) annual sales of cars produced in Canada by General Motors? Why?

Building Your Marketing Plan

Your marketing plan (*a*) needs a market-product grid to focus your marketing efforts, and (*b*) leads to a forecast of sales for the company. Use these steps:

1. Define the market segments (the rows of your grid) using the factors in Figures 9–4 or 9–5. Also see Figure 9–2 for how to form the market-product grid.

2. Define the groupings of related products (the columns in your grid).

3. Form your grid and estimate the size for the market in each market-product cell.

4. Select the target market segments on which to focus your marketing program efforts.

5. Use the information and the lost-horse forecasting technique to make a sales forecast (company forecast).

6. Also, take an initial shot at crafting your positioning statement.

PRINCE SPORTS, INC.: TENNIS RACQUETS FOR EVERY SEGMENT

"Over the last decade we've seen a dramatic change in the media to reach consumers," says Linda Glassel, vice president of sports marketing and brand image of Prince Sports, Inc.

Prince Sports in Today's Changing World

"Today—particularly in reaching younger consumers— we're now focusing so much more on social marketing and social networks, be it Facebook, Twitter, MySpace, and internationally with Hi5, Bebo, and Orkut," she adds.

Linda Glassel's comments are a snapshot look at what Prince Sports faces in the changing world of tennis in the 2010s.

Prince Sports is a racquet sports company whose portfolio of brands includes Prince (tennis, squash, and badminton), Ektelon (racquetball), and Viking (platform/paddle tennis). Its complete line of tennis products alone is astounding: more than 150 racquet models; more than 50 tennis strings; over 50 footwear models; and countless types of bags, apparel, and other accessories.

Prince prides itself on its history of innovation in tennis—including inventing the first "oversize" and "longbody" racquets, the first "synthetic gut" tennis string, and the first "Natural Foot Shape" tennis shoe. Its challenge today is to continue to innovate to meet the needs of all levels of tennis players.

"One favourable thing for Prince these days is the dramatic growth in tennis participation—higher than it's been in many years," says Nick Skally (centre in the photo above), senior marketing manager. A recent study by the Sporting Goods Manufacturers Association confirms this point: Tennis participation in the U.S. was up 43 percent from 2000 to 2008—the fastest growing traditional individual sport in the country.

Taming Technology to Meet Players' Needs

Every tennis player wants the same thing: to play better. But they don't all have the same skills, or the same ability to swing a racquet fast. So adult tennis players fall very broadly into three groups, each with special needs:

- *Those with shorter, slower strokes.* They want maximum power in a lightweight frame.
- *Those with moderate to full strokes.* They want the perfect blend of power and control.
- *Those with longer, faster strokes.* They want greater control with less power.

To satisfy all these needs in one racquet is a big order.

"When we design tennis racquets, it involves an extensive amount of market research on players at all levels," explains Tyler Herring, global business director for Performance Tennis Racquets. In 2005, Prince's research led it to introduce its breakthrough O^3 technology. "Our O^3 technology solved an inherent contradiction between racquet speed and sweet spot," he says. Never before had a racquet been designed that simultaneously delivers faster racquet speed with a dramatically increased "sweet spot." The "sweet spot" in a racquet is the middle of the frame that gives the most power and consistency when hitting. In 2009 Prince introduced their latest evolution of the O^3 platform called EXO^3. Its newly patented design suspends the string bed from the racquet frame—thereby increasing the sweet spot by up to 83 percent while reducing frame vibration up to 50 percent.

Segmenting the Tennis Market

"The three primary market segments for our tennis racquets are our performance line, our recreational line, and our junior line," says Herring. He explains that within each of these segments Prince makes difficult design trade-offs to balance (1) the price a player is willing to pay, (2) what playing features (speed versus spin, sweet spot versus control, and so on) they want, and (3) what technology can be built into the racquet for the price point.

Within each of these three primary market segments, there are at least two sub-segments—sometimes overlapping! Figure 1 gives an overview of Prince's market segmentation strategy and identifies sample racquet models. The three right-hand columns show the design variations of length, unstrung weight, and head size. The table shows the complexities Prince faces in converting its technology into a racquet with physical features that satisfy players' needs.

Distribution and Promotion Strategies

"Prince has a number of different distribution channels—from mass merchants like Walmart and Target, to sporting goods chains, to smaller specialty tennis shops," says

Nick Skally. For the large chains Prince contributes co-op advertising for their in-store circulars, point-of-purchase displays, in-store signage, consumer brochures, and even "space planograms" to help the retailer plan the layout of Prince products in their tennis area. Prince aids for small tennis specialty shops include a supply of demo racquets, detailed catalogues, posters, racquet and string guides, merchandising fixtures, and hardware, such as racquet hooks and footwear shelves, in addition to other items. Prince also provides these shops with "player standees," which are corregated life-size cutouts of professional tennis players.

Prince reaches tennis players directly through its Web site (**www.princetennis.com**), which gives product information, tennis tips, and the latest tennis news. Besides using social networks like Facebook and Twitter, Prince runs ads in regional and national tennis publications, and develops advertising campaigns for online sites and broadcast outlets.

In addition to its in-store activities, advertising, and online marketing, Prince invests heavily in its Teaching

● **FIGURE 1**

Prince Targets Racquets at Specific Market Segments

Market Segments			Product Features in Racquet			
Main Segments	**Sub-Segments**	**Segment Characteristics (Skill level, age)**	**Brand Name**	**Length (Inches)**	**Unstrung Weight (Ounces)**	**Head Size (Sq. In.)**
Performance	Precision	For touring professional players wanting great feel, control, and spin	EXO³ Ignite 95	27.0	11.8	95
	Thunder	For competitive players wanting a bigger sweet spot and added power	EXO³ Red 95	27.25	9.9	105
Recreational	Small head size	Players looking for a forgiving racquet with added control	AirO Lightning MP	27.0	9.9	100
	Larger head size	Players looking for a larger sweet spot and added power	AirO Maria Lite OS	27.0	9.7	110
Junior	More experienced young players	Ages 8 to 15; somewhat shorter and lighter racquets than high school adult players	AirO Team Maria 23	23.0	8.1	100
	Beginner	Ages 5 to 11; much shorter and lighter racquets; tennis balls with 50% to 75% less speed for young beginners	Air Team Maria 19	19.0	7.1	82

Pro program. These sponsored teaching pros receive all the latest product information, demo racquets, and equipment from Prince, so they can truly be Prince ambassadors in their community. Aside from their regular lessons, instructors and teaching professionals hold local "Prince Demo events" to give potential customers a hands-on opportunity to see and try various Prince racquets, strings, and grips.

Prince also sponsors over 100 professional tennis players who appear in marquee events such as the four Grand Slam tournaments (Wimbledon and the Australian, French, and U.S. Opens). TV viewers can watch Russia's Maria Sharapova walk onto a tennis court carrying a Prince racquet bag or France's Gael Monfils hit a service ace using his Prince racquet.

Where is Prince headed in the 2010s? "As a marketer, one of the biggest challenges is staying ahead of the curve," says Glassel. And she stresses, "It's learning, it's studying, it's talking to people who understand where the market is going."

Questions

1 In the 2010s what trends in the environmental forces (social, economic, technological, competitive, and regulatory) (*a*) work for and (*b*) work against success for Prince Sports in the tennis industry?

2 Because sales of Prince Sports in tennis-related products depends heavily on growth of the tennis industry, what marketing activities might it use in North America to promote tennis playing?

3 What promotional activities might Prince use to reach (*a*) recreational players and (*b*) junior players?

4 What might Prince do to help it gain distribution and sales in (*a*) mass merchandisers like Target and Walmart and (*b*) specialty tennis shops?

5 In reaching global markets outside North America (*a*) what are some criteria that Prince should use to select countries in which to market aggressively, (*b*) what three or four countries meet these criteria best, and (*c*) what are some marketing actions Prince might use to reach these markets?

chapter 10

Developing New Products and Services

APPLE'S NEW-PRODUCT INNOVATION MACHINE

The stage in front of the huge auditorium is empty except for a desk with an iMac and a huge screen with a large white logo. Then in walks a legend ready for his annual magic show in his standard uniform—black turtleneck, jeans, and grey sneakers.

The legend is Steve Jobs, co-founder and chief executive officer (CEO) of Apple, Inc., rated by *BusinessWeek* as one of most innovative companies on the globe. The magic shows Jobs has put on over the years have introduced many of Apple's market-changing innovations. Some of these new-product innovations include the following:

- Apple II—the first personal computer
- Macintosh—the first personal computer with a mouse and a graphical user interface
- iPod—the first commercially successful MP3 digital music player
- MacBook Air—the world's thinnest notebook, it uses a solid state drive instead of a hard disk
- iTunes—the innovative online digital music store
- iPhone—the revolutionary multi-touch mobile phone and media player that can do everything from calling and text messaging to taking photos and Web browsing

learning objectives

After reading this chapter, you should be able to:

 LO1 Recognize the various terms that pertain to products and services.

LO2 Identify the ways in which consumer and business goods and services can be classified.

LO3 Explain the implications of alternative ways of viewing "newness" in new products and services.

 LO4 Describe the factors contributing to a product's or service's failure.

 LO5 Explain the purposes of each step of the new-product process.

- iPod Nano—the digital media player with built-in video camera to shoot and play video
- iPod Touch—a combination iPod, pocket computer, and game player
- iPad—a device that Apple calls revolutionary and magical. It allows users to connect with their apps, content, and the Internet in a more intimate, intuitive, and fun way than ever before. Users can browse the Web, read and send e-mail, enjoy and share photos, watch high-definition videos, listen to music, play games, read e-books, and much more, all using iPad's revolutionary multi-touch user interface. iPad is 0.5 inches thin and weighs just 1.5 pounds—thinner and lighter than any laptop or netbook![1]

Within just 80 days of its release, Apple sold over 3 million iPad units. Apple believes that the iPad is re-defining the future of mobile media and computing devices. And according to Steve Jobs, "People are loving iPad as it becomes a part of their daily lives. We're working hard to get this magical product into the hands of even more people around the world." Developers have already created over 11,000 new apps for iPad to take advantage of its multi-touch™ user interface, large screen, and high-quality graphics. And, according to Apple, iPad will run almost all of the more than 225,000 apps on the App Store, including apps already purchased for your iPhone.[2]

product

A good, service, or idea consisting of a bundle of tangible and intangible attributes that satisfies consumers and is received in exchange for money or some other unit of value.

The essence of marketing is in developing products such as Apple's new, technologically advanced iPad to meet buyer needs. A **product** is a good, service, or idea consisting of a bundle of tangible and intangible attributes that satisfies consumers and is received in exchange for money or some other unit of value. Tangible attributes include physical characteristics such as colour or sweetness, and intangible attributes include becoming healthier or wealthier. Hence, a product may be the breakfast cereal you eat, the accountant who fills out your tax return, or quitting smoking.

The life of a company often depends on how it conceives, produces, and markets new products, the topic of this chapter. This chapter covers decisions involved in developing and marketing new products and services. Chapters 11 and 12 discuss the process of managing existing products, services, and brands.

(L01) THE VARIATIONS OF PRODUCTS

A product varies in terms of whether it is a consumer or business good. For most organizations, the product decision is not made in isolation because companies often offer a range of products. To better appreciate the product decision, let us first define some terms pertaining to products.

product line

A group of products that are closely related because they satisfy a class of needs, are used together, are sold to the same customer group, are distributed through the same outlets, or fall within a given price range.

Product Line and Product Mix

A **product line** is a group of products that are closely related because they satisfy a class of needs, are used together, are sold to the same customer group, are distributed through the same type of outlets, or fall within a given price range. Polaroid Canada has two major product lines consisting of cameras and film; Nike's product lines are shoes and clothing; the Toronto Hospital for Sick Children's product lines consist of in-patient hospital care, outpatient physician services, and medical research. Each product line has its own marketing strategy.

Within each product line is the *product item,* a specific product as noted by a unique brand, size, or price. For example, Downy softener for clothes comes in 360-mL and 700-mL sizes; each size is considered a separate item and assigned a distinct ordering code, or *stock-keeping unit (SKU),* which is a unique identification number that defines an item for ordering or inventory purposes.

product mix

The number of product lines offered by a company.

The third way to look at products is by the **product mix,** or the number of product lines offered by a company. Cray, Inc., has a small product mix of four supercomputer lines that are sold mostly to governments and large businesses. Fortune Brands, however, has a large product mix that includes many product lines, including sporting equipment (Titleist golf balls) and plumbing products (Moen faucets).

Classifying Products

consumer goods

Products purchased by the ultimate consumer.

business goods

Products that assist directly or indirectly in providing products for resale (also known as *B2B goods, industrial goods,* or *organizational goods*).

Both the federal government and companies classify products, but for different purposes. The government's classification method helps it collect information on industrial activity. Companies classify products to help develop similar marketing strategies for the wide range of products offered. Two major ways to classify products are by type of user and degree of product tangibility.

Type of User   A major type of product classification is based on the type of user. **Consumer goods** are products purchased by the ultimate consumer, whereas **business goods** (also called B2B goods, industrial goods, or organizational goods) are products that assist directly or indirectly in providing products for resale.

There are difficulties, however, with this classification because some products can be considered both consumer and business items. An Apple computer can be sold to consumers for personal use or to business firms for office use. Each classification results in different marketing actions. Viewed as a consumer product, the Apple computer would be sold through computer stores or directly from the company Web site. As a business product, the HP Compaq computer might be sold by a salesperson offering discounts for multiple purchases.

Specialty goods, such as Raymond Weil watches, require distinct marketing programs to reach narrow target markets.

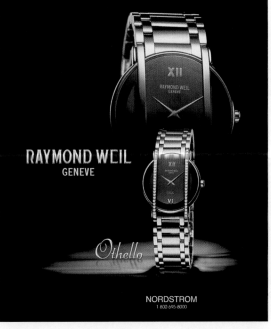

Degree of Tangibility   Classification by degree of tangibility divides products into one of three categories. First is a *nondurable good,* an item consumed in one or a few uses, such as food products and fuel. A *durable good* is one that usually lasts over an extended number of uses, such as appliances, automobiles, and stereo equipment. *Services* are defined as activities, deeds, or other basic intangibles offered for sale to consumers in exchange for money or something else of value. According to this classification, government data indicate that Canada has a service economy, the reason for a separate chapter (Chapter 12) on the topic.

This classification method also provides direction for marketing actions. For nondurable products like Wrigley's gum, inexpensive and purchased frequently, consumer advertising and wide distribution in retail outlets is essential. Durable products such as cars, however, generally cost more than nondurable goods and last longer, so personal selling is an important marketing activity in answering consumer questions and concerns. Because services are intangible, special marketing effort is usually needed to communicate their benefits to potential buyers.

LO2 CLASSIFYING CONSUMER AND BUSINESS GOODS

convenience goods
Items that the consumer purchases frequently and with a minimum of shopping effort.

shopping goods
Items for which the consumer compares several alternatives on such criteria as price, quality, or style.

specialty goods
Items that a consumer makes a special effort to search out and buy.

unsought goods
Items that the consumer either does not know about or knows about but does not initially want.

Because the buyer is the key to marketing, consumer and business product classifications are discussed in greater detail.

Classification of Consumer Goods

Convenience, shopping, specialty, and unsought products are the four types of consumer goods. They differ in terms of (1) effort the consumer expends on the decision, (2) attributes used in purchase, and (3) frequency of purchase.

Convenience goods are items that the consumer purchases frequently, conveniently, and with a minimum of shopping effort. **Shopping goods** are items for which the consumer compares several alternatives on criteria, such as price, quality, or style. **Specialty goods** are items, such as Tiffany sterling silver, that a consumer makes a special effort to search out and buy. **Unsought goods** are items that the consumer either does not know about or knows about but does not initially want. Figure 10–1 shows how the classification of a consumer product into one of these four types results in different aspects of the marketing mix being stressed. Different degrees of brand loyalty and amounts of shopping effort are displayed by the consumer for a product in each of the four classes.

The manner in which a consumer good is classified depends on the individual. One person may view a camera as a shopping good and visit several stores before

● **FIGURE 10–1**
Classification of consumer goods

BASIS OF COMPARISON	TYPE OF CONSUMER GOOD			
	CONVENIENCE	**SHOPPING**	**SPECIALTY**	**UNSOUGHT**
Product	Toothpaste, cake mix, hand soap, laundry detergent	Cameras, TVs, briefcases, clothing	Rolls Royce cars, Rolex watches	Burial insurance, thesaurus
Price	Relatively inexpensive	Fairly expensive	Usually very expensive	Varies
Place (distribution)	Widespread; many outlets	Large number of selective outlets	Very limited	Often limited
Promotion	Price, availability, and awareness stressed	Differentiation from competitors stressed	Uniqueness of brand and status stressed	Awareness is essential
Brand loyalty of consumers	Aware of brand, but will accept substitutes	Prefer specific brands, but will accept substitutes	Very brand loyal; will not accept substitutes	Will accept substitutes
Purchase behaviour of consumers	Frequent purchases; little time and effort spent shopping	Infrequent purchases; needs much comparison shopping time	Infrequent purchases; needs extensive search and decision time	Very infrequent purchases; some comparison shopping

deciding on a brand, whereas a friend may view cameras as a specialty good and will only buy a Nikon.

Classification of Business Goods

A major characteristic of business goods is that their sales are often the result of *derived demand;* that is, sales of business goods frequently result (or are derived) from the sale of consumer goods. For example, if consumer demand for Ford cars (a consumer product) increases, the company may increase its demand for paint-spraying equipment (a business good). Business goods may be classified as production or support goods.

production goods
Items used in the manufacturing process that become part of the final product.

Production Goods   Items used in the manufacturing process that become part of the final product are **production goods.** These include raw materials, such as grain or lumber, as well as component parts. For example, a company that manufactures door hinges used by GM in its car doors is producing a component part. As noted in Chapter 6, the marketing of production goods is based on such factors as price, quality, delivery, and service. Marketers of these products tend to sell directly to business users.

support goods
Items used to assist in producing other goods and services.

Support Goods   The second class of business goods is **support goods,** which are items used to assist in producing other goods and services. Support goods include installations, accessory equipment, supplies, and services.

- *Installations* consist of buildings and fixed equipment. Because a significant amount of capital is required to purchase installations, the business buyer deals directly with construction companies and manufacturers through sales representatives. The pricing of installations is often by competitive bidding.
- *Accessory equipment* includes tools and office equipment and is usually purchased in small-order sizes by buyers. As a result, instead of dealing directly with buyers, sellers of business accessories use distributors to contact a large number of buyers.
- *Supplies* are similar to consumer convenience goods and consist of such products as stationery, paper clips, and brooms. These are purchased with little effort, using the straight rebuy decision sequence discussed in Chapter 6. Price and delivery are key factors considered by the buyers of supplies.
- *Services* are intangible activities to assist the business buyer. This category can include maintenance and repair services and advisory services, such as tax or legal counsel, where the seller's reputation is critical.

---

learning review

1. Explain the difference between product mix and product line.
2. What are the four main types of consumer goods?
3. To which type of good (business or consumer) does the term derived demand generally apply?

LO3 WHAT IS A NEW PRODUCT?

The term *new* is difficult to define. Is Sony's PlayStation Portable (PSP) *new* when there was a PlayStation 3? Is Nintendo's Wii a new product given the company had many previous video game consoles in the past? Or is Microsoft's Xbox *new* when Microsoft has not been a big player in video games before? What does *new* mean for new-product marketing? Newness from several points of view and some marketing implications of this newness are discussed below.

Newness Compared with Existing Products   If a product is functionally different from existing products, it can be defined as new. Sometimes this newness is revolutionary and creates a whole new industry, as in the case of the Apple II computer. At other times additional features are added to an existing product to try to make it appeal to more customers. And as microprocessors now appear not only in computers and cellphones but also in countless applications in vehicles and appliances, consumers' lives get far more complicated. In fact, this proliferation of extra features—sometimes called "feature bloat"—can often overwhelm consumers.[3] Thus, while adding more features seems like a no-brainer, the feature bloat can lead to mind-boggling complexity for the consumer. As we will see later in the chapter, this is why a "less-is-more"—taking features out of a product—can be a new-product success strategy.

Newness in Legal Terms   Industry Canada, the federal government's department that regulates business practices, has determined that a product can be called "new" for only up to 12 months.

Newness from the Company's Perspective   Successful companies are starting to view newness and innovation in their products at three levels. At the lowest level, which usually involves the least risk, is a product line extension. This is an incremental improvement of an existing product for the company, such as Tic Tac Bold or Coke Zero—extensions of the original Tic Tac or the original Coke. At the next level is a significant jump in innovation or technology, such as from a land-line telephone to a cellphone. The third level is true innovation, a truly revolutionary new product, like the first Apple computer in 1976. Effective new-product programs in large firms deal at all three levels.

Newness from the Consumer's Perspective   A fourth way to define new products is in terms of their effects on consumption. This approach classifies new products according to the degree of learning required by the consumer, as shown in Figure 10–2.

Are these products really new?

	LOW Degree of New Consumer Learning Needed HIGH		
BASIS OF COMPARISON	**CONTINUOUS INNOVATION**	**DYNAMICALLY CONTINUOUS INNOVATION**	**DISCONTINUOUS INNOVATION**
Definition	Requires no new learning by consumers	Disrupts consumer's normal routine but does not require totally new learning	Establishes new consumption patterns among consumers
Examples	Sensor and New Improved Tide	Electric toothbrush, compact disc player, and digital cameras	Automobile, home computer, speech recognition software
Marketing emphasis	Generate awareness among consumers and obtain widespread distribution	Advertise benefits to consumers, stressing point of differentiation and consumer advantage	Educate consumers through product trial and personal selling

● **FIGURE 10–2**

Consumption effects define newness

With *continuous innovation,* no new behaviours must be learned. Toothpaste manufacturers can add new attributes or features like "whitens teeth" or "removes plaque," as when they introduce a new or improved product. But the extra features in the new toothpaste do not require buyers to learn new tooth-brushing behaviours, so it is a continuous innovation. The benefit of this simple innovation is that effective marketing mainly depends on generating awareness and not completely re-educating customers.

With *dynamically continuous innovation,* only minor changes in behaviour are required. Heinz launched its EZ Squirt Ketchup in an array of unlikely hues—from green and orange to pink and teal—with kid-friendly squeeze bottles and nozzles. Encouraging kids to write their names on hot dogs or draw dinosaurs on burgers as they use this new product requires only minor behavioural changes. So the marketing strategy is to educate prospective buyers on the product's benefits, advantages, and proper use.

A *discontinuous innovation* involves making the consumer learn entirely new consumption patterns in order to use the product. After decades of research, IBM introduced speech recognition software. If you use this software you are able to speak to your computer and watch your own words appear on your computer screen, and you can also open Windows programs with your voice. The risk that IBM faced in introducing this discontinuous innovation was that people had to learn new behaviours in

For how the kind of innovation present in this ketchup bottle and the innovation present in the Amazon Kindle affects marketing strategy, see the text.

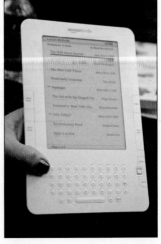

producing word-processed memos and reports. Hence, marketing efforts for discontinuous innovations involve educating consumers on both the benefits and proper use of the innovative product—activities that can cost millions of dollars. A more recent example of a discontinuous innovation are e-book devices such as Kindle by Amazon. These devices are changing the way we read! For example, the Kindle is a software and hardware platform that requires you to learn how to use this technology, whether you buy the Kindle reader device or have the content sent to your iPhone. Really interesting is that the e-books on Kindle are licensed for use, not purchased. Thus, unlike paper books, you do not really own your e-books. Amazon is investing very heavily on advertisements to show you how the Kindle works and how you benefit from its use over traditional books. Millions of Kindle units have already been sold. Moreover, according to Amazon, e-book sales on Amazon.com actually surpassed paper book sales during the past Christmas season!

WHAT ARE NEW SERVICES?

Many services-marketing experts suggest that creating and delivering new services is much more difficult than creating new tangible products. Furthermore, new services differ from product innovations in several important ways. First, for labour-intensive, interactive services, the actual providers (the service delivery staff) are part of the customer experience and thus are part of the innovation. Second, many services require the physical presence of the customer, which demands local decentralized production of the service. Third, new services usually do not have a tangible product to carry a brand name. The new-service development process is also difficult to map out for the service company and often difficult for the service customer to observe.

Services-marketing experts generally agree that there is a hierarchy of new-service categories that is somewhat similar to the continuous, dynamically continuous, and discontinuous innovation continuum discussed previously for physical products. There are seven categories of new services in this hierarchy ranging from major innovations to simple style changes.[4]

1. *Major service innovations* are new core products for markets that have not been previously defined. These services include both new-service offerings and radical new processes. For example, FedEx's overnight express delivery, CNNs 24/7 global news service, and eBay's online auction services would be examples of major service innovations.
2. *Major process innovations* consist of innovative new processes to deliver existing core services in new ways with greater value enhancement to the customer. An example would be a Canadian university or college offering a totally online MBA program where you never have to visit the campus to complete your degree.
3. *Service-line extensions* are additions to existing lines of services. For example, many Canadian banks now offer their customers insurance offerings.
4. *Process-line extensions* are less innovative than major process innovations, but are new ways of delivering existing services so that they offer greater convenience or a different experience to the customer. A common example is a bank offering telephone or Internet banking.
5. *Supplementary-service innovations* take the form of adding new elements to the core service or improving existing supplementary services that accompany the core service. FedEx Office, for example, offers high-speed Internet access at its locations for its customers. Another example would be a hospital that adds valet parking when you visit a family member who is being treated there.
6. *Basic service improvements* are the most common type of new-service innovation. This involves modest changes in the performance of the current service, like serving customers quicker.

7. *Style changes* are the simplest type of new-service innovation, and require no change in the service core or service process. Examples would be new uniforms for service personnel, new colour schemes for the service facilities, or way scripts for employees to use when servicing customers.

Most services companies, like their counterpart product-based companies, focus on creating only incremental improvements (continuous innovation) to their current core offerings. But the few service firms that focus on breakthrough or truly disruptive innovations can create entirely new markets or can dramatically reshape existing markets so that they can enjoy the benefits of unforeseen profits for a considerable length of time.[5] Can you say Google?

LO4 WHY NEW PRODUCTS OR SERVICES SUCCEED OR FAIL

We all know of giant product or service success stories, such as Microsoft Windows, Apple iPods, and Google. Yet thousands of product failures that occur every year cost Canadian businesses millions of dollars. Recent research suggests that it takes about 3,000 raw unwritten ideas to produce a single commercially successful new product.[6] To learn marketing lessons and convert potential failures to successes, we can analyze why new products fail and then study several failures in detail. As we go through the new-product process later in the chapter, we can identify ways such failures might have been avoided—admitting, of course, that hindsight is clearer than foresight.

Marketing Reasons for New-Product Failures

Both marketing and non-marketing factors contribute to new-product failures, as shown in the accompanying Marketing Matters box, "What Separates New-Product Winners and Losers." Using the research results from several studies[7] on new-product success and failure, and also those described in the Marketing Matters box, we can identify critical marketing factors—sometimes overlapping—that often separate new product winners and losers:

1. *Insignificant "point of difference."* Shown as the most important factor in the Marketing Matters box, a distinctive "point of difference" is essential for a new product to defeat competitive ones—through having superior characteristics that deliver unique benefits to the user. For example, General Mills introduced "Fingos," a sweetened cereal flake about the size of a corn chip. Consumers were supposed to snack on them dry, but they did not.[8] The point of difference was not important enough to get consumers to give up eating competing snacks, such as popcorn, potato chips, or Cheerios, from the box late at night.

2. *Incomplete market and product definition before product development starts.* Ideally, a new product needs a precise **protocol**, a statement that, before product development begins, identifies (1) a well-defined target market; (2) specific customers' needs, wants, and preferences; and (3) what the product will be and do. Without this precision, loads of money disappear as research and development (R&D) tries to design a vague product for a phantom market. Apple Computer's hand-sized Newton computer, which intended to help keep the user organized, fizzled badly because no clear protocol existed.

3. *Too little market attractiveness.* Market attractiveness refers to the ideal situation every new-product manager looks for: a large target market with high growth and real buyer need. But often, when looking for ideal market niches, the target

protocol

A statement that, before product development begins, identifies (1) a well-defined target market; (2) specific customers' needs, wants, and preferences; and (3) what the product will be and do.

market is too small and too competitive to warrant the research and development (R&D), production, and marketing expenses necessary to reach it. In the early 1990s, Kodak discontinued its Ultralife lithium battery. With its 10-year shelf life, the battery was touted as lasting twice as long as an alkaline battery. Yet, the product was available only in the 9-volt size, which accounts for less than 10 percent of the batteries sold in North America.

4. *Poor execution of the marketing mix (name, package, price, promotion, distribution).* Coca-Cola thought its Minute Maid Squeeze-Fresh frozen orange juice concentrate in a squeeze bottle was a hit. The idea was that consumers could make one glass of juice at a time, and the concentrate stayed fresh in the refrigerator for more than a month. After two test markets, the product was finished. Consumers loved the idea, but the product was messy to use, and the advertising and packaging did not educate them effectively on how much concentrate to mix.

5. *Poor product quality on critical factors.* This factor stresses that problems on one or two critical factors can kill the product, even though the general quality is high. For example, the Japanese, like the British, drive on the left side of the road. Until the late 1990s, North American car makers sent Japan few right-drive cars—unlike German car makers, who exported right-drive models in a number of their brands.

6. *Bad timing.* The product is introduced too soon, too late, or at a time when consumer tastes are shifting dramatically. Bad timing gives new-product managers

Marketing Matters

What Separates New-Product Winners and Losers

What makes some products winners and others losers? Knowing this answer is a key to a new-product strategy. R. G. Cooper and E. J. Kleinschmidt studied 203 new products to find the answers shown below.

The researchers defined the "product success rate" of new products as the percentage of products that reached the company's own profitability criteria. Product "winners" are the best 20 percent of performers, and "losers" are the worst 20 percent. For example, for the first factor in the table below, 98 percent of the winners had a major point of difference compared with only 18 percent of the losers.

Note that the table below includes only marketing-related factors. Most of the marketing factors tie directly to the reasons cited in the text for new-product success and failures that are taken from a number of research studies.

FACTOR AFFECTING PRODUCT SUCCESS RATE	PRODUCT "WINNERS" (BEST 20%)	PRODUCT "LOSERS" (WORST 20%)	% DIFFERENCE (WINNERS–LOSERS)
1. Point of difference, or uniquely superior product	98%	18%	80%
2. Well-defined product before actual development starts	85	26	59
3. Quality of execution of activities before actual development starts	75	31	44
4. Synergy, or fit, with marketing mix activities	71	31	40
5. Quality of execution of marketing mix activities	71	32	39
6. Market attractiveness, ones with large markets and high growth	74	43	31

nightmares. IBM, for example, killed several laptop computer prototypes because competitors introduced better, more advanced machines to the marketplace before IBM could get there.

7. *No economical access to buyers.* Grocery products provide an example. Today's mega-supermarkets carry 30,000 different SKUs. With new food products introduced each day, the fight for shelf space is tremendous in terms of costs for advertising, distribution, and shelf space.[9] Because shelf space is determined in terms of sales per square foot, Thirsty Dog! (a zesty beef-flavoured, vitamin-enriched, mineral-loaded, lightly carbonated bottled water for your dog) must displace an existing product on the supermarket shelves, a difficult task with the precise measures of revenues per square foot these stores use.

A Look at Some Failures

Before reading further, study the product failures described in Figure 10–3, and try to identify which of the reasons is the most likely explanation for their failure. The two examples are discussed in greater detail below.

Kimberly-Clark's Avert Virucidal tissues lasted 10 months in a test market before being pulled from the shelves. People did not believe the claims and were frightened by the name. So the tissue probably failed because of not having a clear point of difference, a bad name, and, hence, bad marketing mix execution.

Out! International's "Hey! There's A Monster In My Room" spray was creative and cute when introduced in 1993. But the name probably kept the kids awake at night more than their fear of the monsters because it suggested the monster was still hiding in the room. Question: Wouldn't calling it the "Monster-Buster Spray" have licked the name problem? It looks like the spray was never really defined well in a protocol and definitely had poor name execution.

Molson launched a Brazilian imported beer in Canada called A Marca Bavaria. After three years and disappointing sales, the product was removed from the market. Many experts suggest the failure of this product provides a case study on how to do just about everything wrong with a new product. One beverage analyst suggested Canadians did not want a Brazilian beer with a German name and certainly would not pay $20 extra a case for the product. The brand had no identity and the marketing program was underfunded and poorly executed.[10]

Simple marketing research on consumers should have revealed the problems. Developing successful new products may sometimes involve luck, but more often it involves having a product that really meets a need and has significant points of difference over competitive products.

What Were They Thinking? Organizational Problems in New-Product Failure   Besides the marketing reasons for new-product success and failure given above, a number of other organizational problems can cause disasters. Key ones—some that overlap—include:

1. *Not really listening to the "voice of the consumer."* Product managers may believe they "know better" than their customers or feel they "can't afford" the valuable marketing research that could uncover problems.

2. *Skipping steps in the new-product process.* Though details may vary, the seven-step new-product process discussed in the next section is a sequence used in some form by most large organizations. Skipping a step often leads to disaster, the reason that many firms have a "gate" or "milestone" to ensure that one step is completed satisfactorily before going to the next step.[11]

3. *Pushing a poorly conceived product into the market to generate quick revenue.* Today's marketing managers are under incredible pressure from top management to meet quarterly revenue targets. Often this focus on speed also

● **FIGURE 10-3**

Why did these new products fail?

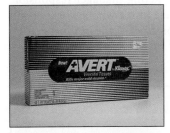

results in overlooking the network of services needed to support the physical product.[12]

4. *"Groupthink" in task force and committee meetings.* Someone in the new-product planning meeting knows or suspects the product concept is a dumb idea. But that person is afraid to speak up for fear of being cast as a "negative thinker" and "not a team player" and then being ostracized from real participation in the group. And a strong public commitment to a new product by its key advocate may make it difficult to kill the product even when the new negative information comes to light.[13]

5. *Not learning critical takeaway lessons from past failures.* The easiest lessons are from "intelligent failures"—ones that happen early in the new-product process so that they are less expensive and that immediately give better understanding of customers' wants and needs.[14]

The text describes some new-product lessons this iRobot co-founder learned the hard way.

Helen Greiner, co-founder and chairman of iRobot, talks about lessons she learned from a key product failure. iRobot manufactures a variety of robots—from the Scooba floor washer to the PackBot bomb-disposal robot. Her lessons came from the Ariel, an amphibious mine-clearing robot that was the most advanced walking robot in the world at the time. Helen Greiner notes Ariel didn't satisfy the user's needs because "it couldn't walk far enough, it couldn't carry the payload it would need to carry, and it was too complex." The result: The failure shifted iRobot's focus from "innovation for innovation's sake" to "building practical and affordable robots that help people.[15]

How Marketing Dashboards Can Reduce New-Product Failures   The Using Marketing Dashboards box shows how marketers measure actual market performance versus the goals set in new-product planning. A new-product success in the marketplace is hardly guaranteed by it being ready to ship from the factory loading dock. The marketing manager responsible tracks its sales and acceptance in the marketplace to see what's working and what's not in the marketing mix actions for the product. Is the product getting on the retailers' shelves okay? Is the price right? Is the advertising effective?

---

learning review

4. From a consumer's viewpoint, what kind of innovation would an improved electric toothbrush be?

5. What does "insignificant point of difference" mean as a reason for new-product failure?

LO5 THE NEW-PRODUCT PROCESS

new-product process
The stages a firm uses to identify business opportunities and convert them to a saleable good or service.

new-product strategy development
The first stage of the new-product process, providing the necessary focus, structure, approach, and guidelines for pursuing innovation.

Such companies as General Electric, Sony, and Procter & Gamble take a sequence of steps before their products are ready for market. Figure 10–4 shows the seven stages of the **new-product process,** the stages a firm uses to identify business opportunities and convert them to a saleable good or service. This sequence begins with new-product strategy development and ends with commercialization.

Stage 1: New-Product Strategy Development

New-product strategy development is the first stage of the new-product process. It provides the necessary focus, structure, approach, and guidelines for pursuing

Using Marketing Dashboards

Monitoring Your New-Product Launch

The goal of new-product introductions is to increase sales. Because sales expectations for new products are usually optimistic, they often are monitored on a month-by-month basis.

Your Challenge   As the CEO, you carefully track the results of new-product launches. The dashboard figures show actual monthly results (blue line) matched up to goals (red line).

Let's say your total potential market contains 100 million (MM) households. In terms of new households buying, your new Super Snack Bar is purchased by 5 million households (HH) in the first month, 4 million in the second month, and 3 million in the third month.

Triers = ((5MM+4MM+3MM)/100MM) × 100 = 12% of HH have tried the new bar in the first three months.

Repeaters in first month: (1MM/5MM) = 20% of triers repeated. In the second month a total of 2MM HH bought again. This is divided into the triers in the first two months (5MM+4MM).

Repeat = [2MM bought again/All who bought to date (5MM + 4MM)] × 100 = 22%

Your Findings   The top figure shows the number of households trying the new flavour (blue line), which is far below the red goal line. To make matters worse, consumers are not repeating to the level of the goal set in the bottom figure. Do you get the sense that this might be a sales train wreck?

Your Action   There could be three different problems. (1) Why are fewer people trying the flavour than expected? This will trace to a marketing, sales, and communication issue. (2) Why are those who bought it not buying it again? This could be a distribution problem (it's not in stock) or it could be a product or packaging problem. (3) Lastly, it is possible that the product is doing fine, and the goals are unrealistic. You decide to tackle the third issue first. You ask the marketing research team for the details on other new-product introductions and make a careful comparison of the assumptions behind the red goals for your new product versus the actual performance of your past new-product launches.

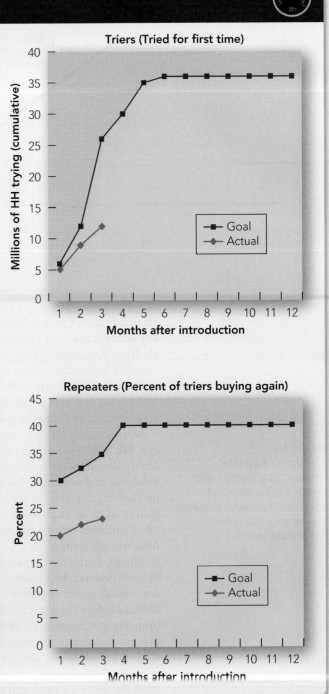

innovation. At this stage a company typically determines the type of innovation it wishes to pursue (its focus). For example, does it wish to only inch out with incremental innovation or attempt to leap out with breakthrough or disruptive innovation? It might also pre-determine the exact role new products will play in terms of the company's overall growth strategy. In other words, how much overall cost and profitability should new products contribute to the company?

● **FIGURE 10-4**
Stages in the new-product process

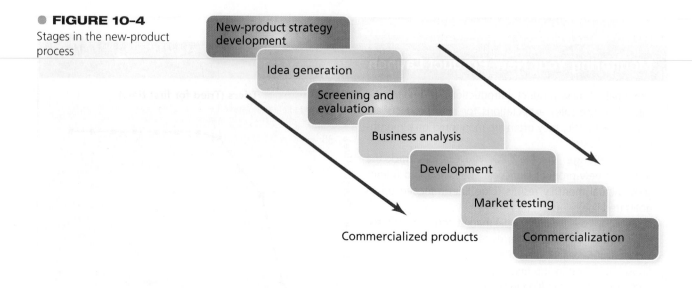

Many companies also develop specific structures, approaches, and guidelines for new-product strategy. For example, many companies utilize *cross-functional teams,* a small number of people from different departments in an organization who are mutually accountable to a common set of performance goals. At 3M, teams of individuals from R&D, marketing, sales, manufacturing, and finance work simultaneously together in a collaborative environment on new-product and market opportunities. In the past, 3M often utilized these department people in sequence—resulting in R&D designing new products that the manufacturing department could not produce economically and that the marketing department could not sell.

Many companies also use Six Sigma protocols as part of their new-product strategy. **Six Sigma** is a means to "delight the customer" by achieving quality through a highly disciplined process that focuses on developing and delivering near-perfect products and services. "Near perfect" here means being 99.9997 percent perfect, or allowing 3.4 defects per million products produced or transactions processed—getting as close as possible to "zero defects." Six Sigma's success lies in determining what variables impact the results, measuring them, and making decisions based on data, not gut feeling.[16]

Finally, many companies now identify and involve lead users as an inherent part of their new-product strategy development process. In consumer markets, *lead users* are a small group of potential product or service users who desire new products or services before the general market recognizes this need. These lead users, if identified properly, can provide valuable information and assistance early in the new-product process in order to properly shape the nature and scope of what is actually to be created or produced. In business markets, *lead users* are buying organizations that are consistently early adopters of new products or services. Like lead users in consumer markets, these adopters can help shape a company's new-product strategy as well as influence the adoption of the newly developed products, services, or technologies. Collaboration or co-participation of lead users in the new-product strategy development process has helped many companies improve the success rate of their new product and services introductions.[17]

Stage 2: Idea Generation

Perhaps one of the most difficult stages of the new-product process is the **idea generation** stage—developing a pool of concepts as candidates for new products. The idea

Six Sigma
A means to "delight the customer" by achieving quality through a highly disciplined process that focuses on developing and delivering near-perfect products and services.

idea generation
Developing a pool of concepts as candidates for new products.

should be made as concrete as possible before moving to the next stage of the new-product process.[18] New-product ideas can be generated by consumers, particularly lead users; suppliers; employees; basic R&D; and competitors. Also, there are other "outsiders": universities, investors, and small technology firms.

Toronto-based Bravado! Designs solicits new-product ideas from its employees.

Customer and Supplier Suggestions

Many researchers suggest that one of the greatest sources of new product or service ideas is the customer. Lead users, in particular, can play a vital role in providing companies with suggestions or ideas about what they need in terms of new products and services as well as how the new products and services should meet those needs.[19] But it is also important for companies to consider what their non-customers may want in terms of new products or services. If these customers are not buying the company's current products or services, there must be a good reason, and perhaps a new innovation might help. Examining customer complaints is another tactic that can lead to new product or service concepts. Many companies actively encourage complaints from customers and then use the complaints as a source of inspiration to innovate. Many companies also engage suppliers to provide ideas for new products or services.

Employee and Co-Worker Suggestions

Many companies think that new product or service ideas come from a few big brains: an inspired founder, an eccentric inventor, or a visionary boss. But every employee or co-worker can contribute new product or service ideas. Some companies, for example, now put their employees through "idea creation and idea management" training programs. Others actively encourage employee suggestions by offering monetary rewards for each successful new product or service launched.[20] Kathryn From, CEO of Bravado! Designs, a Toronto-based company that manufactures and markets maternity and nursing bras, actively solicits ideas and feedback from all her employees. This includes the frontline personnel, such as the people who answer the telephones and talk to customers. She also has regular meetings with employees away from the office to discuss new ideas.[21]

Research and Development Breakthroughs   Another source of new products is a firm's basic research, but the costs can be huge. Sony is a world leader in new-product development in electronics. Sony's research and development breakthroughs have made it a legend in the electronics industry.

But not all R&D labs have Sony's genius for moving electronic breakthroughs into the marketplace. Take Xerox Corporation's Palo Alto Research Center (PARC). In what may be the greatest electronic fumble of all time, by 1979, PARC had what is in your computer system now: graphical user interfaces, mice, windows and pull-down menus, laser printers, and distributed computing. Concerned with aggressive competition from Japan in its core photocopier business, Xerox did not even bother to patent these breakthroughs. Apple Computer's Steven Jobs visited PARC in 1979, adapted many of the ideas for the Macintosh, and the rest is history.

Professional R&D laboratories, sometimes called "innovation labs," that are outside the walls of large corporations also provide new-product ideas. Labs at Arthur D. Little helped put the crunch in Cap'n Crunch cereal and the flavour in Carnation Instant Breakfast. As described in the Going Online box, IDEO is a world-class new-product development firm, having designed more than 4,000 of them. Brainstorming sessions run at IDEO can generate 100 new ideas in an hour. Its "shop-a-long" visits with managers of client firms let the managers experience firsthand what the customers do.[22]

Competitive Products   New-product ideas can also be found by analyzing the competition. A six-person intelligence team from the Marriott Corporation spent six months travelling around the United States staying at economy hotels. The team assessed the competition's strengths and weaknesses on everything from the soundproof qualities of the rooms to the softness of the towels. Marriott then budgeted $500 million for a new economy hotel chain, Fairfield Inns.

Universities, Inventors, and Small Technology Firms   Texas Instruments (TI) manager Gene Franz spends his time looking for visionaries—a lot of them outside his company—with ideas TI could turn into products. Some examples:

- *Universities.* Their technology transfer centres often partner with firms like TI to commercialize inventions of their faculty.
- *Inventors.* Even today lone inventors and entrepreneurs exist with brilliant ideas—like the Israeli entrepreneur who invented a device a bit like the "tricoder" you saw on Star Trek: Point it at a patient and see his vital signs.[23]
- *Small technology firms.* Hewlett-Packard, Google, and Geek Squad were tiny start-up businesses until a venture capital firm or large corporation found them, invested money in them, and helped them grow.

Great ideas can come from almost anywhere—if one can only recognize them.

Stage 3: Screening and Evaluation

screening and evaluation
The stage of the new-product process that involves internal and external evaluations of the new-product ideas to eliminate those that warrant no further effort.

Screening and evaluation is the stage of the new-product process that involves internal and external evaluations of the new-product ideas to eliminate those that warrant no further effort.

Internal Approach   Internally, the firm evaluates the technical feasibility of the proposal and whether the idea meets the objectives defined in the new-product strategy development step. In a recent project, 3M researcher David Windorski worked

---

Going Online

IDEO—the Innovation Lab Superstar in Designing New Products

The Apple mouse. The Palm V PDA. The Crest Neat Squeeze toothpaste dispenser. The Steelcase Leap adjustable office chair. These are just some of the thousands of new products designed by an innovation lab you've probably never heard of but benefit from everyday. For David Kelley, co-founder of IDEO, product design includes both artistic and functional elements. And to foster this creativity, IDEO allows its designers and engineers much freedom—its offices look like schoolrooms; employees can hang their bicycles from the ceiling; there are rubber-band fights; and on Monday mornings, there are show-and-tell sessions.

Visit IDEO's Web site (**www.ideo.com**) to view its recent inventions and innovations for clients, such as McDonald's self-ordering kiosk, the Zyliss Mandolin fruit and vegetable slicer, LifePort's kidney transporter, Pepsi's High Visibility vending machine, and Nike's all-terrain sunglasses.

3M Post-It® Flags

+

Felt Tip Highlighters

=

3M Post-It® Flag Highlighters

For the creative way a student project helped lead to 3M's new Post-it® Flag Highlighter, see the text.

with a team of local university students to find new applications for Post-it® Flags in their studying activities. Student suggestions reinforced some ideas Windorski had been working on in his laboratory. Students said that by combining Post-it® Flags with coloured felt-tip highlighters they could bookmark on key pages in their textbooks that they highlighted. Windorski and the team worked on a few different prototypes: Post-it® Flags on top, on the side, and so on. He knew the basic idea was sound, but the designs were not.

Windorski then hit on his breakthrough idea: put small Post-it® Flags *inside* pens and highlighters that students use! After much engineering, consumer testing, and evaluation, the result was the launch of 3M's Post-it® Flag Highlighter and Post-it® Flag Pen—a credit to global cross-functional collaboration among research, manufacturing, and marketing. In these two 3M products, the pen and highlighter components were sourced worldwide. The new product development team then coordinated the commercialization for a global introduction.

The final, marketable Post-it® Flag Highlighter version is shown in the photo above. But earlier prototypes were first mocked up in cardboard, then modelling clay, and then components screwed together—a far cry from the final product you see in your student bookstore. The product has been a success for 3M with millions of units sold to date.[24]

External Approach   *Concept tests* are external evaluations that consist of preliminary testing of the new-product idea (rather than the actual, final product) with consumers. Generally, these tests are more useful with minor modifications of existing products than with new, innovative products that are not familiar to consumers. Concept tests usually rely on written descriptions of the product but may be augmented with sketches, mockups, or promotional literature. With food products, consumers may actually be asked to taste-test the products. Several key questions

The use of online concept tests: an external evaluation method for new-product ideas.

are asked during concept testing: How does the customer perceive the product? Who would buy it? How would it be used? Frito-Lay, for example, spent a year interviewing 10,000 consumers about the concept of a new multigrain snack chip before introducing its highly successful Sun Chips. Many companies also leverage the power of the Internet to conduct online concept tests. As we saw in Chapter 8, the Internet has enabled this type of research to be conducted quickly, inexpensively, and accurately. For example, Ipsos Canada, a major marketing research firm, offers its clients online concept testing to determine whether a new product or service can be successful. The company combines online interviewing, rich visuals of the concepts, and discrete choice modelling to test concepts and products effectively. In many cases, the concepts can be altered in real-time based on consumer feedback and then re-tested.[25]

---

learning review

6. What is the first step in the new-product process?

7. What are the main sources of new-product ideas?

8. What is the difference between internal and external screening and evaluation approaches used by a firm in the new-product process?

Stage 4: Business Analysis

business analysis
The stage of the new-product process that involves specifying the product features and marketing strategy and making financial projections needed to commercialize a product.

Business analysis is the stage of the new-product process that involves specifying the product features and marketing strategy and making financial projections needed to commercialize a product. This is the last checkpoint before significant capital is invested in creating a *prototype,* a full-scale operating model of the product under development. Economic analysis, marketing strategy review, and legal examination of the proposed product are conducted at this stage.

The marketing strategy review studies the new-product idea in relation to the marketing program to support it. The proposed product is assessed to determine whether it will help or hurt the sales of existing products. Likewise, the product is examined to assess whether it can be sold through existing channels or if new outlets will be needed. Profit projections involve estimating the number of units expected to be sold but also the costs of R&D, production, and marketing and whether it can be protected with a patent or copyright.

Stage 5: Development

development
The stage of the new-product process that involves turning the idea on paper into a prototype.

Product ideas that survive the business analysis proceed to actual **development,** the stage of the new-product process that involves turning the idea on paper into a prototype. This results in a demonstrable, producible product in hand, which involves not only manufacturing the products but also performing laboratory and consumer tests to ensure it meets the standards set for it.

The new product must be able to be manufactured at reasonable cost with the required quality. A brainstorming session at Procter & Gamble produced the idea of printing pop culture images on Pringles chips. So P&G often partners with movie or game companies for timely special promotions—like the appearance of *Spiderman 3.* But how do you print sharp images using edible dyes on thousands and thousands of chips each minute? Internal development would take too long and cost too much. P&G circulated the description of its unusual printing need globally. It discovered a university professor in Bologna, Italy, who had invented an ink-jet method for printing edible images on cakes and cookies. In less than a year P&G adapted the process and launched its new "Pringle Prints"—at a fraction of the time and cost internal development would have taken.[26] So an increasing new-product challenge—from physical products to computer software—is to manage a global development process that operates 24 hours a day.[27]

Some new products can be so important and costly that the company is betting its very existence on success. And creative, out-of-the-box thinking can be critical. In the pharmaceutical industry, no more than one out of every 5,000 to 10,000 new compounds developed in the labs emerges as an approved drug.[28] With the success rate on new drug compounds so low, pharmaceutical giant Eli Lilly has initiated "failure parties" to recognize excellent scientific work that unfortunately resulted in products that failed anyway. These parties result in Lilly naming a team to learn the specific reasons for the failure. This "failure analysis" has resulted in Lilly sometimes finding ways to make the compound succeed in addressing the original disease for which it was designed.

More surprisingly, a number of successful Lilly drugs trace their origins back to trials that demonstrated the drug was a flop for the initial medical problem it was intended to address but works well to treat a different disease. Some of these breakthroughs come from researchers using a Lilly "blue sky" fund that enables them to spend up to a day a week on projects with no clear immediate commercial value.[29] Google, too, stimulates creativity by letting its engineers spend a day a week to develop their own pet projects—a strategy that led to Google News.[30]

During development, laboratory tests like this one on Barbie result in safer dolls and toys for children.

Lilly's drug prototypes go through exhaustive lab and clinical tests to see if they meet design criteria set for them if used the way intended. But safety tests are also critical for when the product isn't used as planned. To make sure 7-year-olds can't bite Barbie's head off and choke, Mattel clamps her foot in steel jaws in a test stand and then pulls on her head with a wire. Similarly, car manufacturers have done extensive safety tests by crashing their cars into concrete walls.

Stage 6: Market Testing

market testing
Exposing actual products to prospective consumers under realistic purchase conditions to see if they will buy.

The **market testing** stage of the new-product process involves exposing actual products to prospective consumers under realistic purchase conditions to see if they will buy. Often, a product is developed, tested, refined, and then tested again to get consumer reactions through either test marketing or purchase laboratories.

Test Marketing Test marketing involves offering a product for sale on a limited basis in a defined area. This test is done to determine whether consumers will actually buy the product and to try different ways of marketing it. Only about a third of the products test marketed do well enough to go on to the next phase. These market tests are usually conducted in cities that are viewed as being representative of Canadian consumers. Test marketing gives the company an indication of potential sales volume and market share. Market tests are also used to check other elements of the marketing mix besides the product itself, such as price, level of advertising support, and distribution. Market tests are time-consuming and expensive because production lines as well as promotion and sales programs must be set up. Costs can run to more than a million dollars. Market tests also reveal information to competitors, sometimes enabling them to get their products into national distribution first. Competitors can also try to sabotage test markets. With such problems, some firms skip test markets completely or use simulated test markets.

Simulated Test Markets   Because of the time, cost, and confidentiality problems of test markets, consumer packaged goods companies often turn to *simulated* (or *laboratory*) *test markets (STM)*, a technique that simulates a full-scale test market but in a limited fashion. STMs are often run in shopping malls, where consumers are questioned to identify who uses the product class being tested. Willing participants are questioned on usage, reasons for purchase, and important product attributes. Qualified persons are then shown TV commercials or print ads for the test product along with competitors' advertising and are given money to make a decision to buy or not buy a package of the product (or the competitors') from a real or simulated store environment. STMs are used early in the development process to screen new-product ideas and later in the process to make sales projections.

Virtual Reality Market Testing   Again, the power of technology, including the Internet, allows companies to engage in a new type of simulated test markets called *virtual reality market testing*. Several consulting companies have developed the capabilities that enable them to test market their clients' products in virtual space, or in virtual reality (VR). For example, researchers are able to create virtual markets and test how well the new products perform in those markets. A variety of simulated market environments can be created, including grocery stores and auto showrooms. It is even possible to create individually simulated store shelves. Virtual reality market testing can be less expensive and more flexible, and can radically decrease time to market compared to real market testing. However, virtual reality is just that, virtual or a simulation, and is not the real thing, and this may be a limitation in that virtual reality markets may not be analogous to what will actually happen in a real test market.

When Test Markets Do Not Work   Test marketing is a valuable step in the new-product process, but not all products can use it. Testing a service beyond the concept level is very difficult because the service is intangible and consumers cannot see what they are buying. For example, how could Google easily have test marketed its launch of Gmail, an e-mail service users get free in exchange for accepting ads with its Gmail?

Similarly, test markets for expensive consumer products, such as cars or consumer electronics, or costly business products, such as jet engines or computers, are impractical. For these products, consumer reactions to mockup designs or one-of-a-kind prototypes are all that are feasible. Car makers, for example, test new style designs on early adopters (discussed in Chapter 11) who are more willing than the average customer to buy new designs or products.[31]

Stage 7: Commercialization

commercialization
The stage of the new-product process that involves positioning and launching a new product in full-scale production and sales.

Finally, the product is brought to the point of **commercialization**—the stage of the new-product process that involves positioning and launching a new product in full-scale production and sales. Companies proceed very carefully at the commercialization stage because this is the most expensive stage for most new products, especially consumer products. If competitors introduce a product that leapfrogs the firm's own new product, or if cannibalization of its own existing products looks significant, the firm may halt the new-product launch permanently.[32] Large companies often use regional rollouts, introducing the product sequentially into certain geographical areas to allow production levels and marketing activities to build up gradually in order to minimize the risk of new-product failure. Grocery product manufacturers and some telecommunications service providers are two examples of firms that use this strategy.

Grocery product manufacturers, in fact, are also exposed to other special commercialization problems. Because shelf space is so limited, many supermarkets require a **slotting fee** for new products, a payment a manufacturer makes to place a new item on a retailer's shelf. This can run to several million dollars for a single product. But there is yet another potential expense. If a new grocery product does not achieve a predetermined sales target, some retailers require a **failure fee,** a penalty payment a manufacturer makes to compensate a retailer for failed sales from its valuable shelf space. These costly slotting fees and failure fees are further examples of why large grocery product manufacturers use regional rollouts.

In recent years, companies have been trying to move very quickly from the idea generation or product concept stage to the commercialization stage of the new-product process. This is because speed or *time to market (TtM)* has been found to be correlated to new-product success. Recent studies, for example, have shown that high-tech products coming to market on time are far more profitable than those arriving late. So some companies—such as Sony, Honda, BMW, 3M, and Hewlett-Packard—have overlapped the sequence of stages described in this chapter.

With this approach, termed *parallel development,* cross-functional team members, who conduct the simultaneous development of both the product and the product process, stay with the product from concept to production. This has enabled Hewlett-Packard (HP) to reduce the development time for notebook computers from 12 months to 7.[33] In software development, *fast prototyping* uses a "do it, try it, fix it" approach—encouraging continuous improvements after the initial design. To speed up time to market many large companies are building "fences" around their new product teams to keep them from getting bogged down in red tape.[34]

Hewlett-Packard's new-product success can be traced to its founders' innovative management style that shunned traditional rigid hierarchical structures. Instead, HP uses a decentralized system where the brainpower of its employees is freed so that they can get whoever is needed to get the job done.[35]

Figure 10–5 identifies the purpose of each stage of the new-product process and the kinds of marketing information and methods used. The third column of the figure also suggests information that might help avoid some new-product failures. Although using the new-product process does not guarantee the success of products, it does increase a firm's success rate.[36]

slotting fee
A payment a manufacturer makes to place a new item on a retailer's shelf

failure fee
A penalty payment a manufacturer makes to compensate a retailer for failed sales from its valuable shelf space.

---

learning review

9. How does the development stage of the new-product process involve testing the product inside and outside the firm?

10. What is a test market?

11. What is commercialization of a new product?

STAGE OF PROCESS	PURPOSE OF STAGE	MARKETING INFORMATION AND METHODS USED
New-product strategy development	Identify focus, structure, approach, and guidelines for innovation	Company objectives; use of cross-functional teams, Six Sigma, and lead users
Idea generation	Develop concepts for possible products	Ideas from employees and co-workers, consumers, R&D, and competitors; methods of brainstorming and focus groups
Screening and evaluation	Separate good product ideas from bad ones inexpensively	Screening criteria, concept tests, and weighted point systems
Business analysis	Identify the product's features and its marketing strategy, and make financial projections	Product's key features, anticipated marketing mix strategy; economic, marketing, production, legal, and profitability analyses
Development	Create the prototype product, and test it in the laboratory and on consumers	Laboratory and consumer tests on product prototypes
Market testing	Test product and marketing strategy in the marketplace on a limited scale	Test markets, simulated test markets (STMs), virtual reality market testing
Commercialization	Position and offer product in the marketplace	Perceptual maps, product positioning, regional rollouts

● **FIGURE 10–5**
Marketing information and methods used in the new-product process

LEARNING OBJECTIVES REVIEW

LO1 Recognize the various terms that pertain to products and services.

A product is a good, service, or idea consisting of a bundle of tangible and intangible attributes that satisfies consumers and is received in exchange for money or some other unit of value. Firms can offer a range of products, which involve decisions regarding the product item, product line, and product mix.

LO2 Identify the ways in which consumer and business goods and services can be classified.

Products can be classified by type of user and tangibility. By user, the major distinctions are consumer goods, which are products purchased by the ultimate consumer, and business goods, which are products that assist in providing other products for resale. By degree of tangibility, products may be classified as (a) nondurable goods, which are consumed in one or a few uses; (b) durable goods, which are items that usually last over an extended number of uses; or (c) services, which are activities, deeds, or other basic intangibles offered for sale. Consumer goods can further be broken down on the basis of the effort involved in the purchase decision process, marketing mix attributes used in the purchase, and the frequency of purchase: (a) convenience goods are items that consumers purchase frequently and with a minimum of shopping effort, (b) shopping goods are items for which consumers compare several alternatives on selected criteria, (c) specialty goods are items that consumers make special efforts to seek out and buy, and (d) unsought goods are items that consumers do not either know about or initially want. Business goods can further be broken down into (a) production goods, which are items used in the manufacturing process that become part of the final product, such as raw materials or component parts; and (b) support goods, which are items used to assist in producing other goods and services and include installations, accessory equipment, supplies, and services.

LO3 Explain the implications of alternative ways of viewing "newness" in new products and services.

A product may be defined as "new" if it (*a*) is functionally different from the firm's existing products; (*b*) falls within the Industry Canada definition; (*c*) is a product line extension, a significant innovation, or a revolutionary new product; or (*d*) affects the degree of learning that consumers must engage in to use the product. With a continuous innovation, no new behaviours must be learned. With a dynamically continuous innovation, only minor behavioural changes are needed. With a discontinuous innovation, consumers must learn entirely new consumption patterns. New services can be defined similarly from major service innovations to simple style changes.

LO4 Describe the factors contributing to a product's or service's failure.

A new product often fails for these marketing reasons: (*a*) insignificant points of difference, (*b*) incomplete market and product definition before product development begins, (*c*) too little market attractiveness, (*d*) poor execution of the marketing mix, (*e*) poor product quality on critical factors, (*f*) bad timing, and (*g*) no economical access to buyers.

LO5 Explain the purposes of each step of the new-product process.

The new-product process consists of seven stages a firm uses to develop a salable good or service. (*1*) New-product strategy development involves defining the role for the new product within the firm's overall objectives. (*2*) Idea generation involves developing a pool of concepts from consumers, employees, basic R&D, and competitors to serve as candidates for new products. (*3*) Screening and evaluation involve evaluating new-product ideas to eliminate those that are not feasible from a technical or consumer perspective. (*4*) Business analysis involves defining the features of the new product, developing the marketing strategy and marketing program to introduce it, and making a financial forecast. (*5*) Development involves not only producing a prototype product but also testing it in the laboratory and on consumers to see that it meets the standards set for it. (*6*) Market testing involves exposing actual products (or virtual products) to prospective consumers under realistic (or virtual reality) purchasing conditions to see if they will buy the product. (*7*) Commercialization involves positioning and launching a product in full-scale production and sales with a specific marketing program.

FOCUSING ON KEY TERMS

business analysis p. 270
business goods p. 255
commercialization p. 272
consumer goods p. 255
convenience goods p. 256
development p. 270
failure fee p. 273
idea generation p. 266
market testing p. 271
new-product process p. 264
new-product strategy development p. 264
product p. 254

product line p. 254
product mix p. 255
production goods p. 257
protocol p. 261
screening and evaluation p. 268
shopping goods p. 256
Six Sigma p. 266
slotting fee p. 273
specialty goods p. 256
support goods p. 257
unsought goods p. 256

APPLYING MARKETING KNOWLEDGE

1 Products can be classified as either consumer or business goods. How would you classify the following products? (*a*) Johnson's baby shampoo, (*b*) a Black & Decker two-speed drill, and (*c*) an arc welder.

2 Are such products as Nature Valley granola bars and Eddie Bauer hiking boots convenience, shopping, specialty, or unsought goods?

3 Based on your answer to question 2, how would the marketing actions differ for each product and the classification to which you assigned it?

4 In terms of the behavioural effect on consumers, how would a PC, such as an Apple iMac be classified? In light of this classification, what actions would you suggest to the manufacturers of these products to increase their sales in the market?

5 Several alternative definitions were presented for a new product. How would a company's marketing strategy be affected if it used (*a*) the legal definition, or (*b*) a behavioural definition?

6 What methods would you suggest to assess the potential commercial success for the following new products? (*a*) a new, improved ketchup, (*b*) a three-dimensional television system that took the company ten years to develop, and (*c*) a new children's toy on which the company holds a patent.

7 Concept testing is an important step in the new-product process. Outline the concept tests for (*a*) an electrically powered car, and (*b*) a new loan payment system for automobiles that is based on a variable interest rate. What are the differences in developing concept tests for products as opposed to services?

Building Your Marketing Plan

In fine-tuning the product/service strategy for your marketing plan, do these two things:

1. Develop a simple three-column table in which (a) market segments of potential customers are in the first column and (b) the one of two key points of difference

of the product/service to satisfy the segment's needs are in the second column.

2. In the third column of your table, write ideas for specific new products/services for your business in each of the rows in your table.

Video Case 10

3M™ GREPTILE GRIP™ GOLF GLOVE: GREAT GRIPPING!

"Marketing is not brain surgery," says Dr. George Dierberger, marketing and international manager of 3M's Sports and Leisure Products Project. "We tend to make it a lot more difficult than it is. 3M wins with its technology. We're not in the 'me-too' business, and in marketing we've got to remember that."

3M's Micro-Replication Technology and Its Greptile Golf Glove

3M is a $20 billion global, diversified technology company. Among its well-known brands are Post-it Notes, Scotch tape, Scotch Brite scouring pads, and Nexcare bandages. The key to 3M's marketing successes is its commitment to innovation. For more than a century, 3M's management has given its employees the freedom to try new ideas. This "culture of creativity" has led to the commercialization of more than 50,000 products.

The Sports and Leisure Products Project is a business unit managed by Dierberger and his marketing staff. Recently, Dierberger and his staff changed the conventional thinking about golfing. Using 3M's proprietary "micro-replication" technology, and applying it to a golf glove, the new Greptile gripping material consists of thousands of tiny "gripping fingers" sewn into the upper palm and lower fingers of a golf glove. According to Dierberger, "It is the only glove on the market that actively improves a golfer's hold on the club by allowing a more relaxed grip, leading to greater driving distance with less grip pressure, even under wet conditions." Laboratory tests found that the Greptile material offers 610 percent greater gripping power than leather and 340 percent greater than tackified (sticky) grips. The result? On drives, the golf ball travels an average 10.5 feet farther!

Introduced in 2004, the new 3M Greptile Grip golf glove is made primarily of high-quality Cabretta sheep leather to give it a soft feel. Initially, 3M sold the Greptile

Grip golf glove through Walmart and other mass merchandisers for a suggested retail price of $11.95 to $15.95. And now it is also being stocked by golf retailers across the country, such as Nevada Bob's, Golfsmith, and Austad's. The golf glove is available in both men's and women's left-hand versions and in small, medium, medium/large, large, and extra-large hand sizes. A right-hand version for both genders appeared in 2005. 3M projected first-year sales of $1 million in the United States.

The Golf Market

Several socio-economic and demographic trends impact the golf glove market favourably. First, the huge baby boomer population (those born between 1946 and 1964) has matured, reaching its prime earning potential. This allows for greater discretionary spending on leisure activities, such as golf. According to the National Golf Foundation (NGF), most spending on golf equipment (clubs, bags, balls, shoes, gloves, etc.) is by consumers 50 and older—today's baby boomers. Second, according to the U.S. Census, the American population has shifted regionally from the East and North to the South and West, where golfing is popular year-round due to the temperate weather. Third, the number of golf courses in the U.S. has been growing, totalling about 15,000 at the end of 2004.

Finally, golf is becoming an increasingly popular leisure activity for all age groups and ethnic backgrounds. According to the NGF, golf participants in the United States totalled 37.9 million in 2003, an all-time high. Female golfers now account for about 25 percent of all golfers, while minority participation has increased to over 10 percent. According to the National Sporting Goods Association, sales of golf equipment was $3.1 billion in 2004, an increase of 2 percent from 2003.

The Golf Glove Market

The global market for golf gloves is estimated at $300 million, with the United States at $180 million or 60 percent of worldwide sales. Historically, about 80 percent of golf gloves are sold through public and private on- and off-course golf pro specialty shops, golf superstores, and sporting good superstores. However, mass merchandisers have recently increased their shares due to the typically lower prices offered by these retailers. FootJoy (46 percent) and Titleist (9 percent), both owned by Acushnet, are the top two golf glove market share leaders. Nike, which recently entered the golf equipment market with Tiger Woods as its spokesperson, has vaulted to a 7 percent share of the golf glove market. These golf glove marketers focus on technology and comfort to create points of difference from its competitors, such as the recently introduced FootJoy SciFlex™ glove ($18), the Titleist Perma-Tech™ glove ($19), and the Nike DriFit glove ($18).

3M's New Product Process

Since about half of 3M's products are less than five years old, the process used by 3M to develop new product innovations is critical to its success and continued growth. Every innovation must meet 3M's new product criteria: (1) be a patentable or trademarked technology; (2) offer a superior value proposition to consumers; and (3) change the basis of competition by achieving a significant point of difference.

When developing a new product innovation such as the 3M Greptile Grip golf glove, 3M uses a rigorous seven-step process: (1) ideas, (2) concept, (3) feasibility, (4) development, (5) scale-up, (6) launch, and (7) post-launch. "But innovation is not a linear path—not just A, then B, then C," says Dierberger. "It's the adjustments you make after you've developed the product that determines your success. And it's learning lessons from testing on real customers to make the final 'tweaks'—changing the price points, improving the benefits statement on the packaging, and sharpening the advertising appeals."

In the case of the 3M Greptile Grip golf glove, countless other examples of these adjustments appeared. Mike Kuhl, marketing coordinator at 3M, points out, "Consumer testing labs said the information on the back of our package was incomplete, so we had dozens of golfers hit drives using our glove and competitive gloves to compare driving distance." And 3M packaging engineer Travis Strom says, "Our first glove package 'pillowed'— bulked up—on the shelf, had hard-to-read text, and wasn't appealing to golfers, so we had to redesign it. After all, you only have a few seconds to capture the customer's attention with the package and make a sale."

The Future of 3M Golf and Greptile

In 2005, 3M Golf launched a premium golf glove consisting of the highest quality Cabretta leather and selling for a suggested retail price of $16.95 to $19.95. On the drawing board: 3M Greptile Grip golf tape that can be applied to golf club grips and possibly a line of Greptile Grip golf grips to double the gripping power when used in conjunction with the Greptile Grip golf glove. In 2006, 3M launched versions of its Greptile Grip golf gloves in Japan and Europe, the second and third largest golf markets behind the United States. Finally, 3M has developed and marketed baseball and softball batting gloves using the Greptile material.

Questions

1 What are the characteristics of the target market for the 3M Greptile Grip golf glove?

2 What are the key points of difference of the 3M Greptile Grip golf glove when compared with competitors' products, such as FootJoy and Nike? Substitute products, such as golf grips?

3 How does the Greptile Grip golf glove meet 3M's three criteria for new products?

4 Because 3M has no prior products for the golf market, what special promotion and distribution problems might 3M have?

5 What would be some new markets and new applications of the greptile grip technology that 3M could pursue?

chapter 11

Managing Products and Brands

GATORADE: SATISFYING THE UNQUENCHABLE THIRST

The thirst for Gatorade is unquenchable. This brand powerhouse has posted yearly sales gains over four decades and commands about 82 percent of the sports beverage market in North America.

Like Kleenex in the tissue market, Jello among gelatin desserts, and iPod for digital music players, Gatorade has become synonymous with sports beverages. Concocted in 1965 as a rehydration beverage for a university football team, the drink was coined "Gatorade" by an opposing team's coach after watching his team lose to the University of Florida Gators in the Orange Bowl. The name stuck, and a new beverage product class was born.

Stokely-Van Camp Inc. bought the Gatorade formula in 1967 and commercialized the product. The original Gatorade was a liquid with a lemon-lime flavour. An orange flavour was introduced in 1971 and a fruit punch flavour in 1983. Instant Gatorade arrived in 1979.

The Quaker Oats Company acquired Stokely-Van Camp in 1983. Quaker Oats executives quickly grew sales through a variety of means. More flavours were added and multiple package sizes were offered using different containers—glass and plastic bottles and aluminum cans. Distribution coverage expanded from convenience stores and supermarkets to vending machines, fountain service, and mass merchandisers such as Walmart. Consistent advertising and promotion effectively conveyed the product's unique benefits and links to

learning objectives

After reading this chapter, you should be able to:

LO1 Explain the product life cycle.

LO2 Identify ways that marketing executives manage a product's life cycle.

LO3 Recognize the importance of branding and alternative branding strategies.

LO4 Describe the role of packaging, labelling, and warranties in the marketing of a product.

athletic competition. International opportunities were vigorously pursued. Today, Gatorade is sold in more than 90 countries in North America, Europe, Latin America, the Middle East, Africa, Asia, and Australia, and has become a global brand.

Brand development spurred Gatorade's success. Gatorade Frost was introduced in 1997, with a "lighter, crisper" taste aimed at expanding the brand's reach beyond organized sports to other usage occasions. Gatorade Fierce with a "bolder" taste appeared in 1999. In the same year, Gatorade entered the bottled-water category with Propel Fitness Water, a lightly flavoured water fortified with vitamins. The Gatorade Performance Series was introduced in 2001, featuring a Gatorade Energy Bar, Gatorade Energy Drink, and Gatorade Nutritional Shake.

Brand development accelerated after PepsiCo, Inc., purchased Quaker Oats and the Gatorade brand in 2001. Gatorade All Stars, designed for teens, and Gatorade Xtremo, developed for Latino consumers with an exotic blend of flavours and a bilingual label, were introduced in 2002. Gatorade X-Factor followed in 2003 with three flavours. In 2005, Gatorade Endurance Formula was introduced for serious runners, construction workers, and other people doing long, sweaty workouts. Gatorade Rain, a lighter tasting version of regular Gatorade, arrived in 2006 with berry, lime, and tangerine flavours. In 2007, Gatorade A.M. debuted for the morning workout consumer with three morning-friendly flavours and no caffeine. A low-calorie Gatorade drink called G2 was launched in 2008. And now there is the "G Series," a system designed to fuel the body before, during, and after practice, training, or competition.

Currently, Gatorade is available in over 50 flavours internationally. Some 45 years after its creation, Gatorade remains a vibrant, multi-billion dollar growth brand with seemingly unlimited potential.[1] The marketing of Gatorade illustrates effective product and brand management in a dynamic marketplace. This chapter shows how the actions taken by Gatorade executives are typical of those made by successful marketers.

Gatorade's success is a direct result of masterful product and brand management over 45 years.

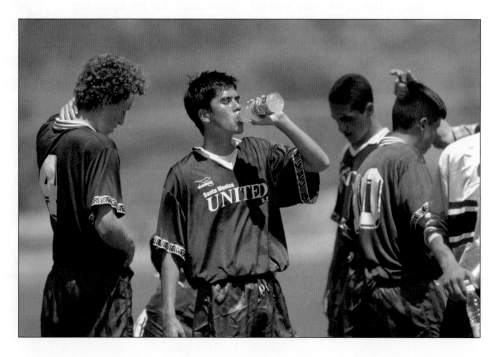

PRODUCT LIFE CYCLE

product life cycle

The stages a new product goes through in the marketplace: introduction, growth, maturity, and decline.

Products, like people, have been viewed as having a life cycle. The concept of the **product life cycle** describes the stages a new product goes through in the marketplace: introduction, growth, maturity, and decline (Figure 11–1).[2] There are two curves shown in this figure: total industry sales revenue and total industry profit, which represent the sum of sales revenue and profit of all firms producing the product. The reasons for the changes in each curve and the marketing decisions involved are discussed on the following pages.

● **FIGURE 11–1**

How stages of the product life cycle relate to a firm's marketing objectives and marketing mix actions

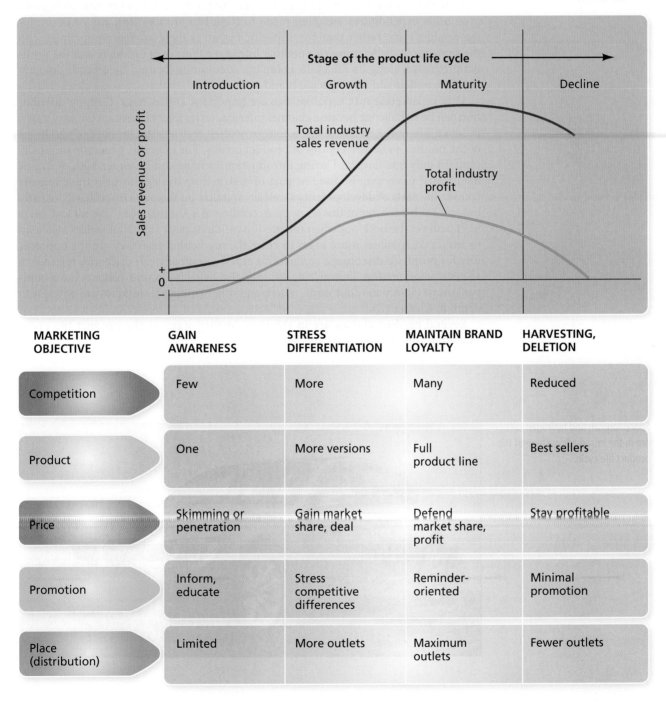

MARKETING OBJECTIVE	GAIN AWARENESS	STRESS DIFFERENTIATION	MAINTAIN BRAND LOYALTY	HARVESTING, DELETION
Competition	Few	More	Many	Reduced
Product	One	More versions	Full product line	Best sellers
Price	Skimming or penetration	Gain market share, deal	Defend market share, profit	Stay profitable
Promotion	Inform, educate	Stress competitive differences	Reminder-oriented	Minimal promotion
Place (distribution)	Limited	More outlets	Maximum outlets	Fewer outlets

Introduction Stage

The *introduction* stage of the product life cycle occurs when a product is first introduced to its intended target market. During this period, sales grow slowly and profit is minimal. The lack of profit is often the result of large investment costs in product development, such as the millions of dollars spent by Gillette to develop and launch the Gillette Fusion razor shaving system. The marketing objective for the company at this stage is to create consumer awareness and stimulate *trial*—the initial purchase of a product by a consumer.

Companies often spend heavily on advertising and other promotion tools to build awareness and stimulate product trial among consumers in the introductory stage. For example, Gillette budgeted millions in advertising alone to introduce the Fusion to male shavers. The result? Over 60 percent of male shavers became aware of the new razor within six months and 26 percent tried the product.[3] However, advertising and promotion expenditures are often made to stimulate *primary demand,* or desire for the product class, rather than for a specific brand, as there are few competitors with the same product. As more competitors introduce their own products and the product progresses along its life cycle, company attention is focused on creating *selective demand,* or demand for a specific brand.

Other marketing mix variables also are important at this stage. Gaining distribution can be a challenge because channel intermediaries may be hesitant to carry a new product. Moreover, in this stage, a company often restricts the number of variations of the product to ensure control of product quality. For example, Gatorade originally came in only one flavour. During introduction, pricing can be either high or low. A high initial price may be used as part of a *skimming* strategy to help the company recover the costs of development as well as capitalize on the price insensitivity of early buyers. 3M is a master of this strategy. According to a 3M manager, "We hit fast, price high, and get the heck out when the me-too products pour in."[4] High prices also tend to attract competitors more eager to enter the market because they see the opportunity for profit. To discourage competitive entry, a company can price low, referred to as *penetration pricing.* This pricing strategy also helps build unit volume, but a company must closely monitor costs. These and other pricing techniques are covered in depth in Chapter 13.

Several product classes are in the introductory stage of the product life cycle. These include space tourism and hydrogen cars.

Space tourism and hydrogen cars are in the introductory stage of the product life cycle.

Growth Stage

The second stage of the product life cycle, *growth,* is characterized by rapid increases in sales. It is in this stage that competitors appear. The result of more competitors and more aggressive pricing is that profit usually peaks during the growth stage. At this stage, the emphasis of advertising shifts to stimulating selective demand, in which product benefits are compared with those of competitors' offerings for the purpose of gaining market share.

Product sales in the growth stage grow at an increasing rate because of new people trying or using the product and a growing proportion of *repeat purchasers*—people who tried the product, were satisfied, and bought again. For the Gillette Fusion razor, over 60 percent of men who tried the razor adopted the product permanently. For successful products, the ratio of repeat to trial purchases grows as a product moves through the life cycle.

Changes start to appear in the product during the growth stage. To help differentiate a company's brand from those of its competitors, an improved version is created or new features added to the original design, and product proliferation occurs.

In the growth stage, it is important to gain as much distribution for the product as possible. In the retail store, for example, this often means that competing companies fight for display and shelf space.

Numerous product classes or industries are in the growth stage of the product life cycle. Examples include HDTVs and hybrid cars.

Maturity Stage

The third stage, *maturity,* is characterized by a slowing of total industry sales or product class revenue. Also, marginal competitors begin to leave the market. Most consumers who would buy the product are either repeat purchasers of the item or have tried and abandoned it. Sales increase at a decreasing rate in the maturity stage as fewer new buyers enter the market. Profit declines because there is fierce price competition among many sellers and the cost of gaining new buyers at this stage increases.

Marketing attention in the maturity stage is often directed toward holding market share through further product differentiation and finding new buyers. Still, a major

Hybrid automobiles are in the growth stage of the product life cycle. Products as well as the companies that manufacture them face unique challenges based on their product life-cycle stage.

consideration in a company's strategy in this stage is to reduce overall marketing costs by improving promotional and distribution efficiency.

Numerous product classes and industries are in the maturity stage of their product life cycle. These include soft drinks, gas-powered automobiles, and DVD players.

Decline Stage

The *decline* stage occurs when sales and profits begin to drop. Frequently, a product enters this stage not because of any wrong strategy on the part of the company but because of environmental changes. Technological innovation often precedes the decline stage as newer technologies replace older technologies. The word-processing capability of personal computers pushed typewriters into decline. Compact discs did the same to cassette tapes in the prerecorded music industry.

Products in the decline stage tend to consume a disproportionate share of management time and financial resources relative to their potential future worth. A company will follow one of two strategies to handle a declining product: deletion or harvesting.

Deletion Product *deletion*, or dropping a product from a company's product line, is the most drastic strategy for a declining product. Because a residual core of consumers still consume or use a product even in the decline stage, product elimination decisions are not taken lightly. For example, Sanford continues to sell its Liquid Paper correction fluid for use in typewriters, even in the era of word-processing equipment.

Harvesting A second strategy, *harvesting*, occurs when a company retains the product but reduces marketing support costs. The product continues to be offered, but salespeople do not allocate time in selling nor are advertising dollars spent. The purpose of harvesting is to maintain the ability to meet customer requests. Coca-Cola, for instance, still sells Tab, its first diet cola, to a small group of die-hard fans. According to Coke's CEO, "It shows you care. We want to make sure those who want Tab get Tab."[5]

Four Dimensions of the Product Life Cycle

Some important aspects of product life cycles are (1) their length, (2) the shape of their curves, (3) how they vary with different levels of the products, and (4) the rate at which consumers adopt products.

Length of the Product Life Cycle There is no exact time that a product takes to move through its life cycle. As a rule, consumer products have shorter life cycles than do business products. For example, many consumer food products, such as Frito-Lay's Baked Lay's potato chips, move from the introduction stage to maturity in 18 months. The availability of mass communication vehicles informs consumers faster and shortens life cycles. Also, the rate of technological change tends to shorten product life cycles as new-product innovation replaces existing products.

The Shape of the Product Life Cycle The product life-cycle curve shown in Figure 11–1 is the *generalized life cycle,* but not all products have the same shape to their curve. In fact, there are several different life-cycle curves, each type suggesting different marketing strategies. Figure 11–2 shows the shape of life-cycle curves for four different types of products: high-learning, low-learning, fashion, and fad products.

A *high-learning product* is one for which significant education of the customer is required and there is an extended introductory period (Figure 11–2A). It may surprise you, but personal computers had this type of life-cycle curve in the 1980s because consumers had to understand the benefits of purchasing the product or be educated in a new way of performing a familiar task. Convection ovens also necessitated that

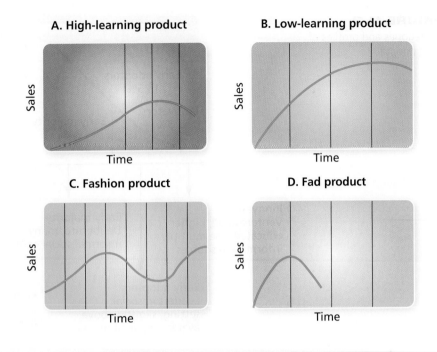

the consumer learn a new way of cooking and alter familiar recipes. As a result, these ovens spent years in the introductory period.

In contrast, for a *low-learning product,* sales begin immediately because little learning is required by the consumer, and the benefits of purchase are readily understood (Figure 11–2B). This product often can be easily imitated by competitors, and so the marketing strategy is to broaden distribution quickly. In this way, as competitors rapidly enter, most retail outlets already have the innovator's product. It is also important to have the manufacturing capacity to meet demand. A recent example of a successful low-learning product is Gillette's Fusion razor. This product achieved $1 billion in worldwide sales in less than three years.[6]

A *fashion product* (Figure 11–2C), such as hemline lengths on skirts or lapel widths on sports jackets, is introduced, declines, and then seems to return. Life cycles for fashion products most often appear in women's and men's clothing styles. The length of the cycles may be years or decades.

A *fad* experiences rapid sales on introduction and then an equally rapid decline (Figure 11–2D). These products are typically novelties and have a short life cycle.

The Product Level: Class and Form   The product life cycle shown in Figure 11–1 is a total industry or product class sales curve. Yet, in managing a product, it is important to often distinguish among the multiple life cycles (class and form) that may exist. **Product class** refers to the entire product category or industry, such as video game consoles and software. **Product form** pertains to variations within the class. For video games, product form exists in the computing capability of game consoles or the portability of the machines such as Sony's PSP, Nintendo's Wii, and Microsoft's Xbox. Game consoles and software have life cycles of their own. They typically move from the introduction stage to maturity in five years.

The Life Cycle and Consumers   The life cycle of a product depends on sales to consumers. Not all consumers rush to buy a product in the introductory stage, and the shapes of the life-cycle curves indicate that most sales occur after the product has been on the market for some time. In essence, a product diffuses, or spreads, through the population, a concept called the *diffusion of innovation.*[7]

product class
The entire product category or industry.

product form
Variations of a product within the product class.

● **FIGURE 11-3**

Five categories and profiles of
product adopters

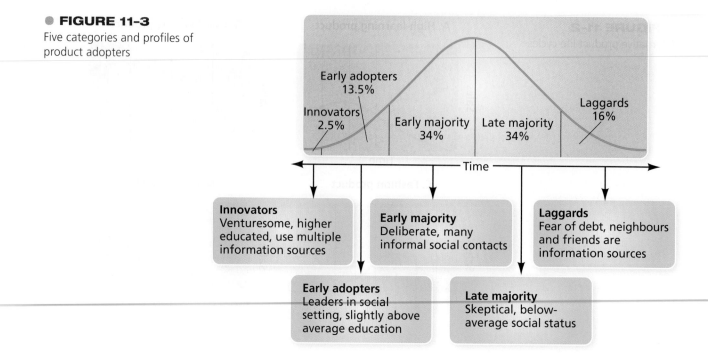

Some people are attracted to a product early, while others buy it only after they
see their friends with the item. Figure 11–3 shows the consumer population divided
into five categories of product adopters based on when they adopt a new product.
Brief profiles accompany each category. For any product to be successful, it must be
purchased by innovators and early adopters. This is why manufacturers of new pharmaceuticals try to gain adoption by leading hospitals, clinics, and physicians that are
widely respected in the medical field. Once accepted by innovators and early adopters, the adoption of new products moves on to the early majority, late majority, and
laggard categories.

Several factors affect whether a consumer will adopt a new product. Common reasons for resisting a product in the introduction stage are usage barriers (the product
is not compatible with existing habits), value barriers (the product provides no incentive to change), risk barriers (physical, economic, or social), and psychological barriers (cultural differences or image).[8]

Companies attempt to overcome these barriers in numerous ways. They provide
warranties, money-back guarantees, extensive usage instructions, demonstrations,
and free samples to stimulate initial trial of new products. For example, software
developers offer demonstrations downloaded from the Internet. Maybelline allows
consumers to browse through the Cover Girl Color Match system on its Web site to
find out how certain makeup products will look. Free samples are one of the most
popular means to gain consumer trial. For example, some Ontario winemakers from
the Niagara region believe that sampling (via taste testing) is critical in order for a
new wine product to be successful in the crowded and competitive Canadian market.[9]

learning review

1. Advertising plays a major role in the _____ stage of the product
   life cycle, and _____ plays a major role in maturity.

2. How do high-learning and low-learning products differ?

3. What does the life cycle for a fashion product look like?

LO2 MANAGING THE PRODUCT LIFE CYCLE

An important task for a firm is to manage its products through the successive stages of their life cycles. This section discusses the role of the product manager, who is usually responsible for this, and analyzes three ways to manage a product through its life cycle: modifying the product, modifying the market, and repositioning the product.

Role of a Product Manager

The product manager (sometimes called *brand manager*) manages the marketing efforts for a close-knit family of products or brands.[10] Introduced by Procter & Gamble (P&G) in 1928, the product manager–style of marketing organization is used by consumer goods firms, such as General Mills and PepsiCo, and by business firms, such as Intel and Hewlett-Packard. All product managers are responsible for managing existing products through the stages of the life cycle, and some are also responsible for developing new products. Product managers' marketing responsibilities include developing and executing a marketing program for the product line described in an annual marketing plan and approving ad copy, media selection, and package design.

Product managers also engage in extensive data analysis related to their products and brands. Sales, market share, and profit trends are closely monitored. Managers often supplement these data with two measures: (1) a category development index (CDI), and (2) a brand development index (BDI). These indexes help to identify strong and weak market segments (usually demographic or geographic segments) for specific consumer products and brands and provide direction for marketing efforts. The calculation, visual display, and interpretation of these two indexes for Hawaiian Punch are described in the Using Marketing Dashboards box.

product modification
Altering a product's characteristics, such as its quality, performance, appearance, features, or package to try to increase and extend the product's sales.

market modification
Strategy in which a company tries to find new customers, increase a product's use among existing customers, or create new-use situations.

Modifying the Product

Product modification involves altering a product's characteristics, such as its quality, performance, appearance, features, or package to try to increase and extend the product's sales. Wrinkle-free and stain-resistant clothing made possible by nanotechnology has revolutionized the men's and women's apparel business and stimulated industry sales of casual pants, shirts, and blouses. Nokia's global leadership position among cellphone handset manufacturers is due to continuous product modification.

New features, ingredients, packages, or scents can be used to change a product's characteristics and give the sense of a revised product. Procter & Gamble revamped Pantene shampoo and conditioner with a new vitamin formula and relaunched the brand with a multi-million dollar advertising and promotion campaign. The result? Pantene, a brand first introduced in the 1940s, is now a top-selling brand! Finally, Heinz Canada has modified its original red ketchup and now offers a light version, a reduced-sugar version, and an organic version of its product.

Modifying the Market

With **market modification** strategies, a company tries to find new customers, increase a product's use among existing customers, or create new-use situations.

Finding New Users   Produce companies have begun marketing and packaging prunes as "dried plums" for the purposes of attracting younger buyers. Ocean Spray offers sweetened dried cranberries, called Craisins, as a healthy snack for younger consumers. Harley-Davidson tailored its marketing program to encourage women to take up cycling, thus doubling the number of potential customers for its motorcycles.

Using Marketing Dashboards

Knowing Your CDI and BDI

Where are sales for my product category and brand strongest and weakest? Data related to this question are often displayed in a marketing dashboard using two indexes: (1) a category development index (CDI), and (2) a brand development index (BDI).

Your Challenge You have joined the marketing team for Hawaiian Punch, the number-one fruit punch drink sold in the market. The brand has been marketed to mothers with children under 12 years old. The majority of Hawaiian Punch sales are in gallon and two-litre bottles. Your assignment is to examine the brand's performance and identify growth opportunities for the Hawaiian Punch brand among households that consume prepared fruit drinks (the product category).

Your marketing dashboard displays a category development index and a brand development index provided by a syndicated marketing research firm. Each index is based on the calculations below:

Category Development Index (CDI) =
$$\frac{\text{Percent of a Product Category's Total Market Sales in a Market Segment}}{\text{Percent of the Total Market Population in a Market Segment}} \times 100$$

Brand Development Index (BDI) =
$$\frac{\text{Percent of a Brand's Total Market Sales in a Market Segment}}{\text{Percent of the Total Market Population in a Market Segment}} \times 100$$

A CDI over 100 indicates above-average product-category purchases by a market segment. A number under 100 indicates below-average purchases. A BDI over 100 indicates a strong brand position in a segment; a number under 100 indicates a weak brand position.

You are interested in CDI and BDI displays for four household segments that consume prepared fruit drinks: (1) households without children; (2) households with children 6 and under; (3) households with children 7 to 12; and (4) households with children 13 to 18.

Your Findings The BDI and CDI measures displayed below show that Hawaiian Punch is consumed by households with children, and particularly households with children 12 and under. The Hawaiian Punch BDI is over 100 for both segments—not surprising because the brand is marketed to these segments. Households with children 13 to 18 years old evidence high fruit drink consumption with a CDI over 100. But Hawaiian Punch is relatively weak in this segment with a BDI under 100.

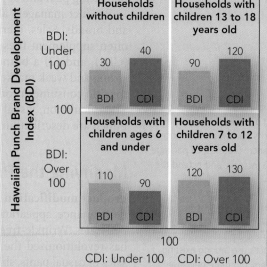

Fruit Drink Category Development Index (CDI)

Your Action An opportunity for Hawaiian Punch exists among households with children 13 to 18 years old—teenagers. You might propose that Hawaiian Punch be repositioned for teens. In addition, you might recommend that Hawaiian Punch be packaged in single-serve cans or bottles to attract this segment, much like soft drinks. Teens might also be targeted for advertising and promotions.

Increasing Use Promoting more frequent usage has been a strategy of Campbell Soup Company. Because soup consumption rises in the winter and declines during the summer, the company now advertises more heavily in warm months to encourage consumers to think of soup as more than a cold-weather food. Similarly, orange juice producers advocate drinking orange juice throughout the day rather than for breakfast only. And the Canadian Turkey Marketing Agency tells Canadians that turkey meat is a good option for everyday meals, not just for Thanksgiving and Christmas.

Nothing says barbeque quite like ~~beef~~ Turkey

BBQ Turkey Burgers

1 1/2 lb	fresh ground Turkey	750 g
1/2 cup	chopped onion	125 mL
1/2 cup	BBQ sauce	125 mL
1/2 cup	dried bread crumbs	125 mL
1/2 tsp	salt	2 mL
	ground black pepper, to taste	

Preparation Time: 5 minutes
Cooking Time: 12 minutes

Combine all ingredients in a large bowl. Mix thoroughly. Shape into 6 patties. Place on oiled grill. Grill over medium heat 4 - 6 minutes on each side, or until no longer pink in centre, basting with additional BBQ sauce if desired.

Turkey makes a good recipe taste better.™

CTMA
CANADIAN TURKEY MARKETING AGENCY

turkeyfordinner.ca

© Canadian Turkey Marketing Agency 2004

product repositioning
Changing the place a product occupies in a consumer's mind relative to competing products.

trading up
Adding value to a product (or line) through additional features or higher-quality materials.

trading down
Reducing the number of features, quality, or price.

Creating New-Use Situations Finding new uses for an existing product has been the strategy behind Woolite, a laundry soap. Originally intended for handwashing of woollen fabric, Woolite now promotes itself for use with all fine clothing items. Mars, Inc. suggests a new-use situation when it markets its M&M's candy as a replacement for chocolate chips in baked goods.

Repositioning the Product

Often, a company decides to reposition its product or product line in an attempt to bolster sales. **Product repositioning** is changing the place a product occupies in a consumer's mind relative to competing products. A firm can reposition a product by changing one or more of the four marketing mix elements. Four factors that trigger a repositioning action are discussed next.

Reacting to a Competitor's Position One reason to reposition a product is that a competitor's entrenched position is adversely affecting sales and market share. New Balance, Inc. successfully repositioned its athletic shoes to focus on fit and comfort rather than competing head-on against Nike and Reebok on fashion and sport. The company offers an expansive range of shoe widths with the message, "N is for fit," and it networks with podiatrists, not sport celebrities.[11]

Reaching a New Market When Unilever introduced iced tea in the United Kingdom in the mid-1990s, sales were disappointing. British consumers viewed it as leftover hot tea, not suitable for drinking. The company made its tea carbonated and repositioned it as a cold soft drink to compete as a carbonated beverage, and sales improved. Johnson & Johnson effectively repositioned St. Joseph Aspirin from one for infants to an adult low-strength aspirin to reduce the risk of heart problems or strokes.[12]

Catching a Rising Trend Changing consumer trends can also lead to repositioning. Growing consumer interest in foods that offer health and dietary benefits is an example, and many products have been repositioned to capitalize on this trend. Quaker Oats makes the claim that oatmeal, as part of a low-saturated-fat, low-cholesterol diet, may reduce the risk of heart disease. Calcium-enriched products, such as Uncle Ben's Calcium Plus rice, emphasize healthy bone structure for children and adults. Weight-conscious consumers have embraced low-fat diets in growing numbers. Today, every major consumer food and beverage company in Canada offers and advertises reduced-fat versions of its products.[13]

Changing the Value Offered In repositioning a product, a company can decide to change the value it offers buyers and trade up or down. **Trading up** involves adding value to the product (or line) through additional features or higher-quality materials. Michelin has done this with its "run-flat" tire, which can keep going up to 70 kilometres after suffering total air loss. Dog food manufacturers, such as Ralston Purina, also have traded up by offering super-premium foods based on "life-stage nutrition." Mass merchandisers, such as Sears Canada, Zellers, and The Bay, can trade up by adding designer clothes sections to their stores.

Trading down involves reducing the number of features, quality, or price. For example, airlines have added more seats, thus reducing leg room, and eliminated

Making Responsible Decisions

Consumer Economics of Downsizing: Get Less, Pay More

For more than 30 years, Starkist put 185 grams of tuna into its regular-size can. Today, Starkist puts 175 grams of tuna into its can but charges the same price. Frito-Lay (Doritos and Lay's snack chips), Procter & Gamble (Pampers and Luvs disposable diapers), and Nestlé (Poland Spring and Calistoga bottled waters) have whittled away at package contents 5 to 10 percent while maintaining their products' package size, dimensions, and prices. Kimberly-Clark cut the retail price on its jumbo pack of Huggies diapers, but also reduced the number of diapers per pack from 48 to 42.

Consumer advocates charge that downsizing the content of packages while maintaining prices is a subtle and unannounced way of taking advantage of consumer buying habits. They also say downsizing is a price increase in disguise and deceptive, but legal. Manufacturers argue that this practice is a way of keeping prices from rising beyond the psychological barriers for their products.

Is downsizing an unethical practice if manufacturers do not inform consumers that the package contents are less than they were previously?

---

downsizing

Reducing the content of packages without changing package size and maintaining or increasing the package price.

extras, such as snack service and food portions. Trading down often exists when companies engage in **downsizing**—reducing the content of packages without changing package size and maintaining or increasing the package price. Firms have been criticized for this practice, as described in the accompanying Making Responsible Decisions box, "Consumer Economics of Downsizing: Get Less, Pay More."[14]

---

learning review

4. How does a product manager help manage a product's life cycle?

5. What does "creating new-use situations" mean in managing a product's life cycle?

6. Explain the difference between trading up and trading down in repositioning.

LO3 BRANDING AND BRAND MANAGEMENT

According to a study by the Canadian Marketing Association, building and managing brands is critically important for marketers but also very difficult in a complex marketplace environment. The study suggests several environmental forces are impacting on just how Canadian marketers can effectively build and manage brands. These forces include the empowered consumer, new media and new technologies, increased pressure to demonstrate a return on investment, the importance of changing demographics, ethics in business, organizational change, and globalization. The Canadian Marketing Association cites the empowered consumer as having the most critical impact on marketers and their branding strategies.[15] As you have already learned, in this new marketing era of customer experience management, marketers must focus on creating brands that can deliver the experiences that the customer is now demanding. In short, the goal is to create and deliver positive experiences with the brand in order to ensure customer satisfaction and strong customer loyalty to the brand. The basic starting point is the decision by the marketer to actually create a brand.

branding

Activity in which an organization uses a name, phrase, design, symbols, or combination of these to identify its products and distinguish them from those of competitors.

brand name

Any word, device (design, shape, sound, or colour), or combination of these used to distinguish a seller's goods or services.

Branding is an activity in which an organization uses a name, phrase, design, symbols, or combination of these to identify its products and distinguish them from those of competitors. A **brand name** is any word, "device" (design, sound, shape, or colour), or combination of these used to distinguish a seller's goods or services. Some brand names can be spoken, such as Gatorade or Bauer. Other brand names cannot be spoken, such as the rainbow-coloured apple (the *logotype* or *logo*) that Apple Inc. puts on

trade name
A commercial, legal name under which a company does business.

trademark
Identifies that a firm has legally registered its brand name or trade name so that the firm has its exclusive use.

brand personality
A set of human characteristics associated with a brand name.

brand equity
The added value that a given brand name gives to a product beyond the functional benefits provided.

Can you describe the personality traits of this brand? Not sure? Try visiting the Web site for more information.

got2b
www.got2b.us

its products and in its ads. A **trade name** is a commercial, legal name under which a company does business. The Campbell Soup Company is the trade name of that firm.

A **trademark** identifies that a firm has legally registered its brand name or trade name so that the firm has its exclusive use, thereby preventing others from using it. In Canada, trademarks are registered under the *Trade-marks Act* with Industry Canada. A well-known trademark can help a company advertise its offerings to customers and develop their brand loyalty.

Because a good trademark can help sell a product, *product counterfeiting,* which involves low-cost copies of popular brands not manufactured by the original producer, has been a growing problem. Counterfeit products can steal sales from the original manufacturer or hurt the company's reputation.

Trademark protection is a significant issue in global marketing. For instance, the breaking up of the Soviet Union into individual countries meant that many firms, such as Xerox, had to re-register trademarks in each of the republics to prohibit misuse and generic use ("xeroxing") of their trademarks by competitors and consumers.

Consumers may benefit most from branding. Recognizing competing products by distinct trademarks allows them to be more efficient shoppers. Consumers can recognize and avoid products with which they are dissatisfied while becoming loyal to other, more satisfying brands. As discussed in Chapter 5, brand loyalty often eases consumers' decision making by eliminating the need for an external search. CanWest Global TV System uses a single brand, "Global," which it says makes it easier for viewers to identify the network's stations and to find the schedule they have.

Brand Personality and Brand Equity

Product managers recognize that brands offer more than product identification and a means to distinguish their products from competitors. Successful and established brands take on a **brand personality,** a set of human characteristics associated with a brand name.[16] Research shows that consumers often assign personality qualities to products—traditional, romantic, rugged, sophisticated, rebellious—and choose brands that are consistent with their own or desired self-image. Marketers can and do imbue a brand with a personality through advertising that depicts a certain user or usage situation and conveys certain emotions or feelings to be associated with the brand. For example, the personality traits associated with Coca-Cola are *real* and *cool;* with Pepsi, *young, exciting,* and *hip;* and with Dr. Pepper, *nonconforming, unique,* and *fun.* The traits often linked to Harley-Davidson are masculinity, defiance, and rugged individualism.

Brand name importance to a company has led to a concept called **brand equity,** the added value that a given brand name gives to a product beyond the functional benefits provided. This value has two distinct advantages. First, brand equity provides a competitive advantage, such as the Sunkist label, which implies quality fruit, and the Disney name, which defines children's entertainment. A second advantage is that consumers are often willing to pay a higher price for a product with brand equity. Brand equity, in this instance, is represented by the premium that a consumer will pay for one brand over another when the functional benefits provided are identical. Intel microchips, Bose audio systems, Duracell batteries, Microsoft computer software, and Louis Vuitton luggage all enjoy a price premium arising from brand equity.

Creating Brand Equity   Brand equity does not just happen. It is carefully crafted and nurtured by marketing programs that forge strong, favourable, and unique consumer associations and experiences with a brand. Brand equity resides in the minds of consumers and results from what they have learned, felt, seen, and heard about a brand over time. Marketers recognize that brand equity is not easily or quickly achieved. Rather, it arises from a sequential building process consisting of four steps (Figure 11–4).[17]

- The first step is to develop positive brand awareness and an association of the brand in consumers' minds with a product class or need to give the brand an identity. Gatorade and Kleenex have done this in the sports drink and facial tissue product classes, respectively.
- Next, a marketer must establish a brand's meaning in the minds of consumers. Meaning arises from what a brand stands for and has two dimensions—a functional, performance-related dimension and an abstract, imagery-related dimension. Nike has done this through continuous product development and improvement, and its links to peak athletic performance in its integrated marketing communications program.
- The third step is to elicit the proper consumer responses to a brand's identity and meaning. Here, attention is placed on how consumers think and feel about a brand. Thinking focuses on a brand's perceived quality, credibility, and superiority relative to other brands. Feeling relates to the consumer's emotional reaction to a brand. Michelin elicits both responses for its tires. Not only is Michelin thought of as a credible and superior-quality brand, but consumers also acknowledge a warm and secure feeling of safety, comfort, and self-assurance without worry or concern about the brand.
- The final, and most difficult, step is to create a consumer–brand resonance evident in an intense, active loyalty relationship between consumers and the brand. A deep psychological bond characterizes consumer–brand resonance and the

● **FIGURE 11–4**

Customer-based brand equity pyramid

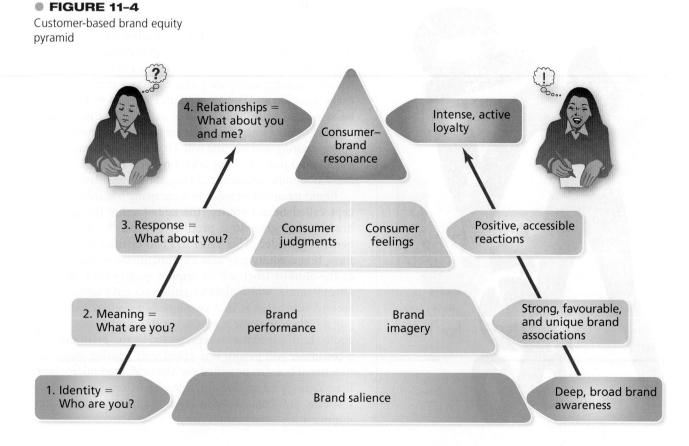

Maple Leaf Sports & Entertainment Ltd. focuses on building bonds between fans and its sports teams.

personal identification that consumers have with the brand. Examples of brands that have achieved this status include Harley-Davidson, Apple, and eBay.

Researchers have demonstrated that forging an emotional connection between the brand and the consumer can lead to brand differentiation, consumer loyalty, and evangelical promotion of the brand. This is particularly true for service brands.[18] The intangible nature of services often makes brand building more difficult. But like their product counterparts, marketers of services also need to actively build their brand names and to create brand equity. Whether they market financial services or sports entertainment, the goal is the same—connect with customers, offer a positive experience, and encourage them to become "brand ambassadors," or people who will spread the word about the brand. For example, Maple Leaf Sports & Entertainment Ltd. (MLSE), which owns the Toronto Maple Leafs and the Toronto Raptors, markets its brand names diligently, focusing on building bonds between the fans and these sports teams. According to Tom Anselmi of MLSE, "Brand building is just as important in the business of sports as it is in selling laundry soap." After the customer has an experience with the Leafs or Raptors, MLSE wants these customers to spread the word about the brands. Recent Canadian research on business start-ups also suggests that building the brand is a key imperative for new venture success. In crowded and competitive markets, the entrepreneur must be able to develop a brand that resonates with the consumer and encourage that consumer to talk about the brand.[19]

Valuing Brand Equity   Brand equity also provides a financial advantage for the brand owner. Successful, established brand names, such as Google, Nike, Gatorade, and Nokia, have an economic value in the sense that they are intangible assets. Unlike physical assets that depreciate with time and use, brands can actually appreciate in value when marketed effectively. However, brands can also lose value when they are not managed properly. Attaching monetary value to brands can often be complicated, and there is little agreement among experts concerning the optimal way to calculate brand equity. Therefore, marketers often use a variety of direct and indirect measures to determine the equity of a brand, including communication investment in the brand and customer loyalty to the brand. Read the accompanying Marketing Matters box, "Top Global and Top Canadian Brands," to find out who are the top global brands and the top Canadian brands in the marketplace today.[20]

General Motors is the worldwide leader in licensed product sales among automakers. A recent licensing arrangement is for Hummer® Footwear made by Roper Footwear & Apparel.

General Motors
www.hummer.com

IT IS RECOMMENDED THAT YOU CHANGE YOUR SOCKS EVERY 3,000 MILES.

Introducing the only full line of footwear tough enough to be called HUMMER. Now you can sell your customers comfort, style, and performance that's like nothing else.

HUMMER
FOOTWEAR • LIKE NOTHING ELSE.

Marketing Matters

Top Global and Top Canadian Brands

BRANDZ is a quantitative brand equity study carried out annually by Millward Brown. The brand values reported in their study are based on the intrinsic value of the brand, which is derived from its ability to generate demand. The dollar value of each brand is the sum of all future earnings that the brand is forecast to generate, discounted to a present-day value.

The number-one brand in the 2009 BRANDZ study was Google, followed by Microsoft (2), Coca-Cola (3), IBM (4), McDonald's (5) and Apple Inc. (6). Only one Canadian company cracked the top 50 global brands; RBC was ranked 48th. TD Canada Trust made the list ranked 61st overall. There are also rankings by specific product categories. For example, H&M was ranked number one in the apparel category, Bud Light was number one in the beer category, Nescafé was number one in the coffee category, Toyota was number one in the car category, and Louis Vuitton was number one in the luxury goods category. The study calculated that the top 100 global brands have an equity value of over $2 trillion. The study also found that building an emotional bond with the customer adds significant brand value.

Back in Canada, a consulting company called Brand Finance Canada released its report, "Canada's Most Valuable Brands." According to the study, the top ten were RBC, BlackBerry, TD Canada Trust, Manulife, Bell, Scotiabank, Loblaws, Bombardier, BMO, and CIBC. A key implication from this study is that companies must do a better job building and sustaining brand value because brand value is driving overall enterprise value.

Overall, what these studies reveal is that brands are vitally important to companies. In fact, some experts suggest that brands, as intangible assets, account for more than one-third of the total value of the Fortune 500 today. Therefore, brands need to be managed strategically and on a company-wide basis. Importantly, companies can increase the value of their brands. The starting point is to create and communicate to the customer a valuable brand promise (what the brand will do for the customer) and then deliver on that promise with a great brand experience.

---

brand licensing

A contractual agreement whereby a company allows another firm to use its brand name, patent, trade secret, or other property for a royalty or fee.

Financially lucrative brand licensing opportunities can also arise from brand equity. **Brand licensing** is a contractual agreement whereby one company (licensor) allows its brand name(s) or trademark(s) to be used with products or services offered by another company (licensee) for a royalty or fee. For example, Playboy earns millions of dollars licensing its name for merchandise ranging from wallpaper in Europe to cooking classes in Brazil. Disney makes billions of dollars each year licensing its characters for children's toys, apparel, and games. Licensing fees for Winnie the Pooh alone exceed $3 billion annually. General Motors sells more than $2 billion in licensed products each year.[21]

Successful brand licensing requires careful marketing analysis to assure a proper match between the licensor's brand and the licensee's products. World-renowned designer Ralph Lauren earns over $140 million each year by licensing his Ralph Lauren, Polo, and Chaps brands for dozens of products, including paint by Sherwin-Williams, furniture by Henredon, footwear by Rockport, and fragrances by Cosmair. Such mistakes as Kleenex diapers, Bic perfume, and Domino's fruit-flavoured bubble gum represent a few examples of poor matches and licensing failures.

Picking a Good Brand Name

We take such brand names as Red Bull, iPod, and Adidas for granted, but it is often a difficult and expensive process to choose a good name. Companies will spend between $25,000 and $100,000 to identify and test a new brand name. For instance, Intel spent $45,000 for the Pentium name given to its family of microchips. There are five criteria mentioned most often when selecting a good brand name:[22]

- The name should suggest the product benefits. For example, Accutron (watches), Easy Off (oven cleaner), Glass Plus (glass cleaner), Cling-Free (antistatic cloth for drying clothes), PowerBook (laptop computer), and Tidy Bowl (toilet bowl cleaner) all clearly describe the benefits of purchasing the product.

- The name should be memorable, distinctive, and positive. In the auto industry, when a competitor has a memorable name, others quickly imitate. When Ford named a car Mustang, others soon followed with Pintos, Colts, and Broncos. The Thunderbird name led to Phoenix, Eagle, Sunbird, and Firebird.

- The name should fit the company or product image. Sharp is a name that can apply to audio and video equipment. Excedrin, Anacin, and Nuprin are scientific-sounding names, good for an analgesic. Eveready, Duracell, and DieHard suggest reliability and longevity. However, naming a personal computer PCjr, as IBM did with its first computer for home use, fit neither the company nor the product. PCjr sounded like a toy and stalled IBM's initial entry into the home-use market.

- The name should have no legal or regulatory restrictions. Legal restrictions produce trademark infringement suits, and regulatory restrictions can arise through improper use of words. Increasingly, brand names need a corresponding address on the Internet. This further complicates name selection because millions of domain names are already registered.

- Finally, the name should be simple (such as Bold laundry detergent, Sure deodorant, and Bic pens) and should have emotional appeal (such as Joy and Obsession perfumes). In the development of names for international use, having a non-meaningful brand name has been considered a benefit. A name such as Esso does not have any prior impressions or undesirable images among a diverse world population with different languages and cultures. The 7UP name is another matter. In Shanghai, China, the phrase means "death through drinking" in the local dialect, and sales have suffered as a result.

Do you have an idea for a brand name? If you do, find out whether the name has been registered with Industry Canada's trademark division. Visit its Web site, described in the accompanying Going Online box, "Have an Idea for a Brand or Trade Name? Check It Out!"

Branding Strategies

Companies can employ several different branding strategies, including multiproduct branding, multibranding, private branding, or mixed branding (Figure 11–5).

multiproduct branding
Use by a company of one name for all its products in a product class.

Multiproduct Branding With **multiproduct branding,** a company uses one name for all its products in a product class. This approach is sometimes called *family branding,* or *corporate branding* when the company's trade name is used. For example,

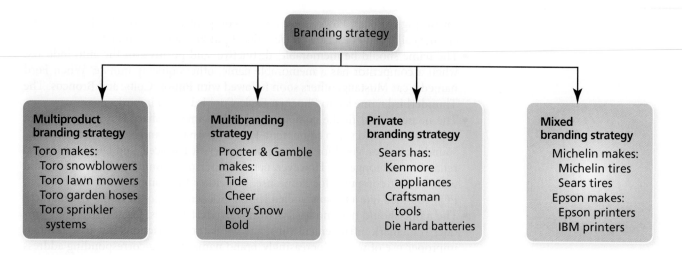

● FIGURE 11–5

Alternative branding strategies

General Electric, Gerber, and Sony engage in corporate branding—the company's trade name and brand name are identical. Church & Dwight employs the Arm & Hammer family brand name for all its products featuring baking soda as the primary ingredient.

There are several advantages to multiproduct branding. Capitalizing again on brand equity, consumers who have a good experience with the product will transfer this favourable attitude to other items in the product class with the same name. Therefore, this brand strategy makes possible *line extensions,* the practice of using a current brand name to enter a new market segment in its product class. Campbell Soup Company effectively employs a multiproduct branding strategy with soup line extensions. It offers regular Campbell's soup, home-cooking style, and chunky varieties, as well as more than 100 soup flavours. This strategy can also result in lower advertising and promotion costs because the same name is used on all products, thus raising the level of brand awareness. A risk with line extensions is that sales of an extension may come at the expense of other items in the company's product line. Therefore, line extensions work best when they provide incremental company revenue by taking sales away from competing brands or attracting new buyers.

Some companies employ *sub-branding,* which combines a corporate or family brand with a new brand. For example, Gatorade has successfully used sub-branding with the introduction of Gatorade A.M. and Gatorade G2.

A strong brand equity also allows for *brand extension,* the practice of using a current brand name to enter a completely different product class. For instance, the equity in the Tylenol name as a trusted pain reliever allowed Johnson & Johnson to successfully extend this name to Tylenol Cold & Flu and Tylenol PM, a sleep aid. Honda's established name for motor vehicles has extended easily to snowblowers, lawn mowers, marine engines, and snowmobiles.

However, there is a risk with brand extensions. Too many uses for one brand name can dilute the meaning of a brand for consumers. Marketing experts claim this has happened to the Arm & Hammer brand given its use for toothpaste, laundry detergent, gum, cat litter, air freshener, carpet deodorizer, and antiperspirant.[23]

co-branding

The pairing of two or more recognized brands on a single product or service.

A variation on brand extensions is the practice of **co-branding,** the pairing of two or more recognized brands on a single product or service.[24] Co-branding benefits firms by allowing them to enter new product classes, capitalize on an already established brand name in a product class, or reach new market segments. Co-branding is particularly popular in the service sector where two or more service companies often bundle their offerings together. For example, Petro-Canada and A&W co-brand; Holiday Inn and Pizza Hut Express co-brand; Renaissance Hotels co-brands with Bath & Body Works; and WestJet and Bell also co-brand in delivering an in-flight experience to WestJet guests.

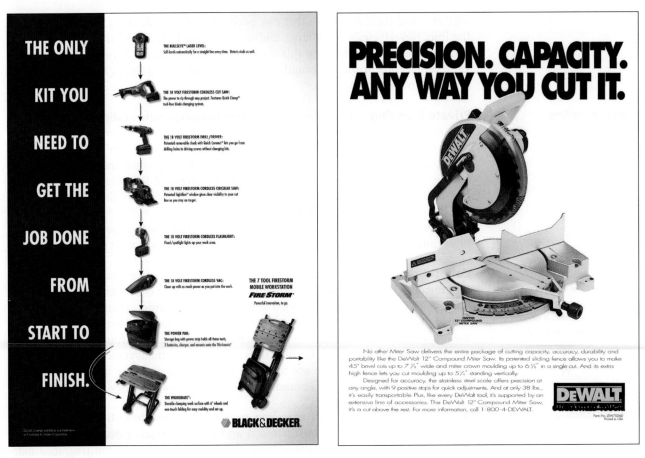

Black & Decker uses a multibranding strategy to reach different market segments. Black & Decker markets its line of tools for the do-it-yourselfer market with the Black & Decker name but uses the DeWalt name for its professional tool line.

Black & Decker
www.blackanddecker.com

multibranding
A manufacturer's branding strategy giving each product a distinct name.

Multibranding Alternatively, a company can engage in **multibranding,** which involves giving each product a distinct name. Multibranding is a useful strategy when each brand is intended for a different market segment. P&G makes Camay soap for those concerned about soft skin and Safeguard for those who want deodorant protection. Black & Decker markets its line of tools for the household do-it-yourselfer segment with the Black & Decker name but uses the DeWalt name for its professional tool line. Disney uses the Miramax and Touchstone Pictures names for films directed at adults and its Disney name for children's films.

Multibranding is applied in a variety of ways. Some companies array their brands on the basis of price–quality segments.[25] Marriott International offers 14 hotel and resort brands, each suited for a particular traveller experience and budget. To illustrate, Marriott Marquis hotels and Vacation Clubs offer luxury amenities at a premium price. Marriott and Renaissance hotels offer medium- to high-priced accommodations. Courtyard hotels and TownePlace Suites appeal to economy-minded travellers, whereas the Fairfield Inn is for those on a very low travel budget. Other multibrand companies introduce new product brands as defensive moves to counteract competition. Called *fighting brands,* their chief purpose is to confront competitor brands. For instance, Frito-Lay introduced Santitas-brand tortilla chip to go head-to-head against regional tortilla chip brands that were biting into the sales of its flagship Doritos- and Tostitos-brand tortilla chips. Mattel launched its Flava brand of hip-hop fashion dolls in response to the popularity of Bratz brand dolls sold by MGA Entertainment, which were attracting the 8- to 12-year-old girl segment of Barbie brand sales.

Compared with the multiproduct approach, promotional costs tend to be higher with multibranding. The company must generate awareness among consumers and retailers for each new brand name without the benefit of any previous impressions. The advantages of this approach are that each brand is unique to each market segment, and there is no risk that one product's failure will affect other products in the line. Nevertheless, some large multibrand firms have found that the complexity and expense of implementing this strategy can outweigh the benefits. For example, Unilever recently pruned its brands from some 1,600 to 400 through product deletion and sales to other companies.[26]

private branding
When a company manufactures products but sells them under the brand name of a wholesaler or retailer (often called *private labelling* or *reseller branding*).

Private Branding   A company uses **private branding,** often called *private labelling* or *reseller branding,* when it manufactures products but sells them under the brand name of a wholesaler or retailer. Radio Shack and Sears are large retailers that have their own brand names. Zellers also launched its Truly private brand hoping to foster the same customer loyalty as Loblaws' very successful President's Choice private brand. Other successful private brands in Canada include Sobeys' Smart Choice brand and Shoppers Drug Mart's Life brand.

Private branding is popular because it typically produces high profits for manufacturers and resellers. Consumers also buy these private brands with regularity.[27]

cohort brand management
The bundling of one company's multiple brands into a single marketing effort aimed at a common consumer group.

Cohort Brand Management   A recent innovation in brand management is the concept of **cohort brand management**—the bundling of one company's multiple brands into a single marketing effort aimed at a common consumer group. It is a collective approach to marketing in contrast to the traditional individualistic brand management approach. Cohort brand management is typically done through online marketing. For example, Proctor & Gamble uses cohort brand management via its Web site HomeMadeSimple.com. The site offers an online guide to home and lifestyle issues while promoting several P&G brands, including Mr. Clean, Swiffer, and Febreze.

mixed branding
A firm markets products under its own name and that of a reseller because the segment attracted by the reseller is different from its own market.

Mixed Branding   A fourth branding strategy is **mixed branding,** where a firm markets products under its own name(s) and that of a reseller because the segment attracted to the reseller is different from its own market. Beauty and fragrance marketer Elizabeth Arden is a case in point. The company sells its Elizabeth Arden brand through department stores and a line of skincare products at Walmart with the "skin-simple" brand name. Kodak uses a mixed branding approach in Japan to increase its sales of 35-mm film. In addition to selling its Kodak brand, the company now makes "COOP" private-label film for the Japanese Consumer Cooperative Union, which is a group of 2,500 stores. Priced significantly below its Kodak brand, the private label seeks to attract the price-sensitive Japanese consumer.[28]

(LO4) PACKAGING AND LABELLING

packaging
Any container in which a product is offered for sale and on which label information is communicated.

label
An integral part of the package that typically identifies the product or brand, who made it, where and when it was made, how it is to be used, and package contents and ingredients.

The **packaging** component of a product refers to any container in which it is offered for sale and on which label information is conveyed. A **label** is an integral part of the package and typically identifies the product or brand, who made it, where and when it was made, how it is to be used, and package contents and ingredients. To a great extent, the customer's first exposure to a product is the package and label, and both are an expensive and important part of marketing strategy. For Pez Candy, Inc., the character-head-on-a-stick plastic container that dispenses a miniature brick candy is the central element of its marketing strategy, as described in the accompanying Marketing Matters box, "Creating Customer Value through Packaging: Pez Heads Dispense More Than Candy."[29]

Creating Customer Value through Packaging and Labelling

Today's packaging and labelling cost Canadian companies billions of dollars, and an estimated 15 cents of every dollar spent by a consumer goes to packaging.[30] Despite the cost, packaging and labelling are essential because both provide important benefits

Marketing Matters

Creating Customer Value through Packaging: Pez Heads Dispense More Than Candy

Customer value can assume numerous forms. For Pez Candy, Inc. (**www.pez.com**), customer value manifests itself in some 450 Pez character candy dispensers. Each refillable dispenser ejects tasty candy tablets in a variety of flavours that delight preteens and teens alike in more than 60 countries.

Pez was formulated in 1927 by Austrian food mogul Edward Haas III and successfully sold in Europe as an adult breath mint. Pez, which comes from the German word for peppermint, *Pfefferminz,* was originally packaged in a hygienic, headless plastic dispenser. Pez first appeared in North America in 1953 with a headless dispenser marketed to adults. After conducting extensive marketing research, Pez was repositioned with fruit flavours, repackaged with licensed character heads on top of the dispenser, and remarketed as a children's product in the mid-1950s. Since then, most top-level licensed characters and hundreds of other characters have become Pez heads. Consumers eat more than three billion Pez tablets annually, and company sales growth exceeds that of the candy industry as a whole.

The unique Pez package dispenses a "use experience" for its customers beyond the candy itself—namely, fun. And fun translates into a 98-percent awareness level for Pez among teenagers and 89 percent among mothers with children. Pez has not advertised its product for years. With that kind of awareness, who needs advertising?

Which chip stacks up better? Frito-Lay's recent introduction of Lay's Stax potato crisps to compete against Procter & Gamble's Pringles illustrates the role of packaging in product and brand management.

Lay's Stax
www.fritolay.com

Pringles
www.pringles.com

for the manufacturer, retailer, and ultimate consumer. Packaging and labelling can also provide a competitive advantage.

Communication Benefits   A major benefit of packaging is the label information on it conveyed to the consumer, such as directions on how to use the product and the composition of the product, which is needed to satisfy legal requirements of product disclosure. This is particularly important in light of federal legislation requiring the listing of product ingredients on the product's package. Many packaged foods contain informative recipes to promote usage of the product. Campbell Soup estimates that the green bean casserole recipe on its cream of mushroom soup can accounts for $20 million in soup sales each year.[31] Other information consists of seals and symbols, either government-required or commercial seals of approval (such as the Good Housekeeping seal or the CSA seal).

Functional Benefits   Packaging often plays an important functional role, such as storage, convenience, protection, or product quality. Storing food containers is one example, and beverage companies have developed lighter and easier ways to stack products on shelves and in refrigerators. Examples include Coca-Cola beverage packs designed to fit neatly into refrigerator shelves and Ocean Spray Cranberries' rectangular juice bottles that allow ten units per package versus eight of its former round bottles.[32]

Can you name this soft drink brand?

The convenience dimension of packaging is becoming increasingly important. Kraft Miracle Whip salad dressing, Heinz ketchup, and Skippy Squeez'It peanut butter are sold in squeeze bottles; microwave popcorn has been a major market success; and Cloverleaf tuna and Folgers coffee are packaged in single-serving portions. Nabisco offers portion-control package sizes for the convenience of weight-conscious consumers. It offers 100-calorie packs of Oreos, Cheese Nips, and other products in individual pouches.

Consumer protection has become an important function of packaging, including the development of tamper-resistant containers. Today, companies commonly use safety seals or pop-tops that reveal previous opening. Nevertheless, no package is truly tamper resistant. There are now laws that provide for prison and fines for package tampering. Consumer protection through labelling also exists in "open dating," which states the expected shelf life of the product.

Functional features of packaging also can affect product quality. Procter & Gamble's Pringles, with its cylindrical packaging, offers uniform chips, minimal breakage, and, for some consumers, better value for the money than flex-bag packages for chips. Not to be outdone, Frito-Lay, the world's leading producer of snack chips decided to "stand up" to Pringles with its line of Lay's Stax potato crisps.[33] The consumers will be the final judge of which chip stacks up better.

Perceptual Benefits   A third component of packaging and labelling is the perception created in the consumer's mind. Package and label shape, colour, and graphics distinguish one brand from another, convey a brand's positioning, and build brand equity. In fact, packaging and labelling have been shown to enhance brand recognition and facilitate the formation of strong, favourable, and unique brand associations.[34] This logic applies to Celestial Seasonings' packaging and labelling, which uses delicate illustrations, soft and warm colours, and quotations about life to reinforce the brand's positioning as a New Age, natural herbal tea.

Successful marketers recognize that changes in packages and labels can update and uphold a brand's image in the customer's mind. Just Born Inc., a candy manufacturer of such brands as Jolly Joes and Mike and Ike Treats is a case in point. For many years,

The distinctive design of Celestial Seasonings tea boxes reinforces the brand's positioning as a New Age, natural herbal tea.

the brands were sold in old-fashioned black and white packages, but when the packaging was changed to four-colour, with animated grape and cherry characters, sales increased 25 percent. Coca-Cola brought back its famous and universally recognized contoured bottle shape to further differentiate itself from competitors.

Because labels list a product's source, brands competing in the global marketplace can benefit from "country of origin or manufacture" perceptions as described in Chapter 7. Consumers tend to have stereotypes about country–product pairings that they judge "best"—English tea, French perfume, Italian leather, and Japanese electronics—which can affect a brand's image. Increasingly, Chinese firms are adopting the English language and Roman alphabet for their brands' labels. This is being done because of the perception in many Asian countries that "things Western are good," even if consumers do not understand the meaning of the English words![35]

Contemporary Packaging and Labelling Challenges

Package and label designers face four challenges. They are (1) the continuing need to connect with customers; (2) environmental concerns; (3) health, safety, and security issues; and (4) cost reduction.

Connecting with Customers   Packages and labels must be continually updated to connect with customers. The challenge lies in creating aesthetic and functional design features that attract customer attention and deliver customer value in their use. If done right, the rewards can be huge.[36]

For example, the marketing team responsible for Kleenex tissues converted its standard rectangular box into an oval shape with colourful seasonal graphics. Sales soared with this aesthetic change in packaging. After months of in-home research, Kraft product managers discovered that consumers often transferred Chips Ahoy! cookies to jars for easy access and to avoid staleness. The company solved both problems by creating a patented resealable opening on the top of the bag. The result? Sales of the new package doubled that of the old package with the addition of this functional feature.

Environmental Concerns   Because of widespread worldwide concern about the growth of solid waste and the shortage of viable landfill sites, the amount, composition, and disposal of packaging material continues to receive much attention. Recycling packaging material is a major thrust.[37] Procter & Gamble now uses recycled cardboard in over 70 percent of its paper packaging and is packaging its detergents in jugs that contain 25 percent recycled plastic. Spic and Span liquid cleaner is packaged in 100 percent recycled material. Other firms, such as Walmart, are emphasizing the use of less packaging material. The company is working with its 600,000 global suppliers to reduce overall packaging and shipping material by 5 percent by 2013.

European countries have been trendsetters concerning packaging guidelines and environmental sensitivity. Many of these guidelines now exist in provisions governing trade to and within the European Union. In Germany, 80 percent of packaging material must be collected, and 80 percent of this amount must be recycled or reused to reduce solid waste in landfills. Canadian firms marketing in Europe have responded to these guidelines and ultimately benefited Canadian consumers.

Health, Safety, and Security Issues   A third challenge involves the growing health, safety, and security concerns of packaging materials. Today, most Canadian and European consumers believe companies should make sure products and their packages are safe and secure, regardless of the cost, and companies are responding in numerous ways. Most butane lighters sold today, like those made by Scripto, contain a child-resistant safety latch to prevent misuse and accidental fire. Child-proof caps on pharmaceutical products and household cleaners and sealed lids on food packages are now common. New packaging technology and materials that extend a product's *shelf life* (the time a product can be stored) and prevent spoilage continue to be developed with special applications for developing countries.

Cost Reduction   About 80 percent of packaging material used in the world consists of paper, plastics, and glass. As the cost of these materials rise, companies are constantly challenged to find innovative ways to cut packaging costs while delivering value to their customers. As an example, Hewlett-Packard reduced the size and weight of its Photosmart product package and shipping container. Through design and material changes, packaging material costs fell by more than 50 percent. Shipping costs per unit dropped 41 percent.[38]

PRODUCT WARRANTY

warranty
A statement indicating the liability of the manufacturer for product deficiencies.

A final component for product consideration is the **warranty,** which is a statement indicating the liability of the manufacturer for product deficiencies. There are various degrees of product warranties with different implications for manufacturers and customers.

Some companies offer *express warranties,* which are written statements of liabilities. In recent years, government has required greater disclosure on express warranties to indicate whether the warranty is a limited-coverage or full-coverage alternative. A *limited-coverage warranty* specifically states the bounds of coverage and, more importantly, areas of non-coverage, whereas a *full warranty* has no limits of non-coverage. Cadillac is a company that boldly touts its warranty coverage. Also, in an effort to improve its image with Canadian consumers, Hyundai offers what it claims to be the best automobile warranty in the industry.

With greater frequency, manufacturers are being held to *implied warranties,* which assign responsibility for product deficiencies to the manufacturer. Studies show that warranties are important and affect a consumer's product evaluation. Brands that have limited warranties tend to receive less positive evaluations compared with full-warranty items.[39]

Warranties are important in light of increasing product liability claims. In the early part of the twentieth century, the courts protected companies, but the trend now is toward "strict liability" rulings, where a manufacturer is liable for any product defect, whether it followed reasonable research standards or not. This issue is hotly contested by companies and consumer advocates.

Warranties represent much more to the buyer than just protection from negative consequences—they can hold a significant marketing advantage for the producer. Sears has built a strong reputation for its Craftsman tool line with a simple warranty: If you break a tool, it is replaced with no questions asked. Zippo has an equally simple guarantee: "If it ever fails, we'll fix it for free."

---

learning review

7. How does a generic brand differ from a private brand?

8. Explain the role of packaging in terms of perception.

9. What is the difference between an expressed warranty and an implied warranty?

LEARNING OBJECTIVES REVIEW

LO1 **Explain the product life cycle.**

The product life cycle describes the stages a new product goes through in the marketplace: introduction, growth, maturity, and decline. Product sales growth and profitability differ at each stage, and marketing managers have marketing objectives and marketing mix strategies unique to each stage based on consumer behaviour and competitive factors. In the introductory stage, the need is to establish primary demand, whereas the growth stage requires selective demand strategies. In the maturity stage, the need is to maintain market share; the decline stage necessitates a deletion or harvesting strategy. Some important aspects of product life cycles are (*a*) their length, (*b*) the shape of the sales curve, (*c*) how they vary by

product classes and forms, and (*d*) the rate at which consumers adopt products.

LO2 **Identify ways that marketing executives manage a product's life cycle.**

Marketing executives manage a product's life cycle in three ways. First, they can modify the product itself by altering its characteristics, such as product quality, performance, or appearance. Second, they can modify the market by finding new customers for the product, increasing a product's use among existing customers, or creating new use situations for the product. Finally, they can reposition the product using any one or a combination of marketing mix elements. Four factors trigger a repositioning action. They include reacting to a competitor's position, reaching a new market, catching a rising trend, and changing the value offered to consumers.

 Recognize the importance of branding and alternative branding strategies.

A basic decision in marketing products is branding, in which an organization uses a name, phrase, design, symbols, or a combination of these to identify its products and distinguish them from those of its competitors. Product managers recognize that brands offer more than product identification and a means to distinguish their products from competitors. Successful and established brands take on a brand personality and acquire brand equity—the added value a given brand name gives to a product beyond the functional benefits provided—that is crafted and nurtured by marketing programs that forge strong, favourable, and unique consumer associations with a brand. A good brand name should suggest the product benefits, be memorable, fit the company or product image, be free of legal restrictions, and be simple and emotive. Companies can and do employ several different branding strategies. With multiproduct branding, a company uses one name for all its products in a product class. A multibranding strategy involves giving each product a distinct name. A company uses private

branding when it manufactures products but sells them under the brand name of a wholesaler or retailer. A company can also employ mixed branding, where it markets products under its own name(s) and that of a reseller. Finally, a recent trend in brand management is cohort brand management, or the bundling of multiple brands into a single marketing effort aimed at a common consumer group.

 Describe the role of packaging, labelling, and warranties in the marketing of a product.

Packaging, labelling, and warranties play numerous roles in the marketing of a product. The packaging component of a product refers to any container in which it is offered for sale and on which label information is conveyed. Manufacturers, retailers, and consumers acknowledge that packaging and labelling provide communication, functional, and perceptual benefits. Contemporary packaging and labelling challenges include (*a*) the continuing need to connect with customers, (*b*) environmental concerns, (*c*) health, safety, and security issues, and (*d*) cost reduction. Warranties indicate the liability of the manufacturer for product deficiencies and are an important element of product and brand management.

FOCUSING ON KEY TERMS

brand equity   p. 291
brand licensing   p. 294
brand name   p. 290
brand personality   p. 291
branding   p. 290
co-branding   p. 296
cohort brand management   p. 298
downsizing   p. 290
label   p. 298
market modification   p. 287
mixed branding   p. 298
multibranding   p. 297
multiproduct branding   p. 295

packaging   p. 298
private branding   p. 298
product class   p. 285
product form   p. 285
product life cycle   p. 281
product modification   p. 287
product repositioning   p. 289
trade name   p. 291
trademark   p. 291
trading down   p. 289
trading up   p. 289
warranty   p. 302

APPLYING MARKETING KNOWLEDGE

1   Listed here are four different products in various stages of the product life cycle. What marketing strategies would you suggest to these companies? (*a*) Canon digital cameras—maturity stage, (*b*) Panasonic high-definition televisions—growth stage, (*c*) handheld manual can openers—decline stage, and (*d*) BMW hydrogen-fuelled cars—introduction stage.

2   It has often been suggested that products are intentionally made to break down or wear out. Is this strategy a planned product modification approach?

3   The product manager of GE is reviewing the penetration of trash compactors in Canadian homes. After more than two decades in existence, this product is in relatively few homes. What problems can account for this poor acceptance? What is the shape of the trash compactor life cycle?

4   For years, Ferrari has been known as the manufacturer of expensive luxury automobiles. The company plans to attract

the major segment of the car-buying market of those who purchase medium-priced automobiles. As Ferrari considers this trading-down strategy, what branding strategy would you recommend? What are the trade-offs to consider with your strategy?

5   The nature of product warranties has changed as the federal court system reassesses the meaning of warranties. How does the regulatory trend toward warranties affect product development?

6   Suppose that you were launching a new service venture, perhaps a marketing consulting company that would cater to small and medium-size Canadian companies. Determine your brand promise (what the brand will do for the customer), create a name, and describe how you communicate the brand and how you would deliver on your brand promise.

Building Your Marketing Plan

For the product offering in your marketing plan:

- Identify (a) its stage in the product life cycle and (b) key marketing mix actions that might be appropriate, as shown in Figure 11–1.

- Develop (a) branding and (b) packaging strategies, if appropriate for your offering.

Video Case 11

SLOW COW

Background

You are probably well aware of the energy-drink product category, which includes such players as Red Bull, Jolt, Monster, and Rockstar. But now there is an "anti-energy" or relaxation drink product category that is jockeying for retail shelf space and consumer patronage. Some experts suggest that the anti-energy drink may be a product whose time has come. While energy drinks have fuelled the hypertensive, party-never-stops mindset over the past few years, anti-energy drinks promise a "vacation in a bottle" or an "acupuncture session in every can." In short, makers of anti-energy drinks believe that some Canadians would rather chill out than tweak out. So these new anti-energy drinks are filled with ingredients such as chamomile, melatonin, valerian root, and/or L-Theanine—all known for their purported calming effects. One Canadian product designed to tap into this trend is Canada's Slow Cow. Slow Cow will be the focus of this case. But first, let's take a brief look at this new anti-energy market segment overall.

The Anti-Energy of the Relaxation Drink Market

According to beverage experts, anti-energy or relaxation drinks currently represent a small niche of the overall beverage market. The number of products sold can be counted in the mere millions of cans whereas the energy-drink market, globally, has an estimated value of $8 billion. And Red Bull, a major energy-drink marketer, is selling over 4 billion units alone. In short, the energy-drink market is considered to be 600 times larger than the anti-energy drink market. However, these same beverage experts suggest that the energy-drinks' high-growth days may be behind them while the anti-energy drink market is the new emerging growth segment. As a category, energy drinks have been around for more than a dozen years while the anti-energy drink category is in its infancy, roughly three years. At first it did not appear that consumers seemed to be thirsty for this new offering. However, sales have begun to take off recently. Jenny Foulds, a food and beverage consultant, suggests that the growth in sales is probably a result of "lifestyles becoming increasingly hectic and a realization that this can't be sustainable." Thus, consumers may be looking for an alternative such as anti-energy or relaxation drinks. She expects the anti-energy drink sales growth to be high over the next few years.

Other experts agree with her assertion. Peter Bianchi, CEO of Innovative Beverage Group Holdings, developed an anti-energy drink called "Drank." He observed people becoming more and more hurried and on the verge of burnout. He believed that some people simply wanted to "relax." His company already markets AriZona Iced Tea and Sweet Leaf Tea, but saw a 228 percent increase in sales in one quarter and attributes this to Drank's growing popularity.

Marketed as a way to "slow your roll"—slang for slow down your life—Drank contains melatonin (a natural hormone used to treat insomnia and jet lag), valerian root (an herb used to counter sleeplessness, anxiety, and depression), and rose hip (a source of vitamin C and antioxidants derived from rose plants). But now Drank has some new competitors in the category, including the Canadian brand Slow Cow.

Slow Cow

Canada's Slow Cow just recently hit store shelves. The name is an allusion to the far more aggressive bovines—two bulls locking horns—that grace Red Bull cans. In fact, to fend off a potential lawsuit from Red Bull, Slow Cow had to redesign its logo. The cans now feature a cow relaxing on the ground. The product is currently available in a variety of retailers, including 7-11, Metro, and Giant Tiger. The Slow Cow promise is "to soothe the mind and body."

According to the company, the product is designed to improve concentration, memory, and learning capacity without causing sleepiness. It contains no calories, no caffeine, no sugar, and no preservatives. But it does contain natural ingredients that are purported to deliver the benefits promised by the drink. These include the amino acid L-Theanine (found in tea), which is supposed to promote relaxation; improve the brain's capacity to concentrate, learn, and memorize; and increase cerebral levels of dopamine, the neurotransmitter responsible for pleasure. It also contains chamomile, which is reputed to treat insomnia, and passiflora, which reportedly induces relaxation. It also contains valerian, linden, and hops, which are supposed to reduce nervousness. According to the company, Slow Cow's effects kick in about 45 minutes after consumption.

However, these claims have not been objectively or scientifically verified. Thus, to succeed, experts argue that anti-energy or relaxation drinks like Slow Cow will have to work as advertised. In short, Slow Cow's ability to deliver on its promise will ultimately be determined by the consumer. Whether that's the case, of course, will be determined by the degree to which consumers embrace the beverage. So far consumers seem to be embracing the beverage, with sales of 1.2 million cans in just eight months. Still, while consumers appear to be open to trying the product, they will not likely continue to purchase it if the product does not meet their needs, whether it is taste or the functional benefit purportedly being offered.

Also, the medical community has expressed concern over the possible side effects of certain ingredients found in the drink. For example, valerian root has been known to cause mild headache or upset stomach in certain individuals. Other individuals can experience abnormal heartbeats and, interestingly enough, insomnia! So, some experts in the medical field are urging consumers to consult their physician before consuming products with such ingredients.

Another issue for Slow Cow could be the entrance of energy-drink companies into the anti-energy category. For example, Red Bull could decide to offer the consumer its energy drink to start the day and an anti-energy drink to help relax at the end of the day. Thus, energy and anti-energy drinks could prove not to be mutually exclusive, and a large well-known energy-drink brand like Red Bull could trump Slow Cow in its own space!

Questions

1 Where are energy and anti-energy drinks in terms of the product life cycle? What are the marketing implications that relate to that position in the life cycle?

2 If you are a marketing or brand manager for Slow Cow, what should be your focus in terms of growing the brand?

3 Who would be a key target market for Slow Cow?

4 What happens if an established energy-drink company decides to enter the anti-energy space? How does the marketing game change for a company like Slow Cow?

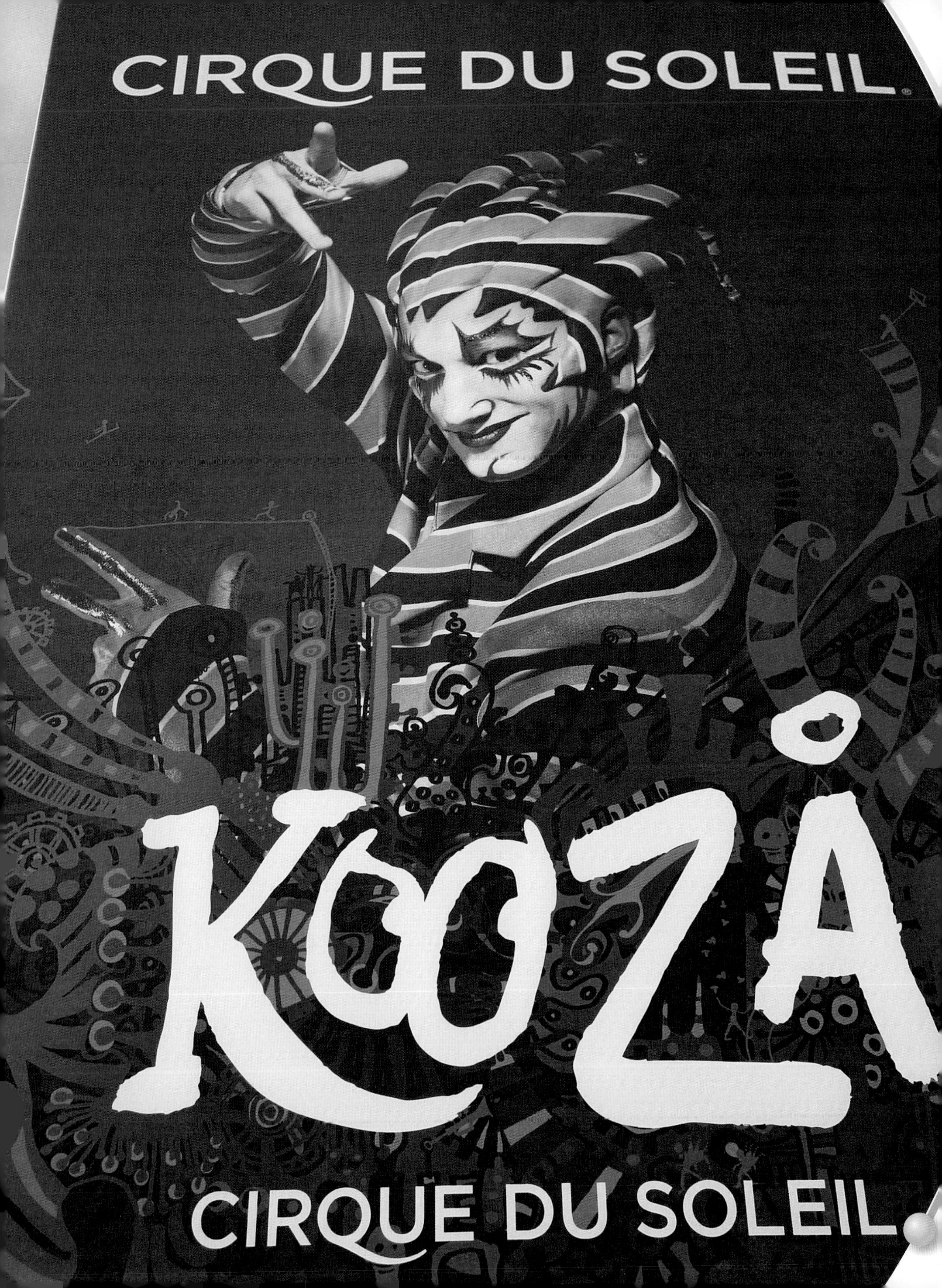
CIRQUE DU SOLEIL
KOOZÅ
CIRQUE DU SOLEIL

chapter 12

Managing Services

SERVICES GET REAL

Have you recently heard someone use the words fake or phony or even counterfeit? It's a common concern of many consumers today and part of a growing trend that will change most services. As authors James Gilmore and Joseph Pine explain, "The more contrived the world seems, the more we all demand what is real." In their book, *Authenticity,* they suggest that what consumers really want are engaging, personal, memorable, and authentic offerings. Canada's Cirque du Soleil, for example, offers a completely new art form, but manages the perception of authenticity by combining the original elements of street performance, the circus, and live theatre.[1]

As you know, a basic theme running throughout this text is the importance of *customer experience management (CEM).* This concept is particularly important for marketers of services. In fact, many services marketers have recognized the emergence of the "experience economy" and now focus on performing services that provide a unique experience. Disneyland, for example, was one of the first organizations to recognize the importance of sights, sounds, tastes, aromas, and textures in creating experiences for consumers. The Hard Rock Cafe uses a similar approach to sell dining experiences that include food, music, entertainment, and a fun environment. Many other companies such as Starbucks and Apple stores also have strategies designed to provide compelling experiences. The growth of produced, sometimes contrived experiences, however, has led consumers to search for sincere, or authentic, offerings.

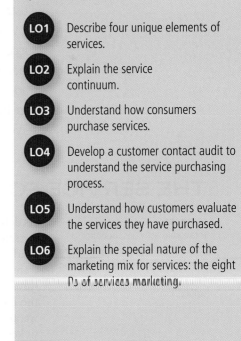

learning objectives

After reading this chapter, you should be able to:

LO1 Describe four unique elements of services.

LO2 Explain the service continuum.

LO3 Understand how consumers purchase services.

LO4 Develop a customer contact audit to understand the service purchasing process.

LO5 Understand how customers evaluate the services they have purchased.

LO6 Explain the special nature of the marketing mix for services: the eight Ps of services marketing.

Consumers are no longer content with affordable, high-quality purchases; they want offerings that reflect their self-image—who they are or who they aspire to be. How can service providers ensure that they are offering authentic experiences? There are many options.

First, services that facilitate customization increase authenticity. Creating custom playlists for iPods, for example, allows consumers to participate in the production process. Another option is to provide personal interaction rather than automation. Automated bank machines (ABMs), kiosks, credit card readers, and many Web sites are not viewed as authentic. Authenticity can also result from a social process that allows consumers to share their interests. YouTube, MySpace, and Facebook are obvious outlets, although companies can create their own social networking opportunities. Finally, institutions that provide services must manage any dimension of their reputation that might influence perceptions of authenticity.

If you look closely you'll see that many services are adding dimensions of authenticity. Nike's customization service, NIKEiD.com, allows customers to design shoes according to their exact preferences. Progressive Insurance provides personal attention by sending "Immediate Response Vehicles" to the site of an accident so that an adjuster can handle emergencies, arrange for new transportation, and provide the policyholder with a cheque—in person. Retailers now facilitate the social aspects of shopping by providing dressing rooms large enough for friends and electronic mirrors that allow texting anyone whose opinion might be needed.

As the actions of Cirque du Soleil, Disneyland, Hard Rock Cafe, and others illustrate, the marketing of services is dynamic and exciting. Importantly, services providers who can create and deliver authentic experiences can achieve much success. For example, Cirque du Soleil sells out over 97 percent of its available seats at every performance.[2] In this chapter, we discuss how services differ from traditional products (goods), how service consumers make purchase decisions, and the important aspects of developing and managing the marketing mix for services in order to create and deliver exceptional customer experiences.

THE SERVICE ECONOMY

services

Intangible activities, benefits, or satisfactions that an organization provides to consumers in exchange for money or something else of value.

As defined in Chapter 1, **services** are activities, deeds, or other basic intangibles offered for sale to consumers in exchange for money or something else of value. One services-marketing expert suggests that services permeate every aspect of our lives.[3] We use transportation services, such as Via Rail, Air Canada, and Thrifty car rental, when we travel. We use restaurant services, such as McDonald's, to feed us, and hotels, such as the Four Seasons, to put a roof over our heads when we are away from home. When we are at home, we rely on electricity providers, such as Ontario Power Generation, to keep the lights on, and telephone services from Bell Canada to keep in touch with family. We also use Sympatico to keep us connected to the Net and Molly Maid to keep our houses clean.

At work, we rely on Canada Post to deliver our mail, and Purolator courier to get our urgent documents to their destinations overnight. And we use ServiceMaster to keep our offices clean and Intercon Security services to keep them safe. Our employers use public relations firms, such as Edelman Public Relations, and advertising agencies, such as Cossette Communications, to maintain their corporate images, while we use the services of First Choice Haircutters to maintain our personal appearances. We use colleges and universities to improve our minds, and online employment services, such as Workopolis, to find us better jobs. We use financial institutions, such as Scotiabank, to safeguard our money, and we buy peace of mind with life insurance from Canada Life. We use lawyers to draw up our wills, and Questrade.com to trade our shares. In our leisure time, we pop in to Blockbuster Video to rent a DVD or stop by a Cineplex Odeon theatre to catch a flick. We might even visit one of the casinos run by the Great Canadian Gaming Corporation.

We might use an online travel service, such as Travelocity, to book our well-deserved vacation and stay and ski at Whistler Resort. While we are there, we might use the ING Direct card to pay for everything. Of course, we always need to stay in touch, and so the wireless telecommunications services provided by Rogers come in handy. Because Whistler Resort does not allow dogs, we have to use a boarding kennel or a personal pet-watching service to care for our border collie. When we get home, we realize the car needs an oil change, and so we drive to Mr. Lube to get it done. The washing machine also sounds a little funny, and so we call the Maytag repairman. After a long day, we just might watch some digital cable and order in a pizza. Because the television looks a little blurry, we decide that it is time to get rid of our eyeglasses and contact TLC Laser Eye Centres to see if they might help. And because we believe in future planning, we have already decided on a nursing home for our parents and even pre-purchased their funerals and burial plots. Services—from the cradle to the grave, we rely on them.

Services have become one of the most important components of the Canadian as well as the global economy. The services sector is now responsible for over 70 percent of Canada's total economic output as well as over 75 percent of its workforce. Moreover, the service sector generates nine of ten new jobs in Canada. At this rate, most experts predict that almost all Canadians will be working in services by 2025.[4] In other words, Canadians will simply be doing things (performing services) rather than making things (producing goods). And while Canada is still suffering a trade deficit in terms of service importation versus exportation, the country is experiencing greater growth in the export of services.

In terms of service job growth, much of it will be created by small and medium-sized businesses, both business-to-consumer (B2C) and business-to-business (B2B). And according to the Canadian Franchise Association, many of these businesses that will be franchise-based will offer personal, professional, and informational services.[5] Many of these services companies will also rely heavily on technology to create and deliver their services, including online travel services, people locator services, information technology services, and financial services.

 ## The Uniqueness of Services

As we noted in Chapter 10, when consumers buy products, they are purchasing a bundle of tangible and intangible attributes that deliver value and satisfaction. In general, it is very difficult to define a pure good or a pure service. A *pure good* implies that the consumer obtains benefits from the good alone without any added value from service, conversely, a *pure service* assumes there is no "goods" element to the service that the customer receives. In reality, most services contain some goods element. For example, at McDonald's you receive a hamburger; at the Royal Bank you are provided with a bank statement. And most goods offer some service—even if it is only delivery. In fact, many goods-producing firms are adding service offerings as a way to differentiate their products from those of their competitors.

four Is of services

Four unique elements to services: intangibility, inconsistency, inseparability, and inventory.

But there are certain commonalities between services as products that set them apart from tangible goods. The four unique elements to services are *intangibility, inconsistency, inseparability,* and *inventory.* These elements are sometimes referred to as the **four Is of services.**

Why do many services emphasize their tangible benefits? The answer appears in the text.

Fairmont Hotels & Resorts
www.fairmont.com

Intangibility Services are intangible; that is, they cannot be held, touched, or seen before the purchase decision. In contrast, before purchasing a traditional product, a consumer can touch a box of laundry detergent, kick the tire of an automobile, or sample a new breakfast cereal. A major marketing need for services is to make them tangible or to show the benefits of using a service. American Express emphasizes the gifts available to cardholders through its Membership Rewards program; a leading insurance company says, "You're in Good Hands with Allstate"; Fairmont Hotels tells business travellers that they will have the convenience of their offices away from their offices, including computer hookups and personal services.

Inconsistency Developing, pricing, promoting, and delivering services is challenging because the quality of a service is often inconsistent. Because services depend on the people who provide them, their quality varies with each person's capabilities and day-to-day job performance. Inconsistency is much more of a problem with services than it is with tangible goods. Tangible products can be good or bad in terms of quality, but with modern production lines, the quality will at least be consistent. On the other hand, the Toronto Maple Leafs hockey team may look like potential Stanley Cup winners on a particular day but lose by ten goals the next day. Or a cello player with the Vancouver Symphony may not be feeling well and give a less-than-average performance. Whether the service involves tax assistance at Ernst & Young or guest relations at the Sheraton, organizations attempt to reduce inconsistency through standardization and training. Standardization through automation is becoming increasingly popular in many service industries, including banking.

Inseparability A third difference between services and goods is inseparability. There are two dimensions to inseparability. The first is inseparability of production and consumption. Whereas goods are first produced, then sold, and then consumed, services are sold first, and then produced and consumed simultaneously. For example, you can buy a ticket at AirCanada.com, then fly and consume in-flight service as it is being produced. The second dimension of inseparability is that, in most cases, the consumer cannot (and does not) separate the deliverer of the service from the service itself. For example, to receive an education, a person may attend a college or university. The quality of the education may be high, but if the student has difficulty interacting

People play an important role in the delivery of many services.

Allstate
www.allstate.com

with instructors, finds counselling services poor, or does not receive adequate library or computer assistance, he or she may not be satisfied with the educational experience. In short, a student's evaluations of education will be influenced primarily by how the instructors, counsellors, librarians, and other people at the college or university responsible for delivering the education are perceived.

The amount of interaction between the consumer and the service deliverer or provider depends on the extent to which the consumer must be physically present to receive the service. Some services, such as golf lessons and medical diagnoses, require the customer to participate in the delivery process. Other services that process tangible objects, such as car repair or dry cleaning, require less involvement from the customer. Finally, many services, such as banking and insurance, can now be delivered electronically, often requiring no face-to-face customer interaction, as with, for example, Bank of Montreal's Web-based banking service.[6]

idle production capacity
When the service provider is available but there is no demand.

Inventory   Inventory of services is different from that of goods. Inventory problems exist with goods because many items are perishable and because there are costs associated with handling inventory. With services, inventory carrying costs are more subjective and are related to **idle production capacity,** which occurs when the service provider is available but there is no demand. The inventory cost of a service is the cost of paying the person used to provide the service along with any needed equipment. If a physician is paid to see patients but no one schedules an appointment, the fixed cost of the idle physician's salary is a high inventory-carrying cost. In some service businesses, however, the provider of the service is on commission (the Merrill Lynch stockbroker) or is a part-time employee (a counterperson at McDonald's). In these businesses, inventory-carrying costs can be significantly lower or nonexistent because the idle production capacity can be cut back by reducing hours or not having to pay salary because of the commission compensation system.

Figure 12–1 shows a scale of inventory-carrying costs, represented on the high end by airlines and hospitals and on the low end by real estate agencies. The inventory-carrying costs of airlines are high because of high-salaried pilots and very expensive equipment. In contrast, real estate agencies have employees who work on commission and need little expensive equipment to conduct business. One reason why service providers must maintain production capacity is because of the importance of time to today's customers. People do not want to wait long for service.

LOW COST   Cost of inventory   HIGH COST

| Real estate agency | Insurance company | Dry cleaner | Auto repair | Restaurant | Hotel | Amusement park | Airline |

● **FIGURE 12–1**

Inventory-carrying costs of services

(LO2) The Service Continuum

The four Is differentiate services from goods in most cases, but as we mentioned earlier, most products sold cannot be defined as pure goods or pure services. For example, does IBM Canada sell goods or services? While the company sells computers and software, a major component of its business is information technology services, including consulting and training. Does Rogers Communications provide only goods when it publishes *Marketing Magazine,* or does it consider itself a service because it presents up-to-date Canadian business information? As companies look at what they bring to the market, there is a range from the tangible to the intangible or good-dominant to service-dominant offerings referred to as the **service continuum** (Figure 12–2).

Teaching, nursing, and the theatre are intangible, service-dominant activities, and intangibility, inconsistency, inseparability, and inventory are major concerns in their marketing. Salt, neckties, and dog food are tangible goods, and the problems represented by the four Is are not relevant in their marketing. However, some businesses are a mix of intangible-service and tangible-good factors. A clothing tailor provides a service but also a good, the finished suit. How pleasant, courteous, and attentive the tailor is to the customer is an important component of the service, and how well the clothes fit is an important part of the product. As shown in Figure 12–2, a fast-food restaurant is about half tangible goods (the food) and half intangible services (courtesy, cleanliness, speed, convenience).

service continuum

A range from the tangible to the intangible or goods-dominant to service-dominant offerings available in the marketplace.

● **FIGURE 12–2**

Service continuum

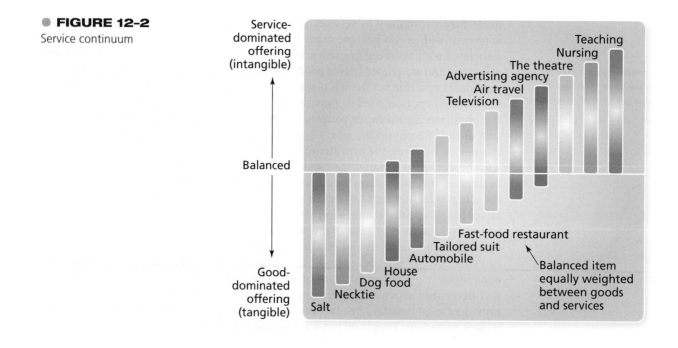

For many businesses today, it is useful to distinguish between their core service and their supplementary services. A core service offering—a bank account, for example— also has supplementary services, such as deposit assistance, parking or drive-through availability, ABMs, and monthly statements. Supplementary services often allow service providers to differentiate their offering from competitors, and they may add value for consumers. While there are many potential supplementary services, key categories of supplementary services include information delivery, consultation, order taking, billing procedures, and payment options.[7]

---

learning review

1. What are the four Is of services?

2. Would inventory-carrying costs for an accounting firm employing chartered accountants be (a) high, (b) low, or (c) nonexistent?

3. To eliminate inconsistencies, organizations rely on _____ and _____.

LO3 HOW CONSUMERS PURCHASE SERVICES

Universities, hospitals, hotels, and lawyers are facing an increasingly competitive environment. Successful service organizations, like successful goods-producing firms, must understand how the consumer makes a purchase decision and a post-purchase evaluation. Service companies will be better able to position themselves effectively if they understand why a consumer chooses to use a particular service. Moreover, by understanding the consumer's post-purchase evaluation process, service companies can identify sources of customer satisfaction or dissatisfaction.

Purchasing a Service

Because of their intangible nature, it is generally more difficult for consumers to evaluate services before purchase than it is to evaluate goods (Figure 12–3). Tangible goods, such as clothes, jewellery, and furniture, have *search* qualities, such as colour, size, and

● **FIGURE 12–3**

Services are more difficult to evaluate than goods before a purchase

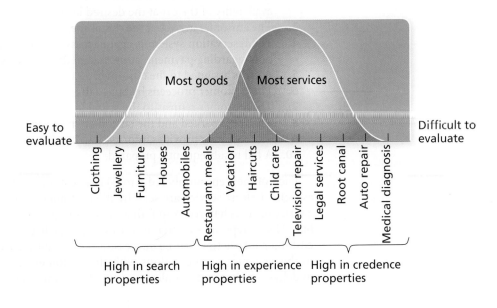

style, which can be determined before purchase. But rarely can a consumer inspect, try out, or test a service in advance. This is because some services, such as restaurants and child care, have *experience* qualities, which can be discerned only after purchase or consumption. Other services provided by specialized professionals, such as medical diagnosis and legal services, have *credence* qualities, or characteristics that the consumer may find impossible to evaluate even after purchase and consumption.[8]

The experience and credence qualities of services force consumers to make a prepurchase examination of the service by assessing the tangible characteristics that are part of, or surround, the service.[9] In other words, consumers will evaluate what they cannot see by what they can see. For example, you might consider the actual appearance of the dentist's office, or its physical location, when making a judgment about the possible quality of dental services that might be provided there. Many service organizations go to great lengths to ensure that the tangible aspects of the services convey the appropriate image and serve as surrogate indicators of the intangible service to be provided.

Services marketers recognize that because of the uncertainty created by experience and credence qualities, consumers turn to personal sources of information, such as early adopters, opinion leaders, and reference group members, during the purchase decision process. Accordingly, services marketers work to ensure customer satisfaction in order to ensure positive word-of-mouth referral.

(LO4) Customer Contact Audit

customer contact audit

A flow chart of the points of interaction between consumer and service provider.

To better understand the service purchasing process, service firms can develop a **customer contact audit**—a flow chart of the points of interaction between consumer and service provider.[10] These points of interaction are often referred to as *contact points, touchpoints,* or *service encounter elements.* Constructing a customer contact audit is particularly important in high-contact services, such as educational institutions, health care, and even automobile rental agencies. Figure 12–4 illustrates a customer contact audit for renting a car from Hertz. The interactions identified in a customer contact audit often serve as the basis for developing better services and delivering them more efficiently and effectively. In other words, it can help to ensure the customer has a positive experience with the service.

When a customer decides to rent a car, the following occurs:

1. He or she contacts the rental company by phone or goes online (see Figure 12–4).
2. A customer service representative receives the information and checks the availability of the car at the desired location.
3. The customer arrives at the rental site.
4. The reservation system is again accessed, and the customer provides information regarding payment, address, and driver's licence.
5. A car is assigned to the customer.
6. The customer proceeds by bus to the car pickup.
7. The customer returns to the rental location.
8. The car is parked and the customer checks in.
9. The customer provides information on mileage, gas consumption, and damages.
10. A bill is subsequently prepared.

Each of the steps numbered 1 to 10 is a customer contact point where the tangible aspects of Hertz service are seen by the customer. Figure 12–4, however, also shows a series of steps lettered A to E that involves two levels of inspections on the automobile. These steps are essential in providing a car that runs, but they are not points of customer interaction. To be successful, Hertz must create a competitive advantage in the sequence of interactions with the customer. In essence, Hertz must attempt to deliver the car in a seamless and timely manner, limiting the amount of time and

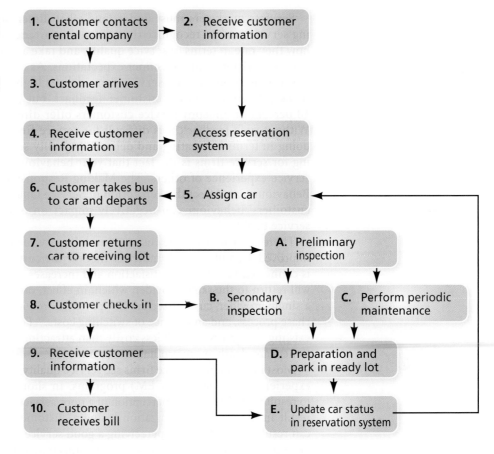

● **FIGURE 12–4**

Customer contact in car rental (green shaded boxes indicate customer activity)

SOURCE: Adapted from W. Earl Sasser, R. Paul Olsen, and D. Daryl Wyckoff, *Management of Service Operations: Text, Cases and Readings* (Boston: Allyn & Bacon, 1978).

effort required on the part of the customer. The customer contact audit is one tool that may help create that competitive advantage for Hertz or any other service firm.

 ## LO5 Post-Purchase Evaluation

Once a consumer tries a service, how is it evaluated? The primary method is by comparing expectations about the service offering with the actual experience a consumer has with the service.[11] Differences between a consumer's expectations and experience are often identified through **gap analysis.** This type of analysis asks consumers to assess their expectations and experiences on various dimensions of service quality. Expectations are influenced by word-of-mouth communications, personal needs, past experience, and marketing communications activities, while actual experiences are determined by the way an organization delivers the service.

One popular instrument developed by researchers to measure service quality and to conduct gap analysis is called SERVQUAL.[12] Researchers measure consumers' expectations and their actual service experience using a multi-item instrument. Consumers are asked to rate the importance of various dimensions of service quality and to score the service in terms of their expectations and actual experience. SERVQUAL provides the services marketer with a consumer rating of service quality and an indication of where improvements can be made.

Using SERVQUAL, these researchers have found that consumers judge service quality along five key dimensions: tangibles, reliability, responsiveness, assurance, and empathy (Figure 12–5). However, the relative importance of these various dimensions of service quality has been found to vary by type of service. For example, a recent Canadian study found that responsiveness and empathy were the most important dimensions of overall service quality in the Canadian banking context. But, for physician services, empathy and reliability were considered most important.[13]

gap analysis

An evaluation tool that compares expectations about a service offering to the actual experience a consumer has with the service.

Services marketers must understand what dimensions consumers use in judging service quality, recognize the relative importance of each dimension, find out how they rate in terms of service quality, and take actions to deliver service quality that is consistent with consumer expectations. As a consumer, you play an important role in ensuring that service firms deliver high service quality. Many service firms actively encourage customer feedback but research shows that only 5 to 10 percent of unhappy service customers offer direct feedback to service firms.[14] Without such feedback it is difficult for service firms to gauge how well they are doing in terms of creating and delivering quality service. What is even more vexing for service firms is the fact that your behaviour, as a customer, can affect the service experience of others. The Making Responsible Decisions box, "Customer Behaviour Can Affect the Perception of Service Quality," points out just how some customers' behaviour can negatively impact on other customers' perception of service quality.[15]

There are benefits to the customer and the service provider when service quality is improved. Recent research indicates that for the customer, improved service quality is connected to customer satisfaction and increases the likelihood that the customer will return to the same provider, which, in effect, offers the benefits of continuity of a single provider, customized service potential, reduced stress due to repetitive purchase process, and an absence of switching costs.[16] For the service provider, retaining existing customers is much less costly than attracting new customers, and repeat customers are clearly more profitable over time.

Most importantly, service firms see service quality as the cornerstone for customer experience management (CEM) programs. In short, poor service quality is likely to result in the customer's perception of a poor service experience, which, in turn, can result in the service organization losing a customer. But excellent service quality can result in the customer perceiving a good service experience and therefore would be more likely to return to the service organization again in the future.[17]

● **FIGURE 12-5**

Dimensions of service quality

SOURCE: Adapted with the permission of The Free Press, a Division of Simon & Schuster Adult Publishing Group, from *ON GREAT SERVICE; A Framework for Action* by Leonard L. Berry. Copyright © 1995 by Leonard L. Berry. All rights reserved.

DIMENSION	DEFINITION	EXAMPLES OF QUESTIONS AIRLINE CUSTOMERS MIGHT ASK
Tangibles	Appearance of physical facilities, equipment, personnel, and communications materials.	Are the plane, the gate, and the baggage area clean?
Reliability	Ability to perform the promised service dependably and accurately.	Is my flight on time?
Responsiveness	Willingness to help customers and provide prompt service.	Are the flight attendants willing to answer my questions?
Assurance	Respectful, considerate personnel who listen to customers and answer their questions.	Are the employees knowledgeable?
Empathy	Knowing the customer and understanding their needs. Approachable and available.	Do the employees know that I have special seating and meal requirements?

Making Responsible Decisions

Customer Behaviour Can Affect the Perception of Service Quality

Picture this. You are flying first-class from Halifax to Vancouver for a well-deserved vacation. You are impressed with the amenities offered by the airline, including the courtesy and friendliness of the personnel on-board. Just when you are starting to settle in and take a quick nap, right behind you in economy class is a man with very poor hygiene, who obviously has had too much to drink and who now begins to play a harmonica as loud and as poorly as possible. His behaviour is clearly disruptive and he is obviously disturbing the peace and quiet of other passengers in economy class, as well as those adjacent to him in first class, including yourself. But to your amazement, the flight attendants do not request that the drunken passenger cease his harmonica playing. He persists in his behaviour and you suffer the consequences. Your service experience with the airline has been compromised and you now rethink your perception of the airline, including its perceived quality. This is a true story.

Other customers and how they behave can contribute negatively to the functioning of service quality delivery processes and service quality outcomes. Customers who misbehave, who are uncooperative or abusive, or who simply break established social etiquette can pose serious problems for service organizations that wish to maintain service quality. You know from your own experience that the behaviour of other customers can affect your enjoyment of a service.

Customers who misbehave in a service environment are sometimes called "jaycustomers"—individuals who act thoughtlessly or abusively, causing problems for the firm, employees, and other customers. You know who they are: people who make or receive wireless phone calls during musical or theatre performances; people who cut in line in front of you as you are queuing to enter a sporting event; careless skiers who pose a risk to your health and safety; or belligerent drunks on airplanes. These people break rules designed to protect the comfort and enjoyment of all customers, including unwritten social norms like not jumping the queue.

What should a service firm do about such customer misbehaviour? What should you do about it?

---

learning review

4. What are the differences between search, experience, and credence qualities?

5. What is gap analysis?

6. An instrument or approach used to measure service quality is _____.

LO6 MANAGING THE MARKETING OF SERVICES: THE EIGHT Ps

eight Ps of services marketing
Product, price, place, and promotion, as well as people, physical evidence, process, and productivity that constitute the services-marketing mix.

Just as the unique aspects of services necessitate changes in the consumer's purchase process, the marketing management process requires special adaptation. As we have seen in earlier chapters, the traditional marketing mix is composed of the four Ps: product, price, place, and promotion. Careful management of the four Ps is important when marketing services. However, the distinctive nature of services requires that other additional variables be effectively managed by services marketers. The concept of an expanded marketing mix for services has been adopted by many services-marketing organizations. In addition to the traditional four Ps, the services-marketing mix includes people, physical evidence, process, and productivity, or the **eight Ps of services marketing.** Importantly, it has been found that the proper blending of these eight Ps is important in attracting customers and ensuring customer satisfaction.[18] Let us now discuss the special nature of the marketing mix for services.

Logos create service identities.

Product (Service)

To a large extent, the concepts of the product component of the marketing mix discussed in Chapters 10 and 11 apply equally to Cheerios (a good) and to Royal Bank Visa (a service). Managers of goods and services must design the product concept, whether a good or a service, with the features and benefits desired by customers. An important aspect of the product concept is branding. Because services are intangible and, therefore, more difficult to describe, the brand name or identifying logo of the service organization is particularly important when a consumer makes a purchase decision. Therefore, service organizations, such as banks, hotels, rental car companies, and restaurants, rely on branding strategies in order to distinguish themselves in the minds of the consumers. Strong brand names and symbols are important for services marketers, not only for differentiation purposes but also for conveying an image of quality. A service firm with a well-established brand reputation will also find it easier to market new services than firms without such brand reputation.[19]

Take a look at the images on this page to determine how successful some companies have been in branding their services by name, logo, or symbol.

Price

In service industries, price is often referred to in many ways. Hospitals refer to *charges;* consultants, lawyers, physicians, and accountants to *fees;* airlines to *fares;* hotels to *rates;* and colleges and universities to *tuition*. Because of the intangible nature of services, price is often perceived by consumers as a possible indicator of the quality of the service. For example, would you be willing to risk a $10 dental surgery? Or a $50 divorce lawyer? In many cases, there may be few other available cues for the customer to judge a service, and so price becomes very important as a quality indicator.[20]

Pricing of services also goes beyond the traditional tasks of setting the selling price. When customers buy services they consider non-monetary costs, such as the time as well as the mental and physical efforts required to consume the service. Therefore, services marketers must also try to minimize the non-monetary costs customers may bear in purchasing and using a service. Finally, as we will see later in this chapter, pricing also plays a role in balancing consumer demand for services.

Place (Distribution)

Place or distribution is a major factor in developing a services-marketing strategy because of the inseparability of services from the producer. Rarely are intermediaries involved in the distribution of a service; the distribution site and the service deliverer are the tangible components of the service. And, until recently, customers generally had to go to the service provider's physical location to purchase the service. Increased competition has forced many service firms to consider the value of convenient distribution and to find new ways of distributing services to demanding customers. Hairstyling chains such as First Choice Haircutters, legal firms, and accounting firms all use multiple locations for the distribution of services. Technology is also being used to deliver services beyond the provider's physical locations. For example, in the banking industry, customers of participating banks using the Interac system can access any one of thousands of ABMs across Canada and need not visit their own specific bank branch. The availability of electronic distribution of services over the Internet also allows for global reach and coverage for a variety of services, including travel services, banking, education, entertainment, and many other information-based services. With speed and convenience becoming increasingly important to customers when they select service providers, service firms can leverage the use of the Internet to deliver services on a 24/7 basis, in real time, on a global scale. In short, forward-looking firms no longer see face-to-face delivery of services as the only distribution option.[21]

Price influences perceptions of services.

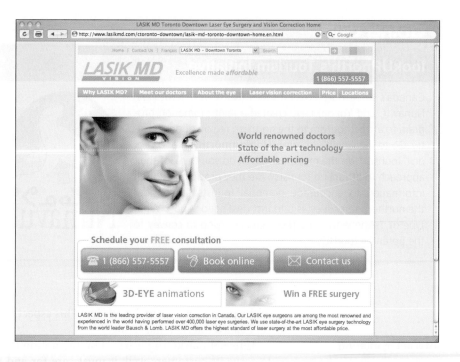

Promotion

The value of promotion, especially advertising, for many services is to show consumers the benefits of purchasing the service. For example, advertising can be an effective way to demonstrate such attributes as availability, location, consistent quality, efficient and courteous service, and assurance of satisfaction.[22] While many service firms are using the Internet as an alternative distribution channel, they are also using it as an advertising or promotional medium. Many colleges and universities, for example, have their own well-designed Web sites to convey their messages to prospective students. Many of these Web sites are highly interactive offering prospective students virtual tours and simulating the type of educational experience they should expect when they arrive on campus. Tourism marketers are also finding the Internet a valuable tool in reaching their prospective target markets; check out how Canada's northern territories are doing exactly that in the accompanying Going Online box, "lookUPnorth's Tourism Initiative."

Public relations is an important promotional tool for service firms. It is particularly useful in conveying a proper image and in helping to support a firm's positioning strategy. Public relations tools, such as event sponsorship or public-service activities, are very popular among service companies. This is particularly true for professional service firms, which are often restricted in the use of advertising by their professional governing bodies.

Personal selling also plays an important role in services marketing. It has been said that when a consumer buys a service, he or she is buying the person selling the service. Personal selling is valuable not only in attracting customers but also in retaining them. Increasingly, many services marketers are following the path set by packaged-goods firms; that is, they are developing integrated marketing communications plans.[23]

People

Many services heavily depend on people for the creation and delivery of the customer service experience.[24] The nature of the interaction between employees and customers strongly influences the customer's perceptions of a service experience. In short, customers will often judge the quality of the service experience based on the performances

of the people providing the service. This aspect of services marketing has led to a concept called internal marketing.[25]

internal marketing
The notion that in order for a service organization to serve its customers well, it must care for and treat its employees like valued customers.

    Internal marketing is based on the notion that in order for a service organization to serve its customers well, it must care for and treat its employees like valued customers. In essence, it must focus on its employees (or its internal market) before successful marketing efforts can be directed at customers.[26] Internal marketing involves creating an organizational climate in general, and jobs in particular, that will lead to the right service personnel performing the service in the right way. The organization must properly select, train, and motivate all of its employees to work together to provide service quality, excellent customer experiences, and customer satisfaction. Research has shown that service organizations that want to be truly customer oriented must be employee oriented.[27] Finally, customer behaviour influences not only their own service outcomes but also other customers. Whether at a hockey game or in a classroom, customers can influence the perceived quality of service by their actions. Therefore, the *people* element in services includes not only the employees and the customer but also other customers.

Physical Evidence

The appearance of the environment in which the service is delivered and where the firm and customer interact can influence the customer's perception of the service. The physical evidence of the service includes all the tangibles surrounding the service: the buildings, landscaping, vehicles, furnishings, signage, brochures, and equipment. Service firms need to manage physical evidence carefully and systematically in order to convey the proper impression of the service to the customer. This is sometimes referred to as *impression management,* or evidence management.[28] With highly tangible services, physical evidence provides an opportunity for the firm to send consistent and strong messages about the nature of the service to be delivered.

Process

In services marketing, *process* refers to the actual procedures, mechanisms, and flow of activities by which the service is created and delivered. The actual creation and delivery steps that the customer experiences provide customers with evidence on which to judge the service. In services marketing, process involves not only "what" gets created but also "how" it gets created. The customer contact audit discussed earlier in the chapter is relevant to understanding the service process discussed here. The customer contact audit—the flow chart of the points of interaction between customer and service provider—can serve as a basis for ensuring better service creation and delivery processes. Badly designed processes are likely to create unhappy customers, and poorly conceived operational processes can make it difficult for front-line employees to do their jobs well. Mr. Lube believes that it has the right process in the vehicle oil change and fluid exchange service business. Customers do not need appointments, most stores are open seven days a week, and customers are in and out in 15 to 20 minutes. While the service is being performed, customers can drink a coffee and read the newspaper.

Productivity

Most services have a limited capacity due to the inseparability of the service from the service provider and the perishable nature of the service. For example, a patient must be in the hospital at the same time as the surgeon to receive an appendectomy, and only one patient can be helped at that time. Similarly, no additional surgery can be conducted tomorrow because of an unused operating room or an available surgeon today—the service capacity is lost if it is not used. So if services marketers have a relatively fixed capacity to produce a service, they must make that capacity as productive as possible without compromising service quality.[29] This is referred to as **capacity management.** The accompanying Using Marketing Dashboards box demonstrates how an airline can use a capacity management measure called *load factor* to assess its productivity and profitability.

Service organizations must manage the availability of the offering so that (1) demand matches capacity over the duration of the demand cycle (e.g., one day, week, month, year), and (2) the organization's assets are used in ways that will maximize the return on investment.[30] Figure 12–6 shows how a hotel tries to manage its capacity during the high and low seasons. Differing price structures are assigned to each segment of consumers to help moderate or adjust demand for the service. Airline contracts fill a fixed number of rooms throughout the year. In the slow season, when more rooms are available, tour packages at appealing prices are used to attract groups or conventions, such as an offer for seven nights at a reduced price. Weekend packages are also offered to buyers. In high-demand season, groups are less desirable because more individual guests will be available and willing to pay higher prices. The use of **off-peak pricing,** which consists of charging different prices during different

capacity management

Making service capacity as productive as possible without compromising service quality.

off-peak pricing

Charging different prices during different times of the day or days of the week to reflect variations in demand for the service.

● **FIGURE 12–6**

Managing capacity in a hotel

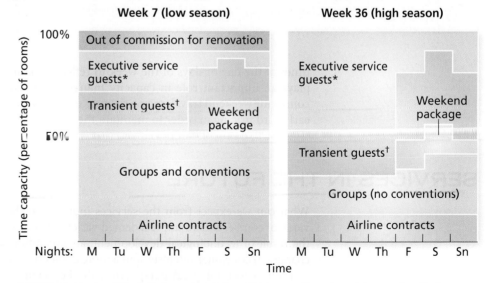

* Employees of corporations called upon by salesforce (book rooms through special reservations line).
† Customers reserving rooms via public telephone number or by just "walking in."

Using Marketing Dashboards

Are Airline Flights Profitably Loaded?

Capacity management is critical in the marketing of many services. For example, having the right number of airline seats or hotel rooms available at the right time, price, and place can spell the difference between a profitable or unprofitable service operation.

Airlines often focus on *load factor* as a capacity management measure on their marketing dashboards, along with two other measures: the operating cost per available seat flown one mile, and the revenue generated by each seat flown one mile, called *yield*. Load factor is the percentage of available seats flown one mile occupied by a paying customer.

These three measures combine to show airline operating income or loss per available seat flown one mile.

Operating income (loss) per available seat flown one mile
= (Yield × Load Factor) − Operating expenses

Your Challenge   As a marketing analyst for a regional Canadian airline, you have been asked to determine the operating income or loss per available seat flown one mile in the first six months of 2010. In addition, you have been asked to determine what load factor the airline must reach to break even, assuming its current yield and operating expense will not change in the immediate future.

Your Findings   The airline's yield, load factor, and operating expense marketing dashboard displays are shown below. You can conclude from these measures that the airline posted about a 0.21 cent loss per available seat flown one mile in the first six months in 2010.

Operating loss per available seat flown one mile
= (9.83 cents × 82.1%) − 8.28 cents = −0.2096 cents

Assuming the airline's yield and operating expenses will not change and using a little math, the airline's load factor will have to increase from 82.1% to 84.23% to break even.

Operating income (loss) per available seat flown one mile
= (9.83 cents × Load factor) = 8.28 cents = 0 cents
(Load factor = 84.23%)

Your Action   Assuming yield and operating expenses will not change, you should recommend that the airline consider revising its flight schedules to better accommodate traveller needs and advertise these changes. Consideration might also be given to how the airline utilizes its existing airline fleet to serve its customers and produce a profit.

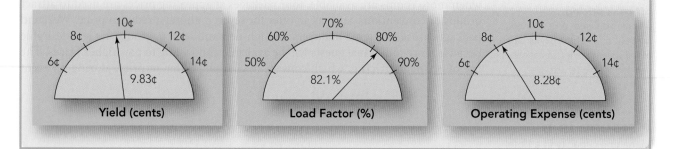

times of the day or days of the week to reflect variations in demand for the service, plays an important role in capacity management. For example, airlines offer discounts for weekend travel, movie theatres offer matinee pricing, and restaurants offer early-bird pricing in order to maintain the productivity of their service capacity.

SERVICES IN THE FUTURE

What can we expect from the services industry in the future? New and better services, of course, and an unprecedented variety of choices. Many of the changes will be the result of technological development, an expanding scope in the global economy, changes in consumer interests, and a more competitive landscape.

From a technological perspective, the key elements of future services include mobility, convergence, personalization, and collaboration. Mobility will be provided by new generations of networks that will allow TV, GPS, high-speed data transfer, and audio programming on portable digital devices. Products such as the Apple iPhone and iPad are indications of the convergence of voice, video, and data in a single device. Personalization of services such as Amazon.ca where past transactions are analyzed to customize information seen by customers are emerging. Collaboration services that allow Web-conferencing, dating, and matchmaking, and even remote involvement of friends when someone is shopping are appearing. Other new e-services based on technology will be innovative security and identification services, such as retinal scanning.[31]

The expanding global economy is also changing the services industries landscape. Services have become the dominant part of the Canadian economy, and now global marketing of services has also increased at a dramatic rate. Technology is assisting this growth, and consumers around the globe can consume services 24/7, in real time. In fact, many services experts predict that global economic exchange has shifted and will continue to shift away from tangible goods to intangible services, especially experiential services.[32]

Other changes in services will be driven by changes in consumer interests. Experts suggest that "time will be the currency of the future." Consumers are searching for new services that reduce the time needed to go to the post office, bank, or supermarket or to prepare food, clean clothes, or maintain their homes. Consumers are placing increased demand on service companies, expecting greater choice, convenience, information, responsiveness, and access to service. Technology will also play a key role in satisfying those demands. Many banking customers, for example, prefer to visit their banks as little as possible, and many are now doing more business by phone or over the Internet. Virtual banks, such as ING Direct, are available to Canadian banking customers, who now have the choice of doing everything electronically or dealing with a real person at a traditional bricks-and-mortar bank.

Finally, both today and the future belong to service firms that can successfully create and deliver unique, personable, and memorable customer experiences. As a result of increased competition, many services have become commoditized or are seen by most consumers to be virtually identical. In that case, price often becomes the driver when making a service selection. But many consumers want something more than just a commoditized service and are prepared to pay for it. If a service firm can customize a service, it turns it into a genuine experience. For example, Pizza Hut can offer a customer more than a meal; it will host your child's birthday party and customize it the way you want it.[33] Read the accompanying Marketing Matters box, "Seven Steps

The Ritz-Carlton does not just market accommodations; it creates and markets experiences.

YJM Photography

Marketing Matters

Seven Steps to Creating Great Service Experiences!

According to Ian Stuart, designing services that deliver memorable personal experiences is a science and an art. Using a theatre analogy, Stuart provides seven critical steps required for services managers to make the leap from merely satisfying the customer to delivering great service experiences.

1. Stay narrowly focused and within your defined resource capabilities. This focus will ensure consistency of performance.
2. Communicate and share the service vision extensively, particularly with those with management responsibilities. This is vital for buy-in at all levels of the organization.
3. Be ever vigilant to ensure consistency and authenticity in all aspects of the service product, from the largest to smallest detail.
4. Integrate across all elements (including technical, performance, and business), using structured and unstructured communication mechanisms. Importantly, there should be an emphasis on supporting front-line service providers.
5. Create a spirit of experimentation and innovation for all service employees by encouraging everyone's involvement in the creative process. Constantly innovating to find better ways to excite the customer is key.
6. Strive for total role and performance immersion from all front-line service providers through extensive training and rehearsals.
7. Facilitate, do not direct. Integrate and lead, do not command and control.

Stuart suggests that if services marketers follow these seven steps, customers will be delighted with the service experience and remain loyal to the service organization.

to Creating Great Service Experiences!" to see just how services marketers can create real and distinctive customer experiences that differentiate themselves from commoditized services providers.[34] For instance, the Ritz-Carlton follows these guidelines, taking your vision of your ultimate wedding and make it a reality—creating what they promise to be an "unforgettable experience." Successful service firms like the Ritz-Carlton embrace comprehensive point-to-point customer experience management approaches. To do so they place special emphasis on high-quality employee interaction with customers. Therefore, hiring, training, and motivating service-minded employees must be part of the service firm's overall customer experience management program.[35]

---

learning review

7. Matching demand with capacity is the focus of _____ management.

8. What factors will influence the services industries in the future?

LEARNING OBJECTIVES REVIEW

 Describe four unique elements of services.

The four unique elements of services—the four Is—are intangibility, inconsistency, inseparability, and inventory. Intangibility refers to the tendency of services to be a performance that cannot be held or touched. Inconsistency is a characteristic of services because they depend on people to deliver them, and people vary in their capabilities and in their day-to-day performance. Inseparability refers to the difficulty of separating the deliverer of the service (hair stylist) from the service itself

(haircut). And services are produced and consumed simultaneously, requiring the consumer to be present for both the production and consumption processes. Inventory refers to the need to have service production capability when there is service demand.

LO2 **Explain the service continuum.**

Many organizations do not market pure services or pure goods. In general, companies market products that have tangible and intangible characteristics. As companies look at what they bring to market, there is a range from the tangible to the intangible or good-dominant to service-dominant offerings, referred to as a service continuum.

 Understand how consumers purchase services.

Because services are intangible, pre-purchase evaluation is difficult for consumers. To choose a service, consumers use search, experience, and credence qualities to evaluate the good and service elements of a service offering. Because of the uncertainty created by experience and credence qualities, consumers often turn to personal sources of information, such as early adopters, opinion leaders, and reference group members, during the purchase decision process.

 Develop a customer contact audit to understand the service purchasing process.

A customer contact audit is a flow chart of the points of interaction between a consumer and a service provider. The interactions identified in the contact audit can help better understand the purchasing purchase and help create and deliver better services that ensure a satisfying experience for the customer.

LO5 **Understand how customers evaluate the services they have purchased.**

Once the consumer tries a service, it is evaluated by comparing expectations with the actual service experience on five

dimensions of service quality: reliability, tangibles, responsiveness, assurance, and empathy. Differences between expectations and experience are identified through gap analysis.

 Explain the special nature of the marketing mix for services: the eight Ps of services marketing.

In addition to the traditional marketing mix (the four Ps) mentioned frequently throughout this text, the distinctive nature of services require that other variables be effectively managed by services marketers. These include people, physical evidence, process, and productivity. Collectively, the marketing mix for services is referred to as the eight Ps. Many services depend on people to create and deliver services, and thus people must be hired, trained, and motivated correctly. The physical environment (physical evidence) where the services are created must be managed to convey the proper impression to the customer. The process by which services are created and delivered must also be managed effectively in order for customers to receive the service in a timely and appropriate manner. And finally, because of the perishable nature of services, capacity management—managing productivity—of the services system is important.

FOCUSING ON KEY TERMS

APPLYING MARKETING KNOWLEDGE

1 Explain how the four Is of services would apply to a branch office of the Royal Bank.

2 Idle production capacity may be related to inventory or capacity management. How would the pricing component of the marketing mix reduce idle production capacity for (*a*) a car wash, (*b*) stage theatre group, and (*c*) a university?

3 Look back at the service continuum in Figure 12–2. Explain how the following points on the continuum differ in terms of consistency: (*a*) salt, (*b*) automobile, (*c*) advertising agency, and (*d*) teaching.

4 What are the search, experience, and credence properties of an airline for the business traveller and pleasure traveller? What properties are most important to each group?

5 Outline the customer contact audit for a typical check-in experience at a local hotel.

6 The text suggests that internal marketing is necessary before a successful marketing program can be directed at consumers. Why is this particularly true for service organizations?

7 Outline the capacity management strategies that an airline must consider.

8 How does off-peak pricing influence demand for services?

9 Physical evidence of one of the eight Ps of services marketing. How would a physician go about managing the physical evidence of her practice to convey the proper image to her patients?

10 This chapter suggests that consumers judge service quality along five key dimensions: tangibles, reliability, responsiveness, assurance, and empathy. Which dimension is most important to you when you judge the following services: (*a*) a physician, (*b*) a bank, (*c*) car rental, and (*d*) dry cleaning?

Building Your Marketing Plan

In this section of your marketing plan you should distinguish between your core product—a good or a service—and supplementary services.

1. Develop an internal marketing program that will ensure that employees are prepared to deliver the core and supplementary services.

2. Conduct a customer contact audit and create a flow chart to identify specific points of interaction with customers.

3. Describe marketing activities that will (a) address each of the eight Ps as they relate to your service and (b) encourage the development of relationships with your customers.

Add this as an appendix to your marketing plan and use the results in developing your marketing mix strategy.

Video Case 12

THE CANADIAN FOOTBALL LEAGUE

Introduction

The Canadian Football League (CFL) is the oldest professional football league in North America. Its history can be traced back to 1892. The league, as it exists today, broke loose from the amateur Canadian Rugby Union in 1958. But Canadian football is different from American football. The most notable differences are that the CFL has 12 players on the field per team, not 11; there are three downs instead of four; and the Canadian field is much larger than the American field. Unlike its American counterpart, the Canadian version of football offers a more wide open, and often unpredictable, style of play.

Currently, the league consists of eight teams in two divisions. In the Eastern Division, the teams are from Montreal, Hamilton, Toronto, and Winnipeg. In the Western Division, the teams are from Saskatchewan, Calgary, Edmonton, and British Columbia. There is a playoff format and the winner in each division meet in the league championship game called the Grey Cup.

But in the mid-2000s, the league believed it had reached a critical point in its history. Research revealed that the CFL was a mature brand that was either underdeveloped or negatively developed and that the league faced critical obstacles to growth. It decided that a new consumer-validated brand would be required to resuscitate and renew the organization.

The CFL Brand Situation

The league's research revealed the following facts about the CFL brand. The CFL brand was not viewed as a cornerstone asset for the league. The league was, in fact, a collection of disparate team brands. The CFL was perceived as a tier-two sports league with unrecognizable players, a weak stadium experience in some markets, and an absence of a visible youth franchise. In fact, the aging fan base could be problematic with regard to sustaining the league in the future. The league symbols (trademark, logos) were also perceived as dated and inconsistent with a professional sport, and the league was failing to consistently deliver brand value to the fan. In essence, the research revealed that the CFL was lacking in terms of perceived "big league" attributes that were important to many prospective fans. Additionally, major market weaknesses in Vancouver, Hamilton, and Toronto were negatively impacting on the brand. In particular, weakness in the Toronto market, North America's fifth-largest media market, was casting a shadow on the CFL.

On the other hand, despite being a mature brand, the CFL was found to have some strong and exploitable core brand equities. These included a strong Canadian heritage, an exciting game, approachable and relatable players, and an affordable entertainment experience. Also, the Grey Cup championship game was a positive ritual associated with the brand.

Perceptual mapping research indicated that the CFL was perceived more as a "game" that operated at a more "localized level" compared to some of its competitors that were perceived as more "national/international sports" that offered more of a "show" (entertainment) when compared to the CFL (Figure 1). For the CFL this perceptual mapping research would have to be considered. Did it wish to reposition itself as a league that offered more of a national sport? And did it wish to migrate to a brand space where it would be perceived as more of a "show" than a "game"? It seemed, based on the research, that a stronger national CFL brand would be necessary in

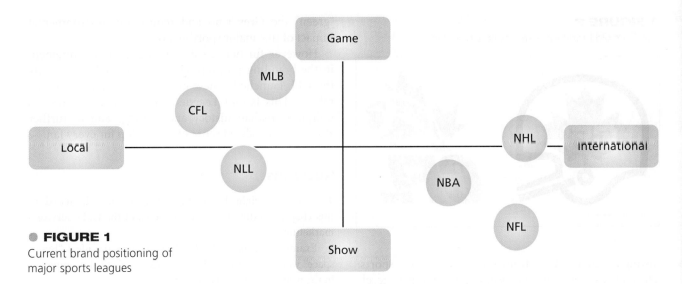

● **FIGURE 1**
Current brand positioning of
major sports leagues

order to strengthen and grow its business in the competitive professional sports market. Moreover, it seemed that striking a balance between "show" and "game" would also be important.

In the end, the CFL believed it reached several basic conclusions from the research. These were as follows:

1. The CFL needed to create a single and unified brand.
2. The CFL needed a compelling brand platform to distinguish its brand from other professional sports.
3. The CFL needed to develop a common brand identity that could be shared across all stakeholders and implement it consistently at all points of consumer contact.
4. The CFL needed to provide brand value, perceived quality, consistency, credibility, and stability to its stakeholders.
5. Team brands must extend the league brand, distinctively but consistently.
6. The CFL must control its brand and its brand message and not allow others to control them.
7. The CFL must address the challenges in underdeveloped markets if the new branding strategy was to be effective.
8. The CFL must proactively build brand trial and loyalty via broadcast, stadium experience, marketing/media relations and trademarking.

The CFL Brand Narrative

The CFL tested a number of brand narratives (brand positionings) that might appeal to new and current fans. After quantitative testing of various possible options, one particular brand positioning seemed to resonate with the consumer: *"The CFL is a hard-hitting celebration of Canadian sport. The game experience exhilarates me and connects me to people who share my passion."* The league

and its clubs would now have to deliver on this positioning and bring it to life. This would require managing very closely the point-of-contact experiences in broadcast, the stadium, marketing and media relations, and trademarks. In essence, the CFL would have to become a brand-centric organization and implement its re-branding effort carefully, consistently, and in a compelling way.

Results of the Re-Branding Efforts

The CFL with its new branding strategy, including its new logo/trademark (Figure 2) saw increases in fan attendance to stadiums across the country. In fact, attendance at games increased to an average of 29,000 fans per game. The league also saw an increase in commitment from its broadcast partners in terms of the number of games provided to CFL football fans. At the same time, there has also been an increase in television audience numbers. The number of fans engaging online through CFL.ca increased, and the league expanded its digital footprint by leveraging Facebook, Twitter, and YouTube, as well as providing a CFL mobile app for BlackBerry users. This was particularly important for the CFL as it wanted to build a younger fan base, particularly kids who would be the fans of the future. Moreover, sponsorships and co-branding partnerships also grew, including firms such as Scotiabank, Rona, Nissan, and Holiday Inn, to name a few.

However, while the re-branding results were impressive, further research revealed that the CFL could benefit from a sharpening in the brand positioning. Consequently, the CFL fine-tuned the brand positioning to be: "The CFL delivers a football experience that puts you right at the centre so that you feel part of the game and everything around it because it is accessible, affordable, and authentic." This positioning, the CFL believed, punctuated the most strategic aspects of the game that

● **FIGURE 2**

The CFL's old brand logo and its new brand logo

distinguished the CFL from other competitive sports. The CFL also felt that this positioning would help accelerate the growth of the brand while creating a truly ownable brand asset.

Finally, to build and deliver the new brand, the league also engaged in grassroots community development work, particularly in franchise cities where the league and local teams are involved in social causes. The CFL also started the "CFL Green Drive," a commitment to "green" the Grey Cup and reduce the environmental impact of this major sporting event.

However, further research indicated more refinement in the branding positioning was warranted, so recently the CFL launched a new branding campaign and narrative. "This Is Our League" was intended to stress its unique Canadian history and heritage and to further stress a personalized sense of ownership for every fan.

Questions

1 Using the eight Ps of services marketing discussed in this chapter, outline the basic elements of the CFL's services-marketing mix.

2 Examine Figure 1. Where do you think the ideal "brand space" would be for the CFL in terms of effectively competing in the professional sports market?

3 What advice would you provide the CFL with regard to strengthening its brand with potential fans? Will the new narrative, "This Is Our League," be effective here?

4 Revisit the Marketing Matters box, "Seven Steps to Creating Great Service Experiences," on page 324 of this chapter. What specific actions could the CFL take to ensure its customers (fans) would be delighted with its offerings?

13

Pricing Products and Services

HERE'S A PRICING PROBLEM FOR YOU!

Imagine you are part of the management team for Strait Crossing Bridge Ltd. (SCBL), a subsidiary company of Strait Crossing Development Inc. You know—the company that built the Confederation Bridge (**www.confederationbridge .com**), the bridge that joins Borden-Carleton, Prince Edward Island, and Cape Jourimain, New Brunswick? Yes, that one. It is 12.9 kilometres long and is the longest bridge over ice-covered waters in the world. And it cost you $1 billion to build it. Now you must determine what price to charge users who might want to cross it.

Well, you have many things to ponder. First, you must consider what it is that you are offering customers. You have a pretty good handle on that. Your bridge carries two lanes of traffic 24 hours a day, seven days a week, and it takes approximately 10 minutes to cross at normal travelling speed, which is 80 km/hr. So, compared with ferry service, which often involved a wait and a much longer travel time to cross, you believe consumers will want to use the bridge. But how many customers and how often are two key questions. In this case, things are not so clear. You do know, however, that consumer demand for your product clearly affects the price that can be charged.

So you hire a consulting firm that does some demand estimates for you. The problem is, you must consider the type of user for the bridge or, more specifically, the type of vehicle being driven across the bridge. Why? Because traffic volume is made up of a variety of different

learning objectives

After reading this chapter, you should be able to:

 LO1 Understand the nature and importance of pricing products and services.

LO2 Recognize the constraints on a firm's pricing latitude and the objectives a firm has in setting prices.

LO3 Explain what a demand curve is and what price elasticity of demand means.

LO4 Perform a break-even analysis.

LO5 Understand approaches to pricing as well as factors considered to establish prices for products and services.

LO6 Describe basic laws and regulations affecting pricing practices.

vehicles, from passenger cars and buses to recreational vehicles and motorcycles. Some vehicles, particularly heavy trucks, put more wear and tear on the bridge, and therefore you believe that these types of vehicles should pay more to use the bridge. So now you try to crunch some numbers: traffic volume by type of vehicle.

But wait a minute. Before you can set prices to make some revenue projections, you must consult the federal government of Canada. The federal government, through its regulatory agency, Transport Canada, must approve the price you charge, or in this case, the toll users will pay. The agency agrees that you can use a toll structure based on the number of axles per vehicle. In essence, there will be a base fee for the first two axles plus a fixed fee for every additional axle the vehicle has. With all this information, you must come up with a pricing strategy for the bridge—a pricing strategy that will cover your capital and operating costs as well as provide some long-run profits for the firm. Wow, it is a pricing problem![1]

So, what is the price to cross the bridge? Well, the current base toll rate for a two-axle vehicle (a passenger vehicle), round-trip, is $42.50, and it is collected on exiting PEI. If you are riding a motorcycle, it is a little cheaper at $17.00. But if you are driving a seven-axle vehicle (a tractor trailer), you pay $77.50. If you are in a hurry, you can use the StraitPass Transportation System, an electronic payment system. The transponder will cost you $40.00. And your toll charges are billed to your credit card. You can also buy bridge passes or even use Confederation Bridge electronic gift cards. While the bridge does not allow pedestrians or cyclists to use the bridge, the bridge provides a shuttle service, charging $4.00 per pedestrian and $8.00 per cyclist.[2]

Some who must use the bridge as part of their daily or weekly activities do complain about the cost of using it. However, many tourists who visit PEI are happy to pay the toll just to say that they had the experience of crossing the Confederation Bridge. Welcome to the fascinating—and intense—world of pricing, where myriad forces come together in the specific price that prospective buyers are asked to pay. This chapter covers important factors used in setting prices.

LO1 NATURE AND IMPORTANCE OF PRICE

The price paid for goods and services goes by many names. You pay *tuition* for your education, *rent* for an apartment, *interest* on a bank credit card, and a *premium* for car insurance. Your dentist or physician charges you a *fee,* a professional or social organization charges *dues,* and operators of the Confederation Bridge charge you a *fare* or a *toll* to use their bridge. In business, a consultant may require a *retainer* for services rendered, an executive is given a *salary,* a salesperson receives a *commission,* and a worker is paid a *wage.* Of course, what you pay for clothes or a haircut is termed a *price.*

price
The money or other considerations (including other goods and services) exchanged for the ownership or use of a good or service.

What Is a Price?

These examples highlight the many varied ways that price plays a part in our daily lives. From a marketing viewpoint, **price** is the money or other considerations (including other goods and services) exchanged for the ownership or use of a good or service. For example, Shell Oil recently exchanged one million pest-control devices for sugar from a Caribbean country, and Wilkinson Sword exchanged some of its knives for advertising used to promote its razor blades. This practice of exchanging goods and services for other goods and services rather than for money is called *barter*. These transactions account for billions of dollars annually in domestic and international trade.

For most products and services, money is exchanged, although the amount is not always the same as the list or quoted price because of the discounts, allowances, and extra fees shown in Figure 13–1.

Price as an Indicator of Value

From a consumer's perspective, price is often used to indicate value when it is compared with the benefits of the product. Specifically, *value* is defined as the ratio of perceived benefits to price.[3] At a given price, as perceived benefits increase, perceived value increases. For example, if you are used to paying $12.99 for a medium pizza from Pizza Pizza, wouldn't a large pizza at the same price be more valuable? Many marketers often engage in the practice of *value pricing*—increasing product or service benefits while maintaining or decreasing price.

But marketers must be careful when using price as an indicator of value. For example, for many consumers, a low price might imply possible poor quality, and ultimately, poor perceived value.[4] This is particularly true for services.[5] For example, what would be your perception of a dentist who charges only $25 for a checkup and cleaning when the average dentist charges between $100 and $150? This example also illustrates that consumers will often make comparative value assessments. That is, the consumer will judge one product or service against other alternatives or substitutes. In doing so, a "reference value" emerges, which involves comparing the prices and benefits of substitute items.

However, intense competition in many industries has led to lower prices for consumers. Accordingly, some research indicates that consumers may have changed their attitudes toward lower prices in this new low-cost world. In short, consumers may not always perceive lower prices as connoting poor value or poor quality.[6]

● **FIGURE 13–1**

The price of four different purchases

ITEM PURCHASED	PRICE EQUATION			
	PRICE	**= LIST PRICE**	**INCENTIVES AND − ALLOWANCES**	**+ EXTRA FEES**
New car bought by an individual	Final price	= List price	− Rebate Cash discount Old car trade-in	+ Financing charges Special accessories Destination charges
Term in university bought by a student	Tuition	= Published tuition	− Scholarship Other financial aid Discounts for number of credits taken	+ Special activity fees
Bank loan obtained by a small business	Principal and interest	= Amount of loan sought	− Allowance for collateral	+ Premium for uncertain creditworthiness
Merchandise bought from a wholesaler by a retailer	Invoice price	= List price	− Quantity discount Cash discount Seasonal discount Functional or trade discount	+ Penalty for late payment

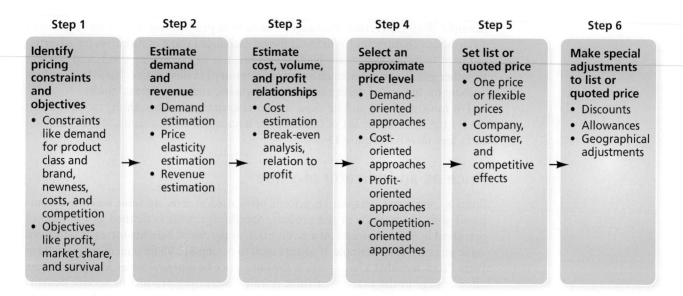

● FIGURE 13–2

Steps in setting price

Price in the Marketing Mix

profit equation

Profit = Total revenue − Total cost, or Profit = (Unit price × Quantity sold) − Total cost.

Pricing is also a critical decision made by a marketing executive because price has a direct effect on a firm's profits. This is apparent from a firm's **profit equation:**

$$\text{Profit} = \text{Total revenue} - \text{Total cost}$$

or

$$\text{Profit} = (\text{Unit price} \times \text{Quantity sold}) - \text{Total cost}$$

What makes this relationship even more important is that price affects the quantity sold, as illustrated with demand curves later in this chapter. Furthermore, because the quantity sold sometimes affects a firm's costs because of efficiency of production, price also indirectly affects costs. Thus, pricing decisions influence both total revenue and total cost, which makes pricing one of the most important decisions marketing executives face.

The importance of price in the marketing mix necessitates an understanding of six major steps involved in the process organizations go through in setting prices (Figure 13–2):

- *Identifying pricing constraints and objectives*
- *Estimating demand and revenue*
- *Estimating cost, volume, and profit relationships*
- *Selecting an approximate price level*
- *Setting list or quoted price*
- *Making special adjustments to list or quoted price*

LO2 STEP 1: IDENTIFYING PRICING CONSTRAINTS AND OBJECTIVES

To define a problem, it is important to consider both the objectives and constraints that narrow the range of alternatives available to solve it. These same principles apply in solving a pricing problem. Let us first review the pricing constraints so that we can better understand the nature of pricing alternatives.

Identifying Pricing Constraints

pricing constraints
Factors that limit the latitude of price a firm may set.

Factors that limit the latitude of prices a firm may set are **pricing constraints**. Consumer demand for the product clearly affects the price that can be charged. Other constraints on price vary from factors within the organization to competitive factors outside the organization. Moreover, legal and regulatory factors, discussed at the end of this chapter, also restrict the prices an organization can set.

Demand for the Product Class, Product, and Brand   The number of potential buyers for the product class (such as cars), product (sports cars), and brand (Dodge Viper) clearly affects the price a seller can charge. So does the question of whether the item is a luxury (a Viper) or a necessity (bread and a roof over your head). In fact, when a consumer is in urgent need of a particular necessity, a marketer may command a premium price. In this case, there may be ethical issues involved (see the accompanying Making Responsible Decisions box, "Getting an Unfair Premium Price?").[7]

Newness of the Product: Stage in the Product Life Cycle   The newer a product and the earlier it is in its life cycle, the higher the price that can usually be charged. Consider the Apple iPhone. With this new technology, Apple has no other direct competition, so it is possible to ask consumers to pay a high initial high price for this innovative product. Are you willing to spend $500 for the Apple iPhone? If not, you may have to wait and hope the price is lowered over time.

Single Product versus a Product Line   When Sony introduced its CD player, not only was it unique and in the introductory stage of its product life cycle but also it was the *only* CD player Sony sold, and so the firm had great latitude in setting a price. Now, with a wide range of Sony CD products and technologies, the price of individual models has to be consistent with the others based on features provided and meaningful price differentials that communicate value to consumers.

Cost of Producing and Marketing the Product   In the long run, a firm's price must cover all the costs of producing and marketing a product. If the price does not cover the cost, the firm will fail, and so in the long term, a firm's costs set a floor under

Making Responsible Decisions

Getting an Unfair Premium Price?

Consumer advocates argue that pharmaceutical companies have a general tendency to command premium prices for necessary drug products knowing that consumers usually have little choice but to pay them. For example, Pompe disease is a neuromuscular disease that is almost always fatal for infants. Genzyme has developed a drug to treat the disease but it costs an American patient over $300,000 per year and it must be used for life. In Canada, the drug costs over $80,000 but Health Canada allows for public funding for "some" sufferers of the disease. But critics of companies who charge premium pricing say the practice is not isolated to pharmaceutical companies. Oil companies, for example, are often criticized for raising prices on home heating oil during the cold Canadian winters. But the oil companies argue it is simply a supply-and-demand issue. Price-gouging claims are also levied against

major airlines during peak travel periods and individual companies are sometimes accused of price gouging during shortages. For example, during water shortages, bottled water suppliers have sometimes increased the price of their product by two to three times its original price. University students also often report paying high and unfair prices for off-campus housing when demand is high and supply is low.

The practice of commanding premium prices for luxuries and necessities appears to be gaining acceptability with marketers. Moreover, recent Canadian research suggests that some corporate executives and entrepreneurs have no ethical issues with knowingly overcharging customers for products and services.

Is the use of premium pricing for necessities fair? Is it ethical? What should be done about this practice?

its price. The operators of the Confederation Bridge are clearly conscious of the fact that the total cost of providing their bridge service must not exceed total revenue, as otherwise they cannot succeed.

Cost of Changing Prices and Time Period They Apply   If Air Canada asks General Electric (GE) to provide spare jet engines to power its Boeing 737s, GE can easily set a new price for the engines to reflect its latest information, as only one buyer has to be informed. But if Sears Canada decides that sweater prices are too low in its winter catalogues after thousands of catalogues have been mailed to customers, it has a big problem, and so it must consider the cost of changing prices and the time period for which they apply in developing the price list for its catalogue items. In actual practice, research indicates that most firms change the price for their major products once a year. But in the online environment, prices can change from minute to minute.

Type of Competitive Markets   The seller's price is constrained by the type of market in which it competes. Economists generally delineate four types of competitive markets: pure monopoly, oligopoly, monopolistic competition, and pure competition. Figure 13–3 shows that the type of competition dramatically influences the latitude of price competition and, in turn, the nature of product differentiation and extent of advertising. A firm must recognize the general type of competitive market it is in to understand the latitude of both its price and non-price strategies. For example, prices can be significantly affected by four competitive situations:

- *Pure monopoly.* In 1994, Johnson & Johnson (J&J) revolutionized the treatment of coronary heart diseases by introducing the *stent*—a tiny mesh tube "spring" that props clogged arteries open. Initially, a monopolist, J&J stuck with its early $2,235 price and achieved $1.4 billion in sales and 91 percent market share in the category. But its reluctance to give price reductions for large-volume purchases antagonized hospitals. When competitors introduced an improved stent at lower prices, J&J's market share plummeted to 8 percent just two years later.[8]
- *Oligopoly.* The few sellers of aluminum (Alcan, Alcoa) try to avoid price competition because it can lead to disastrous price wars in which all lose money. Yet firms in such industries stay aware of a competitor's price cuts or increases and may

● **FIGURE 13-3**
Pricing, product, and advertising strategies available to firms in four types of competitive markets

TYPE OF COMPETITIVE MARKET

STRATEGIES AVAILABLE	PURE MONOPOLY (One seller who sets the price for a unique product)	OLIGOPOLY (Few sellers who are sensitive to each other's prices)	MONOPOLISTIC COMPETITION (Many sellers who compete on non-price factors)	PURE COMPETITION (Many sellers who follow the market price for identical, commodity products)
Extent of price competition	None: sole seller sets price	Some: price leader or follower of competitors	Some: compete over range of prices	Almost none: market sets price
Extent of product differentiation	None: no other producers	Various: depends on industry	Some: differentiate products from competitors	None: products are identical
Extent of advertising	Little: purpose is to increase demand for product class	Some: purpose is to inform but avoid price competition	Much: purpose is to differentiate firm's products from competitors	Little: purpose is to inform prospects that seller's products are available

follow suit. The products can be undifferentiated (aluminum) or differentiated (jetliners), and informative advertising that avoids head-to-head price competition is used.

- *Monopolistic competition.* Dozens of regional, private brands of peanut butter compete with national brands, such as Skippy and Jif. Both price competition (regional, private brands being lower than national brands) and non-price competition (product features and advertising) exist.
- *Pure competition.* Hundreds of local grain elevators sell corn for which price per bushel is set by the marketplace. Within strains, the corn is identical, and so advertising only informs buyers that the seller's corn is available.

Competitors' Prices   Finally, a firm must know or anticipate what specific price its present and potential competitors are charging now or will charge in the future.

Identifying Pricing Objectives

Expectations that specify the role of price in an organization's marketing and strategic plans are **pricing objectives**. To the extent possible, these organizational pricing objectives are also carried to lower levels in the organization, such as in setting objectives for marketing managers responsible for an individual brand. These objectives may change depending on the financial position of the company as a whole, the success of its products, the target segments served by the company, or the competitive environment. For example, H.J. Heinz has specific pricing objectives for its ketchup, which vary by country.

Profit   Three different objectives relate to a firm's profit, usually measured in terms of return on investment (ROI) or return on assets. One objective is *managing for long-run profits,* which is followed by many Japanese firms that are willing to forgo immediate profit in cars, TV sets, or computers to develop quality products that can penetrate competitive markets in the future. A *maximizing current profit* objective, such as during this quarter or year, is common in many firms because the targets can be set and performance measured quickly. Canadian firms are sometimes criticized for this short-run orientation. A *target return* objective involves a firm, such as Irving Oil or Mohawk, setting a goal (such as 20 percent) for pretax ROI. These three profit objectives have different implications for a firm's pricing objectives.

Another profit consideration for such firms as movie studios and manufacturers is to ensure that those firms in their channels of distribution make adequate profits. Without profits for these channel members, the movie studio or manufacturer is cut off from its customers. For example, Figure 13–4 shows where each dollar of your movie ticket goes. The 51 cents the movie studio gets must cover both its production expenses and its profit. While the studio would like more than 51 cents of your dollar, it settles for this amount to make sure theatres and distributors are satisfied and willing to handle their movies. Still, with revenues close to $1 billion, the Canadian movie theatre industry has actually been raising ticket prices to increase its profitability.

Sales   Given that a firm's profit is high enough for it to remain in business, its objectives may be to increase sales revenue. The hope is that the increase in sales revenue will, in turn, lead to increases in market share and profit. Cutting price on one product in a firm's line may increase its sales revenue but reduce those of related products. Objectives related to sales revenue or unit sales have the advantage of being translated easily into meaningful targets for marketing managers responsible for a product line or brand—far more easily than with an ROI target, for example.

Market Share   Market share is the ratio of the firm's sales revenues or unit sales to those of the industry (competitors plus the firm itself). Companies often pursue a

Theatre
19¢

Distributor
30¢

Movie
studio
51¢

10¢ = Theatre
expenses

9¢ = Left for theatre

6¢ = Misc. expenses

24¢ = Left for
distributor

20¢ = Advertising
and publicity
expenses

8¢ = Actors' share
of gross

23¢ = Left for
movie studio

● **FIGURE 13–4**

Where each dollar of your
movie ticket goes

market-share objective when industry sales are relatively flat or declining. The Molson and Labatt breweries have adopted this objective in the beer market, while Pepsi-Cola Canada and Coca-Cola Canada battle for market share in the soft drink category.[9] But although increased market share is the primary goal of some firms, others see it as a means to an end: increasing sales and profits.

Unit Volume   Many firms use unit volume, the quantity produced or sold, as a pricing objective. These firms often sell multiple products at very different prices and need to match the unit volume demanded by customers with price and production capacity. Using unit volume as an objective can be counterproductive if a volume objective is achieved, say, by drastic price cutting that drives down company profitability.[10]

Survival   In some instances, profits, sales, and market share are less important objectives of the firm than mere survival. Continental Airlines has struggled to attract passengers with low fares, no-penalty advance-booking policies, and aggressive promotions to improve the firm's cash flow. This pricing objective has helped Continental to stay alive in the competitive airline industry.

Social Responsibility   A firm may forgo higher profit on sales and follow a pricing objective that recognizes its obligations to customers and society in general. Medtronics followed this pricing policy when it introduced the world's first heart pacemaker. Gerber supplies a specially formulated product free of charge to children who cannot tolerate foods based on cow's milk. Government agencies, which set many prices for services they offer, use social responsibility as a primary pricing objective.

---

learning review

1. What factors impact the list price to determine the final price?

2. How does the type of competitive market a firm is in affect its latitude in setting price?

LO3 **STEP 2: ESTIMATING DEMAND AND REVENUE**

Basic to setting a product's price is the extent of customer demand for it. Marketing executives must also translate this estimate of customer demand into estimates of revenues the firm expects to receive.

Fundamentals of Estimating Demand

Newsweek decided to conduct a pricing experiment at newsstands in 11 cities.[11] In one city, newsstand buyers paid $2.25. In five cities, newsstand buyers paid the regular $2 price. In another city, the price was $1.50, and in four other cities it was only $1. By comparison, the regular newsstand price for *Time* was $1.95. Why did *Newsweek* conduct the experiment? According to a *Newsweek* executive, at that time, "We wanted to figure out what the demand curve for our magazine at the newsstand is." And you thought that demand curves only existed to confuse you on a test in basic economics!

demand curve
The summation of points representing the maximum number of products consumers will buy at a given price.

The Demand Curve   A **demand curve** shows a maximum number of products consumers will buy at a given price. Demand curve D1 in Figure 13–5 shows the newsstand demand for *Newsweek* under existing conditions. Note that as the price falls, people buy more. But price is not the complete story in estimating demand. Economists stress three other key factors:

1. *Consumer tastes.* As we saw in Chapter 3, these depend on many factors, such as demographics, culture, and technology. Because consumer tastes can change quickly, up-to-date marketing research is essential.
2. *Price and availability of other products.* As the price of close substitute products falls (the price of *Time*) and their availability increases, the demand for a product declines (the demand for *Newsweek*).
3. *Consumer income.* In general, as real consumer income (allowing for inflation) increases, demand for a product also increases.

The first of these two factors influences what consumers *want* to buy, and the third affects what they *can* buy. Along with price, these are often called *demand factors,* or factors that determine consumers' willingness and ability to pay for goods and services. As discussed earlier in Chapters 8 and 10, it is often very difficult to estimate demand for new products, especially because consumer likes and dislikes are often difficult to read clearly.

Movement along versus Shift of a Demand Curve   Demand curve D1 in Figure 13–5 shows that as the price is lowered from $2 to $1.50, the quantity demanded increases from 3 million (Q1) to 4.5 million (Q2) units per year. This is an example of a movement along a demand curve and assumes that other factors (consumer tastes, price and availability of substitutes, and consumer income) remain unchanged.

What if some of the factors change? For example, if advertising causes more people to want *Newsweek,* newsstand distribution is increased, and when consumer incomes double, then the demand increases. This is shown in Figure 13–5 as a shift of the demand curve to the right, from D1 to D2. This increased demand means that more *Newsweek* magazines are wanted for a given price: At a price of $2, the demand is 6 million units per year (Q3) on D2 rather than 3 million units per year (Q1) on D1.

price elasticity of demand
The percentage change in quantity demanded relative to a percentage change in price.

Price Elasticity of Demand   Marketing managers are especially interested in **price elasticity of demand,** or the percentage change in quantity demanded relative to a percentage change in price. Price elasticity is central to understanding a product's

● **FIGURE 13–5**
Illustrative demand curves for *Newsweek* magazine

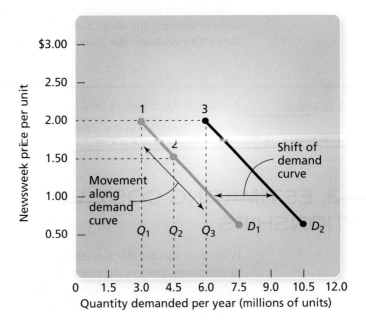

demand curve. It provides an indication of how sensitive consumer demand and the firm's revenues are to changes in the product's price.

For example, a product with elastic demand is one in which a slight decrease in price results in a relatively large increase in demand, or units sold. The reverse is also true. With elastic demand, a slight increase in price results in a relatively large decrease in demand. Typically, the more substitutes a product or service has, the more likely it is to be price elastic. For example, marketing experiments on soft drinks, coffee, and snack foods have been shown to have elastic demand. So marketing managers may cut price to increase the demand of their products depending on what competitors' prices are.

In contrast, a product with inelastic demand means that slight increases or decreases in price will not significantly affect the demand, or units sold, for the product. Typically, products and services considered as necessities usually have inelastic demand, as do products or services with no competitive alternatives. For example, if you have to drive to class in your car and gasoline prices increase one cent per litre, you are probably not going to start using the bus instead. Therefore, gasoline has inelastic demand, which means the increase in price will have a relatively minor impact on the number of litres of gasoline sold and may actually increase the total revenue of your local Petro-Canada or Irving gasoline station.

Fundamentals of Estimating Revenue

total revenue
The total money received from the sale of a product.

While economists may talk about "demand curves," marketing executives are more likely to speak in terms of "revenues generated." Demand curves lead directly to an essential revenue concept critical to pricing decisions: **total revenue**—the total money received from the sale of a product. Total revenue (TR) equals the unit price (P) times the quantity sold (Q). Or TR = P × Q. For example, assume a picture frame shop sets a price of $100 per picture and sells 400 pictures per year. In this case,

$$TR = P \times Q$$
$$= \$100 \times 400$$
$$= \$40,000$$

This combination of price and quantity sold annually shows total revenue of $40,000 per year. But is that shop making a profit? Alas, total revenue is only part of the profit equation that we saw earlier:

$$\text{Total profit} = \text{Total revenue} - \text{Total cost}$$

In order to determine the profitability of the frame shop, we have to examine the costs of running the shop. The following section covers this other important part of the profit equation—the costs of doing business.

---

learning review

3. What is the difference between a movement along and a shift of a demand curve?

4. What does it mean if a product has inelastic demand?

STEP 3: ESTIMATING COST, VOLUME, AND PROFIT RELATIONSHIPS

While revenues are the monies received by a firm from selling its products or services to customers, costs or expenses are the monies the firm pays out to its employees and suppliers. Marketing managers often use break-even analysis to relate revenues and costs, a topic covered in this section.

The Importance of Controlling Costs

total cost
The total expenses incurred by a firm in producing and marketing a product.

fixed cost
The firm's expenses that are stable and do not change with the quantity of product that is produced and cost.

variable cost
The sum of the expenses of a firm that vary directly with the quantity of products that is produced and sold.

Understanding the role and behaviour of costs is critical to all marketing decisions, particularly pricing decisions. Many firms go bankrupt because their costs get out of control, causing their total costs to exceed their total revenues over an extended period of time. This is why smart marketing managers make pricing decisions that balance both their revenues and costs. Three cost concepts are important in pricing decisions: total cost, fixed cost, and variable cost. **Total cost** is the total expenses incurred by a firm in producing and marketing a product. It is the sum of fixed costs and variable costs. **Fixed cost** is the firm's expenses that are stable and do not change with the quantity of product that is produced and cost. These usually include salaries of executives and lease charges on a building. **Variable cost** is the sum of the expenses of a firm that vary directly with the quantity of products that is produced and sold. Variable costs can be direct labour and materials used in producing the product or sales commissions that are tied directly to the quantity sold.

LO4 Break-Even Analysis

break-even analysis
A technique that analyzes the relationship between total revenue and total cost to determine profitability at various levels of output.

Marketing managers often employ an approach that considers cost, volume, and profit relationships, based on the profit equations. **Break-even analysis** is a technique that analyzes the relationship between total revenue and total cost to determine profitability at various levels of output. The *break-even point (BEP)* is the quantity at which total revenue and total costs are equal. Profit comes from any units sold beyond the BEP.

Calculating a Break-Even Point

The break-even point (BEP) is calculated as follows:

$$BEP_{Quantity} = \frac{Fixed\ cost}{Unit\ price - Unit\ variable\ cost}$$

So, consider our frame shop example. Suppose the frame shop owner wanted to identify how many pictures must be sold to cover fixed costs at a given price. Also, assume that the average price a customer will pay for each picture is $100. Suppose the fixed cost (FC) for the business is $28,000 (for real estate rental, interest on a bank loan, and other fixed expenses) and unit variable cost (UVC) for a picture is $30 (for labour, glass, frame, matting). The break-even quanity ($BEP_{Quantity}$) is 400 pictures, as follows:

$$BEP_{Quantity} = \frac{Fixed\ cost}{Unit\ price - Unit\ variable\ cost}$$
$$= \frac{\$28,000}{\$100-30}$$
$$= 400\ pictures$$

The highlighted row in Figure 13–6 shows the break-even quantity for the frame shop at a price of $100 per picture is 400 pictures. At less than 400 pictures, the frame shop incurs a loss, and at more than 400 pictures it makes a profit.

Figure 13–7 shows a graphic presentation of the break-even analysis, called a *break-even chart*. It shows that total revenue and total cost intersect and are equal at a quantity of 400 pictures sold, which is the break-even point at which profit is exactly $0. The frame shop owner would obviously want to do better. So, for example, if the frame shop owner could double the quantity sold annually to 800 pictures, the graph in Figure 13–7 shows that an annual profit of $28,000 could be generated.

Application of Break-Even Analysis

Because of its simplicity, break-even analysis is used extensively in marketing, most frequently to study the impact of profit on changes in price, fixed cost, and variable

QUANTITY OF PICTURES SOLD (Q)	PRICE PER PICTURE (P)	TOTAL REVENUE (TR) = (P × Q)	UNIT VARIABLE COST (UVC)	TOTAL VARIABLE COST (TVC) = (UVC × Q)	FIXED COST (FC)	TOTAL COST (TC) = (FC + TVC)	PROFIT = (TR − TC)
0	$100	$ 0	$30	$ 0	$28,000	$28,000	$28,000
200	100	20,000	30	6,000	28,000	34,000	14,000
400	100	40,000	30	12,000	28,000	40,000	0
600	100	60,000	30	18,000	28,000	46,000	14,000
800	100	80,000	30	24,000	28,000	52,000	28,000
1,000	100	100,000	30	30,000	28,000	58,000	42,000
1,200	100	120,000	30	36,000	28,000	64,000	56,000

● **FIGURE 13-6**

Calculating a break-even point

cost. The mechanics of break-even analysis are the basis of the widely used electronic spreadsheets offered by such computer programs as Microsoft Excel that permit managers to answer hypothetical "what if" questions about the effect of changes in price and cost on their profit.

---

learning review

5. What is the difference between fixed cost and variable cost?

6. What is a break-even point?

STEP 4: SELECTING AN APPROXIMATE PRICE LEVEL

A key to a marketing manager's setting a final price for a product is to find an *approximate price level* to use as a reasonable starting point. Four common approaches to finding this approximate price level are (1) demand-oriented, (2) cost-oriented,

● **FIGURE 13-7**

Break-even analysis chart for picture frame shop

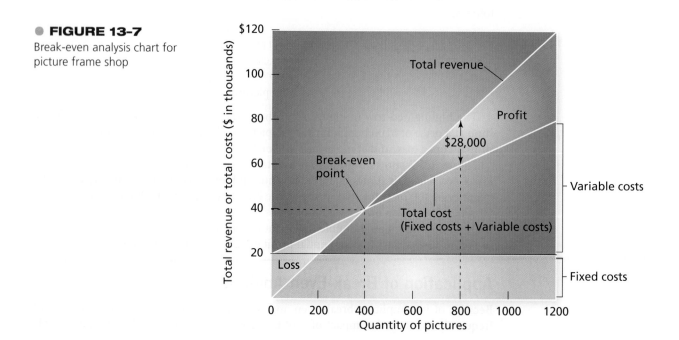

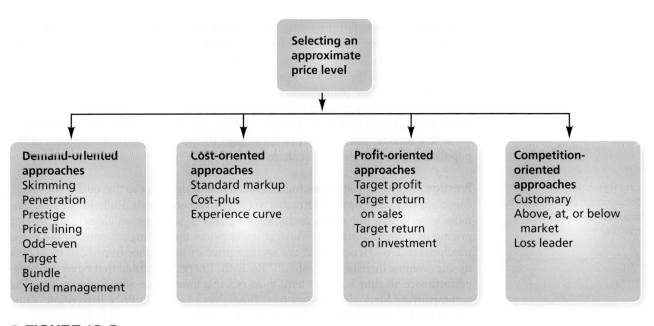

● FIGURE 13–8

Four approaches for selecting an approximate price level

(3) profit-oriented, and (4) competition-oriented approaches (Figure 13–8). Although these approaches are discussed separately below, some of them overlap, and an effective marketing manager will consider several in searching for an approximate price level.

LO5 Demand-Oriented Approaches

Demand-oriented approaches weigh factors underlying expected customer tastes and preferences more heavily than such factors as cost, profit, and competition when selecting a price level.

skimming pricing

The highest initial price that customers really desiring a product are willing to pay.

Skimming Pricing   A firm introducing a new or innovative product can use **skimming pricing,** setting the highest initial price that customers who really desire a product are willing to pay. These customers are not very price sensitive because they weigh the new product's price, quality, and ability to satisfy their needs against the same characteristics of substitutes. As these customers' demands are satisfied, the firm lowers the price to attract another, more price-sensitive segment. Thus, skimming pricing gets its name from skimming successive layers of "cream," or customer segments, as prices are lowered in a series of steps.

Skimming pricing is an effective strategy when (1) enough prospective customers are willing to buy the product immediately at the high initial price to make these sales profitable, (2) the high initial price will not attract competitors, (3) lowering price has only a minor effect on increasing the sales volume and reducing the unit costs, and (4) customers interpret the high price as signifying high quality. These four conditions are most likely to exist when the new product is protected by patents or copyrights or its uniqueness is understood and valued by customers. Duracell adopted a skimming strategy for the Duracell Ultra alkaline battery because many of these conditions applied.

penetration pricing

Setting a low initial price on a new product to appeal immediately to the mass market.

Penetration Pricing   Setting a low initial price on a new product to appeal immediately to the mass market is **penetration pricing,** the exact opposite of skimming pricing. Nintendo consciously chose a penetration strategy when it originally introduced the Nintendo Wii, its popular video game console.

The conditions favouring penetration pricing are the reverse of those supporting skimming pricing: (1) many segments of the market are price sensitive; (2) a low initial price discourages competitors from entering the market; and (3) unit production and marketing costs fall dramatically as production volumes increase. A firm using penetration pricing may (1) maintain the initial price for a time to gain profit lost from its low introductory level, or (2) lower the price further, counting on the new volume to generate the necessary profit.

In some situations, penetration pricing may follow skimming pricing. A company might initially price a product high to attract price-insensitive consumers and recoup initial research and development costs and introductory promotional expenditures. Once this is done, penetration pricing is used to appeal to a broader segment of the population and increase market share.[12]

prestige pricing

Setting a high price on a product to attract quality- or status-conscious consumers.

Prestige Pricing   **Prestige pricing** involves setting a high price so that quality- or status-conscious consumers will be attracted to the product and buy it. Rolls-Royce cars, diamonds, perfumes, fine china, Swiss watches, and crystal have an element of prestige pricing in them and may sell worse at lower prices than at higher ones. When Swiss watchmaker TAG Heuer raised the average price of its watches from $250 to $1,000, its sales volume increased sevenfold![13] Recently, Energizer learned that buyers of high-performance alkaline batteries tend to associate a lower price with lower quality. The accompanying Marketing Matters box, "Energizer's Lesson in Price Perception: Value Lies in the Eye of the Beholder," describes the pricing lesson learned by Energizer.[14]

price lining

Pricing a line of products at a number of different specific pricing points.

Price Lining   Often, a firm that is selling not just a single product but a line of products may price them at a number of different specific pricing points, which is called **price lining**. For example, a discount department store manager may price a line of women's dresses at $59, $79, and $99. In some instances, all the items might be purchased for the same cost and then marked up at different percentages to achieve these price points based on colour, style, and expected demand. In other instances, manufacturers design products for different price points, and retailers apply approximately the same markup percentages to achieve the three or four different price points offered to consumers.

Marketing Matters

Energizer's Lesson in Price Perception: Value Lies in the Eye of the Beholder

Battery manufacturers are as tireless as a certain drum-thumping bunny in their efforts to create products that perform better, last longer, and, not incidentally, outsell the competition. The commercialization of new alkaline battery technology at a price that creates value for consumers is not always obvious or easy. Just ask the marketing executives at Energizer about their experience with pricing Energizer Advanced Formula and Energizer e² AA alkaline batteries.

When Duracell launched its high-performance Ultra brand AA alkaline battery with a 25 percent price premium over standard Duracell batteries, Energizer quickly countered with its own high-performance battery—Energizer Advanced Formula. Believing that consumers would not pay the premium price, Energizer priced its Advanced Formula brand at the same price as its standard AA alkaline battery, expecting to gain market share from Duracell. It did not happen. Why not? According to industry analysts, consumers associated Energizer's low price with inferior quality in the high-performance segment. Instead of gaining market share, Energizer lost market share to Duracell and Rayovac, the number-three battery manufacturer.

Having learned its lesson, Energizer subsequently released its e² high-performance battery, this time priced 4 percent higher than Duracell Ultra and about 50 percent higher than Advanced Formula. The result? Energizer recovered lost sales and market share. The lesson learned? Value lies in the eye of the beholder.

**Occidental Allegro
Punta Cana • 4 ★**

ALL-INCLUSIVE
Standard room
September 3 – 25
1 week

FREE upgrade
to VIP package!

$**879***

PRICE INCLUDES ROUND-TRIP AIRFARE, ACCOMMODATION
AND AIRPORT TRANFERS AT DESTINATION

*PLUS TAXES OF $245, AND DEPARTURE TAX
OF USD$20 (CASH) PAID AT DESTINATION.

The **Dominican**Republic
a land of sensations

odd–even pricing
Setting prices a few dollars or cents under an even number.

target pricing
The practice of deliberately adjusting the composition and features of a product to achieve the target price to consumers.

bundle pricing
The marketing of two or more products in a single "package" price.

yield management pricing
The charging of different prices to maximize revenue for a set amount of capacity at any given time.

Odd–Even Pricing   Sears Canada offers a Craftsman radial saw for $499.99, the individual monthly subscription rate for XM Satellite Radio Canada is $14.99, and Dollarama sells greeting cards for 99 cents. Why not simply price these items at $500, $15, and $1, respectively? These firms are using **odd–even pricing,** which involves setting prices a few dollars or cents under an even number. The presumption is that consumers see the Sears radial saw as priced at "something over $400" rather than "about $500." In theory, demand increases if the price drops from $500 to $499.99. There is some evidence to suggest that this does happen.[15]

Target Pricing   Manufacturers will sometimes estimate the price that the ultimate consumer would be willing to pay for a product. They then work backward through markups taken by retailers and wholesalers to determine what price they can charge wholesalers for the product. This practice, called **target pricing,** results in the manufacturer deliberately adjusting the composition and features of a product to achieve the target price to consumers. Canon uses this practice for pricing its cameras, and Heinz adopted target pricing for its complete line of pet foods.

Bundle Pricing   A frequently used demand-oriented pricing practice is **bundle pricing**—the marketing of two or more products in a single "package" price. For example, Air Canada offers vacation packages that include airfare, car rental, and lodging. Bundle pricing is based on the idea that consumers value the package more than the individual items. This is due to benefits received from not having to make separate purchases and due to enhanced satisfaction from one item given the presence of another. Importantly, recent Canadian research found that the presentation of a bundle sends a powerful message to the customer that "here lies a bargain."[16] Moreover, bundle pricing often means lower marketing costs to sellers.[17]

Yield Management Pricing   Have you noticed that seats on Air Canada flights are priced differently within the economy class? What you observed is **yield management pricing**—the charging of different prices to maximize revenue for a set amount of capacity at any given time.[18] As described in Chapter 12, service businesses engage in capacity management, and an effective way to do this is by varying price by time, day, week, or season. Yield management pricing is a complex approach that continually matches demand and supply to customize the price for a service. Airlines, hotels, cruise ships, and car rental companies use it. The airline industry reports that yield management pricing produces hundreds of millions of dollars of revenue each year that might not ordinarily be produced using traditional pricing practices.[19]

learning review

7. What are the circumstances in pricing a new product that might support skimming or penetration pricing?

8. What is odd–even pricing?

Cost-Oriented Approaches

With cost-oriented approaches, the price setter stresses the supply or cost side of the pricing problem, not the demand side. Price is set by looking at the production and marketing costs and then adding enough to cover direct expenses, overhead, and profit.

standard markup pricing
Adding a fixed percentage to the cost of all items in a specific product class.

Standard Markup Pricing   Managers of supermarkets and other retail stores have such a large number of products that estimating the demand for each product as a means of setting price is impossible. Therefore, they use **standard markup pricing,** which entails adding a fixed percentage to the cost of all items in a specific product class. This percentage markup varies depending on the type of retail store (such as furniture, clothing, or grocery) and on the product involved. High-volume products usually have smaller markups than do low-volume products. Supermarkets, such as Sobeys, Safeway, and Loblaws, have different markups for staple items and discretionary items. The markup on staple items, such as sugar, flour, and dairy products, varies from 10 to 23 percent, whereas markups on discretionary items, such as snack foods and candy, range from 27 to 47 percent. These markups must cover all the expenses of the store, pay for overhead costs, and contribute something to profits. For supermarkets, these markups, which may appear very large, result in only a 1 percent profit on sales revenue if the store is operating efficiently. By comparison, consider the markups on snacks and beverages purchased at your local movie theatre. The markup on soft drinks is 87 percent, 65 percent on chocolate bars, and a whopping 90 percent on popcorn! An explanation of how to compute a markup, along with operating statement data and other ratios, is given in Appendix B following this chapter.

cost-plus pricing
Summing the total unit cost of providing a product or service and adding a specific amount to the cost to arrive at a price.

Cost-Plus Pricing   Many manufacturing, professional services, and construction firms use a variation of standard markup pricing. **Cost-plus pricing** involves summing the total unit cost of providing a product or service and adding a specific amount to the cost to arrive at a price.

Cost-plus pricing is the most commonly used method to set prices for business products. But increasingly, this method is finding favour among business-to-business marketers in the service sector. For example, the rising cost of legal fees has prompted some law firms to adopt a cost-plus pricing approach. Rather than billing business clients on an hourly basis, lawyers and their clients agree on a fixed fee based on expected costs plus a profit for the law firm.[20] Many advertising agencies also use this approach. Here, the client agrees to pay the agency a fee based on the cost of its work plus some agreed-on profit, which is often a percentage of total cost.[21]

experience curve pricing
Pricing method based on production experience, that is, the unit cost of many products and services declines by 10 to 30 percent each time a firm's experience at producing and selling them doubles.

Experience Curve Pricing   The method of **experience curve pricing** is based on the learning effect, which holds that the unit cost of many products and services declines by 10 to 30 percent each time a firm's experience at producing and selling them doubles. This reduction is regular or predictable enough that the average cost per unit can be mathematically estimated. And, because prices often follow costs with experience curve pricing, a rapid decline in price is possible. Japanese firms in the electronics industry often adopt this pricing approach.

Profit-Oriented Approaches

A price setter may choose to balance both revenues and costs to set prices using profit-oriented approaches. These might involve either a target of a specific dollar volume of profit or express this target profit as a percentage of sales or investment.

target profit pricing
Pricing method based on an annual target of a specific dollar volume of profit.

Target Profit Pricing   A firm may set an annual target of a specific dollar volume of profit, which is called **target profit pricing**. Suppose our picture frame shop owner wishes to use target profit pricing to establish a price for a typical framed picture and assumes the following:

- Variable cost is a constant $22 per unit.
- Fixed cost is a constant $26,000.
- Demand is insensitive to price up to $60 per unit.
- A target profit of $7,000 is sought at an annual volume of 1,000 units (framed pictures).

The price can be calculated as follows:

$$\text{Profit} = \text{Total revenue} - \text{Total cost}$$
$$\text{Profit} = (P \times Q) - [FC + (UVC \times Q)]$$
$$\$7,000 = (P \times 1,000) - [\$26,000 + (\$22 \times 1,000)]$$
$$\$7,000 = 1,000P - (\$26,000 + \$22,000)$$
$$1,000P = \$7,000 + \$48,000$$
$$P = \$55$$

Note that a critical assumption is that this higher average price of a framed picture will not cause the demand to fall.

Target Return-on-Sales Pricing   A difficulty with target profit pricing is that although it is simple and the target involves only a specific dollar volume, there is no benchmark of sales or investment used to show how much of the firm's effort is needed to achieve the target. Such firms as supermarket chains often use **target return-on-sales pricing** to set typical prices that will give the firm a profit that is a specified percentage—say, 1 percent of the sales volume.

Target Return-on-Investment Pricing   Such firms as GM and many public utilities set annual return-on-investment (ROI) targets, such as ROI of 20 percent. **Target return-on-investment pricing** is a method of setting prices to achieve this target.

Suppose the shop owner sets a target ROI of 10 percent, which is twice that achieved the previous year. She considers raising the average price of a framed picture to $54 or $58—up from last year's average of $50. To do this, she might improve product quality by offering better frames and higher-quality matting, which will increase the cost but will probably offset the decreased revenue from the lower number of units that can be sold next year.

Competition-Oriented Approaches

Rather than emphasize demand, cost, or profit factors, a price setter can stress what competitors (or "the market") are doing.

Customary Pricing   For some products, when tradition, standardized channels of distribution, or other competitive factors dictate the price, **customary pricing** is used. Tradition prevails in the pricing of Swatch watches. The $40 customary price for the basic model has changed little in 10 years. Chocolate bars offered through standard vending machines have a customary price of 75 cents, and a significant departure from this price may result in a loss of sales for the manufacturer. Hershey typically has changed the amount of chocolate in its chocolate bars depending on the price of raw chocolate rather than vary its customary retail price so that it can continue selling through vending machines.

Above-, At-, or Below-Market Pricing   For most products, it is difficult to identify a specific market price for a product or product class. Still, marketing managers often have a subjective feel for the competitor's price or market price. Using this benchmark, they then may deliberately choose a strategy of **above-, at-, or below-market pricing**.

target return-on-sales pricing
Setting typical prices that will give a firm a profit that is a specific percentage.

target return-on-investment pricing
Setting prices to achieve return-on-investment (ROI) targets.

customary pricing
Setting prices dictated by tradition, standardized channels of distribution, or other competitive factors.

above-, at-, or below-market pricing
Setting prices based on pricing of similar products in the market.

Zellers uses a below-market price strategy for numerous products it retails.

Among watch manufacturers, Rolex takes pride in emphasizing that it makes one of the most expensive watches you can buy—a clear example of above-market pricing. Manufacturers of national brands of clothing, such as Alfred Sung and Christian Dior, and retailers, such as Holt Renfrew, deliberately set premium prices for their products.

Large mass-merchandise chains, such as Sears Canada and The Bay, generally use at-market pricing. These chains often establish the going market price in the minds of competitors. Similarly, Revlon generally prices its products "at market." These companies also provide a reference price for competitors that use above- and below-market pricing.

In contrast, a number of firms, such as Zellers, use a strategy of below-market pricing. Also, manufacturers of all generic products and retailers who offer their own private brands of products deliberately set prices for their products about 8 to 10 percent below the prices of nationally branded competitive products. Below-market pricing also exists in business-to-business marketing.

However, some companies use a "price premium measure" to assess whether their products and brands are above, at, or below the market. An illustration of how the price premium measure is calculated, displayed, and interpreted appears in the Using Marketing Dashboards box.

loss-leader pricing

Selling products below their customary prices to attract attention to them in the hope that customers will buy other products as well.

Loss-Leader Pricing   For special promotions, many retail stores deliberately sell products below their customary prices to attract attention to them. For example, supermarkets will often use produce or paper goods as loss leaders. The purpose of **loss-leader pricing** is not to increase sales of that particular produce but to attract customers in the hope that they will buy other products as well, particularly discretionary items carrying large markups.

Using Marketing Dashboards

Are Cracker Jack Prices Above, At, or Below the Market?

How would you determine whether a firm's retail prices are above, at, or below the market? You might visit retail stores and record what prices retailers are charging for products or brands. This laborious activity can be simplified by combining two consumer market share measures to create a "price premium" display on your marketing dashboard.

Your Challenge Frito-Lay is considering whether to buy the Cracker Jack brand of caramel popcorn from Borden, Inc. Frito-Lay research shows that Cracker Jack has a strong brand equity. But Cracker Jack's dollar sales market share and pound volume market share declined recently and trailed the Crunch 'n Munch brand as shown in the table.

Borden's management used an above-market, premium pricing strategy for Cracker Jack. Specifically, Cracker Jack's suggested retail price was set to yield an average price premium per pound of 28 percent relative to Crunch 'n Munch. As a Frito-Lay marketer studying Cracker Jack, your challenge is to calculate and display Cracker Jack's actual price premium relative to Crunch 'n Munch. A price premium is the percentage by which the actual price charged for a specific brand exceeds (or falls short of) a benchmark established for a similar product or basket of products. This premium can be calculated as follows:

$$\text{Price Premium (\%)} = \frac{\text{Dollar Sales Market Share for a Brand}}{\text{Unit Volume Market Share for a Brand}} - 1$$

Brand	Dollar Sales Market Share	Unit Volume Market Share
Crunch 'n Munch	32%	32%
Cracker Jack	26%	19%
Fiddle Faddle	7%	8%
Private Brands	4%	8%
Seasonal, Specialty, and Regional (S, S, R) Brands	<u>31</u>%	<u>33</u>%
Total	100%	100%

Your Findings Using caramel popcorn brand market share data, the Cracker Jack price premium is 1.368, or 36.8 percent, calculated as follows: (26 percent ÷ 19 percent) − 1 = 0.368. By comparison, Crunch 'n Munch enjoys no price premium. Its dollar sales market share and unit (pound) market share are equal: (32 percent ÷ 32 percent) − 1 = 0, or zero percent. The price premium, or lack thereof, of other brands can be displayed in a marketing dashboard as shown below.

Your Action Cracker Jack's price premium clearly exceeds the 28 percent Borden benchmark relative to Crunch 'n Munch. Cracker Jack's price premium may have overreached its brand equity. Consideration might be given to assessing Cracker Jack's price premium relative to its market position should Frito-Lay purchase the brand.

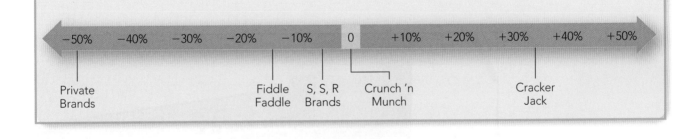

learning review   **9.** What is standard markup pricing?

10. What is the purpose of loss-leader pricing when used by a retail firm?

STEP 5: SETTING THE LIST OR QUOTED PRICE

The first four steps in setting price result in an approximate price level for the product that appears reasonable. But it still remains for the manager to set a specific list or quoted price in light of all relevant factors.

One-Price Policy versus Flexible-Price Policy

A seller must decide whether to follow a one-price policy or a flexible-price policy. A *one-price policy,* also called *fixed pricing,* is setting one price for all buyers of a product or service. For example, when you buy a Wilson Sting tennis racquet from a discount store, you are offered the product at a single price. You can decide to buy it or not, but there is no variation in the price under the seller's one-price policy. Saturn Corporation uses this approach in its stores and features a "no haggle, one price" policy for its cars. Some retailers, such as dollar stores, have married this policy with a below-market approach and sell everything in their stores for $1 or less!

In contrast, a *flexible-price policy,* also called *dynamic pricing,* involves setting different prices for products and services depending on individual buyers and purchase situations. A flexible-price policy gives sellers considerable discretion in setting the final price in light of demand, cost, and competitive factors. For example, recently the Montreal-based Yellow Pages Group, publisher of the Yellow Pages directory, changed from a one-price policy to a flexible or variable pricing policy depending on the advertising category in the Yellow Pages directory. On average, every dollar invested by advertisers in the Yellow Pages directory is worth $26 in sales. But the return varies according to the category. Therefore, the company charges more for advertising in categories that produce more sales for the client, and less for categories that result in lower sales.[22]

While most companies use the one-price policy, flexible pricing has grown in popularity because of increasingly sophisticated information technology. Today, many marketers have the ability to customize a price for an individual on the basis of his or her purchasing patterns, product preferences, and price sensitivity, all of which are stored in company data warehouses. Price customization is particularly prevalent for products and services bought online. Online marketers routinely adjust prices in response to purchase situations and past purchase behaviours of online buyers. Some online marketers monitor an online shopper's "clickstream"—the way that a person navigates through its Web site. If the visitor behaves like a price-sensitive shopper—perhaps by comparing many different products—that person may be offered a lower price. However, as noted at the end of this chapter, flexible pricing carried to the extreme could be considered price discrimination and is a practice prohibited under the *Competition Act.*

Company, Customer, and Competitive Effects

As the final list or quoted price is set, the effects on the company, customers, and competitors must be assessed.

Company Effects For a firm with more than one product, a decision on the price of a single product must consider the price of other items in its product line or related product lines in its product mix. Within a product line or mix, there are usually some products that are substitutes for one another and some that complement each other. Frito-Lay recognizes that its tortilla chip product line consisting of Baked Tostitos, Tostitos, and Doritos brands are partial substitutes for one another and its bean and cheese dip line and salsa sauces complement the tortilla chip line.

A manager's challenge when marketing multiple products is *product-line pricing,* the setting of prices for all items in a product line. When setting prices, the manager seeks to cover the total cost and produce a profit for the complete line, not necessarily for each item.

Product-line pricing involves determining (1) the lowest-priced product and price, (2) the highest-priced product and price, and (3) price differentials for all other products in the line.[23] The lowest- and highest-priced items in the product line play important roles. The highest-priced item is typically positioned as the premium item in quality and features. The lowest-priced item is the traffic builder designed to capture the attention of the hesitant or first-time buyer. Price differentials between items in the line should make sense to customers and reflect the differences in their perceived values of the products offered. Behavioural research also suggests that the price differentials should get larger as one moves up the product line.

Customer Effects In setting prices, retailers weigh factors heavily that satisfy the perceptions or expectations of ultimate consumers, such as the customary prices for a variety of consumer products. Retailers have found that they should not price their store brands 20 to 25 percent below manufacturers' brands. When they do, consumers might view the lower price as signalling lower quality and they do not buy. This is also particularly true in marketing "intangible services," where low price may connote poor quality.[24]

Competitive Effects A manager's pricing decision is immediately apparent to most competitors, who may retaliate with price changes of their own. Therefore, a manager

Frito-Lay recognizes that its tortilla chip products are partial substitutes for one another and its bean and cheese dips and salsa sauces complement tortilla chips. This knowledge is used in Frito-Lay product-line pricing.

Frito Lay, Inc.
www.frito-lay.com

who sets a final list or quoted price must anticipate potential price responses from competitors. Regardless of whether a firm is a price leader or follower, it wants to avoid cutthroat price wars in which no firm in the industry makes a satisfactory profit. A *price war* involves successive pricing by competitors to increase or maintain their unit sales or market share. For example, price wars in the airline industry usually result in losses for all players. Similarly, in the residential long-distance telephone industry, even price reductions as little as 1 percent can have a significant effect on company profitability.[25]

Marketers are advised to consider price cutting only when one or more conditions exist: (1) the company has a cost or technological advantage over its competitors; (2) primary demand for a product class will grow if prices are lowered; and (3) the price cut is confined to specific products or customers (as with airline tickets) and not across the board.

STEP 6: MAKING SPECIAL ADJUSTMENTS TO THE LIST OR QUOTED PRICE

When you pay 75 cents for a bag of M&Ms in a vending machine or receive a quoted price of $10,000 from a contractor to renovate your kitchen, the pricing sequence ends with the last step just described: setting the list or quoted price. But when you are a manufacturer of M&M candies or gas grills and sell your product to dozens or hundreds of wholesalers and retailers in your channel of distribution, you may need to make a variety of special adjustments to the list or quoted price. Wholesalers also must adjust list or quoted prices they set for retailers. Three special adjustments to the list or quoted price are (1) discounts, (2) allowances, and (3) geographical adjustments.

Toro uses seasonal discounts to stimulate consumer demand and smooth out seasonal manufacturing peaks and troughs.

The Toro Company
www.toro.com

Discounts

Discounts are reductions from list price that a seller gives a buyer as a reward for some activity of the buyer that is favourable to the seller. Four kinds of discounts are especially important in marketing strategy: (1) quantity, (2) seasonal, (3) trade (functional), and (4) cash discounts.[26]

Quantity Discounts   To encourage customers to buy larger quantities of a product, firms at all levels in the channel of distribution offer *quantity discounts,* which are reductions in unit costs for a larger order. For example, an instant photocopying service might set a price of 10 cents a copy for 1 to 25 copies, 9 cents a copy for 26 to 100, and 8 cents a copy for 101 or more. Because the photocopying service gets more of the buyer's business and has longer production runs that reduce its order-handling costs, it is willing to pass on some of the cost savings in the form of quantity discounts to the buyer.

Seasonal Discounts   To encourage buyers to stock inventory earlier than their normal demand would require, manufacturers often use seasonal discounts. For example, Toro, which manufactures lawn mowers and snow throwers, offers seasonal discounts to encourage wholesalers and retailers to stock up on lawn mowers in January and February and on snow throwers in July and August—five or six months before the seasonal demand by the ultimate consumers. This enables Toro to smooth out seasonal manufacturing peaks and troughs, thereby contributing to more efficient production. It also rewards wholesalers and retailers for the risk they accept in assuming increased inventory carrying costs and having supplies in stock at the time they are wanted by customers.

Trade (Functional) Discounts   To reward wholesalers and retailers for marketing functions they will perform in the future, a manufacturer often gives trade, or functional, discounts. These reductions off the list or base price are offered to resellers in the channel of distribution on the basis of (1) where they are in the channel, and (2) the marketing activities they are expected to perform in the future.

Traditional trade discounts have been established in various product lines, such as hardware, food, and pharmaceutical items. Although the manufacturer may suggest the trade discounts shown in the example just cited, the sellers are free to alter the discount schedule depending on their competitive situation.

Cash Discounts   To encourage retailers to pay their bills quickly, manufacturers offer them cash discounts. Suppose a retailer receives a bill quoted at $1,000, 2/10 net 30. This means that the bill for the product is $1,000, but the retailer can take a 2 percent discount ($1,000 × 0.02 = $20) if payment is made within 10 days and send a cheque for $980. If the payment cannot be made within 10 days, the total amount of $1,000 is due within 30 days. It is usually understood by the buyer that an interest charge will be added after the first 30 days of free credit.

Retailers also provide cash discounts to consumers as well to eliminate the cost of credit granted. These discounts take the form of discount-for-cash policies. Canadian Tire is famous for its discount-for-cash policy, where consumers receive 3 percent off for cash purchases in the form of cash-bonus coupons that can be used against future purchases. And if you order a computer from Canada Computers.com, you will receive a 2 percent discount if you pay cash or by debit card.

Allowances

Allowances—like discounts—are reductions from list or quoted prices to buyers for performing some activity.

Trade-in Allowances   A new-car dealer can offer a substantial reduction in the list price of a new Toyota Camry by offering you a trade-in allowance of $500 for your Chevrolet. A trade-in allowance is a price reduction given when a used product is part of the payment on a new product. Trade-ins are an effective way to lower the price a buyer has to pay without formally reducing the list price.

Promotional Allowances   Sellers in the channel of distribution can qualify for *promotional allowances* for undertaking certain advertising or selling activities to promote a product. Various types of allowances include an actual cash payment or an extra amount of "free goods" (as with a free case of frozen pizzas to a retailer for every dozen cases purchased). Frequently, a portion of these savings is passed on to the consumer by retailers.

Some companies, such as Procter & Gamble, have chosen to reduce promotional allowances to retailers by using *everyday low pricing (EDLP)*. EDLP is the practice of replacing promotional allowances with lower manufacturer list prices. EDLP promises to reduce the average price to consumers while minimizing promotional allowances that cost manufacturers billions of dollars every year.

Geographical Adjustments

Geographical adjustments are made by manufacturers or even wholesalers to list or quoted prices to reflect the cost of transportation of the products from seller to buyer. The two general methods for quoting prices related to transportation costs are (1) FOB origin pricing, and (2) uniform delivered pricing.

- *FOB origin pricing.* FOB means "free on board" some vehicle at some location, which means the seller pays the cost of loading the product onto the vehicle that is used (such as a barge, railway car, or truck). *FOB origin pricing* usually involves the seller's naming the location of this loading as the seller's factory or warehouse (such as "FOB Toronto" or "FOB factory"). The title to the goods passes to the buyer at the point of loading, and so the buyer becomes responsible for picking the specific mode of transportation, for all the transportation costs, and for subsequent handling of the product. Buyers farthest from the seller face the big disadvantage of paying the higher transportation costs.
- *Uniform delivered pricing.* When a *uniform delivered pricing* method is used, the price the seller quotes includes all transportation costs. It is quoted in a contract as "FOB buyer's location," and the seller selects the mode of transportation, pays the freight charges, and is responsible for any damage that may occur because the seller retains title to the goods until delivered to the buyer.

LO6   Legal and Regulatory Aspects of Pricing

Arriving at a final price is clearly a complex process. The task is further complicated by legal and regulatory restrictions. Five pricing practices receive the most scrutiny: (1) price fixing, (2) price discrimination, (3) deceptive pricing, (4) predatory pricing, and (5) delivered pricing. As you know, the Competition Bureau is responsible for administrating the *Competition Act* in Canada, and this includes pricing practices of businesses. Check out the accompanying Going Online box to see recent price violations by Canadian and international companies and how the Competition Bureau handled these violations.

Price Fixing   A conspiracy among firms to set prices for a product is termed *price fixing.* Price fixing is illegal *per se* (in and of itself) under the *Competition Act.* When two or more competitors explicitly or implicitly set prices, this practice is called *horizontal price fixing.*

    Vertical price fixing involves controlling agreements between independent buyers and sellers (a manufacturer and a retailer) whereby sellers are required not to sell products below a minimum retail price. This practice, called *resale price maintenance,* is also illegal under the provisions of the *Competition Act.*

    It is important to recognize that a manufacturer's "suggested retail price" is not illegal *per se.* The issue of legality arises only when manufacturers enforce such a practice by coercion.

Price Discrimination   The *Competition Act* prohibits *price discrimination*—the practice of charging different prices to different buyers for goods of like grade and quality. The *Competition Act* also covers promotional allowances. To legally offer promotional allowances to buyers, sellers must do so on a proportionally equal basis to all buyers distributing the seller's products. In general, this rule of reason is applied frequently in price discrimination cases and is often applied to cases involving flexible pricing policies of firms. It is not easy to prove price discrimination has actually taken place, especially when firms practise flexible-price policies.

    Under the *Competition Act,* the legislation requires that there be a "practice" of price discrimination, implying more than one instance, or even two or three instances. However, some suggest that the use of flexible pricing may create the potential for some firms to engage in price discrimination. Even if the practice cannot be proven legally as price discrimination, there may be some ethical issues involved.

Deceptive Pricing   Price deals that mislead consumers fall into the category of deceptive pricing. Deceptive pricing is outlawed by the *Competition Act.* The five most common deceptive pricing practices are described in Figure 13–9. Over the past few

DECEPTIVE PRACTICE	DESCRIPTION
Bait and switch	A deceptive practice exists when a firm offers a very low price on a product (the bait) to attract customers to a store. Once in the store, the customer is persuaded to purchase a higher-priced item (the switch) using a variety of tricks, including (1) downgrading the promoted item, and (2) not having the item in stock or refusing to take orders for the item.
Bargains conditional on other purchases	This practice may exist when a buyer is offered "1-Cent Sales," "Buy 1, Get 1 Free," and "Get 2 for the Price of 1." Such pricing is legal only if the first items are sold at the regular price, not a price inflated for the offer. Substituting lower-quality items on either the first or second purchase is also considered deceptive.
Comparable value comparisons	Advertising, such as "Retail Value $100.00, Our Price $85.00," is deceptive if a verified and substantial number of stores in the market area did not price the item at $100.
Comparisons with suggested prices	A claim that a price is below a manufacturer's suggested or list price may be deceptive if few or no sales occur at that price in a retailer's market area.
Former price comparisons	When a seller represents a price as reduced, the item must have been offered in good faith at a higher price for a substantial previous period. Setting a high price for the purpose of establishing a reference for a price reduction is deceptive.

● **FIGURE 13-9**

Five most common deceptive pricing practices

years, companies from Newfoundland to British Columbia have been found guilty and fined for deceptive pricing practices. However, as you examine Figure 13–9, you should remember that it is often difficult for the government to police and enforce all of these laws. It is essential to rely on the ethical standards of those making and publicizing pricing decisions. To determine how the Competition Bureau deals with deceptive pricing practices, check the accompanying Going Online box, "Checking Out Price Violations."

Predatory Pricing Two types of predatory pricing are defined within the Competition Act. The first is called *geographic predatory pricing.* Sellers are prohibited from engaging in a policy of selling products or services in one region in Canada at a price lower than in another region with the intent or effect of lessening competition or of eliminating a competitior.

The second type of predatory pricing offence is committed when a business engages in a policy of selling products or services at "unreasonably low" prices in an attempt to substantially lessen competition. In many cases, the very low prices are designed to drive competitors out of business. Once competitors have been driven out, the firm raises its prices.

Delivered Pricing Delivered pricing is the practice of refusing a customer delivery of an article on the same trade terms as other customers in the same location. It is a non-criminal offence, but the Competition Tribunal can prohibit suppliers from engaging in such a practice.

learning review

11. Why would a seller choose a flexible-price policy over a one-price policy?

12. Which pricing practices are covered by the *Competition Act?*

Going Online

Checking Out Price Violations

As you have read in this chapter, the Competition Bureau is responsible for administering the *Competition Act* in Canada. Competition can be lessened and/or consumers can be harmed by unfair pricing practices. Visit the Competition Bureau's home page at **www.competitionbureau.gc.ca.** Go to the "Media Centre" section on the site and select "Announcements" to search through news releases.

1 What are the types of pricing violations involving Canadian and international companies reported on the site?
2 What types of penalties were imposed?
3 What is your opinion regarding these pricing violations?

LEARNING OBJECTIVES REVIEW

 Understand the nature and importance of pricing products and services.

Price is the money or other considerations exchanged for the ownership or use of a product service. Although price typically involves money, the amount exchanged is often different from the list or quoted price because of allowances and extra fees.

 Recognize the constraints on a firm's pricing latitude and the objectives a firm has in setting prices.

Pricing constraints, such as demand, product newness, costs, competitors, other products sold by the firm, and the type of competitive market, restrict a firm's pricing latitude. Pricing objectives may include profit, sales revenue, market share, unit volume, survival, or some socially responsible price level.

LO3 **Explain what a demand curve is and what price elasticity of demand means.**

A demand curve is a graph relating the quantity sold and price and shows the maximum number of product or service units that will be sold at given price. Three demand factors affect price: (*a*) consumer tastes, (*b*) price and availability of other products, and (*c*) consumer income. These demand factors determine consumers' willingness and ability to pay for products and services. Assuming these demand factors remain unchanged, when the price of a product is lowered or raised, the quantity demanded for it will increase or decrease, respectively. Price elasticity of demand measures the responsiveness of units of a product sold to a change in price, which is expressed as the percentage change in the quantity of a product demanded divided by the percentage change in price. It provides an indication of how sensitive consumer demand and the firm's revenue are to changes in the product's price.

 Perform a break-even analysis.

Break-even analysis shows the relationship between total revenue and total cost at various quantities of output for given conditions of price, fixed cost, and variable cost. At the break-even point, total revenue and total cost are equal.

 Understand approaches to pricing as well as factors considered to establish prices for products and services.

Four general approaches of finding an approximate price level for a product or service are demand-oriented, cost-oriented, profit-oriented, and competition-oriented pricing. Demand-oriented pricing stresses consumer demand; cost-oriented pricing emphasizes the costs aspects; profit-oriented pricing focuses on a balance between revenues and costs; and competition-oriented pricing stresses what competitors or the marketplace are doing. Demand, cost, profit, and competition influence the initial consideration of the price level for a product or service. To set list or quoted price, a marketer must also consider additional factors. First, the marketer must decide whether to follow a one-price policy or a flexible-price policy. And second, the marketer must consider the effects the proposed price will have on the company, customer, and competitors. Finally, list or quoted prices are often modified through discounts, allowances, and geographical adjustments.

 Describe basic laws and regulations affecting pricing practices.

Legal and regulatory issues in pricing focus on price fixing, price discrimination, deceptive pricing, predatory pricing, and delivered pricing. The *Competition Act* in Canada prohibits such practices.

FOCUSING ON KEY TERMS

above-, at-, or below-market pricing   p. 347
break-even analysis   p. 341
bundle pricing   p. 345
cost-plus pricing   p. 346

customary pricing   p. 347
demand curve   p. 339
experience curve pricing   p. 346
fixed cost   p. 341

APPLYING MARKETING KNOWLEDGE

1 How would the price equation apply to the purchase price of (a) gasoline, (b) an airline ticket, and (c) a chequing account?

2 What would be your response to the statement: "Profit maximization is the only legitimate pricing objective for the firm."

3 Touche Toiletries, Inc. has developed an addition to its Lizardman Cologne line tentatively branded Ode d'Toade Cologne. Unit variable costs are 45 cents for a 60-mL bottle, and heavy advertising expenditures in the first year would result in total fixed costs of $900,000. Ode d'Toade Cologne is priced at $7.50 for a 60-mL bottle. How many bottles of Ode d'Toade must be sold to break even?

4 Suppose that marketing executives for Touche Toiletries reduced the price to $6.50 for a 60-mL bottle of Ode d'Toade and the fixed costs were $1,000,000. Suppose further that the unit variable cost remained at 45 cents for a 60-mL bottle. (a) How many bottles must be sold to break even? (b) What dollar profit level would Ode d'Toade achieve if 200 000 bottles were sold?

5 Under what conditions would a digital camera manufacturer adopt a skimming price approach for a new product? A penetration approach?

6 What are some similarities and differences between skimming pricing, prestige pricing, and above-market pricing?

7 Suppose executive estimate that the unit variable costs for their DVD is $100, the fixed cost related to the product is $10 million, and the target volume for next year is 100,000 units. What sales price will be necessary to achieve a target profit of $1 million?

8 Suppose a manufacturer of exercise equipment sets a suggested price to the consumer of $395 for a particular piece of equipment to be competitive with similar equipment. The manufacturer sells its equipment to a sporting goods wholesaler who receives 25 percent of the selling price and a retailer who receives 50 percent of the selling price. What demand-oriented pricing approach is being used? And, at what price will the manufacturer sell the equipment to the wholesaler?

9 To examine the psychology of pricing, we want you to do the following. Take two identical plain plastic containers, label one Brand A and one Brand B. Fill them both with the same "low-priced" hand lotion. Now, go out and find some other students or shoppers. Tell them you are testing Brand A, a $2.99 hand lotion and Brand B, a $12.99 hand lotion. Ask them to compare Brand A and Brand B in terms of perceived quality and value and which one, if any, they prefer. Write up a short report indicating your findings. Did price influence the consumers' perception of the products or not?

Building Your Marketing Plan

In starting to set a final price:

1. List three pricing constraints and two pricing objectives.
2. Think about your customers and competitors and set three possible prices.
3. Assume a fixed cost and unit variable cost and
   (a) calculate the break-even points using the three possible prices, and (b) plot a break-even chart for the three prices (see Figure 13–7).

To arrive at the final price(s) for your offering(s):

1. Modify the three prices in light of (a) pricing considerations for demand-, cost-, profit-, and competition-oriented approaches; and (b) possibilities for discounts, allowances, and geographic adjustments.
2. Prepare another break-even given these modified prices.
3. Choose the final price(s).

Video Case 13

WASHBURN GUITARS: USING BREAK-EVEN POINTS TO MAKE PRICING DECISIONS

"We offer a guitar at every price point for every skill level," explains Kevin Lello, vice president of marketing at Washburn Guitars. Washburn is one of the most prestigious guitar manufacturers in the world, offering instruments that range from one-of-a-kind, custom-made acoustic and electric guitars and basses to less-expensive, mass-produced guitars. Lello has responsibility for marketing Washburn's products and ensuring that the price of each product matches the company's objectives related to sales, profit, and market share. "We do pay attention to break even points," adds Lello. "We need to know exactly how much a guitar costs us, and how much the overhead is for each guitar."

The Company

The modern Washburn Guitars company started in 1977 when a small firm bought the century-old Washburn brand name and a small inventory of guitars, parts, and promotional supplies. At that time, annual company sales of about 2,500 guitars generated revenues of $300,000. Washburn's first catalogue, appearing in 1978, told a frightening truth:

> Our designs are translated by Japan's most experienced craftsmen, assuring the consistent quality and craftsmanship for which they are known.

At that time, the North American guitar-making craft was at an all-time low. Guitars made by Japanese firms, such as Ibane and Yamaha, were in use by an increasing number of professionals.

Times have changed for Washburn. Today, the company sells about 50,000 guitars each year and annual revenues exceed $40 million. All this resulted from Washburn's aggressive marketing strategies to develop product lines with different price points targeted at musicians in distinctly different market segments.

The Products and Market Segments

One of Washburn's early successes was the trendsetting Festival Series of cutaway, thin-bodied flattops, with built-in bridge pickups and controls. This guitar became the standard for live performances as its popularity with rock and country stars increased. Over the years, several generations of musicians have used Washburn guitars. Early artists included Bob Dylan, Dolly Parton, Greg Allman, and the late George Harrison of the Beatles. In recent years, Mike Kennerty of the All American Rejects,

Rick Savage of Def Leppard, and Hugh McDonald of Bon Jovi have been among the many musicians who use Washburn products.

Until 1991, all Washburn guitars were manufactured in Asia. That year Washburn started building its high-end guitars in the United States. Today, Washburn marketing executives divide its product line into four categories to appeal to different market segments. From high end to low end these categories are:

- One-of-a-kind, custom instruments
- Batch-custom instruments
- Mass-customized instruments
- Mass-produced instruments

The one-of-a-kind custom products appeal to the many stars who use Washburn instruments as well as collectors. The batch-custom products appeal to professional musicians. The mass-customized products appeal to musicians with intermediate skill levels who may not yet be professionals. Finally, the mass-produced units are targeted at first-time buyers and are still manufactured in Asian factories.

Pricing Issues

Setting prices for its various lines presents a continuing challenge for Washburn. Not only do the prices have to reflect the changing tastes of its various segments of musicians, but the prices must also be competitive with the prices of other guitars manufactured and marketed globally. The price elasticity of demand, or price sensitivity, for Washburn's products varies between its segments. To reduce the price sensitivity for some of its products Washburn uses endorsements by internationally known musicians who play its instruments and lend their names to lines of Washburn signature guitars. Stars playing Washburn guitars such as Nuno Bettencourt, formerly of Extreme and Population 1; Paul Stanley of KISS; Scott Ian of Anthrax; and Dan Donegan of Disturbed have their own lines of signature guitars—the batch-custom units mentioned earlier. These guitars receive excellent reviews. *Total Guitar* magazine, for example, recently said, "If you want a truly original axe that has been built with great attention to detail . . . then the Washburn Maya Pro DD75 could be the one."

Bill Abel, Washburn's vice president of sales, is responsible for reviewing and approving prices for the company's lines of guitars. Setting a sales target of 2,000 units for a new line of guitars, he is considering a suggested retail price of $349 per unit for customers at one of the hundreds of retail outlets carrying the Washburn line. For planning purposes, Abel estimates half of the final retail price will be the price Washburn nets when it sells its guitar to the wholesalers and dealers in its channel of distribution.

Looking at Washburn's financial data for its present plant, Abel estimates that this line of guitars must bear these fixed costs:

Rent and taxes	= $14,000
Depreciation of equipment	= $ 4,000
Management and quality control program	= $20,000

In addition, he estimates the variable costs for each unit to be:

Direct materials	= $25/unit
Direct labour	= 15 hours/unit @$8/hour

Carefully kept production records at Washburn's plant make Abel believe that these are reasonable estimates. He explains, "Before we begin a production run, we have a good feel for what our costs will be. The domestically built N-4, for example, simply costs more than one of our foreign-produced electrics."

Caught in the global competition for guitar sales, Washburn continually searches for ways to reduce and control costs. For example, Washburn recently purchased Parker Guitar, another guitar manufacturer that designed products for professionals and collectors, and will combine the two production facilities in a new location. Washburn expects the acquisition to lower its fixed and variable costs. Specifically, Washburn projects that its new factory location will reduce its rent and taxes expense by 40 percent, and the new skilled employees will reduce the hours of work needed for each unit by 15 percent.

By managing the prices of its products, Washburn also helps its dealers and retailers. In fact, Abel believes it is another reason for Washburn's success: "We have excellent relationships with the independent retailers. They're our lifeblood, and our outlet to sell our product. We sell through chains and online dealers, but it's the independent dealer that sells the guitars. So we take a smaller margin from them because they have to do more work. They appreciate it, and they go the extra mile for us."

Questions

1 What factors are most likely to affect the demand for the lines of Washburn guitars (*a*) bought by a first-time guitar buyer and (*b*) bought by a sophisticated musician who wants a signature model?

2 For Washburn, what are examples of (*a*) shifting the demand curve to the right to get a higher price for a guitar line (movement of the demand curve) and (*b*) pricing decisions involving moving along a demand curve?

3 In Washburn's factory, what is the break-even point for the new line of guitars if the retail price is (*a*) $349, (*b*) $389, and (*c*) $309? Also, (*d*) if Washburn achieves the sales target of 2,000 units at the $349 retail price, what will its profit be?

4 Assume that the merger with Parker leads to the cost reductions projected in the case. Then, what will be the (*a*) new break-even point at a $349 retail price for this line of guitars and (*b*) new profit if it sells 2,000 units?

5 If for competitive reasons, Washburn eventually has to move all its production back to Asia, (*a*) which specific fixed and variable costs might be lowered and (*b*) what additional fixed and variable costs might it expect to incur?

Financial Aspects
of Marketing

Basic concepts from accounting and finance provide valuable tools for marketing executives. This appendix describes an actual company's use of accounting and financial concepts and illustrates how they assist the owner in making marketing decisions.

THE CAPLOW COMPANY

An accomplished artist and calligrapher, Jane Westerlund, decided to apply some of her experience to the picture framing business. She bought an existing retail frame store, The Caplow Company, from a friend who owned the business and wanted to retire. She avoided the do-it-yourself end of the framing business and chose three kinds of business activities: (1) cutting the frame, mats, and glass for customers who brought in their own pictures or prints to be framed; (2) selling prints and posters that she had purchased from wholesalers; and (3) restoring high-quality frames and paintings.

To understand how accounting, finance, and marketing relate to each other, let us analyze (1) the operating statement for her frame shop, (2) some general ratios of interest that are derived from the operating statement, and (3) some ratios that pertain specifically to her pricing decisions.

The Operating Statement

The *operating statement* (also called an *income statement* or *profit-and-loss statement*) summarizes the profitability of a business firm for a specific time period, usually a month, quarter, or year. The title of the operating statement for The Caplow Company shows it is for a one-year period (Figure B–1). The purpose of an operating statement is to show the profit of the firm and the revenues and expenses that led to that profit. This information tells the owner or manager what has happened in the past and suggests actions to improve future profitability.

The left side of Figure B–1 shows that there are three key elements to all operating statements: (1) sales of the firm's goods and services, (2) costs incurred in making and selling the goods and services, and (3) profit or loss, which is the difference between sales and costs.

Sales Elements   The sales element of Figure B–1 has four terms that need explanation:

- *Gross sales* are the total amount billed to customers. Dissatisfied customers or errors may reduce the gross sales through returns or allowances.
- *Returns* occur when a customer gives the item purchased back to the seller, who either refunds the purchase price or allows the customer a credit on subsequent purchases. In any event, the seller now owns the item again.
- *Allowances* are given when a customer is dissatisfied with the item purchased and the seller reduces the original purchase price. Unlike returns, in the case of allowances the buyer owns the item.
- *Net sales* are simply gross sales minus returns and allowances.

The operating statement for The Caplow Company shows the following:

Gross sales	$80,500
Less: Returns and allowances	$ 500
Net sales	$80,000

The low level of returns and allowances shows the shop generally has done a good job in satisfying customers, which is essential in building the repeat business necessary for success.

Cost Elements   The *cost of goods sold* is the total cost of the products sold during the period. This item varies according to the kind of business. A retail store purchases finished goods and resells them to customers without reworking them in any way. In contrast, a manufacturing firm combines raw and semi-finished materials and parts,

● **FIGURE B–1**

Example of an operating statement

THE CAPLOW COMPANY

Operating Statement
For the Year Ending December 31, 2010

Sales	Gross sales			$80,500
	Less: Returns and allowances			500
	Net sales			$80,000
Costs	Cost of goods sold:			
	Beginning inventory at cost		$ 6,000	
	Purchases at billed cost	$21,000		
	Less: Purchase discounts	300		
	Purchases at net cost	20,700		
	Plus freight-in	100		
	Net cost of delivered purchases		20,800	
	Direct labour (framing)		14,200	
	Cost of goods available for sale		41,000	
	Less: Ending inventory at cost		5,000	
	Cost of goods sold			36,000
	Gross margin (gross profit)			$44,000
	Expenses:			
	Selling expenses:			
	Sales salaries	2,000		
	Advertising expense	3,000		
	Total selling expense		5,000	
	Administrative expenses:			
	Owner's salary	18,000		
	Bookkeeper's salary	1,200		
	Office supplies	300		
	Total administrative expense		19,500	
	General expenses:			
	Depreciation expense	1,000		
	Interest expense	500		
	Rent expense	2,100		
	Utility expenses (heat, electricity)	3,000		
	Repairs and maintenance	2,300		
	Insurance	2,000		
	Canada Pension Plan	2,200		
	Total general expense		13,100	
	Total expenses			37,600
Profit or loss	Profit before taxes			$ 6,400

uses labour and overhead to rework these into finished goods, and then sells them to customers. All these activities are reflected in the cost of goods sold item on a manufacturer's operating statement. Note that the frame shop has some features of a pure retailer (prints and posters it buys that are resold without alteration) and some of a pure manufacturer (assembling the raw materials of moulding, matting, and glass to form a completed frame).

Some terms that relate to cost of goods sold need clarification:

- *Inventory* is the physical material that is purchased from suppliers, may or may not be reworked, and is available for sale to customers. In the frame shop, inventory includes moulding, matting, glass, prints, and posters.
- *Purchase discounts* are reductions in the original billed price for such reasons as prompt payment of the bill or the quantity bought.
- *Direct labour* is the cost of the labour used in producing the finished product. For the frame shop, this is the cost of producing the completed frames from the moulding, matting, and glass.

• *Gross margin (gross profit)* is the money remaining to manage the business, sell the products or services, and give some profit. Gross margin is net sales minus cost of goods sold.

The two right-hand columns in Figure B–1 between "Net sales" and "Gross margin" calculate the cost of goods sold:

Net sales		$80,000
Cost of goods sold		
Beginning inventory at cost	$ 6,000	
Net cost of delivered purchases	20,800	
Direct labour (framing)	14,200	
Cost of goods available for sale	41,000	
Less: ending inventory at cost	5,000	
Cost of goods sold		36,000
Gross margin (gross profit)		$44,000

This section considers the beginning and ending inventories, the net cost of purchases delivered during the year, and the cost of the direct labour going into making the frames. Subtracting the $36,000 cost of goods sold from the $80,000 net sales gives the $44,000 gross margin.

Three major categories of expenses are shown in Figure B–1 below the gross margin:

• *Selling expenses* are the costs of selling the product or service produced by the firm. For The Caplow Company, there are two such selling expenses: sales salaries of part-time employees waiting on customers, and the advertising expense of simple newspaper ads and direct-mail ads sent to customers.

• *Administrative expenses* are the costs of managing the business and, for The Caplow Company, include three expenses: the owner's salary, a part-time bookkeeper's salary, and office supplies expense.

• *General expenses* are miscellaneous costs not covered elsewhere; for the frame shop, these include seven items: depreciation expense (on her equipment), interest expense, rent expense, utility expense, repair and maintenance expense, insurance expense, and employment insurance and Canada Pension Plan.

As shown in Figure B–1, selling, administrative, and general expenses total $37,600 for The Caplow Company.

Profit Element What the company has earned, the *profit before taxes,* is found by subtracting cost of goods sold and expenses from net sales. For The Caplow Company, Figure B–1 shows that profit before taxes is $6,400.

General Operating Ratios to Analyze Operations

Looking only at the elements of The Caplow Company's operating statement that extend to the right column highlights the firm's performance on some important dimensions. Using operating ratios, such as *expense-to-sales ratios,* for expressing basic expense or profit elements as a percentage of net sales gives further insights:

ELEMENT IN OPERATING STATEMENT	DOLLAR VALUE	PERCENTAGE OF NET SALES
Gross sales	$80,500	
Less: Returns and allowances	500	100%
Net sales	80,000	
Less: Cost of goods sold	36,000	45
Gross margin	44,000	55
Less: Total expenses	37,600	47
Profit (or loss) before taxes	$ 6,000	8%

Westerlund can use this information to compare her firm's performance in one time period with that in the next. To do so, it is especially important that she keep the same definitions for each element of her operating statement, also a significant factor in using the electronic spreadsheets discussed in Chapter 13. Performance comparisons between periods are more difficult if she changes definitions for the accounting elements in the operating statement.

She can use either the dollar values or the operating ratios (the value of the element of the operating statement divided by net sales) to analyze the firm's performance. However, the operating ratios are more valuable than the dollar values for two reasons: (1) the simplicity of working with percentages rather than dollars, and (2) the availability of operating ratios of typical firms in the same industry, which are published by Dun & Bradstreet and trade associations. Thus, Westerlund can compare her firm's performance not only with that of *other* frame shops but also with that of *small* frame shops that have annual net sales, for example, of under $100,000. In this way, she can identify where her operations are better or worse than other similar firms. For example, if trade association data showed a typical frame shop of her size had a ratio of cost of goods sold to net sales of 37 percent, compared with her 45 percent, she might consider steps to reduce this cost through purchase discounts, reducing inbound freight charges, finding lower-cost suppliers, and so on.

Ratios to Use in Setting and Evaluating Price

Using The Caplow Company as an example, we can study four ratios that relate closely to setting a price: (1) markup, (2) markdown, (3) stockturns, and (4) return on investment. These terms are defined in Figure B–2 and explained below.

Markup   Both markup and gross margin refer to the amount added to the cost of goods sold to arrive at the selling price, and they may be expressed either in dollar or percentage terms. However, the term *markup* is more commonly used in setting retail prices. Suppose the average price Westerlund charges for a framed picture is $80. Then, in terms of the first two definitions in Figure B–2 and the earlier information from the operating statement,

ELEMENT OF PRICE	DOLLAR VALUE
Cost of goods sold	$36
Markup (or gross margin)	44
Selling price	$80

The third definition in Figure B–2 gives the percentage markup on selling price:

$$\text{Markup on selling price (\%)} = \frac{\text{Markup}}{\text{Selling price}} \times 100$$

$$= \frac{44}{00} \times 100 = 55\%$$

And the percentage markup on cost is obtained as follows:

$$\text{Markup on cost (\%)} = \frac{\text{Markup}}{\text{Cost of goods cold}} \times 100$$

$$= \frac{44}{36} \times 100 = 122.2\%$$

Inexperienced retail clerks sometimes fail to distinguish between the two definitions of markup, which (as the preceding calculations show) can represent a tremendous difference, and so it is essential to know whether the base is cost or selling price. Marketers generally use selling price as the base for talking about "markups" unless they specifically state that they are using cost as a base.

NAME OF FINANCIAL ELEMENT OR RATIO	WHAT IT MEASURES	EQUATION
Selling price ($)	Price customer sees	Cost of goods sold (COGS) + Markup
Markup ($)	Dollars added to COGS to arrive at selling price	Selling price − COGS
Markup on selling price (%)	Relates markup to selling price	$\dfrac{\text{Markup}}{\text{Selling price}} \times 100 = \dfrac{\text{Selling price} - \text{COGS}}{\text{Selling price}} \times 100$
Markup on cost (%)	Relates markup to cost	$\dfrac{\text{Markup}}{\text{COGS}} \times 100 = \dfrac{\text{Selling price} - \text{COGS}}{\text{COGS}} \times 100$
Markdown (%)	Ability of firm to sell its products at initial selling price	$\dfrac{\text{Markdowns}}{\text{Net Sales}} \times 100$
Stockturn rate	Ability of firm to move its inventory quickly	$\dfrac{\text{COGS}}{\text{Average inventory at cost}}$ or $\dfrac{\text{Net Sales}}{\text{Average inventory at selling price}}$
Return on investment (%)	Profit performance of firm compared with money invested in it	$\dfrac{\text{Net profit after taxes}}{\text{Investment}} \times 100$

● **FIGURE B–2**

How to calculate selling price, markup, markdown, stockturn, and return on investment

Retailers and wholesalers that rely heavily on markup pricing (discussed in Chapter 14) often use standardized tables that convert markup on selling price to markup on cost, and vice versa. The two equations below show how to convert one to the other:

$$\text{Markup on selling price (\%)} = \frac{\text{Markup on cost (\%)}}{100\% + \text{Markup on cost (\%)}}$$

$$\text{Markup on cost (\%)} = \frac{\text{Markup on selling price (\%)}}{100\% - \text{Markup on selling price (\%)}}$$

Using the data from The Caplow Company gives the following:

$$\text{Markup on selling price (\%)} = \frac{\text{Markup on cost (\%)}}{100\% + \text{Markup on cost (\%)}} \times 100$$

$$= \frac{122.2}{100 + 122.2} \times 100 = 55\%$$

$$\text{Markup on cost (\%)} = \frac{\text{Markup on selling price (\%)}}{100\% - \text{Markup on selling price (\%)}} \times 100$$

$$= \frac{55}{100} - 55 \times 100 = 122.2\%$$

The use of an incorrect markup base is shown in Westerlund's business. A markup of 122.2 percent on her cost of goods sold for a typical frame she sells gives 122.2% × $36 = $44 of markup. Added to the $36 cost of goods sold, this gives her a selling price of $80 for the framed picture. However, a new clerk working for her who erroneously priced the framed picture at 55 percent of cost of goods sold set the final price at $55.80 ($36 of cost of goods sold plus 55% × $36 × $19.80). The error, if repeated, can be disastrous: Frames would be mistakenly sold at $55.80, or $24.20 below the intended selling price of $80.

Markdown   A markdown is a reduction in a retail price that is necessary if the item will not sell at the full selling price to which it has been marked up. The item might not sell for a variety of reasons: The selling price was set too high or the item is out of style or has become soiled or damaged. The seller "takes a markdown" by lowering the price to sell it, thereby converting it to cash to buy future inventory that will sell faster.

The markdown percentage cannot be calculated directly from the operating statement. As shown in the fifth item of Figure B–2, the numerator of the markdown percentage is the total dollar markdowns. Markdowns are reductions in the prices of goods that are purchased by customers. The denominator is net sales.

Suppose that The Caplow Company had a total of $700 in markdowns on the prints and posters that are stocked and available for sale. Because the frames are custom made for individual customers, there is little reason for a markdown there. Caplow's markdown percentage then is as follows:

$$
\begin{aligned}
\text{Markdown (\%)} &= \frac{\text{Markdown}}{\text{Net sales}} \times 100 \\
&= \frac{\$700}{\$80,000} \times 100 \\
&= 0.875\%
\end{aligned}
$$

Other kinds of retailers often have markdown ratios several times this amount. For example, women's dress stores have markdowns of about 25 percent, and menswear stores have markdowns of about 2 percent.

Stockturn Rate   A business firm is anxious to have its inventory move quickly, or "turn over." Stockturn rate, or simply stockturns, measures this inventory movement. For a retailer, a slow stockturn rate may show it is buying merchandise customers do not want, and so this is a critical measure of performance. When a firm sells only a single product, one convenient way to measure stockturn rate is simply to divide its cost of goods sold by average inventory at cost. The sixth item in Figure B–2 shows how to calculate stockturn rate using information in the following operating statement:

$$
\text{Stockturn rate} = \frac{\text{Cost of goods sold}}{\text{Average inventory at cost}}
$$

The dollar amount of average inventory at cost is calculated by adding the beginning and ending inventories for the year and dividing by 2 to get the average. From Caplow's operating statement, we have the following:

$$
\begin{aligned}
\text{Stockturn rate} &= \frac{\text{Cost of goods sold}}{\text{Average inventory at cost}} \\
&= \frac{\text{Cost of goods sold}}{\dfrac{\text{Beginning inventory + Ending inventory}}{2}} \\
&= \frac{\$36,000}{\dfrac{\$6,000 + \$5,000}{2}} \\
&= \frac{\$36,000}{\$5,500} \\
&= 6.5 \text{ stockturns per year}
\end{aligned}
$$

What is considered a "good stockturn" varies by the kind of industry. For example, supermarkets have limited shelf space for thousands of new products from manufacturers each year, and so they watch stockturn carefully by product line. The stockturn rate in supermarkets for breakfast foods is about 17 times per year, for pet food about 22 times, and for paper products about 25 times per year.

Return on Investment   A better measure of the performance of a firm than the amount of profit it makes in a year is its ROI, which is the ratio of net income to the investment used to earn that net income. To calculate ROI, it is necessary to subtract income taxes from profit before taxes to obtain net income, and then divide this figure by the investment that can be found on a firm's balance sheet (another accounting statement that shows the firm's assets, liabilities, and net worth). While financial and accounting experts have many definitions for "investment," an often-used definition is "total assets."

For our purposes, let us assume that Westerlund has total assets (investment) of $20,000 in The Caplow Company, which covers inventory, store fixtures, and framing equipment. If she pays $1,000 in income taxes, her store's net income is $5,400, and so her ROI is given by the seventh item in Figure B–2:

$$\text{Return on investment} = \text{Net incomes/investment} \times 100$$
$$= \$5,400/\$20,000 \times 100$$
$$= 27\%$$

If Westerlund wants to improve her ROI next year, the strategies she might take are found in this alternative equation for ROI:

$$\text{ROI} = \text{Net sales/investment} \times \text{Net income/net sales}$$
$$= \text{Investment turnover} \times \text{Profit margin}$$

This equation suggests that The Caplow Company's ROI can be improved by raising turnover or increasing profit margin. Increasing stockturns will accomplish the former, whereas lowering cost of goods sold to net sales will cause the latter.

Managing Marketing Channels and Supply Chains

APPLE STORES: CREATING A HIGH-TOUCH CUSTOMER EXPERIENCE IN A HIGH-TECH MARKETING CHANNEL

Apple thrives on innovation . . . in retailing. Yes, retailing! In a short seven-year span, Apple stores have become the gold standard for delivering an unparalleled customer experience. So how did Apple do it?

The vision behind Apple stores was to develop an atmosphere where consumers can experience the thrill of owning and using Apple's complete line of Macintosh computers and an array of digital cameras, camcorders, the entire iPod product family, and more with the assistance of a knowledgeable and customer-friendly staff. In the words of Apple CEO Steven Jobs, Apple stores were to deliver "a buying experience as good as our products." And so it has.

"Apple has changed people's expectations of what retail should be about," says Candace Corlett, a retailing consultant. Product assortments are arranged by customer interests, not product type. Apple products are easily accessible to encourage a customer to "test-drive" them in a shopping environment where clutter is conspicuously absent. Each store's interior design is ultra-modern with a pristine layout and inviting displays. In newer stores, checkout counters have been replaced with Easy Pay, an Apple system that allows salespeople to wander the store with a wireless credit card reader and ask, "Would you like to pay for that?"

But there is more. The customer experience is enhanced with novel in-store features and services. For example, stores contain a Genius Bar

learning objectives

After reading this chapter, you should be able to:

 LO1 Explain what is meant by a marketing channel of distribution and why intermediaries are often needed.

LO2 Distinguish among traditional marketing channels, electronic marketing channels, multichannel distribution, and different types of vertical marketing systems.

LO3 Describe factors considered by marketing executives when selecting and managing a marketing channel.

LO4 Recognize how conflict, cooperation, and legal considerations affect marketing channels' relationships.

LO5 Recognize the relationship among marketing channels, logistics, and supply chain management, and how a company's supply chain aligns with its marketing strategy.

LO6 Identify the major logistics costs and customer service factors that managers consider when making supply chain decisions.

LO7 Describe the key logistics functions in a supply chain.

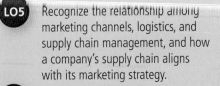

where customers can obtain product information and service on all Apple products from genial technical experts. And Apple also offers a concierge service that enables you to set a personal shopping experience with an Apple specialist.

Has the focus on an innovative customer experience paid off? Apple stores achieved $1 billion in sales faster than any retail business in history, taking just three years to reach that mark. Now, sales exceed $2 billion and the average store generates more than $26 million in annual sales with more than 170 million customers visiting the stores last year. Most importantly, the more-than-270 company-owned stores, including more than a dozen in Canada, are profitable.[1]

This chapter focuses on marketing channels of distribution and supply chains and their importance for marketing success. You will discover that it makes no sense to have good products, like those found in Apple Stores, if they are not accessible to the customer where and when they want them. Most importantly, you'll learn that managing marketing channels and supply chains is extremely important If you really want to deliver an excellent customer experience.

NATURE AND IMPORTANCE OF MARKETING CHANNELS

Reaching prospective buyers, either directly or indirectly, is a prerequisite for successful marketing. At the same time, buyers benefit from distribution systems used by firms.

Defining Marketing Channels of Distribution

marketing channel
Individuals and firms involved in the process of making a product or service available for use or consumption by consumers or industrial users.

You see the results of distribution every day. You may have purchased Lay's Potato Chips at Mac's Milk, a book through Chapters.Indigo.ca, and Levi's jeans at Sears. Each of these items was brought to you by a marketing channel of distribution, or simply a **marketing channel,** which consists of individuals and firms involved in the process of making a product or service available for use or consumption by consumers or industrial users.

Marketing channels can be compared with a pipeline through which water flows from a source to a terminus. Marketing channels make possible the flow of goods from a producer, through intermediaries, to a buyer. Intermediaries go by various names (Figure 14–1) and perform various functions.[2] Some intermediaries actually purchase items from the seller, store them, and resell them to buyers. For example, Sunshine Biscuits produces cookies and sells them to food wholesalers. The wholesalers then sell the cookies to supermarkets and grocery stores, which, in turn, sell them to consumers. Other intermediaries, such as brokers and agents, represent sellers but do not actually take title to products—their role is to bring a seller and buyer together. Century 21 real estate agents are examples of this type of intermediary. The importance of intermediaries is made even clearer when we consider the functions they perform and the value they create for buyers.

Value Created by Intermediaries

Few consumers appreciate the value created by intermediaries. However, producers recognize that intermediaries make selling goods and services more efficient because they minimize the number of sales contacts necessary to reach a target market. Figure 14–2 shows a simple example of how this comes about in the digital camera industry. Without a retail intermediary (such as Future Shop), Kodak, Sony, Panasonic,

TERM   DESCRIPTION

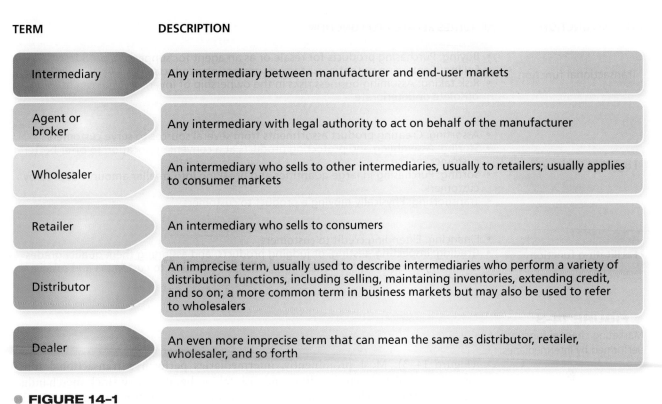

Intermediary	Any intermediary between manufacturer and end-user markets
Agent or broker	Any intermediary with legal authority to act on behalf of the manufacturer
Wholesaler	An intermediary who sells to other intermediaries, usually to retailers; usually applies to consumer markets
Retailer	An intermediary who sells to consumers
Distributor	An imprecise term, usually used to describe intermediaries who perform a variety of distribution functions, including selling, maintaining inventories, extending credit, and so on; a more common term in business markets but may also be used to refer to wholesalers
Dealer	An even more imprecise term that can mean the same as distributor, retailer, wholesaler, and so forth

● **FIGURE 14–1**

Terms used for marketing intermediaries

Source: American Marketing Association. Used by permission.

and Hewlett-Packard would each have to make four contacts to reach the four buyers shown, who are in the target market. However, each producer has to make only one contact when Future Shop acts as an intermediary. Equally important from a macro-marketing perspective, the total number of industry transactions is reduced from 16 to 8, which reduces producer cost and hence benefits the consumer.

Functions Performed by Intermediaries   Intermediaries make possible the flow of products from producers to buyers by performing three basic functions

● **FIGURE 14–2**

How intermediaries minimize transactions

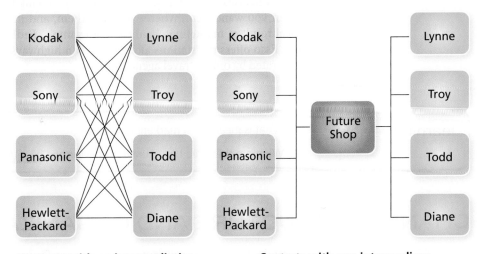

Contacts with no intermediaries
4 producers x 4 buyers = 16 contacts

Contacts with one intermediary
4 producers + 4 buyers = 8 contacts

TYPE OF FUNCTION	ACTIVITIES RELATED TO FUNCTION
Transactional function	• Buying: Purchasing products for resale or as an agent for supply of a product • Selling: Contacting potential customers, promoting products, and soliciting orders • Risk taking: Assuming business risks in the ownership of inventory that can become obsolete or deteriorate
Logistical function	• Assorting: Creating product assortments from several sources to serve customers • Storing: Assembling and protecting products at a convenient location to offer better customer service • Sorting: Purchasing in large quantities and breaking into smaller amounts desired by customers • Transporting: Physically moving a product to customers
Facilitating function	• Financing: Extending credit to customers • Grading: Inspecting, testing, or judging products, and assigning them quality grades • Marketing information and research: Providing information to customers and suppliers, including competitive conditions and trends

◉ FIGURE 14–3

Marketing channel functions performed by intermediaries

(Figure 14–3). Most prominently, intermediaries perform a transactional function that involves buying, selling, and risk taking because they stock merchandise in anticipation of sales. Intermediaries perform a logistical function evident in the gathering, storing, and dispersing of products. Finally, intermediaries perform facilitating functions, which assist producers in making goods and services more attractive to buyers.

All three functions must be performed in a marketing channel, even though each channel member may not participate in all three. Channel members often negotiate about which specific functions they will perform. Sometimes disagreements result, and a breakdown in relationships among channel members occurs. This happened recently when PepsiCo's bottler in Venezuela switched to Coca-Cola. Because all marketing channel functions had to be performed, PepsiCo either had to set up its own bottling operation to perform the marketing channel functions or find another bottler, which it did.[3]

Consumer Benefits from Intermediaries

Consumers also benefit from intermediaries. Having the goods and services you want, when you want them, where you want them, and in the form you want is the ideal result of marketing channels. For example, FedEx provides next-morning delivery, Esso offers gas stations along Canadian highways, and airlines allow tickets to be generated by online travel agencies.

learning review	**1.** What is meant by a marketing channel?
	2. What are the three basic functions performed by intermediaries?

CHANNEL STRUCTURE AND ORGANIZATION

A product can take many routes on its journey from a producer to buyers, and marketers search for the most efficient route from the many alternatives available.

Marketing Channels for Consumer Goods and Services

Figure 14-4 shows the four most common marketing channels for consumer goods and services. It also shows the number of levels in each marketing channel, as evidenced by the number of intermediaries between a producer and ultimate buyers. As the number of intermediaries between a producer and buyer increases, the channel is viewed as increasing in length. Thus, the producer → wholesaler → retailer → consumer channel is longer than the producer → consumer channel.

Channel A represents a **direct channel** because a producer and ultimate consumers deal directly with each other. Many products and services are distributed this way. A number of insurance companies sell their financial services using a direct channel and branch sales offices, and World Book sells its encyclopedias direct to consumers. Schwan's Home Service markets a full line of frozen foods using door-to-door salespeople who sell to customers from refrigerated trucks. Because there are no intermediaries with a direct channel, the producer must perform all channel functions.

The remaining three channel forms are considered **indirect channels** because intermediaries are inserted between the producer and consumers and perform numerous channel functions. Channel B, with a retailer added, is most common when a retailer is large and can buy in large quantities from a producer, or when the cost of inventory makes it too expensive to use a wholesaler. Such manufacturers as General Motors and Ford use this channel, and a local car dealer acts as a retailer. Why is there no wholesaler? So many variations exist in the product that it would be impossible for a wholesaler to stock all the models required to satisfy buyers; in addition, the cost of maintaining an inventory would be too high. However, large retailers, such as Sears Canada, Zellers, and The Bay, buy in sufficient quantities to make it cost effective for a producer to deal with only a retail intermediary.

Adding a wholesaler in Channel C is most common for low-cost, low-unit-value items that are frequently purchased by consumers, such as candy, confectionary items, and magazines. For example, Mars sells its line of candies to wholesalers in case quantities; wholesalers can then break down (sort) the cases so that individual retailers can order in boxes or much smaller quantities.

Channel D, the most indirect channel, is employed when there are many small manufacturers and many small retailers and an agent is used to help coordinate a

direct channel

A marketing channel where a producer and ultimate consumers deal directly with each other.

indirect channel

A marketing channel where intermediaries are inserted between the producer and consumers and perform numerous channel functions.

● **FIGURE 14–4**

Common marketing channels for consumer goods and services

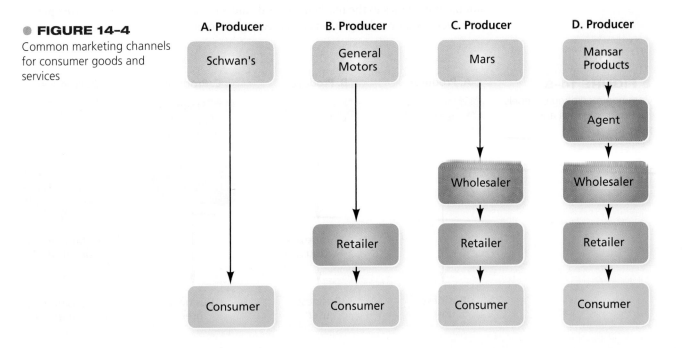

large supply of the product. Mansar Products, Ltd. is a Belgian producer of specialty jewellery that uses agents to sell to wholesalers, which then sell to many small retailers.

Marketing Channels for Business Goods and Services

The four most common channels for business goods and services are shown in Figure 14–5. In contrast to channels for consumer products, business channels typically are shorter and rely on one intermediary or none at all because business users are fewer in number, tend to be more concentrated geographically, and buy in larger quantities (see Chapter 6).

Channel A, represented by IBM's large, mainframe computer business, is a direct channel. Firms using this channel maintain their own salesforce and perform all channel functions. This channel is employed when buyers are large and well defined, the sales effort requires extensive negotiations, and the products are of high unit value and require hands-on expertise in terms of installation or use.

Channels B, C, and D are indirect channels with one or more intermediaries to reach business customers. In Channel B, a **business distributor** performs a variety of marketing channel functions, including selling, stocking, and delivering a full product assortment and financing. In many ways, business distributors are like wholesalers in consumer channels. Caterpillar relies on business distributors to sell its construction and mining equipment in over 200 countries. In addition to selling, Caterpillar distributors stock 40,000 to 50,000 parts, and service equipment using highly trained technicians.[4]

Channel C introduces a second intermediary, an *agent,* who serves primarily as the independent selling arm of producers and represents a producer to industrial users. For example, Stake Fastener Company, a producer of industrial fasteners, has an agent call on business customers rather than employing its own salesforce.

Channel D is the longest channel and includes both agents and distributors. For instance, Culligan, a producer of water treatment equipment, uses agents to call on distributors, who sell to business customers.

Electronic Marketing Channels

These common marketing channels for consumer and business goods and services are not the only routes to the marketplace. Advances in electronic commerce have opened new avenues for reaching buyers and creating customer value.

business distributor

Performs a variety of marketing channel functions, including selling, stocking, delivering a full product assortment, and financing for business goods and services.

● **FIGURE 14–5**

Common marketing channels for business goods and services

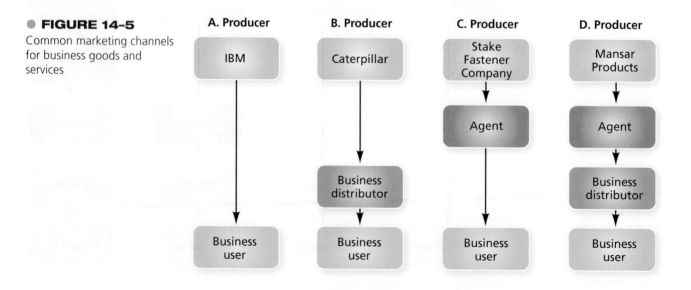

electronic marketing channels

Employ the Internet to make goods and services available for consumption or use by consumers or business buyers.

Interactive electronic technology has made possible **electronic marketing channels** that employ the Internet to make goods and services available for consumption or use by consumers or business buyers. A unique feature of these channels is that they combine electronic and traditional intermediaries to create value for buyers.[5]

Figure 14–6 shows the electronic marketing channels for books (Amazon.ca), automobiles (Cars4u.com), reservation services (Travelocity.ca), and personal computers (Dell.ca). Are you surprised that they look a lot like the common marketing channels? An important reason for the similarity resides in channel functions detailed in Figure 14–3. Electronic intermediaries can and do perform transactional and facilitating functions effectively and at a relatively lower cost than traditional intermediaries because of efficiencies made possible by information technology. However, electronic intermediaries are incapable of performing elements of the logistical function, particularly for such products as books and automobiles. This function remains with traditional intermediaries or with the producer, as evident with Dell, Inc. and its direct channel.

Many services can be distributed through electronic marketing channels, such as travel reservation marketed by Travelocity.ca, financial securities by Scotia iTRADE, and insurance by MetLife.ca. Software, too, can be marketed this way. However, many other services, such as health care and auto repair, still involve traditional intermediaries.

Direct Marketing Channels

direct marketing channels

Allow consumers to buy products by interacting with various advertising media without a face-to-face meeting with a salesperson.

Many firms also use direct marketing channels to reach buyers. **Direct marketing channels** allow consumers to buy products by interacting with various advertising media without a face-to-face meeting with a salesperson. Direct marketing includes mail-order selling, direct-mail sales, catalogue sales, telemarketing, interactive media, and televised home shopping.[6]

Some firms sell products almost entirely through direct marketing channels. These firms include L.L. Bean (apparel) and Dell.ca (personal computers). Such manufacturers as Nestlé and Sunkist, in addition to using traditional channels composed of wholesalers and retailers, employ direct marketing through catalogues and telemarketing to reach more buyers. At the same time, such retailers as Sears Canada use direct marketing techniques to augment conventional store merchandising activities. Some experts believe that direct marketing accounts for 20 percent of all retail transactions in North America and 10 percent of retail transactions in Europe. Direct marketing is covered in greater depth in Chapter 16.

● **FIGURE 14–6**

Representative electronic marketing channels

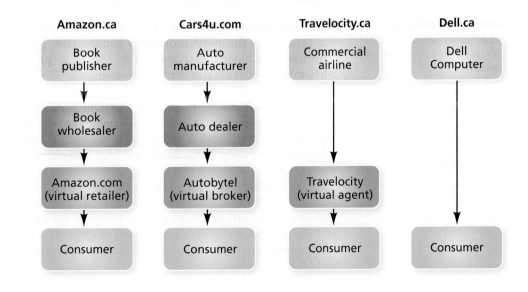

Multiple Channels and Strategic Alliances

multichannel distribution
An arrangement whereby a firm reaches buyers by employing two or more different types of marketing channels.

Historically, most organizations used a single channel of distribution to reach their customers. Today, however, many firms engage in **multichannel distribution**—an arrangement whereby a firm reaches buyers by employing two or more different types of marketing channels. This is sometimes referred to as *hybrid marketing channels* or *dual distribution*. Multichannel distribution can be used to reach similar customers with the same basic product, different customers with the same basic product, or different customers with different products. For example, Apple Inc. sells its products in its own retail stores, through its own Web site, and through other retailers such as Best Buy. On the other hand, GE sells certain appliances directly to home and apartment builders but uses retail stores to sell other appliances to regular homeowners. Finally, Hallmark sells its Hallmark greeting cards through Hallmark stores and select department stores, and its Ambassador brand of cards through discount and drugstore chains, thus reaching different customers with different brands. This is typical of firms that use a multibrand strategy (see Chapter 11), as they wish to minimize cannibalization of the firms' family brand and differentiate the channels.

Many large and small Canadian firms distribute through multiple channels. In fact, multichannel distribution is very common at the manufacturing and retail levels. Retailers that use multiple channels to reach their customers, labelled as *multichannel retailers,* will be discussed in detail in Chapter 15.

strategic channel alliances
A practice whereby one firm's marketing channel is used to sell another firm's products.

Another innovation in marketing channels is the use of **strategic channel alliances,** whereby one firm's marketing channel is used to sell another firm's products. An alliance between Kraft Foods and Starbucks is an example. Kraft distributes Starbucks coffee in supermarkets. Strategic alliances are also popular in global marketing, where the creation of marketing and channel relationships is expensive and time consuming. For example, General Mills and Nestlé have an extensive alliance that spans 75 markets worldwide.[7]

A Closer Look at Channel Intermediaries

Channel structures for consumer and business products assume various forms based on the number and type of intermediaries. Knowledge of the roles played by these intermediaries is important for understanding how channels operate in practice.

The terms *wholesaler, agent,* and *retailer* have been used in a general fashion consistent with the meanings given in Figure 14–1. However, on closer inspection, a variety of specific types of intermediaries emerges. These intermediaries engage in wholesale activities—those activities involved in selling products and services to those who are buying for the purposes of resale or business use. Intermediaries engaged in retailing activities are discussed in detail in Chapter 15.

merchant wholesalers
Independently owned firms that take title to the merchandise they handle.

Merchant Wholesalers   **Merchant wholesalers** are independently owned firms that take title to the merchandise they handle. They go by various names, including industrial distributor (described earlier). About 83 percent of the firms engaged in wholesale activities are merchant wholesalers.

Merchant wholesalers are classified as either full-service or limited-service wholesalers, depending on the number of functions performed. Two major types of full-service wholesalers exist. *General merchandise* (or *full-line*) *wholesalers* carry a broad assortment of merchandise and perform all channel functions. This type of wholesaler is most prevalent in the hardware, drug, and clothing industries. However, these wholesalers do not maintain much depth of assortment within specific product lines. *Specialty merchandise* (or *limited-line*) *wholesalers* offer a relatively narrow range of products but have an extensive assortment within the product lines carried. They perform all channel functions and are found in the health foods, automotive parts, and seafood industries. Four major types of specialty merchandise or limited-service wholesalers exist: (1) rack jobbers, (2) cash-and-carry wholesalers, (3) drop shippers, and (4) truck jobbers.

Agents and Brokers   Unlike merchant wholesalers, agents and brokers do not take title to merchandise and typically provide fewer channel functions. They make their profit from commissions or fees paid for their services, whereas merchant wholesalers make their profit from the sale of the merchandise they own.

Manufacturer's agents and selling agents are the two major types of agents used by producers. **Manufacturer's agents,** or *manufacturer's representatives,* work for several producers and carry non-competitive, complementary merchandise in an exclusive territory. Manufacturer's agents act as a producer's sales arm in a territory and are principally responsible for the transactional channel functions, primarily selling. They are used extensively in the automotive supply, footwear, and fabricated steel industries. By comparison, **selling agents** represent a single producer and are responsible for the entire marketing function of that producer. They design promotional plans, set prices, determine distribution policies, and make recommendations on product strategy. Selling agents are used by small producers in the textile, apparel, food, and home furnishing industries.

Brokers are independent firms or individuals whose principal function is to bring buyers and sellers together to make sales. Brokers, unlike agents, usually have no continuous relationship with the buyer or seller but negotiate a contract between two parties and then move on to another task. Brokers are used extensively by producers of seasonal products (such as fruits and vegetables) and in the real estate industry.

A unique broker that acts in many ways like a manufacturer's agent is a food broker, representing buyers and sellers in the grocery industry. Food brokers differ from conventional brokers because they act on behalf of producers on a permanent basis and receive a commission for their services. For example, Nabisco uses food brokers to sell its candies, margarine, and Planters peanuts, but it sells its line of cookies and crackers directly to retail stores.

Manufacturer's Branches and Offices   Unlike merchant wholesalers, agents, and brokers, manufacturer's branches and sales offices are wholly owned extensions of the producer that perform wholesale activities. Producers assume wholesale functions when there are no intermediaries to perform these activities, customers are few in number and geographically concentrated, or orders are large or require significant attention. A *manufacturer's branch office* carries a producer's inventory and performs the functions of a full-service wholesaler. A *manufacturer's sales office* does not carry inventory, typically performs only a sales function, and serves as an alternative to agents and brokers.

Vertical Marketing Systems and Channel Partnerships

The traditional marketing channels described so far represent a loosely knit network of independent producers and intermediaries brought together to distribute goods and services. However, new channel arrangements have emerged for the purpose of improving efficiency in performing channel functions and achieving greater marketing effectiveness. These new arrangements are called vertical marketing systems and channel partnerships. **Vertical marketing systems (VMS)** are professionally managed and centrally coordinated marketing channels designed to achieve channel economies and maximum marketing impact.[8] Figure 14–7 depicts the major types of vertical marketing systems: corporate, contractual, and administered.

Corporate Systems   The combination of successive stages of production and distribution under a single ownership is a *corporate vertical marketing system.* For example, a producer might own the intermediary at the next level down in the channel. This practice, called *forward integration,* is exemplified by Irving Oil, which refines gasoline and also operates retail gasoline stations. Other examples of forward integration include Goodyear, Singer, Sherwin Williams, and the building materials division of Boise Cascade. Alternatively, a retailer might own a manufacturing operation,

manufacturer's agents
Work for several producers and carry non-competitive, complementary merchandise in an exclusive territory; also called *manufacturer's representatives.*

selling agents
Represent a single producer and are responsible for the entire marketing function of that producer.

brokers
Independent firms or individuals whose principal function is to bring buyers and sellers together to make sales.

vertical marketing systems (VMS)
Professionally managed and centrally coordinated marketing channels designed to achieve channel economies and maximum marketing impact.

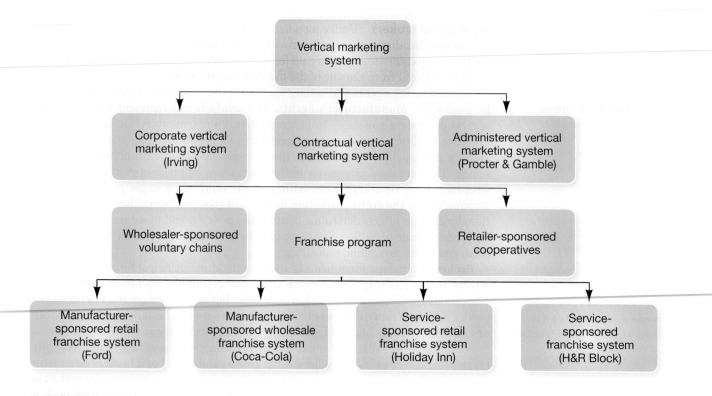

● **FIGURE 14–7**

Types of vertical marketing systems

Sherwin-Williams represents a type of vertical marketing system.

Sherwin-Williams
www.sherwin-williams.com

a practice called *backward integration.* For example, Safeway supermarkets operate their own bakeries, and Tim Hortons operates its own coffee-roasting facilities.

Companies seeking to reduce distribution costs and gain greater control over supply sources or resale of their products pursue forward and backward integration. However, both types of integration increase a company's capital investment and fixed costs. For this reason, many companies favour contractual vertical marketing systems to achieve channel efficiencies and marketing effectiveness.

Contractual Systems Under a *contractual vertical marketing system,* independent production and distribution firms integrate their efforts on a contractual basis to obtain greater functional economies and marketing impact than they could achieve alone. Contractual systems are the most popular among the three types of vertical marketing systems. They account for about 40 percent of all retail sales.

Three variations of contractual systems exist: (1) *wholesaler-sponsored voluntary chains* where a wholesaler develops a contractual relationship with small, independent retailers to standardize and coordinate buying practices, merchandising programs, and inventory management efforts; (2) *retailer-sponsored cooperatives* where small, independent retailers form an organization that operates a wholesale facility cooperatively; and (3) *franchising.* **Franchising** is a contractual arrangement between a parent company (a franchisor) and an individual or firm (a franchisee) that allows the franchise to operate a certain type of business under an established name and according to specific rules. Four types of franchise arrangements are most popular: (1) manufacturer-sponsored retail franchise systems (prominent in the automobile industry), (2) manufacturer-sponsored wholesale systems (evident in the soft-drink industry), (3) service-sponsored retail franchise systems with a unique approach for performing a service (such as McDonald's), and (4) service-sponsored franchise systems where franchisors licence individuals or firms to dispense a service

franchising

Contractual arrangement between a parent company (a franchisor) and an individual or firm (a franchisee) that allows the franchise to operate a certain type of business under an established name and according to specific rules.

under a trade name and specific guidelines (e.g., H&R Block tax services). Service-sponsored franchise arrangements are the fastest-growing type of franchise. Franchising is discussed further in Chapter 15.

Administered Systems In comparison, *administered vertical marketing systems* achieve coordination at successive stages of production and distribution by the size and influence of one channel member rather than through ownership. Procter & Gamble, given its broad product assortment ranging from disposable diapers to detergents, is able to obtain cooperation from supermarkets in displaying, promoting, and pricing its products. Walmart can obtain cooperation from manufacturers in terms of product specifications, price levels, and promotional support, given its position as the world's largest retailer.

---

learning review

3. What is the difference between a direct channel and an indirect channel?

4. What is the principal distinction between a corporate vertical marketing system and an administered vertical marketing system?

LO3 CHANNEL CHOICE AND MANAGEMENT

Marketing channels not only link a producer to its buyers but also provide the means through which a firm implements various elements of its marketing strategy. Therefore, choosing a marketing channel is a critical decision.

Factors Affecting Channel Choice and Management

The final choice of a marketing channel by a producer depends on a number of factors that often interact with each other.

Kensington Florist
www.kensingtonflorist.com

Environmental Factors The changing environment described in Chapter 3 has an important effect on the choice and management of a marketing channel. For example, the Fuller Brush Company, a name synonymous with door-to-door selling, now uses catalogues and telemarketing to reach customers. Rising employment among women, resulting in fewer being at home during working hours, prompted this action. Advances in the technology of growing, transporting, and storing perishable cut flowers has allowed many retailers, such as Calgary's Kensington Florist, to eliminate flower wholesalers and buy direct from flower growers. Additionally, the Internet has created new marketing channel opportunities for online marketing of flowers as well as consumer electronics, books, and music and video products.

Consumer Factors Consumer characteristics have a direct bearing on the choice and management of a marketing channel. Determining which channel is most appropriate is based on answers to some fundamental questions, such as: Who are potential customers? Where do they buy? When do they buy? How do they buy? What do they buy? And what experience are they seeking? The answers to these questions also indicate the type of intermediary best suited to reaching target buyers.

Product Factors In general, highly sophisticated products, such as large, scientific computers; unstandardized products, such as custom-built machinery; and products of high unit value are distributed directly to buyers. Unsophisticated, standardized products with low unit value, such as table salt, are typically distributed through indirect channels. A product's stage in the life cycle also affects marketing channels.

Company Factors   A firm's financial, human, or technological capabilities affect channel choice. For example, firms that are unable to employ a salesforce might use manufacturer's agents or selling agents to reach wholesalers or buyers. If a firm has multiple products for a particular target market, it might use a direct channel, whereas firms with a limited product line might use intermediaries of various types to reach buyers.

Channel Design Considerations

Recognizing that numerous routes to buyers exist and also recognizing the factors just described, marketing executives typically consider three questions when choosing a marketing channel and intermediaries:

1. Which channel and intermediaries will provide the best coverage of the target market?
2. Which channel and intermediaries will best satisfy the buying requirements of the target market?
3. Which channel and intermediaries will be the most profitable?

Target Market Coverage   Achieving the best coverage of the target market requires attention to the density and type of intermediaries to be used at the retail level of distribution. Three degrees of distribution density exist: intensive, exclusive, and selective. *Intensive distribution* means that a firm tries to place its products and services in as many outlets as possible. Intensive distribution is usually chosen for convenience products or services—for instance, candy, fast food, newspapers, and soft drinks. Increasingly, medical services are distributed in this fashion. Cash—yes, cash—is also distributed intensively by Visa. Visit Visa's Web site, described in the Going Online box, "Need Cash Fast? Check the Visa ATM Locator," to locate the nearest Visa automated teller machine.

Exclusive distribution is the extreme opposite of intensive distribution because only one retail outlet in a specified geographical area carries the firm's product. Exclusive distribution is typically chosen for specialty products or services—for example, automobiles, some women's fragrances, men's suits, and yachts. Sometimes, retailers sign exclusive distribution agreements with manufacturers. Gucci, one of the world's leading luxury goods companies, uses exclusive distribution.[9]

Selective distribution lies between these two extremes and means that a firm selects a few retail outlets in a specific geographical area to carry its products. Selective distribution weds some of the market coverage benefits of intensive distribution to the control over resale evident with exclusive distribution. For this reason, selective distribution is the most common form of distribution intensity and is usually associated with shopping goods or services, such as Rolex watches and Ping golf clubs.

Satisfying Buyer Requirements   A second consideration in channel design is gaining access to channels and intermediaries that satisfy at least some of the interests buyers might want fulfilled when they purchase a firm's products or services. These interests fall into four categories: (1) information, (2) convenience, (3) variety, and (4) attendant services.

Information is an important requirement when buyers have limited knowledge or desire specific data about a product or service. Properly chosen intermediaries communicate with buyers through in-store displays, demonstrations, and personal

Going Online

Need Cash Fast? Check the Visa ATM Locator

Short of cash? Visa offers a valuable Web resource in its ATM Locator, which can be accessed at **www.visa.com**. Visa has some 750,000 automated teller machines in 120 countries. One is probably in your neighbourhood, wherever that is in the world! To find the nearest Visa ATM, follow the easy ATM Locator directions and request a site map. You will be in the money in no time. Here is the map for the McGraw-Hill Ryerson Ltd. neighbourhood.

selling. Personal computer manufacturers, such as Apple Inc., have opened their own retail outlets staffed with highly trained personnel to inform buyers how their products can better meet each customer's needs.

Convenience has multiple meanings for buyers, such as proximity or driving time to a retail outlet. For example, Mac's Milk stores, with outlets nationwide, satisfy this interest for buyers, and candy and snack food firms benefit by gaining display space in these stores. For other consumers, convenience means a minimum of time and hassle. Jiffy Lube and Mr. Lube, which promise to change engine oil and filters quickly, appeal to this aspect of convenience. For those who shop on the Internet, convenience means that Web sites must be easy to locate and navigate, and image downloads must be fast.

Variety reflects buyers' interest in having numerous competing and complementary items from which to choose. Variety is evident in both the breadth and depth of products and brands carried by intermediaries, which enhances their attraction to buyers. Thus, manufacturers of pet food and supplies seek distribution through pet superstores, such as Petco and PetsMart, which offer a wide array of pet products.

Services, pre- or post-sale, provided by intermediaries are an important buying requirement for such products as large household appliances that require delivery, installation, and credit. Therefore, Whirlpool seeks dealers that provide such services.

Profitability   The third consideration in designing a channel is profitability, which is determined by the margins earned (revenues minus cost) for each channel member and for the channel as a whole. Channel cost is the critical dimension of profitability. These costs include distribution, advertising, and selling expenses associated with different types of marketing channels. The extent to which channel members share these costs determines the margins received by each member and by the channel as a whole.

Companies routinely monitor the performance of their marketing channels. Read the Using Marketing Dashboards box to see how ABC Furniture views the sales and profit performance of its marketing channels.

Global Dimensions of Marketing Channels

Marketing channels around the world reflect traditions, customs, geography, and the economic history of individual countries and societies. Even so, the basic marketing

Using Marketing Dashboards

Channel Sales and Profit at ABC Furniture

ABC is a mid-size furniture manufacturer. It sells its furniture through furniture store chains, independent furniture stores, and department store chains. The company has traditionally allocated its marketing funds for cooperative advertising, in-store displays, and retail sales support on the basis of dollar sales by channel.

Your Challenge As the vice president of sales and marketing at ABC Furniture, you have been asked to review the company's sales and profit in its three channels and recommend a course of action. The question: Should ABC Furniture continue to allocate its marketing funds on the basis of channel dollar sales or profit?

Your Findings ABC Furniture tracks the sales and profit from each channel (and individual customer) and sales trends on its marketing dashboard. This information is displayed in the marketing dashboard below.

Several findings stand out. Furniture store chains and independent furniture stores account for 85.2 percent of

ABC Furniture sales and 93 percent of company profit. These two channels also evidence growth as measured by annual percentage change in sales. By comparison, department store chains annual percentage sales growth has declined and recorded negative growth in 2007. This channel accounts for 14.8 percent of company sales and 7 percent of company profit.

Your Action ABC Furniture should consider abandoning the practice of allocating marketing funds solely on the basis of channel sales volume. The importance of independent furniture stores to ABC's profitability warrants further spending, particularly given this channel's favourable sales trend. Doubling the percentage allocation for marketing funds for this channel may be too extreme, however. Rather, an objective-task promotional budgeting method should be adopted (see Chapter 16). ABC Furniture might also consider the longer-term role of department store chains as a marketing channel.

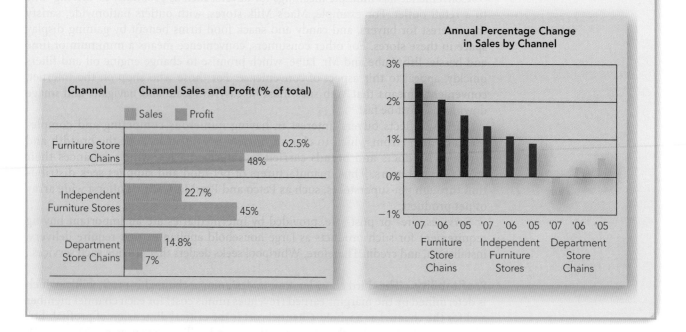

channel functions must be performed. But differences do exist and are illustrated by highlighting marketing channels in Japan.

Intermediaries outside Western Europe and North America tend to be small, numerous, and often owner-operated. Japanese marketing channels tend to include many intermediaries based on tradition and lack of storage space. As many as five intermediaries are involved in the distribution of soap in Japan compared with one or two in North America.

Understanding marketing channels in global markets is often a prerequisite to successful marketing. For example, Gillette attempted to sell its razors and blades through company salespeople in Japan as it does in North America, thus eliminating

For the answer to how Schick became a razor and blade market share leader in Japan, read the text.

Warner Lambert Company
www.warner-lambert.com

channel conflict
Arises when one channel member believes another channel member is engaged in behaviour that prevents it from achieving its goals.

disintermediation
Channel conflict that arises when a channel member bypasses another member and sells or buys products direct.

wholesalers traditionally involved in marketing toiletries. Warner-Lambert Company sold its Schick razors and blades through the traditional Japanese channel involving wholesalers. The result? Schick achieved a commanding lead over Gillette in the Japanese razor and blade market.[10]

Channel relationships also must be considered. In Japan, the distribution *keiretsu* (translated as "alignments") bonds producers and intermediaries together. The bond, through vertical integration and social and economic ties, ensures that each channel member benefits from the distribution alignment. The dominant member of the distribution *keiretsu*, which is typically a producer, has considerable influence over channel member behaviour, including which competing products are sold by other channel members. Well-known Japanese companies, such as Matsushita (electronics), Nissan and Toyota (automotive products), Nippon Gakki (musical instruments), and Kirin (and other brewers and distillers), employ the distribution *keiretsu* extensively. Shiseido and Kanebo, for instance, influence the distribution of cosmetics through Japanese department stores.

LO4 Channel Relationships: Conflict, Cooperation, and Law

Unfortunately, because channels consist of independent individuals and firms, there is always potential for disagreements concerning who performs which channel functions, how profits are allocated, which products and services will be provided by whom, and who makes critical channel-related decisions. These channel conflicts necessitate measures for dealing with them. Sometimes, they result in legal action.

Conflict in Marketing Channels   Channel conflict arises when one channel member believes another channel member is engaged in behaviour that prevents it from achieving its goals. Two types of conflict occur in marketing channels: vertical conflict and horizontal conflict.[11]

Vertical conflict occurs between different levels in a marketing channel—for example, between a manufacturer and a wholesaler or retailer or between a wholesaler and a retailer. Three sources of vertical conflict are most common. First, conflict arises when a channel member bypasses another member and sells or buys products direct, a practice called **disintermediation.** Second, disagreements over how profit margins are distributed among channel members produce conflict. A third conflict situation arises when manufacturers believe wholesalers or retailers are not giving their products adequate attention.

Horizontal conflict occurs between intermediaries at the same level in a marketing channel, such as between two or more retailers (Zellers and Walmart), or between two or more wholesalers that handle the same manufacturer's brands. Two sources of horizontal conflict are common.[12] First, horizontal conflict arises when a manufacturer increases its distribution coverage in a geographical area. For example, a franchised Cadillac dealer might complain to General Motors that another franchised Cadillac dealer has located too close to its dealership. Second, multichannel distribution causes conflict when different types of retailers carry the same brands.

Cooperation in Marketing Channels   Conflict can have destructive effects on the workings of a marketing channel, and so it is necessary to secure cooperation among channel members. One means is through a *channel captain,* a channel member that coordinates, directs, and supports other channel members. Channel captains can be producers, wholesalers, or retailers. P&G assumes this role because it has a strong consumer following in such brands as Crest, Tide, and Pampers. Therefore, it can set policies or terms that supermarkets will follow. Walmart and Home Depot are retail channel captains because of their strong consumer image, number of outlets, and purchasing volume.

A firm becomes a channel captain because it is typically the channel member with the ability to influence the behaviour of other members.[13] Influence can take four forms. First, economic influence arises from the ability of a firm to reward other members given its strong financial position or customer franchise. Microsoft Corporation has such influence. Expertise is a second source of influence over other channel members. Third, identification with a particular channel member may also create influence for that channel member. For instance, retailers may compete to carry the Ralph Lauren line, or clothing manufacturers may compete to be carried by well-known retailers. In both instances, the desire to be associated with a channel member gives that firm influence over others. Finally, influence can arise from the legitimate right of one channel member to direct the behaviour of other members. This situation would occur under contractual vertical marketing systems where a franchisor could legitimately direct how a franchisee behaves. Other means for securing cooperation in marketing channels rest in the different variations of vertical marketing systems.

Channel influence can be used to gain concessions from other channel members. For instance, some large supermarket chains expect manufacturers to pay allowances, in the form of cash or free goods, to stock and display their products. Some manufacturers call these allowances "extortion," as described in the Making Responsible Decisions box, "The Ethics of Slotting Allowances."[14]

Legal Considerations   Conflict in marketing channels is typically resolved through negotiation or the exercise of influence by channel members. Sometimes, conflict produces legal action. Therefore, knowledge of legal restrictions affecting channel strategies and practices is important. Some restrictions were described in Chapter 13, namely, vertical price fixing and price discrimination. However, other legal considerations unique to marketing channels warrant attention.

In general, suppliers have the right to choose the intermediaries that carry or represent their products. However, suppliers can run into legal difficulty over *refusing to deal* with customers who can meet the usual trade terms offered by the supplier. The *Competition Act* looks seriously at cases where a supplier withholds or withdraws products from a customer if such behaviour will adversely affect the customer.

Dual distribution is a situation where a manufacturer distributes through its own vertically integrated channel in direct competition with wholesalers and retailers that also sell its products. If the manufacturer's behaviour is viewed as an attempt to unduly lessen competition by eliminating wholesalers or retailers, then such

Making Responsible Decisions

The Ethics of Slotting Allowances

Have you ever wondered why your favourite cookies are no longer to be found at your local supermarket? Or why that delicious tortilla chip you like to serve at parties is missing from the shelves and replaced by another brand?

Blame it on slotting allowances. Some large supermarket chains demand slotting allowances from food manufacturers, paid in the form of money or free goods, to stock and display products. These allowances can run up to $25,000 per item for a supermarket chain. Not surprisingly, slotting allowances have been labelled "ransom," "extortional allowances," and "commercial bribery" by manufacturers because they already pay supermarkets "trade dollars" to promote and discount their products. Small food manufacturers, in particular, view slotting allowances as an economic barrier to the distribution of their products. Supermarket operators see these allowances as a reasonable cost of handling business for manufacturers.

Is the practice of charging slotting allowances unethical behaviour?

action may violate the *Competition Act* and would be examined by the Competition Bureau.

Vertical integration is viewed in a similar light. Like dual distribution, it is not illegal, but the practice could be subject to legal action if such integration were designed to eliminate or lessen competition unduly.

Exclusive dealing and tied selling are prohibited under the *Competition Act* if they are found to unduly lessen competition or create monopolies. *Exclusive dealing* exists when a supplier requires channel members to sell only its products or restricts distributors from selling directly competitive products. *Tied selling* occurs when a supplier requires a distributor purchasing some products to buy others from the supplier. These arrangements often arise in franchising. Tied selling would be investigated by the Competition Bureau if the tied products could be purchased at fair market value from other suppliers at desired standards of the franchisor and if the arrangements were seen as restricting competition. Full-line forcing is a special kind of tied selling. This is a supplier's requiring that a channel member carry its full line of products to sell a specific item in the supplier's line.

Resale or market restrictions refer to a supplier's attempt to stipulate to whom distributors may resell the supplier's products and in what specific geographical areas or territories they may be sold. These practices could be subject to review under the *Competition Act* if such restrictions were deemed to be restraining or lessening competition.

---

learning review	**5.** What are the three degrees of distribution density?
	6. What are the three questions marketing executives consider when choosing a marketing channel and intermediaries?
	7. What is meant by "exclusive dealing"?

LO5 LOGISTICS AND SUPPLY CHAIN MANAGEMENT

logistics management
The practice of organizing the cost-effective flow of raw materials, in-process inventory, finished goods, and related information from point of origin to point of consumption to satisfy customer requirements.

supply chain
A sequence of firms that perform activities required to create and deliver a good or service to consumers or industrial users.

supply chain management
The integration and organization of information and logistics activities across firms in a supply chain for the purpose of creating and delivering goods and services that provide value to customers.

A marketing channel relies on logistics to actually make products available to consumers and business users—a point emphasized earlier in this chapter. Logistics involves those activities that focus on getting the right amount of the right products to the right place at the right time at the lowest possible cost. The performance of these activities is **logistics management,** the practice of organizing the *cost-effective flow* of raw materials, in-process inventory, finished goods, and related information from point of origin to point of consumption to satisfy *customer requirements*. This perspective is represented in the concept of a supply chain and the practice of supply chain management.

A *supply chain* is a sequence of firms that perform activities required to create and deliver a good or service to consumers or industrial users. It differs from a marketing channel in terms of membership. A supply chain includes suppliers who provide raw material inputs to a manufacturer as well as the wholesalers and retailers who deliver finished goods to you. The management process is also different. **Supply chain management** is the integration and organization of information and logistics activities *across firms* in a supply chain for the purpose of creating and delivering goods and services that provide value to consumers. The relationship among marketing channels, logistics management, and supply chain management is shown in Figure 14–8. An important feature of supply chain management is its application of sophisticated information technology, which allows companies to share and operate systems for order processing, transportation scheduling, and inventory and facility management.

● **FIGURE 14–8**
Logistics management and
supply chain management

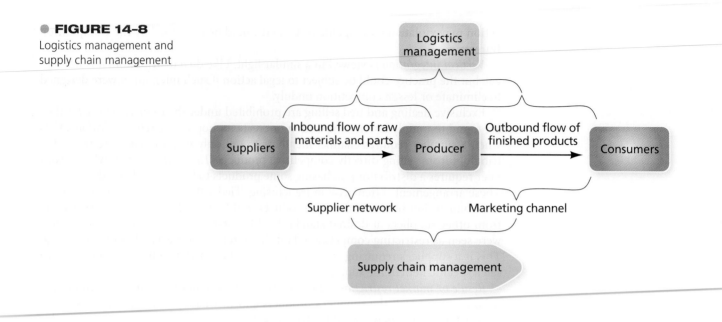

Sourcing, Assembling, and Delivering a New Car: The Automotive Supply Chain

All companies are members of one or more supply chains. A supply chain is essentially a sequence of linked suppliers and customers in which every customer is, in turn, a supplier to another customer until a finished product reaches the final consumer. Even the simplified supply chain diagram for car makers shown in Figure 14–9 illustrates how complex a supply chain can be.[15] A car maker's supplier network includes thousands of firms that provide the 5,000 or so parts in a typical automobile. They provide items ranging from raw materials, such as steel and rubber, to components, including transmissions, tires, brakes, and seats, to complex subassemblies and assemblies evident in chassis and suspension systems that make for a smooth, stable ride. Coordinating and scheduling material and component flows for their assembly into actual automobiles by car makers is heavily dependent on logistical activities, including transportation, order processing, inventory control, materials handling, and information technology. A central link is the car maker supply chain manager, who is responsible for translating customer requirements into actual orders and arranging for delivery dates and financial arrangements for automobile dealers. This is not an easy task, given the different consumer preferences and the amounts consumers are willing to pay.

Logistical aspects of the automobile marketing channel are also an integral part of the supply chain. Major responsibilities include transportation, which involves the selection and oversight of external carriers (trucking, airline, railroad, and shipping companies) for cars and parts to dealers; the operation of distribution centres; the management of finished goods inventories; and order processing for sales. Supply chain managers also play an important role in the marketing channel. They work with extensive car dealer networks to ensure that the right mix of automobiles is delivered to different locations. In addition, they make sure that spare and service parts are available so that dealers can meet the car maintenance and repair needs of consumers. All of this is done with the help of information technology that links the entire automotive supply chain. What does all of this cost? It is estimated that logistics costs represent 25 to 30 percent of the retail price of a typical new car.

Supply Chain Management and Marketing Strategy

The automotive supply chain illustration shows how information and logistics activities are integrated and organized across firms to create and deliver a car for you. What

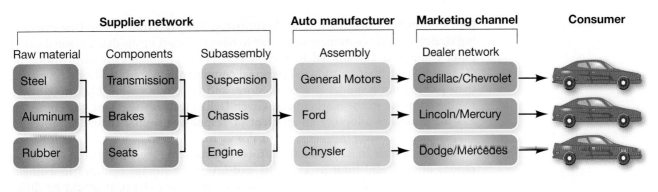

Supplier network   **Auto manufacturer**   **Marketing channel**   **Consumer**

Raw material	Components	Subassembly	Assembly	Dealer network	
Steel	Transmission	Suspension	General Motors	Cadillac/Chevrolet	
Aluminum	Brakes	Chassis	Ford	Lincoln/Mercury	
Rubber	Seats	Engine	Chrysler	Dodge/Mercedes	

● **FIGURE 14–9**
The automotive supply chain

is missing from this illustration is the link between a specific company's supply chain and its marketing strategy. Just as companies have different marketing strategies, they also manage supply chains differently. More specifically, the goals to be achieved by a firm's marketing strategy determine whether its supply chain needs to be more responsive or efficient in meeting customer requirements.

Aligning a Supply Chain with Marketing Strategy   There are a variety of supply chain configurations, each of which is designated to perform a different task well. Marketers today recognize that the choice of a supply chain follows from a clearly defined marketing strategy and involves three steps:[16]

1. *Understand the customer.* To understand the customer, a company must identify the needs of the customer segment being served. These needs, such as a desire for a low price or convenience of purchase, help a company define the relative importance of efficiency and responsiveness in meeting customer requirements.
2. *Understand the supply chain.* Second, a company must understand what a supply chain is designed to do well. Supply chains range from those that emphasize being responsive to customer requirements and demand to those that emphasize efficiency with a goal of supplying products at the lowest possible delivered cost.
3. *Harmonize the supply chain with the marketing strategy.* Finally, a company needs to ensure that what the supply chain is capable of doing well is consistent with the targeted customer's needs and its marketing strategy. If a mismatch exists between what the supply chain does particularly well and a company's marketing strategy, the company will either need to redesign the supply chain to support the marketing strategy or change the marketing strategy. The bottom line is that a poorly designed supply chain can do serious damage to an otherwise brilliant marketing strategy.

How are these steps applied and how are efficiency and responsive considerations built into a supply chain? Let us briefly look at how two market leaders—Dell Computer Corporation and Walmart, Inc.—have harmonized their supply chain and marketing strategies.[17]

World-class marketers Dell Computer and Walmart emphasize responsiveness and efficiency in their supply chains.

Dell Computer Corporation: A Responsive Supply Chain   The Dell marketing strategy targets customers who wish to have the most up-to-date personal computer equipment customized to their needs. These customers are also willing to (1) wait to have their customized personal computer delivered in a few days rather than picking out a model at a retail store, and (2) pay a reasonable, though not the lowest, price in the marketplace. Given Dell's customer segment, the company has the option of adopting an efficient or responsive supply chain. An efficient supply chain may use inexpensive but slower modes of transportation, emphasize economies of scale in its production process by reducing the variety of PC configurations offered, and limit its assembly and inventory storage facilities to a single location. If Dell opted only for efficiency in its supply chain, it would be difficult, if not impossible, to satisfy its target customer's desire for rapid delivery and a wide variety of customizable products. Dell, instead, has opted for a responsive supply chain. It relies on more expensive express transportation for receipt of components from suppliers and delivery of finished products to customers. The company achieves product variety and manufacturing efficiency by designing common platforms across several products and using common components. Dell operates manufacturing facilities in various countries to ensure rapid delivery. Moreover, Dell has invested heavily in information technology to link itself with suppliers and customers.

Walmart, Inc.: An Efficient Supply Chain   Now, let us consider Walmart. Walmart's marketing strategy is to be a reliable, lower-price retailer for a wide variety of mass-consumption consumer goods. This strategy favours an efficient supply chain designed to deliver products to consumers at the lowest possible cost. Efficiency is achieved in a variety of ways. For instance, Walmart keeps relatively low inventory levels, and most inventory is stocked in stores available for sale, not in warehouses gathering dust. The low inventory arises from Walmart's innovative use of *cross-docking*—a practice that involves unloading products from suppliers, sorting products for individual stores, and quickly reloading products onto trucks for a particular store. No warehousing or storing of products occurs, except for a few hours or at most a day. Cross-docking allows Walmart to operate only a small number of distribution centres to service its vast network of Walmart stores, Supercentres, and Sam's Clubs, which contributes to efficiency. On the other hand, the company runs its own fleet of trucks to service its stores. This does increase cost and investment, but the benefits in terms of responsiveness justify the cost, in Walmart's case. Walmart has invested significantly more than its competitors have in information technology to operate its supply chain. The company feeds information about customer requirements and demand from its stores back to its suppliers, which manufacture only what is being demanded. This large investment has improved the efficiency of Walmart's supply chain and made it responsive to customer needs.

Three lessons can be learned from these two examples. First, there is no one best supply chain for every company. Second, the best supply chain is the one that is consistent with the needs of the customer segment being served and complements a company's marketing strategy. And finally, supply chain managers are often called upon to make tradeoffs between efficiency and responsiveness on various elements of a company's supply chain.

learning review	**8.** What is the principal difference between a marketing channel and a supply chain?
	9. What three steps does the choice of a supply chain involve?

LO6 INFORMATION AND LOGISTICS MANAGEMENT OBJECTIVE IN A SUPPLY CHAIN

The objective of information and logistics management in a supply chain is to minimize logistics costs while delivering maximum customer service. The Dell Computer and Walmart examples highlight how two market leaders have realized this objective by different means. An important similarity between these two companies is that both use information to leverage logistics activities, reduce logistics costs, and improve customer service.

Information's Role in Supply Chain Responsiveness and Efficiency

Information consists of data and analysis regarding inventory, transportation, distribution facilities, and customers throughout the supply chain.[18] Continuing advances in information technology make it possible to track logistics activities and customer service variables and manage them for efficiency and responsiveness. For example, information on customer demand patterns allows pharmaceutical companies, such as Eli Lilly and GlaxoSmithKline, to produce and stock medicines in anticipation of customer needs. This improves supply chain responsiveness because customers will find the medicines when and where they want them. Demand information improves supply chain efficiency because pharmaceutical firms are better able to forecast customer needs and produce, transport, and store the required amount of inventory.

A variety of technologies are used to transmit and manage information in a supply chain. *Electronic data interchanges (EDI)* combine proprietary computer and telecommunication technologies to exchange electronic invoices, payments, and information between suppliers, manufacturers, and retailers. When linked with store scanning equipment and systems, EDI provides a seamless electronic link from a retail checkout counter to suppliers and manufacturers. Walmart and Procter & Gamble actually pioneered the use of EDI. EDI is commonly used in the retail, apparel, transportation, pharmaceutical, grocery, health care, and insurance industries, as well as by local, provincial, and federal government agencies. About 95 percent of the companies listed in the *Fortune 1000* use EDI, as do most of the Canadian companies listed in the *Financial Post 500*. At Hewlett-Packard, for example, one million EDI transactions are made every month.

Another technology, the *extranet,* permits secure business-to-business communication between a manufacturer and its suppliers, distributors, and sometimes other partners (such as advertising agencies). Extranets are less expensive and more flexible to operate than EDI because of their connection to the public Internet. This technology is prominent in private electronic exchanges described in Chapter 6.

Whereas EDI and extranets transmit information, other technologies help manage information in a supply chain. Enterprise resource planning (ERP) technology and supply chain management software track logistics cost and customer service variables, both of which are described next.

Total Logistics Cost Concept

total logistics cost
Expenses associated with transportation, materials handling and warehousing, inventory, stockouts, order processing, and return goods handling.

For our purposes, **total logistics cost** includes expenses associated with transportation, materials handling and warehousing, inventory, stockouts (being out of inventory), order processing, and return goods handling. Note that many of these costs are interrelated, and so changes in one will impact the others. For example, as the firm attempts to minimize its transportation costs by shipping in larger quantities, it will also experience an increase in inventory levels. Larger inventory levels will not only increase inventory costs but should also reduce stockouts. It is important, therefore, to study the impact on all of the logistics decision areas when considering a change.

Customer Service Concept

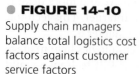

customer service
The ability of logistics management to satisfy users in terms of time, dependability, communication, and convenience.

Because a supply chain is a *flow,* the end of it—or *output*—is the service delivered to customers. Within the context of a supply chain, **customer service** is the ability of logistics management to satisfy users in terms of time, dependability, communication, and convenience. As suggested by Figure 14–10, a supply chain manager's key task is to balance these four customer service factors against total logistics cost factors.

Time   In a supply chain setting, time refers to *lead time* for an item, which means the lag from ordering an item until it is received and ready for use or sale. This is also referred to as *order cycle time* or *replenishment time* and may be more important to retailers or wholesalers than consumers. The various elements that make up the typical order cycle include recognition of the need to order, order transmittal, order processing, documentation, and transportation. A current emphasis in supply chain management is to reduce lead time so that the inventory levels of customers may be minimized. Another emphasis is to make the process of reordering and receiving products as simple as possible, often through electronic data and inventory systems called *quick response* and *efficient consumer response* delivery systems. These inventory management systems are designed to reduce the retailer's lead time for receiving merchandise, thereby lowering a retailer's inventory investment, improving customer service levels, and reducing logistics expense.

Dependability   Dependability is the consistency of replenishment. This is important to all firms in a supply chain and to consumers. It can be broken into three elements: consistent lead time, safe delivery, and complete delivery. Consistent service allows planning (such as appropriate inventory levels), whereas inconsistencies create surprises. Intermediaries may be willing to accept longer lead times if they know about them in advance and can thus make plans.

Communication   Communication is a two-way link between buyer and seller that helps in monitoring service and anticipating future needs. Status reports on orders are a typical example of improved communication between buyer and seller.

● **FIGURE 14–10**

Supply chain managers balance total logistics cost factors against customer service factors

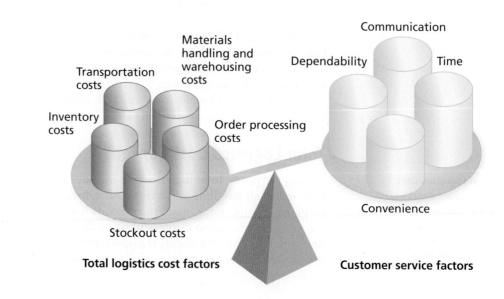

Convenience   The concept of convenience for a supply chain manager means that there should be a minimum of effort on the part of the buyer in doing business with the seller. Is it easy for the customer to order? Are the products available from many outlets? Does the buyer have to buy huge quantities of the product? Will the seller arrange all necessary details, such as transportation? The seller must concentrate on removing unnecessary barriers to customer convenience.

---

learning review

10. The objective of information and logistics management in a supply chain is to _____.

11. How does consumer demand information increase supply chain responsiveness and efficiency?

LO7 KEY LOGISTICS FUNCTIONS IN A SUPPLY CHAIN

The four key logistic functions in a supply chain include (1) transportation, (2) warehousing and materials handling, (3) order processing, and (4) inventory management. These functions have become so complex and interrelated that many companies have outsourced them to third-party logistics providers. *Third-party logistics providers* are firms that perform most or all of the logistics functions that manufacturers, suppliers, and distributors would normally perform themselves.[19] Today, many of Canada's top manufacturers outsource one or more logistics functions, at least on a limited basis. UPS Supply Chain Solutions, FedEx Supply Chain Services, DHL, and Penske Logistics are just a few of the companies that specialize in handling logistics functions for their clients.

The four major logistics functions and the involvement of third-party logistics providers are described in detail next.

FedEx and UPS are two third-party logistics providers that perform most or all of the logistics functions that manufacturers, suppliers, and distributors would normally perform.

FedEx
www.fedex.com

Transportation

Transportation provides the movement of goods necessary in a supply chain. There are five basic modes of transportation: railroads, motor carriers, air carriers, pipelines, and

water carriers, and modal combinations involving two or more modes, such as highway trailers on a rail flatcar.

All transportation modes can be evaluated on six basic service criteria:

- *Cost.* Charges for transportation.
- *Time.* Speed of transit.
- *Capability.* What can be realistically carried with this mode.
- *Dependability.* Reliability of service regarding time, loss, and damage.
- *Accessibility.* Convenience of the mode's routes (such as pipeline availability).
- *Frequency.* Scheduling.

Figure 14–11 summarizes service advantages and disadvantages of five of the modes of transportation available.[20] To read about a unique transportation concept that provides vital supplies to Canada's diamond mines in the north, check out the Marketing Matters box, "Canada's Ice Road, which describes Canada's ice road and the truckers who risk their lives travelling it.[21]

Warehousing and Materials Handling

Warehouses may be classified in one of two ways: (1) storage warehouses, and (2) distribution centres. In *storage warehouses,* the goods are intended to come to rest for some period of time, as in the aging of products or in storing household goods. *Distribution centres,* on the other hand, are designed to facilitate the timely movement of goods and represent a very important part of a supply chain. They represent the second most significant cost in a supply chain after transportation.

Distribution centres not only allow firms to hold their stock in decentralized locations but also are used to facilitate sorting and consolidating products from different plants or different suppliers. Some physical transformation can also take place in distribution centres, for example, mixing or blending different ingredients, labelling, and repackaging. Paint companies, such as Sherwin-Williams and Benjamin Moore, use distribution centres for this purpose. In addition, distribution centres may serve as manufacturer sales offices and order processing centres.

● **FIGURE 14–11**
Advantages and disadvantages of five modes of transportation

MODE	RELATIVE ADVANTAGES	RELATIVE DISADVANTAGES
Rail	• Full capability • Extensive routes • Low cost	• Some reliability, damage problems • Not always complete pickup and delivery • Sometimes slow
Truck	• Complete pickup and delivery • Extensive routes • Fairly fast	• Size and weight restrictions • Higher cost • More weather sensitive
Air	• Fast • Low damage • Frequent departures	• High cost • Limited capabilities
Pipeline	• Low cost • Very reliable • Frequent departures	• Limited routes (accessibility) • Slow
Water	• Low cost • Huge capacities	• Slow • Limited routes and schedules • More weather sensitive

materials handling
Moving goods over short distances into, within, and out of warehouses and manufacturing plants.

Materials handling, which involves moving goods over short distances into, within, and out of warehouses and manufacturing plants, is a key part of warehouse operations. The two major problems with this activity are high labour costs and high rates of loss and damage. Every time an item is handled, there is a chance for loss or damage. Common materials handling equipment includes forklifts, cranes, and conveyors. Today, materials handling in warehouses is automated by using computers and robots to reduce the cost of holding, moving, and recording inventories.

Order Processing

There are several stages in the processing of an order, and a failure at any one of them can cause a problem with the customer. The process starts with transmitting the order by a variety of means, such as the Internet, an extranet, or electronic data interchange (EDI). This is followed by entering the order in the appropriate databases and sending the information to those who need it. For example, a regional warehouse is notified to prepare an order. After checking inventory, a new quantity may need to be reordered from the production line, or purchasing may be requested to reorder from a vendor. If the item is currently out of stock, a *backorder* is created, and the whole process of keeping track of a small part of the original order must be managed. In addition, credit may have to be checked for some customers, all documentation for the order must be prepared, transportation must be arranged, and an order confirmation must be sent. Order processing systems are evaluated in terms of speed and accuracy.

Electronic order processing has replaced manual processing for most large Canadian companies. For example, 96 percent of IBM's purchase transactions with suppliers are conducted on the Internet. Kiwi Brands, the marketer of Kiwi shoe polish, Endust, and Behold, receives 75 percent of its retailers' purchase orders via EDI. The company has also implemented financial EDI, sending invoices to retailers and receiving payment order/remittance advice documents and electronic funds transfer (EFT) payments. Shippers as well are linked to the system, allowing Kiwi to receive shipment status messages electronically.

Materials handling through automation is now common in distribution centres.

Marketing Matters

Canada's Ice Road

When it comes to epic engineering, nothing tops the Tibbitt to Contwoyto Winter Road, a superhighway of ice that extends hundreds of kilometres from Yellowknife into the neighbouring territory of Nunavut over frozen lakes and spongy tundra. To build it, workers from Nuna Logistics put in 20-hour days and fight cold wind chills that dip to 70 below zero. By the end of January, the workers complete the longest heavy-haul ice road in the world. It is as wide as an eight-lane highway, and 75 percent of it is built over frozen lakes. When the ice thickens by late February, it is capable of supporting 70-ton super trucks. This ice road and the trucks that travel it supply the diamond mines of northern Canada. Without the ice road and the vital supplies that travel across it, the diamond mines could not operate effectively. In about a decade, Canada has gone from producing and marketing no diamonds to being the third-largest producer by value in the world, producing more than 12 million carats worth over $1.5 billion. In many ways, the ice road and the truckers who use it have made this industry possible.

To stay in operation, the mines require 300,000 tonnes of fuel, explosives, steel, and concrete, all hauled over the ice each year. If the ice roads do not hold up and truckers cannot make their runs, stranded freight has to be flown in, at six to eight times the cost. This results in added costs to the diamond mines of tens of millions of dollars each year. And, because of weather conditions, many flights are cancelled or delayed, resulting in curtailed operations of the mines. Thus, the ice road plays a vital logistics function in the supply chain of Canada's growing diamond industry. The truckers take great risks driving the ice roads, and people have lost their lives when the ice surface gives way. But the truckers take the risk because they can make almost a year's salary in only nine to ten weeks of work. The ice road only lasts a few months, and close to 10,000 loads must make it through from February to April. Then, the next January, they will rebuild the road all over again, and the supply chain to the diamond mines will be re-established.

Inventory Management

Inventory management is one of the primary responsibilities of the supply chain manager. The major problem is maintaining the delicate balance between too little and too much. Too little inventory may result in poor service, stockouts, brand switching, and loss of market share; too much leads to higher costs because of the money tied up in inventory and the risk that it may become obsolete.

Reasons for Inventory Traditionally, carrying inventory has been justified on several grounds: (1) to offer a buffer against variations in supply and demand, often caused by uncertainty in forecasting demand; (2) to provide better service for those customers who wish to be served on demand; (3) to promote production efficiencies; (4) to provide a hedge against price increases by suppliers; (5) to promote purchasing and transportation discounts; and (6) to protect the firm from such contingencies as strikes and shortages. However, companies today view inventory as something to be moved, not stored, and more of a liability than an asset. The traditional justification for inventory has resulted in excessive inventories that have proven costly to maintain. Consider the North American automobile industry. Despite efforts to streamline its supply chain, industry analysts estimate that more than $230 billion worth of excess inventory piles up annually in the form of unused raw materials, parts waiting to be delivered, and vehicles sitting on dealers' lots.[22]

Inventory Costs   Specific inventory costs are often hard to detect because they are difficult to measure and occur in many different parts of the firm. A classification of inventory costs includes the following:

- *Capital costs.* The opportunity costs resulting from tying up funds in inventory instead of using them in other, more profitable investments; these are related to interest rates.
- *Inventory service costs.* Such items as insurance and taxes that are present in many provinces.
- *Storage costs.* Warehousing space and materials handling.
- *Risk costs.* Possible loss, damage, pilferage, perishability, and obsolescence.

Storage costs, risk costs, and some service costs vary according to the characteristics of the items inventoried. For example, perishable products or highly seasonal items have higher risk costs than a commodity-type product, such as lumber. Capital costs are always present and are proportional to the *values* of the item and prevailing interest rates. The costs of carrying inventory vary with the particular circumstances but quite easily could range from 10 to 35 percent for different firms.

Supply Chain Inventory Strategies   Conventional wisdom a decade ago was that a firm should protect itself against uncertainty by maintaining a reserve inventory at each of its production and stocking points. This has been described as a "just-in-case" philosophy of inventory management and led to unnecessarily high levels of inventory. In contrast is the **just-in-time (JIT) concept,** which is an inventory supply system that operates with very low inventories and requires fast, on-time delivery. When parts are needed for production, they arrive from suppliers "just in time," which means neither before nor after they are needed. Note that JIT is used in situations where demand forecasting is reliable, such as when supplying an automobile production line, and is not suitable for inventories that are to be stored over significant periods of time.

Electronic data interchange and electronic messaging technology coupled with the constant pressure for faster response time in replenishing inventory have also changed the way suppliers and customers do business in a supply chain. The approach, called **vendor-managed inventory (VMI),** is an inventory-management system whereby the *supplier* determines the product amount and assortment a customer (such as a retailer) needs and automatically delivers the appropriate items.

Campbell's Soup's system illustrates how VMI works.[23] Campbell's first establishes EDI links with retailers. Every morning, retailers electronically inform the company of their demand for all Campbell's products and the inventory levels in their distribution centres. Campbell's uses that information to forecast future demand and determine which products need replenishment based on upper and lower inventory limits established with each retailer. Trucks leave the Campbell's shipping plant that afternoon and arrive at the retailer's distribution centres with the required replenishments the same day.

Closing the Loop: Reverse Logistics

The flow of goods in a supply chain does not end with the consumer or industrial user. Companies today recognize that a supply chain can work in reverse. **Reverse logistics** is a process of reclaiming recyclable and reusable materials, returns, and reworks from the point of consumption or use for repair, remanufacturing, redistribution, or disposal. The effect of reverse logistics can be seen in the reduced waste in landfills and lowered operating costs for companies.

Such companies as Eastman Kodak (reusable cameras), Motorola (return and reuse of cellphones), and Caterpillar, Xerox, and IBM (remanufacturing and recycling) have acclaimed reverse logistics programs.[24] Other firms have enlisted third-party logistics providers to handle this process along with other supply chain functions.

---

just-in-time (JIT) concept
An inventory supply system that operates with very low inventories and requires fast, on-time delivery.

vendor-managed inventory (VMI)
An inventory management system whereby the supplier determines the product amount and assortment a customer (such as a retailer) needs and automatically delivers the appropriate items.

reverse logistics
A process of reclaiming recyclable and reusable materials, returns, and reworks from the point of consumption or use for repair, remanufacturing, redistribution, or disposal.

LEARNING OBJECTIVES REVIEW

LO1 **Explain what is meant by a marketing channel of distribution and why intermediaries are often needed.**

A marketing channel of distribution, or simply a marketing channel, consists of individuals and firms involved in the process of making a product or service available for use or consumption by consumers and business users. Intermediaries make possible the flow of products from producers to buyers by performing three basic functions. The transactional function involves buying, selling, and risk taking because intermediaries stock merchandise in anticipation of sales. The logistics function involves the gathering, storing, and dispensing of products. The facilitating function assists producers in making products and services more attractive to buyers.

LO2 **Distinguish among traditional marketing channels, electronic marketing channels, multichannel distribution, and different types of vertical marketing systems.**

Traditional marketing channels describe the route taken by products and services from producers to buyers. This route can range from a direct channel with no intermediaries, because a producer and ultimate consumers deal directly with each other, to indirect channels where intermediaries (agents, wholesalers, distributors, or retailers) are inserted between a producer and consumer and perform numerous channel functions. Electronic marketing channels employ the Internet to make products and services available for consumption and use by consumer or business buyers. Today, many firms engage in multichannel distribution—an arrangement whereby a firm reaches buyers by employing two or more different types of marketing channels. Vertical marketing systems (VMS) are professionally managed and centrally coordinated marketing channels designed to achieve channel economics and maximum marketing impact. There are three types of VMS: corporate, contractual, and administered.

LO3 **Describe factors considered by marketing executives when selecting and managing a marketing channel.**

Four factors affect a company's choice and management of a marketing channel: environmental factors, consumer factors, product factors, and company factors. Recognizing that numerous routes to buyers exist and also recognizing the factors just described, marketers consider three questions when choosing and managing a marketing channel. Which channel and intermediaries will provide the best coverage of the target market? Marketers typically choose one of three levels of coverage: intensive, selective, and exclusive distribution. Which channel and intermediaries will best satisfy the buying requirements of the target market? These buying requirements include information, convenience, variety, and attendant services. Which channel and intermediaries will be the most profitable?

LO4 **Recognize how conflict, cooperation, and legal considerations affect marketing channels' relationships.**

Because marketing channels consist of independent individuals and firms, there is the potential for conflict. Two types of conflict can occur: vertical and horizontal. Vertical conflict occurs between different levels of a marketing channel while horizontal conflict occurs between intermediaries at the same level in a marketing channel. One way to reduce the prospect of conflict is to have a channel captain—a channel member that coordinates, directs, and supports other channel members. However, sometimes channel conflict can result in legal action. Such legal action arises from channel practices that are perceived to restrain competition or to create monopolies.

LO5 **Recognize the relationship between marketing channels, logistics, and supply chain management and how a company's supply chain aligns with its marketing strategy.**

A marketing channel relies on logistics to make products available to consumers and business users. Logistics involves those activities that focus on getting the right amount of the right products to the right place at the right time at the lowest possible cost. The performance of these activities is logistics management—the practice of organizing the cost-effective flow of raw materials, in-process inventory, finished goods, and related information from point of origin to point of consumption to satisfy customer requirements.

A supply chain is a sequence of firms that perform activities required to create and deliver a product or service to consumers or business users. It differs from a marketing channel in terms of membership. A supply chain includes suppliers that provide raw material inputs to a manufacturer as well as the wholesalers and retailers that deliver products and services. The management process is also different. Supply chain management is the integration and organization of information and logistics activities across firms in a supply chain for the purpose of creating and delivering products and services that provide value to consumers.

A company's supply chain follows from its defined marketing strategy. The alignment of a company's supply chain with its marketing strategy involves three steps: (*1*) a supply chain must reflect the needs of the customer being served, (*2*) a company must understand what a supply chain is designed to do well, and (*3*) a supply chain must be consistent with the customer's needs and the company's marketing strategy.

LO6 **Identify the major logistics costs and customer service factors that managers consider when making supply chain decisions.**

Companies strive to provide superior customer service while controlling logistics costs. The major customer service factors include the time between orders and deliveries, dependability in replenishing inventory, communication between buyers and sellers, and convenience in buying from the seller. Logistics

cost factors include transportation, materials handling and warehousing, order processing, inventory, and stockouts.

LO7 **Describe the key logistics functions in a supply chain.**

The four logistics functions in a supply chain include transportation, warehousing and materials handling, order processing, and inventory management. Transportation provides the movement of goods necessary in a supply chain. Five major transport modes are railroads, motor carriers, air carriers, pipelines, and water carriers. Warehousing and materials handling include the storing, sorting, and handling of products at storage warehouse or distribution centres. Order processing includes order receipt, delivery, invoicing, and collection from customers. Inventory management involves minimizing inventory-carrying costs while maintaining sufficient stocks of products to satisfy customer needs. Two popular inventory management practices are just-in-time (JIT) and vendor-managed inventory (VMI) systems.

FOCUSING ON KEY TERMS

brokers p. 377
business distributor p. 374
channel conflict p. 383
customer service p. 390
direct channel p. 373
direct marketing channels p. 375
disintermediation p. 383
electronic marketing channels p. 375
franchising p. 379
indirect channel p. 373
just-in-time (JIT) concept p. 395
logistics management p. 385
manufacturer's agents p. 377

marketing channel p. 370
materials handling p. 393
merchant wholesalers p. 376
multichannel distribution p. 376
reverse logistics p. 395
selling agents p. 377
strategic channel alliances p. 376
supply chain p. 385
supply chain management p. 385
total logistics cost p. 389
vendor-managed inventory (VMI) p. 395
vertical marketing systems (VMS) p. 377

APPLYING MARKETING KNOWLEDGE

1 Suppose that the president of a carpet manufacturing firm has asked you to look into the possibility of bypassing the firm's wholesalers (who sell to carpet, department, and furniture stores) and sell direct to these stores. What caution would you voice on this matter, and what type of information would you gather before making this decision?

2 How does the channel captain idea differ among corporate, administered, and contractual vertical marketing systems with particular reference to the use of different forms of influence available to firms?

3 How do specialty, shopping, and convenience goods generally relate to intensive, selective, and exclusive distribution? Give a brand name that is an example of each goods–distribution matchup.

4 List several companies to which logistical activities might be unimportant. Also list some whose focus is only on the inbound or outbound side.

5 List the logistics customer service factors that would be important to buyers in the following types of companies: (*a*) manufacturing, (*b*) retailers, (*c*) hospitals, and (*d*) construction.

6 The auto industry is a heavy user of just-in-time concept. Why? What other industries would be good candidates for its application? What do they have in common?

7 What are some types of business in which order processing may be among the most important success factors in terms of logistics management?

Building Your Marketing Plan

Does your marketing plan involve selecting channels and intermediaries? If so:

1. Identify which channel and intermediaries will provide the best coverage of the target market for your product and service.
2. Specify which channel and intermediaries will best satisfy the important buying requirements of the target market.
3. Determine which channel and intermediaries will be the most profitable.

Select your channel(s) and intermediary(ies). Now, does your marketing plan involve a product? If so:

1. If inventory is involved, (a) identify the three or four kinds of inventory needed for your organization (retail stock, finished goods, raw materials, supplies, and so on), and (b) suggest ways to reduce their costs.
2. (a) Rank the four customer service factors (time, dependability, communication, and convenience) from most important to least important from your customers' point of view, and (b) identify actions for the one or two most important to serve customers better.

Video Case 14

AMAZON: DELIVERING THE GOODS . . . MILLIONS OF TIMES EACH DAY!

"The new economy means that the balance of power has shifted toward the consumer," explains Jeff Bezos, CEO of Amazon.com, Inc. The global online retailer is a pioneer of fast, convenient, low-cost virtual shopping that has attracted millions of consumers. Of course, while Amazon has changed the way many people shop, the company still faces the traditional and daunting task of creating a seamless flow of deliveries to its customers—often millions of times each day!

The Company

Bezos started Amazon.com with a simple idea: to use the Internet to transform book buying into the fastest, easiest, and most enjoyable shopping experience possible. The company was incorporated in 1994 and opened its virtual doors in July 1995. At the forefront of a huge growth of dot-com businesses, Amazon pursued a get-big-fast business strategy. Sales grew rapidly and Amazon began adding products and services other than books. In fact, Amazon soon set its goal on being the world's most customer-centric company, where customers can find and discover anything they might want to buy online!

Today, Amazon claims to have the "Earth's Biggest Selection" of products and services, including books, CDs, videos, toys and games, electronics, kitchenware, computers, free electronic greeting cards, and auctions. Other services allow customers to:

- search for books, music, and videos with any word from the title or any part of the artist's name;
- browse hundreds of product categories; and

- receive personalized recommendations, based on past purchases, through e-mail or when they log on.

These products and services have attracted millions of people in more than 220 countries and made Amazon.com, along with its international sites in Canada, the United Kingdom, Germany, Japan, France, and China, the leading online retailer.

Despite its incredible success with consumers and continuing growth in sales to more than $3 billion annually, Amazon.com found it difficult to be profitable. Many industry observers questioned the viability of online retailing and Amazon's business model. Then, Amazon shocked many people by announcing its first profit in the fourth quarter of 2001. There are a variety of explanations for the turnaround. Generally, Bezos suggests that "efficiencies allow for lower prices, spurring sales growth across the board, which can be handled by existing facilities without much additional cost." More specifically, the facilities that Bezos is referring to are the elements of its supply chain—which are one of the most complex and expensive aspects of the company's business.

Supply Chain and Logistics Management at Amazon.com

What happens after an order is submitted on Amazon's Web site but before it arrives at the customer's door? A lot! Amazon.com maintains seven huge distribution, or "fulfillment," centres, where it keeps inventory of more than 2.7 million products. This is one of the key differences between Amazon.com and some of its competitors—it actually stocks products. Amazon must manage the flow of products from its suppliers to its distribution centres and the flow of customer orders from the distribution centres to individuals' homes or offices.

The process begins with the suppliers. "Amazon's goal is to collaborate with our suppliers to increase efficiencies and improve inventory turnover," explains Jim Miller, vice-president of supply chain at Amazon.com. "We want to bring to suppliers the kind of interactive relationship that has inspired customers to shop with us," he adds. For example, Amazon is using software to more accurately forecast purchasing patterns by region, which allows it to give its suppliers better information about delivery dates and volumes. Prior to the development of this software, 12 percent of incoming inventory was sent to the wrong location, leading to lost time and delayed orders. Now, only 4 percent of the incoming inventory is mishandled.

At the same time, Amazon has been improving the part of the process that sorts the products into individual orders. Jeffrey Wilke, Amazon's senior vice-president of operations, says, "We spent the whole year really focused on increasing productivity." Again, technology has been essential. "The speed at which telecommunications networks allow us to pass information back and forth has enabled us to do the real-time work that we keep talking about. In the past, it would have taken too long to get this many items through a system," explains Wilke. Once the order is in the system, computers ensure that all items are included in the box before it is taped and labelled. A network of trucks and regional postal hubs then conclude the process with delivery of the order.

The success of Amazon's logistics and supply chain management activities may be most evident during the year-end holiday shopping season. During one past holiday season, Amazon received orders for 37.9 million items between November 9 and December 21, including orders for 450,000 Harry Potter books and products and orders for 36,000 items placed just before the holiday

delivery deadline. Well over 99 percent of the orders were shipped and delivered on time!

Amazon's Challenges

Despite all of Amazon's recent improvements, logistics experts estimate that the company's distribution centres are operating at approximately 40 percent of their capacity. This situation suggests that Amazon must reduce its capacity or increase its sales.

Several sales growth options are possible. First, Amazon can continue to pursue growth through sales of books, CDs, and videos. Expanded lists of books, music, and movies from throughout the world and convenient selection services may appeal to current and potential customers. Second, Amazon can continue its expansion into new product and service categories. This approach would prevent Amazon from becoming a niche merchant of books, music, and movies, and position it as an online department store. Finally, Amazon can pursue a strategy of providing access to its existing operations to other retailers. For example, Amazon took over the Toys "Я" Us Web site, adding it as a store on Amazon's site. Borders, Expedia, and Circuit City have begun similar partnerships.

Amazon.com has come a long way toward proving that online retailing can work. As the company strives to maintain profitability and continue its growth, its future success is likely to depend on the success of its logistics and supply chain management activities!

Questions

1 How do Amazon.com's logistics and supply chain management activities help the company create value for its customers?

2 What systems did Amazon develop to improve the flow of products from suppliers to Amazon distribution centres? What systems improved the flow of orders from the distribution centres to customers?

3 Why will logistics and supply chain management play an important role in the future success of Amazon.com?

Chapter 15

Retailing

TIM HORTONS: SEEKING GROWTH SOUTH OF THE BORDER!

What began as a single donut shop in an Ontario steel town has grown into Canada's top food-service retail chain. With over 3,000 locations coast-to-coast and over $2 billion in restaurant sales, Tim Hortons has become "the people's restaurant." In fact, Tim's accounts for 42 percent of Canadian quick-service restaurant traffic and holds the number one spot for breakfast day part business!

The company also has a long history of community involvement and corporate social responsibility. In short, the company doesn't just serve coffee, it serves its community. Tim Hortons sponsors the Timbits Minor Sports Program, which serves over 200,000 children who play hockey, soccer, lacrosse, and baseball. It also sponsors the Canadian Cycling Association, the Canadian Curling Association, and the national curling championship—The Tim Hortons Brier. It also supports free swim programs and makes a major commitment to environmental events across the nation. And, of course, there is the Tim Horton Children's Foundation, a non-profit organization that sends thousands of economically disadvantaged children to summer camps.

Now the company is setting its sights on growth opportunities south of the border.

Tim Horton opened its first U.S. location in Buffalo, New York, in 1984 but it is picking up its expansion activity very quickly in the American market. For example, Tim Hortons has entered New York City by

learning objectives

After reading this chapter, you should be able to:

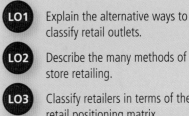

LO1 Explain the alternative ways to classify retail outlets.

LO2 Describe the many methods of non-store retailing.

LO3 Classify retailers in terms of the retail positioning matrix.

LO4 Develop retailing mix strategies over the life cycle of a retail store.

LO5 Identify the challenges Canadian retailers face as they pursue sustainable growth.

buying up old Dunkin' Donuts locations. The move gives it a presence in highly visible locations like Times Square, Penn Station, and Herald Square, capturing the attention of bloggers and media, including several articles in *The New York Times.* According to Tim Hortons' chief operations officer, David Clanachan, the company is seeking out high-traffic areas in airports, hospitals, colleges and universities, and sports stadiums. For example, it opened a restaurant at Fort Knox, the first U.S. military location for the company. Currently, the company has over 500 stores in the U.S., and that number is climbing. As for brand positioning, Tim Hortons is luring Dunkin' Donuts customers by emphasizing quality and value with its ad tag, "Where quality meets value." This is different than the ad tag used in Canada ("Always Fresh, Always Tim Hortons"). However, the company feels the key to success in the U.S. will be its emphasis on making an emotional connection with our American cousins. According to Tim Hortons' vice president of national advertising, Glen Hollis, Canadians feel that Tim Hortons is part of their lives, and this is what the company hopes to accomplish with customers south of the border.[1]

retailing
All activities involved in selling, renting, and providing goods and services to ultimate consumers for personal, family, or household use.

Tim Hortons is just one example of many dynamic and exciting retailers you may encounter today in the Canadian marketplace. This chapter examines the concept of **retailing,** which includes all activities involved in selling, renting, and providing goods and services to ultimate consumers for personal, family, or household use. We will look at the critical role of retailing in the marketplace and the challenging decisions retailers face as they strive to create value and customer satisfaction. In the channel of distribution, retailing is where the customer meets the product. According to the Retail Council of Canada, a non-profit association representing more than 40,000 stores of all formats across Canada, "Retail is the face of Canadian business."[2]

THE VALUE AND SCOPE OF RETAILING

Retailing is an important marketing activity. Not only do producers and consumers meet through retailing actions, but retailing also creates customer value and has a significant impact on the economy. In fact, retailing is critically important to the Canadian and global economies. Retail sales in Canada exceed $460 billion.[3] And the retail sector also employs over two million people in Canada, or one in eight Canadian jobs, making it the second-largest labour force in the country.[4] Major retail categories in Canada include automotive, food, furniture, and clothing.

The magnitude of retail sales is hard to imagine. Some of Canada's top retailers have annual sales revenues that surpass the gross domestic product (GDP) of several nation-states. For example, Canada's top three grocery store rivals (Loblaws, Sobeys, and Metro) have combined sales greater than the GDP of North Korea; Canada's largest department store companies (the Hudson's Bay Company, Walmart Canada, and Sears Canada) have combined sales greater than the GDP of both Iceland and Honduras.

On a global basis, just the top 250 retailers in the world (based on sales) had combined sales of over $3.6 trillion. Walmart is the world's number one retailer with over $375 billion in sales. Some of the other top retailers in the world include Carrefour (France), Metro (Germany), Tesco (U.K.), and Aeon (Japan). Some Canadian retailers also made the top 250 list, including Loblaws (#38), Alimentation Couche-Tard (#53), and Empire Company (#62); Canadian Tire, the Hudson's Bay Company, Metro Inc., Shoppers Drug Mart, and Rona Inc. also made the list. Several Canadian retailers also made the list of the world's Top 50 Fastest Growing Retailers, including Alimentation Couche-Tard, Rona Inc., and Metro.[5]

The scope of retailing has reached all corners of the globe. But the retail market-place is evolving. China, for example, is now the world's third-largest retail market. India, too, is attracting the attention of global retailers, and many South American countries are experiencing strong retail growth, including Argentina and Chile. But despite this changing and competitive global marketplace, leading Canadian retailers are thriving in this new environment.[6] As we will see later in the chapter, in order to sustain their growth, Canadian retailers will have to overcome several challenges in this new global retail arena.

LO1 Classifying Retail Outlets

For manufacturers, consumers, and the economy, retailing is an important component of marketing that has several variations. Because of the large number of alternative forms of retailing, it is easier to understand the differences among retail institutions by recognizing that outlets can be classified in several ways. First, **form of ownership** distinguishes retail outlets based on whether individuals, corporate chains, or contractual systems own the outlet. Second, **level of service** is used to describe the degree of service provided to the customer. Finally, the type of **merchandise line** describes how many different types of products a store carries and in what assortment. A more in-depth discussion of the alternative types of outlets follows.

Form of Ownership

Independent Retailer   One of the most common forms of retail ownership is the independent business, owned by an individual. The independent retailer accounts for over 60 percent of total retail trade in Canada. Small retailers tend to dominate in bakeries, sporting goods, jewellery, and gift stores. They are also popular retailers of auto supplies, books, paint, flowers, and women's accessories. The advantage of this form of ownership for the owner is that he or she can be his or her own boss. For customers, the independent store can offer convenience, quality, personal service, and lifestyle compatibility.

Corporate Chain   A second form of ownership, the corporate chain, involves multiple outlets under common ownership. If you have ever shopped at The Bay, Zellers, or Loblaws, or had your hair cut at First Choice Haircutters, you have shopped at a chain outlet.

In a chain operation, centralization in decision making and purchasing is common. Chain stores have advantages in dealing with manufacturers, particularly as the size of the chain grows. A large chain can bargain with a manufacturer to obtain good service or volume discounts on orders. The buying power of chains allows them to offer consumers competitive prices on merchandise. Walmart's large volume makes it a strong negotiator with manufacturers of most products. Consumers also benefit in dealing with chains because there are multiple outlets with similar merchandise and consistent management policies. The Retail Council of Canada reports tremendous growth in corporate chain stores across the nation.

Contractual System   Contractual systems involve independently owned stores that band together to act like a chain. The three kinds described in Chapter 14 are retailer-sponsored cooperatives, wholesaler-sponsored voluntary chains, and franchises. One retailer-sponsored cooperative is Guardian Drugs, which consists of neighbourhood

form of ownership
Distinguishes retail outlets based on whether individuals, corporate chains, or contractual systems own the outlet.

level of service
The degree of service provided to the customer by self-, limited-, and full-service retailers.

merchandise line
How many different types of products a store carries and in what assortment.

pharmacies that all agree to buy their products from the same wholesaler. In this way, members can take advantage of volume discounts commonly available to chains and also give the impression of being a large chain, which may be viewed more favourably by some consumers. Wholesaler-sponsored voluntary chains, such as Ace Hardware, try to achieve similar benefits.

As noted in Chapter 14, in a franchise system an individual or firm (the franchisee) contracts with a parent company (the franchisor) to set up a business or retail outlet. The franchisor usually assists in selecting the location, setting up the store or facility, advertising, and training personnel. The franchisee usually pays a one-time franchise fee and an annual royalty, usually tied to the franchise's sales. There are two general types of retail franchises: *business-format franchises,* such as McDonald's, and *product-distribution franchises,* such as a Ford dealership or a Coca-Cola distributor. In business-format franchising, the franchisor provides step-by-step procedures for most aspects of the business and guidelines for the most likely decisions a franchisee will face.

Franchising is attractive because it offers an opportunity for people to enter a well-known, established business for which managerial advice is provided. Also, the franchise fee may be less than the cost of setting up an independent business.

Franchise fees paid to the franchisor can range from $15,000 for a Subway franchise to $45,000 for a McDonald's restaurant franchise. When the fees are combined with other costs, such as real estate and equipment, however, the total investment can be much higher. Figure 15–1 shows the top five franchises in North America, as rated by *Entrepreneur* magazine, based on such factors as size, financial strength, stability, growth rate, years in business, and costs.[7] By selling franchises, an organization reduces the cost of expansion but loses some control. A good franchisor, however, will maintain strong control of the outlets in terms of delivery and presentation of merchandise and try to enhance recognition of the franchise name. Canadian entrepreneurs have plenty of franchise opportunities, from automotive care to wine making. You can check it out at the Canadian Franchise Association Web site (**www.cfa.ca**). Or visit CanadianFranchises.com for the latest news on hot franchises in Canada.

Level of Service

Even though most customers perceive little variation in retail outlets by form of ownership, differences among retailers are more obvious in terms of level of service. In some

● **FIGURE 15–1**

The top five franchises in North America

Franchise	Type of Business	Total Investment	Number of Franchises (global)
Subway	Sandwich restaurant	$75,000–$225,000	25,000
Dunkin' Donuts	Doughnut shop	$180,000–$1,600,000	7,500
Jackson Hewitt Tax Service	Income tax preparation	$48,000–$92,000	5,800
7-Eleven	Convenience Store	Varies	30,000
The UPS Store/ Mail Boxes Etc.	Business, communication, and postal services	$155,000–$267,000	5,600

department stores, very few services are provided. Some warehouse grocery stores have customers bag the food themselves. Other retail outlets, such as Holt Renfrew, provide a wide range of customer services from gift wrapping to wardrobe consultation.

Self-Service   Self-service is at the extreme end of the level of service continuum because the customer performs many functions and little is provided by the outlet. Home building-supply outlets and gas stations are often self-service. Warehouse stores, usually in buildings several times larger than a conventional store, are self-service with all non-essential customer services eliminated. Similarly, many gas stations are self-service. New forms of self-service are being developed in grocery stores, airlines, and hotels. For example, when you fly, you can often choose to use self-service kiosks to check in, find a seat, and print a boarding pass without the help of an attendant. In short, with self-service you are actually a co-creator of the value you receive.

Limited Service   Limited-service outlets provide some services, such as return of credit and merchandise, but not others, such as return of custom-made clothes. General merchandise stores, such as Walmart and Zellers, are usually considered limited-service outlets. Customers are responsible for most shopping activities, although salespeople are available in such departments as consumer electronics, jewellery, and lawn and garden.

Full-Service   Full-service retailers, which include most specialty stores and some department stores, provide many services to their customers. Services can include more knowledgeable and friendly salespeople on the floor assisting the customer with purchases or offering special delivery of purchases to customers' homes. Often, this full-service strategy can serve as a competitive advantage for such stores, especially in this new customer experience management era.

Merchandise Line

depth of product line
The store carries a large assortment of each item.

breadth of product line
The variety of different items a store carries.

Retail outlets also vary by their merchandise lines, the key distinction being the breadth and depth of the items offered to customers (Figure 15–2). **Depth of product line** means that the store carries a large assortment of each item, such as a shoe store that offers running shoes, dress shoes, and children's shoes. **Breadth of product line** refers to the variety of different items a store carries.

Depth of Line   Stores that carry a considerable assortment (depth) of a related line of items are limited-line stores. Black's photography stores carry considerable depth in photography equipment. Stores that carry tremendous depth in one primary line of merchandise are single-line stores. La Senza carries great depth in women's lingerie while Lids is a retail outlet that specializes in selling hats to teens. Both limited- and single-line stores are often referred to as *specialty outlets*.

● **FIGURE 15–2**
Breadth versus depth of merchandise lines

Breadth: Number of different product lines

	Shoes	Appliances	CDs	Men's clothing
Depth: Number of items within each product line	Nike running shoes Florsheim dress shoes Top Sider boat shoes Adidas tennis shoes	Sony TV sets Sanyo DVD players General Electric dishwashers Sharp microwave ovens	Classical Rock Jazz Country Rap Christian	Suits Ties Jackets Overcoats Socks Shirts

Specialty discount outlets focus on one type of product, such as electronics, business supplies, or books, at very competitive prices. These outlets are referred to in the trade as *category killers* because they often dominate the market.

Breadth of Line   Stores that carry a broad product line, with limited depth, are referred to as *general merchandise stores*. For example, large department stores carry a wide range of different types of products but not unusual sizes. The breadth and depth of merchandise lines are important decisions for a retailer. For example, Bulk Barn is Canada's largest bulk food retailer. Its tagline emphasizes the breadth of its product line: "At Bulk Barn we carry over 4,000 products—everything from soup to nuts." Traditionally, outlets carried related lines of goods. Today, however, **scrambled merchandising,** offering several unrelated product lines in a single store, is common. The modern drugstore carries food, camera equipment, magazines, paper products, toys, small hardware items, and pharmaceuticals. Supermarkets rent DVDs, develop film, and sell flowers.

A form of scrambled merchandising, the **hypermarket,** has been successful in Europe. These hypermarkets are large stores (more than 200,000 square feet) based on a simple concept: Offer consumers everything in a single outlet, eliminating the need to stop at more than one location. The stores provide variety, quality, and low price for food and groceries and general merchandise. In France, the concept is so successful that hypermarkets maintain a 51 percent share of the grocery market. Carrefour, one of the largest hypermarket retailers, has over 200 hypermarkets in France and over 400 stores in the rest of Europe, and it has expanded into China with close to 100 hypermarkets.[8]

In North America, retailers discovered that many shoppers were uncomfortable with the huge size of hypermarkets. So they developed a variation of the hypermarket called the *supercentre,* which combines a typical merchandise store with a full-size grocery. These supercentres tend to range in size between 100,000 and 200,000 square feet. Loblaws, one of Canada's top retail grocery chains, uses the supercentre concept very successfully. Its McCowan Market in Markham, Ontario, is 115,000 square feet and offers its traditional grocery line along with other merchandise selection, including housewares, office supplies, cosmetics, and electronics. Walmart Canada is also a major player in the supercentre category.

Scrambled merchandising is convenient for consumers because it eliminates the number of stops required in a shopping trip. However, for the retailer, this merchandising policy means that there is competition between very dissimilar types of retail outlets, or **intertype competition.** A local bakery may compete with a department store, discount outlet, or even a local gas station. Scrambled merchandising and intertype competition make it more difficult to be a retailer.

scrambled merchandising
Offering several unrelated product lines in a single retail store.

hypermarket
A large store (more than 200,000 square feet) offering consumers everything in a single outlet.

intertype competition
Competition between very dissimilar types of retail outlets.

---

learning review

1. Centralized decision making and purchasing are an advantage of _____ ownership.

2. What are some examples of new forms of self-service retailers?

3. Would a shop for big men's clothes carrying pants in sizes 40 to 60 have a broad or deep product line?

LO2 NON-STORE RETAILING

Most of the retailing examples discussed earlier in the chapter, such as corporate chains, department stores, and limited- and single-line specialty stores, involve store retailing. Many retailing activities today, however, are not limited to sales in a store. Non-store

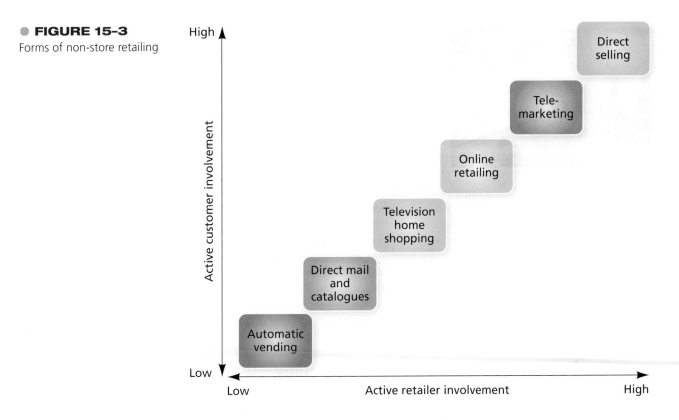

retailing occurs outside a retail outlet through activities that involve varying levels of customer and retailer involvement. Figure 15–3 shows six forms of non-store retailing: automatic vending, direct mail and catalogues, television home shopping, online retailing, telemarketing, and direct selling.

Automatic Vending

Non-store retailing includes vending machines, which make it possible to serve customers when and where stores cannot. Maintenance and operating costs are high,

and so product prices in vending machines tend to be higher than those in stores. Typically, small convenience products are available in vending machines. In fact, most of the machines in use in Canada are soft-drink or beverage machines.

Improved technology is making vending machines easier to use by reducing the need for cash. Many machines already accept credit cards, and some even accept cashless purchases using cellphones. Another improvement in vending machines is the use of wireless technology to notify vendors when their machines are empty. Nestlé, for example, is installing hundreds of ice cream vending machines in France and England that send wireless messages to supply-truck drivers. Finally, there are "smart-interactive" vending machines such as Coca-Cola's new 100-flavour interactive soda fountain (called Freestyle) that allows you to mix your own flavoured soda. Plus, this machine sends sales data back to headquarters, and Coke corporate can also talk to the machine telling it whether certain flavours need to be discontinued.[9]

Direct Mail and Catalogues

Direct mail and catalogue retailing is attractive because it eliminates the cost of a store and clerks. In addition, it improves marketing efficiency

through segmentation and targeting and creates customer value by providing a fast and convenient means of making a purchase. Canadians have been increasing the amount they spend on direct mail catalogue merchandise. Internationally, catalogue shopping is also popular. For example, Swedish furniture retailer IKEA delivers 160 million copies of its catalogue to over 30 countries in over 25 languages, including several million to Canada.[10]

As consumers' direct mail and catalogue purchases have increased, the numbers of direct mailings, catalogues, and products sold have also increased. A typical household now receives dozens of catalogues per year. The competition, combined with higher paper and postal costs, however, has caused direct retailers to focus on proven customers rather than "prospects." A successful approach now used by many catalogue retailers is to send specialty catalogues to market niches identified in their databases. L.L. Bean, a long-standing catalogue retailer, has developed an individual catalogue for fly-fishing enthusiasts.

Creative forms of catalogue retailing are also being developed. Hallmark, for example, offers cards for businesses in its colourful 32-page "Business Expressions" catalogue. Victoria's Secret mails as many as 45 catalogues a year to its customers to generate mail-order and 800-number business and to increase traffic in its 900 stores. Many catalogue retailers, such as Sharper Image, now accept telephone orders, mail orders, and online orders!

Television Home Shopping

Television home shopping is possible when consumers watch a shopping channel on which products are displayed; orders are then placed over the telephone or on the Internet. Two popular networks, the Home Shopping Network and QVC, reach millions of Canadian households. A limitation of TV shopping has been the lack of buyer–seller interaction and the inability of consumers to control the items they see. But new technologies now allow consumers to simultaneously shop, chat, and interact with their favourite show host while watching TV.

Online Retailing

Online retailing allows consumers to search for, evaluate, and order products through the Internet. For many consumers, the advantages of this form of retailing, sometimes called *e-tailing,* are 24-hour access, the ability to comparison shop, in-home privacy, and variety. Online retail sales are estimated at over $13 billion.[11]

Online retail purchases can occur in several ways. Consumers can pay a fee to become a member of an online discount service; they can use an online shopping agent or "bot," such as MySimon (**www.mysimon.com**); or they can go directly to

online malls or online shopping directories (portals), such as the Canadian Online Shopping Mall (**http://homer.ca/shopping/index.htm**). Online retailing can also be done via auction on such sites as **www.ebay.ca.** And, finally, you could simply go to a specific online retailer's site. Currently, 50 percent of all Canadian retailers have a Web site and over 90 percent of large Canadian retailers sell via the Internet.[12]

One interesting shopping portal is Cangive.ca. It allows shoppers to donate up to 15 percent of their online purchases to a cause or charity designated by the shopper. Popular causes or charities include Mothers Against Drunk Driving (MADD) and the Canadian Diabetes Association. Many major Canadian retail companies are part of this portal including Amazon.ca, Canadian Tire, and Chapters-Indigo.[13]

Online retailing has also had an impact in terms of physical cross-border shopping. For example, many Americans now use the Internet to order prescription drugs from online Canadian pharmacies, avoiding the hassle of travelling across the border to do their shopping in person. Sales by Canadian online pharmacies are estimated at $500 million but this is down substantially from a few years ago due to the rising Canadian dollar, improvements in the U.S. health insurance industry pertaining to prescription drug coverage, and governmental pressure on both sides of the border over the safety concerns of marketing and distributing prescription drugs online. At the same time, the online retailing is enabling Canadians to buy from American merchants. For example, for every $100 spent online, only $56 is going to Canadian retailers with most to the rest going south of the border.[14]

Online retailers are working hard at improving the online retailing experience by adding experiential or interactive activities on their Web sites. Research shows that almost 75 percent of Canadians treasure the social aspect of shopping, and so e-tailers are integrating their online experiences with the real thing.[15] For example, many apparel stores use virtual models or avatars to involve consumers in the purchase process and help with product selection.[16] Similarly, car manufacturers, such as BMW, Mercedes, and Jaguar, encourage Web site visitors to "build" a vehicle by selecting interior and exterior colours, packages, and options and then view the customized virtual car. In addition, the merger of television home shopping and online retailing is possible through TV-based Web platforms, such as Microsoft's MSN TV. Finally, owning a computer is not a necessity for online retailing. There are thousands of Internet cafes in more than 170 countries that provide guests with access to the Internet.

Telemarketing

telemarketing
Using the telephone to interact with and sell directly to consumers.

Another form of non-store retailing, called **telemarketing,** involves using the telephone to interact with and sell directly to consumers. Compared with direct mailing, telemarketing is often viewed as a more efficient means of targeting consumers. Insurance companies, brokerage firms, and newspapers have often used this form of retailing as a way to cut costs but still maintain access to their customers. According to the Canadian Marketing Association, annual telemarketing sales exceed $16 billion.[17]

The telemarketing industry has gone through some changes as a result of past and proposed legislation related to telephone solicitations. Such issues as consumer privacy, industry standards, and ethical guidelines have encouraged discussion among consumer groups, government, and businesses. New legislation and regulation has evolved to provide a balance between consumer privacy and the right to engage in ethical business practices.

Direct Selling

Direct selling, sometimes called door-to-door retailing, involves direct sales of goods and services to consumers through personal interactions and demonstrations in their homes or offices. A variety of companies, including such familiar names as Fuller Brush, Avon, World Book, and Mary Kay Cosmetics, have created a multi-billion dollar industry by providing consumers with personalized service and convenience. In Canada, however, sales have been declining as retail chains such as Walmart begin to carry similar products at discount prices and as the increasing number of dual-career households reduces the number of potential buyers at home.

In response to the changes, many direct-selling retailers are expanding into other markets. Avon, for example, has millions of sales representatives in more than 100 countries, including Mexico, Poland, Argentina, and China. Direct selling is likely to continue to grow in markets where the lack of effective distribution channels increases the importance of door-to-door convenience and where the lack of consumer knowledge about products and brands will increase the need for a person-to-person approach.

RETAILING STRATEGY

This section identifies how a retailer develops and implements a retailing strategy by positioning the store and taking specific retailing mix actions. Figure 15–4 identifies the relationship between positioning and the retailing mix.

 Positioning a Retail Store

The classification alternatives presented in the previous sections help determine one store's position relative to its competitors.

retail positioning matrix
Positions retail outlets on two dimensions: breadth of product line and value added.

Retail Positioning Matrix The **retail positioning matrix** was developed by the MAC Group, Inc., a management consulting firm.[18] This matrix positions retail outlets on two dimensions: breadth of product line and value added. As defined previously, breadth of product line is the range of products sold through each outlet. The second dimension, *value added,* includes such elements as location (as with 7-Eleven stores), product reliability (as with Holiday Inn or McDonald's), or prestige (as with Birks).

The retail positioning matrix in Figure 15–5 shows four possible positions. An organization can be successful in any position, but unique strategies are required within each quadrant. Consider the four stores shown in the matrix:

1. *The Bay has high value added and a broad product line.* Retailers in this quadrant pay great attention to store design and product lines. Merchandise often has a high margin of profit and is of high quality. The stores in this position typically provide high levels of service.
2. *Zellers has low value added and a broad line.* Zellers and similar firms typically trade a lower price for increased volume in sales. Retailers in this position

● **FIGURE 15–4**
Elements of a retailing strategy

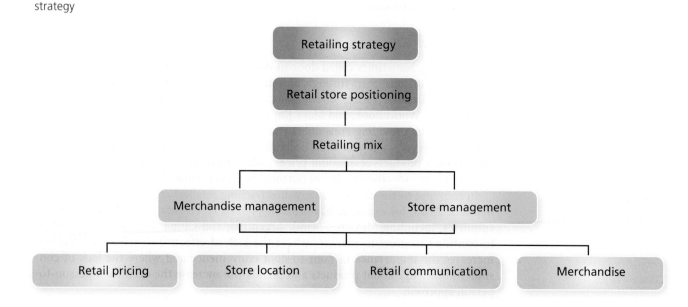

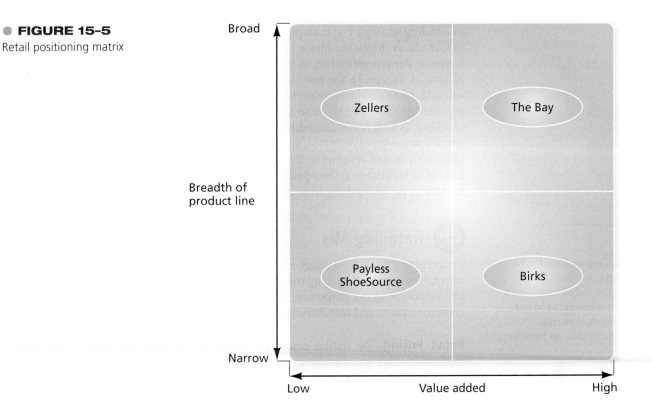

● **FIGURE 15–5**
Retail positioning matrix

Broad

Breadth of
product line

Narrow

Low   Value added   High

Zellers   The Bay

Payless
ShoeSource   Birks

focus on price with low service levels and an image of being a place for good buys.

3. *Birks has high value added and a narrow line.* Retailers of this type typically sell a very restricted range of products that are of high-status quality. Customers are also provided with high levels of service.

4. *Payless ShoeSource has low value added and a narrow line.* Such retailers are specialty mass merchandisers. Payless, for example, carries attractively priced shoes for the entire family. These outlets appeal to value-conscious consumers. Economies of scale are achieved through centralized advertising, merchandising, buying, and distribution. Stores are usually the same in design, layout, and merchandise; hence, they are often referred to as "cookie-cutter" stores.

Keys to Positioning To successfully position a store, it must have an identity that has some advantages over the competitors and yet is recognized by consumers. A company can have outlets in several positions on the matrix, but this approach is usually done with different store names. The Hudson's Bay Company, for example, owns The Bay department stores (with high value added and a broad line) and Zellers stores (low value added and a broad line). Shifting from one box in the retail positioning matrix to another is also possible, but all elements of retailing strategy must be re-examined. In fact, as the competitive landscape in retailing has shifted, Zellers has now responded and adjusted its positioning by altering several aspects of

Zellers has made a shift in its retail positioning.

its retailing strategy. For example, Zellers, the number two discount department store in Canada, is migrating into a new space, between a discount department store and a regular department store, to become a "junior department store." In other words, instead of occupying the low value and broad line space as seen in Figure 15–5, it will add more products, including higher-end offerings. It will still offer low prices on many products but will also offer the customer more fashion-oriented apparel and jewellery, as well home furnishings and appliances. Zellers is renovating its stores to give them a more stylish look and will be using more of its signature red colour in its interior. It is also revamping its flyers to give them a cleaner, more organized look. Instead of its historical "low price" promise, Zellers new communications message to customers is, "Everything from A to Z."[19]

 ## Retailing Mix

retailing mix
Activities related to managing the store and the merchandise in the store—including retail pricing, store location, retail communication, and merchandise.

In developing retailing strategy, managers work with the **retailing mix,** which includes activities related to managing the store and the merchandise in the store. The retailing mix is similar to the marketing mix and includes retail pricing, store location, retail communication, and merchandise.

Retail Pricing   In setting prices for merchandise, retailers must decide on the markup, markdown, and timing for markdowns. As mentioned in the appendix to Chapter 13 (Appendix B), the *markup* refers to how much should be added to the cost the retailer paid for a product to reach the final selling price. Retailers decide on the *original markup,* but by the time the product is sold, they end up with a *maintained markup.* The original markup is the difference between retailer cost and initial selling price. When products do not sell as quickly as anticipated, their price is reduced. The difference between the final selling price and retailer cost is the maintained markup, which is also called the *gross margin.*

Discounting a product, or taking a *markdown,* occurs when the product does not sell at the original price and an adjustment is necessary. Often, new models or styles force the price of existing models to be marked down. Discounts may also be used to increase demand for complementary products. For example, retailers might take a markdown on stereos to increase sales of CDs or reduce the price of cake mix to generate frosting purchases. The *timing* of a markdown can be important. Many retailers take a markdown as soon as sales fall off to free up valuable shelf space and cash. However, other stores delay markdowns to discourage bargain hunters and maintain an image of quality. There is no clear answer, but retailers must consider how the timing might affect future sales.

Although most retailers plan markdowns, many retailers use price discounts as part of their regular merchandising policy. Walmart and Home Depot, for example, emphasize consistently low prices and eliminate most markdowns with a strategy often called *everyday low pricing.* Because consumers often use price as an indicator of product quality, however, the brand name of the product and the image of the store become important decision factors in these situations. Another strategy, *everyday fair pricing,* is advocated by retailers that may not offer the lowest price but try to create value for customers through service and the total buying experience. A special issue for retailers trying to keep prices low is **shrinkage,** or theft of merchandise by customers and employees. Retail theft costs Canadian retailers over $3 billion a year, and the cost of this theft gets passed along to the consumer in the form of higher retail prices. The Retail Council of Canada is working with its members on numerous loss-prevention programs.[20]

shrinkage
Breakage and theft of merchandise by customers and employees.

Off-price retailing is a retail pricing practice that has become quite common. **Off-price retailing** involves selling brand-name merchandise at lower than regular prices. The difference between the off-price retailer and a discount store is that off-price merchandise is bought by the retailer from manufacturers with

off-price retailing
Selling brand-name merchandise at lower than regular prices.

excess inventory at prices below wholesale prices, while the discounter buys at full wholesale price (but takes less of a markup than do traditional department stores). Because of this difference in the way merchandise is purchased by the retailer, selection at an off-price retailer is unpredictable, and searching for bargains has become a popular activity for many consumers where savings can often make up for the search effort.

There are several variations of off-price retailing. One is the warehouse club. These large stores (more than 100,000 square feet) are rather stark outlets with no elaborate displays, customer service, or home delivery. They require an annual membership fee (usually $40) for the privilege of shopping there. While a typical Zellers store stocks 30,000 items, warehouse clubs carry about 3,500 items and usually stock just one brand name of appliance or food product. Service is minimal, and customers usually must pay by cash or cheque. However, the extremely competitive pricing of merchandise makes warehouse clubs attractive. Some major warehouse clubs you may be familiar with include Costco, Walmart's Sam's Club, and BJ's Wholesale Club. Sales of these off-price retailers have grown dramatically over the past decade.

A second variation is the outlet store. Factory outlets, such as Van Heusen Factory Store, Bass Shoe Outlet, and Oneida Factory Store, offer products for 25 to 30 percent off the suggested retail price. Manufacturers use the stores to clear excess merchandise and to reach consumers who focus on value shopping. Some retail outlets, such as Brooks Brothers Outlet Store, allow retailers to sell excess merchandise and still maintain an image of offering merchandise at full price in their primary store.

A third variation of off-price retailing is offered by single-price, or extreme value, retailers, such as Family Dollar, Dollar General, and Dollar Tree. These stores average about 6,000 square feet in size and attract customers who want value and a "corner store" environment rather than a large supercentre experience.

Store Location   A second aspect of the retailing mix involves deciding where to locate the store and how many stores to have. Most stores today locate near each other in one of several settings: the central business district, the regional centre, the community shopping centre, the strip location, the power centre, off-mall, or in a lifestyle centre.

central business district
The oldest retail setting, the community's downtown area.

The **central business district** is the oldest retail setting, the community's downtown area. Until the regional outflow to suburbs it was the major shopping area, but the suburban population has grown at the expense of the downtown area. However, recently, there has been some downtown revitalization, with even some "big box" retailers, such as Home Depot and Costco, locating in the downtown core. But some consumers are put off by big-box stores and large department stores. So, some downtowns are revitalizing themselves by offering smaller boutiques and specialty stores where product quality and customer service are the focus.

regional shopping centre
Consists of 50 to 150 stores that typically attract customers who live within an 8- to 16-km range, often containing two or three anchor stores.

A **regional shopping centre** consists of 50 to 150 stores that typically attract customers who live or work within an 8- to 16-km range. These large shopping areas often contain two or three anchor stores, which are well-known national or regional stores, such as Sears and The Bay. The largest variation of a regional centre is the West Edmonton Mall in Alberta. This shopping centre is a conglomerate of 800 stores, an indoor amusement park, 110 restaurants, and a world-class hotel.

Another new concept in regional shopping centres is Vaughan Mills, a 1.2 million-square-foot complex with more than 200 retailers and a unique merchandising concept. It is the first new enclosed regional shopping centre built in Canada in more than a decade. It is distinctive in that it is organized into six "themed neighbourhoods," each emphasizing an aspect of Ontario culture. One focuses on urban cities and contains urban youth-oriented retailers, such as Bluenotes and West 49. Another focuses on fashion and houses stores, such as Aritzia and BCBG Max Azria Outlet. The complex also houses Bass Pro Shops Outdoor World—which features an indoor trout pond—NASCAR SpeedPark go-cart track, and the largest Tommy Hilfiger outlet in the world.

community shopping centre
A retail location that typically has one primary store (usually a department store branch) and 20 to 40 smaller outlets, serving a population of consumers who are within a 10- to 20-minute drive.

strip location
A cluster of stores serving people who live within a 5- to 10-minute drive.

power centre
A huge shopping strip with multiple anchor (or national) stores, a convenient location, and a supermarket.

lifestyle centre
An open-air cluster of specialty retailers, along with theatres, restaurants, fountains, play areas, and green spaces.

Lifestyle centres are emerging as a popular retail concept in Canada.

A more limited approach to retail location is the **community shopping centre,** which typically has one primary store (usually a department store branch) and often about 20 to 40 smaller outlets. Generally, these centres serve a population of consumers who are within a 10- to 20-minute drive.

Not every suburban store is located in a shopping mall. Many neighbourhoods have clusters of stores, referred to as a **strip location,** to serve people who are within a 5- to 10-minute drive. Gas station, hardware, laundry, grocery, and pharmacy outlets are commonly found in a strip location. Unlike the larger shopping centres, the composition of these stores is usually unplanned. A variation of the strip shopping location is called the **power centre,** which is a huge shopping strip with multiple anchor (or national) stores. Power centres are seen as having the convenient location found in many strip centres and the additional power of national stores. These large strips often have two to five anchor stores and usually contain a supermarket, which brings the shopper to the power centre on a weekly basis. Power centres are being built all over Canada. For example, Hopewell Development is completing an $80 million power centre in Winnipeg, anchored by Rona and Costco; when completed, the power centre will have 1.5 million square feet of retail space.[21]

Another trend in Canada in terms of locating stores is "off-mall retailing." In this case, retailers who traditionally locate in malls are building on stand-alone sites. For example, Sears Canada, a common anchor at malls, has opened new-format stores across Canada away from the malls, while the Hudson's Bay Company has launched Designer Depot outlets as free-standing stores.

Another retail location that is growing in popularity in Canada is the **lifestyle centre**—an open-air cluster of specialty retailers, along with theatres, restaurants, fountains, play areas, and green spaces. These lifestyle centres offer the consumer a back-to-community feel and a shopping and entertainment "experience." The Village at Park Royal in West Vancouver was Canada's first lifestyle centre. It has a lighthouse, old-fashioned gas lamps, and West Coast–style architecture where each store differs in appearance, height, design, and colour. Customers do not go there to comparison shop; instead they go to visit the specialty shops, get a bite to eat, or meet friends for a drink. To learn more about lifestyle centres, read the accompanying Marketing Matters box, "Canada's Lifestyle Centres: It's All about the Experience."[22]

Finally, other types of retail locations include carts, kiosks (including electronic kiosks), and wall units. These forms of retailing have been popular in airports and mall common areas because they provide consumers with easy access and also provide rental income for the property owner. Retailers benefit from the relatively low cost compared with a regular store.

In Canada, there has been a shift in the retail landscape in terms of store location and consumer patronage. For example, power centres and lifestyle centres are attracting customers away from traditional shopping centres, especially the large regional shopping centres. In response, these regional shopping centres are reinventing themselves as "mix use" communities where consumers can shop, be entertained, dine, and participate in sports and leisure, as well as other activities.[23]

Retail Communication   A retailer's communication activities can play an important role in positioning a store and creating its image. While the traditional elements of communication and promotion are discussed in Chapter 17 (advertising) and Chapter 18 (personal selling), the message communicated by the many other elements of the retailing mix is also important.

Deciding on the image of a retail outlet is an important retailing mix factor that has been widely recognized and studied since the late 1950s. Pierre Martineau described image as

Marketing Matters

Canada's Lifestyle Centres: It's All about the Experience

Lifestyle centres are popping up all the across the country as retail developers try to create a unique shopping experience for the customer, typically in a back-to-the-community atmosphere. Unlike a power centre, which is also open-air, a lifestyle centre relies less on big-box retailers that sell on price and more on restaurants, cafes, one-location retailers, and other specialty retailers. At the Village at Park Royal, for example, the stores include Lululemon Athletics, Kiss & Makeup, and Urban Barn. You can get a bite to eat at the Cactus Club or meet friends for a drink. You can buy food at the Whole Foods Market, grab a latte at Starbucks, or relax in one of the sidewalk cafes. Or, at Grandview Corners, a 700,000-square-foot centre, you can walk the main street lined with with one-storey chains such as H&M and Garage, and upscale clothiers such as Calvin Klein. There's also a bookstore, ice cream parlour, banks, medical offices, home accessory shops, and a variety of eateries, from Cupcakes to the Memphis Blues BBQ House with its famous pulled pork sandwiches

Lifestyle centres began in the United States about 15 years ago, but the trend has finally caught fire in Canada. In the U.S., there are over 150 lifestyle centres with 15 to 20 opening every year. They range in size from 150,000 to 500,000 square feet. The key to the success of lifestyle centres depends on the ability of the developer to locate in affluent residential neighbourhoods. Having good restaurants in the retail mix is also important. The open-air lifestyle centres not only are cheaper to build but also offer another shopping platform for national specialty chains looking for expansion. But critically important is the ability of the lifestyle centre to offer the customer a satisfying shopping experience.

Experts suggest that consumers no longer want to drive to vast climate-controlled malls with ubiquitous anchors. They don't want to park long distances away and don't want to trek along confusing layouts to find a product they've already researched on the Internet. What they want instead is easy access to retailers, a distinctive destination, and a place to linger and enjoy themselves, whether it is over a latte, lunch, or a beer.

In Toronto, you can visit the Shops at Don Mills, Ontario's first lifestyle centre, offering a variety of retail stores and services in an open-air setting surrounded by a town square. Or, if you are in Nova Scotia, you can visit Dartmouth Crossing, a lifestyle centre located in Dartmouth. There you can stroll through the streets, take a walk on one of the trails, or relax by the brook and enjoy the fresh air. Experts predict numerous centres to emerge across the country as more and more Canadian consumers seek unique and satisfying shopping experiences.

"the way in which the store is defined in the shopper's mind," partly by its functional qualities and partly by an aura of psychological attributes.[24] In this definition, *functional* refers to such elements as price ranges, store layouts, and breadth and depth of merchandise lines. The psychological attributes are the intangibles, such as a sense of belonging, excitement, style, or warmth. Image has been found to include impressions of the corporation that operates the store, the category or type of store, the product categories in the store, the brands in each category, merchandise and service quality, and the marketing activities of the store.[25]

Closely related to the concept of image is the store's atmosphere or ambience. Many retailers believe that sales are affected by layout, colour, lighting, and music in the store, as well as by how crowded it is. In addition, the physical surroundings that influence customers may affect the store's employees.[26] In creating the right image and atmosphere, a retail store tries to attract its target audience with what those consumers seek from the buying experience, and so the store will fortify the beliefs and the emotional reactions that buyers are seeking.[27] Sears, for example, is attempting to shift from its appliance and tool image with advertising that speaks to all members of a family, emphasizing a broad range of brand-name merchandise and one-stop shopping.[28]

Merchandise   A final element of the retailing mix is the merchandise offering. Managing the breadth and depth of the product line requires retail buyers who are familiar with the needs of the target market and the alternative products available from the many manufacturers that might be interested in having a product available in the store. A popular approach to managing the assortment of merchandise today is called

category management
An approach that assigns a manager with the responsibility for selecting all products that consumers in a market segment might view as substitutes for each other, with the objective of maximizing sales and profits in the category.

category management. This approach assigns a manager with the responsibility for selecting all products that consumers in a market segment might view as substitutes for each other, with the objective of maximizing sales and profits in the category. For example, a category manager might be responsible for shoes in a department store or paper products in a grocery store.

Many retailers are developing an advanced form of category management called *consumer marketing at retail (CMAR).* Recent surveys show that as part of their CMAR programs, retailers are conducting research, analyzing the data to identify shopper problems, translating the data into retailing mix actions, executing shopper-friendly in-store programs, and monitoring the performance of the merchandise. Walmart, for example, has used the approach to test baby-product and dollar-product categories. Some grocery stores, such as Safeway and Kroger, use the approach to determine the appropriate mix of brand name and private label products. Specialty retailer Barnes & Noble won a best practice award for its application of the approach to the selection, presentation, and promotion of magazines.[29]

---

learning review

7. What are the two dimensions of the retail positioning matrix?

8. How does original markup differ from maintained markup?

9. A huge shopping strip with multiple anchor stores is a _____ centre.

LO5 THE CHANGING NATURE OF RETAILING

Retailing is the most dynamic aspect of a channel of distribution. Such stores as factory outlets show that new retailers are always entering the market, searching for a new position that will attract customers. The reason for this continual change is explained by two concepts: the wheel of retailing and the retail life cycle.

The Wheel of Retailing

wheel of retailing
A concept that describes how new retail outlets enter the market as low-status, low-margin stores and gradually add embellishments that raise their prices and status. They now face a new low-status, low-margin operator, and the cycle starts to repeat itself.

The **wheel of retailing** describes how new forms of retail outlets enter the market.[30] Usually, they enter as low-status, low-margin stores, such as a drive-through hamburger stand with no indoor seating and a limited menu (Figure 15–6, box 1). Gradually, these outlets add fixtures and more embellishments to their stores (in-store seating, plants, and chicken sandwiches as well as hamburgers) to increase the attractiveness for customers. With these additions, prices and status rise (see box 2). As time passes, these outlets add still more services, and their prices and status increase even further (see box 3). These retail outlets now face some new form of retail outlet that again appears as a low-status, low-margin operator (see box 4), and the wheel of retailing turns as the cycle starts to repeat itself.

In the 1950s, McDonald's had a very limited menu of hamburgers and french fries. Most stores had no inside seating for customers. Over time, the wheel of retailing for fast-food restaurants has turned. These chains have changed by altering their stores and expanding their menus. Today, McDonald's has new format stores and many new products including specialty coffees and more healthful offerings such as salads. In fact, it recently opened a new coffee chain in Japan, called McCafé, which it believes will compete effectively with Starbucks. These changes are leaving room for new forms of outlets that offer only the basics—burgers, fries, and cola; a drive-through window; and no inside seating. For still others, the wheel has come full circle. Taco Bell

● **FIGURE 15-6**
The wheel of retailing

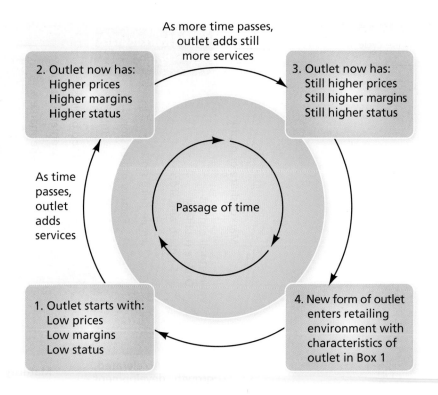

● **FIGURE 15-6**
The wheel of retailing

is now opening small, limited-offering outlets in gas stations or "wherever a burrito and a mouth might possibly intersect."

Discount stores were a major new retailing form in the 1960s and priced their products below those of department stores. As prices in discount stores rose, in the 1980s, they found themselves overpriced compared with a new form of retail outlet — the warehouse retailer. Today, off-price retailers and factory outlets are offering prices even lower than warehouses!

The Retail Life Cycle

retail life cycle
The process of growth and decline that retail outlets, like products, experience.

The process of growth and decline that retail outlets, like products, experience is described by the **retail life cycle.**[31] Figure 15–7 shows the retail life cycle and the position of various current forms of retail outlets on it. *Early growth* is the stage of emergence of a retail outlet, with a sharp departure from existing competition. Market share rises gradually, although profits may be low because of start-up costs. In the next stage, *accelerated development*, both market share and profit achieve their greatest growth rates. Usually, multiple outlets are established as companies focus on the distribution element of the retailing mix. In this stage, some later competitors may enter. Wendy's, for example, appeared on the hamburger chain scene almost 20 years after McDonald's had begun operation. The key goal for the retailer in this stage is to establish a dominant position in the fight for market share.

The battle for market share is usually fought before the *maturity* phase, and some competitors drop out of the market. New retail forms enter in the maturity phase, stores try to maintain their market share, and price discounting occurs. For example, when McDonald's introduced its Extra Value Meal, a discounted package of burger, fries, and drink, Wendy's followed with its 99¢ Value Menu.

The challenge facing retailers is to delay entering the *decline* stage, in which market share and profit fall rapidly. Specialty apparel retailers, such as The Gap, Benetton, and Ann Taylor, have noticed a decline in market share after a decade of growth. To prevent further decline, these retailers will need to find ways of discouraging their customers from moving to low-margin, mass-volume outlets or high-price, high-service boutiques.

● **FIGURE 15-7**
The retail life cycle

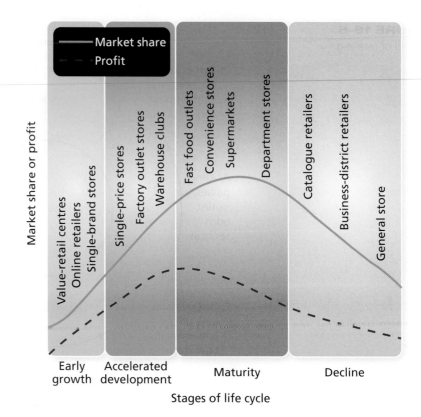

CHALLENGES CANADIAN RETAILERS FACE AS THEY PURSUE SUSTAINABLE GROWTH

The retail marketplace is fast-evolving and competitive. Canadian retailers face numerous challenges as they pursue sustainable growth including: (1) the use of integrated multichannel retailing, (2) embracing technology and using it wisely, (3) better understanding of the complex Canadian shopper, (4) demonstrating corporate social responsibility and going green, (5) providing a satisfying customer experience to the shopper, (6) improving the bottom-line and managing risk, and (7) effective use of human capital.[32] You can also check out other relevant trends facing Canadian retailers by completing the Going Online exercise and checking out the Retail Council of Canada.

Going Online

Welcome to the Retail Council of Canada

Founded in 1963, Retail Council of Canada (RCC) is the "Voice of Retail." RCC is a not-for-profit association representing all retail formats, including national and regional department stores, mass merchants, specialty chains, independent stores, and online merchants. It speaks for an industry that touches the daily lives of Canadians in every corner of the country—by providing jobs, consumer value, world-class product selection, and the colour, sizzle, and entertainment of the marketplace. RCC promotes retail as a career, as an economic driver, and as a barometer of consumer tastes and confidence. Go to its Web site at **www.retailcouncil.org.** At the home page, click on the heading "Media Centre" and then select "Current News Releases." Read about the latest trends and developments in retailing in Canada.

The Use of Integrated Multichannel Retailing

The retailing formats described previously in this chapter allow retailers to offer unique benefits and meet particular needs of various customer groups. While each format has many successful applications, Canadian retailers will need to integrate many of the formats to offer a broader spectrum of benefits and experiences. **Integrated multichannel retailing** utilizes a seamless combination of traditional store formats and non-store formats, such as catalogues, television, electronic kiosks, and online retailing.[33] For example, Canadian Tire markets via its retail stores, catalogues, and online, while Chapters-Indigo offers customers both traditional retail stores as well as online shopping.

Integrated multichannel retailing can make shopping simpler and more convenient for the consumer. A consumer can research choices online or in a catalogue and then make a purchase online, over the telephone, or at the closest store. In addition, the use of multichannel retailing allows retailers to reach a broader profile of customers. And integrated multichannel retailers will also benefit from the synergy of sharing information among the different channel operations. Importantly, to stay competitive, retailers must create a consistently positive cross-channel experience for the customer. In fact, there is tremendous growth in what is called the *cross-channel shopper*—a consumer who researches products online and then purchases them in a retail store. These cross-channel shoppers want the right product at the best price, don't want to wait for delivery, and want a retail to provide a seamless experience across channels.[34]

Embracing Technology and Using It Wisely

Technology will play a key role for a Canadian retailer pursuing sustainable growth. Technology will allow the Canadian retailer to improve productivity, which has lagged behind U.S. retailers who now compete here on Canadian soil. Technology will enable the Canadian retailer to better manage costs and inventories. It will also enable the retailer to better understand and better serve the customer. The technology will include customer relationship management (CRM) tools, including innovative POS systems such as *e-till*, and other simple front-end technologies such as self-checkouts.

One technology that will help the retailer at both the back-end and front-end is *radio frequency identification (RFID)*. RFID are tiny microchip tags that can be attached to pallets, cases, cartons, or even individual items. They allow manufacturers, distributors, and retailers to collect detailed information about a product's origin, distribution path, and price, eliminating the need for the current bar codes used to track goods. RFID can play a vital role in inventory management as well as serve as a new marketing tool. For example, Walmart Canada uses RFID to reduce stockouts. Other retailers are using RFID to track and influence consumers in-store shopping behaviour. For example, one golf-equipment maker tags specific clubs so that if a shopper picks up a particular club, the unique benefits of that piece of equipment will be shown on a display monitor. The Retail Council of Canada reports that there has been a dramatic increase in the use of RFID technology in the Canadian retail environment.[35]

Retailers must also embrace new technologies that will make it more convenient for customers to pay for their purchases, including the use of smart cards and biometric payment systems. *Smart cards* store information on computer chips instead of magnetic strips, including information about bank accounts and amounts of available funds. They also contain customer purchase information, such as airline seat preferences, clothing sizes, and even health information. Smart cards are already very popular in Europe and Asia. Benefits for consumers include faster service—a smart card transaction is much faster than having a cheque or credit card approved—and they are a convenient method of payment for small-dollar-amount transactions. Merchants also benefit because they save the 5 to 7 percent usually paid to credit card

integrated multichannel retailing

Utilizing a seamless combination of traditional store formats and non-store formats, such as catalogues, television, electronic kiosks, and online retailing.

companies or avoid funds lost in handling. New versions of smart cards are now available for use in the memory slot in cellphones and PDAs.

Another new technology is also now available, called *biometric payment systems,* which use thumbprint, fingerprint, or iris scanning as a way to identify a customer, and make a payment automatically from an established account.

Better Understanding of the Complex Canadian Shopper

The Canadian shopper is older, more ethnically diverse, time pressured, connected to the Internet, discerning, and focused on his or her well-being. Experts suggest that the Canadian shopper is far more complex for retailers to serve than U.S. shoppers due to demographic factors, high levels of cultural diversity, and changing family dynamics. Canadians also have 30 percent less disposable income than Americans and consider price carefully when they purchase. Yet, because of a close relationship with Europe, Canadians tend to be fashion and food conscious.[36] And Canadian expectations about quality for the price paid is also rising. Additionally, the market is becoming increasingly fragmented in terms of lifestyles. This will require retailers to focus on specific niche households and offer them new niche-oriented retail formats, fascias, offerings, and customized experiences. In short, a one-size-fits-all retail strategy will no longer be effective. Canadian retailers will need to gain a better understanding of their customer, and craft-specific strategies to cater to that customer. Armed with a better understanding of the shopper, the retailer can act in a more customer-centric manner.

Demonstrating Corporate Social Responsibility and Going Green

As you know from previous chapters, corporate social responsibility (CSR) means that an organization is part of a larger society and is accountable to that society for its actions. The Retail Council of Canada suggests that CSR is fast becoming an important ingredient for retail success. CSR can provide an opportunity for the retailer to differentiate itself and gain a competitive advantage. But retailers must not simply use CSR as a public relations tool as this will alienate customers. In fact, customers are demanding that retail establishments demonstrate in a tangible way that they are fulfilling the social duties and obligations. This socially responsible behaviour includes ethical business practices, respect of employees and customers, giving back to the community by assisting worthy causes and charities, adopting responsible trade practices, and environmental sustainability—"going green." Long-term sustainable green strategies can actually result in savings for the retailer over the long run, increase net sales from scrupulous consumers, and prevent consumer backlash by activists. Shoppers want clean, energy-efficient products, and will respond positively to retailers that are good stewards of the environment. Walmart Canada, for example, has a green plan that includes boosting energy efficiency, cutting down on waste, and reducing greenhouse gas emissions.[37] Of the Top 250 global retailers, over 66 percent currently have CSR programs as part of their overall retail strategies, and the Retail Council of Canada is urging all its members to integrate CSR into their everyday operations.[38] To read more about green activities of several retailers, see the accompanying Making Responsible Decisions box.[39]

Providing a Satisfying Customer Experience

As you have read in previous chapters, consumers no longer simply buy products or services; they buy the end-to-end experience around what is sold. Accordingly, retailers must understand that good products or good services at good prices may no longer be enough to stay competitive. Consumers can often find numerous substitutes in the crowded retail space. Therefore, successful retailers must focus on providing a

Environmentally Friendly Retailing Takes Off!

Sustainability has been a topic of interest for some retailers for many years. Recently, however, it has become a movement for the entire industry. What happened? A combination of factors contributed to the change: Environmental consciousness among consumers has reached an all-time high; publicity related to global warning has increased; "green" has become an important element of company image and reputation; and most environmental initiatives save retailers money!

When consumers learned that food packaging creates 50 percent of all household waste, they added packaging to their purchase decision criteria. Walmart responded by requiring its suppliers to trim one square inch of packaging from its toy lines and reduced packaging by 3,500 tonnes.

Electronics retailer Best Buy recently began using solar energy in some of its stores with the goal of reducing CO_2 emissions by 8 percent by 2012. Mountain Equipment Co-op company is building on its green image by collecting rainwater to water grass at the store and to use in its toilets. When Home Depot switched its in-store light fixtures to compact fluorescent light bulbs, it saved $16 million per year. IKEA Canada no longer offers customers plastic bags in any of their stores and reserves prime parking spaces for customers driving hybrid vehicles. Other companies are using motion detectors to turn lights on and off, improving the fuel economy of delivery vehicles, and designing "zero waste" stores.

Are your favourite retailers "green"? Do sustainability efforts influence your retail purchase decisions?

satisfying customer experience. By offering a compelling shopping experience through improved customer service, store layout and design, and effective personalized marketing, the retailer can differentiate itself with strong experiential branding. Currently, most Canadians do not believe they are receiving satisfying customer experiences. Yet, there is strong evidence that offering a satisfying customer experience can lead to improved profitability for the retailer because positive customer experiences leads to evangelistic customer loyalty.[40] A new type of experience that is emerging is the concept of *social retailing* where retailers are offering bars and restaurants, and using technology to allow customers to send images and messages to friends from the fitting rooms. The combination of being in the store and interacting with friends who are there with you and those in other locations is part of this new social retailing experience that is particularly appealing to young consumers.[41]

Improving the Bottom Line and Managing Risk

Leading retailers not only must focus on top-line growth but also must concentrate on improving their bottom-line performance. This will include cutting operating costs by consolidating support functions and even reducing payroll. In addition, retailers must examine their cost of goods more carefully. This may require new negotiations to obtain better deals with suppliers and re-negotiation of leases on facilities. Retailers must also more closely analyze the mix of businesses they operate and may choose to eliminate formats, fascias, and merchandise categories that are underperforming. They may also have to take a hard look at their locations, choosing to exit some markets and shut down stores to eliminate cannibalization. The best retailers are also very likely to revisit their business focus and redefine what their core business should be in order to improve bottom-line performance.

Additionally, retailers will also have to focus more attention on the issue of risk management. Retailers must be prepared for changes in their external environment where risks abound. These risks include disruptions to supply chains, currency volatility, natural disasters, man-made disasters, legal liability, and financial market disruption. The latter is a critical concern. The recent meltdown in credit markets has demonstrated the importance of having sufficient cash on hand and having strong financial service and supplier relationships. Forward-thinking retailers will likely employ chief risk officers and develop more comprehensive plans for dealing with business disruption. In addition, an important part of risk mitigation will involve diversifying risk. For example, retailers with supply chains concentrated in one location or with one major supplier may choose to re-think such business design and build in diversification of sourcing.[42]

Effective Use of Human Capital

Providing a satisfying customer experience will be nearly impossible unless the retailer has the right employees engaging in the right behaviour. What many customers remember from their retail encounters are the employees with whom they interacted. The "moment of truth" where customer and employee meet is the greatest opportunity to win or lose that retail customer. Many retailers suggest that the retail labour force is the number one challenge facing their business. For them, attracting and retaining the right employees is now their number one priority.

Currently, the retail sector is the second-largest employer in Canada. But just as the consumer landscape is changing, so, too, is the labour market. Specifically, it is getting older, more culturally diverse, and shrinking dramatically. In fact, in many markets there is a shortage of retail workers. To fill vacant positions, many retailers have looked beyond traditional sources to new pools of labour, such as retirees and immigrant populations. Others are creating innovative recruitment plans that include signing bonuses, flexible schedules, in-depth training, and career pathing. In an effort to make retail a career choice for more young workers, the Retail Council of Canada has created the Canadian Retail Institute's professional designation programs and Retail as a Career Scholarship Program.[43] Major Canadian retailers have also helped establish Canada's first bachelor of commerce degree in retail management at Ryerson University in Toronto.

Without employees, retailers cannot sustain growth. At the same time, the wrong employees can also truncate a retailer's growth. For the retailer who is pursuing sustained growth, the goal must be to hire right, train right, compensate right, and motivate right. Only then will it be possible to create and deliver the satisfying experience that customers expect in the retail marketplace.

It is clear that Canadian retailers face many challenges as they pursue sustainable growth. We have identified several that the retailer must understand and respond to if they wish to ensure their future. Ultimately, the retailers with the willingness and ability to overcome these challenges will achieve sustainable growth. Those who are unwilling or unable to do so will inevitably exit the retail marketplace.

---

learning review

10. According to the wheel of retailing, when a new retail form appears, how would you characterize its image?

11. Market share is usually fought out before the _____ stage of the retail life cycle.

12. What is a smart card?

LEARNING OBJECTIVES REVIEW

 LO1 **Explain the alternative ways to classify retail outlets.**
Retail outlets can be classified by form of ownership, level of service, and type of merchandise line. The forms of ownership include independent retailers, corporate chains, and

contractual systems that include retailer-sponsored cooperatives, wholesaler-sponsored voluntary chains, and franchises. The levels of service include self-service, limited-service, and full-service outlets. Stores classified by their merchandise line include stores with depth, such as sporting good specialty stores, and stores with breadth, such as large department stores.

Describe the many methods of non-store retailing.

Non-store retailing includes automatic vending, direct mail and catalogues, television home shopping, online retailing, telemarketing, and direct selling. The methods of non-store retailing vary by the level of involvement of the retailer and the level of involvement of the customer. Vending, for example, has low involvement, whereas both the consumer and the retailer have high involvement in direct selling.

 Classify retailers in terms of the retail positioning matrix.

The retail positioning matrix positions retail outlets on two dimensions: breadth of product line and value added. There are four possible positions in the matrix. Such stores as The Bay have a broad product line and high value added. Such stores as Zellers also have a broad product line but have low value added because they offer fewer services. Birks represents a narrow product line and high value added. Finally, such stores as Payless ShoeSource offer a narrow product line and low value added.

LO4 **Develop retailing mix strategies over the life cycle of a retail store.**

The retail life cycle describes the process of growth and decline for retail outlets through four stages: early growth, accelerated development, maturity, and decline. The retail mix—pricing, store location, communication, and merchandise—can be managed to match the retail strategy with the stage of the life cycle. The challenge facing retailers is to delay entering the decline stage, where market share and profit fall rapidly.

LO5 **Identify the challenges Canadian retailers face as they pursue sustainable growth.**

The retail marketplace is fast-evolving and competitive. Canadian retailers face numerous challenges as they pursue sustainable growth including: (*1*) the use of integrated multi-channel retailing, (*2*) embracing technology and using it wisely, (*3*) better understanding of the complex Canadian shopper, (*4*) demonstrating corporate social responsibility and going green, (*5*) providing a satisfying customer experience to the shopper, (*6*) improving the bottom line and managing risk, and (*7*) effective use of human capital.

FOCUSING ON KEY TERMS

breadth of product line   p. 405
category management   p. 416
central business district   p. 413
community shopping centre   p. 414
depth of product line   p. 405
form of ownership   p. 403
hypermarket   p. 406
integrated multichannel retailers   p. 419
intertype competition   p. 406
level of service   p. 403
lifestyle centre   p. 414
merchandise line   p. 403

off-price retailing   p. 412
power centre   p. 414
regional shopping centre   p. 413
retailing   p. 402
retailing mix   p. 412
retail life cycle   p. 417
retail positioning matrix   p. 410
scrambled merchandising   p. 406
shrinkage   p. 412
strip location   p. 414
telemarketing   p. 409
wheel of retailing   p. 416

APPLYING MARKETING KNOWLEDGE

1 Discuss the impact of the growing number of dual-income households on (*a*) non-store retailing, and (*b*) the retail mix.

2 How does value added affect a store's competitive position?

3 In retail pricing, retailers often have a maintained markup. Explain how this maintained markup differs from original markup and why it is so important.

4 What are the similarities and differences between product and retail life cycles?

5 How would you classify Zellers in terms of its position on the wheel of retailing versus that of an off-price retailer?

6 Develop a chart to highlight the role of each of the three main elements of the retailing mix across the four stages of the retail life cycle.

7 In Figure 15–5, Payless was placed on the retail positioning matrix. What strategies should Payless follow to move itself into the same position as Birks?

8 Breadth and depth are two important components in distinguishing among types of retailers. Discuss the breadth and depth implications of the following retailers: (*a*) La Senza, (*b*) Walmart, (*c*) L.L. Bean, and (*d*) Future Shop.

9 According to the wheel of retailing and the retail life cycle, what will happen to factory outlet stores?

10 The text discusses the development of online retailing. How does the development of this retailing form agree with the implications of the retail life cycle?

Building Your Marketing Plan

Does your marketing plan involve using retail? If the answer is no, read no further and do not include a retailing element in your plan. If the answer is yes:

1. Use Figure 15–4 to develop your retailing strategy by (a) selecting a position in the retail positioning matrix, and (b) specifying the details of the retailing mix.

2. Develop a positioning statement describing the breadth of the product line (broad versus narrow) and value added (low versus high). See Figure 15–5.

3. Describe an appropriate combination of retail pricing, store location, retail communications, and merchandise assortment.

Video Case 15

WEST EDMONTON MALL

Introduction

West Edmonton Mall is considered the world's largest shopping and entertainment complex, and Alberta's number one tourist attraction. It features over 800 stores and services and over 110 eating establishments, plus several major attractions including Galaxyland, the largest indoor amusement park. West Edmonton Mall is often called the "8th Wonder of the World" and spans the equivalent of 48 city blocks in the west end of the City of Edmonton. With a world-class hotel, a variety of one-of-a-kind stores, attractions, games, entertainment, and restaurants, West Edmonton Mall was designed to offer consumers a one-stop shopping and entertainment experience all within a climate-controlled indoor environment. In fact, the developers' vision for the mall was to create "The Greatest Indoor Show on Earth."

History and Development

West Edmonton Mall has evolved over four phases as its developers, Triple Five Group of Companies, assembled ideas on retail and entertainment from other projects and tourist attractions, creating a distinct and unique project. In Phase I (1981), a 25-hectare site (62 acres) was developed. The original mall size was more than 1.1 million square feet, and there were three major department store anchors—Eaton's, Sears, and The Bay, along with 220 other retail stores and services. The cost of Phase I was $200 million.

In Phase II (1983), the site was expanded to 32 hectares (79 acres) and the mall was expanded by an additional 1.1 million square feet. Another 240 stores and services, including Zellers, were added. Recreation and entertainment facilities were also added, including Galaxyland Amusement Park and the Ice Palace skating rink. The estimated costs for Phase II were $250 million.

In 1985, Phase III expanded the mall site to 48 hectares (119 acres), and new major retailers, including The Brick and London Drugs, were added. More entertainment facilities were also added, including World Waterpark, Deep Sea Adventure, Dolphin Lagoon, Sea Life Caverns, and Professor Wem's Adventure Golf. New retail theme streets were also introduced, including Bourbon Street and Europa Boulevard. This phase cost over $1 billion to complete. Finally, Phase IV (1998) expanded the mall site to 49 hectares (121 acres) and added new retail goods and services such as Chapters, Starbucks, HMV, Famous Players, and IMAX 3-D.

A Shopping and Entertainment Mecca

The West Edmonton Mall attracts over 22 million visitors annually. And to accommodate these visitors, the mall has the world's largest parking lot. But the mall is not designed simply for shopping. The developers want visitors to stay at the mall, even vacation there. In short, they want shoppers to have a personal and memorable experience. Accordingly, they offer world-class accommodations, including the Fantasyland Hotel; dinner theatres; casinos; movie theatres; and other activities designed to entertain the entire family. Some of the malls key attractions are Galaxyland Amusement Park, the world's largest indoor amusement park equipped with a roller-coaster and other rides; World Waterpark, a 2-hectare (5-acre) indoor facility that includes watersliders and even bungee jumping; Deep Sea Derby, where visitors can ride boats on an indoor lake; Sea Lions' Rock, where real sea lions entertain visitors; Sea Life Caverns, which houses over 200 species of fish, sharks, and even penguins; Ice Palace which offers public skating and shinny hockey; and Professor Wem's Adventure Golf, an 18-hole miniature golf course.

The West Edmonton Mall also offers its visitors a themed street concept such as Bourbon Street, with dining rooms, lounges, and bars, in an open, airy atmosphere with a starry sky, complete with mannequins that depict street people of New Orleans. There is also Europa Boulevard, fashioned after various European city streets, with exclusive fashion boutiques and designer stores. The mall even has its own Chinatown, an offering designed to reflect a traditional Chinese marketplace, anchored by T&T Supermarket.

There are also numerous other design features throughout the mall such as water fountains, aquariums, a crown jewels display, Chinese vases from thc Ching Dynasty, and numerous statues. A key design element is the Mall's sky ceiling, which provides an atmosphere of a never-ending sky, and one that actually changes from dawn to day to dusk to dark. And to make sure its visitors can stay in touch with home or the office, the West Edmonton Mall also offers WEMiSphere, a WiFi service that provides high-speed wireless Internet access. The system is available throughout the Fantasyland Hotel, as well as in the mall food court and waterpark and throughout the mall.

The Future

The mall currently contains over 4.2 million square feet of shopping and entertainment space. But a 10-year expansion plan is underway where the developer is planning to add 300,000 square feet of new retail space, a third hotel, an 8,000-seat sports/exhibition facility, and 500 apartments. To learn more about the West Edmonton Mall, go to its Web site at **www.wem.ca.**

Questions

1   What (*a*) retail and (*b*) consumer trends helped drive the development and expansion of the West Edmonton Mall?

2   How can the West Edmonton Mall keep its retail concept fresh and offer the visitor a memorable experience?

3   What further actions can the mall take to ensure visitors continue to patronize the mall?

chapter 16

Integrated Marketing Communications and Direct Marketing

KNOWING YOUR CUSTOMER AND REACHING THEM IN A CREATIVE AND INTEGRATED MANNER

The Canadian Tourism Commission (CTC) is tasked with the job of attracting tourists to Canada. To do so, the CTC first turned to Explorer Quotient—a process developed by Environics that links social values with travel preferences. This process helped determine what type of traveller to go after and what message to use. For example, there was a specific segment looking for a "unique" and "authentic" vacation—something that Canada could offer. The CTC then focused its $40 million budget on reaching this segment. But they used a very creative campaign—a campaign consisting of nine 15-second clips of user-generated content found by creative teams on YouTube and other social networking sites, including a man surfing the Lachine rapids near Montreal, a zip-trekker rushing through the treetops at Whistler, and an iceberg collapsing to the amazement of those aboard a nearby boat. The CTC added the tagline, "Canada, Keep Exploring." The videos ran in Europe (France, Germany, and the U.K.) and throughout North America on television, online, and posted to the CTC's YouTube channel. The spots were also promoted through target online groups, bloggers, and forums.

Hyundai developed its "Smart is in" campaign based on consumer research that found Canadians felt increasingly uneasy about gloomy

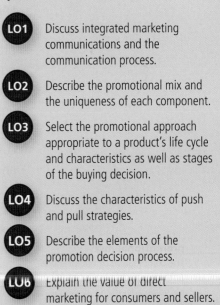

learning objectives

After reading this chapter, you should be able to:

LO1 Discuss integrated marketing communications and the communication process.

LO2 Describe the promotional mix and the uniqueness of each component.

LO3 Select the promotional approach appropriate to a product's life cycle and characteristics as well as stages of the buying decision.

LO4 Discuss the characteristics of push and pull strategies.

LO5 Describe the elements of the promotion decision process.

LO6 Explain the value of direct marketing for consumers and sellers.

economic forecasts and the rising cost of daily necessities. So instead of targeting a particular demographic, the car company focused on a particular mindset—the savvy shopper who isn't concerned with brand image. Hyundai then launched six national TV commercials, as well as radio and print ads under its "Smart is in" umbrella to appeal to this specific car shopper. Hyundai also leveraged its Web site as part of this campaign, allowing consumers to "request a quote" and "schedule a test drive" online. The site saw 2.9 million visitors in the first half of the year alone and has accounted for more than 2,000 test-drive bookings. Hyundai is also the title sponsor of CBC's *Hockey Night in Canada* with a deal that guarantees Hyundai three 30-second commercials within the first period of the game. The program delivers almost four million viewers and is the number-one TV show on Saturday night in Canada. With this integrated campaign, Hyundai expects to sell over 100,000 vehicles by its year-end.

When Kraft Canada was determining the best way to promote its Cheez Whiz brand, It discovered that Cheez Whiz users happened to be big fans of the CTV comedy show, *Corner Gas!* So, Kraft realized this would be a good place to promote the brand. But Kraft wanted to do more than just placing ads during the program's commercial breaks—it wanted the brand integrated into the program. So, it worked closely with Brent Butt, the show's writer/producer/star, so that Cheez Whiz would be an integral part of the final season send-off of Canada's number-one comedy. The iconic brand was placed strategically on the series' corner store shelves and cleverly woven into plot lines. Butt even wrote a hilarious segment where he expounded on the virtues of Cheez Whiz. Kraft augmented this promotion technique with in-store promotions, with winners attending the *Corner Gas* finale cast party as VIP guests. Week after week, thanks to the show's record-breaking viewership, Cheez Whiz reported an increase in sales, as well as top-of-mind awareness among its target audience.[1]

The examples discussed above demonstrate the importance of knowing your customer (or potential customer) and the need for reaching them in a creative and integrated manner. Promotion represents the fourth element in the marketing mix. The promotional element consists of specific communications tools, including advertising, personal selling, sales promotion, public relations, and direct marketing. The combination of one or more of these communications tools is called the **promotional mix.** All of these tools can be used to (1) inform prospective buyers about the benefits of the product, (2) persuade them to try it, and (3) remind them later about the benefits they enjoyed by using the product. And, importantly, more and more often, marketing communications is becoming highly interactive in an effort to engage the customer and connect with him/her in a highly personal manner.

In the past, marketers often viewed the communications tools as separate and independent. The advertising department, for example, often designed and managed its activities without consulting departments or agencies that had responsibility for sales promotion or public relations. The result was often an overall communications effort that was uncoordinated and, in some cases, inconsistent.

promotional mix
The combination of one or more of these communications tools, including advertising, personal selling, sales promotion, public relations, and direct marketing.

Today, the concept of designing marketing communications programs that coordinate all promotional activities—advertising, personal selling, sales promotion, public relations, and direct marketing—to provide a consistent message across all audiences and to maximize the promotional budget and impact of the communications is referred to as **integrated marketing communications (IMC).** Increasingly, the growth of social media has impacted the way organizations communicate with their customers and, indeed, how customers communicate with each other. Therefore, many organizations are now using social media as part of their integrated marketing communications efforts to attract attention, generate online conversations, and encourage consumers to spread the organizations' messages. Importantly, social media also allows organizations to receive direct feedback from their customers.

integrated marketing communications (IMC)
The concept of designing marketing communications programs that coordinate all promotional activities—advertising, personal selling, sales promotion, public relations, and direct marketing—to provide a consistent message across all audiences and to maximize the promotional budget and impact of the communications.

This chapter provides an overview of the communications process, a description of the promotional mix elements, several tools for integrating the promotional mix, and a process for developing a comprehensive promotion program. One of the promotional mix elements, direct marketing, is also discussed in this chapter. Chapter 17 covers advertising, sales promotion, and public relations, and Chapter 18 discusses personal selling.

LO1 THE COMMUNICATION PROCESS

communication
The process of conveying a message to others, which requires six elements: a source, a message, a channel of communication, a receiver, and the processes of encoding and decoding.

source
A company or person who has information to convey.

message
The information sent by a source to a receiver in the communication process.

channel of communication
The means of conveying a message to a receiver.

receivers
Consumers who read, hear, or see the message sent by a source in the communication process.

Communication is the process of conveying a message to others and requires six elements: a source, a message, a channel of communication, a receiver, and the processes of encoding and decoding (Figure 16–1).[2] The **source** may be a company or person who has information to convey. The information sent by a source, such as a description of a new wireless telephone, forms the **message.** The message is conveyed by means of a **channel of communication,** such as a salesperson, advertising media, or public relations tools. Consumers who read, hear, or see the message are the **receivers.**

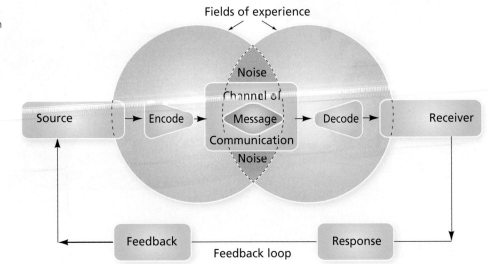

● **FIGURE 16-1**
The communication process

Encoding and Decoding

encoding
The process of having the sender transform an abstract idea into a set of symbols.

decoding
The process of having the receiver take a set of symbols, the message, and transform them back to an abstract idea.

field of experience
Similar understanding and knowledge; to communicate effectively, a sender and a receiver must have a mutually shared field of experience.

A source and a message.

HUMMER
www.hummer.com

Encoding and decoding are essential to communication. **Encoding** is the process of having the sender transform an abstract idea into a set of symbols. **Decoding** is the reverse, or the process of having the receiver take a set of symbols, the message, and transform them back to an abstract idea. Look at the accompanying automobile advertisement: Who is the source, and what is the message? Decoding is performed by the receivers according to their own frame of reference: their attitudes, values, and beliefs.[3] In the nearby ad, HUMMER is the source, and the message is the advertisement, which appeared in *Wired* magazine (the channel). How would you interpret (decode) this advertisement? The picture and text in the advertisement show that the source's intention is to generate interest in a vehicle "Like Nothing Else"—a statement the source believes will appeal to the readers of the magazine.

The process of communication is not always a successful one. Errors in communication can happen in several ways. The source may not adequately transform the abstract idea into an effective set of symbols, a properly encoded message may be sent through the wrong channel and never make it to the receiver, the receiver may not properly transform the set of symbols into the correct abstract idea, or finally, feedback may be so delayed or distorted that it is of no use to the sender. Although communication appears easy to perform, truly effective communication can be very difficult.

For the message to be communicated effectively, the sender and receiver must have a mutually shared **field of experience**—similar understanding and knowledge. Figure 16–1 shows two circles representing the fields of experience of the sender and receiver, which overlap in the message. For example, some communication problems have occurred when Canadian companies have taken their messages to cultures with different fields of experience, resulting in translation problems or misinterpretations.

SAME DNA. SMALLER CHROMOSOMES.
THE ALL-NEW MIDSIZE H3. LIVING UP TO THE OFF-ROAD REPUTATION HUMMER MADE FAMOUS.
STARTING AT $29,500. VEHICLE SHOWN $33,450. HUMMER.COM
*MSRP. TAX, TITLE, LICENSE, DEALER FEES, INSTALLATION AND OPTIONAL EQUIPMENT ARE EXTRA. 1-800-REAL-4WD.
© GENERAL MOTORS CORPORATION, 2005.

HUMMER
LIKE NOTHING ELSE.

For example, Esso found that its name pronounced phonetically meant "stalled car" in Japanese while Kellogg's Bran Buds translates to "burnt farmer" in Swedish.[4]

Feedback

response
The impact the message had on the receiver's knowledge, attitudes, or behaviours.

Figure 16–1 shows a line labelled *feedback loop*, which consists of a response and feedback. A **response** is the impact the message had on the receiver's knowledge, attitudes, or behaviours. **Feedback** is the sender's interpretation of the response and indicates whether the message was decoded and understood as intended. Chapter 17 reviews approaches called *pre-testing* that ensure that messages are decoded properly.

feedback
The communication flow from receiver back to the sender that helps the sender know whether the message was decoded and understood as intended.

Noise

noise
Extraneous factors that can work against effective communication by distorting a message or the feedback received.

Noise includes extraneous factors that can work against effective communication by distorting a message or the feedback received (see Figure 16–1). Noise can be a simple error, such as a printing mistake that affects the meaning of a newspaper advertisement, or using words or pictures that fail to communicate the message clearly. Noise can also occur when a salesperson's message is misunderstood by a prospective buyer, such as when a salesperson's accent, use of slang terms, or communication style makes hearing and understanding the message difficult.

---

learning review

1. What are the six elements required for communication to occur?

2. A difficulty for Canadian companies advertising in foreign markets is that the audience does not share the same _____.

3. A misprint in a newspaper ad is an example of _____.

LO2 THE PROMOTIONAL ELEMENTS

To communicate with consumers, a company can use one or more of five promotional alternatives: advertising, personal selling, public relations, sales promotion, and direct marketing. Figure 16–2 summarizes the distinctions among these five elements. Three of these elements—advertising, sales promotion, and public relations—are often said to use *mass selling* because they are used with groups of prospective buyers. In contrast, personal selling uses *customized interaction* between a seller and a prospective buyer. Personal-selling activities include face-to-face, telephone, and interactive electronic communication. Direct marketing also uses messages customized for specific customers.

Advertising

advertising
Any paid form of non-personal communication about an organization, good, service, or idea by an identified sponsor.

Advertising is any paid form of non-personal communication about an organization, good, service, or idea by an identified sponsor. The *paid* aspect of this definition is important because the space for the advertising message normally must be bought. An occasional exception is the public service announcement, where the advertising time or space is donated. A full-page, four-colour ad in *Canadian Living* magazine, for example, costs over $40,000, and over $36,000 in *MacLean's*. The *non-personal* component of advertising is also important. Advertising involves mass media (such as TV, radio, and magazines), which are non-personal and do not have an immediate feedback loop as does personal selling. So, before the message

PROMOTIONAL ELEMENT	MASS VERSUS CUSTOMIZED	PAYMENT	STRENGTHS	WEAKNESSES
Advertising	Mass	Fees paid for space or time	• Efficient means for reaching large numbers of people	• High absolute costs • Difficult to receive good feedback
Personal selling	Customized	Fees paid to salespeople as either salaries or commissions	• Immediate feedback • Very persuasive • Can select audience • Can give complex information	• Extremely expensive per exposure • Messages may differ between salespeople
Public relations	Mass	No direct payment to media	• Often most credible source in the consumer's mind	• Difficult to get media cooperation
Sales promotion	Mass	Wide range of fees paid, depending on promotion selected	• Effective at changing behaviour in short run • Very flexible	• Easily abused • Can lead to promotion wars • Easily duplicated
Direct marketing	Customized	Cost of communication through mail, telephone, or online	• Messages can be prepared quickly • Facilitates relationship with customer	• Declining customer response • Database management is expensive

● **FIGURE 16–2**

The promotional mix

An attention-getting advertisement.

is sent, marketing research plays a valuable role; for example, it determines that the target market will actually see the medium chosen and that the message will be understood.

There are several advantages to a firm using advertising in its promotional mix. It can be attention-getting—as with the Best Buy ad shown here—and also can communicate specific product benefits to prospective buyers. By paying for the advertising space, a company can control *what* it wants to say and, to some extent, to *whom* the message is sent. If an electronics company wants university students to receive its message about MP3 players, advertising space can be purchased in a campus newspaper. Advertising also allows the company to decide *when* to send its message (which includes how often). The non-personal aspect of advertising also has its advantages. Once the message is created, the same message is sent to all receivers in a market segment. If the message is properly pre-tested, an advertiser can ensure the ad's ability to capture consumers' attention and trust that the same message will be decoded by all receivers in the market segment.[5]

Advertising has some disadvantages. As shown in Figure 16–2 and discussed in depth in Chapter 17, the costs to produce and place a message are significant, and the lack of direct feedback makes it difficult to know how well the message was received. However, direct-response advertising, including television and Internet or online advertising, now offers greater possibility of interactivity between advertiser and customer, including more feedback potential. Direct-response advertising and Internet or online advertising will be discussed further in Chapter 17.

Personal Selling

personal selling
The two-way flow of communication between a buyer and seller, often in a face-to-face encounter, designed to influence a person's or group's purchase decision.

The second major promotional alternative is **personal selling,** defined as the two-way flow of communication between a buyer and seller, designed to influence a person's or group's purchase decision. Unlike advertising, personal selling is usually face-to-face communication between the sender and receiver (although telephone and electronic sales are growing). Why do companies use personal selling?

There are important advantages to personal selling, as summarized in Figure 16–2. A salesperson can control to *whom* the presentation is made. Some control is available in advertising by choosing the medium; for example, some people who are not in the target audience for MP3 players may read the campus newspaper. For the MP3-player manufacturer, those readers outside the target audience are *wasted coverage.* Wasted coverage can be reduced with personal selling. The personal component of selling has another advantage over advertising in that the seller can see or hear the potential buyer's reaction to the message. If the feedback is unfavourable, the salesperson can modify the message.

The flexibility of personal selling can also be a disadvantage. Different salespeople can change the message so that no consistent communication is given to all customers. The high cost of personal selling is probably its major disadvantage. On a cost-per-contact basis, it is generally the most expensive of the five promotional elements.

Public Relations

public relations
A form of communication management that seeks to influence the feelings, opinions, or beliefs held by customers, prospective customers, shareholders, suppliers, employees, and other publics about a company and its products or services.

publicity
A non-personal, indirectly paid presentation of an organization, good, or service.

Public relations is a form of communication management that seeks to influence the feelings, opinions, or beliefs held by customers, prospective customers, shareholders, suppliers, employees, and other publics about a company and its products or services. Many tools, such as special events sponsorship, lobbying efforts, annual reports, and image management, may be used by a public relations department, although publicity often plays the most important role. **Publicity** is a non-personal, indirectly paid presentation of an organization, good, or service. It can take the form of a news story, editorial, or product announcement. A difference between publicity and both advertising and personal selling is the *indirectly paid* dimension. With publicity, a company does not pay for space in a mass medium (such as television or radio) but attempts to get the medium to run a favourable story on the company. In this sense, there is an indirect payment for publicity in that a company must support a public relations staff.

An advantage of publicity is credibility. When you read a favourable story about a company's product (such as a glowing restaurant review), there is a tendency to believe it. Travellers throughout the world have relied on Arthur Frommer's guides, such as *Australia from $60 a Day.* These books outline out-of-the-way, inexpensive restaurants, hotels, inns, and bed-and-breakfast rooms, giving invaluable publicity to these establishments. Such businesses do not (nor can they) buy a mention in the guides, which in recent years have sold millions of copies.

The disadvantages of publicity relate to the lack of the user's control over it. A company can invite a news team to preview its innovative exercise equipment and hope for a favourable mention on the 6 P.M. newscasts. But without buying advertising time, there is no guarantee of any mention of the new equipment or that it will be aired when the target audience is watching. The company representative who calls the station and asks for a replay of the story may be told, "Sorry, it's only news once." With publicity, there is little control over what is said, to whom, or when. As a result, publicity is rarely the main component of a promotional campaign.

sales promotion
A short-term inducement of value offered to arouse interest in buying a good or service.

Sales Promotion

A fourth promotional element is **sales promotion,** a short-term inducement of value offered to arouse interest in buying a good or service. Used in conjunction with advertising or personal selling, sales promotions are offered to intermediaries as well as to ultimate consumers. Coupons, rebates, samples, and sweepstakes are just a few examples of sales promotions discussed in Chapter 17.

The advantage of sales promotion is that the short-term nature of these programs (such as a coupon or sweepstakes with an expiration date) often stimulates sales for their duration. Offering value to the consumer in terms of a cents-off coupon or rebate may increase store traffic from consumers who are not store-loyal.[6]

Sales promotions cannot be the sole basis for a campaign because gains are often temporary and sales drop off when the deal ends.[7] Advertising support is needed to convert the customer who tried the product because of a sales promotion into a long-term buyer.[8] If sales promotions are conducted continuously, they lose their effectiveness. Customers begin to delay purchase until a coupon is offered, or they question the product's value. Some aspects of sales promotions also are regulated by the federal government. These issues are reviewed in detail later in Chapter 17.

Direct Marketing

direct marketing
Promotional element that uses direct communication with consumers to generate a response in the form of an order, a request for further information, or a visit to a retail outlet.

Another promotional alternative, **direct marketing,** uses direct communication with consumers to generate a response in the form of an order, a request for further information, or a visit to a retail outlet.[9] The communication can take many forms, including face-to-face selling, direct mail, catalogues, telephone solicitations, and direct response advertising on television, radio, print, e-mail, social media, or over mobile communication devices. Like personal selling, direct marketing often consists of interactive communication. It also has the advantage of being customized to match the needs of specific target markets. Messages can be developed and adapted quickly to facilitate one-to-one relationships with customers.

While direct marketing has been one of the fastest-growing forms of promotion, it has several disadvantages. First, most forms of direct marketing require a comprehensive and up-to-date database with information about the target market. Developing and maintaining the database can be expensive and time-consuming. In addition, growing concern about privacy has led to a decline in response rates among some customer groups. Companies with successful direct marketing programs are sensitive to these issues and often use a combination of direct marketing alternatives together, or direct marketing combined with other promotional tools, to increase value for customers.

---

learning review	**4.** Explain the difference between advertising and publicity when both appear on television.
	5. Which promotional element should be offered only on a short-term basis?
	6. Cost per contact is high with the _____ element of the promotional mix.

LO2 INTEGRATED MARKETING COMMUNICATIONS— DEVELOPING THE PROMOTIONAL MIX

A firm's promotional mix is the combination of one or more of the promotional elements it chooses to use. In putting together the promotional mix, a marketer must consider several issues. First, the balance of the elements must be determined. Should advertising be emphasized more than personal selling? Should a promotional rebate be offered? Would public relations activities be effective? Would a combination of online and traditional media work best? Several factors affect such decisions: the target

How Combining Online and Traditional Media Create Successful Integration

When Nestlé Canada launched Aero and Kit Kat Singles—a smaller serving of its chocolate bars that are 100 calories or less—to the Canadian market they used an integrated promotional program that would bring the brand to life through an engaging, interactive experience. The key components of the program were traditional print media, a partnered contest, and an online promotion of "hero" characters of the chocolate bar brands, Kit and Bubbles. The goal was to create an environment that played on the theme of "singles," leveraging content integration, viral elements, and Web 2.0.

The campaign was designed to resonate with women by combining delectable chocolate with another indulgence: shoes. Nestlé partnered with retailer Town Shoes to create an online-driven contest that would give lucky winners a chance to win free footwear. Contest awareness was driven through print ads in magazines such as *Hello! Canada* and *LouLou*. To expand the reach of the online contest, entrants received an extra entry when they e-mailed friends about it. To increase consumer engagement with the Web site beyond entering the contest, the site featured user-generated content. Consumers could also interact with the two characters by dressing them up in sunglasses, hats, and jewellery, and placing them in background locales such as a beach or disco. Participants could even tell the characters what to say by using an innovative voice recognition system that added the users' own voices to the characters in real time.

In just five months, sell-through of Nestlé Singles achieved the same levels that a major competitor took 15 months to achieve. Now that is successful integration!

audience for the promotion,[10] the stage of the product's life cycle, the characteristics of the product, the decision stage of the buyer, and even the channel of distribution. Second, because the various promotional elements are often the responsibility of different departments, coordinating a consistent promotional effort is necessary. A promotional planning process designed to ensure integrated marketing communications can facilitate this goal. To see how a combination of online and traditional media helped create successful integration read the accompanying Marketing Matters box, "How Combining Online and Traditional Media Create Successful Integration."[11]

The Target Audience

Promotional programs are directed to the ultimate consumer, to an intermediary (retailer, wholesaler, or industrial distributor), or to both. Promotional programs directed to buyers of consumer products often use mass media because the number of potential buyers is large. Personal selling is used at the place of purchase, generally the retail store. Direct marketing may be used to encourage first-time or repeat purchases. Combinations of many media alternatives are a necessity for many target audiences today.

Advertising directed to business buyers is used selectively in trade publications, such as *Fence Industry* magazine for buyers of fencing material. Because business buyers often have specialized needs or technical questions, personal selling is particularly important. The salesperson can provide information and the necessary support after sales.

Intermediaries are often the focus of promotional efforts. As with business buyers, personal selling is the major promotional ingredient. The salespeople assist intermediaries in making a profit by coordinating promotional campaigns sponsored by the manufacturer and by providing marketing advice and expertise. Intermediaries' questions often pertain to the allowed markup, merchandising support, and return policies.

LO3 The Product Life Cycle

All products have a product life cycle (see Chapter 11), and the composition of the promotional mix changes over the four life-cycle stages, as shown for Purina Dog Chow in Figure 16–3.

● FIGURE 16–3
Promotional tools used over
the product life cycle of Purina
Dog Chow

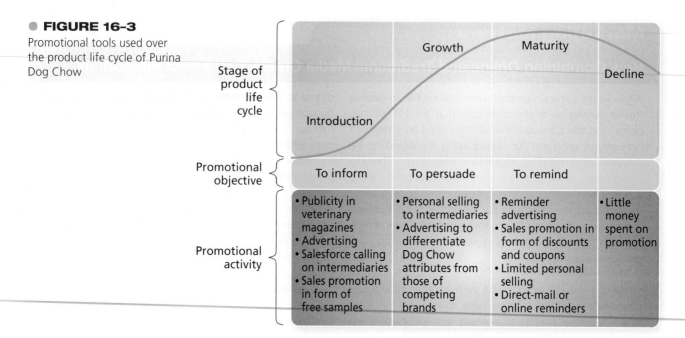

Stage of product life cycle	Introduction	Growth	Maturity	Decline
Promotional objective	To inform	To persuade	To remind	
Promotional activity	• Publicity in veterinary magazines • Advertising • Salesforce calling on intermediaries • Sales promotion in form of free samples	• Personal selling to intermediaries • Advertising to differentiate Dog Chow attributes from those of competing brands	• Reminder advertising • Sales promotion in form of discounts and coupons • Limited personal selling • Direct-mail or online reminders	• Little money spent on promotion

Purina Dog Chow: a product in the
maturity stage of its life cycle.

Introduction Stage Informing consumers in an effort to increase their level of awareness is the primary promotional objective in the introduction stage of the product life cycle. In general, all the promotional mix elements are used at this time, although the use of specific mix elements during any stage depends on the product and situation. News releases about Purina's new nutritional product are sent to veterinary magazines, trial samples are sent to registered dog owners, advertisements are placed in *Dog World* magazine, and the salesforce begins to approach supermarkets to get orders. Advertising is particularly important as a means of reaching as many people as possible to build up awareness and interest. Publicity may even begin slightly before the product is commercially available.

Growth Stage The primary promotional objective of the growth stage is to persuade the consumer to buy the product—Purina Dog Chow—rather than substitutes, and so the marketing manager seeks to gain brand preference and solidify distribution. Sales promotion assumes less importance in this stage, and publicity is not a factor because it depends on novelty of the product. The primary promotional element is advertising, which stresses brand differences. Personal selling is used to solidify the channel of distribution. For consumer products, such as dog food, the salesforce calls on wholesalers and retailers in hopes of increasing inventory levels and gaining shelf space. For business products, the salesforce often tries to get contractual arrangements to be the sole source of supply for the buyer.

Maturity Stage In the maturity stage, the need is to maintain existing buyers, and advertising's role is to remind buyers of the product's existence. Sales promotion, in the form of discounts and coupons offered to both ultimate consumers and intermediaries, is important in maintaining loyal buyers. In a test of one mature consumer product, it was found that 80 percent of the product's sales at this stage resulted from sales promotions.[12] Since 1998, Purina has sponsored the Incredible Dog Challenge, which is now covered by ESPN.[13] Direct marketing actions, such as direct mail, are used to maintain involvement with existing customers and to encourage repeat

How do Gulfstream aircraft and Heinz ketchup differ on complexity, risk, and ancillary services?

Gulfstream
www.gulfstreamvsp.com

Heinz
www.heinz.com

purchases. Price cuts and discounts can also significantly increase a mature brand's sales. The salesforce at this stage seeks to satisfy intermediaries. An unsatisfied customer who switches brands is hard to replace.

Decline Stage   The decline stage of the product life cycle is usually a period of phaseout for the product, and little money is spent in the promotional mix. The rate of decline can be rapid, when a product is replaced by an improved or lower cost product, for example, or slow, if there is a loyal group of customers.

Product Characteristics

The proper blend of elements in the promotional mix also depends on the type of product. Three specific characteristics should be considered: complexity, risk, and ancillary services. *Complexity* refers to the technical sophistication of the product and hence the amount of understanding required to use it. It is hard to provide much information in a one-page magazine ad or 30-second television ad; the more complex the product, the greater is the emphasis on personal selling. Gulfstream asks potential customers to call its senior vice president in its ads. No information is provided for simple products, such as Heinz ketchup.

A second element is the degree of *risk* represented by the product's purchase. Risk for the buyer can be assessed in terms of financial risk, social risk, and physical risk. A private jet, for example, might represent all three risks—it is expensive, employees and customers may see and evaluate the purchase, and safety and reliability are important. Although advertising helps, the greater the risk, the greater is the need for personal selling. Consumers are unlikely to associate any of these risks with, say, cereal.

The level of ancillary services required by a product also affects the promotional strategy. *Ancillary services* pertain to the degree of service or support required after the sale. This characteristic is common to many business products and consumer purchases. Who will provide maintenance for the plane? Advertising's role is to establish the seller's reputation. Direct marketing can be used to describe how a product or service can be customized to individual needs. However, personal selling is essential to build buyer confidence and provide evidence of customer service.

Stages of the Buying Decision

Knowing the customer's stage of decision making can also affect the promotional mix. Figure 16–4 shows how the importance of the promotional elements varies with the three stages in a consumer's purchase decision.

Pre-Purchase Stage   In the pre-purchase stage, advertising is more helpful than personal selling because advertising informs the potential customer of the existence of the product and the seller. Sales promotion in the form of free samples also can play an important role to gain low-risk trial. When the salesperson calls on the customer after heavy advertising, there is some recognition of what the salesperson represents. This is particularly important in business settings in which sampling of the product is usually not possible.

Purchase Stage   At the purchase stage, the importance of personal selling is highest, whereas the impact of advertising is lowest. Sales promotion in the form of coupons, deals, point-of-purchase displays, and rebates can be very helpful in encouraging demand. In this stage, although advertising is not an active influence on the purchase, it is the means of delivering the coupons, deals, and rebates that are often important.

Post-Purchase Stage   In the post-purchase stage, the salesperson is still important. In fact, the more personal contact after the sale, the more the buyer is satisfied. Advertising is also important to assure the buyer that the right purchase was made. Advertising and personal selling help reduce the buyer's post-purchase anxiety.[14] Sales promotion in the form of coupons and direct marketing reminders can help encourage repeat purchases from satisfied first-time users. Public relations plays a small role in the post-purchase stage.

Channel Strategies

Chapter 14 discussed the channel flow from producer to intermediaries to consumer. Achieving control of the channel is often difficult for the manufacturer, and promotional strategies can assist in moving a product through the channel of distribution. This is where a manufacturer has to make an important decision about whether to use a push strategy, a pull strategy, or both in its channel of distribution.[15]

● **FIGURE 16–4**

How the importance of promotional elements varies during the consumer's purchase decision

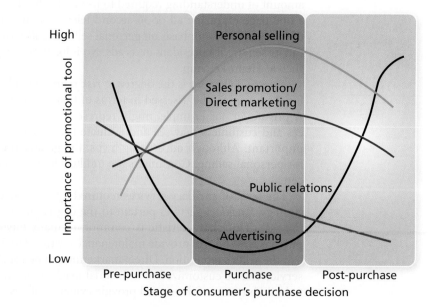

pull strategy

Directing the promotional mix at ultimate consumers to encourage them to ask the retailer for the product.

push strategy

Directing the promotional mix to channel members to gain their cooperation in ordering and stocking a product.

LO4 **Push Strategy** Figure 16–5A shows how a manufacturer uses a **push strategy,** directing the promotional mix to channel members to gain their cooperation in ordering and stocking the product. In this approach, personal selling and sales promotions play major roles. Salespeople call on wholesalers to encourage orders and provide sales assistance. Sales promotions, such as case discount allowances (20 percent off the regular case price), are offered to stimulate demand. By pushing the product through the channel, the goal is to get channel members to push it to their customers.

Canadian firms, such as Pepsi-Cola Canada and Molson, spend a significant amount of their marketing resources on maintaining their relationships with their distributors and, through them, with retailers. In general, Canadian consumer goods firms are allocating greater percentages of their promotional budgets toward intermediaries. In some cases, as much as 60 percent of the promotional budget is being allocated to personal selling and sales promotions designed to reach intermediaries, while 40 percent is spent on promotional activities directed toward ultimate consumers.[16]

Pull Strategy In some instances, manufacturers face resistance from channel members who do not want to order a new product or increase inventory levels of an existing brand. As shown in Figure 16–5B, a manufacturer may then elect to implement a **pull strategy** by directing its promotional mix at ultimate consumers to encourage them to ask the retailer for the product. Seeing demand from ultimate consumers, retailers order the product from wholesalers and thus the item is pulled through the intermediaries. Such firms as Procter & Gamble and Heinz Canada, use pull strategies, including e-mail marketing campaigns, directed at ultimate consumers to create consumer pull. The Pampers Parenting Institute Web site at **www.pampers.ca** is also an example of how P&G engages in pull strategy activities.[17]

A novel pull strategy is one being used by B.C. hemlock producers and their Coastal Forest and Lumber Association as they seek greater market share in Japan. B.C. hemlock, now rebranded as Canada Tsuga, uses a Japanese sumo wrestler in its advertising that is directed toward home builders, who are now, in turn, demanding the product from lumber suppliers. The product is now the preferred product in post-and-beam construction, and the Japanese consumer now views the Canadian Tsuga very positively.[18]

● **FIGURE 16–5**

A comparison of push and pull promotional strategies

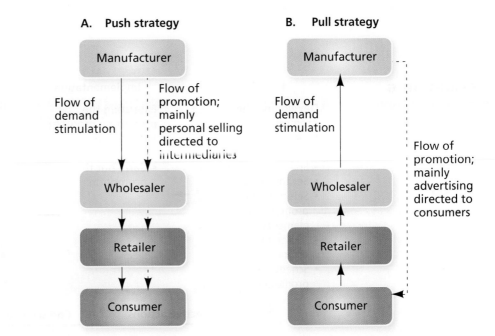

LO5 DEVELOPING THE IMC PROGRAM

Because media costs are high, promotion decisions must be made carefully, using a systematic approach. Paralleling the planning, implementation, and control steps described in the strategic marketing process (Chapter 2), the promotion decision process is divided into (1) developing, (2) executing, and (3) evaluating the promotion program (Figure 16–6). Development of the promotion program focuses on the four Ws:

- *Who* is the target audience?
- *What* are (1) the promotion objectives, (2) the amounts of money that can be budgeted for the promotion program, and (3) the kinds of promotion to use?
- *Where* should the promotion be run?
- *When* should the promotion be run?

Identifying the Target Audience

The first decision in developing the promotion program is identifying the *target audience,* the group of prospective buyers toward which a promotion program is directed. To the extent that time and money permit, the target audience for the promotion program is the target market for the firm's product, which is identified from marketing research and market segmentation studies. The more a firm knows about its target audience's profile—including their lifestyle, attitudes, and values—the easier it is to develop a promotion program. If a firm wanted to reach you with television and magazine ads, for example, it would need to know what TV shows you watch and what magazines you read.

● **FIGURE 16–6**

The promotion decision process

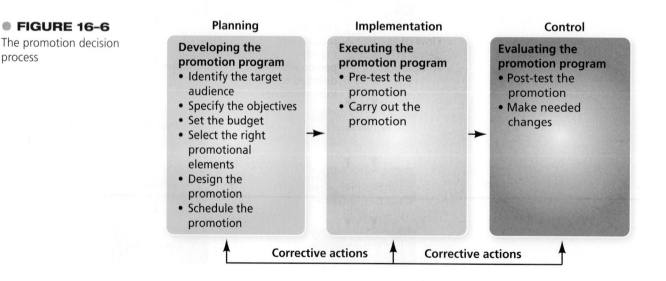

Specifying Promotion Objectives

hierarchy of effects

The sequence of stages a prospective buyer goes through from initial awareness of a product to eventual action.

After the target audience is identified, a decision must be reached on what the promotion should accomplish. Consumers can be said to respond in terms of a **hierarchy of effects,** which is the sequence of stages a prospective buyer goes through from initial awareness of a product to eventual action (either trial or adoption of the product).[19]

- *Awareness.* The consumer's ability to recognize and remember the product or brand name.
- *Interest.* An increase in the consumer's desire to learn about some of the features of the product or brand.
- *Evaluation.* The consumer's appraisal of the product or brand on important attributes.
- *Trial.* The consumer's actual first purchase and use of the product or brand.
- *Adoption.* Through a favourable experience on the first trial, the consumer's repeated purchase and use of the product or brand.

For a totally new product, the sequence applies to the entire product category, but for a new brand competing in an established product category, it applies to the brand itself. These steps can serve as guidelines for developing promotion objectives.

Although sometimes an objective for a promotion program involves several steps in the hierarchy of effects, it often focuses on a single stage. Regardless of what the specific objective might be, from building awareness to increasing repeat purchases,[20] promotion objectives should possess three important qualities. They should (1) be designed for a well-defined target audience, (2) be measurable, and (3) cover a specified time period.

Setting the Promotion Budget

After setting the promotion objectives, a company must decide on how much to spend. The promotion expenditures needed to reach millions of Canadian households are enormous. Canadian companies spent over $14 billion in 2010 on advertising and billions more on sales promotion and direct marketing to reach these households.[21] Some companies, such as McDonald's Canada, Procter & Gamble, General Motors of Canada, and the Royal Bank of Canada, spend hundreds of millions of dollars each year.

Determining the ideal amount for the budget is difficult because there is no precise way to measure the exact results of spending promotion dollars. However, several methods are used to set the promotion budget.[22]

percentage of sales budgeting

Allocating funds to advertising as a percentage of past or anticipated sales, in terms of either dollars or units sold.

Percentage of Sales   In the **percentage of sales budgeting** approach, funds are allocated to promotion as a percentage of past or anticipated sales, in terms of either dollars or units sold. A common budgeting method,[23] this approach is often stated in such terms as, "Our promotion budget for this year is 3 percent of last year's gross sales." The advantage of this approach is obvious: It is simple and provides a financial safeguard by tying the promotion budget to sales. However, there is a major fallacy in this approach, which implies that sales cause promotion. Using this method, a company may reduce its promotion budget because of a downturn in past sales or an anticipated downturn in future sales—situations where it may need promotion the most. See the Using Marketing Dashboards box for an application of the promotion-to-sales ratio for the automotive industry.

competitive parity budgeting

Matching the competitors' absolute level of spending or the proportion per point of market share.

Competitive Parity   A second common approach, **competitive parity budgeting,** is matching the competitor's absolute level of spending or the proportion per point of market share. This approach has also been referred to as *matching competitors* or *share of market.* It is important to consider the competition in budgeting.[24] Consumer responses to promotion are affected by competing promotional activities; thus, if a competitor runs 30 radio ads each week, it may be difficult for another firm to get

Using Marketing Dashboards

How Much Should You Spend on IMC?

Integrated marketing communications programs coordinate a variety of promotion alternatives to provide a consistent message across audiences. The amount spent on the various promotional elements, or on the total campaign, may vary depending on the target audience, the type of product, where the product is in the product life cycle, and the channel strategy selected. Managers often use the promotion-to-sales ratio on their marketing dashboard to assess how effective the IMC program expenditures are at generating sales.

Your Challenge As a manager at General Motors you've been asked to assess the effectiveness of all promotion expenditures during the past year. The promotion-to-sales ratio can be used by managers to make year-to-year

comparisons of their programs, to compare the effectiveness of their program with competitor's programs, or to make comparisons with industry averages. You decide to calculate the promotion-to-sales ratio for General Motors. In addition, to allow a comparison, you decide to make the same calculation for one of your competitors, Ford, and for the entire automobile industry. The ratio is calculated as follows:

Promotion-to-sales ratio = Total promotion expenditures/Total sales

Your Findings The information needed for these calculations is readily available from trade publications and annual reports. The following graph shows the promotion-to-sales ratio for General Motors and Ford and the automotive industry. General Motors spent $3.296 billion on its IMC program to generate $129 billion in sales for a ratio of 2.6 (percent). Ford's ratio was 3.2, and the industry average was 2.7.

Your Action General Motor's promotion-to-sales ratio is substantially lower than Ford's and slightly lower than the industry average. This suggests that the current mix of promotional activities and the level of expenditures are both creating an effective IMC program. In the future you will want to monitor the factors that may influence the ratio. The average ratio for the beverage industry has risen to 9 while the average for grocery stores is about 1.

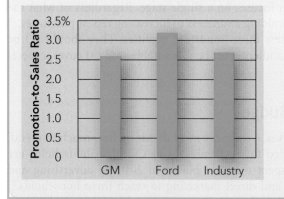

its message across with only five messages.[25] The competitor's budget level, however, should not be the only determinant in setting a company's budget. The competition might have very different promotional objectives, which require a different level of promotion expenditures.

all-you-can-afford budgeting

Allocating funds to promotion only after all other budget items are covered.

All You Can Afford Common to many small businesses is **all-you-can-afford budgeting,** in which money is allocated to promotion only after all other budget items are covered. As one company executive said in reference to this budgeting process, "Why, it's simple. First, I go upstairs to the controller and ask how much they can afford to give us this year. She says a million and a half. Later, the boss comes to me and asks how much we should spend, and I say 'Oh, about a million and a half.' Then we have our promotion appropriation."[26]

Fiscally conservative, this approach has little else to offer. Using this budgeting philosophy, a company acts as though it does not know anything about a promotion–sales relationship or what its promotion objectives are.

objective and task budgeting

A budgeting approach whereby the company (1) determines its promotion objectives, (2) outlines the tasks to accomplish these objectives, and (3) determines the promotion cost of performing these tasks.

Objective and Task The best approach to budgeting is **objective and task budgeting,** whereby the company (1) determines its promotion objectives, (2) outlines the tasks to accomplish these objectives, and (3) determines the promotion cost of performing these tasks.[27]

This method takes into account what the company wants to accomplish and requires that the objectives be specified.[28] Strengths of the other budgeting methods are integrated into this approach because each previous method's strength is tied to the objectives. For example, if the costs are beyond what the company can afford, objectives are reworked and the tasks revised. The difficulty with this method is the judgment required to determine the tasks needed to accomplish objectives. Would two or four insertions in *Time* magazine be needed to achieve a specific awareness level? Figure 16–7 shows a sample media plan with objectives, tasks, and budget outlined. The total amount to be budgeted is $430,000. If the company can afford only $300,000, the objectives must be reworked, tasks redefined, and the total budget recalculated.

Selecting the Right Promotional Tools

Once a budget has been determined, the combination of the five basic integrated marketing communications (IMC) tools—advertising, personal selling, sales promotion, public relations, and direct marketing—can be specified. While many factors provide direction for selection of the appropriate mix, the large number of possible combinations of the promotional tools means that many combinations can achieve the same objective. Therefore, an analytical approach and experience are particularly important in this step of the promotion decision process. The specific mix can vary from a simple program using a single tool to a comprehensive program using all forms of promotion. The Olympics have become a very visible example of a comprehensive IMC program. Because the Games are repeated every two years, the promotion is almost continuous. Included in the program are advertising campaigns; personal selling efforts by the Olympic committee and organizers; sales promotion activities, such as product tie-ins and sponsorships; public relations programs managed by the host cities; and direct marketing efforts targeted at a variety of audiences, including governments, organizations, firms, athletes, and individuals.[29] At this stage, it is also important to assess the relative importance of the various tools. While it may be desirable to utilize and integrate several forms of promotion, one may deserve emphasis. The Olympics, for example, place exceptional importance on public relations and publicity.

Designing the Promotion

The central element of a promotion program is the promotion itself. Advertising consists of advertising copy and the artwork that the target audience is intended to see or hear. Personal selling efforts depend on the characteristics and skills of the salesperson.

FIGURE 16–7

The objective and task approach

OBJECTIVE	
To increase awareness among university students for a new video game. Awareness at the end of one semester should be 20 percent of all students from the existing 0 percent today	
TASKS	
Advertisements once a week for a semester in 500 university papers	$280,000
Direct-mail samples to student leaders on 500 university campuses	50,000
Sponsor a national contest for video-game players	100,000
Total budget	**$430,000**

Sales promotion activities consist of the specific details of inducements, such as coupons, samples, and sweepstakes. Public relations efforts are readily seen in tangible elements, such as news releases; and direct marketing actions depend on written, verbal, and electronic forms of delivery. The design of the promotion will play a primary role in determining the message that is communicated to the audience. This design activity is frequently viewed as the step requiring the most creativity. In addition, successful designs are often the result of insight regarding consumers' interests and purchasing behaviour. All of the promotion tools have many design alternatives. Advertising, for example, can utilize fear, humour, or other emotions in its appeal.[30] Similarly, direct marketing can be designed for varying levels of personal or customized appeals. One of the challenges of IMC is to design each promotional activity to communicate the same message.

Scheduling the Promotion

Once the designs of all of the promotional program elements are complete, it is important to determine the most effective timing of their use. The promotion schedule describes the order in which each promotional tool is introduced and the frequency of its use during the campaign.

Several other factors, such as seasonality and competitive promotion activity, can also influence the promotion schedule. Such businesses as ski resorts, airlines, and professional sports teams are likely to reduce their promotional activity during the off-season. Similarly, restaurants, retail stores, and health clubs are likely to increase their promotional activities when new competitors enter the market.

EXECUTING AND EVALUATING THE IMC PROGRAM

Carrying out the promotion program can be expensive and time-consuming. One researcher estimates that "an organization with sales less than $10 million can successfully implement an IMC program in one year, one with sales between $200 million and $500 million will need about three years, and one with sales between $2 billion and $5 billion will need five years." To facilitate the transition, there are hundreds of IMC agencies, large and small, all across Canada that are available to assist companies that are making the shift to IMC. Moreover, some of the largest global agencies have also adopted approaches that embrace "total communications solutions." While many agencies still have departments dedicated to advertising, direct marketing, and other specialties, the trend is clearly toward a long-term perspective in which all forms of promotion are integrated.[31] Check out the Going Online box, "Canadian Agencies Adopt IMC Approaches," to learn more about how one agency approaches integrated marketing communications.

An important factor in developing successful IMC programs is to create a process that facilitates their design and use. A tool used to evaluate a company's current process is the *IMC audit*. The audit analyzes the internal communication network of the company; identifies key audiences; evaluates customer databases; assesses messages in recent ads, public relations releases, packaging, video news releases, signage, sales promotion programs, direct mail, and online Web sites; and determines the IMC expertise of the company and agency personnel. Still, although many organizations are interested in improving their IMC processes, they have not been successful at implementing them because of lack of expertise, lack of budget, and lack of management approval.

As shown earlier in Figure 16–6, the ideal execution of a promotion program involves pre-testing each design before its actual use to allow for changes and modifications that improve its effectiveness. Similarly, post-tests are recommended to

Going Online

Canadian Agencies Adopt IMC Approaches

Many traditional ad agencies in Canada have shifted their approach away from offering clients only strict advertising solutions to comprehensive marketing communications solutions, including an IMC and interactive advertising approach. Cossette is one such Canadian firm. It offers its Canadian clients a host of marketing communications solutions, many of which combine the promotional elements discussed in this chapter. Go to Cossette's Web site at **www.cossette.com**, click on "Our Work," and then click on "Case Studies."

1 Which campaigns seem to embrace an IMC or interactive approach?

2 How effective do you think these campaigns are? How should they be evaluated in terms of success?

evaluate the impact of each communication and the contribution it makes in achieving program objectives. The most sophisticated pre-test and post-test procedures have been developed for advertising and are discussed in Chapter 17. Testing procedures for sales promotion and direct marketing efforts currently focus on comparisons of different designs and/or responses to programs by the target audience and even different segments within the target audience. To fully benefit from IMC programs, companies must create and maintain a test result database that allows comparisons of the relative impact of the promotional tools and their execution options in varying situations. Information from the database allows informed design and execution decisions and provides support for IMC activities during internal reviews by financial or administrative personnel.

Currently, about one-fourth of all businesses assess promotion program effectiveness by measuring "most of their communication tactics."[32] For most organizations, the assessment focuses on trying to determine which element of promotion works better or which ones work best in combination. In an integrated program, for example, media advertising might be used to build awareness, sales promotion to generate trial, direct marketing to generate additional information on individual prospects, and personal sales to complete a transaction. These tools are obviously used for different reasons to achieve specific objectives, but their combined use creates a synergy that should be the focus of the assessment. Another level of assessment is necessary when firms have global IMC programs.

learning review

10. What are the characteristics of good promotion objectives?

11. What is the weakness of the percentage of sales budgeting approach?

12. How have advertising agencies changed to facilitate the use of IMC programs?

LO6 DIRECT MARKETING

Direct marketing has many forms and utilizes a variety of media. Several forms of direct marketing—direct mail and catalogues, television home shopping, telemarketing, and direct selling—were discussed as methods of non-store retailing in Chapter 15. In addition, although advertising is discussed in Chapter 17, a form of advertising—direct response advertising—is an important form of direct marketing, as is direct mail advertising, also discussed in Chapter 17. Finally, online advertising, especially interactive online advertising, is also discussed in Chapter 17 and is now an important part of many Canadian companies' direct marketing activities. In this section, the growth of direct marketing, its value to consumers and sellers, and key global, technological, and ethical issues are discussed.

The Growth of Direct Marketing

The increasing interest in customer relationship management (CRM) is reflected in the dramatic growth of direct marketing in Canada. The ability to customize communication efforts and create one-to-one interactions is appealing to most marketers, particularly those with IMC programs. While direct marketing methods are not new (e.g., direct mail), the ability to design and use them has increased with the availability of databases. In recent years, direct marketing growth—in terms of spending, revenue generation, and employment—has outpaced total economic growth. The Canadian Marketing Association (CMA) reports that its members employ over 480,000 people and generate more than $51 billion in annual sales through direct marketing activities in Canada.[33] Telemarketing, including call-centre-based direct marketing is responsible for close to one-half of that employment.

However, a major component of the growth in direct marketing is due to the increasing popularity of the newest direct marketing channel—the Internet. As discussed in Chapter 15, online sales have risen from close to nothing in the mid-1990s to over $13 billion. Continued growth is expected as more and more Canadians gain Internet access and the number of businesses with Web sites and electronic commerce offerings increase. According to the CMA, one of the fastest-growing direct marketing mediums in Canada is *e-mail marketing*.[34] E-mail marketing is considered a fast and easy way to stay in touch with customers. Marketers use e-mail to promote special offers and announce new products and upgrades. E-mail is also often used as a component of well-designed IMC programs. For example, the Hudson's Bay Company utilizes e-mail marketing as part of its IMC program. Many Canadian companies are also using e-mail newsletters, or *ezines,* as a way to increase their contact points with customers.

Others communicate with customers through text messaging via cellphones and PDAs. In fact, *direct mobile marketing,* which involves text messages or short message service (SMS) to such devices, has grown dramatically in Canada. Another important element of direct mobile marketing is *common short code (CSC) marketing.* In fact, many direct marketing experts consider short codes to be the foundation of direct mobile marketing. Instead of sending or receiving messages to a 10-digit phone number, a short code is used, which is five or six digits long and often spells a word or brand name. Molson Canada, for example, owns the short code "665766," which spells out Molson. Molson sends messages to consumers' cellphones to promote sponsored events or asking consumers to participate in a promotion. Mobile Internet browsing has also grown significantly with one in five Canadian wireless consumers engaging in the practice, which provides another vehicle for marketers to reach consumers on the go. Finally, many Canadian companies are using social media platforms such as Facebook, MySpace, YouTube, and Twitter to reach their targeted customers.

Just about any offer communicated through traditional direct marketing methods can be promoted through an electronic or digital channel. However, the proliferation of unsolicited (often unwanted) e-mail—called spam—has become an increasing concern for Canadian consumers, so much so that the Canadian government introduced new legislation: Bill C-27, the *Electronic Commerce Protection Act* (ECPA). It is designed to deter the most dangerous forms of spam, such as identity theft, phishing, and spyware, from occurring in Canada. Spam and related online threats are a real concern to all Internet users as they can lead to the theft of personal data, such as credit card information (identity theft), online fraud involving counterfeit Web sites (phishing), the collection of personal information through illicit access to computer systems (spyware), and false or misleading representations in the online marketplace. The legislation would also treat unsolicited text messages, or "cellphone spam," as

Direct mobile marketing, especially via cellphone, is growing in popularity in Canada.

direct orders

The result of offers that contain all the information necessary for a prospective buyer to make a decision to purchase and complete the transaction.

lead generation

The result of an offer designed to generate interest in a product or service and a request for additional information.

traffic generation

The outcome of an offer designed to motivate people to visit a business.

"unsolicited commercial electronic messages." This bill will allow businesses and consumers to take civil action against anyone who violates the ECPA. The Canadian Radio-television and Telecommunications Commission (CRTC), the Competition Bureau, and the Office of the Privacy Commissioner will be given the power to share information and evidence with their counterparts in other countries who enforce similar laws internationally so that violators beyond our borders cannot use Canada as a spam safe haven. The proposed ECPA would allow the CRTC and the Competition Bureau to charge offenders with administrative monetary penalties of up to $1 million for individuals, and $10 million for all other offenders.[35]

The Value of Direct Marketing

One of the most visible indicators of the value of direct marketing for consumers is the level of use of the various forms of direct marketing. For example, over one-half of the Canadian population has ordered merchandise or services by phone or mail; millions purchase items from television offers; about 20 percent of Canadian adults purchase from a catalogue each year; and over 50 percent of Canadian households order goods and services online.[36] Consumers report many benefits purchasing via direct marketing, including the following. They do not have to go to a store; they can usually shop 24/7; buying direct saves time; they avoid hassles with salespeople; they can save money; it is fun and entertaining; and direct marketing offers more privacy than does in-store shopping. Many consumers also believe that direct marketing companies provide excellent customer service. Toll-free telephone numbers, customer service representatives with access to information regarding purchase preferences, overnight delivery services, and unconditional guarantees all help create value for direct marketing customers.

The value of direct marketing for marketers can be described in terms of the responses it generates.[37] **Direct orders** are the result of offers that contain all the information necessary for a prospective buyer to make a decision to purchase and complete the transaction. Club Med, for example, uses e-mail marketing to sell "last-minute specials" to people in its database. The messages, which are sent midweek, describe rooms and air transportation available at 30 to 40 percent discount if the customer can make the decision to travel on such short notice. **Lead generation** is the result of an offer designed to generate interest in a product or service and a request for additional information. Finally, **traffic generation** is the outcome of an offer designed to motivate people to visit a business. Mitsubishi mailed a sweepstakes offer to prospective buyers to encourage them to visit a Mitsubishi dealer and test drive the new vehicles. The names of prospects who took test drives were entered in the sweepstakes to win cars, trips, and high-definition plasma TVs.

Technological, Global, and Ethical Issues in Direct Marketing

The information technology and databases described in Chapter 8 are key elements of any direct marketing program. Databases are the result of organizations' efforts to collect demographic, media, and consumption profiles of customers so that direct marketing tools, such as catalogues, direct mail, and telemarketing, can be directed at specific customers.

While most companies try to keep records of their customers' past purchases, many other types of data are needed in direct marketing to develop one-to-one relationships with customers. Data, however, have little value by themselves. To translate data into information, the data must be unbiased, timely, pertinent, accessible, and organized in a way that helps the marketing manager make decisions that lead to direct marketing actions. Some data, such as lifestyles, media use, and consumption behaviour, must be collected from consumers. Other types of data can be collected from the stores where purchases are made. Today, technology such as the optical scanner helps collect data with as little intrusion on the customer as possible. Safeway supermarkets, for example, use scanners to capture and track customer purchases in its database. Other marketers capture online customer data, including clickstream behaviour (how someone navigates a Web site), and some direct marketers rely on cookies to focus their direct marketing efforts. *Cookies* are computer files that a marketer can upload onto the computer of an online shopper who visits the marketer's Web site. Cookies allow the marketer to record a user's visit, track visits to other Web sites, and store and retrieve this information in the future. Cookies can also contain information provided by the visitors, such as expressed product preferences, personal data, passwords, and financial information. Clearly, cookies make it possible for customized direct marketing including targeted online advertising. And there is some controversy over the use of this practice. See the accompanying Making Responsible Decisions box, "Privacy Concerns Driving Opposition to Targeted Online Advertising."[38]

Technology may also prove to be important in the global growth of direct marketing. Compared with Canada, many other countries' direct marketing systems are underdeveloped. The mail and telephone systems in many countries are likely to improve, however, creating many new direct marketing opportunities. Developments in global marketing research and database management will also facilitate global growth in direct marketing.

Global and domestic direct marketers also face ethical challenges. For example, considerable attention has been given to some annoying direct marketing activities, such as telephone solicitations during dinner and evening hours. And concerns about consumer privacy have also been raised. In fact, the Canadian government established the Office of Privacy Commissioner of Canada (**www.priv.gc.ca**) and enacted

Making Responsible Decisions

Privacy Concerns Driving Opposition to Targeted Online Advertising

According to a study by the Canadian Marketing Association (CMA), privacy concerns trump perceived value when it comes to a consumer's acceptance of targeted ads based on their online behaviour. "An underlying driver is the sense of control," notes Wally Hill, vice-president of public affairs and communications at CMA. "Most Canadian consumers are aware that some of their online browsing information may be collected but want more transparency and control over the ads being presented to them." Other study findings include:

- Seven in ten Canadians (69 percent) are aware their browsing information may be collected for advertising purposes when they are online.
- With the exception of cases where there is an existing relationship, most Canadian consumers feel online advertising is irrelevant to their needs—half (53 percent) indicate that fewer than one in ten ads are relevant.
- Canadians who consider online privacy to be a very important issue (58 percent) are not being driven by

an underlying opposition to online advertising; indeed, they like seeing ads for coupons or promotions from companies they have dealt with before.

- But most Canadians (79 percent) do not see the Internet as a well-regulated and safe place, and many would like to have the means to ensure that they have choice and control over ads presented to them as a result of their Web-browsing activity.

There is also a strong correlation between a user's technical expertise and amount of time spent online and taking actions to be anonymous when online—technically savvy consumers spend more time online and take steps more frequently than their less-skilled counterparts to be anonymous when surfing Web sites.

What do you think about this targeted online advertising practice? Are you concerned about your privacy and your control over your online browsing activity?

legislation, including the *Personal Information Protection and Electronic Documents Act* (PIPEDA), as a way of protecting the privacy of Canadians. Industry associations, such as the CMA, have also developed guidelines for their members to follow when it comes to consumer privacy, including online privacy.

---

learning review

13. The ability to design and use direct marketing programs has increased with the availability of _____ and _____.

14. The fastest-growing direct market medium in Canada is _____.

15. What are the three types of responses generated by direct marketing activities?

LEARNING OBJECTIVES REVIEW

LO1 Discuss integrated marketing communications and the communication process.

Integrated marketing communication is the concept of designing marketing communications programs that coordinate all promotional activities—advertising, personal selling, sales promotion, public relations, and direct marketing—to provide a consistent message across all audiences and to maximize the promotional budget and impact of communication. The communication process conveys messages with six elements: a source, a message, a channel of communication, a receiver, and encoding and decoding. The communication process also includes a feedback loop and can be distorted by noise.

LO2 Describe the promotional mix and the uniqueness of each component.

There are five promotional alternatives. Advertising, sales promotion, and public relations are mass-selling approaches, whereas personal selling and direct marketing use customized messages. Advertising can have high absolute costs but reaches large numbers of people. Personal selling has a high cost per contact but provides immediate feedback. Public relations is often difficult to obtain but is very credible. Sales promotion influences short-term consumer behaviour. Direct marketing can help develop customer relationships, although maintaining a database can be very expensive.

LO3 Select the promotional approach appropriate to a product's life cycle and characteristics as well as stages of the buying decision.

The promotional mix changes over the four product life-cycle stages. During the introduction stage, all the promotional mix elements are used. In the growth stage, the primary promotional element is advertising. The maturity stage utilizes sales promotion and direct marketing. During the decline stage, little money is spent on the promotional mix. Product

characteristics also help determine the promotion mix. The level of complexity, risk, and ancillary services required will determine which element is needed. Knowing the customer's stage in the buying process can help select appropriate promotions. Advertising and public relations can create awareness in the pre-purchase stage, personal selling and sales promotion can facilitate the purchase, and advertising can help reduce anxiety in the post-purchase stage

LO4 Discuss the characteristics of push and pull strategies.

A push strategy directs the promotional mix to channel members to gain their cooperation in ordering and stocking the product. Personal selling and sales promotion are commonly used in push strategies. A pull strategy directs the promotional mix at ultimate customers to encourage them to ask the retailer for the product. Direct-to-consumer advertising is typically used in pull strategies.

LO5 Describe the elements of the promotion decision process.

The promotion decision process consists of three steps: planning, implementation, and control. The planning step consists of six elements: identifying the target audience, specifying the objectives, setting the budget, selecting the right promotional elements, designing the promotion, and scheduling the promotion. The implementation step includes pre-testing. The control step includes post-testing.

LO6 Explain the value of direct marketing for consumers and sellers.

The value of direct marketing for consumers is indicated by its level of use. The value of direct marketing for sellers can be measured in terms of three types of responses: direct orders, lead generation, and traffic generation. Growth in electronic forms of direct marketing, including e-mail marketing, and direct mobile marketing is evident in Canada.

FOCUSING ON KEY TERMS

advertising p. 431
all-you-can-afford budgeting p. 442
channel of communication p. 429
communication p. 429
competitive parity budgeting p. 441
decoding p. 430
direct marketing p. 434
direct orders p. 447
encoding p. 430
feedback p. 431
field of experience p. 430
hierarchy of effects p. 441
integrated marketing communications (IMC) p. 429
lead generation p. 447
message p. 429

noise p. 431
objective and task budgeting p. 442
percentage of sales budgeting p. 441
personal selling p. 433
promotional mix p. 428
public relations p. 433
publicity p. 433
pull strategy p. 439
push strategy p. 439
receivers p. 429
response p. 431
sales promotion p. 433
source p. 429
traffic generation p. 447

APPLYING MARKETING KNOWLEDGE

1 After listening to a recent sales presentation, Mary Smith signed up for membership at the local health club. On arriving at the facility, she learned there was an additional fee for racquetball court rentals. "I don't remember that in the sales talk; I thought they said all facilities were included with the membership fee," complained Mary. Describe the problem in terms of the communication process.

2 Develop a matrix to compare the five elements of the promotional mix on three criteria—to whom you deliver the message, what you say, and when you say it.

3 Explain how the promotional tools used by an airline would differ if the target audience were (a) consumers who travel for pleasure, and (b) corporate travel departments that select the airlines to be used by company employees.

4 Suppose you introduced a new consumer food product and invested heavily both in national advertising (pull strategy) and in training and motivating your field salesforce to sell the product to food stores (push strategy). What kinds of feedback would you receive from both the advertising and your salesforce? How could you increase both the quality and quantity of each?

5 Fisher-Price Company, long known as a manufacturer of children's toys, has introduced a line of clothing for children. Outline a promotional plan to get this product introduced in the marketplace.

6 Many insurance companies sell health insurance plans to companies. In these companies, the employees pick the plan, but the set of offered plans is determined by the company. Recently Blue Cross–Blue Shield, a health insurance company, ran a television ad stating, "If your employer doesn't offer you Blue Cross–Blue Shield coverage, ask why." Explain the promotional strategy behind the advertisement.

7 Identify the sales promotion tools that might be useful for (a) Tastee Yogourt, a new brand introduction; (b) 3M self-sticking Post-it notes; and (c) Wrigley's Spearmint Gum.

8 Design an integrated marketing communications program—using each of the five promotional elements—for Music Boulevard, the online music store.

9 BMW introduced the activity vehicle, the X5, to compete with other popular 4 × 4 vehicles, such as the Mercedes-Benz M-class and Jeep Grand Cherokee. Design a direct marketing program to generate (a) leads, (b) traffic in dealerships, and (c) direct orders.

10 Develop a privacy policy for database managers that provides a balance of consumer and seller perspectives. How would you encourage voluntary compliance with your policy? What methods of enforcement would you recommend?

Building Your Marketing Plan

To develop the promotion strategy for your marketing plan, follow the steps suggested in the planning phase of the promotion decision process described in Figure 16–6.

1. You should (a) identify the target audience, (b) specify the promotion objectives, (c) set the promotion budget, (d) select the right promotion tools, (e) design the promotion, and (f) schedule the promotion.

2. Also specify the pre-testing and post-testing procedures needed in the implementation and control phases.

3. Finally, describe how each of your promotion tools is integrated to provide a consistent message.

UNDER ARMOUR: USING IMC TO CREATE A BRAND FOR THIS GENERATION'S ATHLETES

"Under Armour sees itself as the athletic brand of this generation. Everything that we create, every message that we put out, that's what we want to be," observes Marcus Stevens, senior creative director for Under Armour. Stevens is responsible for the complete brand aesthetic across all media, including broadcast, print, Web, and point-of-sale. His responsibility is to attract new customers and increase sales of the brand. When the company introduced its first product, a form-fitting moisture-wicking T-shirt to be worn under sportswear, the branding efforts were limited by a very small budget. Today, Under Armour is undertaking the challenge of creating an integrated marketing campaign that utilizes a much larger pool of resources and still delivers a consistent message. As a result of Under Armour's communication activities, "We are poised for growth in the future," explains Stevens.

The Company

Under Armour was founded by Kevin Plank, a University of Maryland football player who didn't like changing out of the sweat-soaked T-shirts he wore under his jersey during practice and games. In 1996 he developed a moisture-wicking fabric and modelled his first product after a typical cotton T-shirt. After several trips to the patent office, and some input from his brother, Kevin decided on the name Under Armour and set up the business in his grandmother's basement. Early sales depended entirely on word-of-mouth advertising that was generated by events such as a *USA Today* photo of an Oakland Raider football player wearing an Under Armour shirt, and Georgia Tech ordering more than 300 shirts for its entire football team. The turning point for the company came when Under Armour products were used in the movie *Any Given Sunday*. Plank decided to build on the exposure provided by the movie and purchased a full-page ad in *ESPN The Magazine*. That ad generated $750,000 in sales and began the incredible growth of the company.

As the company grew, Plank developed four "Keys of Greatness" to guide him and the Under Armour employees. The keys are:

- Build a great product
- Tell a great story about the product
- Provide great service
- Build a great team

The success of Under Armour's first product soon led to a complete line of performance sports apparel including shirts, pants, shorts, outerwear, gloves, footwear,

and accessories. Telling the story was the responsibility of the marketing department and emphasized the need for integrated marketing communications. Great service required support from sales and service representatives. Finally, building a great team meant that Plank always hired the best and brightest people possible. The focus on athletes led to many applications of sports concepts to the business—meetings are called "huddles," the huddle doesn't end until a "play is called," and rapid response to changes in the environment may require "calling an audible." The approach creates a team atmosphere where everyone works together to act on the play.

Today, Under Armour's mission is to make all athletes better through passion, science, and the relentless pursuit of innovation. It offers its product assortment to men, women, and youth online and through more than 15,000 retail locations including SportChek, Dick's Sporting Goods, the Sports Authority, Hibbett Sporting Goods, and Modell's Sporting Goods. International distribution includes outlets in the United Kingdom, France, Germany, Italy, New Zealand, and Japan. Headquarters has moved from Plank's grandmother's basement to Baltimore, Maryland, and the number of employees has increased to 2,200. Under Armour sales now exceed $700 million!

The IMC Program

Stevens first met Plank at an advertising agency where Stevens worked. Plank's idea for an athletic brand for this generation's athlete was very exciting and Stevens soon left the agency to work with Plank. With a limited budget, the challenge was getting the message out to consumers. According to Stevens, "We didn't come in with a polished business plan—and a calendar to execute against; we came in with an idea and a lot of passion." To compete with much larger apparel manufacturers. Stevens knew that Under Armour's marketing activities would need to provide a consistent message through advertising, public relations, personal selling, and all promotional efforts. Kevin Haley, senior vice president of sports marketing, agrees, "Everything has to be integrated." Integrating all promotion activities allows Under Armour to increase the effectiveness of its budget as it strives to create and maintain its brand.

Advertising

Following the release of *Any Given Sunday* and their first print ad in *ESPN the Magazine,* Under Armour began work on a new television advertising campaign. The ad, featuring Eric Ogbogu as "Big E," introduced the tag-line, "We must protect this house," and was released at the same time as ESPN's new series *Playmakers,* which featured football players wearing Under Armour apparel. According to Steven Battista, senior vice president of brand, the two coinciding events "propelled the brand into the national spotlight, and then soon after that you would see fans at games holding up signs saying, 'Protect this house.'" The phrase was used by sports fans, David Letterman, Oprah Winfrey, and many others and soon became part of American lexicon. Other campaigns also helped develop the Under Armour brand and image. For example, "Click, Clack" featured the familiar sound made by cleated shoes, and appealed to athletes in many sports such as golf, lacrosse, and baseball, in addition to football.

Under Armour decided to advertise on the Super Bowl to introduce a new performance training shoe. The message in the ad focused on the athlete of tomorrow and included the tagline, "The future is ours." The athletes in the ad included Carl Weathers, a NASCAR driver; Ray Lewis, a football linebacker; Kimmie Meissner, a figure skater; and many others. The ad made a statement that Under Armour could help all athletes train like champions. "The future is ours" was a huge success ranking in the top-five ads according to *USA Today*'s Ad Meter. In addition, Web site traffic tripled following the ad and orders for the product began pouring in! The Super Bowl ad also helped make a statement about the Under Armour brand—that the company, the CEO, the product, and the consumers all represented a new prototype for the future.

Public Relations and Promotion

According to Battista, "half the benefit of a 60-second ad in the Super Bowl is the PR leading up to it and the attention you get" from producing and running the advertisement. Marketing benefits also result from promotion activities such as athlete endorsements, sponsorships, and product placements. These activities play an important role in Under Armour's integrated marketing communications strategy. Each potential athlete endorsement, for example, is evaluated in terms of the products they will be supporting, the media that would be used, and the potential for in-store and on-field visibility. Under Armour signed Alfonso Soriano, a Chicago Cubs baseball player, to support its baseball cleats and baseball apparel, the outdoor advertising at Wrigley Field, and the retail store in the Chicago market. Under Armour looks for athletes that are "all about performance," explains Haley. They "need to be a team player, who is doing everything they can to win on every single play."

Under Armour has also developed many sponsorship relationships with teams and organizations. For example, Under Armour is the official outfitter for the football programs at Auburn University, the University of Delaware, the University of Hawaii, the University of North Texas, the University of South Carolina, and many other schools. The company recently signed a 5-year agreement with the University of Maryland to outfit all of its 27 varsity sports. Similarly, Under Armour is the supplier for all 17 varsity athletic teams at Texas Tech University. Under Armour has also sponsored high school athletes, professional soccer teams, and the NFL.

Product placements in movies, television shows, and video games have reinforced Under Armour's branding efforts and provided exposure to new audiences. In addition to *Any Given Sunday* you may remember seeing Under Armour products in the movies *Gridiron Gang* and *The Replacements.* Television programs with Under Armour product placements include *Friday Night Lights, The Sopranos,* and *MTV Road Rules.* Under Armour even appears in video games such as *Tiger Woods Golf* and *Fight Night 3!*

Retail and Online

When Plank first started Under Armour, its Web site (**www.underarmour.com**) was its only means of sales and distribution. As the company grew it gained

distribution in many retailers. The point-of-sale displays in the retailers, however, offered a unique opportunity to integrate Under Armour's branding. When Under Armour moved into large retailers it noticed that the mannequins in the stores didn't look like the athletes in the advertising because the mannequins did not have muscles. To create a consistent message Under Armour made its own mannequins for the stores so that the displays would look like the athletes in the commercials. Eventually, Under Armour also began opening its own stores. The first Under Armour store opened in Annapolis, Maryland in 2008 and many others soon followed.

The Under Armour Web site remains an important part of the integrated marketing program. Approximately 15 percent of all sales come through the Web site, and many Under Armour consumers use the Web site to learn about new products, study technical details, or view print or television ads. Consumers who register on the site can receive e-mail messages about new or seasonal products and new campaigns. Currently, the Under Armour Web site attracts an average of 35,000 visitors each day. The online program also includes several social networking elements. Under Armour, for example, is building a presence on Facebook and on Xbox Live marketplace. All of these activities help ensure that consumers will be exposed to a consistent message regardless of the medium they utilize.

Future Strategy

How can Under Armour continue its incredible record of growth? Experts observe that future growth will require the company to broaden its appeal without alienating the original segment of athletes interested in performance. There are opportunities to expand exposure in many sports such as the fast-growing lacrosse segment, to attract more men, women, and youth, and to introduce new products to the current line. Under Armour, for example, recently introduced a line of running shoes—a large category with broad appeal to many consumers. Integrating the growth activities will be critical to the company's success. As Battista observes, everything has to "look right and have the same message points and the same type of branding and look and feel!"

The future is likely to be very exciting for Under Armour as it continues to introduce new products and enter new markets. For example, the company recently introduced mouth guards and a body suit that helps athletes recover from a workout faster. To expand in international markets Under Armour is creating distribution networks in Europe and Asia and signing endorsement deals with rugby players, Olympians, and other international athletes. In addition, to change perceptions that Under Armour products are used primarily by football players, the company now sponsors 27 boys' and girls' high school basketball teams. Under Armour's branding and communication strategies have been extraordinarily successful as the company now is the fastest growing performance sports brand. In fact, the company has grown so quickly that it plans to add an additional 135,000 square feet of new space across the street from its headquarters to provide showrooms and new offices. According to one newspaper headline, the company is a "runaway success"!

Questions

1 What promotional opportunities gave Under Armour its initial success?

2 Which of the promotional elements described in Figure 16–2 are used by Under Armour in its IMC campaigns?

3 What are several new strategies Under Armour might pursue as it attempts to continue its extraordinary record of growth?

Driving deeper
into the heart and soul
of agriculture.

ADFarm

chapter 17

Advertising, Sales Promotion, and Public Relations

SO, HOW WOULD YOU LIKE TO BE A CANADIAN ADFARMER?

Although you may see, hear, or read hundreds of advertisements daily, you might not be fully aware of the industry behind these ads. For many students, the advertising business evokes images of glamour, expense accounts, and an exciting lifestyle. This may be partially true. But the advertising business is also demanding, challenging, and a lot of hard work. To be successful in the advertising business requires a mix of personal abilities, considerable business skills, and the capacity to work under pressure to meet deadlines. And compared with other industries, there are actually few entry-level positions available in Canadian advertising agencies. Also, the competition for those jobs is very intense, as there are only a few hundred advertising agencies in Canada. One of the most unique agencies in the business is AdFarm.

AdFarm is Canada's largest agricultural marketing communications firm. It has been recognized as one of the 50 Best Managed Companies in Canada and listed by *Canadian Business* magazine as one of the Best Workplaces in Canada. It focuses exclusively on providing communications solutions for companies and organizations operating in the production agriculture, food, and rural development sectors. It has offices in Calgary and Guelph as well as in Fargo, North Dakota, and Kansas City, Missouri. It operates under a novel "one-agency matrix model" involving functions and teams and has no head office per se. It believes that this model allows AdFarm to create

learning objectives

After reading this chapter, you should be able to:

LO1 Explain the differences between product advertising and institutional advertising and the variations within each type.

LO2 Describe the steps used to develop, execute, and evaluate an advertising program.

LO3 Explain the advantages and disadvantages of alternative advertising media.

LO4 Discuss the strengths and weaknesses of consumer-oriented and trade-oriented sales promotions.

LO5 Recognize public relations as an important form of communication.

and deliver consistently excellent work for its clients, including some of the industry's leading players such as Bayer Cropscience and Dow AgroSciences.

AdFarm is a full-service agency offering a complete range of marketing communications services, including advertising, public relations, issue management, media relations, direct marketing, online marketing, and social media. One of the other unique aspects of the organization is its focus on its employees, which the agency refers to as AdFarmers. All AdFarmers must meet a strict set of hiring criteria, including being able to develop and live AdFarm values such as integrity, excellence, and fun. They must also possess excellent knowledge and skills within their respective function area—creative, public relations, strategy, account services, media, and administration. Moreover, AdFarmers must be willing to embrace their brand's focus on and passion for agriculture, food, and rural development. Finally, the AdFarmers must also be willing to commit to ongoing training to refine their skills and obtain new knowledge. AdFarm, in fact, supports its AdFarmers who wish to continue their studies through additional university and college courses.

How successful is AdFarm? Its growth and financial performance are higher than the majority of competing firms; it has received numerous awards for its work; it has achieved high levels of client satisfaction; and employee retention and work satisfaction are higher than the agency industry average. You will read more about AdFarm in the end-of-chapter video case.

So, do you think you have what it takes to become an AdFarmer, or to work in the advertising industry in general? If you are skilled, bright, articulate, creative, and personable and if you have a well-rounded education and a good business sense, you might. If you want to learn more about working in the Canadian advertising industry, go to the Institute of Communication Agencies (**www.icacanada.ca**), Canada's national association of advertising agencies, and click on "Publications." You will find an interesting publication called, "So. . . . You Want to be in an Advertising Agency." You might also want to check out AdFarm's Web site (**www.adfarmonline.com**) just to see how unique this agency is in the overall Canadian advertising agency landscape. Or, follow the company on Twitter. You never know, maybe some day you will get to become a Canadian AdFarmer after all![1]

advertising

Any paid form of non-personal communication about an organization, good, service, or idea by an identified sponsor.

This chapter introduces you to **advertising**—any paid form of non-personal communication about an organization, good, service, or idea by an identified sponsor. It will also detail the alternative types of advertisement and the advertising decision process as well as introduce you to the concepts of sales promotion and public relations.

TYPES OF ADVERTISEMENTS

As you look through any magazine or watch television, listen to the radio, or browse the Internet, many advertisements you see or hear may give you the impression that they have few similarities. Advertisements are prepared for different purposes, but they basically consist of two types: product and institutional. These two types of ads can

What are the purposes of these ads?

also be classified on the basis of whether they are intended to get the consumer to take immediate action (*direct-response advertising*) or to influence future purchase or actions (*delayed-response advertising*).

LO1 Product Advertisements

product advertisements
Advertisements that focus on selling a good or service and take three forms: (1) pioneering (or informational), (2) competitive (or persuasive), and (3) reminder.

Focused on selling a good or service, **product advertisements** take three forms: (1) pioneering (or informational), (2) competitive (or persuasive), and (3) reminder. Look at the ads on this page by Sony and M&Ms, and determine the type and objective of each ad.

Used in the introductory stage of the product life cycle, *pioneering* advertisements tell people what a product is, what it can do, and where it can be found. The key objective of a pioneering advertisement is to inform the target market. Informative ads have been found to be interesting, convincing, and effective.[2]

Advertising that promotes a specific brand's features and benefits is *competitive*. The objective of these messages is to persuade the target market to select the firm's brand rather than that of a competitor. An increasingly common form of competitive advertising is *comparative* advertising, which shows one brand's strengths relative to those of competitors.[3] The Sony ad, for example, highlights the competitive advantage of the Sony camera over its primary competitors Canon and Nikon. Studies indicate that comparative ads attract more attention and increase the perceived quality of the advertiser's brand.[4] Firms that use comparative advertising need market research to provide legal support for their claims.[5]

Reminder advertising is used to reinforce previous knowledge of a product. The M&Ms ad shown reminds consumers about the association between its product and a special event—in this case, Valentine's Day. Reminder advertising is good for products that have achieved a well-recognized position and are in the mature phase of their product life cycle. Another type of reminder ad, *reinforcement*, is used to assure current users they made the right choice. One example: "Aren't you glad you use Dial? Don't you wish everybody did?"

Institutional Advertisements

institutional advertisements
Advertisements designed to build goodwill or an image for an organization, rather than promote a specific good or service.

The objective of **institutional advertisements** is to build goodwill or an image for an organization, rather than promote a specific good or service. Institutional advertising has been used by such companies as the RBC, Pfizer, and IBM Canada to build confidence in the company name.[6] Often, this form of advertising is used to support the public relations plan or to counter adverse publicity. Four alternative forms of institutional advertisements are often used:

- *Advocacy* advertisements state the position of a company on an issue. For example, Molson's "Take Care" ads encourage the responsible use of alcohol.
- *Pioneering institutional* advertisements, like the pioneering ads for products discussed earlier, are used for announcements about what a company is, what it can do, or where it is located. Recent Bayer ads stating "We cure more headaches than you think" are intended to inform consumers that the company produces many products in addition to aspirin.
- *Competitive institutional* advertisements promote the advantages of one product class over another and are used in markets where different product classes compete for the same buyers. The Dairy Farmers of Canada (DFC), made up of more than 13,000 dairy farmers in Canada, promotes the consumption of milk as it competes against other beverages.
- *Reminder institutional* advertisements, like the product form, simply bring the company's name to the attention of the target market again.

A competitive institutional ad by the Dairy Farmers of Canada tries to increase the demand for milk.

As mentioned earlier, advertising can also be classified as either direct-response advertising or delayed-response advertising. *Direct-response advertising* seeks to motivate the customer to take immediate action, such as a television ad asking you to phone a toll-free telephone number and place an order immediately. Lavalife, for example, uses direct-response television ads. The primary objective of the ads is to generate calls to the company about its online dating services.[7] *Delayed-response advertising*, on the other hand, presents images and/or information designed to influence the consumer in the near future when making purchases or taking other actions. Direct marketers often rely on direct-response advertising as part of their direct-marketing efforts. However, more and more often, traditional marketers are using this form of advertising as they attempt to obtain an immediate return on their advertising dollar and measured response in terms of advertising effectiveness.

---

learning review

1. What is the difference between pioneering and competitive ads?

2. What is the purpose of an institutional advertisement?

3. What is direct-response advertising?

LO2 DEVELOPING THE ADVERTISING PROGRAM

The promotion decision process described in Chapter 16 can be applied to each of the promotional elements. Advertising, for example, can be managed by following the three steps (developing, executing, and evaluating) of the process.

Identifying the Target Audience

To develop an effective advertising program, advertisers must identify the target audience. All aspects of an advertising program are likely to be influenced by the characteristics of the prospective consumer. Understanding the lifestyles, attitudes, and demographics of the target market is essential. When Under Armour began advertising to women, the ads did not have the same ending as the men's ads: "We must protect the house!" Women said they wanted similar ads, so Under Armour introduced a new "hard-core athlete" campaign for women.[8] Similarly, the placement of ads depends on the audience. When Hummer, the biggest and most expensive sport-utility vehicle in the market, opened its campaign targeted at "rugged individualists" with incomes above $200,000, It selected *Wired, Spin, Red Herring, Business Week, Skiing,* and *Cigar Aficionado* to carry the ads. Even scheduling can depend on the audience. Claritin, an allergy medication, schedules its use of brochures, in-store displays, coupons, and advertising to coincide with the allergy season, which varies by geographic region.[9] To eliminate possible bias that might result from subjective judgments about some population segments, advertising program decisions should be based on market research about the target audience. For example, Home Depot tweaked its target audience and its message in Quebec after research revealed its ad campaigns were not connecting with French consumers.[10]

A successful ad campaign achieves its objectives.

Specifying Advertising Objectives

The guidelines for setting promotion objectives described in Chapter 16 also apply to setting advertising objectives. This step helps advertisers with other choices in the promotion decision process, such as selecting media and evaluating a campaign. Advertising with an objective of creating awareness, for example, would be better matched with a magazine than a directory, such as the Yellow Pages.[11] Similarly, an advertiser looking to induce consumers to trial or to take other direct action, such as visit a store location, would use a direct-response form of advertising, such as direct mail. The Institute of Communication Agencies, which represents Canada's communications and advertising agencies, believes that establishing advertising objectives is so important that it created the CASSIE Awards, whereby advertisers are recognized for achieving ad campaign objectives. For example, a creative billboard ad campaign increased sales of James Ready beer by 55 percent over the previous year. And IKEA used a television, magazine, and online ad campaign to significantly increase sales of its PAX wardrobe over the previous year.[12]

Setting the Advertising Budget

The methods used to set the overall promotion budget as outlined in Chapter 16 can be used to establish a specific advertising budget. As with the promotional or integrated marketing communications (IMC) budget, the best approach to setting the ad budget is the objective and task approach. There are numerous advertising options available to the advertiser, and most of the alternatives require substantial financial commitments. A formal budgeting process that involves matching the target audience to the available advertising options, evaluating the ability of those options to achieve specified objectives, and weighing the relative costs of the advertising options is definitely a requirement for effective advertising.

Designing the Advertisement

An advertising message usually focuses on the key benefits of the product that are important to a prospective buyer in making trial and adoption decisions. The message depends on the general form or appeal used in the ad and the actual words included in the ad.

Message Content   Most advertising messages are made up of both informational and persuasional elements. These two elements, in fact, are so intertwined that it is sometimes difficult to tell them apart. For example, basic information contained in many ads, such as the product name, benefits, features, and price, is presented in a way that tries to attract attention and encourage purchase. On the other hand, even the most persuasive advertisements must contain at least some basic information to be successful.

Information and persuasive content can be combined in the form of an appeal to provide a basic reason for the consumer to act. Although the marketer can use many different types of appeals, common advertising appeals include fear appeals,[13] sex appeals, and humorous appeals.

Fear appeals suggest to the consumer that he or she can avoid some negative experience through the purchase and use of a product or service, a change in behaviour, or a reduction in the use of a product. Examples with which you may be familiar include fire or smoke detector ads that depict a home burning, or social cause ads warning of the serious consequences of drug and alcohol use or high-risk sexual behaviour. Pacific Blue Cross of Burnaby, B.C., for example, runs ads asking people to think about the adequacy of their health insurance coverage and the "unthinkable" consequences if they do not.[14] However, when using fear appeals, the advertiser must be sure that the appeal is strong enough to get the audience's attention and concern but not so strong that it will cause them to tune out the message.

In contrast, *sex appeals* suggest to the audience that the product will increase the attractiveness of the user. Sex appeals can be found in almost any product category, from automobiles to toothpaste. Unfortunately, many commercials that use sex appeals are successful only at gaining the attention of the audience; they have little impact on how consumers think, feel, or act. Some advertising experts even argue that such appeals get in the way of successful communication by distracting the audience from the purpose of the ad.

Humorous appeals imply either directly or more subtly that the product is more fun or exciting than competitors' offerings. As with fear and sex appeals, the use of humour is widespread in Canadian advertising and can be found in many product categories. In fact, no product sector appears immune. For example, unlike Pacific Blue Cross health insurance, mentioned above, BCAA Life Insurance uses a humorous ad campaign to promote life insurance.[15] However, humour has to be used with care. Jokes tend to wear out quickly, eventually boring the consumer. Moreover, sometimes, the humour may offend the target audience, and some humorous appeals may not travel well across cultures. Still, recent Canadian research reveals that consumers prefer humorous appeals over sex appeals. A full 67 percent of Canadians say humour is the secret ingredient that makes an advertisement most persuasive, compared to only 7 percent who feel that, ultimately, sex sells.[16]

This ad campaign for BCAA Life Insurance uses humour to underscore the importance of life insurance for family security.

Creating the Actual Message   The "creative people" in an advertising agency—copywriters and art directors—have the responsibility to turn appeals and such features as quality, style, dependability, economy, and service into attention-getting, believable advertisements. Translating creative ideas into actual advertisements is a complex process. Designing quality artwork, layout, and production for the advertisements is also often costly and time-consuming. It typically costs more than $200,000 to produce a 30-second high-quality TV commercial. High-visibility integrated ad campaigns can be even more expensive. Other costs can include paying celebrity spokespersons to appear in the ads. In fact, Canadians are seeing many celebrities featured in advertising today, including sports heroes and entertainers. For example, Don Cherry is a spokesperson for Molson's mini-kegs (or Bubbas) while Sidney Crosby represents Gatorade and Reebok. Non-profits also use spokespeople in their ads, but these spokespeople are not compensated. For example, WorldSkills International, a non-profit organization that promotes vocational education and training, uses Canadian astronaut Julie Payette as a spokesperson while the Canadian Cancer Society uses actor Philippe Charbonneau to promote its cause.[17]

---

learning review

4. What are the three common advertising appeals?

5. Who is responsible for turning appeals and product features into attention-getting advertising?

The use of celebrity spokespersons is popular in Canadian advertising.

Selecting the Right Media

Every advertiser must decide where to place its advertisements. The alternatives are the advertising media, the means by which the message is communicated to the target audience. Newspapers, magazines, radio, and TV are examples of *advertising media*. This "media selection" decision is related to the target audience, type of product, nature of the message, campaign objectives, available budget, and the costs of the alternative media. Figure 17–1 shows the distribution of the almost $14 billion spent on advertising in Canada among the many media alternatives.[18] One trend that experts are seeing is advertising dollars being shifted from several traditional media to Internet advertising. In less than ten years, the spending on Internet advertising has gone from virtually zero dollars to over $1.6 billion in Canada.[19] Some of Canada's leading advertisers include General Motors of Canada, Sears Canada, BCE (Bell Canada Enterprises), the Government of Canada, Procter & Gamble, Rogers Communications, the Hudson's Bay Company, and Ford Motor Company of Canada. And many of them are major Internet advertisers.

Choosing a Medium and a Vehicle within That Medium

In deciding where to place advertisements, a company has several media to choose from and a number of alternatives, or vehicles, within each medium. Often, advertisers use a mix of media forms and vehicles to maximize the exposure of the

● **FIGURE 17–1**
Canadian advertising expenditures by medium, as a percentage of total ad spending

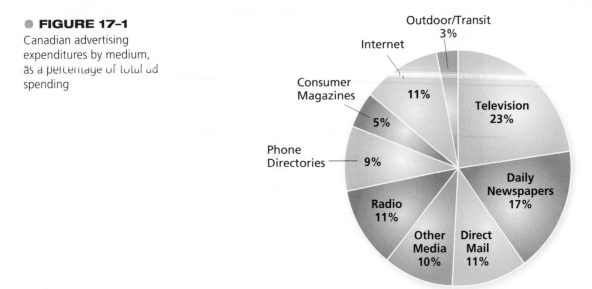

message to the target audience while minimizing costs. These two conflicting goals of (1) maximizing exposure and (2) minimizing costs are of central importance to media planning.

Basic Terms   Media buyers speak a language of their own, and so every advertiser involved in selecting the right media for their campaigns must be familiar with some common terms used in the advertising industry. Figure 17–2 shows the most common terms used in media decisions.

Because advertisers try to maximize the number of individuals in the target market exposed to the message, they must be concerned with reach. **Reach** is the number of different people or households exposed to an advertisement. The exact definition of reach sometimes varies among alternative media. Newspapers often use reach to describe their total circulation or the number of different households that buy the paper. Television and radio stations, in contrast, describe their reach using the term **rating**—the percentage of households in a market that are tuned to a particular TV show or radio station. In general, advertisers try to maximize reach in their target market at the lowest cost.

Like greater reach, greater frequency has been historically viewed by advertisers as desirable. This was because it was believed that consumers often do not pay close attention to the advertising message. Therefore, many advertisers wanted to expose the same audience more than once to their message. This involves **frequency,** or the average number of times a person in the target audience is exposed to a message or advertisement. In fact, the traditional *3 + effective-frequency* model (exposing the target audience 3 + times to an ad) has dominated the advertising industry for years. Now, however, there is evidence that this model may be flawed. So, many Canadian advertisers have turned to a new approach called *recency*—delivering media messages in a way that increases the likelihood of reaching more people with a message close to the time of their purchase. This is sometimes called just-in-time communications.[20]

When reach (expressed as a percentage of the total market) is multiplied by frequency, an advertiser will obtain a commonly used reference number called **gross rating points (GRPs).** To obtain the appropriate number of GRPs to achieve an advertising campaign's objectives, the media planner must balance reach and frequency. The balance will also be influenced by cost. **Cost per thousand (CPM)** refers to the cost of reaching 1,000 individuals or households with the advertising message in a given medium (*M* is the Roman numeral for 1,000). See the accompanying Using Marketing Dashboards box for an example of the use of CPM in media selection.

reach
The number of different people or households exposed to an advertisement.

rating
The percentage of households in a market that are tuned to a particular TV show or radio station.

frequency
The average number of times a person in the target audience is exposed to a message or advertisement.

gross rating points (GRPs)
A reference number for advertisers, created by multiplying reach (expressed as a percentage of the total market) by frequency.

cost per thousand (CPM)
The cost of reaching 1,000 individuals or households with an advertising message in a given medium.

● **FIGURE 17-2**
The language of the media buyer

TERM	WHAT IT MEANS
Reach	The number of different people or households exposed to an advertisement.
Rating	The percentage of households in a market that are tuned to a particular TV show or radio station.
Frequency	The average number of times an individual is exposed to an advertisement.
Gross rating points (GRPs)	Reach (expressed as a percentage of the total market) multiplied by frequency.
Cost per thousand (CPM)	The cost of advertising divided by the number of thousands of individuals or households who are exposed.

Using Marketing Dashboards

What Is the Best Way to Reach 1,000 Customers?

Marketing managers must choose from many advertising options as they design a campaign to reach potential customers. Because there are so many media alternatives (television, radio, magazines, etc.) and multiple options within each of the media, it is important to monitor the efficiency of advertising expenditures on your marketing dashboard.

Your Challenge As the marketing manager for a company about to introduce a new soft drink into the market, you are preparing a presentation in which you must make recommendations for the advertising campaign. You have observed that competitors use magazine ads, newspaper ads, and even Super Bowl ads! To compare the cost of some of the alternatives you decide to use one of the most common measures in advertising: cost per thousand impressions (CPM). The CPM is calculated as follows:

Cost per thousand impressions = Advertising cost ($) / Impressions generated (in 1000s)

Your challenge is to determine the most efficient use of your advertising budget.

Your Findings Your research department helps you collect cost and audience size information for three options: full-page colour ads in *The Globe and Mail* (newspaper) and *MacLean's* magazine, and a 30-second television ad during the Super Bowl (Canada only). With this information you are able to calculate the cost per thousand impressions for each alternative.

Your Action Based on the calculations for these options you see that there is a variation in the cost of reaching 1,000 potential customers (CPM) and also in the absolute cost of the advertising. Although advertising on the Super Bowl has the lowest CPM, $29 for each 1,000 impressions, it also has the largest absolute cost! Your next step will be to consider other factors such as your total available budget, the profiles of the audiences each alternative reaches, and whether the type of message you want to deliver is better communicated in print or on television.

Media Alternative	Cost of Ad	Audience Size	Cost per Thousand Impressions
The Globe and Mail (newspaper)	$13,000	400,000	$32
MacLean's (magazine)	$36,000	385,000	$93
Super Bowl (TV)	$100,000	9,000,000	$11

 Different Media Alternatives

Figure 17–3[21] summarizes the advantages and disadvantages of the important advertising media, which are described in more detail below.

Television Television is a valuable medium because it communicates with sight, sound, and motion. Print advertisements alone could never give you the sense of a new sports car accelerating from a stop or cornering at high speed. In addition, network television is the only medium that can reach 99 percent of the homes in Canada. And 90 percent of Canadian households are cable- or satellite-equipped. *Out-of-home* TV viewing also reaches millions of Canadians in bars, hotels, and university campuses each week. The average Canadian watches over 26 hours of TV per week. Two English national networks, CTV and CBC, share over 33 percent of the national television audience for conventional channels.[22]

Television's major disadvantage is cost. For example, the cost of a 30-second spot on CTV during the Super Bowl can be over $100,000.[23] Because of these high charges, many advertisers have reduced the length of their commercials from 30 seconds to 15 seconds. This practice, referred to as *splitting 30s,* reduces costs but severely restricts the amount of information and emotion that can be conveyed. Research indicates,

MEDIUM	ADVANTAGES	DISADVANTAGES
Television	Reaches extremely large audience; uses picture, print, sound, and motion for effect; can target specific audiences	High cost to prepare and run ads; short exposure time and perishable message; difficult to convey complex information
Radio	Low cost; can target specific local audiences; ads can be placed quickly; can use sound, humour, and intimacy effectively	No visual element; short exposure time and perishable message; difficult to convey complex information
Magazines	Can target specific audiences; high-quality colour; long life of ad; ads can be clipped and saved; can convey complex information	Long time needed to place ad; relatively high cost; competes for attention with other magazine features
Newspapers	Excellent coverage of local markets; ads can be placed and changed quickly; ads can be saved; quick consumer response; low cost	Ads compete for attention with other newspaper features; short lifespan; poor colour
Yellow Pages	Excellent coverage of geographic segments; long use period; available 24 hours/365 days	Proliferation of competitive directories in many markets; difficult to keep up-to-date
Direct mail	High selectivity of audience; can contain complex information and personalized messages; high-quality graphics	High cost per contact; poor image (junk mail)
Internet	Video and audio capabilities; animation can capture attention; ads can be interactive and link to advertiser	Animation and interactivity require time and money; tracking effectiveness
Outdoor	Low cost; local market focus; high visibility; opportunity for repeat exposures	Message must be short and simple; low selectivity of audience; criticized as a traffic hazard
User-generated content	Customers absorb time and cost of promotion efforts	Marketers do not necessarily control what is communicated and how it is communicated

● **FIGURE 17–3**

Advantages and disadvantages of major advertising media

Source: William F. Arens, *Contemporary Advertising*, 9th ed. Copyright © 2004 by The McGraw-Hill Companies; Figure 17.3 from William G. Nickels, James M. McHugh, and Susan M. McHugh, *Understanding Business*, 7th ed. © 2005 by The McGraw-Hill Companies.

however, that two different versions of a 15-second commercial, run back-to-back, will increase recall over long intervals.[24]

Another problem with television is the likelihood of *wasted coverage*—having people outside the market for the product see the advertisement. In recent years, the cost and wasted-coverage problems of TV have been reduced through the introduction of specialized digital or cable and direct broadcast (satellite) channels. Advertising time is often less expensive on cable and direct broadcast channels than on the major networks. There are currently many channel options—such as CMT, MuchMusic, HGTV, YTV, and Food Network Canada—that reach very narrowly defined audiences. Other forms of television are changing television advertising also. On-demand and pay-per-view movie services, as well as personal video recorders (PVRs), for example, offer the potential of commercial-free viewing. Over 15 percent of Canadian households have PVRs.

infomercials

Program-length (30-minute) advertisements that take an educational approach to communication with potential customers.

Another popular form of television advertising is the infomercial. **Infomercials** are program-length (30-minute) advertisements that take an educational approach to communication with potential customers. Volvo, Club Med, General Motors, Mattel, Revlon, and many other companies are using infomercials as a means of providing information that is relevant, useful, and entertaining to prospective customers. In many cases, marketers are using infomercials for direct-response purposes, asking customers to order products and/or to request further information during the airing. Over $25 million is spent on infomercials in Canada.[25]

Radio There are over 600 commercial radio stations in Canada. Radio reaches 92 percent of the population aged 12 and over in an average week. And the average radio listener spends close to 20 hours per week listening to radio. The major advantage of radio is that it is a segmented medium offering distinctive formats. There are jazz stations, classical music stations, all-talk shows, and hard rock stations, all catering to different market segments. The top formats in Canada are news/talk, adult contemporary, country, Hot AC (hot adult contemporary), current hits, and rock.

The disadvantage of radio is that it has limited use for products that must be seen. Another problem is the ease with which consumers can tune out a commercial by switching stations. Radio is also a medium that competes for people's attention as they do other activities, such as driving, working, or relaxing. Peak radio listening time, for example, is during peak rush-hour commuting (6 to 10 A.M. and 4 to 7 P.M.). And now, radio listeners have another radio listening option—satellite radio services (Sirius and XM) that offer digital-quality radio channels for a monthly subscription.[26]

Magazines Magazines have become a very specialized medium. There are over 1,200 consumer magazines in Canada and 1,000 business publications and trade journals. According to the Print Measurement Bureau (PMB), almost 85 percent of Canadians aged 12 or over read a magazine in the past month.[27] The marketing advantage of this medium is the great number of special-interest publications that appeal to narrowly defined segments. Runners read *Runner's World,* golfers buy *Golf Canada,* gardeners subscribe to *Gardening Life,* and children peruse *Famous Kids* or *Owl.* Each magazine's readership often represents a unique profile. Take the *Rolling Stone* reader, who tends to travel, backpack, and ski more than do most people—and so a manufacturer of ski equipment that places an ad in *Rolling Stone* knows that it is reaching the desired target audience. In addition to the distinct audience profiles of magazines, good colour production is an advantage that allows magazines to create strong images.

The cost of advertising in national magazines is a disadvantage, but many national publications, such as *Canadian Living* and *MacLean's,* publish regional and even metro editions, which reduce the absolute cost and wasted coverage. In addition to cost, a limitation to magazines is their infrequency. At best, magazines are printed on a weekly basis, with many specialized publications appearing only monthly or less often.

Newspapers Newspapers are an important local medium with excellent reach potential. There are over 120 daily newspapers in Canada, including more than a dozen French-language papers. There are also over 1,100 community newspapers. Because of the daily publication of most papers, they allow advertisements to focus on specific current events, such as a "24-hour sale." Local retailers often use newspapers as their sole advertising medium.

Newspapers, however, are rarely saved by the purchaser, and so companies are generally limited to ads that call for an immediate customer response (although customers can clip and save the ads they are interested in). Companies also cannot depend on newspapers for the same colour reproduction quality as that in most magazines.

National advertising campaigns rarely include this medium except in conjunction with local distributors of their products. In these instances, both parties often share the advertising costs using a cooperative advertising program, which is described later in this chapter. Another exception is the use of newspapers, such as *The Globe and Mail,* that have national distribution.

In an effort to deliver timely news coverage, many newspapers are delivering online or digital newspapers. For example, *The Globe and Mail* and the *National Post* both offer online or digital papers and continue to make them more interactive as well. This concept is opening up new advertising potential for such newspapers.

Yellow Pages   Yellow Pages represent an alternative advertising medium comparable with radio in terms of expenditures in Canada. Over $1.2 billion is spent on Yellow Pages and phone directory advertising in Canada.[28] Yellow Pages directories reach almost every household in Canada and are a *directional* medium because they help consumers know where purchases can be made after other media have created awareness and demand.

Yellow Pages have several other advantages. First, they are available 24 hours each day and 365 days each year. In addition, Yellow Pages have a long lifespan—directories are typically published once each year and provide advertisers with many advertising size options. A disadvantage of Yellow Pages advertising is the proliferation of similar directories. Many markets now have competing directories for specific neighbourhoods and even ethnic groups. Another disadvantage is the lack of timeliness because Yellow Pages can only be updated with new information once each year. Yellow Pages are typically used for local advertising—more than 80 percent of all Yellow Pages expenditures are local—because of the difficulty of coordinating a nationwide campaign in Yellow Pages directories. However, many of these problems have been overcome with the advent of Internet or online Yellow Pages and phone directories, including **www.canada411.ca.**

Direct Mail   Direct mail advertising is often considered the cornerstone of the efforts of many direct marketers (see Chapters 15 and 16) to reach consumers. But any advertiser looking for good audience selectivity can find direct mail advertising effective. Also, direct mail advertising allows marketers to provide more information to the customer than is possible in a television or radio spot. In many cases, direct mail advertising is being used in conjunction with other media, particularly broadcast, as part of an integrated marketing communications (IMC) solution. Mass media are used to create awareness, while direct mail advertising is used to build a relationship and facilitate a purchase.

One disadvantage of direct mail advertising is its rising costs due to postal rate increases. Another limitation is that people often view direct mail advertising as junk mail and are reluctant to open such mail. A novel approach to overcome that problem is the use of *self-mailers*—simple white envelopes without any promotional messaging—that consumers are more likely to open. Also, the availability of robust databases now allows the advertiser to send mail only to well-defined targets with very specific and appealing offers, which is helping to improve consumer response rates.

Internet   Internet advertising is the fastest-growing advertising medium in Canada. *Internet advertising,* sometimes referred to as *online* or *Web advertising,* now exceeds over $1.6 billion in total ad spending. This form of advertising includes online classified and directory advertising, online e-mail, search engine, social media advertising, and traditional display ads. Quebecor Media, for example, has a classified advertising site called classifiedextra.ca, which integrates ads from more than 200 daily and community newspapers and the Canoe.ca portal.

One of the major reasons for this explosive growth is the trend toward integrated marketing communications with traditional advertisers now using Internet advertising more and more often as part of their integrated campaigns.[29]

Internet advertising is similar to print advertising in that it offers a visual message, but it has additional advantages because it can also use the audio and video capabilities of the Internet. Sound and movement may attract more attention or make the message more entertaining. Online advertising also has the unique feature of being interactive. Interactive online advertising, sometimes called *rich media,* has dropdown menus, built-in games, videos, short films, or search engines to engage viewers.

There are a variety of venues to advertise online, including (1) portal sites, such as Sympatico.ca or Canoe.ca; (2) network buys through multi-site vendors, such as 24/7 Canada; (3) individual site advertising; (4) and search engines, such as Google.ca. Advertisers also have a choice of the type of online ads that they wish to present to the customer. The most common is the banner ad. Other forms of online advertising include skyscrapers, pop-ups, interstitials, and microsites, which use streaming video and audio and are very similar to traditional television advertising. And, of course, growing in popularity is advertising on social media sites.

One concern many advertisers have had with Internet advertising is measuring the effectiveness of the medium. But several companies are now involved in attempting to measure Internet advertising effectiveness. For example, Nielsen Media Research measures click-by-click behaviour through meters installed on the computers of hundreds of thousands of individuals in more than two dozen countries both at home and at work (see **www.nielsennetratings.com** for recent ratings). Another method being tested to provide some indication of the effectiveness of online advertising is *permission-based* advertising, where viewers agree to watch a commercial online in exchange for points, samples, or access to premium content, and advertisers only pay for completed views. The Interactive Advertising Bureau of Canada is also working to advance the use and effectiveness of Internet advertising in Canada. For example, it has a research program called the Canadian Media Optimization (CMOST) designed to measure the impact of online advertising. It has already conducted research for Molson, RBC Insurance, General Motors, Canadian Tire, and AIM Trimark. For example, it discovered that when Canadian Tire combined its radio campaign with online advertising, its awareness levels among its customers went up by 6 percent.[30]

Outdoor   A very effective medium for reminding consumers about your product is outdoor advertising. Outdoor and transit advertising expenditures in Canada are estimated at over $400 million.[31] The most common form of outdoor advertising, called *billboards,* often results in good reach and frequency. The visibility of this medium is good supplemental reinforcement for well-known products, and it is a relatively low-cost and flexible alternative. A company can buy space just in the desired geographical market. A disadvantage of billboards, however, is that no opportunity exists for long advertising copy. Also, the effectiveness of a billboard site depends on traffic patterns and sight lines. In many areas, environmental laws have limited the use of this medium.

If you have ever lived in a metropolitan area, chances are you might have seen another frequently used form of outdoor advertising: *transit advertising.* This medium includes messages on the interior and exterior of buses, subway cars, taxis, and transit shelters. In fact, the advertiser can actually purchase an entire bus, called a *superbus,* for about $100,000 and place its message over the entire vehicle. If selectivity is important, space can be bought in specific neighbourhoods or even transit routes. One disadvantage to this medium is that anxious travel times, when audiences are largest, are not conducive to reading advertising copy. People are standing shoulder to shoulder, hoping not to miss their stop, and little attention is paid to the advertising.

An effective billboard ad for Dairy Queen featuring its Blizzard treat.

But billboards can play an important part of an integrated marketing communications campaign. For example, Harley-Davidson motorcycles used billboards in an integrated campaign, along with radio, newspapers, direct marketing, and point-of-purchase media, to market its bikes in Quebec. It poked fun at the hundreds of "Saint"-named villages across Quebec while promoting the freedom-loving image of the Harley-Davidson.

user-generated content (UGC)

Media generated by users (customers) and disseminated via various channels, in particular, the Internet.

User-Generated Content A growing trend in the advertising business is **user-generated content (UGC),** also referred to as user-generated media. This is media generated by users (customers) and disseminated via various channels, in particular, the Internet. There are numerous ways marketers can interface with such media. They can (1) simply advertise on user-generated content sites such as YouTube; (2) allow the user to create the content themselves, and then sponsor that content and allow it to be shared with others online; (3) sponsor an actual contest encouraging the user to create media; or (4) partner with the consumer to co-create the media and the message and then disseminate it. The "Become the Doritos Guru" campaign is an example of a very successful UGC campaign. Basically, consumers were asked to "name the new Doritos flavour and create an ad to support it." In return the company would pay one winner $25,000 plus 1% of the flavour's sales, forever. The company used an online platform strategy to engage their target (teens) and encourage them to participate. They created a brand Web site DoritosGuru.ca and integrated it with Facebook and YouTube. Over 75,000 people registered as users at DoritosGuru.ca; over 30,000 fans registered on Facebook; and over 1.7 million people viewed the user-generated ads. In the end, there were over 2,000 approved submissions, and after 500,000 votes, Ryan Coopersmith's "Scream Cheese" entry was declared the winner. Sales results were impressive, up 25 percent over the previous year.[32]

Other Media As traditional media have become more expensive and cluttered, advertisers have been attracted to a variety of non-traditional advertising options, called *place-based media*. Messages are placed in locations that attract a specific target audience, such as airports, doctors' offices, health clubs, theatres (where ads are played on the screen before the movies are shown), even bathrooms of bars, colleges

Advertisers can buy space on the inside of a bathroom stall door—captive audiences.

and universities, restaurants, and nightclubs! You have probably also seen advertising on video screens on gas pumps, ATMs, in elevators, and even within video games (in-game advertising, or "advergaming"). St. Joseph's Healthcare in Hamilton, Ontario, for example, uses place-based media by advertising in theatres or cinemas to recruit health-care workers. Finally, another new form of advertising is growing very quickly in Canada—mobile advertising—where companies are reaching consumers on their mobile phones.[33] Check out the Going Online exercise to read about the trends in mobile advertising.

Selection Criteria   Choosing among these alternative media is difficult and depends on several factors. First, knowing the media habits of the target audience is essential. Second, occasionally, product attributes necessitate that certain media be used. For example, if colour is a major aspect of product appeal, radio is excluded. Newspapers allow advertising for quick actions to confront competitors, and magazines are more appropriate for complicated messages because the reader can spend more time reading the message. The final factor in selecting a medium is cost. When possible, alternative media are compared using a common denominator that reflects both reach and cost—a measure such as CPM.

Scheduling the Advertising

There is no correct schedule to advertise a product, but three factors must be considered. First is the issue of *buyer turnover*, which is how often new buyers enter the market to buy the product. The higher the buyer turnover, the greater the amount of advertising required. A second issue in scheduling is the *purchase frequency*; the more frequently the product is purchased, the less repetition is required. Finally, companies must consider the *forgetting rate*, the speed with which buyers forget the brand in the absence of advertising.

Setting schedules requires an understanding of how the market behaves. Most companies tend to follow one of three basic approaches:

- *Continuous (steady) schedule.* When seasonal factors are unimportant, advertising is run at a continuous or steady schedule throughout the year.
- *Flighting (intermittent) schedule.* Periods of advertising are scheduled between periods of no advertising to reflect seasonal demand.
- *Pulse (burst) schedule.* A flighting schedule is combined with a continuous schedule because of increases in demand, heavy periods of promotion, or the introduction of a new product.

For example, such products as dry breakfast cereals have a stable demand throughout the year and would typically use a continuous schedule of advertising. In contrast, such products as snow skis and suntan lotions have seasonal demands and receive flighting-schedule advertising during the seasonal demand period. Some products, such as toys or automobiles, require pulse schedule advertising to facilitate sales throughout the year and during special periods of increased demand (such as holidays or new car introductions). Some evidence suggests that pulsing schedules are superior to other advertising strategies. In addition, findings indicate that the effectiveness of a particular ad "wears out" quickly and, therefore, many alternative forms of an advertisement may be more effective, particularly in light of new evidence concerning recency, discussed earlier.

---

learning review

6. You see the same ad in *Time* and *Maclean's* magazines and on billboards and TV. Is this an example of reach or frequency?

7. Why has the Internet become a popular advertising medium?

8. What factors must be considered when choosing among alternative media?

EXECUTING THE ADVERTISING PROGRAM

Executing the advertising program involves pre-testing the advertising copy and actually carrying out the advertising program. An advertiser once remarked, "I know half my advertising is wasted, but I don't know what half." By evaluating advertising efforts, marketers can try to ensure that their advertising expenditures are not wasted. Evaluation is done usually at two separate times: before and after the advertisements are run in the actual campaign. Several methods used in the evaluation process at the stages of idea formulation and copy development are discussed below. Post-testing methods are reviewed in the section on evaluation.

Pre-Testing the Advertising

pre-tests
Tests conducted before an advertisement is placed to determine whether it communicates the intended message or to select among alternative versions of an advertisement.

To determine whether the advertisement communicates the intended message or to select among alternative versions of the advertisement, **pre-tests** are conducted before the advertisements are placed in any medium.

Portfolio Tests   *Portfolio tests* are used to test copy alternatives. The test ad is placed in a portfolio with several other ads and stories, and consumers are asked to read through the portfolio. Subsequently, subjects are asked for their impressions of the ads on several evaluative scales, such as ranging from "very informative" to "not very informative."

Jury Tests   *Jury tests* involve showing the ad copy to a panel of consumers and having them rate how they liked it, how much it drew their attention, and how attractive they thought it was. This approach is similar to the portfolio test in that consumer reactions are obtained. However, unlike the portfolio test, a test advertisement is not hidden within other ads.

Theatre Tests   *Theatre testing* is the most sophisticated form of pre-testing. Consumers are invited to view new television shows or movies in which test commercials are also shown. Viewers register their feelings about the advertisements either on handheld electronic recording devices used during the viewing or on questionnaires after the viewing.

full-service agency
An advertising agency providing the most complete range of services, including market research, media selection, copy development, artwork, and production.

Carrying Out the Advertising Program

The responsibility for actually carrying out the advertising program can be handled in one of three ways, as shown in Figure 17–4. The **full-service agency** provides the most complete range of services, including market research, media selection, copy

● **FIGURE 17–4**

Alternative structures of advertising agencies used to carry out the advertising program

TYPE OF AGENCY	SERVICES PROVIDED
Full-service agency	Does research, selects media, develops copy, and produces artwork; also coordinates integrated companies with all marketing efforts
Limited-service specialty agency	Specializes in one aspect of creative process; usually provides creative production work; buys previously unpurchased media space
In-house agency	Provides range of services, depending on company needs

development, artwork, and production. Some of Canada's leading full-service ad agencies include Cossette Communications, MDC Partners, Maritz Canada, Carlson Marketing, and Nerun. But as we saw in Chapter 16, many clients are looking to develop and execute IMC programs. Almost all of the major full-service agencies in Canada now offer totally integrated marketing communications capabilities. And some agencies are taking novel approaches to stay in touch with the marketplace to ensure that they are reaching the right audience with the right message. For example, Bleu Blanc Rouge opened a new agency in a downtown Montreal store in an attempt to get straight opinions from trendy youth. The new agency, BW (for black and white), is housed on the retail floor of Off the Hook, a second-storey St. Catherine Street retailer. According to the agency, "You can do all the focus groups in the world, but nothing beats some kid looking over your shoulder and saying 'that's crap.'"[34]

limited-service agency
Specializes in one aspect of the advertising process, such as providing creative services to develop the advertising copy or buying previously unpurchased media space.

Limited-service agencies specialize in one aspect of the advertising process, such as providing creative services to develop the advertising copy or buying previously unpurchased media space. Limited-service agencies that deal in creative work are compensated by a contractual agreement for the services performed. Finally, **in-house agencies** made up of the company's own advertising staff may provide full services or a limited range of services.

in-house agency
A company's own advertising staff, which may provide full services or a limited range of services.

EVALUATING THE ADVERTISING PROGRAM

The advertising decision process does not stop with executing the advertising program. The advertisements must be post-tested to determine whether they are achieving their intended objectives, and results may indicate that changes must be made in the advertising program.

Post-Testing the Advertising

post-tests
Tests conducted after an advertisement has been shown to the target audience to determine whether it has accomplished its intended purpose.

An advertisement may go through **post-tests** after it has been shown to the target audience to determine whether it accomplished its intended purpose. Five approaches common in post-testing are discussed here.[35]

Aided Recall (Recognition-Readership)   After being shown an ad, respondents are asked whether their previous exposure to it was through reading, viewing, or listening. The Starch test shown in the accompanying photo on page 472 uses aided recall to determine the percentage (1) who remember seeing a specific magazine ad (*noted*), (2) who saw or read any part of the ad identifying the product or brand (*seen-associated*),

Starch scores an advertisement.

and (3) who read at least half of the ad (*read most*). Elements of the ad are then tagged with the results, as shown in the picture.

Unaided Recall   Such questions as, "What ads do you remember seeing yesterday?" are asked of respondents without any prompting to determine whether they saw or heard advertising messages.

Attitude Tests   Respondents are asked questions to measure changes in their attitudes after an advertising campaign, such as whether they have a more favourable attitude toward the product advertised.

Inquiry Tests   Additional product information, product samples, or premiums are offered to an ad's readers or viewers. Ads generating the most inquiries are presumed to be the most effective.

Sales Tests   Sales tests involve such studies as controlled experiments (e.g., using radio ads in one market and newspaper ads in another and comparing the results) and consumer purchase tests (measuring retail sales that result from a given advertising campaign). The most sophisticated experimental methods today allow a manufacturer, a distributor, or an advertising agency to manipulate an advertising variable (such as schedule or copy) through cable systems and observe subsequent sales effects by monitoring data collected from checkout scanners in supermarkets.

Making Needed Changes

Results of post-testing the advertising copy are used to reach decisions about changes in the advertising program. If the post-test results show that an advertisement is doing poorly in terms of awareness or cost efficiency, it may be dropped and other ads run in its place. Sometimes, advertisers drop their ads as a result of complaints

Marketing Matters

What Canadians Think about Advertising!

According to an Ipsos Reid poll commissioned by the Institute of Communication Agencies (ICA), most Canadians have a favourable view of advertising, including the role it plays in our economy. For example, 69 percent of Canadians say that ads play an important role in encouraging consumer spending and thus can help a troubled economy. Additionally, most Canadians believe that advertising promotes the green movement (71 percent), elicits national pride (77 percent), and keeps drunk drivers off the road (78 percent). This is the first survey of its kind for the ICA, says Claude Carrier, a vice president at the Bos Toronto advertising agency, and its purpose is to reaffirm the importance of the advertising industry and help attract new creative talent to the business. He believes the overwhelming support for advertising comes from a "newfound understanding of the role it plays in fostering a healthy economy."

Another reason for the consumers' positive attitude toward advertising is the ability for consumers to now enter into a dialogue with advertisers. "If a company has a misstep in advertising, they get nailed overnight. You get fast and immediate input from all the audiences," Carrier says. "TV and Internet are the most prone to that now—TV because of its reach and Internet because of YouTube."

Brands that most consumers think of when asked about Canadian pride are Molson, The Bay, Tim Hortons, and Canadian Tire. However, Carrier thinks this has more to do with those companies' ubiquitous media presence than specific campaigns, because it helps consumers think of those companies as successful. The Bay's top-of-mind status with consumers is certainly no accident, says Hudson's Bay Company vice president of marketing Patrick Dickinson. The Bay has been running a highly targeted, multi-faceted media campaign to promote its new brands and new look, using a mix of traditional and untraditional media to redefine the brand in consumer's minds.

When it comes to brands that had most memorable or persuasive ads, humour and emotional connection are cited as key ingredients (78 percent). Brands such as Budweiser, Telus, Pepsi, Coke, and IKEA are all mentioned.

they receive from consumers. Sometimes, the ads are dropped as a result of Advertising Standards Canada (ASC) receiving complaints about the ads. ASC is the body that administers the industry's self-regulatory code, the Canadian Code of Advertising Standards. In the past year, the ASC received over 1,100 complaints about advertising, of which about 50 percent involved TV advertisements, and 14 percent involved Internet ads. But of those 1,100-plus complaints, only 126 were found to actually contravene the code of standards. Those that did were found to have unacceptable depictions or portrayals, accuracy and clarity problems or involved safety.[36] Still, despite the fact that some Canadian consumers complain about specific advertisements, a recent study shows that Canadians, overall, view advertising favourably and actually believe it can actually help support the Canadian economy! Read the Marketing Matters box to find out more.[37]

---

learning review

9. Explain the difference between pre-testing and post-testing advertising copy.

10. What is the difference between aided and unaided recall post-tests?

SALES PROMOTION

The Importance of Sales Promotion

At one time, sales promotion was considered by many to be a supplemental ingredient of the promotional mix. But more recently, the use of sales promotion has increased, and so has its perceived importance to marketers. In fact, in Canada, more money is now spent on sales promotion than on advertising.[38]

There are several reasons for the growth in importance of sales promotion. For one, many marketers are looking for measurable results from their promotional efforts. Sales promotion is viewed as an effective tool in this regard. Second, consumers and the trade (e.g., retailers) have become more value-conscious and thus more responsive to sales promotion activities. Third, some suggest that the use of sales promotion has grown because it has become contagious. In short, many marketers are simply responding to the increased use of sales promotion by competitors. Finally, the availability of information technology, such as computerized scanning equipment, has also served as a stimulus for the growth of sales promotion.

While sales promotion techniques have grown in use and in stature, they are rarely used in isolation or as a stand-alone promotional tool. With the trend toward IMC, sales promotion techniques are used more commonly in conjunction with other promotional activities. However, the selection and integration of the many sales promotion techniques requires a good understanding of the relative advantages and disadvantages of each kind of sales promotion.

Consumer-Oriented Sales Promotions

consumer-oriented sales promotions
Sales tools used to support a company's advertising and personal selling efforts directed to ultimate consumers; examples include coupons, sweepstakes, and samples.

Directed to ultimate consumers, **consumer-oriented sales promotions,** or simply *consumer promotions,* are sales tools used to support a company's advertising and personal selling efforts. Consumer-oriented sales promotion tools include coupons, deals, premiums, contests, sweepstakes, samples, loyalty programs, point-of-purchase displays, rebates, and product placement (Figure 17–5).

Coupons Coupons are typically printed certificates that give the bearer a savings or a stated price reduction when purchasing a specific product. Coupons can be used to

KIND OF SALES PROMOTION	OBJECTIVES	ADVANTAGES	DISADVANTAGES
Coupons	Stimulate demand	Encourage retailer support	Consumers delay purchases
Deals	Increase trial; retaliate against competitor's actions	Reduce consumer risk	Consumers delay purchases; reduce perceived product value
Premiums	Build goodwill	Consumers like free or reduced-price merchandise	Consumers buy for premium, not product
Contests	Increase consumer purchases; build business inventory	Encourage consumer involvement with product	Require creative or analytical thinking
Sweepstakes	Encourage present customers to buy more; minimize brand switching	Get customer to use product and store more often	Sales drop after sweepstakes
Samples	Encourage new-product trial	Low risk for consumer	High cost for company
Loyalty programs	Encourage repeat purchases	Help create loyalty	High cost for company
Point-of-purchase displays	Increase product trial; provide in-store support for other promotions	Provide good product visibility	Hard to get retailer to allocate high-traffic space
Rebates	Encourage customers to purchase; stop sales decline	Effective at stimulating demand	Easily copied; steal sales from future; reduce perceived product value
Product placement	Introduce new products; demonstrate product use	Positive message in a non-commercial setting	Little control over presentation of product

● **FIGURE 17–5**

Sales promotion alternatives

stimulate demand for mature products or to promote the early trial of a new brand. Billions of direct-to-consumer coupons are distributed annually in Canada. Canadians redeem millions of these coupons resulting in savings of over $100 million on products.[39]

Studies show that when coupons are used, a company's market share does increase during the period immediately after they are distributed.[40] There are indications, however, that couponing can reduce gross revenues by lowering the price paid by already-loyal consumers.[41] Therefore, manufacturers and retailers are particularly interested in coupon programs directed at potential first-time buyers. One means of focusing on these potential buyers is through electronic in-store coupon machines that match coupons to your most recent purchases.

Deals   Deals are short-term price reductions, commonly used to increase trial among potential customers or to retaliate against a competitor's actions. There are two basic types of deals: cents-off deals and price-pack deals. Cents-off deals offer a brand at less than a regular price, and the reduced prices are generally marked directly on the label or package. Cents-off deals can be very effective, even more so than coupons in stimulating short-term sales.

Price-pack deals offer consumers something extra, such as "20 percent more for the same price," or "Two packages for the price of one." Price-pack deals can be very effective in retaliating against or pre-empting a competitor's actions. For example, if a rival manufacturer introduces a new cake mix, the company could respond with the price-pack deal (e.g., 2 for 1), building up the stock on the kitchen shelves of cake mix buyers and making the competitor's introduction more difficult. Marketers must be careful, however, of overusing deals. If consumers expect a deal, they may delay a purchase until the deal occurs. Moreover, frequent deals may erode the perceived value of the brand to the consumer.

Premiums   Premiums are items offered free or at significant savings as incentives to buy a product. A premium offered at below its normal price is known as *self-liquidating* because the cost charged to the consumers covers the cost of the item. Offering premiums at no cost or at low cost encourages customers to return frequently or to use more of the product. However, the company must be careful that the consumer does not just buy the premium.

Contests   In the fourth sales promotion shown in Figure 17–5—the contest—consumers apply their analytical or creative thinking to try to win a prize. Most often, a consumer submits an entry to be judged by a panel. Many companies use contests not only to increase consumer purchases but also to obtain the names and addresses of consumers for direct marketing purposes. Many contests have gone online and are often highly interactive. For example, M&M Meat Shops ran an "M&M Meat Shops Saves a Day" contest, based on a series of television ads. For the contest, consumers were invited to visit a microsite and view all the commercials. They then had to answer multiple-choice questions based on the spots and also indicate which one was their favourite. Those who answered the five questions correctly were entered into a draw to win $1,000 of M&M gift cards. In another example, Teletoon created a site for Maynards candy that included an online game and details for a contest where winners received a variety of prizes, including MP3 players.[42]

Sweepstakes   Sweepstakes require participants to submit some kind of entry forms but are purely games of chance requiring no analytical or creative effort from the consumer. Tim Hortons's Roll Up the Rim to Win, *Reader's Digest,* and Publisher's Clearing House are examples of well-known sweepstakes. Canada has federal and provincial regulations covering sweepstakes, contests, and games regarding fairness, to ensure that the chance of winning is represented honestly and to guarantee that the prizes are awarded.

Samples   Another common consumer sales promotion is sampling, or offering the product free or at a greatly reduced price. Often used for new products, sampling puts the product in the consumer's hands; a trial size is generally offered that is smaller than the regular package size. If consumers like the sample, it is hoped they will remember and buy the product. Many Canadian firms have successfully used sampling as part of their marketing strategy.

Loyalty Programs   Loyalty programs are a sales promotion tool used to encourage and reward repeat purchases by acknowledging each purchase made by a consumer and offering a premium as purchases accumulate. The most popular loyalty programs today are frequent-flyer and frequent traveller programs used by airlines, hotels, and car rental companies to reward loyal customers. Some programs are free, such as Air Canada's Aeroplan, while others require the customer to pay an annual

membership fee. For example, Rogers Video offers its customers the Star Rewards loyalty program for a $10 membership fee, while Chapters-Indigo offers its iRewards loyalty program that provides online and in-store discounts on purchases for a $25 membership fee. But perhaps the most famous and most successful loyalty program in Canada is the Canadian Tire money program. Now, in addition to receiving your Canadian Tire money at the checkout when you make your purchases, you can also collect "virtual" money through the use of a Canadian Tire credit card, and even through the use of the company's Web site. Recently, more and more loyalty programs are going mobile. That is, companies are leveraging mobile smartphones to deliver and maintain loyalty programs.

Point-of-Purchase Displays   In a store aisle, you often encounter a sales promotion called a point-of-purchase display. These product displays take the form of advertising signs, which sometimes actually hold or display the product, and are often located in high-traffic areas near the cash register or the end of an aisle. The accompanying picture shows a point-of-purchase display for Nabisco's annual Back-to-School program. The display is designed to maximize the consumer's attention to lunch-box and after-school snacks and to provide storage for the products.

Some studies estimate that two-thirds of a consumer's buying decisions are made in the store. This means that grocery product manufacturers want to get their message to you at the instant you are next to their brand in your supermarket aisle—perhaps through a point-of-purchase display.

Rebates   Another consumer sales promotion in Figure 17–5—the cash rebate—offers the return of money based on proof of purchase. This tool has been used heavily by car manufacturers facing increased competition. When the rebate is offered on lower-priced items, the time and trouble of mailing in a proof-of-purchase to get the rebate cheque means that many buyers—attracted by the rebate offer—never take advantage of it. However, this "slippage" is less likely to occur with frequent users of rebate promotions.

product placement
Using a brand-name product in a movie, television show, video, or a commercial for another product.

Product Placement   A final consumer promotion, **product placement,** involves the use of a brand-name product in a movie, television show, video, or commercial for another product. Companies are usually eager to gain exposure for their products, and the studios believe that product placements add authenticity to the film or program. You have probably noticed numerous examples of product placement like Ford Explorers on the hit series *24,* Knorr Brand products on the TV program *The Next Great Chef,* or *Corner Gas* placing the Sears Wish Book Catalogue into its program.[43] Another form of product placement uses new digital technology, which can make "virtual" placements in any existing program. Reruns of *Seinfeld,* for example, could insert a Pepsi on a desktop, a Lexus parked on the street, or a box of Tide on Jerry's kitchen countertop! The global "paid" product placement market is valued at over $2.2 billion. If "non-paid" placement is included, the market would be valued at over $6 billion.[44] The U.S. is the world's largest paid product placement market, but product placement is also growing in popularity around the world, including Canada.

Trade-Oriented Sales Promotions

trade-oriented sales promotions
Sales tools used to support a company's advertising and personal selling efforts directed to wholesalers, distributors, or retailers. Three common approaches are allowances and discounts, cooperative advertising, and salesforce training.

Trade-oriented sales promotions, or simply *trade promotions,* are sales tools used to support a company's advertising and personal selling directed to wholesalers, retailers, or distributors. Some of the sales promotions just reviewed are used for this purpose, but there are three other common approaches targeted uniquely to these intermediaries: (1) allowances and discounts, (2) cooperative advertising, and (3) training of distributors' salesforces.

Allowances and Discounts   Trade promotions often focus on maintaining or increasing inventory levels in the channel of distribution. An effective method for encouraging such increased purchases by intermediaries is the use of allowances and discounts. However, overuse of these "price reductions" can lead to retailers changing their ordering patterns in the expectation of such offerings. Although there are many variations that manufacturers can use with discounts and allowances, three common approaches include the merchandise allowance, the case allowance, and the finance allowance.[45]

Reimbursing a retailer for extra in-store support or special featuring of the brand is a *merchandise allowance*. Performance contracts between the manufacturer and trade member usually specify the activity to be performed, such as a picture of the product in a newspaper with a coupon good at only one store. The merchandise allowance then consists of a percentage deduction from the list case price ordered during the promotional period. Allowances are not paid by the manufacturer until it sees proof of performance (such as a copy of the ad placed by the retailer in the local newspaper).

A second common trade promotion, a *case allowance,* is a discount on each case ordered during a specific time period. These allowances are usually deducted from the invoice. A variation of the case allowance is the "free goods" approach whereby retailers receive some amount of the product free based on the amount ordered, such as one case free for every ten cases ordered.

A final trade promotion, the *finance allowance,* involves paying retailers for financing costs or financial losses associated with consumer sales promotions. This trade promotion is regularly used and has several variations. One type is the floor stock protection program—manufacturers give retailers a case allowance price for products in their warehouses, which prevents shelf stock from running down during promotional periods. Also common are freight allowances, which compensate retailers that transport orders from the manufacturer's warehouse.

Cooperative Advertising   Resellers often perform the important function of promoting the manufacturer's products at the local level. One common sales promotional activity is to encourage both better quality and greater quantity in the local advertising efforts of resellers through **cooperative advertising.** These are programs by which a manufacturer pays a percentage of the retailer's local advertising expense for advertising the manufacturer's products.

Usually, the manufacturer pays a percentage, often 50 percent, of the cost of advertising up to a certain dollar limit, which is based on the amount of the purchases the retailer makes of the manufacturer's products. In addition to paying for the advertising, the manufacturer often furnishes the retailer with a selection of different ad executions, sometimes suited for several different media. A manufacturer may provide, for example, several different print layouts as well as a few broadcast ads for the retailer to adapt and use.

cooperative advertising
Advertising programs by which a manufacturer pays a percentage of the retailer's local advertising expense for advertising the manufacturer's products.

Training of Distributors' Salesforces   One of the many functions the intermediaries perform is customer contact and selling for the producers they represent. Both retailers and wholesalers employ and manage their own sales personnel. A manufacturer's success often rests on the ability of the reseller's salesforce to represent its products.

Thus, it is in the best interests of the manufacturer to help train the reseller's salesforce. Because the reseller's salesforce is often less sophisticated and less knowledgeable about the products than the manufacturer might like, training can increase their sales performance. Training activities include producing manuals and brochures to educate the reseller's salesforce. The salesforce then uses these aids in selling situations. Other activities include national sales meetings sponsored by the manufacturer and field visits to the reseller's location to inform and motivate the salesperson to sell the products. Manufacturers also develop incentive and recognition programs to motivate reseller's salespeople to sell their products.

---

learning review

11. Which sales promotional tool is most common for new products?

12. What's the difference between a coupon and a deal?

13. Which trade promotion is used on an ongoing basis?

LO5 PUBLIC RELATIONS

As noted in Chapter 16, public relations is a form of communication management that seeks to influence the feelings, opinions, or beliefs held by various publics about a company and its products or services. PR efforts may utilize a variety of tools and may be directed at many distinct audiences. While public relations personnel usually focus on communicating the positive aspects of the business, they may also be called on to minimize the negative impact of a problem or crisis, sometimes called crisis management.

Public Relations Tools

In developing a public relations campaign, several tools and tactics are available to the marketer. The most frequently used public relations tool is publicity, which we defined in Chapter 16 as a non-personal, indirectly paid presentation of an organization, good, or service. Publicity usually takes the form of a *news release,* consisting of an announcement regarding changes in the company, or the product line.

The objective of a news release is to inform a newspaper, radio station, or other medium of an idea for a story. A study found that more than 40 percent of all free mentions of a brand name occur during news programs.[46] A second common publicity tool is the *news conference.* Representatives of the media are invited to an informational meeting, and advance materials regarding the content are sent. This tool is often used when negative publicity requires a company response.

Non-profit organizations rely heavily on publicity to spread their messages. *Public service announcements (PSAs),* for which free space or time is donated by the media, are a common mode of publicity for these organizations. For example, ABC Canada Literacy Foundation uses televised PSAs to promote adult literacy, while the Canadian Cancer Society and the Heart and Stroke Foundation of Canada use both television and radio PSAs to encourage Canadians to eat more fruits and veggies.

A growing area of public relations is event or cause sponsorship, sometimes referred to as *sponsorship marketing.* The goal of sponsorship marketing is to create a forum to disseminate company information and/or to create brand identification for the company or its product with members of the target audience. For example, the FIFA Under-20 World Cup Canada soccer tournament was sponsored by BMO Insurance, Bell Canada, and Winners, and annual CIAU sports championships are sponsored by some of Canada's leading companies. Petro-Canada is an official sponsor of the Trans Canada Trail project, and CIBC is the official sponsor the Canadian Breast Cancer Foundation's "Run for Life" campaign.

But perhaps the biggest and most visible sponsorship opportunity in the world is the Olympic Games. For example, for the Vancouver 2010 Winter Olympic Games, there were a variety of ways for companies to participate. Some companies signed on as "worldwide partners" such as McDonald's, Coca Cola, and Visa, while others were "national partners" including Bell Canada, HBC, RBC, Chevrolet, Petro-Canada, and RONA. Some companies inked agreements to be "official supporters," such as Air Canada, Bombardier, and the Royal Canadian Mint, while others were named "official suppliers," such as Birks, EPCOR, Saputo, and Weston. The Vancouver Organizing Committee (VANOC)—the group responsible for planning and staging the games—designed its sponsorship marketing program to secure partners with shared values to generate sufficient revenue to host the games and leave a financial legacy for sport in Canada.

Sponsorship marketing has become so popular that there is now a national organization that has been created to help enhance the development of this concept. Check out the Sponsorship Marketing Council of Canada at **www.sponsorshipmarketing.ca.** The council sponsors an annual sponsorship marketing awards show to showcase the effectiveness of sponsorship marketing programs. For example, recent winners include Quebec microbrewery Unibroue's high-profile sponsorship tie-in with Quebec City's 400th Anniversary. The company used its sponsorship to breathe new life into the brand and to stimulate trial and sales. As a result of the sponsorship, sales increased over 13 percent. Additionally, Cadillac sponsored the Toronto International Film Festival in order to generate sales leads and make Cadillac the desired brand of choice for affluent car buyers. Also, Campbell Company sponsors the Canadian Association of Food Banks and sponsors a "Help Hunger Disappear" event, thus showing its commitment to worthy social causes while also increasing its brand visibility. Finally, Kraft Canada's annual "Hockeyville" program, a program designed to find Canada's most passionate hockey community, continues to win sponsorship marketing awards based on metrics such as brand loyalty, community responsibility, and retail sales gains.[47]

Making Responsible Decisions

What Do You Think about PETA's PR Activities?

Many organizations realize that most consumers view public relations, particularly news-oriented publicity, as more credible than advertising per se. As such, organizations have turned to well-managed public relations programs in order to influence the perceptions that relevant segments of the public have toward them or their causes. Many organizations disseminate information that will cast them only in the best possible light or to ensure that their view on a particular issue is conveyed to the public. However, there is growing concern about the public relations activities of organizations that may or may not be presenting all of the relevant information or facts surrounding a particular issue. Additionally, there are concerns about certain organizations engaging in inappropriate activities in order to garner media coverage. One organization that is viewed with some skepticism by some is the People for the Ethical Treatment of Animals (PETA).

PETA has had a history of using PR to win the hearts of minds of Canadians concerning their views on the treatment of animals. It has clashed with the Canadian Cattlemen's Association, making claims that eating meat causes impotence. The medical community discredited this claim. PETA has also issued PR releases stating that eating meat causes cancer. Again, experts have suggested that PETA is overstating acknowledged scientific facts and omitting relevant information about the subject.

PETA also waged a PR war with KFC Canada asking people to boycott KFC restaurants because the company tolerated abuses of the chicken it serves. KFC denied the claims in its news and press releases. In the end, both parties ended up engaged in legal action over the matter. PETA has also been telling Canadians to stop eating fish, suggesting it contains unsafe levels of toxins. Fishermen's unions have denied this claim and suggest that fish is still a healthy food. Now, PETA has a new campaign asking Canadians to boycott Canadian maple syrup, suggesting that by buying this product consumers are actually supporting Canada's seal-hunting industry. The campaign does not make it clear whether there is, or ever has been, a connection between seal hunters, in Canada mostly based in the Maritime provinces, and the producers of maple syrup, the majority of which comes from Quebec. In response to the PETA campaign, Simon Trepanier, the vice-director of the Federation of Quebec Maple Syrup Producers, noted that "maple syrup producers work with the environment, with trees and nature." He added that "it's kind of weird that they are associating maple syrup with (seal) hunting." Finally, some of PETAs tactics to garner PR are also under fire, such as a PETA activist pushing a pie into the face of Fisheries Minister Gail Shea's face to protest the seal-hunting industry. PETA received tremendous media coverage over this incident, but many are asking whether the media should cover such activities. What do you think?

Finally, the development of collateral materials, such as annual reports, brochures, newsletters, corporate Web sites, or videos about the company and its product, are also basic public relations tools. These materials provide information to target publics and often generate good publicity.

Good public relations activities, however, should always be carefully planned and made part of an organization's IMC effort. This also includes recognizing that social media is allowing public discussions online about every possible company, product, or brand. While these discussions are seemingly uncontrollable, many public relations departments are now facilitating and responding to what happens on social media sites. McDonald's, for example, responds to comments about its products and corporate behaviour using a blog called "Open for Discussion." Finally, public relations activities must be used wisely and in an ethical and socially responsible manner (see the Making Responsible Decisions box, "What Do You Think about PETA's PR Activities?").[48]

---

learning review **14.** What is a news release?

15. A growing area of public relations is _____

LEARNING OBJECTIVES REVIEW

LO1 **Explain the differences between product advertising and institutional advertising and the variations within each type.**

Product advertisements focus on selling a good or service and take three forms: Pioneering advertisements tell people what a product is, what it can do, and where it can be found; competitive advertisements persuade the target market to select the firm's brand rather than a competitor's; and reminder advertisements reinforce previous knowledge of a product. Institutional advertisements are used to build goodwill or an image for an organization. They include advocacy advertisements, which state the position of a company on an issue, and pioneering, competitive, and reminder advertisements, which are similar to the product ads but focus on the institution.

LO2 **Describe the steps used to develop, execute, and evaluate an advertising program.**

The promotion decision process can be applied to each advertising element. The steps to develop an advertising program include identify the target audience, specify the advertising objectives, set the advertising budget, design the advertisement, create the message, select the media, and schedule the advertising. Executing the program requires pre-testing, and evaluating the program requires post-testing.

LO3 **Explain the advantages and disadvantages of alternative advertising media.**

Television advertising reaches large audiences and uses picture, print, sound, and motion; its disadvantages, however, are that it is expensive and ephemeral. Radio advertising is inexpensive and can be placed quickly, but it has no visual element and is also ephemeral. Magazine advertising can target specific audiences and can convey complex information, but it takes a long time to place the ad and is relatively expensive. Newspapers provide excellent coverage of local markets and can be changed quickly, but they have a short lifespan and poor colour. Yellow Pages advertising has a long use period and is available 24 hours per day; its disadvantages, however, are that there is a proliferation of directories and they cannot be updated frequently. Internet advertising can be interactive, and used with traditional media for integrated communications purposes. However, work is still being done to measure its effectiveness. Outdoor advertising provides repeat exposures, but its message must be very short and simple. Direct mail can be targeted at very selective audiences, but its cost per contact is high. Finally, user-generated content (UGC), media generated by consumers and disseminated via various channels, in particular, the Internet, is growing in popularity as companies attempt to engage and interact with their customers. The consumer absorbs the costs of the activity, but companies do not always have control over what is communicated and how it is communicated.

LO4 **Discuss the strengths and weaknesses of consumer-oriented and trade-oriented sales promotions.**

Coupons encourage retailer support but may delay consumer purchases. Deals reduce consumer risk but also reduce perceived value. Premiums offer consumers additional merchandise they want, but they may be purchasing only for the premium. Contests create involvement but require creative thinking. Sweepstakes encourage repeat purchases, but sales drop after the sweepstakes. Samples encourage product trial but are expensive. Loyalty programs help create loyalty but are expensive to run. Displays provide visibility but are difficult to place in retail space. Rebates stimulate demand but are easily copied. Product placement provides a positive message in a non-commercial setting but is difficult to control. Trade-oriented sales promotions include (*a*) allowances and discounts, which increase purchases but may change retailer ordering patterns; (*b*) cooperative advertising, which encourages local advertising; and (*c*) salesforce training, which helps increase sales by providing the salespeople with product information and selling skills.

 Recognize public relations as an important form of communication.

Public relations activities usually focus on communicating positive aspects of the business. A frequently used public relations tool is publicity, which includes news releases and news conferences or public service announcements. A growing area of public relations is sponsorship marketing.

FOCUSING ON KEY TERMS

advertising p. 456
consumer-oriented sales promotions p. 473
cooperative advertising p. 477
cost per thousand (CPM) p. 462
frequency p. 462
full-service agency p. 470
gross rating points (GRPs) p. 462
infomercials p. 465
in-house agency p. 471
institutional advertisements p. 457

limited-service agency p. 471
post-tests p. 471
pre-tests p. 470
product advertisements p. 457
product placement p. 476
rating p. 462
reach p. 462
trade-oriented sales promotions p. 476
user-generated content (UGC) p. 468

APPLYING MARKETING KNOWLEDGE

1 How does competitive product advertising differ from competitive institutional advertising?

2 Suppose you are the advertising manager for a new line of children's bath products. Which form of media would you use for this new product?

3 You have recently been promoted to be director of advertising for the Timkin Tool Company. In your first meeting with Mr. Timkin, he says, "Advertising is a waste! We've been advertising for six months now and sales haven't increased. Tell me why we should continue." Give your answer to Mr. Timkin.

4 A large life insurance company has decided to switch from using a strong fear appeal to a humorous approach. What are the strengths and weaknesses of such a change in message strategy?

5 Which medium has the lowest cost per thousand?

MEDIUM	COST	AUDIENCE
TV show	$5,000	25,000
Magazine	2,200	6,000
Newspaper	4,800	7,200
FM radio	420	1,600

6 Some national advertisers have found that they can have more impact with their advertising by running a large number of ads for a period and then running no ads at all for a period. Why might such a flighting schedule be more effective than a continuous or steady schedule?

7 Each year, managers at Bausch and Lomb evaluate the many advertising media alternatives available to them as they develop their advertising program for contact lenses. What advantages and disadvantages of each alternative should they consider? Which media would you recommend to them?

8 What are two advantages and two disadvantages of the advertising post-tests described in the chapter?

9 The RBC is interested in consumer-oriented sales promotions that would encourage senior citizens to direct-deposit their Canada Pension cheques with the bank. Evaluate the sales promotion options, and recommend two of them to the bank.

Building Your Marketing Plan

To augment your promotion strategy from Chapter 16:

1. Use Figure 17–3 to select the advertising media you will include in your plan by analyzing how combinations of media (e.g., television and Internet advertising, radio, Yellow Pages, etc.) can complement each other.

2. Use Figure 17–5 to select your consumer-oriented sales promotion activities.

3. Specify which trade-oriented sales promotions and public relations activities you will use.

Video Case 17

ADFARM

Introduction

AdFarm is the largest marketing communications firm in Canada focused exclusively on production agriculture, food, and rural development. It is recognized as one of Canada's 50 Best Managed Companies and listed by *Canadian Business* magazine as one of the nation's best workplaces. AdFarm is a full-service agency offering a complete range of marketing communications services, including advertising, public relations, issue management, media relations, direct marketing, and online marketing.

AdFarm is a collection of four successful agricultural marketing communications agencies that saw the opportunity to respond to the changing needs and expectations of industry leaders operating in a highly competitive global market. These four firms believed that a combined organization operating with a single focus could compete successfully in serving the multinational, multi-billion-dollar agricultural industry. AdFarm has offices in Calgary and Guelph as well as in Fargo, North Dakota, and Kansas City, Missouri. AdFarm's past and current clients include some of the world's premiere agricultural leaders, including Bayer CropScience, Dow AgroSciences, RBC Royal Bank (the largest bank serving agriculture in North America), Novartis, Bayer Animal Health, Nitragin-Ontario Pork Producers, and UFA (United Farmers of Alberta).

The AdFarm Business Model

The AdFarm business model is somewhat unique for the agency business because of its single industry focus and its "one-agency matrix model" involving *Functions* and *Teams* and no head office per se. This structure encourages employees to look for insights from many sources. Combined with the strict rule of hiring (and firing) to company values, the model ensures greater consistency and excellence across all office locations and enables greater business growth.

The AdFarm Brand Promise

Branding is a key part of the marketing communications services that AdFarm offers its clients. AdFarm takes its work so seriously that they have their own internal brand committee, which is assigned the responsibility of leading and monitoring the development of the AdFarm brand. AdFarm expresses its brand in a variety of ways, most importantly through its people. AdFarm brand expression also extends to the company Web site (**www.adfarmonline.com**), logo, stationery, promotional materials, corporate sponsorships, and even office design.

The AdFarm brand promise centres around three strategic anchors:

- Total focus on production agriculture, food, and rural development (the agency likes to say that it is "Crazy about Farming").
- Commitment to "drive deeper" and provide greater insights to clients as a result of specialized knowledge of the industry and marketing communications.
- Connections within the industry that enable it to open doors and gain greater insights that are of value to its clients.

AdFarm's Vision

AdFarm has articulated its vision and communicated it to all its employees and clients:

- To be the world's most respected agricultural marketing communications firm within 30 years—what it calls its BHAG (Big Hairy Audacious Goal).
- To be a catalyst for the advancement of agriculture.
- To hire and fire according to its values.
- To be the industry's most respected employer.
- To have fun along the way.

AdFarm has also outlined its strategy to achieve and fulfill this vision:

- Grow revenue—through existing clients, by attracting new clients, and through acquisitions and mergers that meet the AdFarm acquisition and merger policy.
- Grow service offering—by adapting to the continual changing needs of clients and the market with new product/service offering, including public affairs, consulting, and traceability/transparency technology.

Attracting and Retaining Quality People

The marketing communications business is both an idea business and a service business, and AdFarm understands that employing quality people is imperative to delivering on both. To attract and retain clients as well as to create products and services that resonate with consumers and differentiate it from competitors, the company looks for people who bring a balance of "ag-ness" and "ad-ness," that is, skills and knowledge that display excellence in agriculture or communications or both.

In terms of hiring, the first criterion that all potential AdFarmers must meet is a willingness to grow into the company's values. These include the desire to build strong business relationships, excellence, passion, integrity, fun, personal accountability, and "thinking outside the box." Individuals looking to join AdFarm must also demonstrate an ability to deliver excellence in his or her respective function area—creative, public relations, strategy, account service, media, online marketing, or finance and administration. And because AdFarm is totally focused on agriculture, some positions require that candidates bring or develop a great deal of knowledge about and appreciation of this industry and its potential.

Once hired, AdFarmers take part in a combination of ongoing internal and external training initiatives to help guide their growth and ensure their peak performance. One unique example of training is Farm Days, a one- or two-day event that provides first-hand experience for all AdFarmers in some aspect of production agriculture, food, or rural development.

Training and brand building at Adfarm also include operating its own real farms; one outside Calgary and one outside Fargo, North Dakota. AdFarmers from all offices are invited to purchase shares in one or both of these farms and to participate in their management. While the company retains a farm manager, AdFarmers make the decisions on what crops to grow, what inputs to use, and how and when they will market the crops.

"Off the farm," AdFarmers also participate in a variety of external training programs specific to their profession. The firm supports employees taking university and college programs as well as training offered through the Communications and Advertising Accredited Professional (CAAP) program through the Institute of Communication Agencies.

Another method of attracting and retaining quality people involves flexibility. Not only does AdFarm offer flexible hours, it also has something called "the summertime option." This provides AdFarmers, who have gained the support of their teammates to cover for them, the opportunity to take a period of time off during the slower summer months. This flexibility is also used to retain key AdFarmers who might have left its employ for family reasons. The barriers of time zones and distance disappear, giving the company a growing nucleus of global freelancers and employees.

One additional management tool used principally to retain employees is profit sharing. Rather than an expectation, profit sharing is seen for what it is: one more indication that management truly values the contribution of every employee. This focus on employees has led to retention rates that are considerably higher than the agency industry average. Morale is excellent, and contribution per employee is also considerably higher than industry average.

Performance

AdFarm is the largest agency serving the Canadian agricultural industry, the largest agency in Alberta, and one of the largest agencies between Toronto and Vancouver. Its performance to date has been outstanding on a number of measures:

1. *Growth and financial performance.* Its growth and financial performance are substantially greater than the majority of marketing communications agencies operating in Canada.
2. *Market share.* AdFarm has a dominant position and is estimated to be involved in approximately 40 percent of the agricultural communications spending in Canada.
3. *Corporate reputation.* AdFarm has developed an excellent corporate reputation within its industry.
4. *Awards.* AdFarm has received numerous local, national, and international creative and public relations awards for its work.
5. *Employee pride.* This is measured by employee involvement in company events, the ideas employees bring forward to improve the organization's growth and performance, the number of people they invite to visit the firm's unique offices, and the enthusiasm they convey to people in both the agricultural and marketing communications communities.

Future Growth

AdFarm's strategic plan calls for continued growth. It is pursuing new business in high growth areas, such as the horticulture markets of California, the cotton markets of the southern United States, the public affairs markets in both Canada and the United States, and the rapidly emerging food safety and traceability technology field. It is also carefully pursuing new opportunities and requests for business expansion outside North America, but in the short term, this will only occur at the request of its clients who are asking AdFarm to grow with them.

Questions

1 Comment on the rationale for AdFarm's focus of its business so fully on agriculture. What are the pros and cons of this decision?

2 What do you think about AdFarm's corporate culture and focus on employees? Why does it emphasize the importance of attracting and retaining excellent employees?

3 Many people argue that the advertising business is an "idea business." How does AdFarm reinforce this notion?

chapter 18

Personal Selling and Sales Management

MEET JULIE ROBERTSON, *i*LEARNING SALES SPECIALIST!

Julie Robertson is an *i*Learning Sales Specialist with McGraw-Hill Ryerson, the publisher of this textbook. She is responsible for sales and customer relationship management with business and economics professors who make the decisions about which books should be used in their classes and, of course, read by their students. Her territory is basically the greater Toronto area and includes colleges and universities such as the University of Toronto, Ryerson University, UOIT, and Durham College.

Julie graduated from her marketing program in 1996. Her very first job after graduation was as a marketing assistant with Brands Computers, a computer hardware company in Richmond Hill, Ontario. She then spent the next four years with Corporate Express/Hermann Marketing as an inside sales representative and as a supervisor of the inside sales team. She then moved on to be a sales account manager with AirIQ Inc., a telematics company in Pickering, Ontario, where she worked with large corporate rental vehicle companies and businesses in the commercial transport industry. Julie then joined McGraw-Hill Ryerson and has achieved tremendous success in her position as an *i*Learning sales specialist.

We asked Julie what she liked best about her job at McGraw-Hill Ryerson. She told us, "I enjoy working with various people, including

learning objectives

After reading this chapter, you should be able to:

LO1 Discuss the nature and scope of personal selling and sales management in marketing.

LO2 Identify the different types of personal selling.

LO3 Explain the stages in the personal selling process.

LO4 Describe the major functions of sales management.

those inside my company, and, of course, with my clients. In particular, I really enjoy dealing with the different types of situations that are inherent in every sales call. For example, I realize that each of my clients has different needs and teaches their courses based on their own personal style. Therefore, I have to be able to adapt to their personality and style, and cater to their specific needs. This changing of 'hats' and adapting to the various situations that I experience throughout the day is something I truly enjoy." She added, "Being constantly on the move and not being restricted to a regular 'desk job' setting is another thing a really enjoy about my sales career."

Julie has achieved much success in her job at McGraw-Hill Ryerson, so we asked her what was the basis of this success? She told us, "I believe I am successful because I take the time to get to know my customers, to understand them and their needs. Importantly, I recognize that every customer is special and unique and I do my best to make sure each one has a positive customer experience." She gave us a few details on her sales process. For example, she researches her clients (the professors) before ever meeting with them. When she meets them, she asks them questions to better understand their needs, the goals that they want to achieve in a particular course, details about students' that they serve, and how a particular textbook may help both the instructor and the student.

She noted, as you also discovered in previous chapters, that the decision to buy often involves more than one person. In fact, sometimes even a buying committee of professors is involved in the process and therefore she has to find a way to satisfy the needs of everyone involved in the process. Thus, she demonstrates how her products can meet the various needs of all those involved. In order to do so, she spends time analyzing the competitors' offerings as well as the products she sells in order to present the client with the best possible product option given the client's specific needs.

"But it is not just the product I emphasize," she told us. "I also point out to the client that McGraw-Hill Ryerson can provide training, advanced learning technology and resources, and responsive customer service to ensure that both the instructor and student have a positive experience with the product." Finally, she emphasized, "I really do not sell textbooks per se; I sell solutions to my customers' problems. And the sale is just the beginning of the relationship. I work with the customer and build a relationship based on service, trust, and care. I want my customers to know that I want them to be successful in the classroom with my products and I am there to support their efforts. In this way, I can ensure total customer satisfaction."[1]

This chapter examines the scope and significance of personal selling and sales management in marketing. It highlights the many forms of personal selling, outlines the selling process, discusses important sales management functions, and describes how technology is affecting the sales function in most forward-thinking companies.

SCOPE AND SIGNIFICANCE OF PERSONAL SELLING AND SALES MANAGEMENT

Chapter 16 described personal selling and management of the sales effort as being part of the firm's promotional mix. Although it is important to recognize that personal selling is a useful vehicle for communicating with present and potential buyers, it is much more. Take a moment to answer the questions in the personal selling and sales management quiz in Figure 18–1. As you read on, compare your answers with those in the text.

 Nature of Personal Selling and Sales Management

personal selling

The two-way flow of communication between a buyer and seller, often in a face-to-face encounter, designed to influence a person's or group's purchase decision.

Personal selling involves the two-way flow of communication between a buyer and seller, often in a face-to-face encounter, designed to influence a person's or group's purchase decision. However, with advances in telecommunications, personal selling also takes place over the telephone, through video teleconferencing, and via the Internet.

However, personal selling remains a highly human-intensive activity despite the use of technology. Accordingly, the people involved must be managed. **Sales management** involves planning the selling program and implementing and controlling the personal selling effort of the firm. The tasks involved in managing personal selling include setting objectives; organizing the salesforce; recruiting, selecting, training, and compensating salespeople; and evaluating the performance of individual salespeople.

sales management

Planning the selling program and implementing and controlling the personal selling effort of the firm.

Pervasiveness of Selling

"Everyone lives by selling something," wrote author Robert Louis Stevenson a century ago. His observation still holds true today. In Canada, more than one million people are employed in sales positions.[2] Included in this number are manufacturing sales personnel, real estate brokers, stockbrokers, and salesclerks who work in retail stores. In reality, however, virtually every occupation that involves customer contact has an element of personal selling. For example, lawyers, accountants, bankers, and company personnel recruiters perform sales-related activities, whether or not they acknowledge it.

Many executives in major companies have held sales positions at some time in their careers. Selling often serves as a stepping-stone to top management, as well as being a career path in itself.

● **FIGURE 18-1**

Personal selling and sales management quiz

> 1. What percentage of the average field sales representative's time each workweek is spent actually selling to customers? (check one)
>   45% _____   55% _____   65%
>
> 2. "A salesperson's job is finished when a sale is made." True or false? (circle one)
>   True   False
>
> 3. About what percentage of companies include customer satisfaction as a measure of salesperson performance? (check one)
>   10% _____   30% _____   50% _____
>   20% _____   40% _____   60% _____

Could this be a salesperson in the operating room? Read the text to find why Medtronic salespeople visit hospital operating rooms.

Medtronic
www.medtronic.com

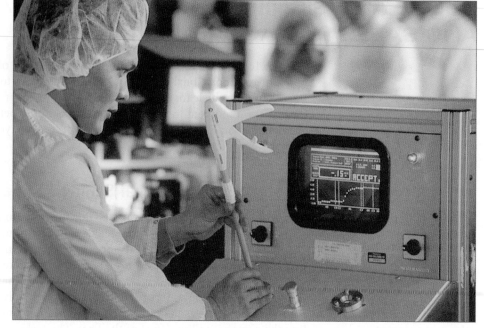

Personal Selling in Marketing

Personal selling serves three major roles in a firm's overall marketing effort. First, salespeople are the critical link between the firm and its customers. This role requires that salespeople match company interests with customer needs to satisfy both parties in the exchange process. Second, salespeople *are* the company in a consumer's eyes. They represent what a company is or attempts to be and are often the only personal contact that a customer has with the company. For example, the "look" projected by Gucci salespeople is an important factor in communicating the style of the company's apparel line. Third, personal selling may play a dominant role in a firm's marketing program. This situation typically arises when a firm uses a push marketing strategy, described in Chapter 16. Avon, for example, pays almost 40 percent of its total sales dollars for selling expenses. Pharmaceutical firms and office and educational equipment manufacturers also rely heavily on personal selling in the marketing of their products.

Creating Customer Value through Salespeople: Relationship and Partnership Selling

As the critical link between the firm and its customers, salespeople can create customer value in many ways. For instance, by being close to the customer, salespeople can identify creative solutions to customer problems. Salespeople at Medtronic, Inc., the world leader in the heart pacemaker market, are in the operating room for more than 90 percent of the procedures performed with their product, and are on call, through pagers, 24 hours a day. "It reflects the willingness to be there in every situation, just in case a problem arises—even though nine times out of ten the procedure goes just fine," notes a satisfied customer.[3] Salespeople can create value by easing the customer buying process. This happened at AMP, Inc., a producer of electrical products. Salespeople and customers had a difficult time getting product specifications and performance data on AMP's 70,000 products quickly and accurately. The company now records all information on CD-ROMs that can be scanned instantly by salespeople and customers. Customer value is also created by salespeople who follow through after the sale. At Jefferson Smurfit Corporation, a multi-billion dollar supplier of packaging products, one of its salespeople juggled production from three of the company's plants to satisfy

relationship selling
The practice of building ties to customers based on a salesperson's attention and commitment to customer needs over time.

partnership selling
The practice, sometimes called *enterprise selling,* whereby buyers and sellers combine their expertise and resources to create customized solutions; to commit to joint planning; and to share customer, competitive, and company information for their mutual benefit, and ultimately the customer.

an unexpected demand for boxes from General Electric. This person's action led to the company being given GE's "Distinguished Supplier Award."

Customer value creation is made possible by **relationship selling,** the practice of building ties to customers based on a salesperson's attention and commitment to customer needs over time. Relationship selling involves mutual respect and trust among buyers and sellers. It focuses on creating long-term customers, not a one-time sale. In fact, research shows that successful sales executives do focus on building long-term relationships with customers.[4] Such companies as Merck Frosst Canada, IBM Canada, National Bank, Bell Canada, and Kraft Canada have made relationship building a core focus of their sales effort.

Some companies have taken relationship selling a step further and forged partnerships between buyer and seller organizations. With **partnership selling,** sometimes called *enterprise selling,* buyers and sellers combine their expertise and resources to create customized solutions; to commit to joint planning; and to share customer, competitive, and company information for their mutual benefit, and ultimately the customer. As an approach to sales, partnership selling relies on cross-functional business specialists who apply their knowledge and expertise to achieve higher productivity, lower cost, and greater customer value. Partnership selling complements supplier and channel partnering described in Chapters 6 and 14. This practice is embraced by such companies as IBM Canada, 3M Canada, DuPont, and Honeywell, which have established partnerships with their customers, such as Air Canada, Ford, and McDonald's.

Relationship and partnership selling represent another dimension of customer relationship management (CRM). Both emphasize the importance of learning about customer needs and wants and tailoring solutions to customer problems as a means to create customer value. Finally, in the customer experience management (CEM) era, sales personnel can play a critical role in ensuring customers perceive a positive experience with the company and its brands.

| **learning review** | **1.** What is personal selling? |
| | **2.** What is involved in sales management? |

LO2 THE MANY FORMS OF PERSONAL SELLING

Personal selling assumes many forms based on the amount of selling done and the amount of creativity required to perform the sales task. Broadly speaking, three types of personal selling exist: order taking, order getting, and sales support activities. While some firms use only one of these types of personal selling, others use a combination of all three.

Order Taking

order taker
Processes routine orders or reorders for products that have already been sold by the company.

Typically, an **order taker** processes routine orders or reorders for products that have already been sold by the company. The primary responsibility of order takers is to preserve an ongoing relationship with existing customers and maintain sales. Two types of order takers exist. *Outside order takers* visit customers and replenish inventory stocks of resellers, such as retailers or wholesalers. For example, Frito-Lay salespeople call on supermarkets, neighbourhood grocery stores, and other establishments to ensure that the company's line of snack products is in adequate supply. In addition, outside order takers often provide assistance in arranging displays. *Inside order takers,* also called *order clerks* or *salesclerks,* typically answer simple questions, take orders, and complete

Portable communications technology enables Frito-Lay salespeople with the order-taking process

Frito-Lay, Inc.
www.fritolay.com

transactions with customers. Many retail clerks are inside order takers. Inside order takers are often employed by companies that use *inbound telemarketing,* the use of toll-free telephone numbers that customers can call to obtain information about products or services and make purchases. In business-to-business settings, order taking arises in straight rebuy situations. Order takers generally do little selling in a conventional sense and engage in only modest problem solving with customers. They often represent products that have few options, such as confectionary items, magazine subscriptions, and highly standardized industrial products. Inbound telemarketing is also an essential selling activity for more "customer service" driven firms, such as Dell Computer. Order takers in such firms undergo extensive training so that they can better assist callers with their purchase decisions.

Order Getting

order getter

A salesperson who sells in a conventional sense and identifies prospective customers, provides customers with information, persuades customers to buy, closes sales, and follows up on customers' use of a product or service.

An **order getter** sells in a conventional sense and identifies prospective customers, provides customers with information, persuades customers to buy, closes sales, and follows up on customers' use of a product or service. Like order takers, order getters can be inside (an automobile salesperson) or outside (a Xerox salesperson). Order getting involves a high degree of creativity and customer empathy and is typically required for selling complex or technical products with many options, and so considerable product knowledge and sales training are necessary. In modified-rebuy or new-buy purchase situations in organizational selling, an order getter acts as a problem solver who identifies how a particular product may satisfy a customer's need. Similarly, in the purchase of a service, such as insurance, a Metropolitan Life insurance agent can provide a mix of plans to satisfy a buyer's needs depending on income, stage of the family's life cycle, and investment objectives.

Order getting is not a 40-hour-per-week job. Industry research indicates that outside order getters, or field service representatives, often work over 50 hours per week. As shown in Figure 18–2, 55 percent of their time is spent selling. What percent did you check for question 1 in Figure 18–1? Another 10 to 20 percent is devoted to customer service calls. The remainder of their work time is occupied by getting to customers and performing numerous administrative tasks.[5]

● **FIGURE 18-2**
How outside order-getting salespeople spend their time each week

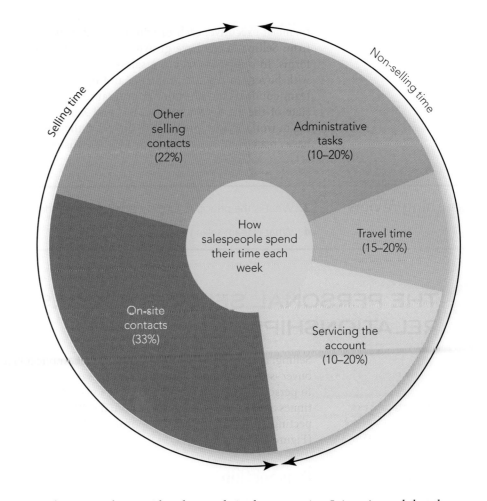

Order getting by outside salespeople is also expensive. It is estimated that the average cost of a single field sales call on a business customer is about $350, factoring in salespeople compensation, benefits, and travel and entertainment expenses. This cost illustrates why outbound telemarketing is so popular today. *Outbound telemarketing* is the practice of using the telephone rather than personal visits to contact customers. A significantly lower cost per sales call (in the range of $20 to $25) and little or no field expense accounts for its widespread appeal. Accordingly, outbound telemarketing has grown significantly.

Customer Sales Support Personnel

Customer sales support personnel augment the selling effort of order getters by performing a variety of services. For example, **missionary salespeople** do not directly solicit orders but rather concentrate on performing promotional activities and introducing new products. They are used extensively in the pharmaceutical industry, where they persuade physicians to prescribe a firm's product. Actual sales are made through wholesalers or directly to pharmacists who fill prescriptions. A **sales engineer** is a salesperson who specializes in identifying, analyzing, and solving customer problems and who brings know-how and technical expertise to the selling situation but often does not actually sell products and services. Sales engineers are popular in selling industrial products, such as chemicals and heavy equipment. In many situations, firms engage in cross-functional **team selling,** the practice of using an entire team of professionals in selling to and servicing major customers.[6]

Team selling is used when specialized knowledge is needed to satisfy the different interests of individuals in a customer's buying centre. For example, a selling team might consist of a salesperson, a sales engineer, a service representative, and a

missionary salespeople
Sales support personnel who do not directly solicit orders but rather concentrate on performing promotional activities and introducing new products.

sales engineer
A salesperson who specializes in identifying, analyzing, and solving customer problems and who brings know-how and technical expertise to the selling situations but does not actually sell goods and services.

team selling
Using an entire team of professionals in selling to and servicing major customers.

financial executive, each of whom would deal with a counterpart in the customer's firm. Selling teams have grown in popularity due to partnering and take different forms. In *conference selling,* a salesperson and other company resource people meet with buyers to discuss problems and opportunities. In *seminar selling,* a company team conducts an educational program for a customer's technical staff, describing state-of-the-art developments. IBM and Xerox pioneered cross-functional team selling in working with prospective buyers. Other firms have embraced this practice and have created and sustained value for their customers.[7]

---

learning review

3. What is the principal difference between an order taker and an order getter?

4. What is team selling?

[LO3] THE PERSONAL SELLING PROCESS: BUILDING RELATIONSHIPS

personal selling process
Sales activities occurring before and after the sale itself, consisting of six stages: (1) prospecting, (2) preapproach, (3) approach, (4) presentation, (5) close, and (6) follow-up.

Selling, and particularly order getting, is a complicated activity that involves building buyer–seller relationships. Although the salesperson–customer interaction is essential to personal selling, much of a salesperson's work occurs before this meeting and continues after the sale itself. The **personal selling process** consists of six stages: (1) prospecting, (2) preapproach, (3) approach, (4) presentation, (5) close, and (6) follow-up (Figure 18–3).

Prospecting

Personal selling begins with *prospecting*—the search for and qualification of potential customers. For some products that are one-time purchases, such as encyclopedias, continual prospecting is necessary to maintain sales. There are three types of prospects.

Trade shows are a popular source for leads and prospects.

● **FIGURE 18-3**
Stages and objectives of the
personal selling process

STAGE	OBJECTIVE	COMMENTS
1. Prospecting	Search for and qualify prospects	Start of the selling process; prospects produced through advertising, referrals, and cold canvassing.
2. Preapproach	Gather information and decide how to approach the prospect	Information sources include personal observation, other customers, and own salespeople.
3. Approach	Gain prospect's attention, stimulate interest, and make transition to the presentation	First impression is critical; gain attention and interest through reference to common acquaintances, a referral, or product demonstration.
4. Presentation	Begin converting a prospect into a customer by creating a desire for the product or service	Different presentation formats are possible; however, involving the customer in the product or service through attention to particular needs is critical; important to deal professionally and ethically with prospect skepticism, indifference, or objections.
5. Close	Obtain a purchase commitment from the prospect and create a customer	Salesperson asks for the purchase; different approaches include the trial close and assumptive close.
6. Follow-up	Ensure that the customer is satisfied with the product or service	Resolve any problems faced by the customer to ensure customer satisfaction and future sales possibilities.

A *lead* is the name of a person who may be a possible customer. A *prospect* is a customer who wants or needs the product. If an individual wants the product, can afford to buy it, and is the decision maker, this individual is a *qualified prospect*.

Leads and prospects are generated using several sources. For example, advertising may contain a coupon or a toll-free number to generate leads. Some companies use exhibits at trade shows, professional meetings, and conferences to generate leads or prospects. Staffed by salespeople, these exhibits are used to attract the attention of prospective buyers and disseminate information. Others use lists and directories or the Internet for generating leads and prospects. Web sites, e-mail, bulletin boards, and newsgroups are used by salespeople to connect with individuals and companies that may be prospects. Another approach for generating leads is through *cold canvassing* in person or by telephone. This approach simply means that a salesperson may open a directory, pick a name, and visit or call that individual or business. Although the refusal rate is high with cold canvassing, this approach can be successful. For example, 41 brokers at a major brokerage firm identified 18,004 prospects, qualified 1,208 of them, made 659 sales presentations, and opened 40 new accounts in four working days.[8] However, cold canvassing is frowned upon in most Asian and Latin American societies. Personal visits, based on referrals, are expected.

Cold canvassing is also often criticized by Canadian consumers. Many consumers see cold canvassing as an intrusion into their privacy, and many find it simply distasteful.[9] Many trade associations, including the Canadian Marketing Association, have codes of ethics for dealing with this issue, such as adhering to consumers' "do not call," "do not mail," or "do not visit" requests. The Canadian government has also attempted to more closely regulate cold canvassing with the Canadian Radio-television and Telecommunications Commission (CRTC) requiring telemarketers to inform consumers that they have the right to say no to such solicitations.

Preapproach

Once a salesperson has identified a qualified prospect, preparation for the sale begins with the preapproach. The *preapproach* stage involves obtaining further information on the prospect and deciding on the best method of approach. Knowing how the prospect prefers to be approached, and what the prospect is looking for in a product or service, is essential regardless of cultural setting. For example, a Merrill Lynch stockbroker will need information on a prospect's discretionary income, investment objectives, and preference for discussing brokerage services over the telephone or in person. For business product companies, such as Texas Instruments, the preapproach involves identifying the buying role of a prospect (for example, influencer or decision maker), important buying criteria, and the prospect's receptivity to a formal or informal presentation. Identifying the best time to contact a prospect is also important. For example, insurance companies have discovered the best times to call on people in different occupations: dentists before 9:30 a.m., lawyers between 11 a.m. and 2 p.m., and university professors between 7 and 8 p.m.

This stage is very important in global selling where customs dictate appropriate protocol. In many South American countries, for example, buyers expect salespeople to be punctual for appointments. However, prospective buyers are routinely 30 minutes late. South Americans take negotiating seriously and prefer straightforward presentations, but a hard-sell approach will not work.[10]

Successful salespeople recognize that the preapproach stage should never be short-changed. Their experience coupled with research on customer complaints indicates that failure to learn as much as possible about the prospect is unprofessional and the ruin of a sales call.

Approach

The *approach* stage involves the initial meeting between the salesperson and prospect, where the objectives are to gain the prospect's attention, stimulate interest, and build the foundation for the sales presentation itself and the basis for a working relationship. The first impression is critical at this stage, and it is common for salespeople

to begin the conversation with a reference to common acquaintances, a referral, or even the product or service itself. Which tactic is used will depend on the information obtained in the prospecting and preapproach stages.

The approach stage is very important in international settings. In many societies outside Canada, considerable time is devoted to non-business talk designed to establish a rapport between buyers and sellers. For instance, it is common for two or three meetings to occur before business matters are discussed in the Middle East and Asia. Gestures are also very important. The initial meeting between a salesperson and a prospect in Canada customarily begins with a firm handshake. Handshakes also apply in France, but they are gentle, not firm. Forget the handshake in Japan. A bow is appropriate. What about business cards? Business cards should be printed in English on one side and the language of the prospective customer on the other. Knowledgeable Canadian salespeople know that their business cards should be handed to Asian customers using both hands, with the name facing the receiver. In Asia, anything involving names demands respect.[11]

Presentation

The *presentation* is at the core of the order-getting selling process, and its objective is to convert a prospect into a customer by creating a desire for the product or service. Three major presentation formats exist: (1) stimulus-response format, (2) formula selling format, and (3) need-satisfaction format.

stimulus-response presentation
A selling format that assumes the prospect will buy if given the appropriate stimulus by a salesperson.

Stimulus-Response Presentation   The **stimulus-response presentation** format assumes that given the appropriate stimulus by a salesperson, the prospect will buy. With this format, the salesperson tries one appeal after another, hoping to "hit the right button." A counter clerk at McDonald's is using this approach when he or she asks whether you would like an order of french fries or a dessert with your meal. The counter clerk is engaging in what is called *suggestive selling*. Although useful in this setting, the stimulus-response format is not always appropriate, and for many products, a more formalized format is necessary.

formula selling presentation
Providing information in an accurate, thorough, and step-by-step manner to inform the prospect.

Formula Selling Presentation   The **formula selling presentation** format, a more formalized presentation, is based on the view that a presentation consists of information that must be provided in an accurate, thorough, and step-by-step manner to inform the prospect. A popular version of this format is the *canned sales presentation,* which is a memorized, standardized message conveyed to every prospect. Used frequently by firms in telephone and door-to-door selling of consumer products (for example, Hoover vacuum cleaners), this approach treats every prospect the same, regardless of differences in needs or preference for certain kinds of information. Canned sales presentations can be advantageous when the differences between prospects are unknown or with novice salespeople who are less knowledgeable about the product and the selling process than are experienced salespeople. Although it guarantees a thorough presentation, it often lacks flexibility and spontaneity and, more importantly, does not provide for feedback from the prospective buyer—a critical component in the communication process and the start of a relationship.

need-satisfaction presentation
A selling format that emphasizes probing and listening by the salesperson to identify the needs and interests of prospective buyers.

Need-Satisfaction Presentation   The stimulus-response and formula selling formats share a common characteristic: the salesperson dominates the conversation. By comparison, the **need-satisfaction presentation** format emphasizes probing and listening by the salesperson to identify the needs and interests of prospective buyers. Once these are identified, the salesperson tailors the presentation to the prospect and highlights product benefits that may be valued by the prospect. The need-satisfaction format, which emphasizes problem solving, is the most consistent with the marketing concept and relationship building.

adaptive selling
A need-satisfaction sales presentation that involves adjusting the presentation to fit the selling situation.

Two selling styles are associated with this format.[12] **Adaptive selling** involves adjusting the presentation to fit the selling situation, such as knowing when to offer solutions and when to ask for more information. Sales research and practice show that knowledge of the customer and sales situation are key ingredients for adaptive selling. Many consumer service firms, such as brokerage and insurance firms (e.g., ING Canada) and consumer product firms (e.g., Gillette), effectively apply this selling style. **Consultative selling** focuses on problem identification, where the salesperson serves as an expert on problem recognition and resolution. With consultative selling, problem solution options are not simply a matter of choosing from an array of existing products or services. Rather, novel solutions often arise thereby creating unique value for the customer. Consultative selling is prominent in business-to-business marketing.

consultative selling
Focuses on problem definition, where the salesperson serves as an expert on problem recognition and resolution.

Marketing Matters

Imagine This . . . Putting the Customer into Customer Solutions!

Solutions for problems are what companies are looking for from suppliers. At the same time, suppliers focus on customer solutions to differentiate themselves from competitors. So what is a customer solution and what does it have to do with selling?

Sellers view a solution as a customized and integrated combination of products and services for meeting a customer's business needs. But what do buyers think? From a buyer's perspective, a solution is one that (1) meets their requirements, (2) is designed to uniquely solve their problem, (3) can be implemented, and (4) ensures follow-up. This insight arose from a field study conducted by three researchers at Emory University. Their in-depth study also yielded insight into what an effective customer solution

offers. According to one buyer interviewed in their study: They (the supplier) make sure that their sales and marketing guys know what's going on. The sales and technical folks know what's going on, and the technical and support guys know what's going on with me. All these guys are in the loop, and it's not a puzzle for them. So what does putting the customer into customer solutions have to do with selling? Three things stand out. First, considerable time and effort is necessary to fully understand a specific customer's requirements. Second, effective customer solutions are based on relationships among sellers and buyers. And finally, consultative selling is central to providing novel solutions for customers, thereby creating value for them.

IBM Canada is often recognized for its consultative selling style as is Xerox. In fact, according to a senior Xerox sales executive, "Our business is no longer about selling boxes. It's about selling digital, networked-based information management solutions, and this requires a highly customized and consultative process." But what does a customer solution really mean? The Marketing Matters box offers a unique answer.[13]

Handling Objections   A critical concern in the presentation stage is handling objections. *Objections* are excuses for not making a purchase commitment or decision. Some objections are valid and are based on the characteristics of the product or service or price. However, many objections reflect prospect skepticism or indifference. Whether valid or not, experienced salespeople know that objections do not put an end to the presentation. Rather, techniques can be used to deal with objections in a courteous, ethical, and professional manner. The following six techniques are the most common:[14]

- *Acknowledge and convert the objection.* This technique involves using the objection as a reason for buying. For example, a prospect might say, "The price is too high." The reply: "Yes, the price is high because we use the finest materials. Let me show you . . ."
- *Postpone.* The postpone technique is used when the objection will be dealt with later in the presentation: "I'm going to address that point shortly. I think my answer would make better sense then."
- *Agree and neutralize.* Here, a salesperson agrees with the objection, then shows that it is unimportant. A salesperson would say, "That's true, and others have said the same. However, they concluded that this issue was outweighed by the other benefits."
- *Accept the objection.* Sometimes, the objection is valid. Let the prospect express such views, probe for the reason behind it, and attempt to stimulate further discussion on the objection.
- *Denial.* When a prospect's objection is based on misinformation and clearly untrue, it is wise to meet the objection head on with a firm denial.
- *Ignore the objection.* This technique is used when it appears that the objection is a stalling mechanism or is clearly not important to the prospect.

Each of these techniques requires a calm, professional interaction with the prospect and is most effective when objections are anticipated in the preapproach stage. Handling objections is a skill requiring a sense of timing, appreciation for the prospect's state of mind, and adeptness in communication. Objections also should be handled ethically. Lying or misrepresenting product or service features are grossly unethical practices.

Close

The *closing stage* in the selling process involves obtaining a purchase commitment from the prospect. This stage is the most important and the most difficult because the salesperson must determine when the prospect is ready to buy. Telltale signals indicating a readiness to buy include body language (prospect re-examines the product or contract closely), statements ("This equipment should reduce our maintenance costs"), and questions ("When could we expect delivery?").

The close itself can take several forms. Three closing techniques are used when a salesperson believes a buyer is about ready to make a purchase: (1) trial close, (2) assumptive close, and (3) urgency close. A *trial close* involves asking the prospect to make a decision on some aspect of the purchase: "Would you prefer the blue or grey model?" An *assumptive close* entails asking the prospect to consider choices concerning delivery, warranty, or financing terms under the assumption that a sale has been finalized. An *urgency close* is used to commit the prospect quickly by making reference to the timeliness of the purchase: "The low-interest financing ends next week" or "That is the last model we have in stock." Of course, these statements should be used only if they accurately reflect the situation; otherwise, such claims would be unethical. When a prospect is clearly ready to buy, the final close is used, and a salesperson asks for the order.

Follow-Up

The selling process does not end with the closing of a sale; rather, professional selling requires customer follow-up. One marketing authority equated selling and follow-up with courtship and marriage, by observing ". . . the sale merely consummates the courtship. Then the marriage begins. How good the marriage is depends on how well the relationship is managed."[15] The *follow-up stage* includes making certain that the customer's purchase has been properly delivered and installed and that any difficulties experienced with the use of the item are addressed. Attention to this stage of the selling process solidifies the buyer–seller relationship. Moreover, research shows that the cost and effort to obtain repeat sales from a satisfied customer is roughly half of that necessary to gain a sale from a new customer.[16] In short, today's satisfied customers become tomorrow's qualified prospects or referrals. (What was your answer to question 2 in the quiz?)

---

learning review

5. What are the six stages in the personal selling process?

6. What is the distinction between a lead and a qualified prospect?

7. Which presentation format is most consistent with the marketing concept? Why?

LO4 THE SALES MANAGEMENT PROCESS

Selling must be managed if it is going to contribute to a firm's overall objectives. Although firms differ in the specifics of how salespeople and the selling effort are managed, the sales management process is similar across firms. Sales management consists of three interrelated functions: (1) sales plan formulation, (2) sales plan implementation, and (3) evaluation and control of the salesforce (Figure 18–4).

● **FIGURE 18–4**
The sales management process

Sales plan formulation	Sales plan implementation	Evaluation and control of the salesforce
Setting objectives	Salesforce recruitment and selection	Quantitative assessment
Organizing the salesforce	Salesforce training	Behavioural evaluation
Developing account management policies	Salesforce motivation and compensation	

● **FIGURE 18–4**
The sales management process

Sales Plan Formulation: Setting Direction

Formulating the sales plan is the most basic of the three sales management functions. According to the vice president of the Harris Corporation, a global communications company, "If a company hopes to implement its marketing strategy, it really needs a detailed sales planning process."[17] The **sales plan** is a statement describing what is to be achieved and where and how the selling effort of salespeople is to be deployed. Formulating the sales plan involves three tasks: (1) setting objectives, (2) organizing the salesforce, and (3) developing account management policies.

sales plan

A statement describing what is to be achieved and where and how the selling effort of salespeople is to be deployed.

Setting Objectives   Setting objectives is central to sales management because this task specifies what is to be achieved. In practice, objectives are set for the total salesforce and for each salesperson. Selling objectives can be output related and focus on dollar or unit sales volume, number of new customers added, and profit. Alternatively, they can be input related and emphasize the number of sales calls and selling expenses. Output- and input-related objectives are used for the salesforce as a whole and for each salesperson. A third type of objective that is behaviourally related is typically specific for each salesperson and includes his or her product knowledge, customer service, and selling and communication skills. Increasingly, firms are also emphasizing knowledge of competition as an objective, as salespeople are calling on customers and should see what competitors are doing.[18] But should salespeople explicitly ask their customers for information about competitors? Read the accompanying Making Responsible Decisions box, "The Ethics of Asking Customers about Competitors," to find out how salespeople view this practice.[19]

Whatever objectives are set, they should be precise and measurable and specify the time period over which they are to be achieved. Once established, these objectives serve as performance standards for the evaluation of the salesforce—the third function of sales management.

Organizing the Salesforce   Organizing a selling organization is the second task in formulating the sales plan. Three questions are related to organization. First, should the company use its own salesforce, or should it use independent agents, such as manufacturer's representatives? Second, if the decision is made to employ company salespeople, then should they be organized according to geography, customer type, or product or service? Third, how many company salespeople should be employed?

The decision to use company salespeople or independent agents is made infrequently. However, recently, Coca-Cola's Food Division replaced its salesforce with independent agents (food brokers). The Optoelectronics Division of Honeywell, Inc. has switched back and forth between agents and its own salesforce over the last 25 years and now uses both. The decision is based on an analysis of economic and behavioural factors. An economic analysis examines the costs of using both types of salespeople and is a form of break-even analysis.

Consider a situation in which independent agents would receive a 5 percent commission on sales, and company salespeople would receive a 3 percent commission,

Making Responsible Decisions

The Ethics of Asking Customers about Competitors

Salespeople are a valuable source of information about what is happening in the marketplace. By working closely with customers and asking good questions, salespeople often have first-hand knowledge of customer problems and wants. They also are able to spot the activities of competitors. However, should salespeople explicitly ask customers about competitor strategies, such as pricing practices, product development efforts, and trade and promotion programs?

Gaining knowledge about competitors by asking customers for information is a ticklish ethical issue. Research indicates that 25 percent of North American salespeople engaged in business-to-business selling consider this practice unethical, and their companies have explicit guidelines for this practice. It is also noteworthy that Japanese salespeople consider this practice to be more unethical than do salespeople in North America.

Do you believe that asking customers about competitor practices is unethical? Why, or why not?

salaries, and benefits. In addition, with company salespeople, sales administration costs would be incurred for a total fixed cost of $500,000 per year. At what sales level would independent or company salespeople be less costly? This question can be answered by setting the costs of the two options equal to each other and solving for the sales level amount, as shown in the following equation:

$$\underbrace{\frac{\text{Total cost of company salespeople}}{0.03(X)+\$500,000}} = \underbrace{\frac{\text{Total cost independent agents}}{0.05(X)}}$$

where X = sales volume. Solving for X, sales volume equals $25 million, indicating that below $25 million in sales, independent agents would be cheaper, but above $25 million, a company salesforce would be cheaper. This relationship is shown in Figure 18–5.

Economics alone does not answer this question, however. A behavioural analysis is also necessary and should focus on issues related to the control, flexibility, effort, and availability of independent and company salespeople.[20] An individual firm must weigh the pros and cons of the economic and behavioural considerations before making this decision.

● **FIGURE 18–5**

Break-even chart for comparing independent agents and a company salesforce

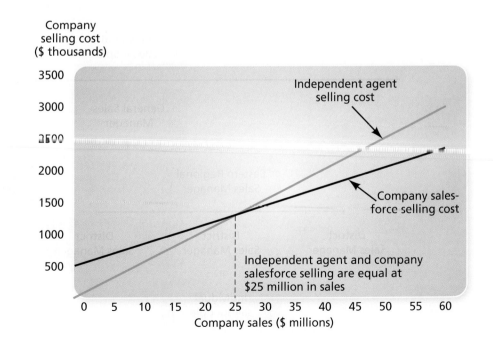

If a company elects to employ its own salespeople, then it must choose an organizational structure based on (1) geography, (2) customer, or (3) product (Figure 18–6). A geographical structure is the simplest organization, where Canada or, indeed, the

● **FIGURE 18–6**

Organizing the salesforce by customer, product, and geography

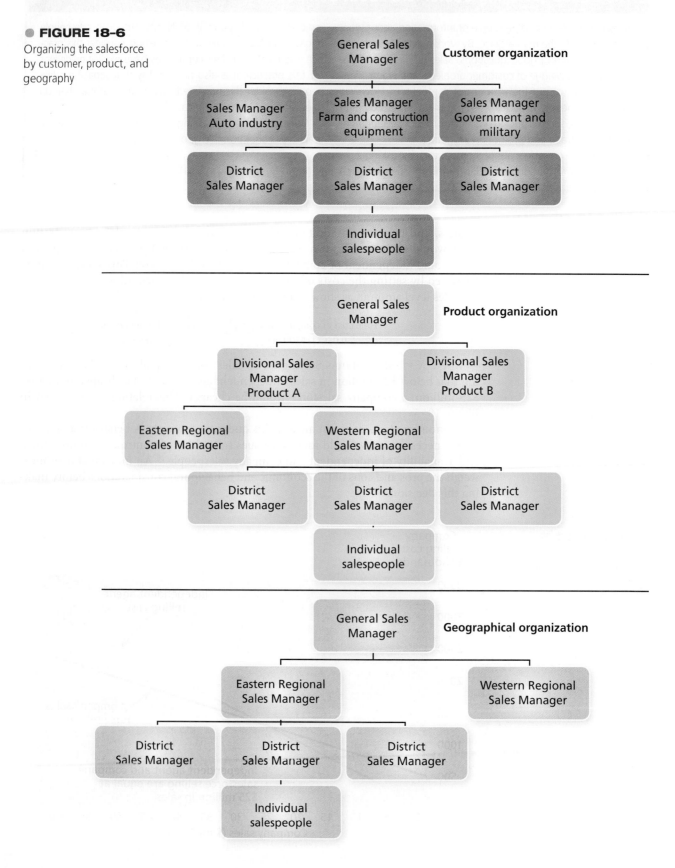

globe is first divided into regions and each region is divided into districts or territories. Salespeople are assigned to each district with defined geographical boundaries and call on all customers and represent all products sold by the company. The principal advantage of this structure is that it can minimize travel time, expenses, and duplication of selling effort. However, if a firm's products or customers require specialized knowledge, then a geographical structure is not suitable.

When different types of buyers have different needs, a customer sales organizational structure is used. In practice, this means that a different salesforce calls on each separate type of buyer or marketing channel. For example, Kodak switched from a geographical to a marketing channel structure, with different sales teams serving specific retail channels: mass merchandisers, photo specialty outlets, and food and drug stores. The rationale for this approach is that more effective, specialized customer support and knowledge are provided to buyers. However, this structure often leads to higher administrative costs and some duplication of selling effort because two separate salesforces are used to represent the same products.

An important variation of the customer organizational structure is **key account management**—the practice of using team selling to focus on important customers so as to build mutually beneficial, long term, cooperative relationships.[21] Key account management involves teams of sales, service, and often technical personnel who work with purchasing, manufacturing, engineering, logistics, and financial executives in customer organizations. This approach, which often assigns company personnel to a customer account, results in "customer specialists" who can provide exceptional service. Procter & Gamble uses this approach with Walmart, as does Black & Decker with Home Depot.

When specific knowledge is required to sell certain types of products, then a product sales organization is used. For example, a steel manufacturer has a salesforce that sells drilling pipe to oil companies and another that sells specialty steel products to manufacturers. The primary advantage of this structure is that salespeople can develop expertise with technical characteristics, applications, and selling methods associated with a particular product or family of products. However, this structure also produces high administrative costs and duplication of selling effort because two company salespeople may call on the same customer.

In short, there is no one best sales organization for all companies in all situations. Rather, the organization of the salesforce should reflect the marketing strategy of the firm. Each year, about 10 percent of firms change their sales organizations to implement new marketing strategies.

The third question related to salesforce organization involves determining the size of the salesforce. For example, why does Frito-Lay have about 17,500 salespeople who call on supermarkets, grocery stores, and other establishments to sell snack foods? The answer lies in the number of accounts (customers) served, the frequency of calls on accounts, the length of an average call, and the amount of time a salesperson can devote to selling.

A common approach for determining the size of a salesforce is the **workload method.** This formula-based method integrates the number of customers served, call frequency, call length, and available selling time to arrive at a figure for the salesforce size. For example, Frito-Lay needs about 17,500 salespeople according to the following workload method formula:

$$NS = \frac{NC \times FC \times CL}{AST}$$

where:
    NS = Number of salespeople
    NC = Number of customers
    CF = Call frequency necessary to service a customer each year
    CL = Length of an average call
    AST = Average amount of selling time available per year

key account management
The practice of using team selling to focus on important customers so as to build mutually beneficial, long-term, cooperative relationships.

workload method
A formula-based method for determining the size of a salesforce that integrates the number of customers served, call frequency, call length, and available selling time to arrive at a salesforce size.

Frito-Lay sells its products to 350,000 supermarkets, grocery stores, and other establishments. Salespeople should call on these accounts at least once a week, or 52 times a year. The average sales call lasts an average of 81 minutes (1.35 hours). An average salesperson works 2,000 hours a year (50 weeks × 40 hours a week), but 12 hours a week are devoted to non-selling activities, such as travel and administration, leaving 1,400 hours a year. Using these guidelines, Frito-Lay would need:

$$NS = \frac{350,000 \times 52 \times 1.35}{1,400} = 17,550 \text{ salespeople}$$

The value of this formula is apparent in its flexibility; a change in any one of the variables will affect the number of salespeople needed. Changes are determined, in part, by the firm's account management policies.

account management policies

Policies that specify whom the salespeople should contact, what kinds of selling and customer service activities should be engaged in, and how these activities should be carried out.

Developing Account Management Policies   The third task in formulating a sales plan involves developing **account management policies** that specify whom the salespeople should contact, what kinds of selling and customer service activities should be engaged in, and how these activities should be carried out. These policies might state which individuals in a buying organization should be contacted, the amount of sales and service effort that different customers should receive, and the kinds of information that the salespeople should collect before or during a sales call.

An example of an account management policy in Figure 18–7 shows how different accounts or customers can be grouped according to level of opportunity and the firm's competitive sales position.[22] When specific account names are placed in each cell, salespeople clearly see which accounts should be contacted, with what level of selling and service activity, and how to deal with them. Accounts in cells 1 and 2 might have high frequencies of personal sales calls and increased time spent on a call. Cell 3 accounts will have lower call frequencies, and cell 4 accounts might be contacted through telemarketing or direct mail rather than in person.[23]

Sales Plan Implementation: Putting the Plan into Action

The sales plan is put into practice through the tasks associated with sales plan implementation. Whereas sales plan formulation focuses on "doing the right things,"

● **FIGURE 18–7**
Account management policy grid

Competitive position of sales organization

	High	Low
High	**1** *Attractiveness:* Accounts offer a good opportunity because they have high potential and sales organization has a strong position. *Account management policy:* Accounts should receive high level of sales calls and service to retain and possibly build accounts.	**3** *Attractiveness:* Accounts may offer a good opportunity if sales organization can overcome its weak position. *Account management policy:* Emphasize a heavy sales organization position or shift resources to other accounts if a stronger sales organization position is impossible.
Low	**2** *Attractiveness:* Accounts are somewhat attractive because sales organization has a strong position, but future opportunity is limited. *Account management policy:* Accounts should receive moderate level of sales and service to maintain current position of sales organization.	**4** *Attractiveness:* Accounts offer little opportunity, and sales organization position is weak. *Account management policy:* Consider replacing personal calls with telephone sales or direct mail to service accounts. Consider dropping account.

Account opportunity (vertical axis label)

implementation emphasizes "doing things right." The three major tasks involved in implementing a sales plan are (1) salesforce recruitment and selection, (2) salesforce training, and (3) salesforce motivation and compensation.

Salesforce Recruitment and Selection   Effective recruitment and selection of salespeople is one of the most crucial tasks of sales management. It entails finding people who match the type of sales position required by a firm. Recruitment and selection practices would differ greatly between order-taking and order-getting sales positions, given the differences in the demands of these two jobs. Therefore, recruitment and selection begin with a carefully crafted job analysis and job description followed by a statement of job qualifications.[24]

A *job analysis* is a study of a particular sales position, including how the job is to be performed and the tasks that make up the job. Information from a job analysis is used to write a *job description,* a written document that describes job relationships and requirements that characterize each sales position. It explains (1) to whom a salesperson reports, (2) how a salesperson interacts with other company personnel, (3) the customers to be called on, (4) the specific activities to be carried out, (5) the physical and mental demands of the job, and (6) the types of products and services to be sold. The job description is then translated into a statement of job qualifications, including the aptitudes, knowledge, skills, and a variety of behavioural characteristics considered necessary to perform the job successfully. Qualifications for order-getting sales positions often mirror the expectations of buyers: (1) imagination and problem-solving ability, (2) honesty, (3) intimate product knowledge, and (4) attentiveness reflected in responsiveness to buyer needs and customer loyalty and follow-up.[25] Firms use a variety of methods for evaluating prospective salespeople. Personal interviews, reference checks, and background information provided on application forms are the most frequently used methods.

emotional intelligence
The ability to understand one's own emotions and the emotions of people with whom one interacts on a daily basis.

Successful selling also requires a high degree of emotional intelligence. **Emotional intelligence** is the ability to understand one's own emotions and the emotions of people with whom one interacts on a daily basis. These qualities are important for adaptive selling and may spell the difference between effective and ineffective order getting salespeople.[26] Are you interested in what your emotional intelligence might be? Read the accompanying Going Online box, "What Is Your Emotional Intelligence?" and test yourself.

The search for qualified salespeople has produced an increasingly diverse salesforce in Canada. Women now represent half of all professional salespeople, and minority representation is growing.

Salesforce Training   Whereas recruitment and selection of salespeople is a one-time event, salesforce training is an ongoing process that affects both new and seasoned salespeople. Sales training covers much more than selling practices. For example, IBM Global Services salespeople, who sell consulting and various information technology

Going Online

What Is Your Emotional Intelligence?

A person's success at work depends on many talents, including intelligence and technical skills. Recent research indicates that an individual's emotional intelligence is also important, if not more important! Emotional intelligence (E-IQ) has five dimensions: (1) self-motivation skills; (2) self-awareness, or knowing one's own emotions; (3) the ability to manage one's emotions and impulses; (4) empathy, or the ability to sense how others are feeling; and (5) social skills, or the ability to handle the emotions of other people.

What is your E-IQ? Visit the Web site **www.ihhp.com/quiz.php**. Answer 20 questions to learn what your emotional intelligence is and obtain additional insights.

Marketing Matters

Sales Training Should Include Gender Intelligence

A recent study asked Canadian women to name a company that actually markets or sells well to women. Twenty-five percent of respondents could not come up with an answer. Moreover, respondents then went on to fail all 22 industries examined in the study based on their inability to satisfy women's needs. Women gave poor marks, for example, to the banking, investment, and insurance industries, citing the poor treatment they received because of their gender. Additionally, they ranked car dealers at 21 out of 22 industry categories in terms of meeting their needs as buyers.

Many experts are suggesting that Canadian companies should start focusing their efforts on training their salespeople to become more gender intelligent. Fortunately, some companies are heeding the call and are investing in gender intelligent salesforces. For example, RBC Financial Group

trained 1,500 account managers on how to meet the specific requirements of female clients. The results? After just one year, RBC reported a 10-point jump in market share and a 29-percent increase in customer satisfaction levels of women entrepreneurs with their account managers. Toyota Canada also created a new sales process called Access, designed specifically to meet the needs of women consumers. All salespeople are trained to be gender sensitive and to understand and approach women in such a way as to ensure a satisfying car-shopping experience. According to Toyota Canada, Access has been a major success, and its women-friendly program has driven market share and customer satisfaction numbers. Finally, Rona has also seen close to a 40 percent annual compounded growth rate in revenue since it implemented gender-intelligent sales strategies.

---

services, take at least two weeks of in-class and Web-based training on both consultative selling and the technical aspects of business.

On-the-job training is the most popular type of training, followed by individual instruction provided by experienced salespeople. Formal classes and seminars conducted by sales trainers and computer-based training are also popular.

Two areas with regard to salesforce training in Canada are training salespeople to respect and connect with female buyers, and training salespeople for their new roles in enterprise-wide customer relationship management (CRM). Evidence suggests that many Canadian companies are failing to do both.[27] Read the accompanying Marketing Matters box, "Sales Training Should Include Gender Intelligence," about some insight into the state of salesforce training when it comes to female Canadian consumers.[28]

Mary Kay Cosmetics recognizes a top salesperson at its annual sales meeting

Mary Kay Cosmetics, Inc.
www.marykay.com

Salesforce Motivation and Compensation   A sales plan cannot be successfully implemented without motivated salespeople. Research on salesperson motivation suggests that (1) a clear job description, (2) effective sales management practices, (3) a personal need for achievement, and (4) proper compensation, incentives, or rewards will produce a motivated salesperson.[29]

The importance of compensation as a motivating factor means that close attention must be given to how salespeople are financially rewarded for their efforts. Salespeople are paid using one of three plans: (1) straight salary, (2) straight commission, or (3) a combination of salary and commission. Under a *straight salary compensation plan,* a salesperson is paid a fixed fee per week, month, or year. With a *straight commission compensation plan,* a salesperson's earnings are directly tied to the sales or profit generated. For example, an insurance agent might receive a 2 percent commission of $2,000 for selling a $100,000 life insurance policy. A *combination compensation plan* contains a specified salary plus a commission on sales or profit generated.

Each compensation plan has its advantages and disadvantages.[30] A straight salary plan is easy to administer and gives management a large measure of control over how salespeople allocate their efforts. However, it provides little incentive to expand sales volume. This plan is used when salespeople engage in many non-selling activities, such as account servicing. A straight commission plan provides the maximum amount of selling incentive but can detract salespeople from providing customer service. This plan is common when non-selling activities are minimal. Combination plans are most preferred by salespeople and attempt to build on the advantages of salary and commission plans while reducing the potential shortcomings of each. Today, a majority of companies use combination plans.

Nonmonetary rewards are also given to salespeople for meeting or exceeding objectives. These rewards include trips, honour societies, distinguished salesperson awards, and letters of commendation. Some unconventional rewards include the new pink Cadillacs and Pontiacs, fur coats, and jewellery given by Mary Kay Cosmetics to outstanding salespeople. Mary Kay, with 10,000 cars, has the largest fleet of General Motors cars in the world![31]

Effective recruitment, selection, training, motivation, and compensation programs combine to create a productive salesforce. Ineffective practices often lead to costly salesforce turnover. Canadian and American firms experience an annual 11.6 percent turnover rate, which means that more than one of every ten salespeople are replaced each year.[32] The expense of replacing a salesperson and training a new one, including the cost of lost sales, can be high. Moreover, new recruits are often less productive than established salespeople.

Salesforce Evaluation: Measuring Results

The final function in the sales management process involves evaluating the salesforce. It is at this point that salespeople are assessed as to whether sales objectives were met and account management policies were followed. Both quantitative and behavioural measures are used to tap different selling dimensions.[33]

Quantitative Assessments   Quantitative assessments, called quotas, are based on input- and output-related objectives set forth in the sales plan. Input-related measures focus on the actual activities performed by salespeople, such as those involving sales calls, selling expenses, and account management policies. The number of sales calls made, selling expense related to sales made, and the number of reports submitted to superiors are frequently used input measures.

sales quota

Contains specific goals assigned to a salesperson, sales team, branch sales office, or sales district for a stated time period.

Output measures often appear in a sales quota. A **sales quota** contains specific goals assigned to a salesperson, sales team, branch sales office, or sales district for a stated time period. Dollar or unit sales volume, last year/current year sales ratio, sales of specific products, new accounts generated, and profit achieved are typical goals. The time period can range from one month to one year.

Behavioural Evaluation   Behavioural measures are also used to evaluate salespeople. These include assessments of a salesperson's attitude, attention to customers, product knowledge, selling and communication skills, appearance, and professional demeanour. Even though these assessments are sometimes subjective, they are frequently considered and, in fact, inevitable, in salesperson evaluation. Moreover, these factors are often important determinants of quantitative outcomes.

Almost 60 percent of companies now include customer satisfaction as a behavioural measure of salesperson performance.[34] (What percentage did you check for question 3 in Figure 18–1?) IBM Canada has been the most aggressive in using this behavioural measure. Forty percent of an IBM salesperson's evaluation is linked to customer satisfaction; the remaining 60 percent is linked to profits achieved. Eastman Chemical Company surveys its customers with eight versions of its customer satisfaction questionnaire printed in nine languages. Some 25 performance items are studied, including on-time and correct delivery, product quality, pricing practice, and sharing of market information. The survey is managed by the salesforce, and salespeople review the results with customers. Eastman salespeople know that "the second most important thing they have to do is get their customer satisfaction surveys out to and back from customers," says Eastman's sales training director. "Number one, of course, is getting orders."

Increasingly, companies are using marketing dashboards to track salesperson performance for evaluation purposes. An illustration appears in the accompanying Using Marketing Dashboards box.

Using Marketing Dashboards

Tracking Salesperson Performance at Moore Chemical & Sanitation Supply, Inc.

Moore Chemical & Sanitation Supply, Inc. (MooreChem) is a large supplier of cleaning chemicals and sanitary products. MooreChem sells to janitorial companies that clean corporate and professional office buildings.

MooreChem recently installed a sales and account management planning software package that included a dashboard for each of its sales representatives. Salespeople had access to their dashboards as well. These dashboards included seven measures—sales revenue, gross margin, selling expense, profit, average order size, new customers, and customer satisfaction. Each measure was gauged to show actual salesperson performance relative to target goals.

Your Challenge   As a newly promoted district sales manager at MooreChem, your responsibilities include tracking each salesperson's performance in your district. You are also responsible for directing the sales activities and practices of district salespeople.

In anticipation of a performance review with one of your salespeople, Brady Boyle, you review his dashboard for the previous quarter. Provide a constructive review of his performance.

Your Findings   Brady Boyle's quarterly performance is displayed below. Boyle has exceeded targeted goals for sales revenue, selling expenses, and customer satisfaction. All of these measures show an upward trend. He has met his target for gaining new customers and average order size. But Boyle's gross margin and profit are below targeted goals. These measures evidence a downward trend as well. Brady Boyle's mixed performance requires a constructive and positive correction.

Your Action   Brady Boyle should already know how his performance compares with targeted goals. Remember, Boyle has access to his dashboard. Recall that he has exceeded his sales target, but is considerably under his profit target. Boyle's sales trend is up, but his profit trend is down.

You will need to focus attention on Boyle's gross margin and selling expense results and trend. Boyle, it seems, is spending time and money selling lower margin products that produce a targeted average order size. It may very well be that Boyle is actually expending effort selling more products to his customers. Unfortunately, the product mix yields lower gross margins, resulting in a lower profit.

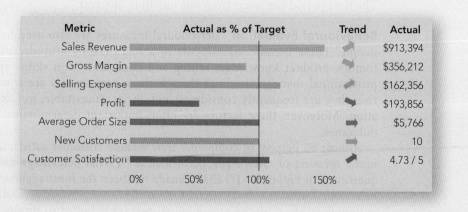

Metric	Actual as % of Target	Trend	Actual
Sales Revenue		↗	$913,394
Gross Margin		↘	$356,212
Selling Expense		↗	$162,356
Profit		↘	$193,856
Average Order Size		→	$5,766
New Customers		→	10
Customer Satisfaction		↗	4.73 / 5

Salesforce Automation and Customer Relationship Management

Personal selling and sales management are undergoing a technological revolution with the integration of salesforce automation and customer relationship management processes. In fact, the emergence of information and communication technologies (ICTs) has transformed the sales function in many companies and made the promise of customer relationship management a reality. **Salesforce automation (SFA)** is the use of technology to make the sales function more effective and efficient. SFA applies to a wide range of activities, including each stage in the personal selling process and management of the salesforce itself.

Salesforce automation exists in many forms. Examples of SFA applications include computer hardware and software for account analysis, lead management, contact management, time management, territory management, order processing and follow-up, sales presentations, proposal generation, and product and sales training. Each application is designed to ease administrative tasks and free up time for salespeople to be with customers building relationships and providing service.

salesforce automation (SFA)
The use of technology to make the sales function more effective and efficient.

Salesforce Technology Technology has become an integral part of field selling. Today, most companies supply their field salespeople with laptop or notebook computers. For example, salespeople for Godiva Chocolates use their laptop computers to process orders, plan time allocations, forecast sales, and communicate with other Godiva personnel and with customers. While in a department store candy buyer's office, a salesperson can calculate the order cost, transmit the order, and obtain a delivery date within a few minutes from Godiva's order processing department.[35]

Toshiba America Medical System salespeople use laptop computers with built-in CD-ROM capabilities to provide interactive presentations for their computerized tomography (CT) and magnetic resonance imaging (MRI) scanners. In it the customer sees elaborate three-dimensional animations, high-resolution scans, and video clips of the company's products in operation as well as narrated testimonials from satisfied customers. Toshiba has found this application to be effective both for sales presentations and for training its salespeople.[36]

Salesforce Communication Technology has changed the way salespeople communicate with customers, other salespeople and sales support personnel, and management. Electronic mail, text messaging, and voice mail are common communication technologies used by salespeople today. In particular, Web-enabled smartphones now allow salespeople to exchange data, text, and voice transmissions in an instant. Whether travelling or in a customer's office, this type of technology provides information at the salesperson's fingertips to answer customer questions and solve problems.

Advances in communication and computer technologies have made possible the mobile and home sales office. Some salespeople now equip minivans with a fully functional desk, swivel chair, light, computer, printer, fax machine, cellular phone, and a satellite dish. Other sales representatives, like those at Symetra Financial, for example, use their BlackBerries to look up customers' addresses and to retrieve notes on past visits. They can even get maps and directions from MapQuest so that they don't get lost! After they visit with the customer, they enter information on the visit into the customer files stored on the device as well as into the company's database.[37] At EDS, a professional services firm, salespeople access its intranet to download client material, marketing content, account information, technical papers, and competitive profiles. In addition, EDS offers 7,000 training classes that salespeople can take anytime and anywhere.

Home offices are now common. Hewlett-Packard is a case in point. The company shifted its salesforce into home offices, closed several regional sales offices, and saved millions of dollars in staff salaries and office rent. A fully equipped home office for each salesperson includes a notebook computer, fax/copier, mobile phone, VOIP (Voice over Internet Protocol) phones, and office furniture.

Salesforce automation is clearly changing how selling is done and how salespeople are managed. Its numerous applications promise to boost selling productivity, improve customer relationships, and decrease selling cost. But importantly, along with this technology is the realization that all organizations must empower their salesforces to use the technology wisely and ethically in order to build long-term profitable relationships with the customers. It is also apparent that in this new era of customer experience management, organizations must recognize that the experience the customer has with a salesperson might be the greatest opportunity to win or lose customers, and therefore, organizational support for the salespeople must be a major priority.[38]

---

learning review	**8.** What are the three types of selling objectives?
	9. What three factors are used to structure sales organizations?
	10. How does emotional intelligence tie to adaptive selling?

LEARNING OBJECTIVES REVIEW

LO1 **Discuss the nature and scope of personal selling and sales management in marketing.**

Personal selling involves the two-way flow of communication between a buyer and seller, often in a face-to-face encounter, designed to influence a person's or group's purchase decision. Sales management involves planning the selling program and implementing and controlling the personal selling effort of the firm. The scope of selling and sales management is apparent in three ways. First, virtually every occupation that involves customer contact has an element of personal selling. Second, selling plays a significant role in a company's overall marketing effort. Salespeople occupy a boundary position between buyers and sellers; they *are* the company to many buyers and account for a major cost of marketing in a variety of industries; and they can create value for customers. Finally, through relationship and partnership selling, salespeople play a central role in tailoring solutions to customer problems as a means to customer value creation.

LO2 **Identify the different types of personal selling.**

Three types of personal selling exist: (*a*) order taking, (*b*) order getting, and (*c*) customer sales support activities. Each type differs from the others in terms of actual selling done and the amount of creativity required to perform the sales task. Order takers process routine orders or reorders for products that were already sold by the company. They generally do little selling in a conventional sense and engage in only modest problem solving with customers. Order getters sell in a conventional sense and identify prospective customers, provide customers with information, persuade customers to buy, close sales, and follow up on customers' use of a product or service. Order getting involves a high degree of creativity and customer empathy and is typically required for selling complex or technical products

with many options. Customer sales support personnel augment the sales effort of order getters by performing a variety of services. Sales support personnel are prominent in cross-functional team selling, the practice of using an entire team of professionals in selling to and servicing major customers.

LO3 **Explain the stages in the personal selling process.**

The personal selling process consists of six stages: (*a*) prospecting, (*b*) preapproach, (*c*) approach, (*d*) presentation, (*e*) close, and (*f*) follow-up. Prospecting involves the search for and qualification of potential customers. The preapproach stage involves obtaining further information on the prospect and deciding on the best method of approach. The approach stage involves the initial meeting between the salesperson and prospect. The presentation stage involves converting a prospect into a customer by creating a desire for the product or service. The close involves obtaining a purchase commitment from the prospect. The follow-up stage involves making certain that the customer's purchase has been properly delivered and installed and difficulties experienced with the use of the item are addressed.

LO4 **Describe the major functions of sales management.**

Sales management consists of three interrelated functions: (*a*) sales plan formulation, (*b*) sales plan implementation, and (*c*) evaluation and control of the salesforce. Sales plan formulation involves setting objectives, organizing the salesforce, and developing account management policies. Sales plan implementation involves salesforce recruitment, selection, training, motivation, and compensation. Finally, evaluation and control of the salesforce focuses on quantitative assessments of sales performance and behavioural measures, such as customer satisfaction that are linked to selling objectives and account management policies.

FOCUSING ON KEY TERMS

account management policies p. 502
adaptive selling p. 495
consultative selling p. 495
emotional intelligence p. 503
formula selling presentation p. 495
key account management p. 501
missionary salespeople p. 491
need-satisfaction presentation p. 495
order getter p. 490
order taker p. 489
partnership selling p. 489

personal selling p. 487
personal selling process p. 492
relationship selling p. 489
sales engineer p. 491
salesforce automation (SFA) p. 507
sales management p. 487
sales plan p. 498
sales quota p. 505
stimulus-response presentation p. 495
team selling p. 491
workload method p. 501

APPLYING MARKETING KNOWLEDGE

1 Jane Dawson is a new sales representative for the Charles Schwab brokerage firm. In searching for clients, Jane purchased a mailing list of subscribers to the *Financial Post* and called them all regarding their interest in discount brokerage services. She asked if they had any stocks and if they had a regular broker. Those people without a regular broker were asked about their investment needs. Two days later, Jane called back with investment advice and asked if they would like to open an account. Identify each of Jane Dawson's actions in terms of the personal selling process.

2 For the first 50 years of business, the Johnson Carpet Company produced carpets for residential use. The salesforce was structured geographically. In the past five years, a large percentage of carpet sales has been to industrial users, hospitals, schools, and architects. The company also has broadened its product line to include area rugs, Oriental carpets, and wall-to-wall carpeting. Is the present salesforce structure appropriate, or would you recommend an alternative?

3 Where would you place each of the following sales jobs on the order taker/order getter continuum shown below? (*a*) Tim Hortons counter clerk, (*b*) automobile insurance salesperson, (*c*) IBM salesperson, (*d*) life insurance salesperson, and (*e*) shoe salesperson.

Order taker ——————————————— Order getter

4 Listed here are two different firms. Which compensation plan would you recommend for each firm, and what reasons would you give for your recommendations? (*a*) A newly formed company that sells lawn care equipment on a door-to-door basis directly to consumers; and (*b*) the Nabisco Company, which sells heavily advertised products in supermarkets by having the salesforce call on these stores and arrange shelves, set up displays, and make presentations to store buying committees.

5 The TDK company services 1,000 electronic stores throughout the country. Each store is called on 12 times a year, and the average sales call lasts 30 minutes. Assuming a salesperson works 40 hours a week, 50 weeks a year, and devotes 75 percent of the time to actual selling, how many salespeople does TDK need?

6 A furniture manufacturer is currently using manufacturer's representatives to sell its line of living room furniture. These representatives receive a 4 percent commission. The company is considering hiring its own salespeople and has estimated that the fixed cost of managing and paying their salaries would be $1 million annually. The salespeople would also receive a 4 percent commission on sales. The company has sales of $25 million dollars, and sales are expected to grow by 15 percent next year. Would you recommend that the company switch to its own salesforce? Why, or why not?

7 Suppose someone said to you, "The only real measure of a salesperson is the amount of sales produced." How might you respond?

Building Your Marketing Plan

Does your marketing plan involve a personal selling activity? If the answer is no, read no further and do not include a personal selling element in your plan. If the answer is yes:

1. Identify likely prospects for your product or service.
2. Determine what information you should obtain about the prospect.

3. Describe how you would approach the prospect.
4. Outline the presentation you would make to the prospect for your product or service.
5. Develop a sales plan, focusing on the organizational structure you would use for your salesforce (geography, product, or customer).

XEROX: BUILDING CUSTOMER RELATIONSHIPS THROUGH PERSONAL SELLING

"I'm like the quarterback of the team. I manage 250 accounts, and anything from billing issues, to service issues, to selling the products. I'm really the face to the customer," says Alison Capossela, a Washington, D.C.– based Xerox sales representative.

As the primary company contact for Xerox customers, Alison is responsible for developing and maintaining customer relationships. To accomplish this she uses a sophisticated selling process that requires many activities, from making presentations, to attending training sessions, to managing a team of Xerox personnel, to monitoring competitors' activities. The face-to-face interactions with customers, however, are the most rewarding for Capossela. "It's an amazing feeling; the more they challenge me the more I fight back. It's fun!" she explains.

The Company

Xerox Corporation's mission is to "help people find better ways to do great work by constantly leading in document technologies, products, and services that improve customers' work processes and business results." To accomplish this mission Xerox employs 53,700 people in 160 countries. With annual sales of $16 billion, Xerox is the world's leading document management enterprise and a Fortune 500 company. Xerox offers a wide range of products and services. These include printers, copiers and fax machines, multifunction and network devices, high-speed color presses, digital imaging and archiving products and services, and supplies such as toner, paper, and ink. The entire company is guided by customer-focused and employee-centred core values (e.g., "We succeed through satisfied customers") and a passion for innovation, speed, and adaptability.

Xerox was founded in 1906 as a manufacturer of photographic paper called The Haloid Company. In 1947, the company purchased the licence to basic xerographic patents. The following year it received a trademark for the word "Xerox." By 1973 Xerox had introduced the automatic, plain-paper copier, opened offices in Japan, and its Palo Alto Research Center (PARC) had invented the world's first personal computer (the Alto), the "mouse," and graphical user interface software. In 1994, Xerox adopted "The Document Company" as its signature and the partially digitized red "X" as its corporate symbol. Despite this extraordinary history of success, Xerox was $19 billion in debt by 2000 and was losing business rapidly. Many experts predicted that the company would fail.

The Xerox board of directors knew a change was needed and it asked Anne M. Mulcahy to serve as the company's CEO. Mulcahy had begun her career as a sales representative at Xerox and observed that "we had lost our way in terms of delivering value to customers." Mulcahy reduced the size of the workforce by one-third and invested in new technologies, while keeping the Xerox culture and values. The changes, coupled with Mulcahy's commitment to a sales organization that focused on customer relationships, reversed Xerox's decline. As Kevin Warren, vice president of sales explains: "One of the reasons she has been so successful is that she absolutely resonates with all the people. I think [because of] the fact that she started out as a sales rep, people feel like she is one of them." The turnaround has been such an extraordinary success that Mulcahy was recently recognized by *Forbes* magazine as the fifth most powerful woman in the world!

The Selling Process at Xerox

When Mulcahy became CEO, Xerox began a shift to a consultative selling model that focused on helping customers solve their business problems rather than just placing more equipment in their office. The shift meant that sales reps needed to be less product-oriented and more relationship- and value-oriented. Xerox wanted to be a provider of total solutions. Today, Xerox has more than 8,000 sales professionals throughout the world who spend a large amount of their day developing customer relationships. Capossela explains: "Fifty percent of my day is spent with my customers, twenty-five percent is following up with phone calls or emails, and another twenty-five percent involves preparing proposals." The approach has helped Xerox attract new customers and keep existing customers.

The sales process at Xerox typically follows the six stages of the personal selling process identified in Figure 18–3: (1) Xerox identifies potential clients through responses to advertising, referrals, and telephone calls; (2) the salesforce prepares for a presentation by familiarizing themselves with the potential client and its document needs; (3) a Xerox sales representative approaches the prospect and suggests a meeting and presentation; (4) as the presentation begins, the salesperson summarizes relevant information about potential solutions Xerox can offer, states what he or she hopes to get out of the meeting, explains how the products and services work, and reinforces the benefits of working with Xerox; (5) the salesperson engages in an action close (gets a signed document or a firm confirmation of the sale); and then (6) continues to meet and communicate with the client to provide assistance and monitor the effectiveness of the installed solution.

Xerox sales representatives also use the selling process to maintain relationships with existing customers. In today's competitive environment it is not unusual to have customers who have been approached by competitors or who are required to obtain more than one bid before renewing a contract. Xerox has teams of people who collect and analyze information about competitors and their products. The information is sent out to sales reps or offered to them through workshops and seminars. The most difficult competitors are the ones that have also invested in customer relationships. The selling process allows Xerox to continually react and respond to new information and take advantage of opportunities in the marketplace.

The Sales Management Process at Xerox

The Xerox salesforce is divided into four geographic organizations: North America, which includes the United States and Canada; Europe, which includes 17 countries; Global Accounts, which manages large accounts that operate in multiple locations; and Developing Markets, which includes all other geographic territories that may require Xerox products and services. Within each geographic area, the majority of Xerox products and services are typically sold through its direct salesforce. Xerox also utilizes a variety of other channels, including value-added resellers, independent agents, dealers, systems integrators, telephone, and Internet sales channels.

Motivation and compensation is an important aspect of any salesforce. At Xerox there is a passion for winning that provides a key incentive for sales reps. In addition, the compensation plan plays an important role. As Warren explains, "Our compensation plans are a combination of salary as well as an opportunity to leverage earnings through sales commissions and bonuses." Xerox also has a recognition program called the President's Club where the top performers are awarded a five-day trip to one of the top resorts in the world. The program has been a huge success and has now been offered for more than 30 years.

Perhaps the most well-known component of Xerox's sales management process is its sales representative training program. For example, Xerox developed the

"Create and Win" program to help sales reps learn the new consultative selling approach. The components of the program consisted of interactive training sessions and distance-learning Webinars. Every new sales representative at Xerox receives eight weeks of training development in the field and at the Xerox Corporate University in Virginia. "The training program is phenomenal!" according to Capossela. The training and its focus on the customer is part of the Xerox culture outside of the sales organization also. Every senior executive at Xerox is responsible for working with at least one customer. They also spend a full day every month responding to incoming customer calls and inquiries.

What Is in the Future for the Xerox Salesforce?

The recent growth and success at Xerox is creating many opportunities for the company and for its sales representatives. For example, Xerox is accelerating the development of its top salespeople. Mentors are used to provide advice for day-to-day issues and long-term career planning. In addition, globalization has become such an important initiative at Xerox that experienced and successful sales representatives are quickly given opportunities to manage large global accounts. Xerox is also moving toward an approach that empowers sales representatives to make decisions about how to handle accounts. The large number of Xerox customers means there are a variety of different corporate styles, and the sales reps are increasingly the best qualified to manage the relationship. This approach is just one more example of Xerox's commitment to customers and creating customer value.

Questions

1 Why was Anne Mulcahy's experience as a sales representative an important part of Xerox's growth in recent years?

2 How did the sales approach change after Mulcahy became the CEO of Xerox?

3 How does Xerox create customer value though its personal selling process? How does Alison Capossela provide solutions for Xerox customers?

4 Why is the Xerox training program so important to the company's success?

Pulling It All Together:
The Strategic Marketing Process

WESTJET: CRAFTING STRATEGY IN AN EVOLVING MARKETING ENVIRONMENT

WestJet was founded in 1996 by four Calgary entrepreneurs led by Clive Beddoe. WestJet's original strategy was simple: offer low-fare air travel across western Canada. The WestJet founders studied the success of Southwest Airlines and determined that a similar concept could be successful in western Canada. The team developed a business plan and raised the capital to start the business. The airline started flight operations with 220 employees and three 737 aircraft to the cities of Vancouver, Kelowna, Calgary, Edmonton, and Winnipeg. The company then added Victoria, Regina, and Saskatoon to its route network. In 1997, WestJet began service to Abbotsford/Fraser Valley, and in 1999, WestJet added Thunder Bay, Prince George, and Grande Prairie to its service area.

In July 1999, WestJet became a publicly traded company and extended its airline service across Canada. In June 2000, the company added service to the eastern Canadian cities of Hamilton, Moncton, and Ottawa, creating an eastern network with Hamilton as the hub. In 2001, WestJet added new service to Fort McMurray, Comox, and Brandon. In 2001, WestJet also added its first four Next-Generation Boeing 737-700 aircraft. In 2002, WestJet added service to two new Ontario destinations, London and Toronto. In February 2002, the corporation successfully offered 3 million common shares yielding net proceeds of $78.9 million. The proceeds were used to fund aircraft additions, spare parts, and a third flight simulator. In 2002, WestJet added service

learning objectives

After reading this chapter, you should be able to:

LO1 Explain how marketing managers allocate their limited resources.

LO2 Describe three marketing planning frameworks: Porter's generic strategies, profit enhancement options, and market–product synergies.

LO3 Explain what makes an effective marketing plan and some problems that often exist with it.

LO4 Describe the alternatives for organizing a marketing department and the role of a product manager.

LO5 Explain how marketing ROI, metrics, and dashboards relate to evaluating programs.

to the new markets of Halifax, Windsor, Montreal, St. John's, and Gander. As the Canadian airline market evolved, WestJet looked to continue its growth and found an opportunity to expand its routes into the United States. Cross-border service commenced in the fall of 2004 to the cities of Los Angeles, San Francisco, Phoenix, Fort Lauderdale, Tampa, Orlando, and New York. In 2005, service was commenced to Palm Springs, San Diego, and Hawaii. In 2006, WestJet began flying to the Bahamas and in 2007 it added services to Newfoundland, New Brunswick, and Kitchener-Waterloo. It also began international service to Jamaica, the Dominican Republic, and Mexico. In 2008, it began service to Quebec City and New York City via Newark, New Jersey. In 2009, it began service to Yellowknife, Northwest Territories, and Sydney, Nova Scotia. In 2010, it began service to Bermuda. It also has agreements in place with KLM and Air France for travel to Europe and a codeshare deal with Southwest Airlines for expanded travel to the U.S. Finally, it has a frequent-flyer program with RBC and MasterCard. Now in its second decade of business, WestJet currently employs more than 7,500 people and flies to close to 70 destinations in North America. Its market share of the Canadian airline industry has grown from 7 percent in 2000 to 36 percent in 2009. It has carried over 10 million passengers, whom they refer to as "guests," and has a $1.2 billion (US) market capitalization value.

So, what are the ingredients to WestJet's success? Well, as you will discover in this chapter, four basic business practices are fundamental to business success: strategy, execution, culture, and structure. From the beginning, WestJet had a clear and focused strategy, and it executed it well. The company also developed a strong organizational and entrepreneurial culture with its employees (who are shareholders) as key architects to its success. The company also built and maintains a flat, flexible organization, with its employees empowered to make corporate decisions and solve problems.

WestJet also continuously adapts to the fast-paced airline industry looking for new opportunities as well as responding to changing guests' needs. By 2016, WestJet intends to be one of the five most successful international airlines in the world. The company believes it will achieve this goal by providing its guests with a friendly and caring experience that will change the air travel industry forever. According to Sean Durfy, former president and CEO of WestJet, the company's continued success will be based on offering a great service experience at a great value.[1]

Chapter 19 discusses issues and techniques related to the planning, implementation, and evaluation phases of the strategic marketing process, the kind of topics marketing managers and executives deal with every day. Throughout the chapter, you will be able to obtain insights into the marketing strategies used by many successful Canadian and global companies.

MARKETING BASICS: DOING WHAT WORKS AND ALLOCATING RESOURCES

As noted in Chapter 2, corporate and marketing executives search continuously to find a competitive advantage—a unique strength relative to competitors. Having identified this competitive advantage, they must figure out how to exploit it.[2] This involves (1) finding and using what works for their organization and industry, and (2) allocating resources effectively.

Finding and Using What Really Works

Costco achieves excellence in what really matters.

In a five-year study, researchers conducted in-depth analysis of 160 companies and more than 200 management tools and techniques, such as supply chain management, customer relationship management (CRM), or the use of information and communications technologies. The result? Individual management tools and techniques had no direct relationship to superior business performance.[3]

What did matter? The researchers concluded that what matters are four basic business and management practices—"what really works," to use a phrase. These are (1) strategy, (2) execution, (3) culture, and (4) structure. Firms with excellence in all four of these areas are likely to achieve superior business performance. And in terms of individual tools and techniques, the researchers concluded that the firm's choice of a tool or technique is less important than the flawless execution of it.

Industry leaders, such as Walmart, Home Depot, and Dell, do all four of the basic practices extremely well, not just two or three, and are vigilant to keep doing them well even when conditions change. And as the chapter opener indicates, WestJet also performs well on all four dimensions. However, Coca-Cola[4] and Kodak,[5] superstars a decade ago, are struggling today to get these basics right and regain past success. But let us look at some other companies that stand out today in each of the four basics:

- *Strategy: Devise and maintain a clearly stated, focused strategy.* Walmart may be the unstoppable force in mass-merchandise retailing, but among warehouse clubs, its Sam's Club is not. The winner, to date, is Costco, with 60 percent as many stores as Sam's Club but almost twice the sales revenue. A key reason is Costco's focused strategy based on the knowledge that, of all retail channels, warehouse clubs attract the largest proportion of affluent shoppers. Costco's strategy: sell a limited selection of branded high-end merchandise at low prices.[6]

- *Execution: Develop and maintain flawless operational execution.* Toyota is generally acknowledged as the best in the world in revolutionizing the design and manufacture of autos. Toyota managers created the doctrine of *kaizen,* or continuous improvement. For example, by speeding up decisions, Toyota reduced the time to get the Solara from the drawing board to the showroom in 19 months, about half the industry average.[7]

- *Culture: Develop and maintain a performance-oriented culture.* Several high-performing companies point to their culture as central to their success. Janssen-Ortho, for example, promotes leadership development and innovation teams as part of its organizational culture. Flight Centre keeps its organization performing well by promoting from within, thus motivating its employees and perpetuating its winning culture. Spin Master Toys promotes a fun and positive environment that keeps its company humming along, while Defasco leverages employee profit sharing to promote a performance-oriented culture.

- *Structure: Build and maintain a fast, flexible, flat organization.* Successful small organizations often grow into bureaucratic large ones with layers of managers and red tape that slow down the decision-making process. High-performing firms, on the other hand, empower their employees to make decisions and provide an environment where internal communications are encouraged, as is active problem-solving, all within simple and flat organizational structures.

Of course, in practice, a firm cannot allocate unlimited resources to achieving each of these business basics. It must make choices on where its resources can give the greatest return, the topic of the next section.

Allocating Marketing Resources Using Sales Response Functions

sales response function
Relates the expense of marketing effort to the marketing results obtained.

A **sales response function** relates the expense of marketing effort to the marketing results obtained.[8] For simplicity, in the examples that follow, only the effects of annual marketing effort on annual sales revenue will be analyzed, but the concept applies to other measures of marketing success—such as profit, units sold, or level of awareness—as well.

Maximizing Incremental Revenue Minus Incremental Cost   Economists give managers a specific guideline for optimal resource allocation: allocate the firm's marketing, production, and financial resources to the markets and products where the excess of incremental revenues over incremental costs is greatest.

Figure 19–1 illustrates the resource allocation principle that is inherent in the sales response function. The firm's annual marketing effort, such as sales and advertising expenses, is plotted on the horizontal axis. As the annual marketing effort increases, so does the resulting annual sales revenue, which is plotted on the vertical axis. The relationship is assumed to be S-shaped, showing that an additional $1 million of marketing effort, from $3 million to $4 million, results in far greater increases of sales revenue in the midrange ($20 million) of the curve than at either end (an increase from $2 million to $3 million in spending yields an increase of $10 million in sales; an increase from $6 million to $7 million in spending leads to an increase of $5 million in sales).

A Numerical Example of Resource Allocation   Suppose that Figure 19–1 shows the situation for a new General Mills product, such as Fruity Cheerios`, an extension of the Cheerios brand targeted at health-conscious consumers. Each serving of Fruity Cheerios contains at least 23 grams of whole grain and 100 percent of an adult's daily needs of 12 key vitamins and minerals.[9]

Also, assume that the sales response function does not change through time as a result of changing consumer tastes and incomes. Point A shows the position of the firm in year 1, whereas Point B shows it three years later in year 4. Suppose General Mills decides to launch new advertising and sales promotions that, say, increase its marketing effort for the brand from $3 million to $6 million a year. If the relationship in Figure 19–1 holds true and is a good picture of consumer purchasing behaviour, the sales revenues of Fruity Cheerios should increase from $30 million to $70 million a year.

Let us look at the major resource allocation question: What are the probable increases in sales revenue for Fruity Cheerios in year 1 and year 4 if General Mills were to spend an additional $1 million in marketing effort? As Figure 19–1 reveals:

● **FIGURE 19–1**

Sales response function showing the situation for two different years

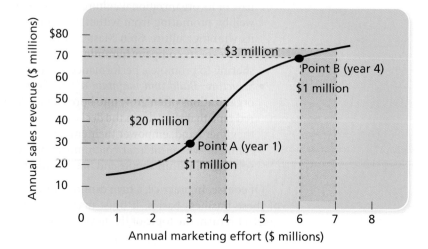

Year 1

Increase in marketing effort from $3 million to $4 million = $1 million

Increase in sales revenue from $30 million to $50 million = $20 million

Ratio of incremental sales revenue to effort = $20,000,000:$1,000,000 = 20:1

Year 4

Increase in marketing effort from $6 million to $7 million = $1 million

Increase in sales revenue from $70 million to $73 million = $3 million

Ratio of incremental sales revenue to effort = $3,000,000:$1,000,000 = 3:1

Thus, in year 1, a dollar of extra marketing effort returned $20 in sales revenue, whereas in year 4, it returned only $3. If no other expenses are incurred, it might make sense to spend $1 million in year 4 to gain $3 million in incremental sales revenue. However, it may be far wiser for General Mills to invest the money in products in one of its other business units, such as its Warm Delights microwaveable desserts. The essence of resource allocation is simple: put incremental resources where the incremental returns are greatest over the foreseeable future. For General Mills this means allocating its available resources efficiently among its broad portfolio of product lines.

Allocating Marketing Resources in Practice   General Mills, like many firms in these businesses, does extensive analysis using **share points,** or percentage points of market share, as the common basis of comparison to allocate marketing resources effectively for different product lines within the same firm. This allows it to seek answers to the question, "How much is it worth to us to try to increase our market share by another 1 (or 2, or 5, or 10) percentage point?"

share points

Percentage points of market share; often used as the common basis of comparison to allocate marketing resources effectively.

This analysis enables higher-level managers to make resource allocation trade-offs among different kinds of business units owned by the company. To make these resource allocation decisions, marketing managers must estimate (1) the market share for the product, (2) the revenues associated with each point of market share (a share point in breakfast cereals may be five times what it is in cake mixes), (3) the contribution to overhead and profit (or gross margin) of each share point, and (4) possible cannibalization effects on other products in the line (for example, new Fruity Cheerios might reduce the sales of regular Cheerios).[10] Fortunately, in the case of Fruity Cheerios, the brand was a success for General Mills.[11]

Resource Allocation and the Strategic Marketing Process   Company resources are allocated effectively in the strategic marketing process by converting marketing information into marketing actions. Figure 19–2 summarizes the strategic marketing process introduced in Chapter 2, along with some details of the marketing actions and information that comprise it. Figure 19–2 is really a simplification of the actual strategic marketing process: While the three phases of the strategic marketing process have distinct separations in the figure and the marketing actions are separated from the marketing information, in practice, these blend together and interact.

The upper half of each box in Figure 19–2 highlights the actions involved in that part of the strategic marketing process and the lower half summarizes the information and reports used. Note that each phase has an output report:

PHASE	OUTPUT REPORT
Planning	Marketing plans (or programs) that define goals and the marketing mix strategies to achieve them
Implementation	Results (memos or computer outputs) that describe the outcomes of implementing the plans
Evaluation	Corrective action memos, triggered by comparing results with goals, often using the firm's marketing metrics and dashboards

Planning phase

	Step 1	Step 2	Step 3	Implementation phase	Evaluation phase
Action	**Situation (SWOT) analysis** • Identify industry trends • Analyze competitors • Assess own company • Research customers	**Market–product focus and goal setting** • Set market and product goals • Select target markets • Find points of difference • Position the product	**Marketing program** • Develop the program's marketing mix • Develop the budget, by estimating revenues, expenses, and profits	• Obtain resources • Design marketing organization • Develop schedules • Execute marketing program	• Compare results with plans to identify deviations • Correct negative deviations; exploit positive ones

Information	• Determine trend in past and current revenues:
	  For industry and competitors in total and by segment
	• Project future revenues, expenses, and profits:
	  For own product in total and by segment
		• Market potential
		  By industry
		  By segment
		• Market-product grids, with ranked targets
		• Product positioning that stresses key features, advantages, and benefits
			• Characteristics and timing of:
			  Product actions
			  Price actions
			  Promotion actions
			  Place actions
			• Projected marketing expenses
			• Detailed plans to execute the marketing program
				• Memos assigning responsibilities for actions and deadlines; Gantt charts
				• Organizational charts and job descriptions
				• Marketing research reports on sales, awareness, and effectiveness
					• Tracking reports measuring results of the marketing actions
					• Deviation reports comparing actual results with plans
					• Action memos to try to correct problems and exploit opportunities

Plans → | ← Results

Corrective actions ←——— | Corrective actions ←———

● **FIGURE 19-2**
The strategic marketing process: actions and information

The corrective action memos become feedback loops in Figure 19–2 that help improve decisions and actions in the earlier phases of the strategic marketing process.

THE PLANNING PHASE OF THE STRATEGIC MARKETING PROCESS

Four aspects of the strategic marketing process deserve special mention: (1) the vital importance of metrics in marketing planning, (2) the varieties of marketing plans, (3) marketing planning frameworks that have proven useful, and (4) some marketing planning and strategy lessons.

The Vital Importance of Metrics in Marketing Planning

In the past decade, measuring the effectiveness of marketing activities has become a central focus in many organizations. This boils down to defining "where the organization is going"—the goals—and "whether it is really getting there"—the marketing metrics used to measure the actual performance.

Planners have a tongue-in-cheek truism: "If you don't know where you're going, any road will get you there." In making marketing plans, the "road" chosen is really the goal plus the metric used to measure whether the goal is achieved.

Even in today's economic turmoil, most firms stress innovation to help achieve growth. Marketing departments work closely with research and development (R&D) departments to complete successful innovation projects. So what marketing metrics might they use to measure their innovation performance? Typically firms use several metrics including input metrics and outputs metrics. An input metric frequently used is the number of ideas in the innovation pipeline while an output metric could be revenue growth from new products or services. It should be noted, however, that it is generally far easier to measure marketing inputs rather than marketing outputs. For example, measuring the number of R&D projects (an input) is far easier than measuring "customer satisfaction with new products and services" (an output). But, as shown in Figure 19–2, the evaluation phase of the strategic marketing process involves comparing actual results—an output metric—with the goals set. So where possible, marketing managers prefer to use effective output metrics if they are available.

The Variety of Marketing Plans

The planning phase of the strategic marketing process usually results in a marketing plan that sets the direction for the marketing activities of an organization. As noted earlier in Appendix A (following Chapter 2), a marketing plan is the heart of a business plan. Like business plans, marketing plans are not all from the same mould; they vary with the length of the planning period, the purpose, and the audience. Let us look briefly at two kinds: long-range plans and annual marketing plans.

Long-Range Marketing Plans   Typically, long-range marketing plans cover marketing activities from two to five years into the future. Except for firms in such industries as autos, steel, or forest products, marketing plans rarely go beyond five years into the future because the tremendous number of uncertainties present make the benefits of planning less than the effort expended. Such plans are often directed at top-level executives and the board of directors.

Annual Marketing Plans   Usually developed by a marketing or product manager (discussed later in the chapter) in a consumer products firm, such as General Mills, annual marketing plans deal with marketing goals and strategies for a product, product line, or entire firm for a single year. Typical steps that such firms as Kellogg's, Coca-Cola, and Johnson & Johnson take in developing their annual marketing plans for their existing products are shown in Figure 19–3.[12] This annual planning cycle typically starts with a detailed marketing research study of current users and ends after 48 weeks, with the approval of the plan by the division general manager—10 weeks before the fiscal year starts. Between these points, there are continuing efforts to uncover new ideas through brainstorming and key-issues sessions with specialists both inside and outside the firm. The plan is fine-tuned through a series of often-excruciating reviews by several levels of management, which leaves few surprises and very little to chance.

---

learning review

1. What is the significance of the S-shape of the sales response function in Figure 19–1?

2. What are the main output reports from each phase of the strategic marketing process?

3. What are two kinds of marketing plans?

 Marketing Planning Frameworks: The Search for Growth

Marketing planning for a firm with many products competing in many markets—a multiproduct, multimarket firm—is a complex process. Three techniques that are useful in helping corporate and marketing executives in such a firm make important

Steps in annual marketing planning process	Weeks before approval of plan

Steps in annual marketing planning process	50	40	30	20	10	0
1. Obtain up-to-date marketing information from marketing research study of product users.	▲					
2. Brainstorm alternatives to consider in next year's plan with marketing research and ad agency.	▰					
3. Meet with internal media specialists to set long-run guidelines in purchase of media.		▰				
4. Obtain sales and profit results from last fiscal year, which ended 16 weeks earlier.			▰			
5. Identify key issues to address by talks with marketing researchers, ad agency, and so on.			▰▰			
6. Hold key issues meeting with marketing director; form task force of line managers, if needed.				▲		
7. Write and circulate key issues memo; initiate necessary marketing research to reduce uncertainty.				▰		
8. Review marketing mix elements and competitors' behaviour with key managers, marketing director.					▰	
9. Draft marketing plan, review with marketing director, and revise, as necessary.					▰	
10. Present plan to marketing director, task force, key line departments; make necessary changes.					▲	
11. Present marketing plan to division general manager for approval, 10 weeks before start of fiscal year.						▲

KEY: ▰ Planned period of work   ▲ Planned completion date

● **FIGURE 19-3**

Steps a large consumer packaged goods firm takes in developing its annual marketing plan

Source: Reprinted with permission from *Journal of Marketing*, published by the American Marketing Association, Summer 1980, p. 82

generic business strategy
Strategy that can be adopted by any firm, regardless of the product or industry involved, to achieve a competitive advantage.

cost leadership strategy
Focuses on reducing expenses and lowering produce prices while targeting a broad array of market segments.

resource allocation decisions are (1) Porter's generic business strategies, (2) profit enhancement options, and (3) market–product synergies. All of these techniques are based on elements introduced in earlier chapters.

Porter's Generic Business Strategies As shown in Figure 19–4, Michael E. Porter has developed a framework in which he identifies four basic, or "generic," strategies.[13] A **generic business strategy** is one that can be adopted by any firm, regardless of the product or industry involved, to achieve a competitive advantage.

Although all of the techniques discussed here involve generic strategies, the phrase is most often associated with Porter's framework. In this framework, the columns identify the two fundamental alternatives firms can use in seeking competitive advantage: (1) becoming the low-cost producer within the markets in which it competes, or (2) differentiating itself from competitors through developing points of difference in its product offerings or marketing programs. In contrast, the rows identify the competitive scope: (1) a broad target by competing in many market segments, or (2) a narrow target by competing in only a few segments or even a single segment. The columns and rows result in four generic business strategies, any one of which can provide a competitive advantage among similar business units in the same industry:

1. A **cost leadership strategy** (cell 1) focuses on reducing expenses and lowering product prices while targeting a broad array of market segments. One way is by securing raw materials from a lower-cost supplier. Also, significant investments in capital equipment may be necessary to improve the production or distribution process and achieve these lower unit costs. The cost leader still must have

Which of Porter's generic strategies is Walmart using? For the answer and a discussion of the strategies, see the text.

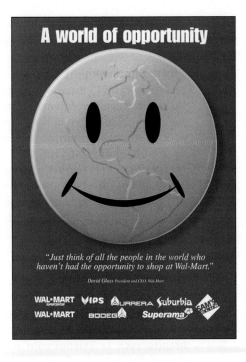

adequate quality levels. Walmart's sophisticated systems of regional warehouses and electronic data interchange with its suppliers have led to huge cost savings and its cost leadership strategy that results in lower prices for customers.

differentiation strategy

Requires products to have significant points of difference in product offerings, brand image, higher quality, advanced technology, or superior service to charge a higher price while targeting a broad array of market segments.

cost focus strategy

Involves controlling expenses and, in turn, lowering product prices targeting a narrow range of market segments.

differentiation focus strategy

Requires products to have significant points of difference to target one or only a few market segments.

2. A **differentiation strategy** (cell 2) requires products to have significant points of difference in product offerings, brand image, higher quality, advanced technology, or superior service to charge a higher price while targeting a broad array of market segments. This allows the firm to charge a price premium. For example, OnStar Canada is the nation's leading provider of in-vehicle safety and security. Using advanced technology and superior customer service, the company ensures that customers have reliable communications while in their vehicles.

3. A **cost focus strategy** (cell 3) involves controlling expenses and, in turn, lowering product prices, targeting a narrow range of market segments. Retail chains targeting only a few market segments in a restricted group of products—such as Office Depot in office supplies—have used a cost focus strategy successfully. Similarly, some airlines have been very successful in offering low fares between very restricted pairs of cities.

4. A **differentiation focus strategy** (cell 4) requires products to have significant points of difference to target one or only a few market segments. Volkswagen has achieved spectacular success by targeting the "nostalgia segment," 35- to 55-year-old baby boomers, with its technology-laden Beetle, while Stratus Vineyards focuses on a niche market of consumers looking for a high-priced, ultra-premium wine.

● **FIGURE 19–4**

Porter's four generic business strategies

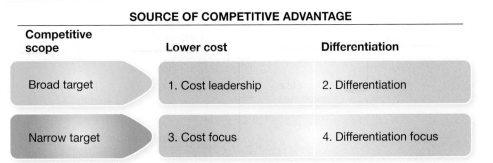

SOURCE OF COMPETITIVE ADVANTAGE		
Competitive scope	Lower cost	Differentiation
Broad target	1. Cost leadership	2. Differentiation
Narrow target	3. Cost focus	4. Differentiation focus

These strategies also form the foundation for Michael Porter's theory about what makes a nation's industries successful, as was discussed in Chapter 7.

Profit Enhancement Options   If a business wants to increase, or "enhance," its profits, it can (1) increase revenues, (2) decrease expenses, or (3) do both. Among these "profit enhancement options," let us look first at the strategy options of increasing revenues and then at those for decreasing expenses.

The strategy option of increasing revenues can be achieved only by using one or a combination of four ways to address present or new markets and products (Figure 19–5): (1) market penetration, (2) product development, (3) market development, and (4) diversification (all of which were described in Chapter 2).

Procter & Gamble has followed a successful strategy of market penetration (present markets, present products) by concentrating its effort on becoming the market leader in each of its more than 30 product categories. It is currently first in market share in more than half these product categories. Efforts to increase customer satisfaction have also helped increase market penetration. It has also increased its market share in 19 of its 20 largest core brands by introducing product improvements and trimming retail prices.[14]

In contrast, Johnson & Johnson has succeeded with a product development strategy—finding new products for its present markets—to complement popular brands, such as Tylenol pain reliever and Acuvue contact lenses. To compete with Bristol-Myers and other companies, Johnson & Johnson developed Tylenol PM, a combination pain killer and sleeping pill, and Acuvue Oasis, a comfortable and disposable contact lens.

Walt Disney Co. pursued a market development strategy (new market, present product) following the success of the original Disneyland in Anaheim, California. The first market expansion was to Orlando, Florida, and then Tokyo and Paris. Disney has also pursued a diversification strategy by entering into the motion picture business with the development of Touchstone Pictures, a film studio, and Disney Cruise Line, a family-oriented cruise ship line.

Canadian Tire has pursued a multipronged strategy, including increased market penetration in existing markets; market development (geographic expansion);

● **FIGURE 19–5**
Profit enhancement options for increasing a firm's profits

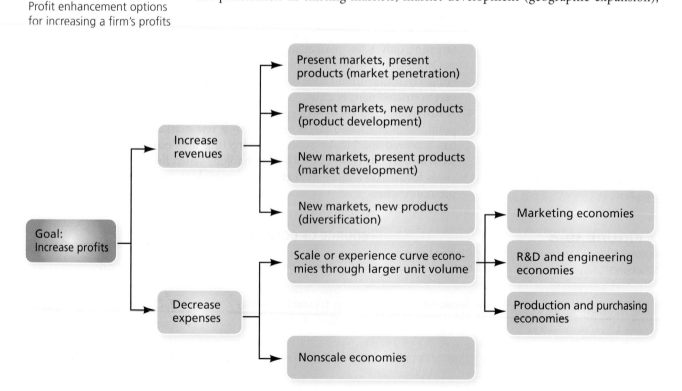

introducing new products to expand its current product line; and diversification through the acquisition of Mark's Work Wearhouse, the establishment of retail gasoline stations and retail car washes, and participation in the financial services business, including banking, insurance, and credit card services.

Strategy options for decreasing expenses fall into two broad categories (see Figure 19–5). One is relying on scale economies or experience-curve benefits from an increased volume of production to drive unit costs down and gross margins up, the best-known examples being consumer electronic devices such as DVD players, prices of which fell by half over a period of just a few years. Scale economies may occur in marketing, as well as in R&D, engineering, production, and purchasing.

The other strategy option to decrease expenses is simply finding other ways to reduce costs, such as cutting the number of managers, increasing the effectiveness of the salesforce through more training, or reducing product rejects by improving quality. Procter & Gamble concluded that the world did not really need 31 varieties of Head & Shoulders shampoo, and so it cut the number of packages, sizes, and formulas and thereby reduced expenses and increased profits.

Market–Product Synergies   Using the market–product grid framework introduced in Chapter 9, we can see two kinds of synergy that are critical in developing corporate and marketing strategies: (1) marketing synergy, and (2) R&D–manufacturing synergy. While the following example involves external synergies through mergers and acquisitions, the concepts apply equally well to internal synergies sought in adding new products or seeking new markets.

A critical step in the external analysis is to assess how these merger and acquisition strategies provide the organization with synergy—the increased customer

Marketing Matters

A Key Strategy Issue: Finding Synergies

The Molson–Coors merger created the fifth-largest brewing company in the world. It also created synergy—with the potential to generate $175 million a year in cost savings and new revenues. This merger follows Molson's acquisition of Kaiser in Brazil and Coors' acquisition of British Carling brands. The companies believe that the merger creates a stronger company in a consolidating global beer industry. Another major merger that created plenty of synergy was the Procter & Gamble–Gillette merger. It resulted in one of the largest packaged goods companies in the world. Finally, Toronto Dominion Bank (TD) acquired BankNorth of New England, and then Commerce Bank of New Jersey to achieve synergy and obtain a presence in the lucrative American retail banking market. This merged firm resulted in cost savings, technology sharing, and increased revenues. TD also acquired Ameritrade to gain a presence in the wealth management and brokerage segment of the financial services market.

To try your hand in this synergy game, assume that you are a vice president of marketing for Great Lawns Corp., which markets a line of nonpowered and powered walking and riding lawn mowers. A market–product grid for your business is shown here. You distribute your nonpowered mowers in all three market segments shown and powered walking mowers

only in suburban markets. However, you do not offer powered riding mowers for any of the three markets.

Here are your strategy dilemmas:

1. Where are the marketing synergies (efficiencies)?
2. Where are the R&D and manufacturing synergies (efficiencies)?
3. What would a market–product grid look like for an ideal company that Great Lawns could merge with for it to achieve both marketing and R&D/manufacturing synergies (efficiencies)?

For answers to these questions, read the text and study Figures 19–6 and 19–7.

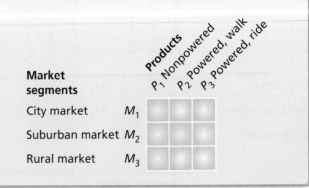

value achieved through performing organizational functions more efficiently. The "increased customer value" can take many forms: more products, improved quality on existing products, lower prices, improved distribution, and so on. But the ultimate criterion is that customers should be better off as a result of the increased synergy. The firm, in turn, should be better off by gaining more satisfied customers.

A market–product grid helps identify important trade-offs in the strategic marketing process. As noted in the nearby Marketing Matters box, "A Key Strategy Issue: Finding Synergies,"[15] assume you are vice president of marketing for Great Lawns Corporation's line of nonpowered lawn mowers and powered walking mowers sold to the consumer market. You are looking for new product and new market opportunities to increase your revenues and profits.

You conduct a market segmentation study and develop a market–product grid to analyze future opportunities. You identify three major segments in the consumer market based on geography: (1) city, (2) suburban, and (3) rural households. These market segments relate to the size of lawn a consumer must mow. The product clusters are (1) nonpowered, (2) powered walking, and (3) powered riding mowers. Five alternative marketing strategies are shown in the market–product grids in Figure 19–6. The important marketing efficiencies—or synergies—run horizontally across the rows in Figure 19–6. Conversely, the important R&D and production efficiencies—or synergies—run vertically down the columns. Let us look at the synergy effects for the five combinations in Figure 19–6:[16]

1. *Market–product concentration.* The firm benefits from "focus" on a single product line and market segment, but it loses opportunities for significant synergies in both marketing and R&D–manufacturing.
2. *Market specialization.* The firm gains marketing synergy through providing a complete product line, but R&D–manufacturing have the difficulty of developing and producing two new products.
3. *Product specialization.* The firm gains R&D–manufacturing synergy through production economies of scale, but gaining market distribution in the three different geographic areas will be costly.
4. *Selective specialization.* The firm does not get either marketing or R&D–manufacturing synergies because of the uniqueness of the market–product combinations.
5. *Full coverage.* The firm has the maximum potential synergies in both marketing and R&D–manufacturing. The question is whether it is spread too thin due to the resource requirements needed to reach all market–product combinations.

The Marketing Matters box, "A Key Strategy Issue: Finding Synergies," posed the question of what the ideal partner for Great Lawns would be if it merged with another firm, given the market–product combinations shown in the box. If, as vice president of marketing, you want to follow a full-coverage strategy, then the ideal merger

● **FIGURE 19-6**

Market–product grid of alternative strategies for a lawn mower manufacturer

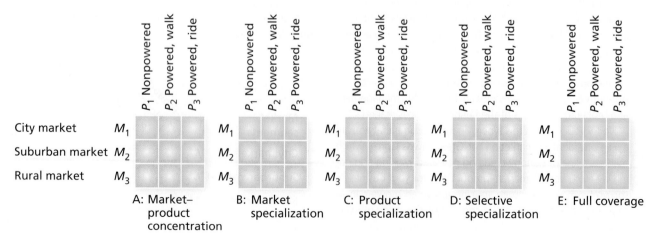

● **FIGURE 19-7**

An ideal merger for Great Lawns to obtain full market–product coverage

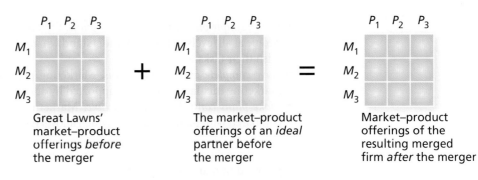

Great Lawns' market–product offerings *before* the merger   The market–product offerings of an *ideal* partner before the merger   Market–product offerings of the resulting merged firm *after* the merger

partner is shown in Figure 19–7. This would give the maximum potential synergies—if you are not spreading your merged companies too thin. Marketing gains by having a complete product line in all regions, and R&D–manufacturing gains by having access to new markets that can provide production economies of scale through producing larger volumes of its existing products.

---

learning review

4. Describe Porter's four generic business strategies.

5. What are four alternative ways to increase a firm's profit when considering profit enhancement options and strategies?

6. Where do (*a*) marketing synergies and (*b*) R&D–manufacturing synergies appear in a market–product grid framework?

LO3 Some Planning and Strategy Lessons

Applying these frameworks is not automatic but requires a great deal of managerial judgment. Common-sense requirements of an effective marketing plan are discussed next, followed by problems that can arise.

Guidelines for an Effective Marketing Plan Dwight D. Eisenhower, when he commanded Allied armies in World War II, made his classic observation, "Plans are nothing; planning is everything." It is the process of careful planning that focuses an organization's efforts and leads to success. The plans themselves, which change with events, are often secondary. Effective planning and plans are inevitably characterized by identifiable objectives, specific strategies or courses of action, and the means to execute them. Here are some guidelines in developing effective marketing plans:

- *Set measurable, achievable goals.* Ideally, goals should be quantified and measurable in terms of what is to be accomplished and by when. "Increase market share from 18 to 22 percent by December 31, 2012" is preferable to "Maximize market share given our available resources." Also, to motivate people, the goals must be achievable.
- *Use a base of facts and valid assumptions.* The more a marketing plan is based on facts and valid assumptions, rather than guesses, the less are the uncertainty and risk associated with executing it. Good marketing research helps. For example, General Mills' research indicates a basic fact that busy consumers on the go want very convenient food products—ones they can eat with one hand. So, when Steve Sanger, CEO of General Mills, receives plans for a new food product from his employees, he asks one question: Does it have the "one-handedness" feature that consumers want? Without that feature, the marketing plan for that product is not likely to be successful.

- *Utilize simple but clear and specific plans.* Effective execution of plans requires that people at all levels in the firm understand what, when, and how they are to accomplish their tasks.
- *Have complete and feasible plans.* Marketing plans must incorporate all the key marketing mix factors and be supported by adequate resources.
- *Make plans controllable and flexible.* Marketing plans must enable results to be compared with planned targets, which allows replanning—the flexibility to update the original plans.
- *Find the right person to implement the plans.* But make sure that person is heavily involved in making the plans.
- *Work toward consensus-building.* "Ownership" of the plan by team members and stakeholders increases the chances for its success.

Problems in Marketing Planning and Strategy   From post-mortems on company plans that did work and on those that did not work, a picture emerges of where problems occur in the planning phase of a firm's strategic marketing process. The following list explores these problems:

1. Plans may be based on very poor assumptions about environmental factors, especially changing economic conditions and competitors' actions. Canadians used to equate the name Listerine with mouthwash. But Scope started an anti-Listerine campaign and successfully convinced Canadians that mouthwash did not have to taste bad to work. The result? Listerine lost its position as market leader.
2. Planners and their plans may have lost sight of their customers' needs. But not the Papa John's pizza chain. The "better ingredients, better pizza" slogan makes the hair stand up on the back of the necks of Pizza Hut executives. The reason is that this slogan of Papa John's reflects the firm's obsessive attention to detail, which is stealing market share from the much bigger Pizza Hut! Sample detail: If the cheese on the pizza shows a single air bubble or the crust is not golden brown, the offending pizza is not served to the customer!
3. Too much time and effort may be spent on data collection and writing the plans. Westinghouse has cut its planning instructions for operating units "that looked like an auto repair manual" to five or six pages.
4. Line operating managers often feel no sense of ownership in implementing the plans. Andy Grove, when he was CEO of Intel, observed, "We had the very ridiculous system . . . of delegating strategic planning to strategic planners. The strategies these [planners] prepared had no bearing on anything we actually did."[17] The solution is to assign more planning activities to line operating managers—the people who actually carry them out.

Balancing Value and Values in Strategic Marketing Plans   Two important trends are likely to influence the strategic marketing process in the future. The first, *value-based planning,* combines marketing planning ideas and financial planning techniques to assess how much a division or strategic business unit (SBU) contributes to the price of a company's shares (or shareholder wealth). Value is created when the financial return of a strategic activity exceeds the cost of the resources allocated to the activity.

The second trend is the increasing interest in *value-driven strategies,* which incorporate concerns for ethics, integrity, employee health and safety, and environmental safeguards with more common corporate values, such as growth, profitability, customer service, and quality. As the nearby Making Responsible Decisions box, "Strategy Includes Good Citizenship and Sustainable Development," points out many Canadian companies are engaging in socially responsible and sustainable development practices and have integrated such activities as central components of their strategic plans.[18]

Making Responsible Decisions

Strategy Includes Good Citizenship and Sustainable Development

Many companies have integrated corporate social responsibility and sustainable development business practices into both their short-term and long-term strategic plans. For example, Transcontinental Inc. of Montreal is Canada's largest printing company. It has embedded the concepts of corporate citizenship and environmental responsibility into the company's strategic planning and implementation processes. Every year it develops a list of worthy causes and makes cash donations or provides free printing services to those causes. The company focuses on health, education, culture, and community development. It supports many hospitals and research centres, provides funds to major universities, and supports Centraide/United Way and the Heritage Canada fund. It also has a comprehensive environmental policy aimed to protect the natural environment. In fact, it establishes corporate objectives to improve its environmental performance in the same way it establishes its more traditional corporate objectives such as revenue and profitability.

Potash Corp. of Saskatchewan also engages in sustainable business practices. It was recently ranked among the top 50 global companies by SustainAbility, Inc, a global think tank that works in partnerships with the United Nations Environment Program. One area of focus for the company is demanding adherence to human rights standards from its suppliers, and this practice is an inherent part of the company's strategic sourcing process. Canadian Tire is another company that integrates good citizenship and

the protection of the environment into its traditional strategic planning and implementation processes. For example, the company has a comprehensive environment, health, and safety program, and managers of this program report to the company's board of directors outlining their activities and the goal-achievement with regard to this program.

Finally, Vancity is Canada's largest credit union. It is guided by its commitment to corporate social responsibility and to improve the quality of life in the communities in which it operates. It has a clear "statement of values" that includes the concepts of integrity, innovation, and responsibility. To ensure that it achieves its objectives with regard to these values, the company conducts a social audit process. It then publishes the results in an "accountability report" to provide a picture of its social and environmental performance. According to the company, "It's the business decisions you make as an organization, the people you hire to make them and the impact you leave on the community in which you do business that matter. And, at the end of day, how you do all these things is based on your organizational values. While [our accountability] report covers everything from our employee engagement scores to how much paper we recycle, it's really about what counts most: our values of integrity, innovation and responsibility."

What are your thoughts on these companies who make value-driven strategies an important part of the strategic focus? Importantly, what about the companies who do not make such a commitment?

Finally, remember that it is easier to talk about planning than to do it well. Try your hand as a consultant to help Trevor's Toys make some strategic decisions, as described in the nearby Going Online box, "Want to Be a BCG Consultant? Solve the Trevor's Toys Online Case."

THE IMPLEMENTATION PHASE OF THE STRATEGIC MARKETING PROCESS

The Monday-morning diagnosis of a losing football coach often runs something like, "We had an excellent game plan; we just didn't execute it."

Is Planning or Implementation the Problem?

The planning-versus-execution issue applies to the strategic marketing process as well: A difficulty when a marketing plan fails is determining whether the failure is due to a poor plan or poor implementation.[19]

Effective managers tracking progress on a struggling plan first try to identify whether the problems involve (1) the plan and strategy, (2) its implementation, or

Marketing implementation	MARKETING PLANNING AND STRATEGY	
	Good (appropriate)	Bad (inappropriate)
Good (effective)	1. *Success:* Marketing program achieves its objectives.	2. *Trouble:* Solution lies in recognizing that only the strategy is at fault and correcting it.
Bad (ineffective)	3. *Trouble:* Solution lies in recognizing that only implementation is at fault and correcting it.	4. *Failure:* Marketing program flounders and fails to achieve its objectives.

(3) both, and then they try to correct the problems. But as discussed earlier in the chapter, research on what really works shows that successful firms have excellence on both the planning and strategy side and the implementation and execution side. For example, General Electric's continuing leadership in lighting combines strong innovative products (planning and strategy) with excellent advertising and distribution (implementation and execution). Figure 19–8 shows the outcomes of (1) good and bad marketing planning, and (2) good and bad marketing implementation.

Increasing Emphasis on Marketing Implementation

The implementation phase of the strategic marketing process has emerged as a key factor to success by moving many planning activities away from the duties of planners to those of line managers.

General Electric's Jack Welch has become a legend in making GE far more efficient and far better at implementation. When Welch became CEO of GE, he faced an organization mired in red tape, turf battles, and slow decision making. Further, Welch saw GE bogged down with 25,000 managers and close to a dozen layers between him and the factory floor. In his "delayering," he sought to cut GE's levels in half and to speed up decision making and implementation by building an atmosphere of trust and autonomy among his managers and employees.

In terms of implementation and meeting key goals, Welch also insisted that GE's departments be "winners"—or #1 or #2 in their industry in terms of revenues and profits. Welch had another mantra for these departments: "Fix, close, or sell!" Under his leadership, more than 100 GE businesses were closed or sold. An example is GE's small appliance division that was sold to Black & Decker. The remaining GE businesses were either running well or were "fixed"—in Welch's terms. Although there are debates on some Welch strategies, businesses around the world are using GE's focus on implementation as a benchmark.

Going Online

Want to Be a BCG Consultant? Solve the Trevor's Toys Online Case

The Boston Consulting Group, or BCG, is probably best known for its "growth–share" portfolio matrix. As a very active and respected management consulting organization, BCG maintains a Web site to describe its services. Included in its Web site is an interactive strategy case that asks potential employees to analyze typical strategic challenges faced by BCG clients.

Go to the BCG Web site and assess the e-commerce strategy for Trevor's Toys. You can access the case by going to **www.bcg.com/join_bcg/interview_prep/interactive_case/default.aspx.** Read the case carefully, solve it within the time limits, and consider becoming a BCG consultant after graduation!

An example of where GE combines both planning and implementation is its much-publicized "ecomagination" initiative. This campaign includes goals of doubling its investment in research and development, reducing greenhouse gas emissions, and increasing revenues from its ecomagination-products that aid the environment—such as more efficient lighting, lower-emission aircraft engines, and solar-energy hybrid locomotives. This ecomagination program led GE to re-lamp 62 of its facilities using the products from its Lighting Division, both to reduce greenhouse emissions and to lower its energy costs.[20]

Improving Implementation of Marketing Programs

No magic formula exists to guarantee effective implementation of marketing plans. In fact, the answer seems to be equal parts of good management skills and practices, from which have come some guidelines for improving program implementation.

Communicate Goals and the Means to Achieving Them   Those called on to implement plans need to understand both the goals sought and how they are to be accomplished. Everyone in Papa John's—from founder John Schnatter to telephone order takers and make-line people—is clear on what the firm's goal is: to deliver better pizzas using better ingredients. The firm's orientation packet for employees lists its six "core values," which executives are expected to memorize. Sample: Core value no. 4 is "PAPA," or "People Are Priority No. 1, Always."[21]

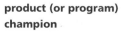

product (or program) champion
A person who is able and willing to cut red tape and move the program forward.

Have a Responsible Program Champion Willing to Act   Successful programs almost always have a **product (or program) champion** who is able and willing to cut red tape and move the program forward. Such people often have the uncanny ability to move back and forth between big-picture strategy questions and specific details when the situation calls for it. Program champions are notoriously brash in overcoming organizational hurdles. In many cases, they adhere to the axiom, "Better to ask forgiveness than permission." Using this strategy, 3M's Art Fry championed Post-it Notes to success, an idea he got when looking for a simple way to mark places in his hymnal while singing in his church choir.

Reward Successful Program Implementation   When an individual or a team is rewarded for achieving the organization's goal, they have maximum incentive to see a program implemented successfully because they have personal ownership and a stake

What are some of the benefits General Electric achieved in its "ecomagination" initiative? For the answer, which shows GE's world-class program planning and implementation, see the text.

General Electric Company
www.ge.com

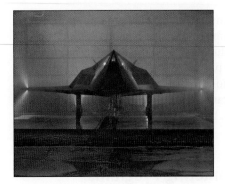

in its success. At a General Electric surge protector plant, employees receive a bonus for each quarter that the facility meets plantwide performance goals.

Take Action and Avoid "Paralysis by Analysis" Management experts warn against paralysis by analysis, the tendency to excessively analyze a problem instead of taking action. To overcome this pitfall, they call for a "bias for action" and recommend a "do it, fix it, try it" approach.[22] Conclusion: Perfectionists finish last, so getting 90 percent perfection and letting the marketplace help in the fine-tuning makes good sense in implementation.

Lockheed Martin's Skunk Works got its name from the comic strip *L'il Abner* and its legendary reputation from achieving superhuman technical feats with a low budget and ridiculously short deadlines by stressing teamwork. Under the leadership of Kelly Johnson, Skunk Works turned out a series of world-class aircraft, from the world's fastest (the SR-71 Blackbird) to the most untraceable aircraft (the F-117 Stealth fighter). Two of Kelly Johnson's basic tenets: (1) make decisions promptly, and (2) avoid paralysis by analysis. In fact, one study showed that Johnson's Skunk Works could carry out a program on schedule with 126 people, whereas a competitor in a comparable program was behind schedule with 3,750 people.[23]

Foster Open Communication to Surface the Problems Success often lies in fostering a work environment that is open enough so that employees are willing to speak out without fear of recrimination when they see problems. The focus is placed on trying to solve the problem as a group rather than finding someone to blame. Solutions are solicited from anyone who has a creative idea to suggest—from the caretaker to the president—without regard to status or rank in the organization.

Two more Kelly Johnson axioms from Lockheed Martin's Skunk Works apply here: (1) When trouble develops, surface the problem immediately, and (2) get help; do not keep the problem to yourself. This may mean getting ideas from competitors. Moreover, it may also mean combing your own entire firm as well as key suppliers and distributors to find talented people with solutions.

Schedule Precise Tasks, Responsibilities, and Deadlines Successful implementation requires that people know the tasks for which they are responsible and the deadline for completing them. To implement the tasks required to carry out its marketing plans, the Royal Canadian Mint prepares an **action item list** that has three columns: (1) the task, (2) the name of the person responsible for accomplishing that task, and (3) the date by which the task is to be finished. Action item lists are forward looking, clarify the targets, and put strong pressure on people to achieve their designated tasks by the deadline.

Related to the action item lists are formal *program schedules,* which show the relationships through time of the various program tasks. Scheduling an action program involves (1) identifying the main tasks, (2) determining the time required to complete each, (3) arranging the activities to meet the deadline, and (4) assigning responsibilities to complete each task.

Scheduling program activities can be done efficiently with *Gantt charts* developed by Henry L. Gantt. This method is the basis for the scheduling techniques used today, including elaborate computerized methods. The key to all scheduling techniques is to distinguish tasks that must be done sequentially from those that *can* be done concurrently. Scheduling tasks concurrently often reduces the total time required for a program. Software programs, such as Microsoft Project, simplify the task of developing a schedule or a Gantt chart.

action item list

An aid to implementing a market plan, consisting of three columns: (1) the task, (2) the name of the person responsible for completing that task, and (3) the date by which the task is to be finished.

7. Why is it important to include line operating managers in the planning process?

8. What is the meaning and importance of a program champion?

9. Explain the difference between sequential and concurrent tasks in a Gantt chart.

 ## Organizing for Marketing

A marketing organization is needed to implement the firm's marketing plans. Basic issues in today's marketing organizations include understanding (1) how line versus staff positions and divisional groupings interrelate to form a cohesive marketing organization, and (2) the role of the marketing or product manager.

line positions

People in line positions, such as senior marketing managers, who have the authority and responsibility to issue orders to the people who report to them, such as product managers.

staff positions

People in staff positions who have the authority and responsibility to advise people in the line positions but cannot issue direct orders to them.

Line versus Staff and Divisional Groupings   Although simplified, Figure 19–9 shows the organization of a typical business unit in a consumer packaged goods firm, such as Kraft Canada. This business unit shown in Figure 19–9 consists of Dinner Products, Baked Goods, and Desserts. It highlights the distinction between **line positions** and **staff positions** in marketing. People in line positions, such as senior marketing manager for Biscuits, have the authority and responsibility to issue orders to the people who report to them, such as the two product managers shown in Figure 19–9.

In this organizational chart, line positions are connected with solid lines. Those in staff positions (shown by dotted lines) have the authority and responsibility to advise people in line positions but cannot issue direct orders to them.

● **FIGURE 19–9**
Organization of a Pillsbury business unit, showing product or brand groups

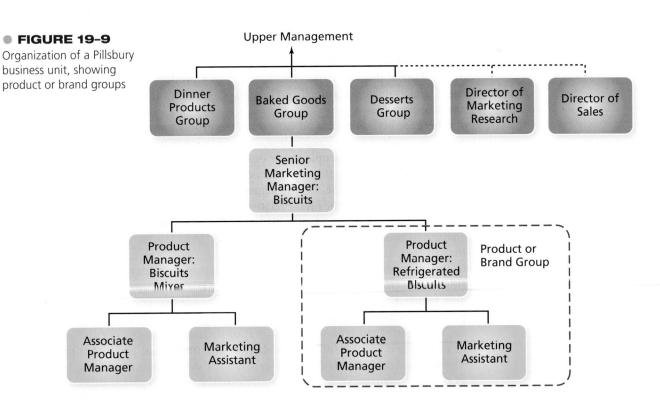

product line groupings
Organizational groupings in which a unit is responsible for specific product offerings.

functional groupings
Organizational groupings, such as manufacturing, marketing, and finance, which are the different business activities within a firm.

geographical groupings
Organizational groupings in which a unit is subdivided according to geographical location.

market-based groupings
Organizational groupings that utilize specific customer segments.

Most marketing organizations use divisional groupings—such as product line, functional, geographical, and market-based—to implement plans and achieve their organizational objectives. Some of these appear in some form in the organizational chart in Figure 19–9. The top of the chart shows organization by **product line groupings,** in which a unit is responsible for specific product offerings, such as Dinner Products or Baked Goods.

At levels higher than those shown in Figure 19–9, firms may be organized by **functional groupings,** such as manufacturing, marketing, and finance, which are the different business activities within a firm.

Many packaged goods firms use **geographical groupings,** in which sales territories are subdivided according to geographic location. Each director of sales has several regional sales managers reporting to him or her, such as western, eastern, and so on. These, in turn, have district managers reporting to them, with the field sales representatives at the lowest levels.

A fourth method of organizing a company is to use **market-based groupings,** which utilize specific customer segments, such as the banking, health care, or manufacturing segments. When this method of organizing is combined with product groupings, the result is a *matrix organization.*

A relatively recent position in consumer products firms is the *category manager* (senior marketing manager in Figure 19–9). Category managers have profit-and-loss responsibility for an entire product line—all biscuit brands, for example. They attempt to reduce the possibility of one brand's actions hurting another brand in the same category. Procter & Gamble uses category managers to organize by "global business units," such as baby care and beauty care. Cutting across country boundaries, these global business units implement standardized worldwide pricing, marketing, and distribution.[24]

Role of the Product Manager   The key person in the product or brand group shown in Figure 19–10 is the manager who heads it. This person is often called the *product manager* or *brand manager.* This person and the assistants in the product group are the basic building blocks in the marketing department of most consumer and industrial product firms. The function of a product manager is to plan, implement, and evaluate the annual and long-range plans for the products for which he or she is responsible.

There are both benefits and dangers to the product manager system. On the positive side, product managers become strong advocates for the assigned products, cut red tape to work with people in various functions both inside and outside the organization (see Figure 19–10), and assume profit-and-loss responsibility for the performance of the product line. On the negative side, even though product managers have major responsibilities, they have relatively little direct authority, and so most groups and functions shown in Figure 19–10 must be coordinated to meet the product's goals.[25] To coordinate the many units, product managers must use persuasion rather than orders.

But as more Canadian firms embrace customer-intimacy, customer relationship management (CRM), and customer experience management (CEM) strategies, product managers are no longer the only ones responsible for managing the product or customer base. Some Canadian firms have created new positions, such as "manager of student segment," "VP of financial services clients," or "director of customer management," which shadow the traditional product manager roles. These firms have divided their organizations into "customer-facing roles" (such as segment managers). More and more often, it is the segment managers, not the product managers, who make the final decisions on product, price, promotion, and place (distribution).

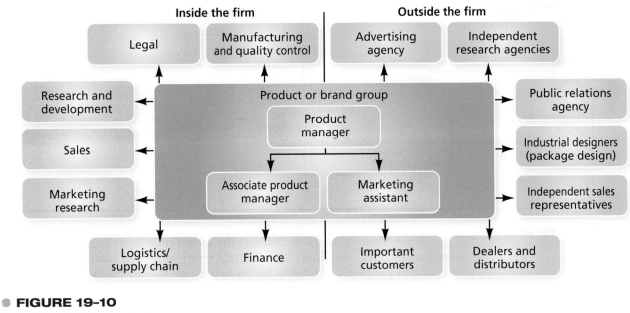

● FIGURE 19-10
Units with which the product manager and product group work

LO5 THE EVALUATION PHASE OF THE STRATEGIC MARKETING PROCESS

The essence of evaluation, the final phase of the strategic marketing process, is to compare results with planned goals for the marketing program in order to take necessary corrective actions.

The Marketing Evaluation Process

Ideally, quantified goals from the marketing plans developed in the planning phase have been accomplished by the marketing actions taken in the implementation phase (Figure 19–11) and measured as results in the evaluation phase. A marketing manager then uses management by exception, which means identifying results that deviate from plans to diagnose their causes and take new actions.

Often, results fall short of plans, and a corrective action is needed. For example, after 50 years of profits, Caterpillar accumulated losses of $1 billion. To correct the problem, Caterpillar focused its marketing efforts on core products and reduced its manufacturing costs. When results are better than plans, the marketing manager tries to identify the reason and move quickly to exploit the unexpected opportunity.

Evaluation Involves Marketing ROI, Metrics, and Dashboards

In the past decade, measuring the performance of marketing activities has become a central focus in many organizations. This boils down to some form of the question, "What measure can I use to determine if my company's marketing is effective?"

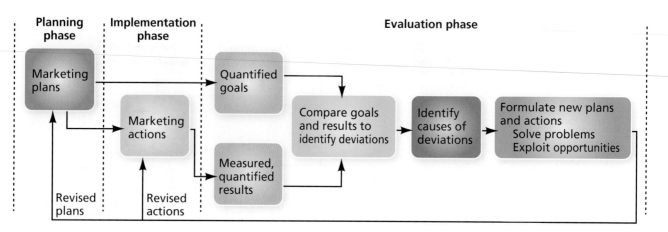

Planning phase | **Implementation phase** | **Evaluation phase**

● FIGURE 19–11

The evaluation phase of the strategic marketing process

marketing ROI

The application of modern measurement technologies to understand, quantify, and optimize marketing spending.

Strange. It's only breakfast and your toothpaste has already called it a day.

Unless you use Colgate Total.

Colgate *Total*

12-Hour Protection

No single measure exists. In finance, the return on investment (ROI) measure relates the total investment made to the total return generated from the investment. The concept has been extended to trying to measure the effectiveness of marketing expenditures with **marketing ROI,** the application of modern measurement technologies to understand, quantify, and optimize marketing spending.[26]

The evaluation phase of the strategic marketing process tries to improve marketing ROI through the effective use of marketing metrics and dashboards:

- *Marketing metrics.* Depending on the specific objective sought, one or a few key marketing metrics are chosen, such as market share, cost per lead, retention rate, cost per click, sales per square foot, and so on.[27] This is the "quantified goals" step in Figure 19–11.
- *Marketing dashboards.* If the financial resources and technology are available, the marketing metrics are displayed—often hourly or daily on the manager's computer. With today's syndicated scanner data, Internet clicks, and TV viewership tracking, the typical manager faces information overload. So effective marketing dashboard displays highlight—often in colour—where actual results vary significantly from plans. This alerts the manager to potential problems.[28]

These highlighted exceptions, or deviations from plans in Figure 19–11, are the immediate focus of the marketing manager. Marketing managers then try to improve their marketing ROI by correcting shortfalls and exploiting results that exceed plans.

Taking Marketing Actions   The sole reason for marketing metrics and dashboards is to provide managers useful, timely information that leads to logical actions. Beaten badly for years in the U.S. toothpaste market by P&G's Crest, in the late 1990s Colgate went on the offensive. It used new technology and aggressive marketing actions to introduce its Total toothpaste. Not only does Total clean teeth, but also its germ-fighting feature helps heal gingivitis, a bleeding-gum disease. This has helped Colgate achieve the highest market share in the U.S. toothpaste market.[29]

A Dashboard Look at a Career in Marketing

Let's see how marketing dashboards and metrics affect the everyday work life of a marketer.

If you choose a career in marketing, you will soon find that the on-the-job strategic marketing process discussed in the book is really a whirlwind of ideas, issues, and concerns that are volunteered to you by your bosses, the salesforce, market research analysts, operations professionals, your distributor partners, happy and unhappy customers, and even friends and family. These people are all genuinely interested in giving their opinion. More importantly, they all want to help you and your business succeed. Let's apply the challenge–findings–action steps from the book's Using Marketing Dashboards boxes to what your life will look like if you choose a career in marketing.

Your Challenge   Most of the issues and concerns that will be shared with you as a marketing professional are *not* carefully researched, evaluated, or considered. There simply isn't time. And your colleagues will ask you, "Isn't that your job?"

The exciting challenge you have, as a marketing professional, is to evaluate what you hear, distill out important themes, and set in motion actions that grow the business. Almost always the problem starts in some way with increasing revenues and profits, or "growing the business." For example, as marketing manager for Nike, you discover sales of your new, just-launched sneakers aren't up to company expectations.

Your Findings   Many factors impact your business, including pricing, distribution, sales velocity, new products, other marketing variables, and competition. Analyzing sales by region, you discover most regions are doing well but the western region is lagging badly. Further research shows that many western retailers are out of stock.

Your Action   In many marketing positions, you will find that you have little time to reflect and ponder in your busy workday. Many marketplace changes are simply out of your control, and your opinion and decisions will be sought quickly on what to do. In growing your sneaker business, you make calls and write e-mails to overcome your distribution problems in the western region and get your sneakers on those shelves—ASAP!

After all the data collection and analysis, marketing professionals always ask the same question: "What's our action?"

Marketing Careers Are Exciting

What does it take to be a good marketer? If you are considering going into marketing, the "Planning a Career in Marketing" appendix that accompanies this text gives a practical guide to career alternatives, résumés, information steps, and the job search process.

A career in marketing is exciting but is not for everyone. It can take the patience of a career counsellor, the mathematical rigour of an economist, and an undying passion to understand and provide what the consumer wants to buy. And let's not forget the confidence to make decisive decisions on incomplete information, learning from past mistakes, and having a continuing focus on the consumer.

And . . . it's always a challenge!

---

learning review

10. What is the difference between line and a staff positions in a marketing organization?

11. What are four groupings used within a typical marketing organization?

12. What two components of the strategic marketing process are compared to evaluate a marketing program?

LEARNING OBJECTIVES REVIEW

LO1   **Explain how marketing managers allocate their limited resources.**

Marketing managers use the strategic marketing process and marketing information, such as marketing plans, sales reports, and action memos, to effectively allocate their scarce resources to exploit the competitive advantages of their products. Marketers may use either sales response functions or market share (share point) analysis to help them assess what the market's response will be to additional marketing efforts.

LO2 Describe three marketing planning frameworks: Porter's generic strategies, profit enhancement options, and market-product synergies.

Three useful frameworks to improve marketing planning are (*a*) Porter's generic business strategies, (*b*) profit enhancement options, and (*c*) market–product synergies. Porter identifies four generic business strategies that firms can adopt: (*1*) a cost leadership strategy, which focuses on reducing expenses to lower product prices while targeting a broad array of market segments; (*2*) a differentiation strategy, which requires products to have significant points of difference to charge a premium price while targeting a broad array of market segments; (*3*) a cost focus strategy, which involves controlling costs to lower prices of products targeted at a narrow range of market segments; and (*4*) a differentiation focus strategy, which requires products to have significant points of difference to reach one or only a few market segments.

A second marketing planning framework is to use profit enhancement options to increase sales revenues, decrease costs, or both. To increase revenues, marketers can use one or a combination of four strategies to focus on present or new products or markets: (*1*) market penetration (selling more of a product to existing markets); (*2*) market development (selling an existing product to new markets); (*3*) product development (selling a new product to existing markets); and (*4*) diversification (selling a new product to new markets). To reduce expenses, marketers can (*a*) generate additional economies of scale in marketing and production costs, and (*b*) reduce personnel and other non-marketing costs, product rejects through improved quality, and so forth.

The third framework is to use a market–product grid that results in two kinds of synergies: marketing synergies (efficiencies), which run horizontally across the row of the various products offered by the firm to a single market segment; and R&D–manufacturing synergies (efficiencies), which run vertically down a column of the various market segments targeted for a given product or product class. The interactions or synergy effects of these marketing and production efficiencies results in five alternative combinations: market–product concentration, market specialization, product specialization, selective specialization, and full coverage.

LO3 Explain what makes an effective marketing plan and some problems that often exist with it.

An effective marketing plan has measurable, achievable goals; uses facts and valid assumptions; is simple, clear, and specific; is complete and feasible; and is controllable and flexible. Some problems that arise with marketing plans are that marketers (*a*) base them on poor assumptions about the marketing environment; (*b*) lose sight of their customers' needs; (*c*) spend too much time and effort on data collection for and writing the actual plan; and (*d*) do not seek ownership of the plan by operating managers and others charged with its implementation.

LO4 Describe the alternatives for organizing a marketing department and the role of a product manager.

A marketing department must be organized to effectively implement a marketing plan. First, marketing organizations must distinguish between line positions, those individuals in the marketing organization who have the authority and responsibility to issue orders to people that report to them to carry out a particular aspect of the marketing plan, and staff positions, those individuals who have the authority and responsibility to advise but not directly order people in line positions to do something.

The role of the product manager is to interact with numerous people and groups both inside and outside the firm to coordinate the planning, implementation, and evaluation of the marketing plan and its budget on an annual and long-term basis for the products responsible.

LO5 Explain how marketing ROI, metrics, and dashboards relate to evaluating programs.

The evaluation phase of the strategic marketing process involves measuring the results of the actions from the implementation phase and comparing them with goals set in the planning phase. The marketing manager then takes action to correct negative deviations from the plan and to exploit positive ones. Today, managers want an answer to the question, "Are my marketing activities effective?" One answer is in using marketing ROI, which is the application of modern measurement technologies to understand, quantify, and optimize marketing spending. Quantifying a marketing goal with a carefully defined marketing metric and tracking this metric on a marketing dashboard can improve marketing ROI.

FOCUSING ON KEY TERMS

action item list p. 530
cost focus strategy p. 521
cost leadership strategy p. 520
differentiation focus strategy p. 521
differentiation strategy p. 521
functional groupings p. 532
generic business strategy p. 520
geographical groupings p. 532

line positions p. 531
market-based groupings p. 532
marketing ROI p. 534
product line groupings p. 532
product (or program) champion p. 529
sales response function p. 516
share points p. 517
staff positions p. 531

APPLYING MARKETING KNOWLEDGE

1 Assume a firm faces an S-shaped sales response function. What happens to the ratio of incremental sales revenue to incremental marketing effort at the (a) bottom, (b) middle, and (c) top of this curve?

2 What happens to the ratio of incremental sales revenue to incremental marketing effort when the sales response function is an upward-sloping straight line?

3 Assume General Mills has to decide how to how millions of dollars to try and expand its cereal and yogourt businesses. To allocate this money between these two businesses, what information would General Mills like to have?

4 Suppose your Great States lawn mower company has the market–product concentration situation shown in

Figure 19–6A. What are both the synergies and potential pitfalls of following expansion strategies of (a) market specialization and (b) product specialization?

5 Are value-driven strategies inconsistent with value-based planning? Give an example that supports your position.

6 The first Domino's Pizza restaurant was near a college campus. What implementation problems are (a) similar and (b) different for restaurants near a college campus versus a military base?

7 A common theme among managers who succeed repeatedly in program implementation is fostering open communication. Why is this so important?

8 Why are quantified goals in the planning phase of the strategic marketing process important for the evaluation phase?

Building Your Marketing Plan

Do the following activities to complete your marketing plan:

1. Draw a simple organization chart for your organization.

2. In terms of evaluation, list (a) the four or five critical factors (such as revenues, number of customers, variable costs) and (b) how frequently (monthly, quarterly)

you will monitor them to determine if special actions are needs to exploit opportunities or correct deviations.

3. Read Appendix A, "Creating an Effective Marketing Plan." Then, write a 600-word executive summary for your marketing plan using the numbered headings shown in Appendix A.

Video Case 19

GENERAL MILLS WARM DELIGHTS™: INDULGENT, DELICIOUS, AND GOOEY!

Vivian Milroy Callaway, vice president for the Center for Learning and Experimentation at General Mills, retells the story for the "indulgent, delicious, and gooey" Warm Delights™. She summarizes, "When you want something that is truly innovative, you have to look at the rules you have been assuming in your category and break them all!"

When a new business achieves a breakthrough, it looks easy to outsiders. The creators of Betty Crocker Warm Delights stress that if the marketing decisions had been based on the traditions and history of the cake category, a smaller, struggling business would have resulted. The team chose to challenge the assumptions and expectations of accumulated cake category business experience. The team took personal and business risks, and Warm Delights is a roaring success.

Planning Phase: Innovation, but a Shrinking Market

"In the typical grocery store, the baking mix aisle is a quiet place," says Callaway. Shelves sigh with flavours, types, and brands. Prices are low, but there is little consumer traffic. Cake continues to be a tradition for birthdays and social occasions. But consumer demand declines. The percentage of U.S. households that bought at least one baking mix in 2000 was 80 percent. Four years later, the percentage of households was 77 percent, a very significant decline.

Today, a promoted price of 89 cents to make a 9×12 inch cake is common. Many choices, but little differentiation, gradually falling sales, and low uniform prices are the hallmarks of a mature category. But it's not that consumers don't buy cake-like treats. In fact, indulgent treats are growing. The premium prices for ice cream ($3.00 a pint) and chocolate ($3.00 a bar) are not slowing consumer purchases.

The Betty Crocker marketing team challenged the food scientists at General Mills to create a great-tasting, easy-to-prepare, single-serve cake treat. The goal: Make it indulgent, delicious, and gooey. The team focused the scientists on a product that would have:

- Consistent great taste,
- Quick preparation,
- A single portion, and
- No cleanup.

The food scientists delivered the prototype! Now, the marketing team began hammering out the four Ps. They started with a descriptive name "Betty Crocker Dessert Bowls" (see photo) and a plan to shelve it in the "quiet" cake aisle. This practical approach would meet the consumer need for a "small, fast, microwave cake" for dessert. Several marketing challenges emerged:

- *The comparison problem.* The easy shelf price comparison to 9×12 inch cakes selling for 89 cents would make it harder to price Dessert Bowls at $2.00.
- *The communication problem.* The product message "a small, faster-to-make cake" wasn't compelling. For example, after-school snacks should be fast and small, but "dessert" sounds too indulgent.
- *The quiet aisle problem.* The cake-aisle shopper is probably not browsing for a cake innovation.
- *The dessert problem.* Consumer's on-the-go, calorie conscious meal plans don't generally include a planned dessert.
- *The microwave problem.* Consumers might not believe it tastes good.

In sum, the small, fast-cake product didn't resonate with a compelling consumer need. But it would be a safe bet because the Dessert Bowl positioning fit nicely with the family-friendly Betty Crocker brand.

Implementation Phase: Leaving the Security of Family Behind

The consumer insights team really enjoyed the hot, gooey cake product. They feared that it would languish in the cake aisle under the Dessert Bowl name because it didn't fully describe the essence of what the food delivered. They explored who really are the indulgent treat customers. The data revealed that the heaviest buyers of premium treats are women without children. This focused the team on a target consumer: "What does she want?" They enlisted an ad agency and consultants to come up with a name that would appeal to "her." Several independently suggested the "Warm Delights" name, which became the brand name.

An interesting postscript to the team's brand name research: A competitor apparently liked not only the idea of a quick, gooey, microwavable dessert but also the "Dessert Bowls" name! You may now see its competitive product on your supermarket's shelves.

Targeting the on-the-go women who want a small, personal treat had marketing advantages:

- The $2.00 Warm Delights price compared favourably to the price of many single-serve indulgent treats.
- The product food message "warm, convenient, delightful" is compelling.
- On-the-go women's meal plans do include the occasional delicious treat.

One significant problem remained: the cake-aisle shopper is probably not browsing for an indulgent, single-serve treat.

The marketing team solved this shelving issue by using advertising and product displays outside the cake aisle. This would raise women's awareness of Warm Delights. Television advertising and in-store display programs are costly, so Warm Delights sales would have to be strong to pay back the investment.

Vivian Callaway and the team turned to market research to fine-tune the plan. The research put Warm Delights (and Dessert Bowls) on the shelf in real (different) stores. A few key findings emerged. First, the name "Warm Delights" beat "Dessert Bowls." Second, the Warm Delights with nuts simply wasn't easy to prepare, so nuts were removed. Third, the packaging with a disposable bowl beat the typical cake-mix packaging involving using your own bowl. Finally, by putting the actual product on supermarket shelves and in displays in the stores, sales volumes could be analyzed.

Evaluation Phase: Turning the Plan into Action!

The marketing plan isn't action. Sales for "Warm Delights" required the marketing team to: (1) get the retailers to stock the product, preferably somewhere other than the cake aisle, and (2) appeal to consumers enough to have them purchase, like, and repurchase the product.

The initial acceptance of a product by retailers is important. But each store manager must experience good sales of Warm Delights to be motivated to keep its shelves restocked with the product. Also, the Warm Delights team must monitor the display activity in the store. Are the displays occurring as expected? Do the sales increase when a display is present? Watching distribution and display execution on a new product is very important so that sales shortfalls can be addressed proactively.

Did the customer buy one or two Warm Delights? Did the customer return for a second purchase a few weeks later? The syndicated services that sell household panel purchase data provide the answer. The Warm Delights team evaluates these reports to see if the number of people who tried the product matches with expectations and how the repeat purchases occur. Often, the "80/20 rule" applies. So, in the early months, is there a group of consumers that buys repeatedly and will fill this role?

For ongoing feedback, calls by Warm Delights consumers to the free consumer information line are monitored. This is a great source of real-time feedback. If a pattern emerges and these calls are mostly about the same problem, that is bad. However, when consumers call to say "thank you" or "it's great," that is good. This is an informal quick way to identify if the product is on track or further investigation is warranted.

Good Marketing Makes a Difference

The team took personal and business risks by choosing a Warm Delights plan over the more conservative Dessert Bowl plan. Today, General Mills has loyal Warm Delights consumers who are open to trying new flavours, new sizes, and new forms. If you were a consultant to the Warm Delights team, what would you do to grow this brand?

Questions

1 What is the competitive set of desserts in which Warm Delights is located?

2 (*a*) Who is the target market? (*b*) What is the point of difference on the positioning for Warm Delights? (*c*) What are the potential opportunities and hindrances of the target market and positioning?

3 (*a*) What marketing research did Vivian Callaway execute? (*b*) What were the critical questions that she sought research and expert advice to get answers to? (*c*) How did this affect the product's marketing mix price, promotion, packaging, and distribution decisions?

4 (*a*) What initial promotional plan directed to consumers in the target market did Callaway use? (*b*) Why did this make sense to Callaway and her team when Warm Delights was launched?

5 If you were a consultant to Vivian Callaway, what product changes would you recommend to increase sales of Warm Delights?

GLOSSARY

80/20 rule   A concept that suggests 80 percent of a firm's sales are obtained from 20 percent of its customers. p. 237

above-, at-, or below-market pricing   Setting prices based on pricing of similar products in the market. p. 347

account management policies   Policies that specify whom the salespeople should contact, what kinds of selling and customer service activities should be engaged in, and how these activities should be carried out. p. 502

action item list   An aid to implementing a market plan, consisting of three columns: (1) the task, (2) the name of the person responsible for completing that task, and (3) the date by which the task is to be finished. p. 530

adaptive selling   A need-satisfaction sales presentation that involves adjusting the presentation to fit the selling situation. p. 495

advertising   Any paid form of non-personal communication about an organization, good, service, or idea by an identified sponsor. pp. 431, 456

all-you-can-afford budgeting   Allocating funds to promotion only after all other budget items are covered. p. 442

attitude   A learned predisposition to respond to an object or class of objects in a consistently favourable or unfavourable way. p. 132

baby boomers   The generation of those born between 1946 and 1964. p. 79

back translation   Retranslating a word or phrase into the original language by a different interpreter to catch errors. p. 184

balance of trade   The difference between the monetary value of a nation's exports and imports. p. 171

barriers to entry   Business practices or conditions that make it difficult for new firms to enter a market. p. 90

beliefs   A consumer's subjective perception of how well a product or brand performs on different attributes. p. 132

benchmarking   Discovering how others do something better than your own firm so that you can imitate or leapfrog competition. p. 35

bidders' list   A list of firms believed to be qualified to supply a given item. p. 160

blended family   Family formed by the merging into a single family of two previously separated units. p. 80

blog   A personal Web site or Web page that contains the online personal journal of an individual. p. 88

bottom of the pyramid   The largest, but poorest socio-economic group of people in the world consisting of 4 billion people who reside in developing countries and live on less than $2 per day. p. 185

brand equity   The added value that a given brand name gives to a product beyond the functional benefits provided. p. 291

branding   Activity in which an organization uses a name, phrase, design, or symbols, or combination of these to identify its products and distinguish them from those of competitors. p. 290

brand licensing   A contractual agreement whereby a company allows another firm to use its brand name, patent, trade secret, or other property for a royalty or fee. p. 294

brand loyalty   A favourable attitude toward and consistent purchase of a single brand over time. p. 131

brand name   Any word, device (design, shape, sound, or colour), or combination of these used to distinguish a seller's goods or services. p. 290

brand personality   A set of human characteristics associated with a brand name. p. 291

breadth of product line   The variety of different items a store carries. p. 405

break-even analysis   A technique that analyzes the relationship between total revenue and total cost to determine profitability at various levels of output. p. 341

brokers   Independent firms or individuals whose principal function is to bring buyers and sellers together to make sales. p. 377

bundle pricing   The marketing of two or more products in a single "package" price. p. 345

business   The clear, broad, underlying industry or market sector of an organization's offering. p. 32

business analysis   The stage of the new-product process that involves specifying the product features and marketing strategy and making financial projections needed to commercialize a product. p. 270

business distributor   Performs a variety of marketing channel functions, including selling, stocking, delivering a full product assortment, and financing for business goods and services. p. 374

business goods   Products that assist directly or indirectly in providing products for resale (also known as *B2B goods*, *industrial goods*, or *organizational goods*). p. 255

business marketing   The marketing of goods and services to companies, governments, and not-for-profit organizations for use in the creation of goods and services that they can produce and market to others. p. 148

buy classes   Three types of organizational buying situations: new buy, straight rebuy, and modified rebuy. p. 157

buying centre   The group of people in an organization who participate in the buying process and share common goals, risks, and knowledge important to a purchase decision. p. 155

buzz marketing   Popularity created by consumer word of mouth. p. 135

capacity management   Making service capacity as productive as possible without compromising service quality. p. 321

category management   An approach that assigns a manager with the responsibility for selecting all products that consumers in a market segment might view as substitutes for each other, with the objective of maximizing sales and profits in the category. p. 416

cause marketing   Occurs when the charitable contributions of a firm are tied directly to the customer revenues produced through the promotion of one of its products. p. 112

caveat emptor   The legal concept of "let the buyer beware" that was pervasive in Canadian business culture before the 1960s. p. 106

census metropolitan areas (CMAs)   Geographic labour markets having a population of 100,000 persons or more. p. 80

central business district The oldest retail setting, the community's downtown area. p. 413

channel conflict Arises when one channel member believes another channel member is engaged in behaviour that prevents it from achieving its goals. p. 383

channel of communication The means of conveying a message to a receiver. p. 429

co-branding The pairing of two or more recognized brands on a single product or service. p. 296

code of ethics A formal statement of ethical principles and rules of conduct. p. 107

cognitive dissonance Feeling of post-purchase psychological tension or anxiety. p. 124

cohort brand management The bundling of one company's multiple brands into a single marketing effort aimed at a common consumer group. p. 298

commercialization The stage of the new-product process that involves positioning and launching a new product in full-scale production and sales. p. 272

communication The process of conveying a message to others, which requires six elements: a source, a message, a channel of communication, a receiver, and the processes of encoding and decoding. p. 429

community shopping centre A retail location that typically has one primary store (usually a department store branch) and 20 to 40 smaller outlets, serving a population of consumers who are within a 10- to 20-minute drive. p. 414

competencies An organization's special capabilities, including skills, technologies, and resources, that distinguish it from other organizations and provide value to its customers. p. 35

competition Alternative firms that could provide a product to satisfy a specific market's needs. p. 89

Competition Act The key legislation designed to protect competition and consumers in Canada. p. 93

competitive advantage A unique strength relative to competitors, often based on quality, time, cost, innovation, customer intimacy, or customer experience management. p. 35

competitive parity budgeting Matching the competitors' absolute level of spending or the proportion per point of market share. p. 441

consideration set The group of brands that a consumer would consider acceptable from among all the brands of which he or she is aware. p. 123

consultative selling Focuses on problem definition, where the salesperson serves as an expert on problem recognition and resolution. p. 495

consumer behaviour The actions that a person takes in purchasing and using products and services, including the mental and social processes that precede and follow these actions. p. 122

consumer ethnocentrism The tendency to believe that it is inappropriate, indeed immoral, to purchase foreign-made products. p. 184

consumer goods Products purchased by the ultimate consumer. p. 255

consumerism A grassroots movement started in the 1960s to increase the influence, power, and rights of consumers in dealing with institutions. p. 94

consumer-oriented sales promotions Sales tools used to support a company's advertising and personal selling efforts directed to ultimate consumers; examples include coupons, sweepstakes, and samples. p. 473

consumer socialization The process by which people acquire the skills, knowledge, and attitudes necessary to function as consumers. p. 136

convenience goods Items that the consumer purchases frequently and with a minimum of shopping effort. p. 256

cooperative advertising Advertising programs by which a manufacturer pays a percentage of the retailer's local advertising expense for advertising the manufacturer's products. p. 477

core values An organization's core values are the fundamental, passionate, and enduring principles that guide its conduct over time. p. 31

corporate level Level at which top management directs overall strategy for the entire organization. p. 29

cost focus strategy Involves controlling expenses and, in turn, lowering product prices targeting a narrow range of market segments. p. 521

cost leadership strategy Focuses on reducing expenses and lowering produce prices while targeting a broad array of market segments. p. 520

cost per thousand (CPM) The cost of reaching 1,000 individuals or households with an advertising message in a given medium. p. 462

cost-plus pricing Summing the total unit cost of providing a product or service and adding a specific amount to the cost to arrive at a price. p. 346

countertrade The practice of using barter rather than money for making global sales. p. 170

cross-cultural analysis Involves the study of similarities and differences among consumers in two or more nations or societies. p. 181

cross-functional teams A small number of people from different departments in an organization who are mutually accountable to accomplish a task or common set of performance goals. p. 30

cultural symbols Things that represent ideas and concepts. p. 182

culture The set of values, ideas, and attitudes that are learned and shared among the members of a group. p. 81

currency exchange rate The price of one country's currency expressed in terms of another country's currency. p. 187

customary pricing Setting prices dictated by tradition, standardized channels of distribution, or other competitive factors. p. 347

customer contact audit A flowchart of the points of interaction between consumer and service provider. p. 314

customer experience management (CEM) Managing the customers' interactions with the organization at all levels and at all touchpoints (direct and indirect contacts of the customer with an organization) so that the customer has a positive impression of the organization, is satisfied with the experience, and will remain loyal to the organization. p. 17

customer lifetime value (CLV) The profit generated by the customer's purchase of an organization's product or service over the customer's lifetime. p. 16

customer relationship management (CRM) The process of building and developing long-term relationships with customers by delivering customer value and satisfaction. p. 16

customer satisfaction The match between customer expectations of the product and the product's actual performance. p. 15

customer service The ability of logistics management to satisfy users in terms of time, dependability, communication, and convenience. p. 390

customer value The unique combination of benefits received by the customer that include quality, price, convenience, on-time delivery, and both before-sale and after-sale service. p. 15

customs Norms and expectations about the way people do things in a specific country. p. 182

data mining The extraction of hidden predictive information from large databases. p. 222

decoding The process of having the receiver take a set of symbols, the message, and transform them back to an abstract idea. p. 430

demand curve The summation of points representing the maximum number of products consumers will buy at a given price. p. 339

demographics The study of the characteristics of a human population. These characteristics include population size, growth rate, gender, marital status, ethnicity, income, and so forth. p. 78

depth interviews Detailed, individual interviews with people relevant to a research project. p. 208

depth of product line The store carries a large assortment of each item. p. 405

derived demand Demand for business products and services is driven by, or derived from, demand for consumer products and services. p. 152

development The stage of the new-product process that involves turning the idea on paper into a prototype. p. 270

differentiation strategy Requires products to have significant points of difference in product offerings, brand image, higher quality, advanced technology, or superior service to charge a higher price while targeting a broad array of market segments. p. 521

differentiation focus strategy Requires products to have significant points of difference to target one or only a few market segments. p. 521

direct channel A marketing channel where a producer and ultimate consumers deal directly with each other. p. 373

direct forecast Estimating the value to be forecast without any intervening steps. p. 246

direct investment A domestic firm actually investing in and owning a foreign subsidiary or division. p. 191

direct marketing Promotional element that uses direct communication with consumers to generate a response in the form of an order, a request for further information, or a visit to a retail outlet. p. 434

direct marketing channels Allow consumers to buy products by interacting with various advertising media without a face-to-face meeting with a salesperson. p. 375

direct orders The result of offers that contain all the information necessary for a prospective buyer to make a decision to purchase and complete the transaction. p. 447

discretionary income The money that remains after paying for taxes and necessities. p. 85

disintermediation Channel conflict that arises when a channel member bypasses another member and sells or buys products direct. p. 383

disposable income The money a consumer has left after paying taxes to use for such necessities as food, shelter, clothing, and transportation. p. 85

downsizing Reducing the content of packages without changing package size and maintaining or increasing the package price. p. 290

dumping Occurs when a firm sells a product in a foreign country below its domestic price or below its actual cost. p. 194

e-business All electronic-based company activities, both within and outside the company. p. 86

e-commerce Specific buying and selling processes on the Internet. p. 86

economic espionage The clandestine collection of trade secrets or proprietary information about a company's competitors. p. 106

economy Pertains to the income, expenditures, and resources that affect the cost of running a business and household. p. 84

eCRM A Web-centric, personalized approach to managing long-term customer relationships electronically. p. 16

eight Ps of service marketing Product, price, place, and promotion, as well as people, physical evidence, process, and productivity that constitute the services-marketing mix. p. 317

electronic marketing channels Employ the Internet to make goods and services available for consumption or use by consumers or business buyers. p. 375

e-marketing Also called *online marketing*, the marketing component of e-commerce. p. 86

e-marketplaces Online trading communities that bring together buyers and supplier organizations. p. 161

emotional intelligence The ability to understand one's own emotions and the emotions of people with whom one interacts on a daily basis. p. 503

encoding The process of having the sender transform an abstract idea into a set of symbols. p. 430

environmental forces The uncontrollable factors involving social, economic, technological, competitive, and regulatory forces. p. 11

environmental scanning The process of continually acquiring information on events occurring outside the organization to identify and interpret potential trends. p. 76

ethics The moral principles and values that govern the actions and decisions of an individual or group. pp. 18, 102

ethnic marketing Combinations of the marketing mix that reflect the unique attitudes, race or ancestry, communication preferences, and lifestyles of ethnic Canadians. p. 81

ethnographic research Observational approach to discover subtle emotional reactions as consumers encounter products in their "natural use environment." p. 216

evaluative criteria Factors that represent both the objective attributes of a brand (such as locate speed) and the subjective ones (such as brand prestige) you use to compare different products and brands. p. 123

experience curve pricing Pricing method based on production experience, that is, the unit cost of many products and services declines by 10 to 30 percent each time a firm's experience at producing and selling them doubles. p. 346

experiment Obtaining data by manipulating factors under tightly controlled conditions to test cause and effect. p. 212

exporting Producing goods in one country and selling them in another country. p. 189

extranet An Internet-based technology that permits communication between a company and its suppliers, distributors, and other partners. p. 86

failure fee A penalty payment a manufacturer makes to compensate a retailer for failed sales from its valuable shelf space. p. 273

family life cycle The distinct phases that a family progresses through from formation to retirement, each phase bringing with it identifiable purchasing behaviours. p. 236

feedback The communication flow from receiver back to the sender that helps the sender know whether the message was decoded and understood as intended. p. 431

field of experience Similar understanding and knowledge; to communicate effectively, a sender and a receiver must have a mutually shared field of experience. p. 430

fixed cost The firm's expenses that are stable and do not change with the quantity of product that is produced and cost. p. 341

focus groups An informal session of six to ten customers—past, present, or prospective—in which a discussion leader, or moderator, asks their opinions about the firm's and its competitors' products. p. 207

form of ownership Distinguishes retail outlets based on whether individuals, corporate chains, or contractual systems own the outlet. p. 403

formula selling presentation Providing information in an accurate, thorough, and step-by-step manner to inform the prospect. p. 495

four Is of services Four unique elements to services: intangibility, inconsistency, inseparability, and inventory. p. 309

franchising Contractual arrangement between a parent company (a franchisor) and an individual or firm (a franchisee) that allows the franchise to operate a certain type of business under an established name and according to specific rules. p. 379

frequency The average number of times a person in the target audience is exposed to a message or advertisement. p. 462

full-service agency An advertising agency providing the most complete range of services, including market research, media selection, copy development, artwork, and production. p. 470

functional groupings Organizational groupings, such as manufacturing, marketing, and finance, which are the different business activities within a firm. p. 532

functional level The level in an organization where groups of specialists actually create value for the organization. p. 30

gap analysis An evaluation tool that compares expectations about a service offering to the actual experience a consumer has with the service. p. 315

Generation X The population of those born between 1965 and 1976. p. 80

Generation Y Those born between 1977 and 1994. p. 80

generic business strategy Strategy that can be adopted by any firm, regardless of the product or industry involved, to achieve a competitive advantage. p. 520

geographical groupings Organizational groupings in which a unit is subdivided according to geographical location. p. 532

global brand A brand marketed under the same name in multiple countries with similar and centrally coordinated marketing programs. p. 180

global competition Exists when firms originate, produce, and market their products and services worldwide. p. 178

global consumers Consumer groups living in many countries or regions of the world that have similar needs or seek similar features and benefits from products or services. p. 180

global marketing strategy The practice of standardizing marketing activities when there are cultural similarities and adapting them when cultures differ. p. 179

goals Statements of an accomplishment of a task to be achieved, often by a specific time. p. 33

government units The federal, provincial, and local agencies that buy goods and services for the constituents they serve. p. 149

green marketing Marketing efforts to produce, promote, and reclaim environmentally sensitive products. p. 111

greenwashing Disinformation disseminated by an organization so as to present an environmentally responsible public image. p. 114

grey market A situation where products are sold through unauthorized channels of distribution. p. 194

gross domestic product (GDP) The monetary value of all goods and services produced in a country during one year. p. 171

gross income The total amount of money made in one year by a person, household, or family unit. p. 85

gross rating points (GRPs) A reference number for advertisers, created by multiplying reach (expressed as a percentage of the total market) by frequency. p. 462

hierarchy of effects The sequence of stages a prospective buyer goes through from initial awareness of a product to eventual action. p. 441

hypermarket A large store (more than 200,000 square feet) offering consumers everything in a single outlet. p. 406

idea generation Developing a pool of concepts as candidates for new products. p. 266

idle production capacity When the service provider is available but there is no demand. p. 311

indirect channel A marketing channel where intermediaries are inserted between the producer and consumers and perform numerous channel functions. p. 373

industrial firm An organizational buyer that, in some way, reprocesses a good or service it buys before selling it again to the next buyer. p. 149

infomercials Program-length (30-minute) advertisements that take an educational approach to communication with potential customers. p. 465

in-house agency A company's own advertising staff, which may provide full services or a limited range of services. p. 471

institutional advertisements Advertisements designed to build goodwill or an image for an organization, rather than promote a specific good or service. p. 457

integrated marketing communications (IMC) The concept of designing marketing communications programs that coordinate all promotional activities—advertising, personal selling, sales promotion, public relations, and direct marketing—to provide a consistent message across all audiences and to maximize the promotional budget and impact of the communications. p. 429

integrated multichannel retailing Utilizing a seamless combination of traditional store formats and non-store formats, such as catalogues, television, electronic kiosks and online retailing. p. 419

interactive marketing Involves two-way buyer–seller electronic communication in which the buyer can control the kind and amount of information received from the seller. p. 16

internal marketing The notion that in order for a service organization to serve its customers well, it must care for and treat its employees like valued customers. p. 320

intertype competition Competition between very dissimilar types of retail outlets. p. 406

intranet An Internet/Web-based network used within the boundaries of an organization. p. 86

involvement The personal, social, and economic significance of the purchase to the consumer. p. 125

ISO 14001 Worldwide standards for environmental quality and green marketing practices. p. 112

ISO 9000 standards Registration and certification of a manufacturer's quality management and quality assurance system. p. 154

joint venture An arrangement in which a foreign company and a local firm invest together to create a local business, sharing ownership, control, and profits of the new company. p. 190

just-in-time (JIT) concept An inventory supply system that operates with very low inventories and requires fast, on-time delivery. p. 395

key account management The practice of using team selling to focus on important customers so as to build mutually beneficial, long-term, cooperative relationships. p. 501

label An integral part of the package that typically identifies the product or brand, who made it, where and when it was made, how it is to be used, and package contents and ingredients. p. 298

laws Society's values and standards that are enforceable in the courts. p. 102

lead generation The result of an offer designed to generate interest in a product or service and a request for additional information. p. 447

learning Those behaviours that result from (1) repeated experience, and (2) thinking. p. 131

level of service The degree of service provided to the customer by self-, limited-, and full-service retailers. p. 403

licensing Offering the right to a trademark, patent, trade secret, or other similarly valued items of intellectual property in return for a royalty or a fee. p. 190

lifestyle A mode of living that is identified by how people spend their time and resources, what they consider important in their environment, and what they think of themselves and the world around them. p. 133

lifestyle centre An open-air cluster of specialty retailers, along with theatres, restaurants, fountains, play areas, and green spaces. p. 414

limited-service agency Specializes in one aspect of the advertising process, such as providing creative services to develop the advertising copy or buying previously unpurchased media space. p. 471

line positions People in line positions, such as senior marketing managers, who have the authority and responsibility to issue orders the people who report to them, such as product managers. p. 531

linear trend extrapolation The pattern is described with a straight line. p. 246

logistics management The practice of organizing the cost-effective flow of raw materials, in-process inventory, finished goods, and related information from point of origin to point of consumption to satisfy customer requirements. p. 385

loss-leader pricing Selling products below their customary prices to attract attention to them in the hope that customers will buy other products as well. p. 348

lost-horse forecast Making a forecast using the last known value and modifying it according to positive or negative factors expected in the future. p. 246

macromarketing The aggregate flow of a nation's goods and services to benefit society. p. 19

make-buy decision An evaluation of whether components and assemblies will be purchased from outside suppliers or built by the company itself. p. 159

manufacturer's agents Work for several producers and carry non-competitive, complementary merchandise in an exclusive territory; also called *manufacturer's representatives*. p. 377

market People with the desire and ability to buy a specific product. p. 6

market-based groupings Organizational groupings that utilize specific customer segments. p. 532

marketing The activity for creating, communicating, delivering, and exchanging offerings that benefit the organization, its stakeholders, and society at large. p. 5

marketing channel Individuals and firms involved in the process of making a product or service available for use or consumption by consumers or industrial users. p. 370

marketing concept The idea that an organization should strive to satisfy the needs of consumers, while also trying to achieve the organization's goals. p. 15

marketing dashboard The visual computer display of the essential information related to achieving a marketing objective. p. 40

marketing metric A measure of the quantitative value or trend of a marketing activity or result. p. 40

marketing mix The marketing manager's controllable factors; the marketing actions of product, price, promotion, and place that he or she can take to create, communicate, and deliver value. p. 11

marketing plan A road map for the marketing activities of an organization for a specified future period of time, such as one year or five years. p. 42

marketing program A plan that integrates the marketing mix to provide a good, service, or idea to prospective buyers. p. 13

marketing research The process of defining a marketing problem and opportunity, systematically collecting and analyzing information, and recommending actions to improve an organization's marketing activities. p. 202

marketing ROI The application of modern measurement technologies and contemporary organizational design to understand, quantify, and optimize marketing spending. p. 534

marketing strategy The means by which a marketing goal is to be achieved, usually characterized by a specified target market and a marketing program to reach it. p. 48

marketing tactics Detailed day-to-day operational decisions essential to the overall success of marketing strategies. p. 48

market modification Strategy in which a company tries to find new customers, increase a product's use among existing customers, or create new-use situations. p. 287

market orientation Focusing efforts on (1) continuously collecting information about customers' needs and competitors' capabilities, (2) sharing this information throughout the organization, and (3) using the information to create value, ensure customer satisfaction, and develop customer relationships. p. 15

market potential The maximum total sales of a product by all firms to a segment during a specified time period under specified environmental conditions and marketing efforts of the firms; also called *industry potential*. p. 245

market-product grid A framework to relate the market segments of potential buyers to products offered or potential marketing actions by the firm. p. 231

market segmentation Aggregating prospective buyers into groups, or segments, that (1) have common needs and (2) will respond similarly to a marketing action. p. 44

market segments The relatively homogeneous groups of prospective buyers that result from the market segmentation process. p. 231

market share The ratio of sales revenue of the firm to the total sales revenue of all firms in the industry, including the firm itself. p. 33

marketspace An information- and communication-based electronic exchange environment. p. 86

market testing Exposing actual products to prospective consumers under realistic purchase conditions to see if they will buy. p. 271

materials handling Moving goods over short distances into, within, and out of warehouses and manufacturing plants. p. 393

merchandise line How many different types of products a store carries and in what assortment. p. 403

merchant wholesalers Independently owned firms that take title to the merchandise they handle. p. 376

message The information sent by a source to a receiver in the communication process. p. 429

microfinance The practice of offering small, collateral-free loans to individuals who otherwise would not have access to the capital necessary to begin small businesses or other income-generating activities. p. 187

micromarketing How an individual organization directs its marketing activities and allocates its resources to benefit its customers. p. 19

mission A statement of the organization's function in society, often identifying its customers, markets, products, and technologies. p. 31

missionary salespeople Sales support personnel who do not directly solicit orders but rather concentrate on performing promotional activities and introducing new products. p. 491

mixed branding A firm markets products under its own name and that of a reseller because the segment attracted by the reseller is different from its own market. p. 298

moral idealism A personal moral philosophy that considers certain individual rights or duties as universal, regardless of the outcome. p. 109

motivation The energizing force that causes behaviour that satisfies a need. p. 127

multibranding A manufacturer's branding strategy giving each product a distinct name. p. 297

multichannel distribution An arrangement whereby a firm reaches buyers by employing two or more different types of marketing channels. p. 376

multidomestic marketing strategy Use of as many different product variations, brand names, and advertising programs as countries in which they do business. p. 179

multiproduct branding Use by a company of one name for all its products in a product class. p. 295

national character A distinct set of personality characteristics common among people of a country or society. p. 128

need-satisfaction presentation A selling format that emphasizes probing and listening by the salesperson to identify the needs and interests of prospective buyers. p. 495

new-product process The stages a firm uses to identify business opportunities and convert them to a saleable good or service. p. 264

new-product strategy development The first stage of the new-product process, providing the necessary focus, structure, approach, and guidelines for pursuing innovation. p. 264

noise Extraneous factors that can work against effective communication by distorting a message or the feedback received. p. 431

nonprobability sampling Using arbitrary judgments to select the sample so that the chance of selecting a particular element may be unknown or zero. p. 218

objective and task budgeting A budgeting approach whereby the company (1) determines its promotion objectives, (2) outlines the tasks to accomplish these objectives, and (3) determines the promotion cost of performing these tasks. p. 442

objectives Statements of an accomplishment of a task to be achieved, often by a specific time. p. 33

observation Watching, either mechanically or in person, how people behave. p. 214

odd–even pricing Setting prices a few dollars or cents under an even number. p. 345

off-peak pricing Charging different prices during different times of the day or days of the week to reflect variations in demand for the service. p. 321

off-price retailing Selling brand-name merchandise at lower than regular prices. p. 412

opinion leaders Those knowledgeable about users of particular products and services, and so their opinions influence others' choices. p. 134

order getter A salesperson who sells in a conventional sense and identifies prospective customers, provides customers with information, persuades customers to buy, closes sales, and follows up on customers' use of a product or service. p. 490

order taker Processes routine orders or reorders for products that have already been sold by the company. p. 489

organizational buyers Those manufacturers, wholesalers, retailers, and government agencies that buy goods and services for their own use or for resale. pp. 7, 148

organizational buying behaviour The decision-making process that organizations use to establish the need for products and services, and to identify, evaluate, and choose among alternative brands and suppliers. p. 152

organizational buying criteria The objective attributes of the supplier's products and services and the capabilities of the supplier itself. p. 153

organizational culture A set of values, ideas, attitudes, and norms of behaviour that is learned and shared among the members of an organization. p. 32

packaging Any container in which a product is offered for sale and on which label information is communicated. p. 298

partnership selling The practice, sometimes called *enterprise selling,* whereby buyers and sellers combine their expertise and resources to create customized solutions; to commit to joint planning; and to share customer, competitive, and company information for their mutual benefit, and ultimately the customer. p. 489

penetration pricing Setting a low initial price on a new product to appeal immediately to the mass market. p. 343

perceived risk The anxiety felt because the consumer cannot anticipate the outcomes of a purchase but believes that there may be negative consequences. p. 130

percentage of sales budgeting Allocating funds to advertising as a percentage of past or anticipated sales, in terms of either dollars or units sold. p. 441

perception The process by which an individual selects, organizes, and interprets information to create a meaningful picture of the world. p. 129

perceptual map A means of displaying or graphing in two dimensions the location of products or brands in the minds of consumers to enable a manager to see how consumers perceive competing products or brands relative to its own and then take marketing actions. p. 244

personality A person's consistent behaviours or responses to recurring situations. p. 128

personal selling The two-way flow of communication between a buyer and seller, often in a face-to-face encounter, designed to influence a person's or group's purchase decision. pp. 433, 487

personal selling process Sales activities occurring before and after the sale itself, consisting of six stages: (1) prospecting, (2) preapproach, (3) approach, (4) presentation, (5) close, and (6) follow-up. p. 492

points of difference Characteristics of a product that make it superior to competitive substitutes. p. 45

post-tests Tests conducted after an advertisement has been shown to the target audience to determine whether it has accomplished its intended purpose. p. 471

power centre A huge shopping strip with multiple anchor (or national) stores, a convenient location, and a supermarket. p. 414

prestige pricing Setting a high price on a product to attract quality- or status-conscious consumers. p. 344

pre-tests Tests conducted before an advertisement is placed to determine whether it communicates the intended message or to select among alternative versions of an advertisement. p. 470

price The money or other considerations (including other goods and services) exchanged for the ownership or use of a good or service. p. 332

price elasticity of demand The percentage change in quantity demanded relative to a percentage change in price. p. 339

price lining Pricing a line of products at a number of different specific pricing points. p. 344

pricing constraints Factors that limit the latitude of price a firm may set. p. 335

pricing objectives Expectations that specify the role of price in an organization's marketing and strategic plans. p. 337

primary data Facts and figures that are newly collected for the project. p. 206

private branding When a company manufactures products but sells them under the brand name of a wholesaler or retailer (often called *private labelling* or *reseller branding*). p. 298

probability sampling Using precise rules to select the sample such that each element of the population has a specific known chance of being selected. p. 218

product A good, service, or idea consisting of a bundle of tangible and intangible attributes that satisfies consumers and is received in exchange for money or some other unit of value. p. 254

product advertisements Advertisements that focus on selling a good or service and take three forms: (1) pioneering (or informational), (2) competitive (or persuasive), and (3) reminder. p. 457

product class The entire product category or industry. p. 285

product differentiation Strategy that involves a firm using different marketing mix activities, such as product features and advertising, to help consumers perceive the product as being different from and better than competing products. p. 231

product form Variations of a product within the product class. p. 285

production goods Items used in the manufacturing process that become part of the final product. p. 257

product life cycle The stages a new product goes through in the marketplace: introduction, growth, maturity, and decline. p. 281

product line A group of products that are closely related because they satisfy a class of needs, are used together, are sold to the same customer group, are distributed through the same outlets, or fall within a given price range. p. 254

product line groupings Organizational groupings in which a unit is responsible for specific product offerings. p. 532

product mix The number of product lines offered by a company. p. 255

product modification Altering a product's characteristics, such as its quality, performance, appearance, features, or package to try to increase and extend the product's sales. p. 287

product (or program) champion A person who is able and willing to cut red tape and move the program forward. p. 529

product placement Using a brand-name product in a movie, television show, video, or a commercial for another product. p. 476

product positioning The place an offering occupies in consumers' minds on important attributes relative to competitive products. p. 243

product repositioning Changing the place a product occupies in a consumer's mind relative to competing products. pp. 243, 289

profit The money left after a business firm's total expenses are subtracted from its total revenue; the reward for the risk it undertakes in marketing its offerings. p. 28

profit equation Profit = Total revenue − Total cost, or Profit = (Unit price × Quantity sold) − Total cost. p. 334

profit responsibility Idea that companies have a simple duty—to maximize profits for their owners or shareholders. p. 110

promotional mix The combination of one or more of these communication tools, including advertising, personal selling, sales promotion, public relations, and direct marketing. p. 428

protectionism The practice of shielding one or more industries within a country's economy from foreign competition through the use of tariffs or quotas. p. 175

protocol A statement that, before product development begins, identifies (1) a well-defined target market; (2) specific customers' needs, wants, and preferences; and (3) what the product will be and do. p. 261

publicity A non-personal, indirectly paid presentation of an organization, good, or service. p. 433

public relations A form of communication management that seeks to influence the feelings, opinions, or beliefs held by customers, prospective customers, shareholders, suppliers, employees, and other publics about a company and its products or services. p. 433

pull strategy Directing the promotional mix at ultimate consumers to encourage them to ask the retailer for the product. p. 439

purchase decision process The stages a buyer passes through in making choices about which products and services to buy. p. 122

push strategy Directing the promotional mix to channel members to gain their cooperation in ordering and stocking a product. p. 439

quality Those features and characteristics of a product that influence its ability to satisfy customer needs. p. 35

quota A restriction placed on the amount of a product allowed to enter or leave a country. p. 175

rating The percentage of households in a market that are tuned to a particular TV show or radio station. p. 462

reach The number of different people or households exposed to an advertisement. p. 462

receivers Consumers who read, hear, or see the message sent by a source in the communication process. p. 429

reciprocity An industrial buying practice in which two organizations agree to purchase each other's products and services. p. 154

reference groups People to whom an individual looks as a basis for self-appraisal or as a source of personal standards. p. 136

regional shopping centre Consists of 50 to 150 stores that typically attract customers who live within an 8- to 16-km range, often containing two or three anchor stores. p. 413

regulation Restrictions that provincial and federal laws place on business with regard to the conduct of its activities. p. 92

relationship selling The practice of building ties to customers based on a salesperson's attention and commitment to customer needs over time. p. 489

resellers Wholesalers or retailers that buy physical products and sell them again without any processing. p. 149

response The impact the message had on the receiver's knowledge, attitudes, or behaviours. p. 431

retailing All activities involved in selling, renting, and providing goods and services to ultimate consumers for personal, family, or household use. p. 402

retailing mix Activities related to managing the store and the merchandise in the store—including retail pricing, store location, retail communication, and merchandise. p. 412

retail life cycle The process of growth and decline that retail outlets, like products, experience. p. 417

retail positioning matrix Positions retail outlets on two dimensions: breadth of product line and value added. p. 410

reverse auction A buyer communicates a need for a product or service, and would-be suppliers are invited to bid in competition with each other. p. 162

reverse logistics A process of reclaiming recyclable and reusable materials, returns, and reworks from the point of consumption or use for repair, remanufacturing, redistribution, or disposal. p. 395

sales engineer A salesperson who specializes in identifying, analyzing, and solving customer problems and who brings know-how and technical expertise to the selling situations but does not actually sell goods and services. p. 491

salesforce automation (SFA) The use of technology to make the sales function more effective and efficient. p. 507

salesforce survey forecast Asking the firm's salespeople to estimate sales during a coming period. p. 246

sales forecast The total sales of a product that a firm expects to sell during a specified time period under specified environmental conditions and its own marketing efforts. Also called *company forecast*. p. 245

sales management Planning the selling program and implementing and controlling the personal selling effort of the firm. p. 487

sales plan A statement describing what is to be achieved and where and how the selling effort of salespeople is to be deployed. p. 498

sales promotion A short-term inducement of value offered to arouse interest in buying a good or service. p. 433

sales quota Contains specific goals assigned to a salesperson, sales team, branch sales office, or sales district for a stated time period. p. 505

sales response function Relates the expense of marketing effort to the marketing results obtained. p. 516

sampling The process of gathering data from subsets of a total population. p. 217

scrambled merchandising Offering several unrelated product lines in a single retail store. p. 406

screening and evaluation The stage of the new-product process that involves internal and external evaluations of the new-product ideas to eliminate those that warrant no further effort. p. 268

secondary data Facts and figures that have been recorded before the project at hand. p. 206

self-concept The way people see themselves and the way they believe others see them. p. 128

self-regulation An alternative to government control where an industry attempts to police itself. p. 94

selling agents Represent a single producer and are responsible for the entire marketing function of that producer. p. 377

semiotics The field of study that examines the correspondence between symbols and their role in the assignment of meaning for people. p. 182

service continuum　A range from the tangible to the intangible or goods-dominant to service-dominant offerings available in the marketplace. p. 312

services　Intangible activities, benefits, or satisfactions that an organization provides to consumers in exchange for money or something else of value. p. 308

share points　Percentage points of market share; often used as the common basis of comparison to allocate marketing resources effectively. p. 517

shopping goods　Items for which the consumer compares several alternatives on such criteria as price, quality, or style. p. 256

shrinkage　Breakage and theft of merchandise by customers and employees. p. 412

situational influences　Have an impact on your purchase decision process: (1) the purchase task, (2) social surroundings, (3) physical surroundings, (4) temporal effects, and (5) antecedent states. p. 126

situation analysis　Taking stock of where the firm or product has been recently, where it is now, and where it is headed in terms of the organization's plans and the external factors and trends affecting it. p. 43

Six Sigma　A means to "delight the customer" by achieving quality through a highly disciplined process that focuses on developing and delivering near-perfect products and services. p. 266

skimming pricing　The highest initial price that customers really desiring a product are willing to pay. p. 343

slotting fee　A payment a manufacturer makes to place a new item on a retailer's shelf. p. 273

social audit　A systematic assessment of a firm's objectives, strategies, and performance in the domain of social responsibility. p. 112

social class　The relatively permanent, homogeneous divisions in a society into which people sharing similar values, lifestyles, interests, and behaviour can be grouped. p. 138

social forces　Forces of the environment that include the demographic characteristics of the population and its values. p. 78

social marketing　Marketing designed to influence the behaviour of individuals in which the benefits of the behaviour accrue to those individuals or to the society in general and not to the marketer. p. 7

social media marketing　Consumer-generated online-marketing efforts to promote brands and companies for which they are fans (or conversely, negatively promoting brands and companies for which they are non-fans), and the use by marketers of online tools and platforms to promote their brands or organizations. p. 18

social responsibility　Individuals and organizations are part of a larger society and are accountable to that society for their actions. p. 19

societal marketing concept　The view that an organization should discover and satisfy the needs of its consumers in a way that also provides for society's well-being. p. 19

societal responsibility　Refers to obligations that organizations have to the (1) preservation of the ecological environment, and (2) the general public. p. 111

source　A company or person who has information to convey. p. 429

specialty goods　Items that a consumer makes a special effort to search out and buy. p. 256

staff positions　People in staff positions who have the authority and responsibility to advise people in the line positions but cannot issue direct orders to them. p. 531

stakeholder responsibility　Focuses on the obligations an organization has to those who can effect achievement of its objectives, including customers, employees, suppliers, and distributors. p. 111

standard markup pricing　Adding a fixed percentage to the cost of all items in a specific product class. p. 346

stimulus-response presentation　A selling format that assumes the prospect will buy if given the appropriate stimulus by a salesperson. p. 495

strategic alliances　Agreements among two or more independent firms to cooperate for the purpose of achieving common goals, such as a competitive advantage or customer value creation. p. 178

strategic business unit level　A business unit level where managers set a more specific strategic direction for their businesses to exploit value-creating opportunities. p. 30

strategic business unit (SBU)　A subsidiary, division, or unit of an organization that markets a set of related offerings to a clearly defined group of customers. p. 30

strategic channel alliances　A practice whereby one firm's marketing channel is used to sell another firm's products. p. 376

strategic marketing process　Process whereby an organization allocates its marketing mix resources to reach its target markets. p. 42

strategy　An organization's long-term course of action designed to deliver a unique customer experience while achieving its goals. p. 29

strip location　A cluster of stores serving people who live within a 5- to 10-minute drive. p. 414

subcultures　Subgroups within the larger, or national, culture with unique values, ideas, and attitudes. p. 139

subliminal perception　Means that you see or hear messages without being aware of them. p. 130

supplier development　The deliberate effort by organizational buyers to build relationships that shape suppliers' products, services, and capabilities to fit a buyer's needs and those of its customers. p. 154

supply chain　A sequence of firms that perform activities required to create and deliver a good or service to consumers or industrial users. p. 385

supply chain management　The integration and organization of information and logistics activities across firms in a supply chain for the purpose of creating and delivering goods and services that provide value to customers. p. 385

supply partnership　A relationship that exists when a buyer and its supplier adopt mutually beneficial objectives, policies, and procedures for the purpose of lowering the cost and/or increasing the value of products and services delivered to the ultimate consumers. p. 154

support goods　Items used to assist in producing other goods and services. p. 257

survey　A research technique used to generate data by asking people questions and recording their responses on a questionnaire. p. 209

survey of buyers' intentions forecast　Asking prospective customers if they are likely to buy the product during some future time period. p. 246

sustainable development　Conducting business in a way that protects the natural environment while making economic progress. p. 112

SWOT analysis An acronym describing an organization's appraisal of its internal **S**trengths and **W**eaknesses and its external **O**pportunities and **T**hreats. p. 43

target market One or more specific groups of potential consumers toward which an organization directs its marketing program. p. 11

target pricing The practice of deliberately adjusting the composition and features of a product to achieve the target price to consumers. p. 345

target profit pricing Pricing method based on an annual target of a specific dollar volume of profit. p. 346

target return-on-investment pricing Setting prices to achieve return-on-investment (ROI) targets. p. 347

target return-on-sales pricing Setting typical prices that will give a firm a profit that is a specific percentage. p. 347

tariff A government tax on goods or services entering a country, which primarily serves to raise prices on imports. p. 175

team selling Using an entire team of professionals in selling to and servicing major customers. p. 491

technology Inventions or innovations from applied science or engineering research. p. 86

telemarketing Using the telephone to interact with and sell directly to consumers. p. 409

total cost The total expenses incurred by a firm in producing and marketing a product. p. 341

total logistics cost Expenses associated with transportation, materials handling and warehousing, inventory, stockouts, order processing, and return goods handling. p. 389

total revenue The total money received from the sale of a product. p. 340

trade feedback effect A country's imports affect its exports and exports affect its imports. p. 171

trademark Identifies that a firm has legally registered its brand name or trade name so that the firm has its exclusive use. p. 291

trade name A commercial, legal name under which a company does business. p. 291

trade-oriented sales promotions Sales tools used to support a company's advertising and personal selling efforts directed to wholesalers, distributors, or retailers. Three common approaches are allowances and discounts, cooperative advertising, and salesforce training. p. 476

trading down Reducing the number of features, quality, or price. p. 289

trading up Adding value to a product (or line) through additional features or higher-quality materials. p. 289

traditional auction A seller puts an item up for sale, and would-be buyers are invited to bid in competition with each other. p. 162

traffic generation The outcome of an offer designed to motivate people to visit a business. p. 447

trend extrapolation Extending a pattern observed in past data into the future. p. 246

triple-bottom-line Recognition of the need for organizations to improve the state of people, the planet, and profit simultaneously, if they are to achieve sustainable, long-term growth. p. 111

ultimate consumers People—whether 80 years or 8 months old—who use the goods and services purchased for a household. p. 7

unsought goods Items that the consumer either does not know about or knows about but does not initially want. p. 256

usage rate Quantity consumed or patronage—store visits— during a specific period; varies significantly among different customer groups. p. 237

user-generated content (UGC) Media generated by users (customers) and disseminated via various channels, in particular, the Internet. p. 468

utilitarianism A personal moral philosophy that focuses on the "greatest good for the greatest number" by assessing the costs and benefits of the consequences of ethical behaviour. p. 109

value analysis A systematic appraisal of the design, quality, and performance of a product to reduce purchasing costs. p. 159

value consciousness The concern for obtaining the best quality, features, and performance of a product or service for a given price. p. 83

values Personally or socially preferable modes of conduct or states of existence that are enduring. p. 132

variable cost The sum of the expenses of a firm that vary directly with the quantity of products that is produced and sold. p. 341

vendor-managed inventory An inventory management system whereby the supplier determines the product amount and assortment a customer (such as a retailer) needs and automatically delivers the appropriate items. p. 395

vertical marketing systems Professionally managed and centrally coordinated marketing channels designed to achieve channel economies and maximum marketing impact. p. 377

viral marketing The online version of word of mouth, involving the use of messages "infectious" enough that consumers wish to pass them along to others through online communication. p. 135

warranty A statement indicating the liability of the manufacturer for product deficiencies. p. 302

wheel of retailing A concept that describes how new retail outlets enter the market as low-status, low-margin stores and gradually add embellishments that raise their prices and status. They now face a new low-status, low-margin operator, and the cycle starts to repeat itself. p. 416

whistle-blowers Employees who report unethical or illegal actions of their employers. p. 108

word of mouth The influencing of people during conversations. p. 135

workload method A formula-based method for determining the size of a salesforce that integrates the number of customers served, call frequency, call length, and available selling time to arrive at a salesforce size. p. 501

yield management pricing The charging of different prices to maximize revenue for a set amount of capacity at any given time. p. 345

CHAPTER NOTES

CHAPTER 1

1. This discussion is based on information provided by WildPlay Element Parks, **www.wildplay.com** (Summer 2010).
2. Regis McKenna, "Marketing Is Everything," *Harvard Business Review* (Jan/Feb 1991), pp. 65–79.
3. "AMA Adopts New Definition of Marketing," *Marketing News* (September 15, 2004), p. 1.
4. Philip Kotler and Sidney J. Levy, "Broadening the Concept of Marketing," *Journal of Marketing* (January 1969), pp. 10–15.
5. George G. Brenkert, "Ethical Challenges in Social Marketing," *Journal of Public Policy & Marketing* (Spring 2002), pp. 14–25; and Alan R. Andreasen, "Marketing Social Marketing in the Social Change Marketplace," *Journal of Public Policy & Marketing* (Spring 2002), pp. 3–13.
6. Robert M. McMath and Thom Forbes, *What Were They Thinking?* (New York: Times Business, 1998), pp. 3–22.
7. Chad Terhune, "Coca-Cola's Low-Carb Soda Loses Its Fizz," *The Wall Street Journal*, October 20, 2004, pp. B1, B9.
8. "Special Issues for Young Children," and "How Marketers Target Kids," **www.media-awareness.ca** (downloaded January 10, 2007).
9. E. Jerome McCarthy, *Basic Marketing: A Managerial Approach* (Homewood, IL: Richard D. Irwin, 1960); and Walter van Waterschoot and Christophe Van den Bulte, "The 4P Classification of the Marketing Mix Revisited," *Journal of Marketing* (October 1992), pp. 83–93.
10. Frederick G. Crane, "Why Corporate America Cannot Innovate," working paper, Northeastern University (2009).
11. Information provided by WildPlay Element Parks, **www.wildplay.com** (Summer 2010).
12. Robert F. Keith, "The Marketing Revolution," *Journal of Marketing* (January 1960), pp. 35–38.
13. *Annual Report* (New York: General Electric Company, 1952), p. 21.
14. Michael Treacy and Fred D. Wiersema, *The Discipline of Market Leaders* (Reading, MA: Addison-Wesley, 1995); Michael Treacy and Fred Wiersema, "How Market Leaders Keep Their Edge," *Fortune* (February 6, 1995), pp. 88–89; and Michael Treacy, "You Need a Value Discipline—But Which One?" *Fortune* (April 17, 1995), p. 195.
15. Frederick G. Crane and Jeffrey E. Sohl, "Imperatives for Venture Success: Entrepreneurs Speak," *International Journal of Entrepreneurship and Innovation* (May 2004), pp. 99–106.
16. "What's a Loyal Customer Worth?" *Fortune* (December 11, 1995), p.182; and Lauren Keller Johnson, "The Real Value of Customer Loyalty," *MIT Sloan Management Review* (Winter 2002), pp. 14–17.
17. G.R. Iyer and David Bejou, *Customer Relationship Management in Electronic Markets* (New York: The Haworth Press Inc. 2004).
18. William Band, *CRM Market Size and Forecast 2006 to 2010* (Boston, MA: Forrester Research, 2006).
19. Mark Whitmore and Jonathan Copulsky, "CRM R.I.P.?" *Marketing* (April 7, 2003), **www.marketingmag.ca** (downloaded June 10, 2005).
20. Bruce Temkin, "Companies Deliver Subpar Customer Experiences," Forrester Research (January 7, 2005).
21. Bob Thompson, *Customer Experience Management: A Winning Business Strategy in a Flat World* (CustomerThinkCorp, 2006).
22. Sharon Morrison and Frederick G. Crane, "Building the Service Brand by Creating and Managing an Emotional Brand Experience," *Journal of Brand Management* (May 1, 2007), pp. 410–21.
23. Rob Gerlsbeck, "Sweeeet," *Marketing Magazine* (December 11/18, 2006), p. 8; and Peter Kim, "Reinventing the Marketing Organization," Forrester Research (July 13, 2006).
24. Kathleen Martin, "Froot Flavoured," *Marketing Magazine* (April 3, 2006), pp. 13 and 16; and Sarah Dobson, "Great Reputations," *Marketing Magazine* (May 8, 2006), pp. 14–18.
25. Erik Qualman, *Socialnomics* (New York: Wiley, 2009).
26. Chuck Bamford and Garry Bruton, "Social Media Networking & the Small Business: Six Tips for Using Social Media Successful," *Starting Up, A Newsletter for Entrepreneurship*, McGraw-Hill, May 2010.
27. Andrew Crane and John Desmond, "Societal Marketing and Morality," *European Journal of Marketing* (Spring 2002), pp. 548–70.
28. Shelby D. Hunt and John Burnett, "The Macromarketing/Micromarketing Dichotomy: A Taxonomical Model," *Journal of Marketing* (Summer 1982), pp. 9–26.

Case: Written by Frederick G. Crane. Sources include Canadian Vintners Association; The Wine Council of Ontario; Stratus Vineyards; Peggy Hope-Ross, "From the Vine to the Glass: Canada's Grape and Wine Industry," Statistics Canada, Ottawa (2006); "The Canadian Wine Industry," Agriculture and Agri-Food Canada (2006); and Statistics Canada, CANSIM, Tables 0510-0001 and 183-0015.

CHAPTER 2

1. Information supplied by Canadian Tire Corporation Limited including Annual Reports (August, 2009).
2. W. Chan Kim and Renee Mauborgne, "Blue Ocean Strategy: From Theory to Practice," *California Management Review*, 47, no. 3, Spring 2005, p. 105.
3. Costas Markides, "What Is Strategy and How Do You Know if You Have One?" *Business Strategy Review*, 15, no. 2, Summer 2004, p. 5.
4. Michael E. Porter, "What Is Strategy?" *Harvard Business Review*, OnPoint Article, November–December, 1996, p.2; and Gerry Johnson, Kevin Scholes, and Richard Wittington, *Exploring Corporate Strategy* (Upper Saddle River, NJ: Prentice Hall, 2005).
5. Roger A. Kerin, "Strategic Marketing and the CMO," *Journal of Marketing*, October 2005, pp. 12–13; and The CMO Council: Biographies of Selected Advisory Board Members. See **www.cmocouncil.org/advisoryboard.html**.
6. Roger A. Kerin, Vijay Mahajan, and P. Rajan Varadarajan, *Contemporary Perspectives on Strategic Marketing Planning* (Boston: Allyn & Bacon, 1990), chap. 1; and Orville C. Walker, Jr., Harper W. Boyd, Jr., and Jean-Claude Larreche, *Marketing Strategy* (Burr Ridge, IL: Richard D. Irwin, 1992), chaps. 1 and 2.
7. Taken in part from Jim Collins and Jerry I. Porras, *Built to Last: Successful Habits of Visionary Companies* (New York: HarperCollins Publishers, 2002), p. 54.
8. Ibid, p. 54; and Jim Collins, *Good to Great: Why Some Companies Make the Leap . . . and Others Don't* (New York: HarperCollins Publishers, 2001), p. 195.
9. Collins and Porras, *Built to Last*, p.73; Patrick M. Lencioni, "Make Your Values Mean Something," *Harvard Business Review*, July 2002, p.6.
10. Catherine M. Dalton, "When Organizational Values Are Mere Rhetoric," *Business Horizons* 49 (September–October 2006), p. 345.
11. Collins and Porras, *Built to Last*, p. 73; and Lencioni, "Make Your Values Mean Something," p. 6.
12. Collins and Porrar, *Built to Last*, pp. 94–95; and Tom Krattenmaker, "Write a Mission Statement that Your Company is Willing to Live," *Harvard Management Communication Letter*, March 2002, pp. 3–4.
13. Nikos Mourkogiannis, "The Realist's Guide to Moral Purpose," *Strategy+Business*, no. 41 (Winter 2005), pp. 42, 45, 47.

14. Sheila M.J. Bonini, Lenny T. Mendonca, and Jeremy M. Oppenheim, "When Social Issues Become Strategic," *The McKinsey Quarterly*, 2006, no. 2, pp. 23, 25, 30–31.

15. Theodore Levitt, "Marketing Myopia," *Harvard Business Review* (July–August 1960), pp. 45–56.

16. Katherine Ellison, "The Bottom Line Redefined," *Nature Conservancy* (Winter 2002), pp. 45–50.

17. George Stalk, Philip Evans and Lawrence E. Shulman, "Competing on Capabilities: The New Rules of Corporate Strategy," *Harvard Business Review*, March–April 1992, pp. 57–69; and Darrell K. Rigby, *Management Tools 2007: An Executive's Guide* (Boston: Bain & Company, 2007), p. 22.

18. Roger A. Kerin and Robert A. Peterson, *Strategic Marketing Problems: Cases and Comments*, 10th edition (Englewood Cliffs, NJ: Prentice Hall, 2004), pp. 2–3; and Derek F. Abell, *Defining the Business* (Englewood Cliffs, NJ: Prentice Hall, 1980), pp. 57–69.

19. Jim Collins, Good to Great: *Why Some Companies Make the Leap . . . and Others Don't*, pp. 13, 90–91, 95–96, 107.

20. W. Chan Kim and Renee Mauborgne, Blue Ocean Strategy: *How to Create Uncontested Market Space and Make the Competition Irrelevant* (Boston: Harvard Business School Press, 2005); and Kim and Mauborgne, "*Blue Ocean Strategy: From Theory to Practice*."

21. Brian Levy, "Value Pioneering—How to Discover Your Own "Blue Ocean": Interview with W. Chan Kim and Renee Mauborgne," *Strategy & Leadership*, 13, no. 6 (2005), p. 14.

22. Adapted from "The Experience Curve Reviewed, IV. The Growth Share Matrix of the Product Portfolio" (Boston: The Boston Consulting Group, 1973).

23. H. Igor Ansoff, "Strategies for Diversification," *Harvard Business Review* (September–October 1957), pp. 113–24.

24. "Dairy Producers Pour More Milk," *Marketing* (September 26, 2006), p. 4.

25. Eve Lazarus, "Tea's Time," *Marketing* (September 26, 2006), p. 6.

26. "Second Cup Adds Music to its Menu," *Marketing* (September 26, 2006), p. 4; **www.mccain.com**; and **www.heinz.com**.

27. The definition is adapted from Stephen Few, *Information Dashboard Design: The Effective Visual Communication of Data* (Sebastopol, CA: O'Reilly Media, Inc. 2006), pp. 2–46.

28. Ibid.; Bruce H. Clark, Andrew V. Abela, and Tim Ambler, "Behind the Wheel," *Marketing Management*, May–June 2006, pp. 19–23; Spencer E. Ante, "Giving the Boss the Big Picture," *Business Week*, February 13, 2006, pp. 48–49; *Dashboard Tutorial* (Cupertino, CA: Apple, Inc, 2006).

29. Stephen Few, *Information Dashboard Design*.

30. Michael Krauss, "Balance Attention to Metrics with Intuition," *Marketing News*, June 1, 2007, pp. 6–8; John Davis, *Measuring Marketing: 103 Key Metrics Every Marketer Needs* (Singapore: John Wiley & Sons, 2007); Paul W. Farris, Neil T. Bendle, Phillip E. Pfeifer and David J. Reibstein, *Marketing Metrics* (Upper Saddle River, NJ: Wharton School Publishing, 2006); and Marcel Corstjens and Jeffrey Merrihue, "Optimal Marketing," *Harvard Business Review*, October 2003, pp. 114–21.

31. The now-classic reference on effective graphic presentation is E. d R. Tufte, *The Visual Display of Quantitative Information*, 2nd Edition (Chesire, CN: Graphic Press, 2001); also see Stephen Few, *Information Dashboard Design*.

32. Linda Swenson and Kenneth E. Goodpaster, *Medtronic in China (A)* (Minneapolis, MN: University of St. Thomas, 1999), pp. 4–5.

33. "Starbucks Gets Personal," *Marketing* (February 8, 2007); and "Zip-Car," *Marketing* (February 6, 2007).

34. Todd Wasserman, "The Mercenary (a.k.a. 'Super') CMO," *BrandWeek* (June 21, 2004), pp. S6–S18.

35. Peter Kim, "Reinventing the Marketing Organization," Forrester Research (July 13, 2006).

36. Information provided by Masterfoods (February, 2007).

Case: This case was written by Frederick G. Crane.

APPENDIX A

1. Personal interview with Arthur R. Kydd, St. Croix Management Group.

2. Examples of guides to writing marketing plans include William A. Cohen, *The Marketing Plan* (New York: Wiley, 1995); Mark Nolan, *The Instant Marketing Plan* (Santa Maria, CA: Puma Publishing Company, 1995); and Roman G. Hiebing, Jr., and Scott W. Cooper, *The Successful Marketing Plan*, 2nd ed. (Lincolnwood, IL: NTC Business Books, 1997).

3. Examples of guides to writing business plans include the following Rhonda M. Abrahms, *The Successful Business Plan: Secrets & Strategies*, 3rd ed. (Grants Pass, OR: Oasis Press/PSI Research, 2000); Joseph A. Covello and Brian J. Hazelgren, *The Complete Book of Business Plans* (Naperville, IL: Sourcebooks, 1995); Joseph A. Covello and Brian J. Hazelgren, *Your First Business Plan*, 3rd ed. (Naperville, IL: Sourcebooks, 1998); and Angela Shupe, ed., *Business Plans Handbook*, vols. 1–4 (Detroit: Gale Research, 1997).

4. Abrahms, *The Successful Business Plan*, p. 30.

5. Some of these points are adapted from Abrahms, pp. 30–38; others are adapted from William Rudelius, *Guidelines for Technical Report Writing* (Minneapolis: University of Minnesota, undated). See also William Strunk, Jr., and E. B. White, *The Elements of Style* (New York, Macmillan, 1979).

CHAPTER 3

1. Jonathan Strickland, "How Web 3.0 Will Work," **http://computer. howstuffworks.com/web 3.0**, accessed August 10, 2009; Jessi Hempel, "Web 2.0 Is So Over: Welcome to Web 3.0," *Fortune*, January 9, 2009; Allison Enright, "Get Clued In: Mystery of 'Web 2.0' Concept Solved," *Marketing News*, January 15, 2007, p. 20; Jeff Howe, "Your Web, Your Way," *Time*, December 25, 2006, pp. 60–61; Bob Greenberg, "On Web 2.0's Impact," Adweek.com, January 1, 2007; Robert D. Hof, "There's Not Enough 'Me' in Myspace," *Business Week*, December 4, 2006, p. 40; and Sebastian Rupley, "You've Heard of Web 2.0. What About Web 3.0?" *PC Magazine*, December 20, 2006.

2. "Food Consumption Highlights," Statistics Canada, Ottawa (Summer 2006).

3. Eve Lazarus, "Tea's Time," *Marketing* (September 26, 2006), p. 6.

4. Fred Vogelstein, "10 Tech Trends to Bet On," *Fortune* (February 23, 2004), pp. 76–88; Alison Stein Wellner, "The Next 25 Years," *American Demographics* (April 2003), pp. 24–27; Stephen B. Shepard, "You Read It Here First," *BusinessWeek* (March 15, 2004), p. 16; Catherine Arnold, "Anti-Smoking Trend Hits Asia," *Marketing News* (January 15, 2004), p. 4; Arundhati Parmar, "Outlook 2004: Competitive Intelligence," *Marketing News* (January 15, 2004), pp. 16–17; and Steve Jarvis, "Internet Privacy at the Plate, Net Names, Taxes on Deck Too," *Marketing News* (January 1, 2001), pp. 12–14.

5. *World Population Prospects: The 2004 Revision*, United Nations, New York.

6. Ibid.

7. Statistics Canada, CANSIM 052-0004, and Catalogue no. 91-520-x; and The 2004 Revision, United Nations, New York.

8. The 2004 Revision, United Nations, New York.

9. "EU's Future Consumers: 3 Groups to Watch," *Marketing News* (June 4, 2001), p. 9.

10. Statistics Canada, "Population Projections of Visible Minority Groups in Canada," 91-541-XIE (March 22, 2005); and Jack Jedwab, "Ethnic Marketing in Canada: The Challenges Ahead," Canadian Marketing Association (August 29, 2006).

11. Jack Jedwab, "Ethnic Marketing in Canada."

12. Rebecca Harris, "Skin Deep," *Marketing* (January 29, 2007), pp. 18–19; and Lou Puim, "How Wal-Mart Learned Diversity," *Marketing* (January 23, 2006), pp. 10–13.

13. Sachi Mukerji, "Three Follies of Multicultural Marketing," *Marketing*, October 13, 2008, pp. 13–14.

14. "Food Consumption in Canada," Statistics Canada, 23f0001XCD (2005).

15. Michelle Halpern, "Flavour Nation," *Marketing* (January 23, 2006), p. 10.

16. Statistics Canada, CANSIM 203-0001 – 203-0020 (January 2007).

17. "Electronic Commerce and Technology," *The Daily,* Statistics Canada (April 20, 2006).

18. *Media Digest 06–07,* Canadian Media Directors' Council, Toronto, p. 75.

19. "Essential Interactive, Vol. 3," *Working Knowledge* (2006).

20. Ibid.

21. "Mobile in Motion," *Working Knowledge* (2006), p. 4.

22. Ibid.

23. Jeromy Lloyd, "Cool Campaigns that Worked," *Marketing,* June 15, 2009, pp. 18–19.

24. *Media Digest 06–07,* Canadian Media Directors' Council, Toronto, pp. 73–75.

25. "Mobile in Motion," p. 4–5.

26. "Essential Interactive, Vol. 3," *Working Knowledge* (2006), pp. 30–31.

27. Erik Qualman, *Socialnomics* (New York: Wiley, 2009); and Erik Qualman, "Statistics Show Social Media Is Bigger Than You Think," **http://socialnomics.net/2009/08/11/statistics-show-social-media-is-bigger-than-you-think** (accessed August 1, 2010).

28. Michael Porter, *Competitive Advantage* (New York: Free Press, 1985); and Michael Porter, *Competitive Strategy* (New York: Free Press, 1980).

29. Bruce H. Clark, Andrew V. Abela and Time Ambler, "Behind the Wheel," *Marketing Management,* June 2006, p. 19–23; and Paul W. Farris, Neil T. Bendle, Phillip E. Pfeifer, and David J. Reibstein, *Marketing Metrics: 50+ Metrics Every Executive Should Master* (Philadelphia: Wharton School Publishing, 2007).

30. Canadian Federation of Independent Business, **www.cfib.ca** (downloaded August 6, 2009); **www.ic.gc.ca/sbstatistics**, July 2009; and Frederick G. Crane, *Marketing for Entrepreneurs* (CA: Sage Publications, 2010).

31. **www.ic.gc.ca**.

32. Lisa D'Innocenzo, "What Privacy Law," *Strategy Magazine* (January 12, 2004), p. 4.

33. Amanda Maltby, "Adapting to Canada's New Privacy Rules," *Marketing* (November 3, 2003), **www.marketingmag.ca** (downloaded June 10, 2005); and Sarah Dobson, "Wake-up Call," *Marketing* (November 14, 2005), pp. 20–21.

Case: This case was written by Steven Hartley. Sources: Mary Ellen Lloyd, "Camp Teaches Power of Geekdom," *The Wall Street Journal,* July 11, 2007; Dean Foust, Michael Mandel, Frederick F. Jespersen and David Henry, "The Business Week 50—The Best Performers," *Business Week,* March 26, 2007, p. 58; Jessica E. Vascellaro, "What's a Cellphone For? Businesses are Finding All Sorts of New Uses for Mobile Devices," *The Wall Street Journal,* March 26, 2007, p. R5; Cade Metz, "Just How Stupid Are You? Geek Squad War Stories," *PC Magazine,* February 1, 2006; Brad Stone, "Lore of the Geek Squad," *Newsweek,* February 20, 2006, p. 44; Michelle Conlin, "Smashing the Clock," *BusinessWeek,* December 11, 2006, p. 60; "Best Buy: How to Break Out of Commodity Hell," *BusinessWeek,* March 27, 2006, p. 76; Pallavi Gogoi, "Meet Jane Geek," *BusinessWeek,* November 28, 2005, p. 94; Desiree J. Hanford, "Geek Squad Is Popular at Best Buy," *The Wall Street Journal,* December 14, 2005, p. 1; Michelle Higgins, "Getting Your Own IT Department," *The Wall Street Journal,* May 20, 2004, p. D1; and information contained on the Geek Squad Web site (**www.geeksquad.com**).

CHAPTER 4

1. **www.generalmotors.ca**, **www.ford.ca**, **www.nissan.ca**, and **www.toyota.ca** (downloaded August 10, 2010).

2. Patrick Murphy and Gene Laczniak, *Marketing Ethics: Cases and Readings* (Upper Saddle River, NJ, Prentice Hall, 2006); and D. Robin and S.J. Vitell, *Theoretical Foundations in Marketing Ethics* (London: Elsevier, 2006).

3. Verne E. Henderson, "The Ethical Side of Enterprise," *Sloan Management Review* (Spring 1982), pp. 37–47. See also, Joseph L. Badaracco, Jr., *Defining Moments: When Managers Must Choose Between Right and Right* (Boston: Harvard Business School Press, 1997).

4. M. Bommer, C. Gratto, J. Grauander, and M. Tuttle, "A Behavioral Model of Ethical and Unethical Decision Making," *Journal of Business Ethics,* vol. 6 (1987), pp. 265–80.

5. F. G. Crane, "What's Ethical and What's Not with Canadian Business Students," working paper (2007).

6. Cornelius von Baeyer, "Ethics in Organizations: A Brief Retrospective," *EPAC-APEC Magazine* (January 2006), 6(1), pp. 2–4.

7. F. G. Crane, "Teaching Business Ethics in B-Schools: A Cross-Cultural Examination," *Journal of the Academy of Business Education, 2005, 6(2), pp. 63–67.*

8. **www.ethicscan.ca** (downloaded August 14, 2009).

9. Lawrence B. Chonko, *Ethical Decision Making in Marketing* (Thousand Oaks, CA: Sage, 1995).

10. See Murphy and Laczniak, *Marketing Ethics;* and Robin and Vitell, *Theoretical Foundations in Marketing Ethics.*

11. Barry R. Shapiro, "Economic Espionage," *Marketing Management* (Spring 1998), pp. 56–58; and Dan T. Swartwood and Richard J. Heffernan, *Trends in Intellectual Property Loss, Survey Report* (Alexandria, VA: American Society for Industrial Security, 1998).

12. Vern Terpstra and Kenneth David, *The Cultural Environment of International Business,* 3rd ed. (Cincinnati: South-Western Publishing, 1991), p. 12.

13. For an extended treatment of ethics in the exchange process, see Gregory T. Gundlach and Patrick E. Murphy, "Ethical and Legal Foundations in Relational Marketing Exchanges," *Journal of Marketing* (October 1993), pp. 35–46.

14. For an extensive examination on slotting fees, see Paul N. Bloom, Gregory T. Gundlach, and Joseph P. Cannon, "Slotting Allowances and Fees: Schools of Thought and Views of Practicing Managers," *Journal of Marketing* (April 2000), pp. 92–109.

15. This discussion contains statistics reported in Carolyn F. Siegel, "Introducing Marketing Students to Business Intelligence Using Project-Based Learning on the World Wide Web," *Journal of Marketing Education* (August 2000), pp. 90–98.

16. John Dalla Costa, "Ethics & Marketing," *Marketing* (May 22/29, 2006), p. 13.

17. Laura Pratt, "Everyday Ethics," *Marketing* (September 11, 2006), pp. 16–17.

18. R. Eric Reidenbach and Donald P. Robin, *Ethics and Profits* (Englewood Cliffs, NJ: Prentice Hall, 1989).

19. "Scotguard Working Out Recent Stain on Its Business," **www.mercurynews.com** (downloaded June 2003).

20. James Q. Wilson, "Adam Smith on Business Ethics," *California Management Review* (Fall 1989), pp. 59–72; and George M. Zinkham, Michael Bisesi, and Mary Jane Saxon, "MBAs: Changing Attitudes Toward Marketing Dilemmas," *Journal of Business Ethics,* vol. 8 (1989), pp. 963–74.

21. **www.nestlecanada.ca** (downloaded April 25, 2001).

22. Robert B. Reich, "The New Meaning of Corporate Social Responsibility," *California Management Review* (Winter 1998), pp. 8–17.

23. Harvey S. James and Farhad Rassekh, "Smith, Friedman, and Self-Interest in Ethical Society," *Business Ethics Quarterly* (July 2000), pp. 659–74.

24. "Drug Firms Gouge After Taking Taxpayer Handouts," *The New Standard* (April 14, 2006), **www.newstandardnews.net** (downloaded February 14, 2007).

25. For an extended description of the Perrier decision, see "Perrier—Overresponding to a Crisis," in Robert F. Hartley, *Marketing Mistakes and Successes*, 8th ed. (New York: Wiley, 2001), pp. 127–37.

26. "Four Canadian Companies Win 2007 Globe Environmental Awards," GreenBiz.com (June 21, 2007); **http://greenbiz.com/news** (downloaded June 22, 2007); Karl Moore, "Environment Rising," *Marketing* (October 9/16, 2006), p. 14; Harvey Meyer, "The Greening of Corporate America," *Journal of Business Strategy* (January–February 2000), pp. 38–43; and Irina Maslennikova and David Foley, "Xerox's Approach to Sustainability," *Interfaces* (May–June 2000), pp. 226–33. Also see Philemon Oyewale, "Social Costs of Environmental Justice Associated with the Practice of Green Marketing," *Journal of Business Ethics*, vol. 29 (2001), pp. 239–51.

27. The ISO Survey of ISO 9000 and ISO 14000 Certificates (Geneva, Switzerland: International Organization for Standardization, 2004).

28. The examples given are found in "The Socially Correct Corporation," *Fortune* (July 24, 2000), special section; and "The Wider Benefits of Backing a Good Cause," *Marketing* (September 2, 1999), pp. 18–22.

29. D. Van den Brink, G. Odekerken-Schroder, and P. Pauwels, "The Effect of Strategic and Tactical Cause-Related Marketing on Consumers' Brand Loyalty," *Journal of Consumer Marketing*, 2006, 23(1), pp. 15–25.

30. These steps are adapted from J. J. Carson and G. A. Steiner, *Measuring Business Social Performance: The Corporate Social Audit* (New York: Committee for Economic Development, 1974). See also Sandra Waddock and Neil Smith, "Corporate Responsibility Audits: Doing Well by Doing Good," *Sloan Management Review* (Winter 2000), pp. 75–84.

31. D.A. Rondinelli and G. Vastag, "International Standards and Corporate Policies: An Integrated Framework," *California Management Review* (November 9, 1998), p. 14.

32. Angela Kryhul, "The Consumer Connection," *Marketing* (June 5, 2006), pp. 12–13.

33. "Corporate America's Social Conscience," *Fortune* (May 26, 2003), p. 147ff.

34. Kryhul, "The Consumer Connection."

35. "Hydro One Tops Best 50 Corporate Citizens in Canada List for 2009," CorporateKnights, **www.corporateknights.ca** (downloaded August 27, 2009); and "Global 100—Most Sustainable Corporations in the World," **www.global100.org** (downloaded August 27, 2009).

36. This discussion is based on Wayne D. Hoyer and Deborah J. MacInnis, *Consumer Behavior*, 3rd ed. (New York: Houghton Mifflin Company, 2004), pp. 535–37; "Factoids," *Research Alert* (December 8, 2002), p. 5; and "Penny for Your Thoughts," *American Demographics* (September 2000), pp. 8–9.

37. Chris Powell, "Downloading Movies not a Serious Offense to Most Canadians," *Marketing Daily* (June 26, 2007).

38. M. Laroche, Jasmin Bergeron, Marc-Alexandre Tomiuk, and Guido Barbaro-Forleo, "Cultural Differences in Environmental Knowledge, Attitudes, and Behaviors of Canadian Consumers," *Canadian Journal of Administrative Sciences*, vol. 8 (2002).

39. Michael Adams, "Smarter than You Think," *Marketing* (August 14/21, 2006), p. 20.

40. "Schism on the Green," *Brandweek* (February 26, 2001), p. 18.

41. Adams, "Smarter than You Think."

42. "CorporateKnights Special Reports," **www.corporateknights.ca** (downloaded August 27, 2009).

Case: Starbucks Corporation: This case is based on information on the company Web site (**www.starbucks.com**) and the following sources: "Living Our Values," *2003 Corporate Social Responsibility Annual Report*; "Starbucks Annual Shareholder Meeting," Starbucks press release

(March 30, 2004); Ranjay Gulati, Sarah Huffman, and Gary Neilson, "The Barista Principle: Starbucks and the Rise of Relational Capital," *Strategy and Business* (3rd Quarter 2002), pp. 58–69; and Andy Serwer, "Hot Starbucks to Go," *Fortune* (January 12, 2004), p. 52ff.

CHAPTER 5

1. Marti Barletta, "Who's Really Buying that Car? Ask Her," *BrandWeek*, September 4, 2006, p. 20; Joan Voight, "The Lady Means Business," *BrandWeek*, April 30, 2006, pp. 28ff; and Jennifer Saranow, "Car Dealers Recruit Saleswomen at the Mall," *The Wall Street Journal*, April 12, 2006, pp. B1, B3. Also see, "Car Dealers Catering to Women," CBC.ca (March 8, 2007), **www.cbc.ca/news/yourview/consumer_life/2007/03/car_dealers_catering_to_women.html** (downloaded March 10, 2007); and also see **driving.ca** and **drivingtvcanada.com**.

2. Roger D. Blackwell, Paul W. Miniard, and James F. Engel, *Consumer Behavior, 10th ed.* (Mason, OH: South-Western Publishing, 2005).

3. For thorough descriptions of consumer expertise, see Joseph W. Alba and J. Wesley Hutchinson, "Knowledge Calibration: What Consumers Know and What They Think They Know," *Journal of Consumer Research* (September 2000), pp. 123–57.

4. For in-depth studies on external information search patterns, see Sridhar Moorthy, Brian T. Ratchford, and Debabrata Tulukdar, "Consumer Information Search Revisited: Theory and Empirical Analysis," *Journal of Consumer Research* (March 1997), pp. 263–77; Joel E. Urbany, Peter R. Dickson, and William L. Wilkie, "Buyer Uncertainty and Information Search," *Journal of Consumer Research* (March 1992), pp. 452–63.

5. "Essential Interactive, Volume 3," *Working Knowledge* (2006), p. 4.

6. For an extended discussion on evaluative criteria, see Del J. Hawkins, David L. Mothersbaugh, and Roger J. Best, *Consumer Behavior*, 10th ed. (Burr Ridge, IL: McGraw-Hill/Irwin, 2007), pp. 572–77.

7. Hawkins, Mothersbaugh, and Best, *Consumer Behavior*, pp. 534–35. For an extended discussion on consumer choice sets, see Allan D. Shocker, Moshe Ben-Akiva, Bruno Boccara, and Prakesh Nedungadi, "Consideration Set Influences on Consumer Decision Making and Choice: Issues, Models, and Suggestions." *Marketing Letters* (August 1991), pp. 181–98.

8. William J. McDonald, "Time Use in Shopping: The Role of Personal Characteristics," *Journal of Retailing* (Winter 1994), pp. 345–66; Robert J. Donovan, John R. Rossiter, Gillian Marcoolyn, and Andrew Nesdale, "Store Atmosphere and Purchasing Behavior," *Journal of Retailing* (Fall 1994), pp. 283–94; and Eric A. Greenleaf and Donald R. Lehman, "Reasons for Substantial Delay in Consumer Decision Making," *Journal of Consumer Research* (September 1995), pp. 186–99.

9. Ruth N. Bolton, "A Dynamic Model of the Duration of the Customer's Relationship with a Continuous Service Provider: The Role of Satisfaction," *Marketing Science* 17 (1998), pp. 45–65.

10. Jagdish N. Sheth, Banwari Mitral, and Bruce Newman, *Consumer Behavior* (Fort Worth: Dryden Press, 1999), p. 22.

11. Frederick F. Reichheld and Thomas Teal, *The Loyalty Effect* (Boston: Harvard Business School Press, 1996), "What's a Loyal Customer Worth?" *Fortune* (December 11, 1995), p. 182; and Patricia Sellers, "Keeping the Buyers You Already Have," *Fortune* (Autumn–Winter 1993), p. 57. For an in-depth examination of this topic, see Werner J. Reinartz and V. Kumar, "On the Profitability of Long-Life Customers in a Noncontractual Setting: An Empirical Investigation and Implications for Marketing," *Journal of Marketing* (October 2000), pp. 17–35.

12. For an overview of research on involvement, see John C. Mowen and Michael Minor, *Consumer Behavior*, 5th ed. (Upper Saddle River, NJ: Prentice Hall, 1998), pp. 64–68; and Wayne D. Hoyer and Deborah J. MacInnis, *Consumer Behavior*, 3rd ed. (Boston: Houghton Mifflin Co., 2004), pp. 57–59.

13. For an overview on the three problem-solving variations, see Hawkins, Mothersbaugh, and Best, *Consumer Behavior*, pp. 510–14.

14. Russell Belk, "Situational Variables and Consumer Behavior," *Journal of Consumer Research* (December 1975), pp. 157–63.

15. A.H. Maslow, *Motivation and Personality* (New York: Harper & Row, 1970). Also see Richard Yalch and Frederic Brunel, "Need Hierarchies in Consumer Judgments of Product Design: Is It Time to Reconsider Maslow's Hierarchy?" in Kim Corfman and John Lynch, eds., *Advances in Consumer Research* (Provo, UT: Association for Consumer Research, 1996), pp. 405–10.

16. Joel B. Cohen, "An Interpersonal Orientation to the Study of Consumer Behavior," *Journal of Marketing Research* (August 1967), pp. 270–78; and Rena Bartos, *Marketing to Women around the World* (Cambridge, MA: Harvard Business School, 1989).

17. Terry Clark, "International Marketing and National Character: A Review and Proposal for an Integrative Theory," *Journal of Marketing* (October 1990), pp. 66–79; and John-Benedict E. M. Steenkamp, "The Role of National Culture in International Marketing Research," *International Marketing Review* 18, no. 1 (2001), pp. 30–44.

18. Jane Spencer, "Lenovo Puts Style in New Laptop," *The Wall Street Journal*, January, 2008, p. B5.

19. This example provided in Michael R. Solomon, *Consumer Behavior*, 4th ed. (Upper Saddle River, NJ: Prentice Hall, 1999), p. 59.

20. For further reading on subliminal perception, see Anthony G. Greenwald, Sean C. Draine, and Richard L. Abrams, "Three Cognitive Markers of Unconscious Semantic Activation," *Science* (September 1996), pp. 1699–701; Dennis L. Rosen and Surendra N. Singh, "An Investigation of Subliminal Embedded Effect on Multiple Measures of Advertising Effectiveness," *Psychology & Marketing* (March–April 1992), pp. 157–73; and Kathryn T. Theus, "Subliminal Advertising and the Psychology of Processing Unconscious Stimuli: A Review of the Research," *Psychology & Marketing* (May–June 1994), pp. 271–90.

21. August Bullock, *The Secret Sales Pitch* (San Jose, CA: Norwich Publishers, 2004); "GOP Commercial Resurrects Debate on Subliminal Ads," *The Wall Street Journal* (September 13, 2000), p. B10; "I Will Love This Story," *U.S. News & World Report* (May 12, 1997), p. 12; and "Firm Gets Message Out Subliminally," *Dallas Morning News* (February 2, 1997), pp. 1H, 6H.

22. Sholnn Freeman, "Brand Breakdown," *The Washington Post*, March 26, 2006, p. F1ff.

23. Martin Fishbein and I. Aizen, *Belief, Attitude, Intention and Behavior: An Introduction to Theory and Research* (Reading, MA: Addison-Wesley 1975), p. 6.

24. Richard J. Lutz, "Changing Brand Attitudes through Modification of Cognitive Structure," *Journal of Consumer Research* (March 1975), pp. 49–59. See also Mowen and Minor, *Consumer Behavior*, pp. 287–88.

25. This discussion is based on Ed Keller and Jon Berry, *The Influentials* (New York: Simon and Schuster, 2003).

26. Lyn Fletcher, "The Buzz on Buzz," *Marketing* (August 23, 2004).

27. F.G. Crane and T.K. Clarke, "The Identification of Evaluative Criteria and Cues Used in Selecting Services," *Journal of Services Marketing* (Spring 1988), pp. 53–59.

28. This example is drawn from **www.matchstick.ca**; **www.buzzcanuck.typepad.com**; **www.the-cma.org**. Also see, Emanuel Rosen, *Anatomy of Buzz Marketing Revisited* (New York: Broadway Business, 2009).

29. For an extensive review on consumer socialization of children, see Deborah Roedder John, "Consumer Socialization of Children: A Retrospective Look at Twenty-Five Years of Research," *Journal of Consumer Research* (December 1999), pp. 183–213.

30. "Special Issues for Young Children," and "How Marketers Target Kids," **www.media-awareness.ca** (downloaded January 10, 2007).

31. J. Paul Peter and Jerry C. Olson, *Consumer Behavior and Marketing Strategy*, 8th ed. (Burr Ridge, IL: McGraw Hill/Irwin, 2008).

32. This discussion is based on Hawkins, Mothersbaugh, and Best, *Consumer Behavior: Building Marketing Strategy*; **www.teenresearch.com**, downloaded April 1, 2007; "Teens Rule," **MediaBuyer.com**, downloaded April 7, 2007; Jennifer Saranow, "This Is the Car We Want, Mommy," *The Wall Street Journal*, November 9, 2006, pp. D1, D4; and "Trillion-Dollar Kids," *The Economist*, December 2, 2006, p. 66.

33. Harold R. Kerbo, *Social Stratification and Inequality* (Burr Ridge, IL: McGraw-Hill, 2000). For an extensive discussion on social class, see Eric Arnould, Linda Price, and George Zinkhan, *Consumers*, 2nd ed. (Burr Ridge, IL: McGraw Hill/Irwin, 2004), chap. 6.

34. Astrid Van Den Broek, "Fighting Cultural Fade," *Strategy Magazine* (February 11, 2004), p. 21.

35. Adapted from "Viva la Difference!?" *Marketing* (October 27, 2008), p. 23; Joel Mitch, "User-Generated Future," *Marketing* (December 4, 2006), p. 1,3; Eric Blais, "The 36 Keys of the Quebecois Revisited," *Marketing* (November 2004); Nicolette Fleming, "The True Meaning of Profitez," *Marketing* (June 10, 2002); **www.environics.ca**, PRIZMCE (downloaded June 10, 2005); Danny Kucharsky, "Most Quebecers Ignoring Online Ads," *Marketing* (December 2006), p.4; Hubert Sacy, "Moderating Effect," *Marketing* (April 10, 2006), p. 17; and Danny Kucharsky, "French Lessons," *Marketing* (March 27, 2006), p. 8.

36. Rebecca Harris, "Embrace and Prosper," *Marketing* (January 23, 2006), p. 11.

37. Rebecca Harris, "Home Away From Home," *Marketing* (February 13, 2006), p. 4.

Case: The case was written by Frederick G. Crane.

CHAPTER 6

1. Information provided by Bombardier (2009).

2. Statistics Canada, **www.statcan.ca**, CANSIM, 304-0014, 304-0015 (September 15, 2009).

3. Statistics Canada, **www.statcan.ca**, CANSIM, 380-0002 and 13-001 XIB (September 15, 2009).

4. Statistics Canada, **www.statcan.ca/english/Subjects/Standard/napcs/napcs.htm** (downloaded March 17, 2007).

5. An argument that consumer buying and organizational buying do not have important differences is found in Edward F. Fern and James R. Brown, "The Industrial/Consumer Marketing Dichotomy: A Case of Insufficient Justification," *Journal of Marketing* (Spring 1984), pp. 68–77. However, most writers on the subject do draw distinctions between the two types of buying. See, for example, Michael D. Hutt and Thomas W. Speh, *Business Marketing Management*, 7th ed. (Fort Worth, TX: Dryden Press, 2001); and H. Michael Hayes, Per V. Jenster, and Nils-Erik Aaby, *Business Marketing: A Global Perspective* (Chicago: Richard D. Irwin, 1996).

6. This listing and portions of the following discussion are based on F. Robert Dwyer and John F. Tanner, Jr., *Business Marketing*, 2nd ed. (Burr Ridge, IL: McGraw-Hill/Irwin, 2002; Edward G. Brierty, Robert W. Eckles, and Robert R. Reeder, *Business Marketing*, 3rd ed. (Upper Saddle River, NJ: Prentice Hall, 1998); Frank G. Bingham, Jr., *Business Marketing Management* (Lincolnwood, IL: NTC, 1998).

7. F. Robert Dwyer and John Tanner, *Business Marketing* (Burr Ridge, ILL: McGraw-Hill, 2002).

8. "Latin Trade Connection," *Latin Trade* (June 1997), p. 72.

9. "Boise Cascade Turns Green," *The Wall Street Journal* (September 3, 2003), p. B6.

10. For a study of buying criteria used by industrial firms, see Daniel H. McQuiston and Rockney G. Walters, "The Evaluative Criteria of Industrial Buyers: Implications for Sales Training," *Journal of Business & Industrial Marketing* (Summer/Fall 1989), pp. 65–75. See also "What Buyers Look For," *Sales & Marketing Management* (August 1995), p. 31.

11. For an overview on ISO 9000 certification, see Thomas H. Stevenson and Frank C. Barnes, "What Industrial Marketers Need to Know about ISO 9000 Certification: A Review, Update, and Integration with Marketing," *Industrial Marketing Management* (November 2002), pp. 695–703.

12. P.K. Humphreys, W.L. Li and L.Y. Chan, "The Impact of Supplier Development on Buyer-Supplier Performance," *Omega,* 32(2), 2004, pp. 131–143.

13. This example is found in Sandy D. Jap and Jakki J. Mohr, "Leverage Internet Technologies in B2B Relationships," *California Management Review* (Summer 2002), pp. 24–38.

14. "Harley-Davidson Company," *Purchasing Magazine Online* (September 4, 2003).

15. "IBM Plans New Supercomputers," *Dallas Morning News* (November 19, 2002), p. 8D.

16. Pratibha A. Dabholkar, Wesley J. Johnston, and Amy S. Cathey, "The Dynamics of Long-Term Business-to-Business Exchange Relationships," *Journal of Academy of Marketing Science,* vol. 22, 2 (1994), pp. 130–45.

17. "EDS Signs $1.7 Billion IT Services Agreement with Kraft Foods," EDS news release, April 28, 2006; and "HP Finalizes $3 Billion Outsourcing Agreement to Manage Procter & Gamble's IT Infrastructure," Hewlett-Packard news release, May 6, 2003.

18. James C. Anderson and James A. Narus, *Business Market Management* (Upper Saddle River, NJ: Prentice Hall, 1999); and Neil Rackham, Lawrence Friedman and Richard Ruff, *Getting Partnering Right* (New York: McGraw-Hill, 1996); and Joseph P. Cannon and Christian Homburg, "Buyer-Supplier Relationships and Customer Firm Costs," *Journal of Marketing* (January 2001), pp. 29–43.

19. Helen Walker and Wendy Phillips, "Sustainable Procurement: Emerging Issues," *International Journal of Procurement Management,* 2 (1), 2009, pp. 41–61.

20. Thomas V. Bonoma, "Major Sales: Who Really Does the Buying?" *Harvard Business Review* (May–June 1982), pp. 11–19. For recent research on buying centres, see Morry Ghinghold and David T. Wilson, "Buying Center Research and Business Marketing Practices: Meeting the Challenge of Dynamic Marketing," *Journal of Business & Industrial Marketing,* vol. 13, no. 2 (1998), pp. 96–108; and Philip L. Dawes, Don Y. Lee, and Grahame R. Dowling, "Information Control and Influence in Emerging Buying Centers," *Journal of Marketing* (July 1998), pp. 55–68.

21. Paul A. Herbig, *Handbook of Cross-Cultural Marketing* (New York: The Halworth Press, 1998).

22. Jule M. Bristor, "Influence Strategies in Organizational Buying: The Importance of Connections to the Right People in the Right Places," *Journal of Business-to-Business Marketing,* vol. 1 (1993), pp. 63–98.

23. These definitions are adapted from Frederick E. Webster, Jr., and Yoram Wind, *Organizational Buying Behavior* (Englewood Cliffs, NJ: Prentice Hall, 1972), p. 6.

24. "Can Corning Find Its Optic Nerve?" *Fortune* (March 19, 2001), pp. 148–50.

25. Representative studies on the buy-class framework that document its usefulness include Erin Anderson, Wujin Chu, and Barton Weitz, "Industrial Purchasing: An Empirical Exploration of the Buy Class Framework," *Journal of Marketing* (July 1987), pp. 71–86; Morry Ghingold, "Testing the 'Buy-Grid' Buying Process Model," *Journal of Purchasing and Materials Management* (Winter 1986), pp. 30–36; P. Matthyssens and W. Faes, "OEM Buying Process for New Components: Purchasing and Marketing Implications," *Industrial Marketing Management* (August 1985), pp. 145–57.

26. See, for example, R. Vekatesh, Ajay Kohli, and Gerald Zaltman, "Influence Strategies in Buying Centers," *Journal of Marketing* (October 1995), pp. 61–72; Gary L. Lilien and Anthony Wong, "An Exploratory Investigation of the Structure of the Buying Center in the Metal Working Industry," *Journal of Marketing Research* (February 1984), pp. 1–11. See also, Christopher P. Puto, Wesley E. Patton III,

and Ronald H. King, "Risk Handling Strategies in Industrial Vendor Selection Decisions," *Journal of Marketing* (Winter 1985), pp. 89–98.

27. "B2B E-Commerce Headed for Trillions," **www.clickz.com** (downloaded September 1, 2009); and "Electronic Commerce and Technology," *The Daily,* Statistics Canada (April 20, 2009).

28. This discussion is based on Jennifer Reinhold, "What We Learned in the New Economy," *Fast Company* (March 4, 2004), pp. 56ff; Mark Roberti, "General Electric's Spin Machine," *The Industry Standard* (January 22–29, 2001), pp. 74–83; "Grainger Lightens Its Digital Load," *Industrial Distribution* (March 2001), pp. 77–79; and **www.boeing.com/procurement** (downloaded February 6, 2004).

29. "B2B, Take 2," *Business Week Online* (November 25, 2003).

30. Mark Krauss, "eBay 'Bids' on Small-Biz Firms to Sustain Growth," *Marketing News* (December 8, 2003), pp. 6, 7; "eBay Realizes Success in Small-Biz Arena," *Marketing News* (May 1, 2004), p. 11; and **www.ebaybusiness.com**.

31. This discussion is based on Robert J. Dolan and Youngme Moon, "Pricing and Market Making on the Internet," *Journal of Interactive Marketing* (Spring 2000), pp. 56–73; and Ajit Kambil and Eric van Heck, *Marking Markets: How Firms Can Benefit from Online Auctions and Exchanges* (Boston: Harvard Business School Press, 2002).

32. Susan Avery, "Supply Management Is Core of Success at UTC," *Purchasing,* September 7, 2006, pp. 36–39.

33. Shawn P. Daley and Prithwiraz Nath, "Reverse Auctions for Relationship Marketers," *Industrial Marketing Management,* February 2005, pp. 157–66; Sandy Jap, "An Exploratory Study of the Introduction of Online Reverse Auctions," *Journal of Marketing,* July 2003, pp. 96–107; and Sandy Jap, "The Impact of Online Reverse Auction Design on Buyer-Supplier Relationships," *Journal of Marketing,* January 2007, pp. 146–59.

Case: This case was written by Frederick G. Crane.

CHAPTER 7

1. **www.inniskillin.com**; **www.cme-mec.ca**; Rebecca Harris, "Innovative Icon," *Marketing,* December 4, 2006, pp. 19–20; Eve Lazarus, "Branching Out," *Marketing,* **www.marketingmag.ca** (downloaded June 22, 2005); **www.spinmaster.com**; and **www.gapaventures.com**.

2. These estimates are based on data from *International Trade Statistics 2010* (Geneva: World Trade Organization). Global trade statistics reported in this chapter also came from this source, unless otherwise indicated.

3. Ibid.

4. Masaaki Kotabe and Kristiaan Helsen, *Global Marketing Management,* 3rd ed. (New York: Wiley, 2004), p. 440.

5. Statistics in this section were derived from Statistics Canada, CANSIM 228-0003, 380-0017, 2010.

6. "Pocket Facts," Foreign Affairs & International Trade Canada; **www.international.gc.ca** (May 2010); and *International Trade Statistics 2010.*

7. Statistics Canada, CANSIM 228-0003 (2010).

8. Kara Asserud, "Your Next Big Thing: Canada's Hottest Export Markets," *Canadian Business Online* (March 3, 2007), **www.canadianbusiness.com**, "Pocket Facts, Foreign Affairs & International Trade Canada;" **www.international.gc.ca** (September, 2009); and *International Trade Statistics 2009.*

9. Michael E. Porter, *The Competitive Advantage of Nations* (New York: Free Press, 1990), pp. 577–615. For another view that emphasizes cultural differences, see David S. Landes, *The Wealth and Poverty of Nations* (New York: Norton, 1998).

10. Roger L. Martin and Michael E. Porter, "Canadian Competitiveness: Nine Years After the Crossroads." **www.mgmt.utoronto.ca/research/competitive.htm** (downloaded May 5, 2002).

11. Dennis R. Appleyard and Alfred J. Field, Jr., *International Economics,* 4th ed. (Burr Ridge, IL: McGraw-Hill/Irwin, 2001), chap. 15; "A Fruit Peace," *The Economist* (April 21, 2001), pp. 75–76; and

Gary C. Hufbauer and Kimberly A. Elliott, *Measuring the Cost of Protection in the United States* (Washington, DC: Institute for International Economics, 1994).

12. This discussion is based on information provided by the World Trade Organization, **www.wto.org** (downloaded March 17, 2007).

13. **www.juniper.net/company** (downloaded March 15, 2004); and "Alliances in Consumer and Packaged Goods," **www.corporatefinance. mckinsey.com** (downloaded Autumn 2003).

14. For an excellent overview of different types of global companies and marketing strategies, see Warren J. Keegan, *Global Marketing Management,* 7th ed. (Upper Saddle River, NJ: Prentice Hall, 2002), chap. 2.

15. Johnny K. Johansson and Ilkka A. Ronkainen, "The Brand Challenge," *Marketing Management* (March–April 2004), pp. 54–55.

16. Kevin Lane Keller, *Strategic Brand Management,* 2nd ed. (Upper Saddle River, NJ: Prentice Hall, 2003), p. 693.

17. For an extensive discussion on identifying global consumers, see Jean-Pierre Jeannet and H. David Hennessey, *Global Marketing Strategies,* 4th ed. (Boston: Houghton Mifflin, 1998).

18. "Worldwide Internet Users Top 1 Billion in 2005," *Computer Industry Almanac;* **www.c-I-a/pro106.htm** (downloaded March 22, 2007).

19. For comprehensive references on cross-cultural aspects of marketing, see Paul A. Herbig, *Handbook of Cross-Cultural Marketing* (New York: Halworth Press, 1998); Jean-Claude Usunier, *Marketing across Cultures,* 2nd ed. (London: Prentice Hall Europe, 1996); and Philip R. Cateora and John L. Graham, *International Marketing,* 12th ed. (Burr Ridge, IL: McGraw-Hill/Irwin, 2005). Unless otherwise indicated, examples found in this section appear in these excellent sources.

20. "Clash of Cultures," *BrandWeek* (May 4, 1998), p. 28. Also see R. L. Tung, *Business Negotiations with the Japanese* (Lexington, MA: Lexington Books, 1993).

21. For examples on cross-cultural marketing see Hawkins, Mothersbaugh, and Best, *Consumer Behavior,* 10th ed. (Burr Ridge, IL: McGraw-Hill, 2007).

22. "Greens Protest Coke's Use of Parthenon," *Dallas Morning News* (August 17, 1992), p. D4.

23. "Japanese Products are Popular in the U.S.," *Research Alert* (November 17, 2000), p. 8; and "Buying American," *American Demographics* (March 1998), pp. 32–38; and Sharon Younger, "Marketing Overseas? Keep it Canadian," *Strategy Magazine* (February 11, 2002), p. 23.

24. "Marketing by Language: Oracle Trims Teams, Sees Big Savings," *Advertising Age International* (July 2000), pp. 4, 38.

25. Terrence A. Shimp and Subhash Sharma, "Consumer Ethnocentrism, Construction and Validation of the CETSCALE," *Journal of Marketing Research* (August 1987), pp. 280–89.

26. Subhash Sharma, Terrence Shimp, and Jeongshin Shin, "Consumer Ethnocentrism: A Test of Antecedents and Moderators," *Journal of the Academy of Marketing Science* (Winter 1995), pp. 26–37; Joel Herche, "A Note on the Predictive Validity of the CETSCALE," *Journal of the Academy of Marketing Science* (Summer 1992), pp. 261–64;

27. Vijay Mahajan and Kamini Banga, *The 86 Percent Solution: How to Succeed in the Biggest Market Opportunity of the Next 50 Years* (Upper Saddle River, NJ: Pearson Education, 2006); and C.K. Pralahad, *The Fortune at the Bottom of the Pyramid: Eradicating Poverty Through Profits* (Upper Saddle River, NJ: Pearson Education, 2005).

28. "Betting on a New Label: Made in Russia," *BusinessWeek* (April 12, 1999), p. 122; "Russia and Central-Eastern Europe: Worlds Apart," *BrandWeek* (May 4, 1998), pp. 30–31; and "We Will Bury You . . . with a Snickers Bar," *U.S. News & World Report* (January 26, 1998), pp. 50–51.

29. **www.wto.com** (downloaded February 15, 2004).

30. Pralahad, *The Fortune at the Bottom of the Pyramid;* and Jay Greene, "Taking Tiny Loans to the Next Level," *BusinessWeek,* November 27, 2006, pp. 76–79.

31. Cateora and Graham, *International Marketing.*

32. For an extensive and recent examination of these market entry options, see, for example, Johnny K. Johansson, *Global Marketing: Foreign Entry, Local Marketing, and Global Management,* 3rd ed. (Burr Ridge, IL: McGraw Hill/Irwin, 2003); Keegan, *Global Marketing Management;* Kotabe and Helson, *Global Marketing Management;* and Cateora and Graham, *International Marketing.*

33. McDonald's 2009 Annual Report.

34. "A Survey of Business in China," *The Economist* (March 20, 2004), special section.

35. This discussion is based on Keller, *Strategic Brand Management,* pp. 709–10; "Machines for the Masses," *The Wall Street Journal* (December 9, 2003), pp. A19, A20; "The Color of Beauty," *Forbes* (November 22, 2000), pp. 170–76; "It's Goo, Goo, Goo, Goo Vibrations at the Gerber Lab," *The Wall Street Journal* (December 4, 1996), pp. A1, A6; Donald R. Graber, "How to Manage a Global Product Development Process," *Industrial Marketing Management* (November 1996), pp. 483–98; and Herbig, *Handbook of Cross-Cultural Marketing.*

36. Jagdish N. Sheth and Atul Parvatiyar, "The Antecedents and Consequences of Integrated Global Marketing," *International Marketing Review* 18, no. 1 (2001), pp. 16–29. Also see D. Szymanski, S. Bharadwaj, and R. Varadarajan, "Standardization versus Adaptation of International Marketing Strategy: An Empirical Investigation," *Journal of Marketing* (October 1993), pp. 1–17.

37. This discussion is based on John Fahy and Fuyuki Taguchi, "Reassessing the Japanese Distribution System," *Sloan Management Review* (Winter 1995), pp. 49–61; and Edward Tse, "The Right Way to Achieve Profitable Growth in the Chinese Consumer Market," *Strategy & Business* (Second Quarter 1998), pp. 10–21.

38. "With Profits Elusive, Wal-Mart to Exit Germany," *The Wall Street Journal,* July 29, 2006, pp. A1, A6.

Case: CNS Breathe Right Strips: This case was prepared by Mary L. Brown based on interviews with Kevin McKenna, vice president, International and Nick Naumann, Sr. Marketing Services Manager of CNS, Inc. (September 2004).

CHAPTER 8

1. Adapted from Joseph Rydholm, "Will Creativity Save Marketing Research," *Quirks* (May 2009), p. 152.

2. For a lengthier, expanded, consult the American Marketing Association's Web site at **www.marketingpower.com**; for a researcher's comments on this and other definitions of marketing research, see Lawrence D. Gibson, "Quo Vadis, Marketing Research?" *Marketing Research* (Spring 2000), pp. 36–41.

3. Joseph Pereira, "Unknown Fruit Takes on Unfamiliar Markets," *The Wall Street Journal* (September 9, 1995), pp. B1, B5.

4. Lisa D'Innocenzo, "Focus Groups for a New Age," *Strategy Magazine* (August 23, 2004), p. 10.

5. Rob Gerlsbeck, "Canadian Forces," *Marketing* (November 26, 2007), p. 22.

6. "Focus on Consumers," *General Mills Midyear Report* (Minneapolis, MN: General Mills, January 8, 1998), pp. 2–3.

7. Michael J. McCarthy, "Stalking the Elusive Teenage Trendsetter," *The Wall Street Journal* (November 19, 1998), pp. B1, B10.

8. **www.trendhunter.com/about-trend-hunter**, accessed July 25, 2010.

9. Joshua Grossnickle and Oliver Raskin, "What's Ahead on the Internet," *Marketing Research* (Summer 2001), pp. 9–13.

10. Scott Moore, "The New Currency," *Marketing* (September 14, 2009), p. 41.

11. Mark Maremont, "New Toothbrush Is Big-Ticket Item," *The Wall Street Journal* (October 27, 1998), pp. B1, B6; Emily Nelson, "P&G Checks Out Real Life," *The Wall Street Journal* (May 17, 2001), pp. B1, B4.

12. Kenneth Chang, "Enlisting Science's Lessons to Entice More Shoppers to Spend More," *The New York Times*, September 19, 2006, p. D3; and Janet Adamy, "Cooking Up Changes at Kraft Foods," *The Wall Street Journal*, February 20, 2007, pp. B1, B4.

13. Dina Elboghdady, "Naked Truth," *Portland Press* (March 5, 2002), pp. C1, C5. For more information on Ethnography, see Hy Mariampolski, *Ethnography for Marketers: A Guide to Consumer Immersion* (Thousand Oaks, CA: Sage Publications, 2006).

14. Laurie Burkitt, "Battle for the Brain," *Forbes* (November 16, 2009), pp. 76–78.

15. Marketing Research and Intelligence Association; **www.mria-arim.ca** (downloaded November 11, 2009).

16. Patrick E. Murphy and Gene R. Lacznick, *Marketing Ethics: Cases and Readings* (Upper Saddle River, NJ: Pearson Education, 2006).

17. "Charter of Respondent Rights," Marketing Research and Intelligence Association, **www.mria-arim.ca** (downloaded March 27, 2007).

Case: This case was written by Frederick G. Crane. Thanks to Mark L. Michelson, "The Differences Between Mystery Shopping and Marketing Research," *Quirk's Marketing Research Review*, January, 2001, for his contribution.

CHAPTER 9

1. Information in the chapter opener was obtained from the Sleep Research Institute, the National Sleep Foundation, and the International Sleep Products Association (March 20, 2007).

2. Liz Torlee, "Not My News," *Marketing* (November 28, 2005), pp. 29, 32.

3. Ken Wong, "Why Johnny Can't Segment," *Marketing*, January 9, 2006, p. 11; Marc H. Meyer, *FASTPATH to Growth* (Oxford: Oxford University Press, 2007); Malcolm McDonald, "The Marketing Leaders," **www.themarketingleaders.com/articles/oct06/malcolm_mcdonald.htm** (downloaded April 24, 2007); and Roger J. Best, *Market-based Management* (Saddle River, NJ: Prentice-Hall, 2000).

4. Patti Summerfield, "The Death of Demographics," *Strategy Magazine* (October 20, 2003).

5. These examples were gleaned from the PRIZM C2 Clusters developed by Environics.

6. The discussion of fast-food trends and market share is based on: *National Consumer Survey© Choices 3 Crosstabulation Report: Fast-Food Restaurants* (New York: Simmons Market Research Bureau, Inc., Spring 2001).

7. Del J. Hawkins, David L. Mothersbaugh, and Roger J. Best, *Consumer Behavior*, 10th ed. (Burr Ridge, IL: McGraw-Hill/Irwin, 2007).

8. Eve Lazarus, "I'm a Big Kid Now," *Marketing* (August 14/21, 2006), p. 6.

9. Eve Lazarus, "Getting Juiced," *Marketing* (June 26, 2006), p. 9.

10. David Menzies, "Being Frank," *Marketing* (July 31/August 7, 2006), pp. 12, 14.

11. This discussion is based on Roger A. Kerin and Robert A. Peterson, *Strategic Marketing Problems: Cases and Comments*, 11th ed. (Upper Saddle River, NJ: Prentice Hall, 2007), pp. 147–49; John M. Mullins, Orville C. Walker Jr., Haper W. Boyd Jr., and Jean-Claude Larreche, *Marketing Management: A Strategic Decision-Marketing Approach*, 5th ed. (Burr Ridge, IL: McGraw-Hill/Irwin, 2005), p. 216; and Carol Traeger, "What Are Automakers Doing for Women? Part III: Volvo," **www.edmund.com**, July 26, 2005.

12. Nicholas Zamiska, "How Milk Got a Major Boost by Food Panel," *The Wall Street Journal*, August 30, 2004, pp. B1, B5.

13. Rebecca Winter, "Chocolate Milk," *Time*, April 30, 2001, p. 20.

14. Mark A. Moon, John T. Mentzer, Carlo D. Smith, and Michael S. Garver, "Seven Keys to Better Forecasting," *Business Horizons* (September –October 1998), pp. 44–52.

Case: This case was written by William Rudelius and is based on personal interviews with Linda Glassel, Tyler Herring, and Nick Skally in 2009.

CHAPTER 10

1. Much of the Apple example opening Chapter 10 is based on Lev Grossman, "The Apple of Your Ear," *Time*, January 22, 2007, pp. 48–54.

2. "Apple Sells Three Million iPads in 80 Days," Apple Inc. Press Release, June 10, 2010.

3. Debora Viana Thompson, Rebecca W. Hamilton, and Roland Rust, "Feature Fatigue: When Product Capabilities Become Too Much of a Good Thing," *Journal of Marketing Research*, November 2005, pp. 431–42; and Roland T. Rust, Debora Viana Thompson, and Rebecca W. Hamilton, "Defeating Feature Fatigue," *Harvard Business Review*, February 2006, pp. 98–107.

4. This discussion is based on Christopher Lovelock and Jochen Wirtz, *Services Marketing*, 5th edition (Upper Saddle River, NJ: Prentice-Hall, 2004).

5. Leonard Berry, Venkatesh Shankar, Janet Turner Parish, Susan Cadwallader, and Thomas Dotzel, "Creating New Markets Through Service Innovation," *MIT Sloan Management Review* (Winter 2006), 56–71.

6. Greg A. Stevens and James Burley, "3,000 Raw Ideas = 1 Commercial Success!" *Research-Technology Management* (May–June 1997), pp. 16–27.

7. R. G. Cooper and E. J. Kleinschmidt, "New Products—What Separates Winners from Losers?" *Journal of Product Innovation Management* (September 1987), pp. 169–84; Robert G. Cooper, *Winning at New Products*, 2nd ed. (Reading, MA: Addison-Wesley, 1993), pp. 49–66; and Thomas D. Kuczmarski, "Measuring Your Return on Innovation," *Marketing Management* (Spring 2000), pp. 25–32.

8. Julie Fortser, "The Lucky Charm of Steve Sanger," *BusinessWeek* (March 26, 2001), pp. 75–76.

9. See Productscan Online at **www.productscan.com**.

10. Paul Brent, "Brewing Blues," *Marketing* (March 13, 2006), p. 8.

11. Robert Cooper, *The Accelerate to Market—Small-Medium Enterprise: A Stage-Gate Roadmap from Idea to Launch* (Ontario, Canada: Product Development Institute, 2002); and Pierre Loewe and Jennifer Dominiquini, "Overcoming the Barriers to Effective Innovation," *Strategy & Leadership* 34, no. 1 (2006), pp. 24–31.

12. Dan P. Lovallo and Olivier Sibony, "Distortions and Deceptions in Strategic Decisions," *The McKinsey Quarterly*, no. 1 (2006), pp. 19–29; and Byron G. Augusto, Eric P. Harmon, and Vivek Pandit, "The Right Service Strategies for Product Companies," *The McKinsey Quarterly*, no. 1 (2006), pp. 41–51.

13. Isabelle Royer, "Why Bad Projects Are So Hard to Kill," *Harvard Business Review*, February 2003, pp. 10–30; John T. Morn, Dan P. Lovallo, and S. Patrick Viguerie, "Beating the Odds in Market Entry," *The McKinsey Quarterly*, no. 4 (2005), pp. 35–45; Leslie Perlow and Stephanie Williams, "Is Silence Killing Your Company?" *Harvard Business Review*, May 2003, pp. 52–58; Beverly K. Brockman and Robert M. Morgan, "The Moderating Effect of Organizational Cohesiveness in Knowledge Use and New Product Development," *Journal of Marketing Science*, no. 3 (Summer 2006), pp. 295–306; Eyal Biyalogorsky, William Boulding, and Richard Staelin, "Stuck in the Past: Why Managers Persist with New Product Failures," *Journal of Marketing*, April 2006, pp. 108–21; and Irwin L. Janis, *Groupthink* (New York: Free Press, 1988).

14. Jena McGregor, "How Failure Breeds Success," *BusinessWeek,* July 10, 2006, pp. 42–52.

15. Ibid.

16. Amy Merrick, "As 3M Chief, McNerney Wastes No Time Starting Systems Favored by Ex-Boss Welch," *The Wall Street Journal* (June 5, 2001), pp. B1, B4; see General Electric's Web site (**www.ge.com**) for an in-depth explanation of Six Sigma that 3M and other Fortune 500 companies use to improve quality: "The Road to Customer Impact: What Is Six Sigma?"

17. Jonas Matthing, Per Kristensson, and Andres Gustafsson, "Developing Successful Technology-based Services: The Issue of Identifying and Involving Innovative Users," *Journal of Services Marketing,* 20 (2006), 288–97.

18. Janice Griffiths-Hemans and Rajiv Grover, "Setting the Stage for Creative New Products: Investigating the Idea Fruition Process," *Journal of the Academy of Marketing Science,* Winter 2006, pp. 27–39.

19. C. K. Prahalad and Venkat Ramswamy, *The Future of Competition* (Boston: Harvard Business School Press, 2004); Steve Hamm, "Adding Customers to the Design Team," *BusinessWeek* (March 1, 2004), pp. 22–23; and Anthony W. Ulwick, "Turn Customer Input into Innovation," *Harvard Business Review* (January 2002), pp. 91–97.

20. Jeffrey Pfeffer, "Why Employees Should Lead Themselves," CCNMoney.com (February 6, 2006), **http://money.cnn.com/ magazines/business2**; "Ideas That Bloom," *BusinessWeek* (Spring 2006), **www.businessweek.com/magazine/content**; and William Taylor, "Here's an Idea: Let Everyone Have Ideas," *The New York Times* (March 26, 2006).

21. "Ideas That Bloom," *BusinessWeek.*

22. Bruce Nussbaum, "The Power of Design," *BusinessWeek* (May 17, 2004), pp. 86–94; the article gives many techniques for idea and concept generation, as do Appendixes A, B, and C in Merle Crawford and Anthony Di Benedetto, *New Products Management,* 7th ed. (Burr Ridge, IL: McGraw-Hill/Irwin, 2003).

23. Peter Lewis, "Texas Instruments' Lunatic Fringe," *Fortune,* September 4, 2006, pp. 121–28.

24. Personal interview with David Windorski, 3M (April 2004).

25. See Ipsos Canada's Web site at **www.ipsos.ca**.

26. Larry Huston and Nobil Sakkab, "Connect and Develop," *Harvard Business Review,* March 2006, pp. 58–66; "Pringles Announces First-of-Its-Kind Technology that Prints Directly on Individual Crisps," **www.pg.com**, accessed April 6, 2004.

27. Ely Dahan and John R. Hauser, "Product Development—Managing a Dispersed Process," in *Handbook of Marketing,* ed. Barton Weitz and Robin Wensley (London: Sage Publications, 2006), pp. 179–222.

28. Gary Hammel, "Innovation's New Math," *Fortune,* July 9, 2001, pp. 130–31.

29. Thomas M. Burton, "By Learning from Failures, Lilly Keeps Drug Pipeline Full," *The Wall Street Journal,* April 21, 2004, pp. A1, A12.

30. Ben Elgin, "Managing Google's Idea Factory," *BusinessWeek,* October 3, 2005, pp. 88–90.

31. Tom Molson and George Sproles, "Styling Strategy," *Business Horizons* (September–October 2000), pp. 45–52.

32. Yuhong Wu, Sridhar Balasubramanian, and Vijay Mahajan, "When Is a Preannounced New Product Likely to Be Delayed?" *Journal of Marketing* (April, 2004), pp. 101–13.

33. Kerry A. Dolan, "Speed: The New X Factor," *Forbes,* December 26, 2005, pp. 74–77.

34. Gail Edmonson, "BMW's Dream Factory," *BusinessWeek,* October 16, 2006, pp. 70–80; Steve Hamm, "Speed Demons," *BusinessWeek,* March 27, 2006, pp. 68–76; and Amy Barrett, "J & J: Reinventing How It Invents," *BusinessWeek,* April 17, 2006, pp. 60–61.

35. Peter Burrows, "Architects of the Info Age," *BusinessWeek,* March 29, 2004, p. 22.

36. For more information on how to reduce the risks of new product development, see Susuma Ogawa, "Reducing the Risks of New Product Development," *MIT Sloan Management Review* (Winter 2006), pp. 65–71.

Case: The 3M Greptile Grip Golf Glove video case was written by Michael J. Vessey based on interviews with Dr. George Dierberger, 3M personnel, 3M sources, and other published sources, including "3M Introduces 3M Golf Glove With Griptile Grip," 3M press release (May 5, 2004); "Who We Are," National Golf Foundation, see **www.ngf.org**; "The Golf 20/20 Vision for the Future Industry Report for 2003" (published June 8, 2004), see **www.golf2020.com**; "Core Golfers Gain Ground in 2003," National Golf Foundation press release (May 21, 2004), see **www.ngf.org**; National Sporting Goods Association e-mail newsletter (received June 21, 2004), see **www.nsga.org**; 3M Golf Griptile Grip Business Plan; and Golf Datatech 2003 Retail Market Share Report, see **www. golfdatatech.com**.

CHAPTER 11

1. Betsy McKay, "Pepsi Launches Low-Calorie Gatorade," *The Wall Street Journal,* September 7, 2007, p. B6; Cheryl Jackson, "Quaker Acquisition a Big Winner for Pepsi," *Chicago Sun-Times,* December 1, 2006, pp. D1, 5; Darren Rovell, *First in Thirst: How Gatorade Turned the Science of Sweat into a Cultural Phenomenon* (New York: AMACOM, 2005); "Cindy Alston: CMO, Gatorade and Propel," *Advertising Age,* November 13, 2006, p. S6; and "Gatorade Works on Endurance," *The Wall Street Journal,* March 21, 2005, p. B6.

2. For an extended discussion of the generalized product life cycle, see Donald R. Lehmann and Russell S. Winer, *Product Management,* 5th ed (Burr Ridge, IL: McGraw-Hill, 2008).

3. Jack Neff, "Six-Blade Blitz," *Advertising Age,* September 19, 2005, pp. 3, 53; and Jack Neff, "Fusion's Nuclear Launch Isn't Good Enough—Yet," *Advertising Age,* July 3, 2006, pp. 3, 23.

4. John W. Mullins, Orville C. Walker, Jr., Harper W. Boyd, Jr., and Jean-Claude Larréché, *Marketing Management: A Strategic Decision-Making Approach,* 5th ed. (Burr Ridge, IL: McGraw-Hill/Irwin, 2005), p. 396.

5. Kate MacArthur, "Coke Energizes Tab, Neville Isdell's Fave," *Advertising Age,* August 29, 2005, pp. 3, 21.

6. Julia Boorstin, "Can Fusion Become a Billion-Dollar Razor?" **MoneyCentral.msn.com**, downloaded January 10, 2007.

7. Everett M. Rogers, *Diffusion of Innovations,* 5th ed. (New York: Free Press, 2003).

8. Jagdish N. Sheth and Banwasi Mitral, *Consumer Behavior: A Managerial Perspective,* 2nd ed. (Mason, OH: South-Western College Publishing, 2003).

9. "When Free Samples Become Saviors," *The Wall Street Journal* (August 14, 2001), pp. B1, B4, and **www.marketingmag.ca** (March 9, 1998).

10. For a historical perspective on the product/brand manager system, see George S. Low and Ronald A. Fullerton, "Brands, Brand Management, and the Brand Manager System: A Critical-Historical Evaluation," *Journal of Marketing Research* (May 1994), pp. 173–90.

11. **www.newbalance.com** (downloaded May 6, 2007).

12. Sheth and Mitral, *Consumer Behavior*; and Marsha Cohen, *Marketing to the 501 Population* (New York: EPM Communications, Inc., 2007).

13. "Food Marketers Latch on to Health," *Advertising Age* (February 23, 2004), pp. 4, 41; and Daniel Kadlec "The Low Carb Frenzy," *Time* (May 3, 2004), pp. 47–54.

14. John Gourville, "How to Avoid a Price Increase," *Working Knowledge for Business Leaders,* Harvard Business School, June 28, 2004; "The Shrink Wrap," *Time,* June 2, 2003, p. 81; "Don't Raise the Price, Lower the Water Award," *BrandWeek,* January 8, 2001, p. 19; and "More For Less," *Consumer Reports,* August 2004, p. 63.

15. "Building Brands in a Complex Environment," Canadian Marketing Association, Ottawa (May 2007).

16. This discussion is based on Kevin Lane Keller, *Strategic Brand Management,* 2nd ed. (Upper Saddle River, NJ: Prentice Hall, 2003).

17. This discussion is based on Kevin Lane Keller, "Building Customer-Based Brand Equity" *Marketing Management* (July–August, 2001), pp. 15–19.

18. Sharon Morrison and Frederick G. Crane, "Building the Service Brand by Creating and Managing an Emotional Brand Experience," *Journal of Brand Management*, (May 2007), pp. 410–21.

19. Susan Heinrich, "The Leafs Budding Brand," *National Post* (June 4, 2001), p. C4; and Frederick G. Crane and Jeffrey E. Sohl, "Imperatives for Venture Success: Entrepreneurs Speak," *The International Journal of Entrepreneurship and Innovation* (May 2004), pp. 99–106.

20. "2009 BRANDZ, Top 100 Most Powerful Brands," Millward Brown Optimor (New York, 2009); "Canada's Most Valuable Brands," Brand Finance Canada (Toronto, 2009); and Alan Middleton, "The Measure of a Brand," *Marketing* (February 20, 2006), p. 8.

21. "Hummer Markets Shoes for Offroad Set," *Advertising Age* (January 12, 2004), pp. 3, 40; Bruce Orwell, "Disney's Magic Transformation?" *The Wall Street Journal* (October 4, 2000), pp. A1, A15; and Keller, *Strategic Brand Management*.

22. Rob Osler, "The Name Game: Tips on How to Get It Right," *Marketing News* (September 14, 1998), p. 50; and Keller, *Strategic Brand Management*. Also see Pamela W. Henderson and Joseph A. Cote, "Guidelines for Selecting or Modifying Logos," *Journal of Marketing* (April 1998), pp. 14–30; and Chiranjeev Kohli and Douglas W. LaBahn, "Creating Effective Brand Names: A Study of the Naming Process," *Journal of Advertising Research* (January–February 1997), pp. 67–75.

23. "When Brand Extension Becomes Brand Abuse," *BrandWeek* (October 26, 1998), pp. 20, 22.

24. Piyush Kumar, "The Impact of Cobranding on Customer Evaluations of Brand Counterextensions," *Journal of Marketing* (July 2005).

25. This discussion is based on David Aaker, *Brand Portfolio Strategy* (New York: Free Press, 2004); and "To Lure Older Girls, Mattel Brings in Hip-Hop Crowd," *The Wall Street Journal* (July 18, 2003), pp. A1, A6.

26. "Unilever Finally Pares Down to Core Brands," *Mergers & Acquisitions* (February 2004), pp. 6–9.

27. "Private Labels Stock on Growth," *The Wall Street Journal*, July 18, 2007, p. B8; and Lien Lamey, Barbara Deleersnyder, Marnik G. Dekimpe, and Jan-Benedict E. M. Steenkamp, "How Business Cycles Contribute to Private-Label Success: Evidence from the United States and Europe," *Journal of Marketing*, January 2007, pp. 1–15.

28. "Elizabeth Arden Unveils Wal-Mart Only Brand," *Advertising Age* (February 9, 2004), p. 2; and **www.Kodak.com/international** (downloaded December 3, 2003).

29. **www.pez.com**, downloaded February 1, 2007; David Welch, *Collecting Pez* (Murphysboro, IL: Bubba Scrubba Publications, 1995); and "Elements Design Adds Dimension to Perennial Favorite Pez Brand," *Package Design Magazine*, May 2006, pp. 37–38.

30. "Market Statistics," **Packaging-Gateway.com**, downloaded March 25, 2007.

31. "Green Bean Casserole Turns 50," *Dallas Morning News*, November 19, 2005, p. 10D.

32. "Packaging Is the Capper," *Advertising Age* (May 5, 2003), p. 22.

33. Theresa Howard, "Frito-Lay's New Stax to Take a Stand," *USA Today* (August 14, 2003), p. 12B.

34. Representative recent scholarly research on packaging and labeling perceptions includes: Priya Raghubir and Eric A. Greenleaf, "Ratios in Proportion: What Should the Shape of the Package Be?" *Journal of Marketing*, April 2006, pp. 95–107; Peter H. Bloch, Frederic F. Brunel, and Todd Arnold, "Individual Differences in the Centrality of Visual Product Aesthetics: Concept and Measurement," *Journal of Consumer Research*, March 2003, pp. 551–65: and Pamela Anderson, Joan Giese, and Joseph A. Cote, "Impression Management Using Typeface Design," *Journal of Marketing*, October 2004, pp. 60–72.

35. "Asian Brands Are Sprouting English Logos in Pursuit of Status, International Image," *The Wall Street Journal* (August 7, 2001), p. B7C.

36. Susanna Hamner, "Packaging that Pays," *Business 2.0*, July 26, 2006, pp. 68–69.

37. "Wal-Mart: Use Less Packaging," *Dallas Morning News*, September 23, 2006, p. 2D. For an overview of Procter & Gamble's environmental efforts, see *Sustainability Report 2005* (Cincinnati, OH: Procter & Gamble Company, 2006).

38. "Packaging," **www.hp.com**, downloaded January 17, 2007.

39. Christian Twigg-Flesner, *Consumer Product Guarantees* (Aldershot, England: Ashgate Publishing, 2003).

Case: This case was written by Frederick G. Crane.

CHAPTER 12

1. James H. Gilmore and B. Joseph Pine II, *Authenticity* (Boston: Harvard Business School Press, 2007).

2. W.C. Kim and R. Mauborgne, "Blue Ocean Strategy," *Harvard Business Review*, 82 (October 2004), pp. 76–84; and G. Keighley, "The Phantasmagoria Factory," *Business 2.0* (February 2004), pp. 103–7.

3. John E. G. Bateson and Douglas Hoffman, *Managing Services Marketing*, 6th ed. (Fort Worth: Dryden, 2004).

4. Statistics Canada, "Services Industries" (February 27, 2008), **www.statcan.gc.ca** (downloaded January 4, 2010); and Hebert G. Grubel and Michael A. Walker, *Services Industry Growth* (Vancouver: The Fraser Institute, 1989).

5. **www.cfa.ca** (downloaded January 5, 2010).

6. Christopher Lovelock and Evert Gummesson, "Whither Services Marketing?" *Journal of Services Research* 7 (August 2004), pp. 20–41.

7. Christopher Lovelock and Jochen Wirtz, *Services Marketing*, 6th ed. (Upper Saddle River, NJ: Pearson, 2007).

8. Valarie A. Zeithhaml, "How Consumer Evaluation Processes Differ Between Goods and Services," in James H. Donnelly and William R. Georges, eds., *Marketing of Services* (Chicago, IL; American Marketing Association, 1981).

9. Keith B. Murray, "A Test of Services Marketing Theory: Consumer Information Acquisition Activities," *Journal of Marketing* (January 1991), pp. 10–25; and F. G. Crane, *Professional Services Marketing: Strategy and Tactics* (New York: The Haworth Press, Inc., 1993).

10. Vicki Clift, "Everyone Needs Service Flow Charting," *Marketing News* (October 23, 1995), pp. 41, 43; Mary Jo Bitner, Bernard H. Booms, and Mary Stanfield Tetreault, "The Service Encounter: Diagnosing Favorable and Unfavorable Incidents," *Journal of Marketing* (January 1990), pp. 71–84; Eberhard Scheuing, "Conducting Customer Service Audits," *Journal of Consumer Marketing* (Summer 1989), pp. 35–41; and W. Earl Susser, R. Paul Olsen, and D. Daryl Wyckoff, *Management of Service Operations* (Boston: Allyn & Bacon, 1978).

11. John Ozment and Edward Morash, "The Augmented Service Offering for Perceived and Actual Service Quality," *Journal of the Academy of Marketing Science* (Fall 1994), pp. 352–63.

12. A. Parasuraman, Valarie A. Zeithaml, and Leonard L. Berry, "Reassessment of Expectations as a Comparison Standard in Measuring Service Quality: Implications for Further Research," *Journal of Marketing* (January 1994), pp. 111–24; and Leonard L. Berry, *On Great Service* (New York: Free Press, 1995).

13. Riadh Ladhari, "Assessment of the Psychometric Properties of SERVQUAL in the Canadian banking industry," *Journal of Financial Services Marketing* (June 2009) vol. 14, no. 1, pp. 70–82, and Jacquelyn Crane, Brenna Crane, and Frederick Crane "Patient Satisfaction with Family Physicians in Canada," *Journal of Medical Marketing*, vol. 6, no. 1 (2006), pp. 63–66.

14. Stephen S. Tax and Stephen W. Brown, "Recovering and Learning from Service Failure," *Sloan Management Review* (Fall 1998), pp. 75–88.

15. Lovelock and Wirtz, *Services Marketing*, 6th ed.

16. Francois Carillat, Fernando Jaramillo, and Jay Mulki, "Examining the Impact of Service Quality: A Meta-Analysis of Empirical Evidence," *Journal of Marketing Theory & Practice* (Spring 2009), vol. 17, no. 2, pp. 95–110; Richard Spreng, Linda Hui Shi, and Thomas Page, "Service Quality and Satisfaction in Business-to-Business Services," *Journal of Business & Industrial Marketing*, 2009,

vol. 24, no. 7/8, pp. 537–48; and Crane, Crane and Crane, "Patient Satisfaction with Family Physicians in Canada," *Journal of Medical Marketing*. Also see Gordon Fullerton and Shirley Taylor, "Mediating, Interactive, and Non-linear Effects in Service Quality and Satisfaction with Services Research," *Canadian Journal of Administrative Sciences* (June 2002).

17. Katherine N. Lemon, Tiffany Barnett White, and Russell S. Winer, "Dynamic Customer Relationship Management: Incorporating Future Considerations into the Service Retention Decision," *Journal of Marketing* (January 2002), pp. 1–14.

18. Lovelock and Wirtz, *Services Marketing*, 5th ed.; Valarie A. Zeithaml and Mary Jo Bitner, *Services Marketing*, 3rd ed. (Burr Ridge, IL: 2003); and Leighann Neilson and Megha Chadha, "International marketing strategy in the retail banking industry: The case of ICICI Bank in Canada." *Journal of Financial Services Marketing* (Dec 2008), vol. 13, no. 3, pp. 204–20.

19. Sundar G. Bharedwaj, P. Rajan Varadarajan and John Fahy, "Sustainable Competitive Advantage in Services Industries: A Conceptual Model and Research Propositions," *Journal of Marketing* (October 1993), pp. 83–99.

20. F. G. Crane, "The Relative Effect of Price and Personal Referral Cues on Consumers' Perceptions of Dental Services," *Health Marketing Quarterly*, vol. 13, no. 4 (1996), pp. 91–105.

21. Christopher Lovelock, *Services Marketing*.

22. Robert E. Hite, Cynthia Fraser, and Joseph A. Bellizzi, "Professional Service Advertising: The Effects of Price Inclusion, Justification, and Level of Risk," *Journal of Advertising Research* 30 (August/September 1990), pp. 23–31; and F. G. Crane, *Professional Services Marketing: Strategy and Tactics*.

23. F. G. Crane, *Professional Services Marketing: Strategy and Tactics*; and Kathleen Mortimer "Services Advertising: The Agency Viewpoint," *Journal of Services Marketing*, No. 2 (2001), pp. 131–46.

24. Patriya Tansuhaj, Donna Randall, and Jim McCullough, "A Services Marketing Management Model: Integrating Internal and External Marketing Functions," *Journal of Services Marketing* (Winter 1988), pp. 31–38.

25. Christian Gronroos, "Internal Marketing Theory and Practice," in Tim Bloch, G. D. Upah, and V. A. Zeithaml, eds., *Services Marketing in a Changing Environment* (Chicago, IL: American Marketing Association, 1984); and Dennis J. Cahill, *Internal Marketing* (New York: The Haworth Press Inc., 1996).

26. Ibid.

27. Stephen W. Brown, "The Employee Experience," *Marketing Management* 12 (March–April 2003), pp. 12–13; Lawrence A. Crosby and Sheree L. Johnson, "Watch What I Do," *Marketing Management* 12 (November–December 2003), pp. 10–11

28. F.G. Crane, *Professional Services Marketing: Strategy and Tactics;* and Leonard L. Berry and Neeli Bendapudi, "Clueing in Customers," *Harvard Business Review* (February 2003), pp. 100–6.

29. Frederick H. deB. Harris and Peter Peacock, "Hold My Place, Please," *Marketing Management* (Fall 1995), pp. 34–46, and Lovelock, p. 17.

30. Lovelock and Wirtz, *Services Marketing*, 6th ed.

32. Stephen L. Vargo and Robert F. Lusch, "Evolving to a New Dominant Logic for Marketing," *Journal of Marketing* 68 (January 2004), pp. 1–17; and Stephen J. Grove, Raymond P. Fisk, and Joby John, "The Future of Services Marketing: Forecasts from Ten Services Experts," *Journal of Services Marketing*, vol. 17, no. 2 (2003), pp. 107–21.

33. Pine and Gilmore, *The Experience Economy*.

34. Ian Stuart, "Designing and Executing Memorable *Service Experiences*: Lights, Camera, Experiment, Integrate, Action!" *Business Horizons*, (Mar/Apr 2006), vol. 49, no. 2, pp. 149–59.

35. Leonard Berry, Venkatesh Shankar, Janet Turner Parish, Susan Cadwallader, and Thomas Dotzel, "Creating New Markets Through Service Innovation," *MIT Sloan Management Review* (Winter 2006), pp. 56–71.

Case: This case was written by Frederick G. Crane.

CHAPTER 13

1. **www.confederationbridge.com**; and interview in CBSL (January, 2010).

2. Ibid.

3. Adapted from Kent B. Monroe, *Pricing: Making Profitable Decisions*, 2nd ed. (New York: McGraw-Hill, 1990), chapter 4. See also David J. Curry, "Measuring Price and Quality Competition," *Journal of Marketing* (Spring 1985), pp. 106–17.

4. Del J. Hawkins, David L. Mothersbaugh, and Roger J. Best, *Consumer Behavior*, 10th ed. (Burr Ridge, IL: McGraw-Hill/Irwin, 2007).

5. Carmer Salvador, Enrique Rebolloso, Baltasar Fernandez-Ramirez and Maria del Pilar Canton, "Service Price Components and their Relationship with Customer Satisfaction," *Journal of Revenue and Pricing Management* (2007), 6, pp. 40–50. Also see F.G. Crane, *Professional Services Marketing: Strategy and Tactics* (New York: The Howard Press, Inc, 1993); and F. G. Crane, "The Relative Effect of Price and Personal Referral Cues on Consumers' Perceptions of Dental Services," *Health Marketing Quarterly*, vol. 13, no. 4 (1996), pp. 91–105.

6. Ian Yeoman and Una McMahon-Beattie, "The UK Low-Cost Economy," *Journal of Revenue and Pricing Management* (2007), 6, pp. 40–50.

7. **www.cadth.ca/media** (downloaded January 15, 2009); and Frederick G. Crane, "Ethics, Entrepreneurs and Corporate Managers: A Canadian Study," *Journal of Small Business & Entrepreneurship*, vol. 22, no. 3 (2009), pp. 267–74. Also see N. Craig Smith and John A. Quelch, *Ethics in Marketing* (Homewood, IL: Richard D. Irwin, 1993).

8. Ron Winslow, "How a Breakthrough Quickly Broke Down for Johnson & Johnson," *The Wall Street Journal* (September 18, 1998), pp. A1, A5.

9. Jeff Lobb, "The Right (Pepsi) Stuff," *Marketing* (July 8, 1996), p. 15.

10. "Price War Is Raging in Europe," *Business Week* (July 6, 1992), pp. 44–45.

11. Michael Garry, "Dollar Strength: Publishers Confront the New Economic Realities," *Folio: The Magazine for Magazine Management* (February 1989), pp. 88–93; Cara S. Trager, "Right Price Reflects a Magazine's Health Goals," *Advertising Age* (March 9, 1987), pp. 5–8ff; and Frank Bruni, "Price of Newsweek? It Depends," *Dallas Times Herald* (August 14, 1986), pp. S1, S20.

12. Wilson, Dominic, "Penetration Pricing," *Blackwell Encyclopedic Dictionary of Marketing*, 2005, p. 259.

13. "Time Is Money," *Forbes* (September 18, 2000), pp. 178–85.

14. "Premium AA Alkaline Batteries," *Consumer Reports* (March 21, 2001), p. 54; Kemp Powers, "Assault and Batteries," *Forbes* (September 4, 2000), pp. 54, 56; "Razor Burn at Gillette," *BusinessWeek* (June 18, 2001), p. 37.

15. "Why That Deal Is Only $9.99," *BusinessWeek* (January 10, 2000), p. 36. For further reading on odd–even pricing, see Jianping Liang and Vinay Kanetkar, "Price Endings: Magic and Math," *Journal of Product & Brand Management*, vol.15, no. 6 (2006), pp. 377–85.

16. Adam Nguyen, Roger Heeler and Cheryl Buff, "Consumer Perceptions of Bundles," *Journal of Product & Brand Management*, vol. 18, no. 3 (2009), pp. 218–25.

17. Thomas T. Nagle and Reed K. Holden, *The Strategy and Tactics of Pricing*, 4th ed. (Englewood Cliffs, NJ: Prentice Hall, 2006), pp. 243–49.

18. Kent B. Monroe, *Pricing: Making Profitable Decisions*, 2nd ed. (New York: McGraw-Hill, 1990), pp. 326–27. For a recent discussion of this topic, see Ramarao Desiraju and Steven M. Shugan, "Strategic

Service Pricing and Yield Management," *Journal of Marketing* (January 1999), pp. 44–56.

19. Robert J. Dolan and Hermann Simon, *Power Pricing: How Managing Price Transforms the Bottom Line* (New York: Free Press, 1996), p. 249.

20. Peter M. Noble and Thomas S. Gruca, "Industrial Pricing: Theory and Managerial Practice," *Marketing Science*, vol. 18, no. 3 (1999), pp. 435–54.

21. George E. Belch and Michael A. Belch, *Introduction to Advertising and Promotion*, 5th ed. (New York: Irwin/McGraw-Hill, 2001), p. 93.

22. "Variable Pricing on the Way for Yellow Pages," *Marketing Daily* (June 14, 2007), **www.marketing.ca.**

23. Monroe, *Pricing*, p. 34.

24. F.G. Crane, "The Relative Effect of Price and Personal Referral Cues on Consumers' Perceptions of Dental Services." Also see, Akshay R. Rao, "The Quality of Price as a Quality Cue," *Journal of Marketing Research*, November 2005, pp. 401–5.

25. Charles Fishman, "Which Price Is Right," *FastCompany* (March 2003), p. 92 (**www.fastcompany.com/magazine/68/pricing.html**).

26. For an extensive discussion on discounts, see Monroe, *Pricing*, chapters 14 and 15.

Case: This case was edited by Steven Hartley. Sources: Burkhard Bilger, "String Theory, Building a Better Guitar," *The New Yorker*, May 14, 2007, p. 79; and the Washburn Guitar Web site (**www.washburn.com**).

CHAPTER 14

1. Jerry Useem, "Simply Irresistible," *Fortune*, March 19, 2007, pp. 107–12; Nick Wingfield, "How Apple's Store Strategy Beat the Odds," *The Wall Street Journal*, May 17, 2006, pp. B1, B10; **www.apple.com/retail,** downloaded January 20, 2010; and **www.macworld.com**, January 22, 2010.

2. See Peter D. Bennett, ed. *Dictionary of Marketing Terms*, 3rd ed. (Chicago, American Marketing Association, 2000).

3. PepsiCo, Inc. Annual Report, 1997.

4. Donald V. Fites, "Make Your Dealers Your Partners," *Harvard Business Review* (March–April 1996), pp. 84–95.

5. Bert Rosenbloom, *Marketing Channels: A Management View*, 7th ed. (Cincinnati, OH: South-Western College Publishing, 2004).

6. **www.the-cma.org.**

7. **www.generalmills.com**, downloaded May 15, 2007; **www.nestle .com**, downloaded May 15, 2007; and Ian Friendly, "Cereal Partners Worldwide: A World of Opportunity," Nestlé Invester Seminar, Vevey, Switzerland, June 8, 2005.

8. For an overview of vertical marketing systems, see Lou Pelton, David Stutton, and James R. Lumpkin, *Marketing Channels*, 2nd ed. (Chicago: Irwin, 2002), chapter 14.

9. Joshua Levine and Matthew Swibel, "Dr. No," *Forbes* (May 28, 2001), pp. 72–76.

10. "Gillette Tries to Nick Schick in Japan," *The Wall Street Journal* (February 4, 1991), pp. B3, B4.

11. Christine B. Bucklin, Pamela A. Thomas-Graham, and Elizabeth Webster, "Channel Conflict: When Is It Dangerous?" *The McKinsey Quarterly*, No. 3, (1997), pp. 36–43.

12. "Dealer Surplus," *Forbes*, October 16, 2006, pp. 50–52; and Kevin Kelleher, "Giving Dealers a Raw Deal," *Business 2.0*, December 2004, pp. 82–83.

13. F. Robert Dwyer and Julie Gassenheimer, "Relational Roles and Triangle Dramas: Effects on Power Play and Sentiments in Industrial Channels," *Marketing Letters*, vol. 3 (1992), pp. 187–200.

14. Paul N. Bloom, Gregory T. Gundlach, and Joseph P. Cannon, "Slotting Allowances and Fees: Schools of Thought and Views of Practicing Managers," *Journal of Marketing*, April 2000, pp. 92–109; and William L. Wilkie, Debra M. Desrochers, and Gregory T. Gundlach,

"Marketing Research and Public Policy: The Case of Slotting Fees," *Journal of Public Policy & Marketing*, Fall 2002, pp. 275–89.

15. Jeffrey McCracken, "Ford Seeks Big Savings by Overhauling Supply System," *The Wall Street Journal*, September 29, 2005, p. All; April Terreri, "Driving Efficiencies in Automotive Logistics," **www.inboundlogistics.com**, January 2004; and Robyn Meredith, "Harder Than Hype," *Forbes*, April 16, 2001, pp. 188–94.

16. Major portions of this discussion are based on Sunil Chopra and Peter Meindl, *Supply Chain Management: Strategy, Planning, and Operations*, 3rd ed. (Upper Saddle River, NJ: Prentice Hall, 2007), chapters 1–3; and Hau L. Lee, "The Triple-A Supply Chain," *Harvard Business Review*, October 2004, pp. 102–12.

17. This discussion is based on Kathryn Jones, "The Dell Way," *Business 2.0* (February 2003), pp. 61–66; Charles Fishman, "The Wal-Mart You Don't Know," *Fast Company* (December 2003), pp. 68–80; and Chopra and Meindl, *Supply Chain Management*.

18. David Simchi-Levi, Philip Kaminsky, and Edith Simchi-Levi, *Designing and Managing the Supply Chain*, 3rd ed. (Burr Ridge, IL: McGraw-Hill/Irwin, 2007). Also, Fan Wu, Sengun Yeniyurt, Daekwan Kim, and S. Tamer Cavusgil, "The Impact of Information Technology on Supply Chain Capabilities and Firm Performance: A Resource-Based View," *Industrial Marketing Management*, October 2006, pp. 593–4.

19. Erik Schonfeld, "The Total Package," *eCompany* (June 2001), pp. 91–97; and Kurt Hoffman, "Snapple Found Handling Logistics In-House Left a Sour Taste," **www.supplychainbrain.com** (April 2002).

20. Douglas M. Lambert, *Supply Chain Management: Processes. Partnerships, and Performance*, 2nd ed. (Sarasota, FL: Supply Chain Management Institute, 2006).

21. Jeff Wise, "Building Canada's Epic Ice Road," *Popular Mechanics* (February 2007), **www.popularmechanics.com**.

22. Jeffrey Davis and Martha Baer, "Some Assembly Required," *Business 2.0* (February 12, 2001), pp. 78–87.

23. Jean Murphy, "Better Forecasting, S&OP Support Transformation at Campbell's Soup Co.," *Global Logistics & Supply Chain Strategies*, June 2004, pp. 28–30.

24. Brian Hindo, "Everything Old is New Again," *BusinessWeek*, September 25, 2006, pp. 64–70.

Case: Amazon.com: This case is based on material available on the company Web site, **www.amazon.com**, and the following sources: Robert D. Hof and Heather Green, "How Amazon Cleared That Hurdle," *BusinessWeek* (February 4, 2002), p. 60; Heather Green, "How Hard Should Amazon Swing?" *BusinessWeek* (January 14, 2002), p. 38: Robert D. Hof, "We've Never Said We Had To Do It All," *BusinessWeek* (October 15, 2001), p. 53; "Amazon.com Selects Mercator E-Business Integration Brokers as Key Technology for Supply Chain Integration," *Business Wire* (November 28, 2000); Bob Walter, "Amazon Leases Distribution Center from Sacramento, Calif., Development Firm," *Sacramento Bee* (July 19, 2001).

CHAPTER 15

1. Noreen O'Leary, "Canada's Tim Hortons Expands Southward," *Convenience Store News*, January 5, 2010, **http://csnews.com**, downloaded January 10, 2010; and Tim Horton's Annual Report (2009);

2. Retail Council of Canada, Annual Report, **www.retailcouncil.org** (downloaded February, 2010)

3. Ibid

4. Retail Fast Facts, Retail Council of Canada (March 2010), **www. retailcouncil.org** (downloaded June 10, 2010).

5. *2009 Global Powers of Retailing*, Deloitte & Touche (2009).

6. Ibid.

7. "Franchise 500," *Entrepreneur* (January 2009).

8. "Crossroads: Carrefour," *The Economist,* March 17, 2007; Harry Maurer, "Wal-Mart: Deeper Into China," *BusinessWeek,* October 30, 2006, p. 32; and Carrefour Web site, **www.carrefour.com/cdc/ group/our-business/our-network-of-stores**, accessed May 31, 2007.

9. Zachary Wilson, "Coca-Cola's 100-Flavour Interactive Freestyle Soda Fountain," *FastCompany*; **www.fastcompany.com**, downloaded January 20, 2010.

10. **www.ikea.com**, accessed January 25, 2010.

11. "Household and Canadian Internet Use Surveys," Statistics Canada, Ottawa, 2009.

12. "Electronic Commerce and Technology," *The Daily,* Statistics Canada (April 20, 2007).

13. **www.cangive.ca**.

14. Canadian Pharmacy News (May 28, 2007), **www.canadianpharmacy news.com** (downloaded June 20, 2007); and "Household and Canadian Internet Use Surveys," Statistics Canada, Ottawa, 2009

15. Kristen Vinakmens, "Digitizing the Experience," *Strategy Magazine* (December 1, 2003), p. 11.

16. "My Virtual Model Inc. Acquires EZsize," *PR Newswire* (June 21, 2001); Steve Casimiro, "Shop Till You Crash," *Fortune* (December 21, 1998), pp. 267–70; and De' Ann Weimer, "Can I Try (Click) That Blouse (Drag) in Blue?" *BusinessWeek* (November 9, 1998), p. 86.

17. **www.the-cma.org**.

18. The following discussion is adapted from William T. Gregor and Eileen M. Friars, *Money Merchandizing: Retail Revolution in Consumer Financial Services* (Cambridge, MA: Management Analysis Center, Inc., 1982).

19. Kristin Laird, "A Stylish Effort from Zellers," *Marketing Daily* (June 20, 2007).

20. "A Changing Attitude: Loss Prevention," from the Annual Report of the Retail Council of Canada, **www.retailcouncil.org** (downloaded June 10, 2007).

21. **www.hopewellrealestateservices.com**.

22. Eve Lazarus, "Main Street Malls," *Marketing* (April 3, 2006), pp. 11–12.

23. *Retail Market Trends, North America,* Grubbs & Ellis (Summer 2007).

24. Pierre Martineau, "The Personality of the Retail Store," *Harvard Business Review* (January–February 1958), p. 47.

25. Julie Baker, Dhruv Grewal, and A. Parasuraman, "The Influence of Store Environment on Quality Inferences and Store Image," *Journal of the Academy of Marketing Science* (Fall 1994), pp. 328–39; and Dhruv Grewal, R. Krishnan, Julie Baker, and Norm Burin, "The Effect of Store Name, Brand Name and Price Discounts on Consumers' Evaluations and Purchase Intentions," *Journal of Retailing* (Fall 1998), pp. 331–52.

26. Mary Jo Bitner, "Servicescapes: The Impact of Physical Surroundings on Customers and Employees," *Journal of Marketing* (April 1992), pp. 57–71.

27. Jans-Benedict Steenkamp and Michel Wedel, "Segmenting Retail Markets on Store Image Using a Consumer-Based Methodology," *Journal of Retailing* (Fall 1991), p. 300; and Philip Kotler, "Atmospherics as a Marketing Tool," *Journal of Retailing*, vol. 49 (Winter 1973–1974), p. 61.

28. Kristen Vinakmens, "How Would You Turn Around Sears," *Strategy Magazine* (October 20, 2003), p. 2.

29. Kusum L. Ailwadi and Bari Harlam, "An Empirical Analysis of the Determinants of Retail Margins: The Role of Store-Brand Share," *Journal of Marketing* (January 2004), pp. 147–65; Joseph Tarnowski, "And the Awards Went to . . ." *Progressive Grocer* (April 15, 2004); Betsy Spethmann, "Shelf Sets," *Promo* (May 1, 2004), p. 6; and "Study Shows Continued Support for Category Management," *CSNews Online* (March 17, 2004).

30. The wheel of retailing theory was originally proposed by Malcolm P. McNair, "Significant Trends and Development in the Postwar Period," in A. B. Smith, ed., *Competitive Distribution in a Free, High-Level Economy and Its Implications for the University* (Pittsburgh:

University of Pittsburgh Press, 1958), pp. 1–25; see also Stephen Brown, "The Wheel of Retailing—Past and Future," *Journal of Retailing* (Summer 1990), pp. 143–49; and Malcolm P. McNair and Eleanor May, "The Next Revolution of the Retailing Wheel," *Harvard Business Review* (September–October 1978), pp. 81–91.

31. William R. Davidson, Albert D. Bates, and Stephen J. Bass, "Retail Life Cycle," *Harvard Business Review* (November–December 1976), pp. 89–96.

32. This discussion is based on "Canadian Retail Trends," Deloitte & Touche (2007); The Retail Council of Canada, Annual Report (2007).

33. Jim Carter and Norman Sheehan, "From Competition to Cooperation: E-Tailing's Integration with Retailing," *Business Horizons* (March–April 2004), pp. 71–78.

34. Carrie Johnson, "Getting Multichannel Marketing Right," **www. forrester.com** (downloaded January 7, 2005); and "Shop Online, Spend Offline," **www.emarketer.com**, July 11, 2007.

35. **www.retailcouncil.org**, Annual Report, 2008; and Paul Brent, "Chip Power," *Marketing*, (August 14/21, 2006), p. 6.

36. Mike Duff, "Hudson's Bay Bridges Gap Between Canada's Discount and Mid-tier Retailers," *DSN Retailing* (October 24, 2005).

37. **www.greenbiz.com** (June 19, 2007)

38. *2009 Global Powers of Retailing,* Deloitte & Touche (2009); and **www.retailcouncil.org**, Annual Report (July 2008).

39. "Best Environmental Practices of Leading Retailers Around the World," **http://www.greeningretail.ca** (accessed August 25,2010). Also see, "Top Green Retailers Find Sustainability Makes Good Business Sense," February 18, 2010, **http://www.ryerson.ca/news/ news/Research_News/20100218_green.html** (accessed August 25, 2010); "Research and Markets: Learn About Sustainability & Retailing, 2008," *Business Wire,* February 23, 2009; "Research and Markets: Going Green Isn't Just Good for the Environment—It's Good for Business Too," *Business Wire,* February 20, 2009; Jason Kirby, "Going Green for Selfish Reasons," *MacLean's,* December 8, 2008, p.39; and Adam Aston, "Wal-Mart," *BusinessWeek,* December 22, 2008, p.48.

40. *2009 Global Powers of Retailing,* Deloitte & Touche (2009).

41. Joseph Olewitz, "Facebook Meets the Mall," Icon Nicholson Media Release, **http://www.iconnicholson.com/news/press_releases/doc/ nrf011407.pdf,** January 14, 2007.

42. *2009 Global Powers of Retailing,* Deloitte & Touche (2009).

43. **www.retailcouncil.org**, Annual Report (July 2008)

Case: This case was written by Frederick G. Crane.

CHAPTER 16

1. Eve Lazarus, "Canadian Tourism Commission," *Marketing,* November 23, 2009, p. 10; Kristin Laird, "Hyundai Auto Canada," *Marketing,* November 23, 2009, pp. 15–17; Kate McCaffery, "Kraft Canada," *Marketing,* November 23, 2009, p.16; and "Best of Show," *Marketing,* November 23, 2009, p. 6.

2. Wilbur Schramm, "How Communication Works," in Wilbur Schramm, ed., *The Process and Effects of Mass Communication* (Urbana, IL: University of Illinois Press, 1955), pp. 3–26.

3. F. G. Crane and T. K. Clarke, *Consumer Behaviour in Canada: Theory and Practice,* 2nd ed. (Toronto: Dryden, 1994), pp. 287–98.

4. Del J. Hawkins, David L. Mothersbaugh, and Roger J. Best, *Consumer Behavior,* 10th ed. (Burr Ridge, IL: McGraw-Hill/Irwin, 2007), p. 56.

5. Rik Pieters and Michel Wedel, "Attention Capture and Transfer in Advertising: Brand Pictorial, and Text-Size Effects," *Journal of Marketing* (April 2004), pp. 36–50.

6. Kusum L Ailawadi, Scott A. Neslin, and Karen Gedenk, "Pursuing the Value-Conscious Consumer: Store Brands versus National Brand Promotions," *Journal of Marketing* (January 2001), pp. 71–89.

7. B. C. Cotton and Emerson M. Babb, "Consumer Response to Promotional Deals," *Journal of Marketing*, vol. 42 (July 1978), pp. 109–13.

8. Robert George Brown, "Sales Response to Promotions and Advertising," *Journal of Advertising Research*, vol. 14 (August 1974), pp. 33–40.

9. Adapted from *Economic Impact: U.S. Direct Marketing Today* (New York: Direct Marketing Association, 1998), p. 25.

10. Siva K. Balasubramanian and V. Kumar, "Analyzing Variations in Advertising and Promotional Expenditures: Key Correlates in Consumer, Industrial, and Service Markets," *Journal of Marketing* (April 1990), pp. 57–68.

11. This example was adapted from "Interactive to the Max," *Interactive Advertising Bureau* and *Marketing Magazine* (2007).

12. Dunn Sunnoo and Lynn Y. S. Lin, "Sales Effects of Promotion and Advertising," *Journal of Advertising Research*, vol. 18 (October 1978), pp. 37–42.

13. John Palmer, "Animal Instincts," *PROMO* (May 2001), pp. 25–33.

14. F. G. Crane and T. K. Clarke, pp. 237–38, 346.

15. James M. Oliver and Paul W. Farris, "Push and Pull: A One-Two Punch for Packages Products," *Sloan Management Review* (Fall 1989), pp. 53–61.

16. Ken Riddell, "Advertising Sees Share of Pie Dwindling," *Marketing* (January 7, 1994), p. 2.

17. David Ciekiewicz, "Wired World," *Marketing* (June 18, 2001), **www.marketingmag.ca** (downloaded June 22, 2005).

18. Eve Lazarus, "Branching Out," *Marketing* (October 20, 2003), **www.marketingmag.ca** (downloaded June 22, 2005).

19. Robert J. Lavidge and Gary A. Steiner, "A Model for Predictive Measurement of Advertising Effectiveness," *Journal of Marketing* (October 1961), p. 61.

20. Brian Wansink and Michael Ray, "Advertising Strategies to Increase Usage Frequency," *Journal of Marketing* (January 1996), pp. 31–46.

21. *Media Digest 2009–2010,* Canadian Media Directors Council, Toronto.

22. Don E. Schultz and Anders Gronstedt, "Making Marcom an Investment," *Marketing Management* (Fall 1997), pp. 41–49; and J. Enrique Bigne, "Advertising Budget Practices: A Review," *Journal of Current Issues and Research in Advertising* (Fall 1995), pp. 17–31.

23. John Philip Jones, "Ad Spending: Maintaining Market Share," *Harvard Business Review* (January–February 1990), pp. 38–42; and Charles H. Patti and Vincent Blanko, "Budgeting Practices of Big Advertisers," *Journal of Advertising Research*, vol. 21 (December 1981), pp. 23–30.

24. James A. Schroer, "Ad Spending: Growing Market Share," *Harvard Business Review* (January–February 1990), pp. 44–48.

25. Jeffrey A. Lowenhar and John L. Stanton, "Forecasting Competitive Advertising Expenditures," *Journal of Advertising Research*, vol. 16, no. 2 (April 1976), pp. 37–44.

26. Daniel Seligman, "How Much for Advertising?" *Fortune* (December 1956), p. 123.

27. James E. Lynch and Graham J. Hooley, "Increasing Sophistication in Advertising Budget Setting," *Journal of Advertising Research*, vol. 30 (February–March 1990), pp. 67–75.

28. Jimmy D. Barnes, Brenda J. Muscove, and Javad Rassouli, "An Objective and Task Media Selection Decision Model and Advertising Cost Formula to Determine International Advertising Budgets," *Journal of Advertising*, vol. 11, no. 4 (1982), pp. 68–75.

29. Don E. Schultz, "Olympics Get the Gold Medal in Integrating Marketing Event," *Marketing News* (April 27, 1998), pp. 5, 10.

30. Cornelia Pechman, Guangzhi Zhao, Marvin E. Goldberg, and Ellen Thomas Reibling, "What to Convey in Antismoking Advertisements for Adolescents: The Use of Protection Motivation Theory to Identify Effective Message Themes," *Journal of Marketing* (April 2003), pp. 1–18.

31. Kate Fitzgerald, "Beyond Advertising," *Advertising Age* (August 3, 1998), pp. 1, 14; Curtis P. Johnson, "Follow the Money: Sell CFO on Integrated Marketing's Merits," *Marketing News* (May 11, 1998).

32. "Measure for Measure," *Marketing Management* (January–February 2004), p. 7.

33. **www.the-cma.org** (downloaded on January 22, 2010).

34. Ibid.

35. "Government of Canada Protects Canadians with Electronic Commerce Protection Act," **www.ic.gc.ca**; downloaded, January 30, 2010.

36. "Essential Interactive, vol. 3," Working Knowledge (2006). Also see "Canadian Internet Use Survey," Statistics Canada (August 15, 2006), Ottawa.

37. Carrie A. Johnson, "Getting Multichannel Retailing Right," **www.forrester.com** (downloaded January 7, 2005).

38. "Privacy Concerns Driving Opposition to Targeted Online Advertising," Canadian Marketing Association (April 29, 2009); **www.the-cma-org**, downloaded, January 30, 2010.

Case: This case was prepared by Steven Hartley. Sources: Jeremy Mullman, "Protecting This Brand While Running Ahead," *Advertising Age*, January 12, 2009, p. 16; Jeremy Mullman, "Under Armour hopes to outrun Nike," *Advertising Age*, April 28, 2008, p. 6; Jeremy Mullman, "No Sugar and Spice Here," *Advertising Age*, June 18, 2007, p. 3; Stanley Holmes, "Under Armour May Be Overstretched," *Business Week*, April 30, 2007, p. 65; interviews with Marcus Stevens, Nathan Shriver, Steven Battista, and Kevin Haley; and information contained on the Under Armour Web site (**www.underarmour.com**).

CHAPTER 17

1. Information supplied by AdFarm (June 2007).

2. David A. Aaker and Donald Norris, "Characteristics of TV Commercials Perceived as Informative," *Journal of Advertising Research*, vol. 22, no. 2 (April–May 1982), pp. 61–70.

3. Larry D. Compeau and Dhruv Grewal, "Comparative Price Advertising: An Integrative Review," *Journal of Public Policy & Marketing* (Fall 1998), pp. 257–73.

4. Jennifer Lawrence, "P&G Ads Get Competitive," *Advertising Age* (February 1, 1993), p. 14; Jerry Gotlieb and Dan Sorel, "The Influence of Type of Advertisement, Price, and Source Credibility on Perceived Quality," *Journal of the Academy of Marketing Science* (Summer 1992), pp. 253–60; and Cornelia Pechman and David Stewart, "The Effects of Comparative Advertising on Attention, Memory, and Purchase Intentions," *Journal of Consumer Research* (September 1990), pp. 180–92.

5. Bruce Buchanan and Doron Goldman, "Us vs. Them: The Minefield of Comparative Ads," *Harvard Business Review* (May–June 1989), pp. 38–50.

6. Lewis C. Winters, "Does It Pay to Advertise to Hostile Audiences with Corporate Advertising?" *Journal of Advertising Research* (June/July 1988), pp. 11–18; and Robert Selwitz, "The Selling of an Image," *Madison Avenue* (February 1985), pp. 61–69.

7. Matt Semansky, "Lavalife Spot Looks on Bright Side of Dating," *Marketing Daily* (July 10, 2007), **www.marketingmag.ca** (downloaded July 18, 2007).

8. Jeremy Mullman, "No Sugar and Spice Here," *Advertising Age*, June 18, 2007, p. 3.

9. "Claritin Springs into Allergy Season with New Consumer Programs," *PR Newswire* (February 20, 2001).

10. Matt Semansky, "Home Depot Tweaks Message in Quebec," *Marketing Daily* (June 11, 2007), **www.marketingmag.ca** (downloaded July 12, 2007).

11. Bob Donath, "Match Your Media Choice and Ad Copy Objective," *Marketing News* (June 8, 1998), p. 6.

12. **www.cassies.ca/winners/2010winners** (downloaded February, 2010).

13. Michael S. LaTour and Herbert J. Rotfeld, "There Are Threats and (Maybe) Fear-Caused Arousal: Theory and Confusions of Appeals to Fear and Fear Arousal Itself," *Journal of Advertising* (Fall 1997), pp. 45–59.

14. Eve Lazarus, "Think About the Unthinkable in New Blue Cross Ads," *Marketing Daily* (June 6, 2007), **www.marketingmag.ca** (downloaded July 4, 2007).

15. This example has been supplied by Rethink Canada, agency of record for BCAA Life Insurance.

16. "If Sex Sells, Humour Sells Way More," Institute of Communication Agencies; **www.icacanada.ca** (downloaded, February 3, 2010).

17. **www.worldskills.org** (downloaded, February 2, 2010); and **www.cancer.ca** (downloaded, February 2, 2010).

18. Canadian Media Directors' Council, Media Digest 2009/2010.

19. Ibid.

20. Lowell L. Lunden, "Secrets for Powerful Advertising: Strategic Implications of Recency," *Canadian Advertising Research Foundation Newsletter* (December 2003), pp. 9–13.

21. William F. Arens, *Contemporary Advertising*, 9th ed (New York: McGraw-Hill/Irwin, 2004); and William G. Nickels, James M. McHugh, and Susan M. McHugh, *Understanding Business*, 7th ed. (Burr Ridge, IL: McGraw-Hill, 2005, p. 493).

22. Canadian Media Directors' Council, Media Digest 2009/2010.

23. **www.ctv.ca**.

24. Surendra N. Singh, Denise Linville, and Ajay Sukhdial, "Enhancing the Efficacy of Split Thirty-Second Television Commercials: An Encoding Variability Application," *Journal of Advertising* (Fall 1995), pp. 13–23; Scott Ward, Terence A. Oliva, and David J. Reibstein, "Effectiveness of Brand-Related 15-Second Commercials," *Journal of Consumer Marketing*, no. 2 (1994). pp. 38–44; and Surendra N. Singh and Catherine Cole, "The Effects of Length, Content, and Repetition on Television Commercial Effectiveness," *Journal of Marketing Research* (February 1993), pp. 91–104.

25. "Net Advertising Revenue by Medium in Canada," Television Bureau of Canada (2010).

26. Canadian Media Directors' Council, Media Digest 2009/2010; and Michelle Halpern, "Ready for Satellite Radio," *Marketing Magazine* (December 13, 2004).

27. Canadian Media Directors' Council, Media Digest, 2009/2010.

28. Ibid.

29. **www.iabcanada.com** (downloaded March 10, 2010).

30. Ibid.

31. Canadian Media Directors' Council, Media Digest 2009/2010;

32. "*Become the Doritos Guru*," **www.cassies.ca/caselibrary** (downloaded March 10, 2010)

33. **www.iabcanada.com**, downloaded, January 30, 2010.

34. Danny Kucharsky, "Agency Opens Inside Clothing Shop," *Marketing Daily* (May 28, 2007), **www.marketingmag.ca** (downloaded July 20, 2007).

35. The discussion of post-testing is based on William F. Arens, *Contemporary Advertising*, 9th ed. (Burr Ridge, IL: Richard D. Irwin, 2004).

36. **www.adstandards.com** (downloaded March 20, 2010).

37. Melita Kuburas, "Can Ads Save the Economy? Consumers Say Yes." *Strategy*, January 22, 2010, **www.strategyonline.ca/articles**, downloaded, February 7, 2010.

38. Lisa D'Innocenzo, "Selling to the Store," *Strategy Magazine* (February 9, 2004), p. 1.

39. *Couponing Trends* (Markham, ON: NCH Promotional Services, 2007).

40. Kapil Bawa and Robert W. Shoemaker, "Analyzing Incremental Sales from a Direct-Mail Coupon Promotion," *Journal of Marketing* (July 1998), pp. 66–78.

41. Roger A. Strang, "Sales Promotion—Fast Growth, Faulty Management," *Harvard Business Review*, vol. 54 (July–August 1976), pp. 115–24; and Ronald W. Ward and James E. Davis, "Coupon

Redemption," *Journal of Advertising Research*, vol. 18 (August 1978), pp. 51–58. Similar results on favorable mail-distributed coupons were reported by Alvin Schwartz, "The Influence of Media Characteristics on Coupon Redemption," *Journal of Marketing*, vol. 30 (January 1966), pp. 41–46.

42. Matt Semansky, "M&M Ads Spawn New Contest," *Marketing Daily* (June 8, 2007), **www.marketingmag.ca** (downloaded July 20, 2007); and Matt Semansky, "Teltoon Contesting with General Mills, Maynards," *Marketing Daily* (June 6, 2007), **www.marketingmag.ca** (downloaded July 20, 2007).

43. Keith McArthur and Grant Robertson, "Product Placement Hits Canadian TV," *The Globe & Mail* (November 21, 2005).

44. "Global Product Placement, Forecast 2006–2010," PQ Media, **www.pqmedia.com** (downloaded July 10, 2007).

45. This discussion is drawn particularly from John A. Quelch, *Trade Promotions by Grocery Manufacturers: A Management Perspective* (Cambridge, MA: Marketing Science Institute, August 1982).

46. Scott Hue, "Free 'Plugs' Supply Ad Power," *Advertising Age* (January 29, 1990), p. 6.

47. **www.sponsorshipmarketing.ca**.

48. "PETA Ads Target of Complaints to ASC," *Marketing* (February 22, 2005), **www.marketingmag.ca** (downloaded June 10, 2005); and Martin O'Hanlon, "Meat Lovers Not Complete Lovers," *The Chronicle-Herald* (August 11, 1999), pp. A1, A2; "KFC vs. PETA," Veg.ca (August 7, 2005), **www.veg.ca** (downloaded July 20, 2007); and "Throw Fish Back from the Dinner Plate," CBC.ca (August 11, 2005), **www.cbc.ca** (downloaded July 25, 2007); Mark Kerstein, "PETA's New Campaign Targets Canadian Maple Syrup," **www.digitaljournal.com**, May 29, 2009 (downloaded, March 5, 2010); and **www.canoe.ca**. January 25, 2010.

Case: This case was written by Frederick G. Crane based on information supplied by AdFarm.

CHAPTER 18

1. Based on an interview with Julie Robertson, McGraw-Hill Ryerson (Summer 2007).

2. Statistics Canada, *Canada Year Book*, (Ottawa, 2007).

3. "America's 25 Best Sales Forces," *Sales & Marketing Management* (July 2000), pp. 57–85.

4. Rick Bauman, "The Sales Solution," *Canadian Underwriter* (January 2005), pp. 57–58; and Mark W. Johnston and Greg W. Marshall, *Relationship Selling and Sales Management* (Burr Ridge, IL: McGraw-Hill/Irwin, 2005).

5. Barton A. Weitz, Stephen B. Castleberry, and John F. Tanner, Jr., *Selling: Building Partnerships*, 6th ed. (Burr Ridge, IL: McGraw-Hill/Irwin, 2007), p. 8.

6. For an overview of team selling, see Eli Jones, Andrea Dickson, Lawrence B. Chonko, and Joseph P. Cannon, "Key Accounts and Team Selling: A Review, Framework, and Research Agenda," *Journal of Personal Selling & Sales Management*, Spring 2005, pp. 181–98.

7. "Group Dynamics," *Sales & Marketing Management*, January/February 2007, p. 8; and Steve Atlas and Elise Atlas, "Team Approach," *Selling Power*, May 2000, pp. 126–28.

8. Carol J. Loomis, "Have You Been Cold-Called?" *Fortune* (December 16, 1991), pp. 109–15.

9. Jim Edwards, "Dinner, Interrupted," *BrandWeek* (May 26, 2003), pp. 28–32.

10. Paul A. Herbing, *Handbook of Cross-Cultural Marketing* (New York: The Haworth Press, 1998).

11. "Japanese Business Etiquette," *Smart Business* (August 2000), p. 55.

12. This discussion is based on Weitz, Castleberry, and Tanner, *Selling*; F. Robert Dwyer and John F. Tanner, *Business Marketing*, 3rd ed. (Burr Ridge, IL: McGraw-Hill/Irwin, 2006); and Jeff Golterman,

"Strategic Account Management in the Age of the Never Satisfied Customer," *Velocity* 2 (2000).

13. Kapil R. Tuli, Ajay K. Kohli, and Sundar G. Bharadwaj, "Rethinking Customer Solutions: From Product Bundles to Relational Processes," *Journal of Marketing*, July 2007, pp. 1–17.

14. For an extensive discussion of objections, see Charles M. Futrell, *Fundamentals of Selling*, 9th ed. (Burr Ridge, IL: McGraw-Hill/Irwin, 2007), chap. 12.

15. Theodore Levitt, *The Marketing Imagination* (New York: Free Press, 1983), p. 111.

16. Weitz, Castleberry, and Tanner, *Selling*.

17. *Management Briefing: Sales and Marketing* (New York: Conference Board, October 1996), pp. 3–4.

18. Ellen Neuborne, "Know Thy Enemy," *Sales & Marketing Management* (January 2003), pp. 29–33.

19. Alan J. Dubinsky, Marvin A. Jolson, Ronald E. Michaels, Masaaki Katobe, and Chae Un Lim, "Ethical Perceptions of Field Sales Personnel: An Empirical Assessment," *Journal of Personal Selling & Sales Management* (Fall 1992), pp. 9–21; and Alan J. Dubinsky, Marvin A. Jolson, Masaaki Katobe, and Chae Un Lim, "A Cross-National Investigation of Industrial Salespeople's Ethical Perceptions," *Journal of International Business Studies* (Fourth Quarter 1991), pp. 651–70.

20. See Gilbert A. Churchill, Jr.; Neil M. Ford; Orville C. Walker, Jr.; Mark W. Johnson; and Greg Marshall, *Sales Force Management*, 8th ed. (Burr Ridge, IL: McGraw-Hill/Irwin, 2006), pp. 100–4; and William T. Ross, Jr.; Frederic Dalsace; and Erin Anderson, "Should You Set Up Your Own Sales Force or Should You Outsource It? Pitfalls in the Standard Analysis," *Business Horizons*, January–February 2005, pp. 23–36.

21. Eli Jones, et al., "Key Accounts and Team Selling." Also see, Arun Sharma, "Success Factors in Key Accounts," *Journal of Business & Industrial Marketing* 21, no. 3 (2006), pp. 141–50.

22. This discussion is based on William L. Cron and Thomas E. DeCarlo, *Dalrymple's Sales Management*, 9th ed. (Hoboken, NJ: John Wiley & Sons, Inc., 2006).Also see Rene Darmon, "Joint Assessment of Optimal Sales Force Sizes and Sales Call Guidelines: A Management-Oriented Tool," *Canadian Journal of Administrative Sciences* (September 2007), pp. 200–19.

23. Darmon, "Joint Assessment of Optimal Sales Force Sizes and Sales Call Guidelines: A Management-Oriented Tool"; and "Look Who's Calling," *Sales & Marketing Management* (May 1998), pp. 43–46.

24. This discussion is based on Dalrymple, Cron, and DeCarlo, *Sales Management*.

25. Julia Chang, "Born to Sell?" *Sales & Marketing Management* (July 2003), pp. 34–38.

26. Weitz, Castleberry, and Tanner, *Selling*, p. 21. For further reading see Daniel Goleman, "What Makes a Leader?" *Harvard Business Review* (November–December 1998), pp. 93–102; A. Fisher, "Success Secret: A High Emotional IQ," *Fortune* (October 26, 1998), pp. 293–98; and Daniel Goleman, *Working with Emotional Intelligence* (New York: Bantam, 1999).

27. Joanne Thomas Yaccato, "Through the Gender Lens," *Marketing Magazine* (June 30, 2003); and Lesley Young, "Strange Hybrids," *Marketing* (February 11, 2002), **www.marketingmag.ca** (downloaded June 22, 2005).

28. Ibid.

29. Rosann L. Spiro, Gregory A. Rich, and William J. Stanton, *Management of the Sales Force*, 12th ed. (Burr Ridge, IL: McGraw-Hill/Irwin, 2008), chap. 7.

30. Ibid, chapter 8.

31. **www.marykay.com/recognition** (downloaded June 21, 2004).

32. "Number Crunching," *Sales & Marketing Management* (September 2000), pp. 79–88.

33. For further reading, see Goutam N. Challagolla and Tasadduq A. Shervani, "A Measurement Model of the Dimensions and Types of Output and Behavior Control: An Empirical Test in the Salesforce Context," *Journal of Business Research* (July 1997), pp. 159–72; and Gregory A. Rich, William H. Bommer, Scott B. McKenzie, Philip M. Podsakoff, and Jonathan L. Johnson, "Apples and Apples or Apples and Oranges? A Meta-Analysis of Objective and Subjective Measures of Salesperson Performance," *Journal of Personal Selling & Sales Management* (Fall 1999), pp. 41–52.

34. "Measuring Sales Effectiveness," *Sales & Marketing Management* (October 2000), p. 136; "Quota Busters," *Sales & Marketing Management* (January 2001), pp. 59–63.

35. "Corporate America's New Sales Force," *Fortune*, August 11, 2003, special advertising section.

36. **www.toshiba.com/technology**, downloaded May 15, 2004.

37. Sue Hildreth, "Mobile CRM Makes its Move," SearchCRM.com (June 13, 2006), **www.searchcrm.com** (downloaded July 29, 2007).

38. Christopher Plouffe and Donald Barcley, "Salesperson Navigation: The Intraorganizational Dimension of the Sales Role," *Industrial Marketing Management* (May 2007), pp. 528–39.

Case: Xerox: This case was written by Steven Hartley and Roger Kerin. Sources: Joseph Kornik, "Table Talk: A Sales Leaders Roundtable," *Sales & Marketing Management*, February, 2007; Philip Chadwick, "Xerox Global Services," *Printweek*, October 11, 2007, p. 32; Kevin Maney, "Mulcahy Traces Steps of Xerox's Comeback," *USA Today*, September 11, 2006, p. 4B; Sarah Campbell, "What It's Like Working for Xerox," *The Times* September 14, 2006, p. 9; "Anne Mulcahy, How I Compete," *BusinessWeek*, August 21, 2006, p 55; Simon Avery, "CEO's HR Skills Turn Xerox Fortunes," *The Globe and Mail*, June 2, 2006, p. B3; Julia Chang, "Ultimate Motivation Guide: Happy Sales Force, Happy Returns," *Sales & Marketing Management*, March 2006; Chris Taylor, "Changing Gears," **www.salesandmarketing.com**, October 1, 2005; and resources available on the Xerox Web site (**www.xerox.com**) including About Xerox, Executive Biographies, the Xerox 2007 Fact Sheet, the Online Fact Book: Historical Highlights, and the Online Fact Book: How Xerox Sells.

CHAPTER 19

1. **www.westjet.com** (downloaded July 15, 2010); interview with Sean Durfy, VP Marketing, WestJet (August 16, 2010); and Norma Ramage, "WestJet on the Fly," *Marketing* (June 20, 2005), **www.marketingmag.ca** (downloaded June 20, 2005).

2. Roger A. Kerin, P. Rajan Varadarajan, and Robert A. Peterson, "First-Mover Advantage: A Synthesis, Conceptual Framework, and Research Proposition," *Journal of Marketing* (October 1992), pp. 33–52; and Pankaj Ghemawat, "Sustainable Advantage," *Harvard Business Review* (September–October 1986), pp. 53–58.

3. Nitin Nohria, William Joyce, and Bruce Roberson, "What Really Works," *Harvard Business Review* (July, 2003), pp. 42–52; and "Who Gets Eaten and Who Gets to Eat," *The Economist* (July 12, 2003), pp. 61–63.

4. Chad Terhune and Betsey McKay, "Behind Coke's Travails: A Long Struggle Over Strategy," *The Wall Street Journal* (May 4, 2004), pp. A1, A6; and Betsy Morris, "The Real Story," *Fortune* (May 31, 2004), pp. 84–98.

5. Faith Arner, "No Excuse Not to Succeed," *BusinessWeek* (May 10, 2004), pp. 96–98.

6. Jack Gordon, "Wall Street Curls Its Lip at Costco's Ungreedy CEO," *Star Tribune* (December 19, 2003), p. A33; and John Helyar, Ann Harrington, and Sol Price, "The Only Company Wal-Mart Fears," *Fortune* (November 24, 2003), pp. 158–63.

7. Kathleen Kerwin and Paul Magnusson, "Can Anything Stop Toyota?" *BusinessWeek* (November 17, 2003), pp. 114–22.

8. Murali K. Mantrala, Prabhakant Sirha, and Andris A. Zoltners, "Impact of Resource Allocation Rules on Marketing Investment-Level Decisions and Profitability," *Journal of Marketing Research* (May 1992), pp. 162–75.

9. **www.generalmills.com**.

10. Vanitha Swaminathan, Richard J. Fox, and Srinivas K. Reddy, "The Impact of Brand Extension Introduction on Choice," *Journal of Marketing* (October 2001), pp. 1–15; Deborah Roedder-John, Barbara Loken, and Christopher Joiner, "The Negative Impact of Extensions: Can Flagship Products Be Diluted?" *Journal of Marketing* (January 1998), pp. 19–32; and Akshay R. Rao, Lu Qu, and Robert W. Ruekert, "Signalling Unobservable Product Quality through a Brand Ally," *Journal of Marketing Research* (May 1999), pp. 258–68.

11. *2010 Annual Report* (Minneapolis: General Mills, Inc., 2010).

12. This discussion and Figure 19–3 are adapted from Stanley F. Stasch and Patricis Longtree, "Can Your Marketing Planning Procedures Be Improved?" *Journal of Marketing* (Summer 1980), p. 82; by permission of the American Marketing Association.

13. Adapted with permission of The Free Press, a Division of Macmillan, Inc., from *Competitive Advantage: Creating and Sustaining Superior Performance* by Michael E. Porter. Copyright 1985 by Michael E. Porter.

14. Patricia Sellers, "P&G: Teaching an Old Dog New Tricks," *Fortune* (May 31, 2004), pp. 167–80.

15. Sandy Shore, "Coors-Molson Would Create No. 5 Brewer," *Portland Press* (July 23, 2004), p. 1C, 8C.

16. Adapted from Philip Kotler and Kevin Lane Keller, *Marketing Management*, 12th ed. (Upper Saddle River, NJ: Prentice Hall, 2006), pp. 262–63.

17. Stratford Sherman, "How Intel Makes Spending Pay Off," *Fortune* (February 22, 1993), pp. 57–61.

18. **www.transcontinental.com**; **www.potashcorp.com**; **www.canadian tire.com**; and **www.vancity.com**.

19. Charles H. Noble and Michael P. Mokwa, "Implementing Marketing Strategies: Developing and Testing a Managerial Theory," *Journal of Marketing* (October 1999), pp. 57–74.

20. "Ecomagination," see **www.ge.com/company/citizenship/ ecomagination/index.html**, July 24, 2007.

21. Daniel Roth, "This Ain't No Pizza Party," *Fortune* (November 9, 1998), pp. 158–64.

22. Thomas J. Peters and Robert H. Waterman, Jr., *In Search of Excellence: Lessons from America's Best-Run Companies* (New York: Harper & Row, 1982).

23. Tom Peters, "Winners Do Hundreds of Percent over Norm," *Minneapolis Star Tribune* (January 8, 1985), p. 5B; and Ben Rich and Leo Janos, *Skunk Works* (Boston: Little Brown, 1994), pp. 51–53.

24. Peter Galuska, Ellen Neuborne, and Wendy Zeliner, "P&G's Hottest New Product: P&G," *BusinessWeek* (October 5, 1998), pp. 92–96.

25. Robert W. Ruekert and Orville C. Walker, Jr., "Marketing's Interaction with Other Functional Units: A Conceptual Framework and Empirical Evidence," *Journal of Consumer Marketing* (Spring 1987), pp. 1–19. Shikhar Sarin and Vijay Mahajan, "The Effect of Reward Structures on the Performance of Cross-Functional Product Development Teams," *Journal of Marketing* (April 2001), pp. 35–53; and Amy Edmondson, Richard Bohmer, and Gary Pisano, "Speeding Up Team Learning," *Harvard Business Review* (October 2001), pp. 125–32.

26. James D. Lenskold, *Marketing ROI* (New York: McGraw-Hill, 2003).

27. Michael Krauss, "Balance Attention to Metrics with Intuition," *Marketing News*, June 1, 2007, pp. 6–8; John Davis, *Measuring Marketing: 103 Key Metrics Every Marketer Needs* (Singapore: John Wiley & Sons, 2007); and Paul W. Farris, Neil T. Bendle, Phillip E. Pfeifer, and David J. Reibstein, *Marketing Metrics* (Upper Saddle River, NJ: Wharton School Publishing, 2006).

28. Malcolm Craig, *Thinking Visually: Business Applications of 14 Core Diagrams* (New York and London: Continuum, 2000).

29. Nelson D. Schwartz, "Colgate Cleans Up," *Fortune,* April 16, 2001, pp. 179–80

Case: This case was prepared by David Ford based on interviews with Vivian Milroy Callaway.

CREDITS

CHAPTER 1

p. 2, Courtesy of Wildplay Ltd.; p. 7, Courtesy of Communications Services Manitoba (left); p. 7, Courtesy of the Registered Nurses' Association of Ontario (right); p. 10, © M. Hruby; p. 14, Courtesy of Wildplay Ltd. (all); p. 16, © Dick Hemingway (left and centre); p. 16, McGraw-Hill Companies; p. 17, Courtesy of Pete's Frootiques and Limelight Group (all); p. 18, The Twitter name, logo, Twitter T, Tweet, and Twitter blue bird are trademarks of Twitter, Inc. (top); p. 18, © MySpace, Inc. (bottom)

CHAPTER 2

p. 26, Courtesy of Canadian Tire Corporation (all); p. 30, Courtesy Yahoo! Inc. (left); p. 30, Courtesy Motorola, Inc. (top right); p. 30, Courtesy FUBU - The Collection and FB Entertainment (bottom right); p. 33, Photography by Sean Lamb; p. 39, Federation des producteurs de lait du Quebec\Agency: BBDO Montreal (left); p. 39, CP/Stuart Nimmo (right); p. 48, 3 MUSKETEERS ® is a registered trademark owned by Mars, Incorporated and its affiliates. This trademark is used with permission. Mars, Incorporated is not associated with McGraw-Hill Ryerson Limited. Advertisement printed with permission of Mars, Incorporated. © Mars, Inc. 2008

CHAPTER 3

p. 74, © Jeff Howe; p. 77, © John A. Rizzo/ Getty Images; p. 83, McGraw-Hill Companies; p. 84, Used with permission of Sobeys Inc.; p. 87, The Twitter name, logo, Twitter T, Tweet, and Twitter blue bird are trademarks of Twitter, Inc. (top); p. 87, CP PHOTO/ Winnipeg Free Press/ George Douklias (bottom)

CHAPTER 4

p. 100, Courtesy of Toyota Canada (top); p. 100, © Bloomberg/Getty Images; p. 107, Courtesy Transparency International; p. 109, *No credit*; p. 112, © George Bartoli/Reuters/ Corbis; p. 113, Courtesy of McDonald's Corporation p. 115, CP/Don Denton; p. 118, Michael Newman/Photo Edit

CHAPTER 5

p. 120, Photodisc; p. 124, The McGraw-Hill Companies Inc., Christopher Kerrigan, photographer; p. 126, Courtesy McNeil P.P.C.; p. 129, Fresh Steps® is a registered trademark of The Clorox Pet Products Company. Used with permission. (left); p. 129, © 2001 Mary

Kay, Inc. Photos by: Grace Huang/for Sarah Laird (right); p. 130, The Secret Sales Pitch: An Overview of Subliminal Advertising. Copyright © 2004 by August Bullock. All Rights Reserved. Used with permission. SubliminalSex.com.; p. 132, Courtesy of Colgate-Palmolive Company (left); p. 132, The Bayer Company; p. 133, CP/Richard Buchan; p. 133, Figure 5-5: © 2008 Environics Analytics Group Ltd. PRIZM is a registered trademark of Claritas Inc., used with permission; p. 138, Courtesy of Haggar Clothing Co.

CHAPTER 6

p. 146, Courtesy of Bombardier; p. 151, Courtesy U.S. Department of Commerce/ Bureau of the Census; p. 155, Jewel Samad/ AFP/Getty Images; p. 156, Stockbyte/Getty Images; p. 160, *No credit*; p. 162, These materials have been reproduced with the permission of eBay, Inc., Copyright © eBay Inc. All Rights Reserved.

CHAPTER 7

p. 168, Inniskillin Wine Inc. Used with permission of Vincor International (main); p. 168, Courtesy of G.A.P. Adventures (inset photo); p. 173, Courtesy of Sharp USA (left); p. 173, Courtesy of Alison Derry (right); p. 177, European Union, www.europa.eu.int; p. 179, Courtesy of ALMAP/BBDO Sao Paulo; p. 180, Courtesy of Nestle S.A.; p. 183, Photodisc (top); p. 183, Courtesy of Hewlett-Packard/ Canada: Publicis Hal Riney (bottom left and right); p. 186, Courtesy of the Coca-Cola Company (photo); p. 186, Figure 7-5: Reprinted with the permission PRIMEDIA Business Magazines & Media, Inc. Copyright © 2002. All rights reserved. (figure); p. 188, Courtesy of The PRS Group, Inc., East Syracuse, NY; p. 190, Courtesy of McDonald's Corporation; p. 194, Courtesy of The Gillette Company (all); p. 197, Courtesy of CNS Inc

CHAPTER 8

p. 200, © John Eder/Getty Images; p. 203, Dairy Farmers of Canada advertisement developed in conjunction with its advertising agency Allard-Johnson Communications; p. 207, Courtesy of Ocean Spray; p. 211, Courtesy of Wendy's International, p. 212–213, Figure 8-5: Product and brand drivers: factors that influence sales. Ford Consulting Group.; p. 214, Photo by Cancun Chu/Getty Images; p. 216, Courtesy of the Gillette Company; p. 221, Figure 8-6: Used by permission of Ford Consulting Group, Inc.

CHAPTER 9

p. 228, Erin Patrice O'Brien/Taxi/Getty Images; p. 233, CP/AP Photo/Elise Amendola; p. 237, Courtesy of Solo Mobile, p. 238, Provided courtesy of Xerox Corporation; p. 241, Courtesy Wendy's International, Inc.; p. 243, © CLEO Photography; p. 245, Figure 9-9: © M. Hruby; p. 246, Courtesy of Wilson Sporting Goods Co.; p. 249, Courtesy Prince Sports; p. 251, Courtesy Prince Sports

CHAPTER 10

p. 252, AP Photo/Paul Sakuma/CP; p. 255, Courtesy of Raymond Weil; p. 258, © Issei Kato/Reuters/Corbis (left); p. 258, CP/AP Photo/LM Otero; p. 259, © M. Hruby (left); p. 259, © James Leynse/Corbis; p. 263, Courtesy of NewProductWorks (all); p. 264, Courtesy iRobot Corporation; p. 265, charts: Reprinted with permission from the July 29, 2001 issue of *Advertising Age*. Copyright 2001 Crain Communications Inc. (all); p. 267, Used with permission of Bravado Designs; p. 269, Courtesy of 3M (top three); p. 269, © Copyright 2007 Ipsos Canada, part of the Ipsos Group (bottom); p. 271, Jose Azel/Aurora; p. 276, Courtesy 3M; p. 277, Courtesy 3M

CHAPTER 11

p. 278, © Kan Photography 2005; p. 280, © David Young-Wolff/PhotoEdit; p. 282, AP Photo/Reed Saxon/CP; p. 283, CP/Nathan Denette; p. 287, © CLEO Photography; p. 289, Courtesy of Canadian Turkey Marketing Agency; p. 291, Courtesy of Advanced Research Labs; p. 293, AP/Douglas C. Pizac/CP (top); p. 293, Courtesy of Roper Footwear and Apparel (bottom); p. 297, Courtesy of Black & Decker (U.S.) Inc. (left); p. 297, Courtesy of DeWalt Industrial Tool Company (right); p. 299, © M. Hruby (all); p. 300, Photo by: Arthur Meyerson, "Coco-Cola, the Conour Bottle design and the Coca-Cola Fridge Pack are trademarks of the Coca-Cola Company. Copyright 1994. All rights reserved (top); p. 300, © 2001 Susan G. Holtz

CHAPTER 12

p. 306, Photo by Angela Weis/Getty Images; p. 310, Courtesy of Fairmont Hotels & Resorts; p. 311, Courtesy of Allstate; p. 315, Figure 12-4: Source: Adapted from W. Earl Sasser, R. Paul Olsen, and D. Daryl Wyckoff, Management of Service Operations: Text, Cases and Readings (Boston: Allyn & Bacon, 1978); p. 316, Figure 12-5: Adapted with the permission of The Free Press, a Division of Simon & Schuster Adult Publishing Group, from *ON GREAT SERVICE, A Framework for Action* by Leonard L. Berry. Copyright © 1995 by Leonard L. Berry. All rights reserved. p. 318, Used with permission from McDonald's Corporation (top); p. 318, Courtesy of Sprint (middle); p. 318, Courtesy of Canadian Blood Services (bottom); p. 319, Photo courtesy of Lasik MD; p. 320, Nunavut logo, used with permission of the Government of Nunavut (left); p. 320, Northwest Territories logo, used with permission of the Government of the Northwest Territories (right); p. 323, YJM Photography; p. 328, Used with permission of the Canadian Football League (all)

CHAPTER 13

p. 330, © Walter Bibikow/JAI/Corbis; p. 338, © Tony Arruza/CORBIS; p. 344, © Terry McElroy; p. 345, Courtesy of Air Canada Vacations; p. 348, Courtesy of Hudson's Bay Company; p. 350, © Tracy Leonard; p. 351, © Sharon Hoogstraten; p. 352, Courtesy of The Toro Company

CHAPTER 14

p. 368, © Dick Hemingway; p. 371, Figure 14-1: American Marketing Association. Used by permission; p. 378, © Tracy Leonard; p. 379, Courtesy of Kensington Florist, Calgary, Alberta. http://www.kensingtonflorist.com; p. 381, Courtesy of Visa; p. 383, Courtesy of Dai-Ichi Kikaku Co. Ltd. and Warner-Lambert; p. 387, Courtesy of Dell, Inc. (left); p. 387, Courtesy of Wal-Mart Stores, Inc. (right); p. 391, Courtesy of FedEx Corporation (left); p. 391, AP Photo/Douglas C. Pizac/CP (right); p. 393, © Chuck Savage/CORBIS; p. 394, James Reeve/Corbis

CHAPTER 15

p. 400, The Canadian Press/Steve White; p. 404, © Tracy Leonard; p. 407, © Nancy Copeland/Ivy Images; p. 408, © Tracy Leonard (top); p. 408, Used with permission of www.cangive.ca (bottom); p. 411, Courtesy of Alison Derry; p. 414, Photo courtesy of Musson Cattell Mackey Partnership and F&A Architecture (Joint Venture Architect) Photographer: Michael Boland Photography; p. 416, Courtesy of Taco Bell

CHAPTER 16

p. 426, © Design Pics/Michael Interisano/Getty Images (top right); p. 426, The Canadian Press/Don Denton (top left); p. 426, The Canadian Press/Keith Srakocic (bottom); p. 430, Courtesy GM Archives; p. 432, Courtesy of Best Buy; p. 433, © 2007 Llewellyn/Frommer's *Australia From $60 a Day*. Reprinted with permission of John Wiley & Sons, Inc.; p. 435, Courtesy of *Fence* Magazine; p. 436, © Bill Ivy/Ivy Images; p. 437, Courtesy of Gulf Stream Aircraft, Inc. (left); p. 437, Courtesy of H.J. Heinz Company. Used with permission (right); p. 447, Photodisc/Flying Colours Ltd.; p. 452, Courtesy Under Armour, Inc.; p. 453, Photo by Joe Robbins/Getty Images

CHAPTER 17

p. 454, Courtesy of AdFarm; p. 457, Courtesy Sony Electronics, Inc. (left); p. 457, Courtesy Mars, Inc.; p. 458, From Dairy Farmers of Canada, © 2010, Luc Robitaille (Photographer), Allard-Johnson (Agency); p. 459, Inter IKEA Systems B.V. 2010; p. 460, Used with permission of Rethink Canada; p. 461, CP/Halifax Daily News/Jeff Harper; p. 464, From

Wllliam F. Arens, Contemporary Advertising, 9th ed. Copyright © 2004 by The McGraw-Hill Companies; Figure 17.3 from William G. Nickels, James M. McHugh, and Susan M. McHugh, *Understanding Business,* 7th ed. © 2005 by The McGraw-Hill Companies; p. 465, Courtesy *Cosmo Girl*; p. 468, CP/Lethbridge Herald - David Rossiter; p. 469, © Will Ivy/Ivy Images; p. 472, Courtesy of Starch™; p. 476, Courtesy of Canadian Tire (top); p. 476, *No credit* (bottom)

CHAPTER 18

p. 484, Courtesy of Julie Robertson; p. 488, Courtesy Medtronic; p. 490, © Corbis; p. 492, © Einzig Photography; p. 494, © Image Source/Corbis; p. 504, © Rex C. Curry; p. 507, Royalty-Free/Corbis; p. 511, Used with permission of Xerox

CHAPTER 19

p. 512, © Lonnie Ganz; p. 515, AP Photo/Don Ryan; p. 516, © M. Hruby; p. 520, Reprinted with permission from *Journal of Marketing*, published by the American Marketing Association, Summer 1980, p. 82.; p. 521, Courtesy of Wal-Mart Inc.; p. 521, Figure 19-4: Adapted with permission from The Free Press, a Division of Simon & Schuster Group, from *COMPETITIVE ADVANTAGE: Creating and Sustaining Superior Performance* by Michael E. Porter. Copyright © 1985, 1998 by Michael E. Porter. All rights reserved; p. 529, Courtesy General Electric Company; p. 530, Courtesy of Lockheed Martin Corp.; p. 534, Courtesy of Colgate-Palmolive Company; p. 538, Courtesy General Mills

NAME INDEX

COMPANY/PRODUCT INDEX

SUBJECT INDEX